Lecture Notes in Computer Science 14021

Founding Editors

Gerhard Goos
Juris Hartmanis

Editorial Board Members

The series Lecture Notes in Computer Science (LNCS), including its subseries Lecture Notes in Artificial Intelligence (LNAI) and Lecture Notes in Bioinformatics (LNBI), has established itself as a medium for the publication of new developments in computer science and information technology research, teaching, and education.

LNCS enjoys close cooperation with the computer science R & D community, the series counts many renowned academics among its volume editors and paper authors, and collaborates with prestigious societies. Its mission is to serve this international community by providing an invaluable service, mainly focused on the publication of conference and workshop proceedings and postproceedings. LNCS commenced publication in 1973.

Margherita Antona · Constantine Stephanidis
Editors

Universal Access in Human-Computer Interaction

17th International Conference, UAHCI 2023
Held as Part of the 25th HCI International Conference, HCII 2023
Copenhagen, Denmark, July 23–28, 2023
Proceedings, Part II

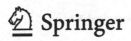

Editors
Margherita Antona
Foundation for Research and Technology
Heraklion, Crete, Greece

Constantine Stephanidis
Foundation for Research and Technology
Heraklion, Crete, Greece

ISSN 0302-9743 ISSN 1611-3349 (electronic)
Lecture Notes in Computer Science
ISBN 978-3-031-35896-8 ISBN 978-3-031-35897-5 (eBook)
https://doi.org/10.1007/978-3-031-35897-5

This Springer imprint is published by the registered company Springer Nature Switzerland AG
The registered company address is: Gewerbestrasse 11, 6330 Cham, Switzerland

Foreword

Human-computer interaction (HCI) is acquiring an ever-increasing scientific and industrial importance, as well as having more impact on people's everyday lives, as an ever-growing number of human activities are progressively moving from the physical to the digital world. This process, which has been ongoing for some time now, was further accelerated during the acute period of the COVID-19 pandemic. The HCI International (HCII) conference series, held annually, aims to respond to the compelling need to advance the exchange of knowledge and research and development efforts on the human aspects of design and use of computing systems.

The 25th International Conference on Human-Computer Interaction, HCI International 2023 (HCII 2023), was held in the emerging post-pandemic era as a 'hybrid' event at the AC Bella Sky Hotel and Bella Center, Copenhagen, Denmark, during July 23–28, 2023. It incorporated the 21 thematic areas and affiliated conferences listed below.

A total of 7472 individuals from academia, research institutes, industry, and government agencies from 85 countries submitted contributions, and 1578 papers and 396 posters were included in the volumes of the proceedings that were published just before the start of the conference, these are listed below. The contributions thoroughly cover the entire field of human-computer interaction, addressing major advances in knowledge and effective use of computers in a variety of application areas. These papers provide academics, researchers, engineers, scientists, practitioners and students with state-of-the-art information on the most recent advances in HCI.

The HCI International (HCII) conference also offers the option of presenting 'Late Breaking Work', and this applies both for papers and posters, with corresponding volumes of proceedings that will be published after the conference. Full papers will be included in the 'HCII 2023 - Late Breaking Work - Papers' volumes of the proceedings to be published in the Springer LNCS series, while 'Poster Extended Abstracts' will be included as short research papers in the 'HCII 2023 - Late Breaking Work - Posters' volumes to be published in the Springer CCIS series.

I would like to thank the Program Board Chairs and the members of the Program Boards of all thematic areas and affiliated conferences for their contribution towards the high scientific quality and overall success of the HCI International 2023 conference. Their manifold support in terms of paper reviewing (single-blind review process, with a minimum of two reviews per submission), session organization and their willingness to act as goodwill ambassadors for the conference is most highly appreciated.

This conference would not have been possible without the continuous and unwavering support and advice of Gavriel Salvendy, founder, General Chair Emeritus, and Scientific Advisor. For his outstanding efforts, I would like to express my sincere appreciation to Abbas Moallem, Communications Chair and Editor of HCI International News.

July 2023   Constantine Stephanidis

HCI International 2023 Thematic Areas and Affiliated Conferences

Thematic Areas

- HCI: Human-Computer Interaction
- HIMI: Human Interface and the Management of Information

Affiliated Conferences

- EPCE: 20th International Conference on Engineering Psychology and Cognitive Ergonomics
- AC: 17th International Conference on Augmented Cognition
- UAHCI: 17th International Conference on Universal Access in Human-Computer Interaction
- CCD: 15th International Conference on Cross-Cultural Design
- SCSM: 15th International Conference on Social Computing and Social Media
- VAMR: 15th International Conference on Virtual, Augmented and Mixed Reality
- DHM: 14th International Conference on Digital Human Modeling and Applications in Health, Safety, Ergonomics and Risk Management
- DUXU: 12th International Conference on Design, User Experience and Usability
- C&C: 11th International Conference on Culture and Computing
- DAPI: 11th International Conference on Distributed, Ambient and Pervasive Interactions
- HCIBGO: 10th International Conference on HCI in Business, Government and Organizations
- LCT: 10th International Conference on Learning and Collaboration Technologies
- ITAP: 9th International Conference on Human Aspects of IT for the Aged Population
- AIS: 5th International Conference on Adaptive Instructional Systems
- HCI-CPT: 5th International Conference on HCI for Cybersecurity, Privacy and Trust
- HCI-Games: 5th International Conference on HCI in Games
- MobiTAS: 5th International Conference on HCI in Mobility, Transport and Automotive Systems
- AI-HCI: 4th International Conference on Artificial Intelligence in HCI
- MOBILE: 4th International Conference on Design, Operation and Evaluation of Mobile Communications

List of Conference Proceedings Volumes Appearing Before the Conference

1. LNCS 14011, Human-Computer Interaction: Part I, edited by Masaaki Kurosu and Ayako Hashizume
2. LNCS 14012, Human-Computer Interaction: Part II, edited by Masaaki Kurosu and Ayako Hashizume
3. LNCS 14013, Human-Computer Interaction: Part III, edited by Masaaki Kurosu and Ayako Hashizume
4. LNCS 14014, Human-Computer Interaction: Part IV, edited by Masaaki Kurosu and Ayako Hashizume
5. LNCS 14015, Human Interface and the Management of Information: Part I, edited by Hirohiko Mori and Yumi Asahi
6. LNCS 14016, Human Interface and the Management of Information: Part II, edited by Hirohiko Mori and Yumi Asahi
7. LNAI 14017, Engineering Psychology and Cognitive Ergonomics: Part I, edited by Don Harris and Wen-Chin Li
8. LNAI 14018, Engineering Psychology and Cognitive Ergonomics: Part II, edited by Don Harris and Wen-Chin Li
9. LNAI 14019, Augmented Cognition, edited by Dylan D. Schmorrow and Cali M. Fidopiastis
10. LNCS 14020, Universal Access in Human-Computer Interaction: Part I, edited by Margherita Antona and Constantine Stephanidis
11. LNCS 14021, Universal Access in Human-Computer Interaction: Part II, edited by Margherita Antona and Constantine Stephanidis
12. LNCS 14022, Cross-Cultural Design: Part I, edited by Pei-Luen Patrick Rau
13. LNCS 14023, Cross-Cultural Design: Part II, edited by Pei-Luen Patrick Rau
14. LNCS 14024, Cross-Cultural Design: Part III, edited by Pei-Luen Patrick Rau
15. LNCS 14025, Social Computing and Social Media: Part I, edited by Adela Coman and Simona Vasilache
16. LNCS 14026, Social Computing and Social Media: Part II, edited by Adela Coman and Simona Vasilache
17. LNCS 14027, Virtual, Augmented and Mixed Reality, edited by Jessie Y. C. Chen and Gino Fragomeni
18. LNCS 14028, Digital Human Modeling and Applications in Health, Safety, Ergonomics and Risk Management: Part I, edited by Vincent G. Duffy
19. LNCS 14029, Digital Human Modeling and Applications in Health, Safety, Ergonomics and Risk Management: Part II, edited by Vincent G. Duffy
20. LNCS 14030, Design, User Experience, and Usability: Part I, edited by Aaron Marcus, Elizabeth Rosenzweig and Marcelo Soares
21. LNCS 14031, Design, User Experience, and Usability: Part II, edited by Aaron Marcus, Elizabeth Rosenzweig and Marcelo Soares

47. CCIS 1836, HCI International 2023 Posters - Part V, edited by Constantine Stephanidis, Margherita Antona, Stavroula Ntoa and Gavriel Salvendy

https://2023.hci.international/proceedings

Preface

The 17th International Conference on Universal Access in Human-Computer Interaction (UAHCI 2023), an affiliated conference of the HCI International (HCII) conference, provided an established international forum for the exchange and dissemination of scientific information on theoretical, methodological, and empirical research that addresses all issues related to the attainment of universal access in the development of interactive software. It comprehensively addressed accessibility and quality of interaction in the user interface development life-cycle from a multidisciplinary perspective, taking into account dimensions of diversity, such as functional limitations, age, culture, background knowledge, etc., in the target user population, as well as various dimensions of diversity which affect the context of use and the technological platform and arise from the emergence of mobile, wearable, ubiquitous, and intelligent devices and technologies.

UAHCI 2023 aimed to help, promote, and encourage research by providing a forum for interaction and exchanges among researchers, academics, and practitioners in the field. The conference welcomed papers on the design, development, evaluation, use, and impact of user interfaces, as well as standardization, policy, and other non-technological issues that facilitate and promote universal access.

Universal access is not a new topic in the field of human-computer interaction and information technology. Yet, in the new interaction environment shaped by current technological advancements, it becomes of prominent importance to ensure that individuals have access to interactive products and services that span a wide variety of everyday life domains and are used in fundamental human activities. The papers accepted to this year's UAHCI conference present research, methods, and practices addressing universal access issues related to user experience and interaction, and approaches targeted to provide appropriate interaction means to individuals with specific disabilities, but also issues related to extended reality – a prominent technological medium presenting novel accessibility challenges, as well as advancements in learning and education.

Two volumes of the HCII 2023 proceedings are dedicated to this year's edition of the UAHCI conference. The first part focuses on topics related to Design for All methods, tools and practice, interaction techniques, platforms and metaphors for Universal Access, understanding the Universal Access User Experience, as well as designing for children with Autism Spectrum Disorders. The second part focuses on topics related to Universal Access to XR, Universal Access to learning and education, and assistive environments and quality of life technologies.

Papers of these volumes are included for publication after a minimum of two single-blind reviews from the members of the UAHCI Program Board or, in some cases, from members of the Program Boards of other affiliated conferences. We would like to thank all of them for their invaluable contribution, support and efforts.

July 2023

Margherita Antona
Constantine Stephanidis

17th International Conference on Universal Access in Human-Computer Interaction (UAHCI 2023)

Program Board Chairs: **Margherita Antona**, *Foundation for Research and Technology - Hellas (FORTH), Greece* and **Constantine Stephanidis**, *University of Crete and Foundation for Research and Technology - Hellas (FORTH), Greece*

Program Board:

- João Barroso, *INESC TEC and UTAD, Portugal*
- Ingo Bosse, *Interkantonale Hochschule für Heilpädagogik (HFH), Switzerland*
- Laura Burzagli, *CNR, Italy*
- Pedro J.S. Cardoso, *University of Algarve, Portugal*
- Silvia Ceccacci, *University of Macerata, Italy*
- Nicole Darmawaskita, *Arizona State University, USA*
- Carlos Duarte, *Universidade de Lisboa, Portugal*
- Pier Luigi Emiliani, *National Research Council, Italy*
- Andrina Granic, *University of Split, Croatia*
- Gian Maria Greco, *Università di Macerata, Italy*
- Simeon Keates, *University of Chichester, UK*
- Georgios Kouroupetroglou, *National and Kapodistrian University of Athens, Greece*
- Barbara Leporini, *CNR-ISTI, Italy*
- John Magee, *Clark University, USA*
- Daniela Marghitu, *Auburn University, USA*
- Jorge Martín-Gutiérrez, *Universidad de La Laguna, Spain*
- Maura Mengoni, *Università Politecnica delle Marche, Italy*
- Silvia Mirri, *University of Bologna, Italy*
- Federica Pallavicini, *Università degli Studi di Milano-Bicocca, Italy*
- João M.F. Rodrigues, *University of Algarve, Portugal*
- Frode Eika Sandnes, *Oslo Metropolitan University, Norway*
- J. Andrés Sandoval-Bringas, *Universidad Autónoma de Baja California Sur, Mexico*
- Volker Sorge, *University of Birmingham, UK*
- Hiroki Takada, *University of Fukui, Japan*
- Philippe Truillet, *Université de Toulouse, France*
- Kevin Tseng, *National Taipei University of Technology, Taiwan*
- Gerhard Weber, *TU Dresden, Germany*

The full list with the Program Board Chairs and the members of the Program Boards of all thematic areas and affiliated conferences of HCII2023 is available online at:

http://www.hci.international/board-members-2023.php

HCI International 2024 Conference

The 26th International Conference on Human-Computer Interaction, HCI International 2024, will be held jointly with the affiliated conferences at the Washington Hilton Hotel, Washington, DC, USA, June 29 – July 4, 2024. It will cover a broad spectrum of themes related to Human-Computer Interaction, including theoretical issues, methods, tools, processes, and case studies in HCI design, as well as novel interaction techniques, interfaces, and applications. The proceedings will be published by Springer. More information will be made available on the conference website: http://2024.hci.international/.

General Chair
Prof. Constantine Stephanidis
University of Crete and ICS-FORTH
Heraklion, Crete, Greece
Email: general_chair@hcii2024.org

https://2024.hci.international/

Contents – Part II

Universal Access to Learning and Education

Assistive Environments and Quality of Life Technologies

Contents – Part I

Interaction Techniques, Platforms and Metaphors for Universal Access

Understanding the Universal Access User Experience

Designing for Children with Autism Spectrum Disorders

Universal Access to XR

A Method and Experimentation to Benchmark XR Technologies Enhancing Archeological Museum Experience

Thomas Agostinelli[1](✉)🆔, Andrea Generosi[1]🆔, Silvia Ceccacci[2]🆔,
Rosita Pretaroli[3]🆔, and Maura Mengoni[1]🆔

[1] Department of Industrial Engineering and Mathematical Sciences,
Università Politecnica delle Marche, via Brecce Bianche, 12, Ancona, AN 60131, Italy
`t.agostinelli@pm.univpm.it`

[2] Department of Education, Cultural Heritage and Tourism, Università degli Studi di
Macerata, Via Luigi Bertelli, 1, Macerata, MC 62100, Italy

[3] Department of Political Sciences, Communication and International Relations,
Università degli Studi di Macerata,
Via Don Giovanni Minzoni, 22/A, Macerata, MC 62100, Italy

Abstract. The use of eXtended Reality (XR) technologies, including
augmented reality (AR), virtual reality (VR), and mixed reality (MR),
has become increasingly popular in museums to enhance the visitor experience. However, the impact of XR technologies on Learning Performance
in the context of archeological museums needs to be better understood.
This study aims to investigate the relationships between Usability, Presence and Learning Performance by developing XR experiences showcasing archeological artefacts and conducting user testing to evaluate their
effectiveness. A laboratory test is conducted to compare a VR application
with a mobile AR one, presenting the digital models of five archeological
findings. Descriptive statistics are used to compare the two case studies, providing valuable insights into the impact of XR technologies on
the visitor experience from a learning perspective. The study confirms
that Usability has a more significant effect on learning than Presence
and can help designers and museum managers better understand the
factors contributing to a successful XR experience. The findings suggest
that while Presence is an important factor in improving visitors' experience, Usability should be the priority when designing XR experiences
for museums.

Keywords: Cultural heritage · XR Technologies · Technological
Benchmarking

1 Introduction

In recent years, the use of eXtended Reality (XR) technologies (which includes
augmented reality (AR), virtual reality (VR), and mixed reality (MR)) in museums have become increasingly popular as a way to enhance the visitor experience [1–5]. XR technologies provide visitors with immersive and interactive

M. Antona and C. Stephanidis (Eds.): HCII 2023, LNCS 14021, pp. 3–16, 2023.
https://doi.org/10.1007/978-3-031-35897-5_1

experiences that can engage them in a way that traditional museum exhibits cannot, offering an immersive experience that can enhance their understanding and appreciation of the historical and cultural significance of the artefacts. Archeological museums are unique cultural spaces that play a significant role in preserving and presenting human history. The challenge for museums is to find a balance between providing visitors with accurate information about the artefacts and making the experience engaging and entertaining. XR technologies can offer visitors a more immersive and engaging experience, enabling them to interact with artefacts in a previously impossible way. These technologies can also help visitors to learn more about archeology and history by making the exhibits more interactive and engaging. However, the impact of XR technologies on Learning Performance at the end of a museum visit needs a better understanding. There is a need to investigate whether an increased level of perceived Presence, i.e., the subjective experience of being in one place or environment, even when one is physically situated in another [6], is enough to improve visitors' ability and willingness to learn, or if designers should focus on other aspects, such as Usability. Furthermore, to the best of our knowledge, there are no studies investigating the relationships between Usability, Presence and Learning Performance in the context of XR technologies applied to the Cultural Heritage field. A method is developed to benchmark the technologies to address these challenges and determine the effectiveness of XR technologies in enhancing archeological museum experiences from a learning perspective. The method includes selecting a set of archeological artefacts, developing XR experiences showcasing the artefacts, and conducting user testing to evaluate the effectiveness of the XR experiences. The user testing includes surveys to gather data on XR experience Usability, conveyed Presence and Learning Performance at the end of the virtual museum visit.

1.1 Usability and Presence Evaluation for XR Technologies

The use of XR technologies in cultural heritage is a relatively new field, and the existing literature is limited. However, evidence suggests that XR technologies can enhance visitors' experience and Learning Performance. XR technologies can be classified based on their ability to convey a different degree of Immersion to the user as non-immersive, semi-immersive and immersive [7]. One of the main technological factors that affect user engagement with XR technologies is immersion [8], which refers to the extent to which a technological system can replicate natural perception and action through multisensory devices and tracking capabilities. Presence is crucial in determining the level of Immersion in a system [9]. Several authors evaluated Presence in XR experiences and assessed whether an increased level somehow affects the experience from a user standpoint. In [10], the authors assessed the effects of Presence (and, therefore, of Immersion) on the recall performance of industry workers trained in their manual assembly operations employing XR technologies. They found that, in such circumstances, a greater Presence is not beneficial to the recall performances. On the other hand, in [11], the authors found that in a similar context (aircraft maintenance training), the user group that showed higher performance was the one that performed the training on a high-level Presence VR platform. In [12], the effects of the use of augmented and virtual reality technologies on the visitor experience in a museum setting are evaluated, going to assess the Social Presence factor, described as "the extent to which other beings (living or synthetic) also exist in the virtual environment" [13]. In this context, Social Presence is evaluated as a strong predictor of the four realms of experience economy, i.e. education, entertainment, escape and aesthetics [14]. Following Pine's theory, museums should focus on providing a memorable experience, focusing on visitors and precisely the visitor experience, instead of marketing campaigns to increase visitor numbers.

Another key aspect affecting users' engagement with XR technologies (and, in general, with technological systems) is Usability. Usability is "the effectiveness, efficiency and satisfaction with which specified users can achieve specified goals in a particular environment" [15]. Schnack et al. [16] investigate the potential of using immersive virtual reality (iVR) technologies in a simulated virtual store to understand how they affect presence and Usability compared to the classic display on a PC screen, finding that the former is augmented while the latter is unchanged from classic keyboard and mouse use. In [17], the authors assessed the Usability of three gait disorders rehabilitation setups (non-immersive, semi-immersive and immersive). They found that using a combination of treadmill training and VR technologies can increase training motivation and outcomes, provided that the system, as a whole, demonstrates a high level of Usability. Similarly, [18], in a research on XR technologies used as a support tool for urban planning professionals, the authors state that among several AR and VR environments, those that have been evaluated as usable in professional practice are the same ones that have the highest Usability. Such environments do not have high usability complexities and resemble common practices and situations encountered in the tools traditionally used by these professionals. In addition, [19] presents a comparative evaluation of different virtual machines through user studies. However, the study is primarily focused on system interface Usability as the basis for comparison.

However, while it is widely understood that Usability and Presence can greatly impact visitor experience, it is still being determined how they can affect one of the key aspects of a museum visit: the Learning Performance. Few studies investigate the relationships between Presence, Usability and Learning Performance. In [20], the authors conducted a study on users watching an interactive drama and found that increasing perceived Presence did not necessarily lead to increased user engagement. In [21], the researchers involved users in a virtual reality training setting to teach them how to perform a procedural task and found that the effects of Usability on Engagement were more statistically significant than those of Presence. Finally, [22] surveyed users of an interactive museum and theorized that Usability positively influences Engagement, which positively influences Learning Performance. While these studies provide interesting theoretical insights, none assessed XR technologies in the Cultural Heritage field or provided a comprehensive model useful to assess the impact of XR technologies on visitor experience and learning outcomes.

1.2 Research Aim

This study investigates the impact of two of the most commercialized XR technologies (Virtual Reality and Augmented Reality) on museum visitors' experience quality and Learning Performance, focusing on the relationships between Usability, Presence, and Learning Performance. This research is a preliminary study to confirm the hypothesis that Usability has a more significant effect on Learning Performance than Presence. The hypothesis is validated through a laboratory test, comparing a VR application with a mobile AR one, simulating a real archeological museum presenting the digital models of five archeological artefacts. Every virtual artefact is accompanied by a written text describing the finding, which the user can choose to show or hide, and an audio guide whose playback is freely playable or stoppable by the user. The two case studies are compared in terms of descriptive statistics, providing useful insights for researchers to improve the experimental setup for future works and especially valuable insights into the impact of XR technologies on the visitor experience from a learning perspective. By investigating the relationships between Usability, Presence and Learning Performance, this study can help designers and museum managers better understand the factors contributing to a successful XR experience.

2   Material and Methods

The developed applications consist of the virtual simulation of a museum environment, one developed using Virtual Reality (VR) technology and the other using Augmented Reality (AR) technology. Both depict five digital archeological artefacts: their original copies are kept at the National Archeological Museum of the Marche in Ancona, Italy. The five artefacts (depicted in Fig. 1), listed in chronological order of antiquity, are:

– Statuette (Venus) of Frasassi, stalactite figurine attributable to a period
  between 28000 and 20000 years ago
– Bronze dagger, datable between 2000 B.C. and 1700 B.C.
– Kylix, datable between 470 B.C. and 460 A.D.
– Pyxis, datable to about 460 B.C.
– Augusto capite velato, datable between 12 BC and 14 AD.

The digital models of the artefacts are obtained from the originals by combining laser scanning for the accurate acquisition of the geometries of the artefacts and photogrammetry, which allows the acquisition of photorealistic textures to be applied to the digital models. The two applications share the same artefacts and, therefore, the same digital reproductions.

The applications are structured from a common base. In addition to sharing digital models of the exhibits, both contain a UI (User Interface) that provides virtual museum visitors with information about the artefact they are viewing. Specifically, there is a brief textual description to the right of each artefact. The description is not always visible on the screen, but users can decide whether to display it according to their taste. A button shows or hides the description: pressing it causes the text to enter the scene with an animation reminiscent of the unrolling of parchment, a metaphor reinforced by the sound effect of unrolling paper. Pressing the button again causes the text to roll upward until it disappears. On the opposite side, a media player allows the visitor to play, pause or stop an audio guide, that is, a recorded voice accompanied by a light musical base that reads the same text in the textual description. There is also a slider that adjusts the volume of the audio. Completing the picture is the sound effect of a hubbub typical of the halls of a museum, which is useful in returning greater immersiveness to the user (since the tests did not take place at the halls of a real museum).

Fig. 1. The included archeological findings. From left to right: Statuette of Frasassi, Bronze dagger, Kylix, Pyxis, Augusto capite velato.

2.1 AR Application

The AR application is an Android app installed on a 10.4-inch diagonal screen RealME Pad tablet, developed on Unity ver. 2020.3.20f1. AR features are implemented through the Vuforia Engine SDK.

During use, the user, holding the tablet with the app open, can frame one of the target images (representing each of the artefacts present) at will. Once the image is framed, the app projects the digital model of the artefact resting on top of a marble plinth above it. Contextually, for the same artefact observed by the user, the application loads an audio track with the audio guide and a textual description. The user can freely explore the artefact by walking around it and moving away or closer to it simply by walking in the real world around the target image. The UI is interacted with via the tablet's touchscreen. A screenshot of the application is depicted in Fig. 2.

Fig. 2. A screenshot of the AR application

2.2 VR Application

The VR application is installed on a Meta Quest 2 headset used in standalone mode. Development is performed on Unity ver. 2020.3.20f1 leveraging the XR Interaction Toolkit plugin to implement motion and interactions and the Oculus XR plugin that supports Meta (formerly Oculus) visor displays and controllers.

The user is fully immersed in a virtual room with a parquet floor, black walls, and roof. A soft, warm light illuminates the room. The environment is designed in a minimalist style to keep the user's attention on the artefacts. Along the four walls and in the centre of the room are five pedestals, above which the artefacts are placed. At the base of each pedestal is a square emitting a faint blue light, so it is distinguishable within the scene. By pointing the left or right controller at one of the squares and pressing the Grab button, the application teleports the user to the vicinity of the artefact. To avoid or at least mitigate possible effects of cybersickness, a tunnelling transition is initiated during teleportation to ease the user's otherwise instantaneous transition from one position to another. Once near the pedestal, the user can freely walk around it within a circumference with a radius of 1 m centred on the pedestal. Outside this boundary, the application stops, and the headset switches to see-through mode, thanks to the cameras installed on it, to avoid the risk of the visitor colliding with other people or physical obstacles that may be present. The VR UI behaves differently than the AR one: it is fixed in space in the virtual world around each artefact rather than fixed to the user's viewpoint and always visible, even when not framing an artefact. There are thus five instances of the UI, one for each artefact, activated only when the user is near one of the exhibits, while the other four remain

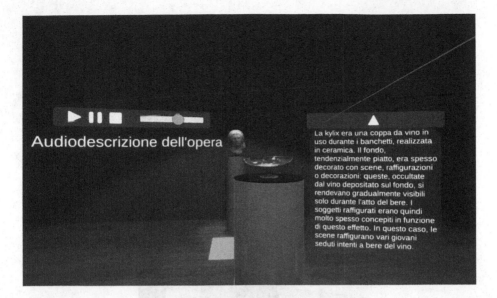

Fig. 3. A screenshot of the VR application

invisible. This solution is adopted to avoid potential cybersickness effects since there is evidence that, when using VR devices, a UI that follows the user and is always present in the user's field of view can cause nausea. The controls in the UI are interacted with by pointing it with either controller and pressing the Trigger button. The two halves of the UI are not parallel but rather slightly tilted toward the users in a way that "surrounds" them, increasing the sense of Immersion. A screenshot of the application is depicted in Fig. 3.

3 Experimental Procedure

The tests occurred at the Polytechnic University of Marche during an outreach event. This event made it possible to select a heterogeneous sample of different cultural backgrounds, although centred around an age range of 20-25 years. The researchers were present at a banquet where they showcased AR and VR technologies, and test users were selected on a voluntary basis from those who approached the banquet to ask questions and express curiosity. The moderately crowded environment of the classrooms at which the event took place provided an opportunity to conduct the tests in an environment full of sounds and possible distractions, as might occur in a real museum. Users were equally split between the two technologies to have an equal distribution. Each group (AR and VR) counted 22 users. Virtual museum visitors could freely explore the applications without time constraints: tests' duration never exceeded 10 min, with an average of 5.

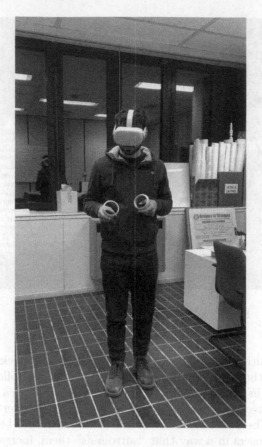

Fig. 4. A user testing the VR application

Usability, Presence and Learning Performance were measured employing a questionnaire divided into four sections, administered at the end of the test of interest. The questionnaire includes four sections:

- section 0: demographic data
- section I: System Usability Scale (SUS)
- section II: Presence
- section III: verification of the learned concepts

Sections I (SUS) [23] and II (Presence) [24] are questionnaires already validated and widely adopted in the literature. Instead, the Section on Learning Performance is a questionnaire developed by the authors, tailored to test the learning of some simple notions regarding the descriptive content of the artefacts. It consists of five questions, one for each displayed artefact, structured in multiple-choice format with only one correct answer for each question. The order of the answers is randomized, so any communication between the subjects could not distort the results. The five questions, and their answers, are listed below (the bold test marks correct answers):

- How was the statuette made?
  - By working a stalagmite
  - **By working a stalactite**
  - By working pure calcite layers found within the Frasassi Caves
  - By reusing a scrap of limestone used for another statuette
- Where was the dagger found?
  - **In the municipality of Ripatransone in the province of Ascoli Piceno**
  - In the municipality of Genga in the province of Ancona
  - Near the church of S. Michele Arcangelo in the province of Ancona
  - In the crypt of the Abbey of S. Firmano in the province of Macerata
- What was the Kylix?
  - A vessel used to hold and pour liquids, mainly water
  - **A wine cup used for drinking**
  - A jar with a lid, used to hold cosmetics
  - A large vessel used for mixing wine and water
- What is the scene depicted on the Pyxis?
  - The birth of Zeus
  - **The birth of Aphrodite**
  - The birth of Athena from the head of Zeus
  - The abduction of Persephone
- Augustus is depicted:
  - Before he assumed the office of pontifex maximus, represented with veiled head
  - **After assuming the office of pontifex maximus, represented with the veiled head**
  - Before assuming the office of pontifex maximus, represented with the lorìca (the armor of the legionaries)
  - After assuming the office of pontifex maximus, represented with the lorìca (the armor of the legionaries)

4   Results

The answers from the questionnaire are analyzed to assess whether the differences between the AR and the VR applications are statistically significant and to investigate possible correlations between Usability, Presence and Learning Performance. Given that the data do not follow a normal distribution, a Mann-Whitney U Test is performed to assess the differences. Results are in Table 1.

The test highlights that Usability (SUS), Presence and Learning Performance (Score) show statistically significant differences between the two groups of users (AR and VR), given that for all three of them, $p-value < 0.05$. In particular, AR is the application that results in the best Learning Performance score, showing a 26% higher mean when compared to the VR application. Moreover, AR also

Table 1. Mann-Whitney U Test

	U-value	p-value	Test results
SUS	312	0.001	$p-value < 0.05$
Presence	187.5	0.010	$p-value < 0.05$
Score	286.5	0.031	$p-value < 0.05$

Table 2. Descriptive statistics for the three measured metrics

Score			
AR		VR	
Mean	2.41	Mean	1.91
Median	2.00	Median	2.00
Standard Deviation	1.50	Standard Deviation	1.48
SUS			
AR		VR	
Mean	85.23	Mean	79.20
Median	86.25	Median	77.50
Standard Deviation	10.41	Standard Deviation	12.04
Presence			
AR		VR	
Mean	4.70	Mean	5.24
Median	4.88	Median	5.38
Standard Deviation	1.36	Standard Deviation	1.26

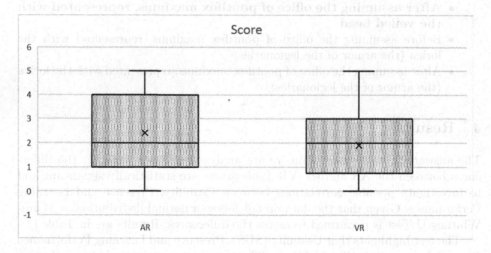

Fig. 5. Comparison between AR and VR Score

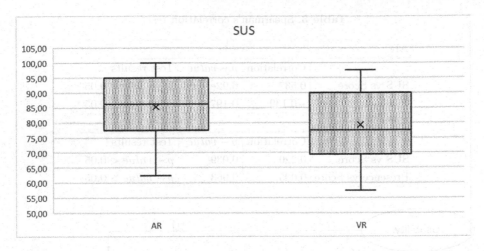

Fig. 6. Comparison between AR and VR SUS

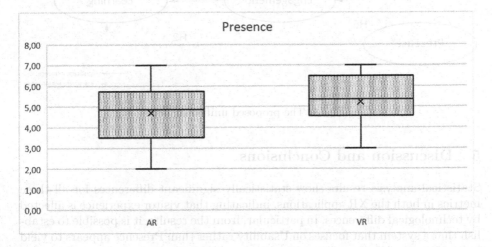

Fig. 7. Comparison between AR and VR Presence

results in the best Usability, with a 7.60% higher performance than VR. Finally, as expected, VR shows a higher Presence level than AR (+11.35%). The results are presented in greater detail in Table 2, while Fig. 5, Fig. 6 and Fig. 7 show a graphical representation of such results.

A Spearman test is performed regarding correlations between SUS and Score and between Presence and Score for AR and VR. As shown in Table 3, the test shows a positive correlation between SUS and Score for both the AR application ($r = 0.537, p-value = 6.92e-8$) and the VR application ($r = 0.220, p-value = 0.039$). However, the latter is a weaker correlation. On the contrary, Presence and Score show no correlations, given that their $p - value$ is higher than 0.05 for both applications. Details are shown in Table 3.

Table 3. Spearman's correlation test

AR			
	Correlation	$p - value$	Test results
SUS vs Score	0.537	$6.92e - 08$	$p - value < 0.05$
Presence vs Score	-0.139	0.197	$p - value > 0.05$
VR			
	Correlation	$p - value$	Test results
SUS vs Score	0.220	0.039	$p - value < 0.05$
Presence vs Score	0.005	0.963	$p - value > 0.05$

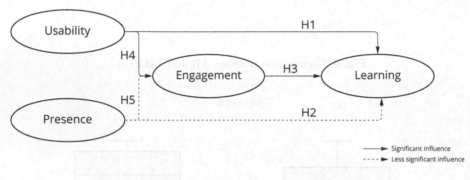

Fig. 8. The proposed unified model

5   Discussion and Conclusions

Statistical analysis results show statistically significant differences for all three metrics in both the XR applications, indicating that visitor experience is affected by technological differences. In particular, from the results, it is possible to establish that a system that focuses on Usability rather than Presence appears to yield better Learning Performance because:

– Usability and Learning Performance show a positive correlation, while Presence and Learning Performance show no correlation
– The system with the greatest Usability also shows the best Learning performance.

The study confirms the hypothesis that Usability has a more significant effect on Learning Performance than Presence. Usability and Learning Performance have a positive correlation. In contrast, Presence does not have a significant effect. Overall, the study provides valuable insights into using XR technologies to enhance museum visitors' experience and Learning Performance. The findings suggest that while Presence is an important factor in improving visitors' experience, the priority in designing XR experiences for museums should be Usability. Additionally, the study highlights the potential of XR technologies in creating immersive and engaging museum experiences. However, further research is needed to explore the effectiveness of different XR technologies in enhancing Learning Performance.

The proposal of a unified model, summarizing the theoretical findings from previous studies, will be the topic of future works. Based on the reviewed literature and the outcomes of the present paper, the authors formulated the following hypothesis: Usability positively influences Learning in museums XR experiences (H1); Presence does not affect Learning in museums XR experiences as much as Usability does (H2); Engagement positively affects Learning in museums XR experiences (H3); Usability positively affects Engagement in museums XR experiences (H4); Presence does not affect Engagement in museums XR experiences as much as Usability does (H5). Engagement, while not included in the present study, will be evaluated in future work, as it is frequently mentioned in related research. The validation of the model will require laboratory tests assessing the four metrics (Usability, Presence, Engagement, and Learning Performance). The hypothesized model is depicted in Fig. 8.

References

1. Carrozzino, M., Bergamasco, M.: Beyond virtual museums: experiencing immersive virtual reality in real museums. J. Cultural Heritage **11**(4), 452–458 (2010)
2. Noh, Z., Sunar, M.S., Pan, Z.: A review on augmented reality for virtual heritage system. In Learning by Playing. Game-based Education System Design and Development: 4th International Conference on E-Learning and Games, Edutainment 2009, Banff, Canada,9-11 August 2009. Proceedings 4, pp. 50-61. Springer Berlin, (2009). https://doi.org/10.1007/978-3-642-03364-3_7
3. Rua, H., Alvito, P.: Living the past: 3D models, virtual reality and game engines as tools for supporting archaeology and the reconstruction of cultural heritage-the case-study of the Roman villa of Casal de Freiria. J. Archaeol. Sci. **38**(12), 3296–3308 (2011)
4. He, Z., Wu, L., Li, X.R.: When art meets tech: The role of augmented reality in enhancing museum experiences and purchase intentions. Tourism Manag. **68**, 127–139 (2018)
5. Leopardi, A., Ceccacci, S., Mengoni, M.: Dynamic projection for the design of an adaptive museum guide. In: Rizzi, C., Andrisano, A.O., Leali, F., Gherardini, F., Pini, F., Vergnano, A. (eds.) ADM 2019. LNME, pp. 85–94. Springer, Cham (2020). https://doi.org/10.1007/978-3-030-31154-4_8
6. Witmer, B.G., Singer, M.J.: Measuring presence in virtual environments: A presence questionnaire. Presence **7**(3), 225–240 (1998)
7. Burdea, G.C., Coiffet, P.: Virtual Reality Technology. John Wiley & Sons (2003)
8. Nilsson, N., Nordahl, R., Serafin, S.: Immersion revisited: A review of existing definitions of immersion and their relation to different theories of presence. Hum. Technol. **12**(2), 108 (2016)
9. Bowman, D.A., McMahan, R.P.: Virtual reality: how much immersion is enough? Computer **40**(7), 36–43 (2007)
10. Generosi, A., Agostinelli, T., Mengoni, M., Ceccacci, S.: Augmented Reality for assembly operation training: does immersion affect the recall performance?. In: 2022 IEEE International Conference on Metrology for Extended Reality, Artificial Intelligence and Neural Engineering (MetroXRAINE), pp. 58–63. IEEE (October 2022)

11. Lee, H., Woo, D., Yu, S.: Virtual reality metaverse system supplementing remote education methods: Based on aircraft maintenance simulation. Appli. Sci. **12**(5), 2667 (2022)
12. Jung, T., tom Dieck, M.C., Lee, H., Chung, N.: Effects of virtual reality and augmented reality on visitor experiences in museum. In: Inversini, A., Schegg, R. (eds.) Information and Communication Technologies in Tourism 2016, pp. 621–635. Springer, Cham (2016). https://doi.org/10.1007/978-3-319-28231-2_45
13. Schuemie, M.J., Van Der Straaten, P., Krijn, M., Van Der Mast, C.A.: Research on presence in virtual reality: A survey. Cyberpsychol. Behav. **4**(2), 183–201 (2001)
14. Pine, B. J., Gilmore, J.H.: Welcome to the experience economy, vol. 76(40), pp. 97–105. Harvard Business Review Press (1998)
15. Brooke, J., Bevan, N., Brigham, F., Harker, S., Youmans, D.: Usability statements and standardisation: Work in progress in ISO. In: Proceedings of the IFIP TC13 Third Interational Conference on Human-Computer Interaction, pp. 357–361 (August 1990)
16. Schnack, A., Wright, M.J., Holdershaw, J.L.: Immersive virtual reality technology in a three-dimensional virtual simulated store: Investigating telepresence and usability. Food Res. Int. **117**, 40–49 (2019)
17. Winter, C., Kern, F., Gall, D., Latoschik, M.E., Pauli, P., Käthner, I.: Immersive virtual reality during gait rehabilitation increases walking speed and motivation: a usability evaluation with healthy participants and patients with multiple sclerosis and stroke. J. Neuroeng. Rehabilit. **18**(1), 68 (2021)
18. Rzeszewski, M., Orylski, M.: Usability of WebXR visualizations in urban planning. ISPRS Int. J. Geo-Inform. **10**(11), 721 (2021)
19. Barbieri, L., Bruno, F., Muzzupappa, M.: Virtual museum system evaluation through user studies. J. Cultural Heritage **26**, 101–108 (2017)
20. Dow, S., Mehta, M., Harmon, E., MacIntyre, B., Mateas, M.: Presence and engagement in an interactive drama. In: Proceedings of the SIGCHI Conference on Human Factors In Computing Systems, pp. 1475–1484 (April 2007)
21. Schroeder, B.L., Bailey, S.K.T., Johnson, C.I., Gonzalez-Holland, E.: Presence and usability do not directly predict procedural recall in virtual reality training. In: Stephanidis, C. (ed.) HCI 2017. CCIS, vol. 714, pp. 54–61. Springer, Cham (2017). https://doi.org/10.1007/978-3-319-58753-0_9
22. Pallud, J.: Impact of interactive technologies on stimulating learning experiences in a museum. Inform. Manag. **54**(4), 465–478 (2017)
23. Brooke, J.: SUS-A quick and dirty usability scale. Usability Evaluat. Indus. **189**(194), 4–7 (1996)
24. Georgiou, Y., Kyza, E.A.: The development and validation of the ARI questionnaire: an instrument for measuring immersion in location-based augmented reality settings. Int. J. Hum.-Comput. Stud. **98**, 24–37 (2017)

Preliminary Findings About an Office Chair as a Low-Threshold Treadmill Substitute

Thomas Keller[1]([⊠]) [iD], Sacha Guyer[1] [iD], Vanessa Manoharan[1], and Ingo Bosse[2] [iD]

[1] ZHAW Institute of Business Information Technology, Winterthur, Switzerland
kell@zhaw.ch
[2] Competence Center ICT for Inclusion, HfH University of Teacher Education in Special Needs, Zürich, Switzerland

Abstract. A treadmill is a peripheral device enabling players in an immersive virtual world a rather intuitive way to move around. The body is fixed and secured around the waist whilst the legs can freely simulate a walking or even running movement. The hands usually hold controllers to interact with the virtual world. Such a human machine interaction is powerful and at the same time demands a high degree of concentration. Usually, a learning phase is required for players that are not familiarized with such a concept. In a project with children with special needs this challenge has prevented an easy introduction of a treadmill. To overcome this problem the children were then asked to use the treadmill without VR-glasses. In a second step VR-glasses were introduced while the children were sitting on a chair. The final step combined then treadmill and glasses but with limited success. This paper introduces another approach based on an ordinary office chair to facilitate and enabling a stepwise learning experience. Children with special needs are equipped with additional tracked markers at their feet. If the children are shuffling feet a movement is calculated. In such a way a risk-free movement in a virtual world is enabled without any costly equipment. At the same time this experience can be considered a promising intermediate step towards the use of a treadmill which will open an even better immersive experience. This paper gives an introduction of the experimental setup and disseminates preliminary findings.

Keywords: Access to education and learning · Accessible Virtual and Augmented Reality · Design for All education and training · Design for Children with and without disabilities · Design for Cognitive Disabilities

1 Introduction

Virtual reality (VR) is slowly making its way into schools for isolated use cases (Berger et al. 2022; Curcio 2022; Keller et al. 2018, 2022). One possible reason is that the investment costs for hardware have only fallen recently and the availability of software has improved and can be considered mature today. At the same time, the importance of VR in the lifeworld of children and adolescents is increasing: In order to be able to get to know the opportunities and risks associated with VR in a safe framework, media education work in schools is a good place to start. It is important to teach competencies

© The Author(s), under exclusive license to Springer Nature Switzerland AG 2023
M. Antona and C. Stephanidis (Eds.): HCII 2023, LNCS 14021, pp. 17–28, 2023.
https://doi.org/10.1007/978-3-031-35897-5_2

for growing up with digital media and specifically for VR in our context. Virtual worlds of experience enable new teaching and learning concepts and are part of the canon of current media education (Buchner 2022). The question of impact also raises the question of a possible increase in learning through this technology. Studies with different results are currently available on this (for an overview, see Zender (2018)). Numerous research results indicate that students and teachers can be significantly supported by VR.

The project "Virtual Reality for Children with Special Needs" (Bosse et al. 2022) addresses students on the autistic spectrum as well as students with other diagnoses in the special focus of mental development. In the field of school-based special and inclusive education, the use of virtual reality is still less widespread than in general education, but is becoming increasingly important, including for students with autism spectrum disorders (Bradley & Newbutt 2018; Schulz & Skeide Fuglerud, 2022) and with intellectual impairments (Bjelic & Keller 2021; Ip et al. 2018).

One of the three use cases concerned safety training in virtual worlds using a treadmill for an intuitive locomotion and the safe accomplishment of daily routine tasks while walking, e.g., independent exploration of places and solving of adapted tasks, safe exploration of waters. This use case was chosen because the school is located somewhat remotely in the rural area of Weinfelden. Therefore, it requires a considerable amount of time and organization to acquire action skills in order to move safely in traffic. Therefore, in addition to the excursions into urban traffic, the students should be offered additional opportunities to experience demanding situations in VR. The introduction of a treadmill turned out to be a challenge which led to the approach described in this paper.

2 Objective

A treadmill (Fig. 1) is a peripheral device enabling players in an immersive virtual world a rather intuitive way to move around. The body is fixed and secured around the waist whilst the legs can freely simulate a walking or even running movement. The hands usually hold controllers to interact with the virtual world. Such a human machine interaction is powerful and at the same time demands a high degree of concentration. Usually, a learning phase is required for players that are not familiarized with such a concept. In the above mentioned project (Bosse et al. 2022) with children with special needs, this challenge has prevented an easy introduction of a treadmill. To overcome this problem the children were then asked to use the treadmill without VR-glasses. In a second step VR-glasses were introduced while the children were sitting on a chair. The final step combined then treadmill and glasses but with limited success. This paper introduces another approach based on an ordinary office chair to facilitate and enabling a stepwise learning experience. Children with special needs are equipped with two additional tracked markers on both of their feet. A third marker is attached to an ordinary office chair which becomes a physical object in the virtual world. If the children are shuffling feet a forward or backward movement is calculated. In such a way a risk-free movement in a virtual world is enabled without any costly equipment. At the same time this experience can be considered a promising intermediate step towards the use of a treadmill which will open an even better immersive experience.

Fig. 1. The omnidirectional treadmill used in (Bosse et al. 2022)

In the context outlined above the research question addresses design criteria for VR applications that facilitate and support the "onboarding" process. Specifically, we investigate in low-cost possibilities that allow a step-by-step introduction to the world of VR. This paper introduces the office chair as a low-cost approach and investigates necessary design criterias that meet the needs of the children and adolescents.

From a computer science perspective an evolutionary prototyping approach is applied. This approach meets very well the inclusion principle (Bosse & Pelka 2020) of the application domain. We follow the steps promoted by the design thinking process (Plattner et al. 2012).

3 Methodology

Methodologically, the prototype development is based on an iterative research and development cycle that is often used in the context of social innovation and was adapted for people with disabilities in the SELFMADE project (Bosse & Pelka 2020). The methodological insights generated in the SELFMADE project can be transferred to this project. The method is also geared towards self-determination and participation of people with disabilities.

The features of the prototype is identified based on a needs analysis. In the needs analysis, the project uses a User Centered Design approach linked to a Design Thinking process (Elizabeth B.-N. Sanders 2002). This allows the prototype to be identified, tested, and adapted through a co-creation process. During the process, experiences gathered during the development of each prototype version are incorporated into the design of the following prototype version. With this process, evolutionary prototypes (Sherrell 2013) are created in an iterative cycle based on the principles of design thinking (Plattner et al. 2012).

A total of 6 people were involved in three design thinking workshops. The girls and boys come from different classes at the Vivala school[1] and are between the ages of 10 and 16. There are often diagnoses on the autism spectrum, as well as frequent developmental delays in mental development, and specific syndromes that affect individual participants. The following steps of design thinking are used.

- Understanding: The first step focuses on understanding the problem. This leads to an appropriate question that defines the needs and challenges.
- Observation: to gain important insights and define the status quo, intensive search and field observation follows.
- Point of view: individual needs are clearly defined in a question.
- Brainstorming to develop and visualize different concepts.
- Prototyping: to test and demonstrate the ideas, first customized virtual reality.
- Refinement: Based on the findings from the prototype, the concept is further improved and refined until a better optimized, user-centric product is developed. This iteration step can be applied to all previous steps.

Design methods are already well established in co-creation contexts. Among other benefits, some of them improve development processes by bringing in a user-centered perspective. This specific approach is a good starting point for an inclusive development process. A user-centered approach makes it possible to consider the perspective and thus the needs and capabilities of a solution's target group.

In the first phase, all participants were introduced to the Design Thinking process in a workshop at the school, which was adapted to the needs and abilities of the students. Technically, the design thinking process is a prototyping approach. Each iteration of the design thinking process is accompanied by an iteration of prototyping the use cases. The evolving experimental prototype is then used as input for the next iteration of the Design Thinking process.

4 State of the Art

Existing reviews of applications of immersive virtual reality in the field of education can be found, e.g., in (Bradley & Newbutt 2018; Jensen & Konradsen 2018; Lorenzo et al. 2019; Maas & Hughes 2020). Reviews with a focus on children with special needs can be found, e.g., in (Carreon et al. 2022; Tzanavari et al. 2015). Older literature concerning this focus are, e.g., (Jeffs 2010; Parsons & Cobb 2011). The above mentioned project (Bosse et al. 2022) which motivated this work also adds to the current state of the art. An even more focused search on immersive virtual reality, children with special needs, and peripheral devices like a treadmill or a motion simulator exhibit works related to medical treatment or rehabilitation after a disease, e.g., as in (Moreira et al. 2013; Peruzzi et al. 2017), which don't cover the main application domain of our work. We only found an older research work focusing on physical fitness of people with special needs (Lotan et al. 2010). Since virtual reality technology has improved considerably since 2010 the findings may be of limited relevance for today's situation.

---

[1] https://www.vivala.ch/.

Obviously, there is no existing work as to our knowledge that covers our field of research. That means how to onboard children with special needs to immersive virtual reality for a use case consisting of an omnidirectional treadmill.

However, literature gives hints about the potentials and challenges related to virtual reality and its impact on the learning process. A comprehensive summary can be found in (Keller et al. 2022) as well as the previous mentioned literature. In short, virtual reality has an added value for action competencies but must be based on a sound didactical concept. Furthermore, virtual reality as a means for learning must be well embedded in existing curricula and necessary infrastructure must be available. Immersive virtual reality in the standard classroom may be prone to failure.

5   Design of the Prototype

The crucial capabilities of our replacement of the treadmill by an office chair was to detect rotation and movement. To implement the prototype, tracking the positions of the feet and the rotation of the chair was necessary. We chose the HTC Vive platform[2] because it supports additional trackers (Fig. 2) next to the normal head and hand trackers. We attached one tracker to each foot of the user (Fig. 3) and one tracker at the back of the office chair (Fig. 4) using elastic bands.

The HTC Vive platform makes use of lasers coming from so called lighthouses mounted above the player. We initially had used the default 2 lighthouses, but the tracker at the back of the chair was often not visible from both lighthouses, leading to errors in the calculation of the chair rotation. By using 3 lighthouses we could overcome this problem.

Fig. 2. Three Vive Trackers with bluetooth dongles

---

[2] https://www.vive.com.

Fig. 3. Vive Trackers attached to feet

Fig. 4. Office chair with Vive Tracker attached to back

On the software side, we used **Unity**[3] (2021.3.9f1) and the **SteamVR_TrackedObject**[4] class of the **OpenVR XR** Plugin for accessing the trackers. Adding SteamVR_TrackedObject as component to a game object will move and rotate it based on the position and orientation of the tracker in the real world.

The SteamVR_TrackedObject can be configured with a device index to specify which of the connected trackers should be used. The device indices are assigned when the trackers are turned on and thus can change after each startup of the machine. This is very tedious because either attention must be paid on the order how the devices are turned on, or the indices have to be adjusted after each startup. To overcome this issue, we found **SteamVR_TrackedObject_Plus**[5] which is an adjusted version of SteamVR_TrackedObject that allows to set the serial number of the trackers. Upon start, all connected trackers are checked, and the device id is set according to the defined serial number. With this, the serial numbers need to be set only once and no configuration is needed upon start of the machine.

To represent the chair in virtual reality, we used a simple office chair model from the unity asset store. For a human to sit on the chair, we used the "pilot" model from the **Final IK**[6] unity asset.

This asset supports additional game objects for the feet and calculates a plausible overall body pose using inverse kinematics. We observed that using the two feet trackers in addition to the two hand controllers and the headset created a realistic pose of the model when the user was sitting in the chair. The position of the chair object was set to the center of the pilot model. One possibility for the rotation of the chair would have been to derive it from the rotation of the pilot model. However, this had the effect that rotating the head would also rotate the chair, which was an unnatural behavior. A better approach was to detect the orientation of the chair from a tracker at the back of the chair. The Euler angle corresponding to the vertical direction was read from the Vive Tracker and applied to the chair model. With the mechanisms described above, the chair model could be rotated and was always placed at the position of the model.

---

[3] https://unity.com.

[4] https://valvesoftware.github.io/steamvr_unity_plugin/api/Valve.VR.SteamVR_TrackedObject.html.

[5] https://gist.github.com/jeffcrouse/50cada719e7b6f9201fc29802a427da4.

[6] https://assetstore.unity.com/packages/tools/animation/final-ik-14290.

Our first approach for detecting a movement from the foot trackers was to define an active state for a foot. This active state was reached when the foot was lifted above and again lowered below a threshold. The threshold was chosen in such a way that the user could reach the active state by lifting its foot from the ground and putting it back at a different position. When in active state, we measured the movement vector in the horizontal plane in each frame. The active state was left if the user changed the movement direction from forward to backward or vice versa. This behavior was applied to both feet independently and the sum of both movement vectors was calculated. We then took the magnitude of this vector and detected if the movement was in forward or backward direction. We used the **CharacterController.Move(Vector3 motion)** method to apply the movement to the pilot model. While it would be possible to move the character in any direction, we restricted ourselves to only move it along the chair forward/backward direction vector. By doing so, the user could navigate forward by iteratively lifting one foot near the chair, putting it down in front of the chair and shuffle it back. Moving backwards was possible by lifting the foot in front of the chair, putting it down close to the chair and shuffle away from the chair. We called this movement mode **Vertical Activation**.

In our second approach we simplified the logic and restricted the movement to the forward direction only. A forward movement was detected as soon as the sum of the movement magnitudes of the feet was above a certain threshold. The direction of the movement was not considered. With this approach, it was not necessary to lift the feet from the ground anymore. The movement magnitude could be configured to either be constant when the feet were moving, or it could be dependent on how fast the feet were moving. This movement mode was called **Wiggle**.

6 The Laboratory Experiments

During the development of the office chair prototype we had in total four children that were giving feedback on the usability. These four children did not have any experience on the treadmill. At the same time we had six children that were exposed to the treadmill and which had some difficulties at various degrees. All of these six children were then invited to test out the office chair. At the same time the four children already trained with the office chair were then exposed to the treadmill. The treadmill scene (Fig. 5) was different from the two scenes with the office chair. The motivation for this scene setup was road safety education for children with special needs. Our findings are based on observations during the intervention and on interviews just after the intervention finished.

6.1 The Virtual Worlds for the Experiments

As a first environment to test the navigation with the office chair we designed a simple playground scene with a pavement around a tree and a sandbox model (Fig. 6). The goal was to walk on the pavement around the objects. With this setup we could test how navigation of the office chair was perceived.

Fig. 5. The city scene for road safety education

We invited four children from Vivala for two separate sessions to test the office chair. They managed to navigate around the objects without problems. However, they found it dull, so that we designed another scene that should be more interesting. The second scene (Fig. 7) was a larger parcours where we added some features to make it more interesting. The user would start the parcours by walking over a bridge and should pay attention not to fall off. After falling from the bridge, the user had to start from the beginning. On the bridge, there were some chickens that ran away as the user approached them. After the bridge, we created a life size bowling alley (Fig. 8). When the user touched the bowling ball it was launched in the direction of the bowling pins. There were two special areas where the bowling pins and the bowling ball could be reset by walking into them. We designed them to be a few steps apart from each other to motivate the user to walk from one place to the other.

6.2 Findings

Additional children from the Vivala school tested the office chair in both worlds (Fig. 9). There was no hesitation to use the office chair and no signs of cyber sickness while using the office chair. Also, none of them were afraid to use the office chair, and all of them were able to quickly start exploring the world.

Using the Vertical Activation movement mode was exhausting after a short time for the legs and consequently the feet were not lifted high enough anymore to activate the movement. The observation of this behavior motivated the implementation of the other mode. The Wiggle mode was less tiring for the legs and was preferred by the users. A limitation of the Wiggle mode is that walking backwards with the office chair is not possible. However, this was not considered as a disadvantage by our test subjects.

Fig. 6. Simple playground scene with gray pavement around a tree and a sandbox

Fig. 7. Vivala Parcours with bridge and bowling alley

One possible benefit of using the office chair is that the movement and rotation is operated by the body so that the head and hands are free to simultaneously do other things. For our test scenarios the hand controllers did not have any functionality apart from tracking the hand position and rotation. This also can be achieved by visual hand

Fig. 8. Detail view of the bowling alley with pin and ball reset areas

Fig. 9. Child using the office chair

tracking which opens up complete freedom for the hands. This may be a very crucial feature for certain disabilities.

Finally, the four children which were involved in the prototyping process of the office chair also tried out the treadmill. Although the virtual world differed from the office chair scenes they showed in general less difficulties to trust the treadmill and wearing the head mounted displays at the same time.

7 Conclusion

The use of virtual reality for children and adolescents with special needs is as diverse as the field of special education itself and the people it serves. People with special needs often have problems with attention, language, spatial skills, memory, reasoning, and knowledge acquisition. Virtual environments specifically promote action-based learning and provide learners with a variety of ways to control their individual learning process. However, to make the potential of VR available, a low-threshold entry point must be offered. For our context, we use the office chair as an element to provide a low-threshold entry point. Our experiments show that an office chair is indeed perceived as lower threshold than a treadmill. Locomotion via the movement of the feet was perceived as intuitive. The possibility of rotation around one's own axis did not lead to any orientation difficulties. Likewise, the risk of cybersickness seems to be lower than with locomotion without movement of the feet. Children with an office chair training profit from an easier onboarding on a treadmill. However, these observations are still based on a very small number of subjects and must therefore be viewed with caution. Additionally, the heterogeneity of the children is high and therefore general statements are difficult to prove.

References

Berger, M., Kraus, K., Keller, T., Brucker-Kley, E., Knaack, R.: Virtuelle Lernumgebungen in der betrieblichen Ausbildung – eine Analyse am Beispiel der Elektrobranche in der Schweiz—Bwp@ Berufs- und Wirtschaftspädagogik—Online (2022). https://www.bwpat.de/ausgabe/43/berger-etal

Bjelic, D., Keller, T.: Preliminary findings of a virtual reality app for children with special needs, pp. 350–354 (2021). https://digitalcollection.zhaw.ch/handle/11475/23504

Bosse, I.K., Haffner, M., Keller, T.: Virtual Reality for Children with Special Needs. ICCHP-AAATE 2022 Open Access Compendium "Assistive Technology, Accessibility and (e)Inclusion" Part I (2022). https://doi.org/10.35011/icchp-aaate22-p1-09

Bosse, I.K., Pelka, B.: Peer production by persons with disabilities – opening 3D-printing aids to everybody in an inclusive MakerSpace. J. Enabling Technol. 14(1), 41–53 (2020). https://doi.org/10.1108/JET-07-2019-0037

Bradley, R., Newbutt, N.: Autism and virtual reality head-mounted displays: A state of the art systematic review. J. Enabling Technol. (2018)

Buchner, J.: Generative learning strategies do not diminish primary students' attitudes towards augmented reality. Educ. Inf. Technol. 27(1), 701–717 (2021). https://doi.org/10.1007/s10639-021-10445-y

Carreon, A., Smith, S.J., Mosher, M., Rao, K., Rowland, A.: A review of virtual reality intervention research for students with disabilities in K–12 settings. J. Spec. Educ. Technol. 37(1), 82–99 (2022). https://doi.org/10.1177/0162643420962011

Curcio, R.: Router Learning Unit (2022). https://osf.io/tvd86/

Sanders, E.B.-N.: From user-centered to participatory design approaches. In: Design and the Social Sciences (S. 18–25). CRC Press (2002). https://doi.org/10.1201/9780203301302-8

Ip, H.H., et al.: Enhance emotional and social adaptation skills for children with autism spectrum disorder: a virtual reality enabled approach. Comput. Educ. 117, 1–15 (2018)

Jeffs, T.L.: Virtual reality and special needs. Themes Sci. Technol. Educ. 2(1–2), Art. 1–2 (2010)

Jensen, L., Konradsen, F.: A review of the use of virtual reality head-mounted displays in education and training. Educ. Inf. Technol. 23(4), 1515–1529 (2017). https://doi.org/10.1007/s10639-017-9676-0

Keller, T., Botchkovoi, S., Brucker-Kley, E.: Findings from a field experiment with a VR learning unit. In: International Conference on Educational Technologies 2022 (2022)

Keller, T., Curcio, R., Brucker-Kley, E.: The Value of Virtual Reality as a Complementary Tool for Learning Success. CELDA (2022)

Keller, T., Glauser, P., Ebert, N., Brucker-Kley, E: Virtual reality at secondary school–first results. In: Proceedings of the 15th International Conference on Cognition and Exploratory Learning in the Digital Age (CELDA 2018), pp. 53–60 (2018)

Lorenzo, G., Lledó, A., Arráez-Vera, G., Lorenzo- Lledó, A.: The application of immersive virtual reality for students with ASD: a review between 1990–2017. Educ. Inf. Technol. **24**(1), 127–151 (2018). https://doi.org/10.1007/s10639-018-9766-7

Lotan, M., Yalon-Chamovitz, S., (Tamar) Weiss, P.L.: Virtual reality as means to improve physical fitness of individuals at a severe level of intellectual and developmental disability. Res. Dev. Disabil. **31**(4), 869–874 (2010). https://doi.org/10.1016/j.ridd.2010.01.010

Maas, M.J., Hughes, J.M.: Virtual, augmented and mixed reality in K–12 education: a review of the literature. Technol. Pedagog. Educ. **29**(2), 231–249 (2020). https://doi.org/10.1080/147 5939X.2020.1737210

Moreira, M.C., de Amorim Lima, A.M., Ferraz, K.M., Benedetti Rodrigues, M.A.: Use of virtual reality in gait recovery among post stroke patients – a systematic literature review. Disabil. Rehabil. Assist. Technol. **8**(5), 357–362 (2013). https://doi.org/10.3109/17483107.2012. 749428

Parsons, S., Cobb, S.: State-of-the-art of virtual reality technologies for children on the autism spectrum. Eur. J. Spec. Needs Educ. **26**(3), 355–366 (2011). https://doi.org/10.1080/08856257. 2011.593831

Peruzzi, A., Zarbo, I.R., Cereatti, A., Della Croce, U., Mirelman, A.: An innovative training program based on virtual reality and treadmill: effects on gait of persons with multiple sclerosis. Disabil. Rehabil. **39**(15), 1557–1563 (2017). https://doi.org/10.1080/09638288.2016.1224935

Plattner, H., Meinel, C., Leifer, L. (Hrsg.): Design Thinking Research. Springer, Heidelberg (2012). https://doi.org/10.1007/978-3-642-21643-5

Schulz, T., Skeide Fuglerud, K.: Creating a robot-supported education solution for children with autism spectrum disorder. In: International Conference on Computers Helping People with Special Needs, pp. 211–218 (2022)

Sherrell, L.: Evolutionary prototyping. In: Runehov, A.L.C., Oviedo, L. (Hrsg.): Encyclopedia of Sciences and Religions, pp. 803–803. Springer, Netherlands (2013). https://doi.org/10.1007/ 978-1-4020-8265-8_201039

Tzanavari, A., Charalambous-Darden, N., Herakleous, K., Poullis, C.: Effectiveness of an immersive virtual environment (CAVE) for teaching pedestrian crossing to children with PDD-NOS. In: 2015 IEEE 15th International Conference on Advanced Learning Technologies, pp. 423–427 (2015). https://doi.org/10.1109/ICALT.2015.85

Zender, R., Weise, M., von der Heyde, M., Söbke, H.: Lehren und Lernen mit VR und AR–Was wird erwartet? Was funktioniert. In: Proceedings der pre-conference-workshops der, 16 (2018)

An Augmented Reality Based Approach for Optimization of Language Access Services in Healthcare for Deaf Patients

Roshan Mathew(✉) ⓘ, Wendy A. Dannels ⓘ, and Aaron J. Parker ⓘ

Rochester Institute of Technology, Rochester, NY, USA
rm1299@rit.edu

Abstract. Deaf adults often rely on sign language interpreters and real-time captioners for language access during healthcare consultations. While deaf adults generally prefer that these access services be offered in person, previous studies have described that many healthcare providers frequently resort to employing video remote interpreting (VRI) or remote captioning services because of the lack of locally available qualified interpreters or captioners and because of a shorter turnaround time for availing these services. VRI equipment typically consists of a tablet mounted on a utility cart, whereas captions are usually displayed on hand-held tablets. These approaches present visibility and cognitive challenges for deaf adults who then need to divide their attention between the interpreting or captioning display and the healthcare provider, thereby affecting their ability to thoroughly access health information shared during consultations. This study proposes augmented reality (AR) smart glasses as an alternative to traditional VRI and remote captioning services for optimizing communication access in healthcare settings. A descriptive study about the perspectives of deaf adults (N = 62), interpreters (N = 25), and captioners (N = 22) on using a smart glasses application for language access in healthcare and biomedical settings are discussed. Results showed that deaf adults who primarily use sign language interpreting and interpreters prefer onsite language access services but identified the benefits of implementing a smart glasses application whenever onsite access services are unavailable or not feasible. Additionally, deaf adults who rely primarily on captioning and captioners prefer the smart glasses application over traditional captioning methods.

Keywords: Human-centered computing · Accessibility design and evaluation methods · Deaf and hard of hearing · Augmented Reality · Communication access · Healthcare and Medical

1 Introduction

According to national health interview surveys, nearly 15% (37.5 million) of adults aged 18 and over in the United States reported some difficulty hearing [1–3]. People who are deaf or hard of hearing (henceforth, deaf) use a range of communication methods and auxiliary aids, such as sign language interpreting, real-time captioning, assistive listening

M. Antona and C. Stephanidis (Eds.): HCII 2023, LNCS 14021, pp. 29–52, 2023.
https://doi.org/10.1007/978-3-031-35897-5_3

devices, and/or written communication. Although federal civil rights laws, such as the Rehabilitation Act of 1973 (Section 504) [4] and the Americans with Disabilities Act of 1990 (amended 2008) [5], prohibits discrimination based on disability, many deaf people struggle with communication barriers, resulting in negative outcomes such as (a) *health disparities* [6–10]; (b) *mental health issues* [11, 12]; (c) *inadequate education* [13–15]; (d) *employment challenges* [16]; and, (e) *poor quality of life* [11, 12]. This study aimed to collect data on improving the quality of language access for deaf adults in healthcare settings.

Prior research has established that deaf patients seldom receive healthcare services that accommodate their preferred language access method, so they are at the highest risk for miscommunication with their healthcare providers [17]. Federal disability discrimination laws dictate that people who are deaf have equal access and opportunity to partake and benefit from healthcare services [18, 19]. These laws require that healthcare providers ensure effective communication so deaf individuals can communicate and receive information critical to access appropriate, effective, and quality healthcare services. While deaf adults largely prefer to have accessibility accommodations offered in person, many healthcare providers often end up utilizing video remote interpreting (VRI) or remote captioning because of the quicker scheduling times and cost efficiency [20]. Healthcare centers often offer remote access services through a computer mounted on utility carts for VRI or handheld tablets for captioning. These approaches may present visibility and cognitive challenges for deaf people who have to continuously divide their attention between the interpreting or captioning display, the healthcare provider, and any demonstrations affecting their ability to thoroughly access health information during consultations [21, 22]. Figures 1(a) and 1(b) demonstrate the visual dispersion experienced by a deaf patient while using onsite interpreting and traditional captioning methods.

Fig. 1. Scenarios showing deaf patients' challenges with full visual access to information and how they can be improved using AR smart glasses

The visibility and cognitive challenges deaf patients encounter for language access during healthcare consultations can be categorized into three key themes: limitation of the line of sight, limitation of sustained attention, and limitation of executing activities. A *limitation of the line of sight* occurs when deaf patients have to simultaneously focus on the interpreters or captions, the healthcare provider, and any other related artifacts. An example would be medical procedures where deaf patients and healthcare providers are required to wear personal protective equipment, such as masks or hoods, and the onsite access service provider, VRI, or captioning screens cannot be in the deaf patient's field of view. A *limitation of sustained attention* arises when deaf individuals have to attend to a stimulus over a long time in the presence of other distracting stimuli. For example, during healthcare consultations, deaf patients may have to view reports or hands-on demonstrations while their healthcare provider explains a diagnosis or a treatment plan. It would be quite challenging for deaf patients to focus on their medical report or a demonstration while simultaneously viewing an onsite interpreter or a handheld device for viewing VRI or real-time captioning. Finally, a *limitation of executing activities* happens when deaf patients have to follow instructions from a healthcare provider, such as a physiotherapist while participating in some movement or physical rehabilitation activity. In such situations, taking their attention away from the movement or activity to look at the interpreter or VRI/captioning display could be unsafe. Moreover, the cost of this divided attention could be critical in many healthcare situations where quick comprehension and time are of the essence.

A possible improvement to overcome these communication access challenges is wearable technology in the form of augmented reality (AR) smart glasses. AR smart glasses can merge virtual information with physical information in a user's field of view [23], and recent advancements in AR technology and hardware have made it possible for smart glasses to achieve form factors almost similar to regular eyeglasses. One example of commercially available lightweight smart glasses is Vuzix Blade, a self-contained pair of AR smart glasses featuring advanced waveguide optics for hands-free connectivity. Vuzix Blade offers developers access to a software development kit (SDK) [24], which we [25, 26] utilized to develop a prototype application called Access on Demand (AoD), that displays remote sign language interpreting and real-time captioning. Figures 1(c) and 1(d) demonstrate how AR smart glasses help minimize the visual dispersion experienced by a deaf patient while using remote interpreting and captioning. Accessing interpreters or captions on smart glasses in their line of sight will allow deaf patients to focus directly on healthcare providers instead of dividing their attention between different individuals and screens while observing hands-on demonstrations, reviewing instructions, and acquiring essential information during consultations.

The purpose of this study is to understand the experiences of three key stakeholder groups: deaf adults, interpreters, and captioners regarding the current state of language access services in healthcare settings and also evaluate their perceptions of implementing an AR smart glasses-based application, such as AoD, for optimizing language access during healthcare interactions. The researchers conducted a descriptive study using surveys to answer the following research questions (RQ):

RQ1: What are the benefits and drawbacks of onsite sign language interpreting, VRI, and onsite or remote captioning services for language access to deaf adult patients in healthcare settings?

RQ2: What are the barriers and facilitators to using an AR smart glasses prototype for optimizing language access services for deaf adult patients in healthcare settings?

Researchers distributed three surveys among the stakeholder groups. The surveys probed the participants' experiences regarding language access in healthcare settings. In addition, the surveys also introduced the concept of using an AR smart glasses application to optimize language access services in healthcare settings to gain participants' observations on its anticipated benefits and challenges. We then discuss the findings from our research to address the research questions and propose recommendations for future work regarding the use of AR smart glasses as an access technology application for the deaf in healthcare settings.

2   Related Works

Prior studies investigating the experiences of deaf adults accessing and receiving health care determined that communication barriers between healthcare providers and deaf patients often led to the misunderstanding of the diagnosis, treatment plans, and medication use [22, 27]. A key contributor to these misunderstandings is the differences in body language and eye contact between deaf patients and healthcare providers because deaf adults depend greatly on facial expressions and their meanings and prefer to look directly at the healthcare provider's face [22]. However, maintaining eye contact and observing facial expressions are not always feasible, such as when healthcare providers wear face masks and surgical hoods or when deaf patients undergo specific procedures like pelvic exams. Sheppard [2014] recommends that deaf patients should be allowed to see the healthcare provider's face during healthcare consultations, and whenever this is not feasible, healthcare centers should provide alternate communication modalities.

Most deaf patients who use sign language as their primary method of communication prefer a sign language interpreter to be present onsite during healthcare interactions [28–31]. However, several deaf patients have reported that they or sometimes the providers do not prefer to have onsite interpreters for reasons of privacy and confidentiality associated with discussing sensitive patient information [32]. A solution to some of the challenges in providing onsite interpreting services is the use of video remote interpreting (VRI), a specially designed translation service that connects the deaf patient and their healthcare provider to a remote sign language interpreter via a webcam, often a computer or a tablet installed on a rolling cart, connected to the Internet [33]. Healthcare providers increasingly prefer VRI over onsite services because of its cost-effectiveness and flexibility with scheduling based on needs [33]. However, VRI also has several limitations. Napier et al. [34] conducted an international survey of sign language interpreters with experience working remotely either for a video relay service (a form of video telecommunication over phones or similar) or as a video remote interpreter and found that only 50% (N = 58) of participants reported positive feedback about video-based services. Some of the main limitations of VRI are that the remote interpreter has to rely on two-dimensional (2D) video formats to translate a three-dimensional (3D) language (sign language), challenges with a variety of sign language styles among deaf adults, audio and video quality issues, technical problems with the equipment, and Internet quality and connectivity issues. Kushalnagar et al. [2019] studied the national trends in the United States regarding deaf patients' satisfaction with the quality of VRI in health settings using secondary data collected using the Health Information National Trends Survey in American Sign Language. Their findings indicated that only 41% of deaf patients who used VRI services between 2016 and 2018 were satisfied with the quality of service. Some of the disadvantages reported were technical issues with slow Internet connections, set-up times to connect to a remote interpreter, restricted viewing angles with VRI, and the limited ability to follow the focus of the conversation between multiple individuals in the consulting environment. This study also pointed out the inability of remote interpreters to simultaneously focus on multiple people in the consulting room while providing VRI services and that troubleshooting technical issues are often challenging because of the healthcare providers' lack of familiarity with the equipment and service. Technical issues as barriers to effective communication access during video-based healthcare consultations were also reported in a study investigating deaf participants' experiences during telehealth visits [35].

While several studies have investigated communication access for deaf patients who use onsite sign language interpreting and VRI in healthcare contexts, only limited research is available that examined language access for deaf adults who use captioning in healthcare settings. A study by Mitchell et al. [36] estimates that only about 2.8% of the population they studied (deaf, hard of hearing, and hearing adult signers) in the United States use American Sign Language (ASL) for communication. This demonstrates that a vast majority of deaf people rely on other auxiliary aids for language access, and it is essential that their access needs are met using their preferred means of communication. People with hearing loss who do not know sign language, but are competent in another spoken or written language, such as English, have used written communication to interact with the hearing world [37]. Recent innovations and advancements in assistive technologies, such as Automatic Speech Recognition (ASR), have opened up new ways for deaf people to communicate with those who are hearing. ASR is nowadays integrated with a host of mobile and wearable devices, such as smartphones, smartwatches, tablets, and laptops. Prior research has established that the visual dispersion that stems from deaf individuals splitting their attention between handheld or desktop screens and communication partners can affect their focus and cognitive effort, leading to misinformation and misunderstanding of captioned and non-captioned information [41, 42]. To overcome visual dispersion, researchers have evaluated the feasibility of leveraging Head Mounted Displays (HMDs)/Head Worn Displays (HWDs) and ASR to provide captioning for deaf people, especially in mobile contexts [21, 43, 44]. Research on deaf individuals' preferences for wearable and mobile sound awareness technologies using smartwatches, smartphones, and HMDs, showed that HMD was the most preferred device for displaying captions as it is easier to glance at captions while maintaining eye contact or line of sight [38]. Another study on conversation greeting detection using HWD found consistently improved average response times to events when HWDs are used as an assistive device compared to smartphones [39, 40]. However, only limited research is available that looked into language access for deaf patients using ASR or other captioning methods in healthcare environments. A study evaluated the feasibility of implementing an interactive multitouch tabletop display, Shared Speech Interface (SSI), to enable conversations between a deaf patient and a healthcare provider using speech recognition and visuals [37]. This study revealed that while SSI was promising in facilitating privacy and independence, the overall experience for deaf patients was limited by inadequacies with the speech recognition engine, which also led to slower communication.

Researchers have also looked into the usability and preferences of ASR among deaf people for conversations [45, 46] and found that ASR services, in their current form, do not reliably provide accurate or usable transcripts. Therefore, it is reasonable to infer that ASR is not suitable for deaf adults in healthcare settings because of the possibility of errors and inconsistencies that could potentially be critical, particularly when more complex terminologies are used during consultations. A Joint Statement on ASR as a form of captioning services issued by the Word Federation of the Deaf and the International Federation of Hard of Hearing stated, "ASR... has difficulty in providing consistently good recognition accuracy, due to poor sound quality... as well as... poor environmental conditions such as noise and an unspecified number of speakers and. In addition, some words, such as proper nouns and technical terms that are unknown to the ASR system, are hard to learn beforehand, and it is still difficult to always ensure reliable recognition. When ASR services are used without human operator, deaf and hard of hearing people are excluded from full participation in society." [47]. Therefore, for this research, we designed AoD so that a human captioner can provide real-time captions in addition to ASR. Specifically, there are two types of Speech-to-Text (STT) services: verbatim and meaning-for-meaning. There is no best system, but C-Print (meaning-to-meaning) [48] is a technology developed at the university where this research project takes place and will be used for AoD.

3 Methods

3.1 Access on Demand (AoD)

Our research team built AoD so that deaf people can view remote real-time captioning and sign language interpreting on AR smart glasses. Using AoD, deaf individuals can view interpreters or captions in their line of sight while interacting with those who use spoken language for communication. AoD is designed to be used as a multimodal application that allows various stakeholders, including deaf individuals, captioners, interpreters, and presenters, to access different tools to support their goals for language access.

Design and Development of Proof of Product. We envision deaf patients using AoD in healthcare settings as follows: The deaf patient arrives at the front desk; they or an office staff creates a user profile on reactive webpages (web portal) to log in to the user's account; next, the deaf patient receives the smart glasses and wears them; real-time data are automatically sent to the video streaming cloud server; the server dispatches a remote on-call interpreter to go to a webcam-enabled laptop or a remote captioner to use the speech-to-text platform; the interpreter begins signing (when the provider speaks); the patient sees the interpreter or captioning in the smart glasses; and the healthcare provider hears the interpreter via their smartphone app. The design objectives of the AoD are:

- Allow deaf patients to easily access remote sign language interpreting or captioning for emergency healthcare visits or when an access service provider is unavailable in person.
- Offer deaf patients the freedom to look around their environment without missing real-time communication information.
- Afford improved mobility for deaf patients using wireless technologies so they can move freely within or between different locations at the clinic or hospital. At the same time, access service providers can remain stationary or even work remotely while providing services.

- Remote access service providers can see exactly what deaf patients are viewing through their AR smart glasses, resulting in better service delivery.

For AoD, we used the Vuzix Blade AR smart glasses. Figure 2 (a) exhibits the Vuzix Blade, Fig. 2 (b) demonstrates a deaf adult wearing the Blade, and Fig. 2 (c) shows how the projected display looks on the right lens of the Blade. AoD supports three modes: remote real-time interpreting, real-time captioning, and auto-captioning (ASR). The application also offers several customization features, such as brightness, font size, font style, and font color. The brightness of the display can be adjusted to three different levels. Currently, three font sizes and four font styles are available for personalization. Font colors can be personalized using six colors – white, yellow, green, blue, red, and purple.

(a)   (b)   (c)

Fig. 2. Vuzix Blade smart glasses with a transparent near-eye display (Color figure online)

Figure 3 shows how a deaf user views interpreting or captioning on the Blade. It should be noted that the container is transparent on the Blade, unlike what is shown as opaque in these figures.

(a)   (b)

Fig. 3. (a) Interpreting and (b) captioning mode on the smart glasses, as viewed by the deaf patient

Figure 4 demonstrates how AoD's web portal looks for access service providers. Interpreters and captioners can also access another web portal, presenter view, to watch the live stream of the deaf patient's consultation session. AoD accommodates team interpreting, a standard practice for interpreters to switch with another interpreter every 15–20 min [49, 50]. The two interpreters can see each other through the portal to communicate with each other to coordinate switching and other session-specific needs. They also can toggle on and off the camera for privacy and expand/collapse the video clip. A red border is shown around the interpreter that the deaf user is currently viewing.

(a)   (b)

Fig. 4. (a) AoD's web portal for remote interpreters (b) C-Print interface for remote captioners (Color figure online)

3.2 Survey Instrument and Participant Sampling

This research was approved by the author's Institutional Review Board. Based on an initial literature review, three surveys were developed using Qualtrics to be distributed among deaf adults, sign language interpreters, and captioners. The surveys were divided into three parts: participants' prior experience receiving (deaf adults) or providing (interpreters and captioners) language access in biomedical and healthcare fields, participant feedback about the AoD application, and demographic information. It should be noted that in the surveys, the researchers only presented the concept of AoD, i.e., language access optimization using AR smart glasses, to the participants without referring specifically to Vuzix Blade or the AoD application. This ensured that participants provided feedback on their general perceptions of how such an application would work in healthcare contexts without focusing on the details of how the technology works.

For the survey of deaf adults, participants had to be 18 years or older and identify as Deaf, deaf, hard of hearing, deafblind, oral deaf, or late-deafened [51]. To participate in the study, interpreters and captioners had to be 18 years or older and have experience providing VRI or captioning services in biomedical and healthcare settings. In addition, interpreters had to be certified. Participants were recruited through purposeful, criterion, convenience, and snowball sampling via email, private social media channels, posters, and in-person recruitment at community events. For the survey of interpreters and captioners, participants were recruited by reaching out to service providers known for providing healthcare interpreting and captioning services.

3.3 Data Collection and Analysis

The survey was open for five months, between May and December 2022. The survey took approximately 15 min to complete, and all eligible participants received a monetary incentive.

Descriptive statistics were used to evaluate participant demographics. Additionally, in each of the three surveys, participants were asked to rank their preferences for communication access during healthcare visits to identify how survey respondents ranked the use of AR smart glasses against the access services they have prior experience with. Non-parametric tests were performed to determine if there were differences in the perceived impact on the quality of language access during healthcare consultations based on the type of access services offered to deaf adult patients. These statistical analyses were performed using SPSS, and the results are presented in our findings.

Thematic analysis was performed using an inductive, semantic approach for the open-text responses. Codes were generated for participant feedback on the benefits and barriers of AoD, onsite, and remote access services to identify themes, which were compared across the samples. Based on the frequency of codes, significant themes were then grouped to generate higher-level categories that described barriers, facilitators, and participants' preferences for language access services in healthcare settings.

4 Findings

4.1 Survey of Deaf Adults

The sample used for data analysis for the survey of deaf adults contained 62 valid responses. The survey participants had a mean age of 31.32 years (Range: 19–67 years). Forty participants (64.5%) identified as male, and 22 (35.5%) identified as female. Most of the participants, 49, identified as White or Caucasian (79%), six identified as Black or African American (9.7%), five identified as Asian (8.1%), and two as Middle Eastern (3.2%). Participants' hearing status is shown in Table 1 below.

Current Preferences for Language Access Services. Thirty-three participants preferred captioning as their communication accessibility accommodation during healthcare interactions, while 27 preferred interpreting services. Two participants used their own assistive technology devices or strategies for communication access.

Deaf Adults Who Use Sign Language Interpreting. Participants (N = 27; Deaf = 9, deaf = 4, hard of hearing = 10, oral deaf = 2, deafblind = 2) who stated that they primarily

Table 1. Participants' Hearing Status

Hearing Status	Frequency	Valid Percent	Cumulative Percent
Deaf	19	30.6	30.6
deaf	14	22.6	53.2
hard of hearing	21	33.9	87.1
deafblind	3	4.8	91.9
oral deaf	2	3.2	95.2
late-deafened	3	4.8	100.0

use sign language interpreting for communication were asked to rank their preferences between onsite interpreting, VRI, and viewing interpreters on AR smart glasses for language access during consultations with a healthcare provider. A Friedman test was used to test against the null hypothesis that all access services are preferred equally. There was a marginally significant difference in the perceived quality of language access depending on which type of access method was used, $\chi 2(2) = 5.63$, p $= 0.06$. A post-hoc analysis using Wilcoxon signed-rank tests was conducted with a Bonferroni correction. There was no difference in any variables with this adjustment. However, the non-adjusted p-value showed that deaf adults preferred onsite interpreting over AR smart glasses at the set significance level. There was no difference between the perceived quality of language access using VRI and smart glasses, with and without this adjustment.

Many deaf adults emphasized that having an onsite interpreter allowed them to clarify any miscommunications. In addition, onsite interpreters could move around with the healthcare provider so that both the deaf adults and interpreters can see each other's signing and body language clearly. Deaf adults also did not have to carry around any screens (for VRI or captioning) if they had to move around. Participants thought onsite interpreting facilitated better rapport between healthcare providers, interpreters, and deaf adult patients. On the other hand, deaf adults recognized that VRI offered the benefits of not having to schedule interpreters ahead of time and that there is more privacy during healthcare consultations, but it presented a lot more challenges, such as with Internet connectivity and equipment issues.

Deaf Adults Who Use Captioning. Participants (N $= 33$; Deaf $= 10$, deaf $= 9$, hard of hearing $= 11$, late-deafened $= 2$, deafblind $= 1$) who reported that they typically use captioning during healthcare interactions were asked to rank their preferences between remote captioning and following captions on AR smart glasses for language access during consultations with a healthcare provider. A Wilcoxon signed-rank test was conducted to determine participants' preferences for the type of language access method used. The difference scores were approximately symmetrically distributed, as assessed by the ranks scored by each participant. There was a statistically significant difference in participants' preferences, and accessing captions using AR smart glasses was preferred over traditional remote captioning, W $= 891$, p < 0.01.

Participants found captioning to be convenient during healthcare consultations but pointed out that it also slows down communication as they have to switch back and forth between the captioning screen and looking at their healthcare providers. Deaf adults also stated that onsite captioning is usually more effective and accurate when compared to remote captioning.

Deaf Adults Who Use Other Access Methods Participants (N $= 2$; deaf $= 1$, late-deafened $= 1$) who noted that they use other language access methods mentioned that they either struggle without access services or use their laptops to type back and forth. According to one participant (DP08), "*I type on my own laptop & doctors write their words because I am not fluent in ASL. I have never ever been offered captioning, and remote interpreters are typically provided by companies that do not make sure their interpreters are qualified. The remote options often do not work in ER or near X-ray or*

CT/MRI due to interference. Also, it is very awkward to have an interpreter you may know in a private exam or medical conversation."

4.2 Survey of Interpreters

A total of 38 participants responded to the survey of interpreters, of which 13 responses were discarded as partial or incomplete surveys. Twenty-five valid responses were used for data analysis. The survey participants had a mean age of 42.32 years (Range: 25–67 years). The majority of the participants, 19, identified as female (76%), and six identified as male (24%). An overwhelming majority of the participants, 22 of them, identified as White or Caucasian (88%), one as Native American/American Indian/Alaskan Native (4%), one as Asian (4%), and one preferred not to disclose their ethnicity (4%).

Current Preferences for Language Access Services. Participants (N = 25) were asked to rank their preferences between onsite interpreting, VRI, interpreting using AR smart glasses, and other interpreting methods or strategies for offering language access services during deaf adults' consultations with healthcare providers. A Friedman test was used to test against the null hypothesis that interpreters preferred all four delivery methods equally. A post-hoc analysis using Wilcoxon signed-rank tests was performed with a Bonferroni correction for multiple comparisons. There was a statistically significant difference in participants' preferences based on the type of access method used, $\chi 2(3) = 46.92$, $p < .0001$. The post-hoc analysis revealed a statistically significant difference in preferences for onsite interpreting but not between VRI and AR smart glasses. Other interpreting methods or strategies were the least preferred. Interpreters found onsite interpreting as the most preferred type of language access service but did not have a preference between VRI and AR smart glasses.

According to interpreters, onsite interpreting allows them to build rapport and personal connections with deaf patients and healthcare providers. This is particularly helpful if the same interpreter regularly works with a healthcare center and their patients. Interpreters also have more contextual information regarding the consultation and better control over the interactions as they can slow down the communication to suit the deaf patients' pace and ask for repetitions and clarifications to avoid misunderstandings. Onsite interpreting also allows ASL interpreters to work alongside certified deaf interpreters (CDI). CDIs are those who themselves identify as deaf or hard of hearing (DHH) and are certified to be assigned to interpret a wide range of scenarios where a DHH interpreter would be beneficial for deaf people [52]. Interpreters also added that they could position themselves better and navigate turn-taking more efficiently when they are onsite.

On the other hand, interpreters acknowledged that it would be taxing for deaf patients to switch their attention between the interpreters and healthcare workers, which can also slow down and hamper the flow of communication. This would also be the case when consultations or medical examinations are performed in smaller rooms, which according to interpreters, is often the case. They also added that positioning themselves when deaf patients are bedridden or have limited mobility is often demanding. Another challenge with onsite interpreting is that it may not be suitable for deaf patients with communicable diseases, such as COVID-19, as it may not always be possible to maintain adequate social distancing in small consulting or treatment rooms. Moreover, many interpreters also reported that deaf patients might not prefer onsite interpreting in several cases, such as during personal examinations, invasive procedures, or while discussing sensitive health information. Interpreters also acknowledged that onsite services are often complex to schedule, especially last-minute or emergency requests such as in emergency rooms and those needing access services overnight. Onsite interpreting may also not be available in rural areas or where qualified local interpreters are unavailable.

Interpreters recognized that some of the challenges with onsite interpreting could be addressed using VRI. It is easier to schedule VRI services as they are usually available 24/7, making them suitable for last-minute or emergency requests. VRI is also a great solution to provide access services for deaf patients in rural areas where they may not have qualified interpreters available locally. VRI also offers better privacy for deaf patients and is less invasive because cameras can be turned off during private or sensitive interactions. VRI also helps reduce the number of personnel physically present in smaller consulting rooms and is better suited for scenarios where appropriate social distancing needs to be maintained.

4.3 Survey of Captioners

A total of 22 responses were collected from captioners. All responses were valid and used for data analysis. The mean age of the respondents was 38.82 years, with a minimum age of 29 years and a maximum age of 62 years. Thirteen participants identified as female (59.1%), and nine as male (40.9%). The majority of participants were White or Caucasian (72.7%).

Current Preferences for Language Access Services. Participants (N = 22) were asked to rank their preferences between remote captioning, captioning using AR smart glasses, and other captioning methods or strategies for offering language access services during deaf adults' consultations with healthcare providers. A Friedman test was performed against the null hypothesis. There was a statistically significant difference in participants' preferences based on the type of access method used, $\chi^2(2) = 34.38$, p < .0001. Post-hoc analysis using Wilcoxon signed-rank tests was performed with a Bonferroni correction for multiple comparisons. The post-hoc analysis revealed statistically significant differences in preferences between the three language access methods even with this adjustment. Captioners ranked offering services using AR smart glasses as the most preferred, followed by remote captioning and other captioning methods.

Several captioners shared that onsite captioning often offers the benefits of better audio and additional contextual information regarding the consultation they may not have access to during remote captioning. At the same time, onsite captioning is logistically more complex to manage. Captioners also added that Internet connections in medical facilities are often spotty, and they are usually not allowed to access a medical facility's network as they are contract workers and not employees. As such, they are forced to use guest networks, which may not be secure for transmitting sensitive patient information. On the other hand, captioners stated that remote captioning generally works well and addresses some of the challenges with onsite captioning if they have a reliable audio source and Internet connection. However, some drawbacks with remote captioning include not having a live feed to view the consultation, technical issues that may arise with equipment, and healthcare providers' lack of familiarity with how remote captioning works.

4.4 Participant Feedback on Using AR Smart Glasses for Language Access

Table 2 encapsulates the major themes from participant feedback on the benefits of using AR smart glasses in healthcare settings. For each participant group, the themes listed are in the order of their top concerns as established during thematic analysis. All three participant groups identified that deaf patients would significantly benefit from viewing the interpreters or captions in their line of sight. Deaf patients can maintain eye contact with the healthcare provider, allowing them to access visual communication cues and build rapport. The ability to view interpreting or captions in their line of sight will help deaf patients maintain communication even while viewing demonstrations or reports or if they need to look away from the healthcare staff, interpreters, or captioning screens. According to a deaf participant who uses captioning in healthcare settings, *DP58*, *"I think it will be really advantageous if I were to wear the proposed smart glass to view captions as I would not have [to] stare at the captioning devices or app all the time and with [the] glass I will also be able to look at person's faces and captions at the same time. It will be like watching movies with captions, except that I am interacting with the characters too."* Participant *DP57*, who uses VRI for healthcare consultations, said, *"Miscommunication might be a bit [of a] hassle by looking back and forth [between] the doctor and the video phone relay (VRI)."* Interpreter IP24 also observed the benefit for deaf patients to maintain the line of sight afforded by the smart glasses, *"I think it would be very good - as long as the interpreter can hear - then it makes a more comfortable way to communicate - allowing the hearing person to feel like they are making eye contact with the patient - even while the patient is listening to them talk."* Captioner *CP05* added, *"Deaf adults would not have to look away to view another screen and miss information from a demonstration. Also, some also lip-read and [by] looking away at another screen, they miss that. It helps build rapport, too, [by] being able to look at the provider while they are communicating with you. It is important to be able to change font size/color/contrast."*

Deaf adults and interpreters noted that using remote access services through smart glasses would ease the logistics of scheduling services, even last-minute or emergency requests. Some captioners also acknowledged that remote services would be logistically less complex, but overall, they identified the communication efficiency afforded by smart glasses as more beneficial. According to captioners, remote services would help streamline the communication between deaf patients and healthcare professionals as fewer people are in the consulting room. Many interpreters thought smart glasses would be a good solution to implement in rural health centers where there may be a lack of qualified interpreters or captioners. According to interpreter *IP11*, *"This technology may be used in parts of the country where providing an in-person interpreter is not always possible. I could also see this being used to provide a CDI when an in-person CDI is not available in person."* Other interpreters also mentioned that smart glasses could be utilized to provide a CDI to work remotely along with a Hearing Interpreter (HI) because the availability of CDIs is much more limited compared to HIs.

Several deaf participants thought using smart glasses would offer them parity in terms of communication access compared to hearing patients. Interpreters also identified this benefit, as interpreter *IP21* noted, *"Love this idea! I see greater parity with hearing people who can look away from the speaker and still receive incoming communication. Would love to see this in action."* Several interpreters thought that remote services using smart glasses would offer more privacy for deaf patients, especially when they do not prefer to have an interpreter they know while discussing sensitive health-related information or undergoing specific medical procedures or personal examinations. Deaf patients also observed that some hospitals have smaller consulting or treatment rooms, such as delivery rooms, where it is difficult to accommodate an onsite interpreter or a captioner. Using smart glasses would be a good workaround in these situations. Captioners also noted that the customization options offered by the AoD application would aid deaf patients in tailoring how they view captions based on individual needs and situations.

Table 2. Participants' Inputs on the Benefits of using AR Smart Glasses – Major Themes

Deaf Adults	Interpreters	Captioners
Line of Sight • Can see interpreters and captions while maintaining eye contact with the healthcare provider or while viewing demos or reports • See interpreters and captions more closely and clearly	Line of Sight • Deaf adults can maintain eye contact with the healthcare provider • Allows deaf adults to follow interpreting while viewing demos or reports	Line of Sight • Deaf adults can maintain eye contact to build rapport with the healthcare provider • Deaf adults can follow captions while viewing demos or reports • Deaf adults can follow visual communication cues while viewing captions
Logistics • Fewer logistical procedures involved in scheduling, and can be utilized for last-minute or emergency requests	Logistics • Beneficial for use in rural areas lacking qualified interpreters • It can be used to offer services of CDI when needed • Suitable for last-minute access services requests	Communication • Reduced communication times • Simplified interaction between healthcare providers and deaf patients with fewer people in the room
Equality in Communication Accessibility • Experience a healthcare consultation comparable to that of hearing patients	Privacy • Fewer people in the room	Customization • Customize technology, such as fonts, font sizes, and font colors

Table 3 summarizes the major themes from participant feedback on the drawbacks of using AR smart glasses in healthcare settings. For each participant group, the themes listed are in the order of their top concerns as established during thematic analysis. Anticipated technical issues with smart glasses were identified as one of the main drawbacks by all three participant groups. These include Internet connectivity issues such as poor Wi-Fi connections leading to a delay or lag in remote sign language translation or captioning. A deaf participant (*DP01*) compared the receiving access services using smart glasses to VRI services and noted, *"VRI interpreters often have a 4–5 s lag plus I have had many VRIs lose connection because of the poor Wi-Fi signals."* Participants were also concerned that the smart glasses might fail during a consultation, and the healthcare staff may not have the technical knowledge to troubleshoot issues or perform preventative maintenance to prevent the glasses from breaking down. An interpreter (*IP09*) observed, *"I could see this being advantageous when compared to VRI. But I fear that these glasses could also suffer from similar issues that VRI stations suffer from. Healthcare staff not knowing how to manage and maintain the equipment to be functional to use when a deaf or hard of hearing patient arrives."* Moreover, interpreters and captioners were also concerned about the video and audio quality being affected due to Wi-Fi issues, thereby affecting their ability to provide the most accurate translation or captions.

The inability of interpreters to see the deaf patients signing and thereby preventing deaf patients who use sign language as the primary language to communicate to the healthcare provider for questions or clarifications, was seen as another significant barrier to using smart glasses in healthcare contexts. In addition, deaf patients and interpreters have to frequently engage in backchannel communication to clarify certain signs or expressions. Similarly, deaf patients who use captioning also need to communicate with their captioner for clarification. The version of AoD presented to the participants did not allow for this two-way communication between deaf patients and their healthcare staff or access service providers. A deaf participant, *DP08*, said, *"Patient cannot ask the interpreter to repeat something or clarify, and medical staff will still refuse to allow the patient to communicate expressively."* An interpreter, *IP24*, had similar concerns and shared, *"The one point I would be uncertain about is how would I see the Deaf person to be able to voice for them. If the Deaf person voices for themselves, then that difficulty is resolved, otherwise, if the interpreter was really "good," they could see the signs from the perspective of the signer (from behind) and voice from that."* While having directional video and audio using smart glasses was an advantage, interpreters and captioners believed that not having access to the live context and background information could prove challenging in certain situations where multiple people are involved in a consultation. For example, deaf patients may be accompanied by their family members and caregivers, who may be deaf or hearing, and interpreters might find it challenging to manage such situations. A captioner (*CP21*) said, *"As the captioner, I would like to see what is going on in the room so I can ensure I have the most complete and accurate captions."* Interpreters also pointed out that while smart glasses allow deaf patients to view interpreters in their line of sight, deaf patients may sometimes still need to choose between focusing on multiple visuals (physical space, provider, AR projection), which could lead to higher visual demand that may be uncomfortable for some deaf patients.

Some participants noted that most AR smart glasses use dark-tinted lenses, which prevent healthcare providers from seeing deaf patients' eyes, which can hinder building rapport and personal connections between them. Additionally, deaf adults and interpreters felt that remote interpreting gets in the way of building personal connections and rapport between them. An interpreter (IP24) remarked, *"the biggest plus to having an in-person interpreter is - you can see each other, you can hear the hearing person well - even when they are not visible. The Deaf person and the interpreter can bond - so the Deaf person does not feel alone when trying to talk about scary medical things. It is hard to provide that bit of culture [using remote services]."*

Table 3. Participants' Inputs on the Drawbacks of using AR Smart Glasses – Major Themes

Deaf Adults	Interpreters	Captioners
Technical Issues • Internet connectivity issues *(b)* • Delay/lag in remote translation and remote captioning *(a)*	Technical Issues • Internet connectivity Issues *(b)* • Device hardware issues or malfunctions *(b)* • Healthcare staff may not have the technical skills to maintain the smart glasses in working order *(b)*	Technical Issues • Internet connectivity Issues *(b)* • Device hardware issues or malfunctions *(b)* • Healthcare staff may not have the technical knowledge to troubleshoot issues with the smart glasses *(b)*
Two-Way Communication • Interpreter cannot voice for the deaf patient *(b)* • The inability of deaf patients to communicate with the healthcare provider for feedback or clarifications *(b)*	Two-Way Communications • Interpreter cannot voice for the deaf patient *(b)* • Interpreter cannot communicate with the deaf patients for clarification *(b)* • Consultations involving multiple deaf patients/families of deaf patients can be challenging for the interpreter *(b)* • Challenges involved with focusing on two visuals simultaneously *(b)*	Two-Way Communications • The inability of deaf patients to communicate with the healthcare provider or captioner for feedback or clarifications *(b)*
Building Rapport • Less "human" connection due to the interpreter being remote *(c)*	Live Context • Interpreter cannot see everything going on in the consultant room *(a)*	Audio quality issues • Poor audio quality leads to missed/incorrect captions *(b)*

(a) no issue (b) feasible solution(s) to be incorporated in AoD (c) future work.

5 Discussion

5.1 Main Findings

Our findings show that, whenever feasible, deaf adults who communicate using ASL preferred onsite interpreting and those who rely on captioning preferred smart glasses over traditional remote captioning services in healthcare settings. Interpreters, too, prefer onsite interpreting over remote interpreting, and they see smart glasses as an effective alternative to VRI whenever onsite interpreting is not feasible or available. Therefore, both interpreters and deaf adults who use sign language for language access favor onsite services over remote services in healthcare contexts, which is consistent with the findings from prior studies [28–31]. Captioners ranked smart glasses higher than traditional captioning services, in line with the feedback from deaf adults who use captioning for communication access. This finding correlates to prior studies demonstrating that HMDs are the most preferred device for displaying captions [38].

5.2 Benefits and Drawbacks of Onsite Language Access Services in Healthcare Contexts

From the access service providers' perspective, one of the main advantages of onsite interpreting and captioning is that they have live context for interpretation or translation. Being in the same location not only helps them have more contextual information and non-verbal cues but also makes it easier for them to ask questions or clarifications for accurate interpretation or translation. This is particularly important when communicating with family members or caregivers. Being in the same room as the deaf patient and healthcare provider helps build rapport, personal connections, and trust among all parties. Deaf adults also noted that communication is much easier and smoother when an onsite interpreter or captioner is available. Interpreters can also move around with the doctor in a consultation room if needed so that deaf patients and interpreters can see each other's body language clearly. Interpreters also stated that being onsite would allow them to use more of their bodies for interpreting (compared to VRI) and control the pace of the conversation to suit the deaf patient better. Captioners and interpreters further pointed out that they have better access to audio quality onsite, which may not always be the case when remote. Interpreters, captioners, and deaf adults agreed that with onsite services, they would not have to be concerned about troubleshooting technical issues with the Internet or equipment, and it is generally a more efficient and less frustrating experience.

One of the biggest drawbacks of onsite language access services is that deaf patients have to focus on the interpreter or captioning devices during consultations, often breaking eye contact with their healthcare providers. As established by other studies [22, 41, 42], dividing their attention between healthcare providers, any demonstrations or artifacts, and the interpreter or captioning devices is often cognitively demanding for deaf adults and leads to miscommunication and misunderstandings. This is also often detrimental to maintaining the flow of conversations and building rapport among healthcare personnel, access service providers, and deaf patients. Consistent with literature [6, 27, 28, 31, 32], logistics and scheduling are other disadvantages of onsite language access services. Study participants noted that scheduling onsite services is often time-consuming and complex. Sometimes, appointments may not start on time or go longer than initially scheduled, which has a domino effect on other appointments as interpreters and captioners often drive around a lot to get to different appointments. Last-minute requests for onsite appointments may not get fulfilled, and qualified interpreters or captioners may not always be available for overnight assignments or in rural areas. Onsite access services may not be feasible in smaller consultation rooms where the interpreter might find it challenging to stay in front of the deaf patient. Correspondingly, onsite services may not be ideal for bedridden patients, especially those who cannot sit up to see the interpreters or caption screens, for deaf patients with limited upper body mobility, or deaf patients with communicable diseases and access service providers will have to maintain social distancing or wear personal protective equipment. Similar to findings from other studies [22, 32], some participants thought that having an onsite interpreter or captioner would result in less privacy for deaf patients, and some prefer not to have another person in the room or someone whom they know personally while discussing sensitive medical information. In addition, captioners raised security concerns with captioning Health Insurance Portability and Accountability Act (HIPAA) [53] protected information on unsecured guest Wi-Fi hospital networks. Such Internet connections are often spotty in many healthcare establishments, resulting in delayed, interrupted, or disconnected transcriptions.

5.3 Benefits and Drawbacks of Remote Language Access Services in Healthcare Contexts

Similar to results from other studies [28, 33], participants noted that one of the significant advantages of remote services is the logistical ease of scheduling them, and they are frequently accepted as a backup or short-term solution if onsite interpreters or captioners are unavailable. Often, last-minute requests for appointments or emergencies can be fulfilled using remote services as a wider pool of qualified interpreters and captioners is available. Interpreters and captioners can offer their services to more deaf patients as they save time not traveling between appointments. Interpreters and captioners disclosed that remote access services are also cost-effective for healthcare providers who pay only for the actual utilized time instead of the minimum required hours with onsite services. VRI and remote captioning may be better options for providing services in rural areas without qualified local interpreters or captioners. Having the interpreter or captioner join remotely may also mean fewer distractions for healthcare providers during the consultations, given the fewer people in the consulting room. Access service providers joining remotely also results in better privacy for deaf patients. As opposed to onsite interpreting and captioning, VRI and remote captioning seem to be better suited for consultations involving deaf patients with communicable diseases or when using smaller consultation rooms where physical space is limited.

One of the critical drawbacks of traditional remote access services was that deaf patients found it challenging to divide their attention between different streams of information, often delayed, which results in reduced eye contact between deaf patients and healthcare staff. Most participants reported technical issues with the service are often a big challenge with VRI and remote captioning services. Internet connectivity issues,

issues with the equipment, and poor audio/video quality were among the technical problems listed by the study participants, which were also reported by previous studies as one of the primary concerns against using VRI [28, 31, 33]. Interpreters and captioners found it tough not to have access to live context and non-verbal communication cues. Deaf adults found using VRI or captioning on tablet screens challenging when bedridden or unable to sit up. They also deemed moving around the equipment needed for VRI services to be cumbersome. Participants also stated that some deaf patients and healthcare staff might be technologically challenged by handling equipment and technology for remote captioning or VRI services.

5.4   Barriers and Facilitators of Using AR Smart Glasses for Language Access Services in Healthcare Contexts

The main advantage of using AR smart glasses for language access in healthcare settings is that it helps overcome the limitation of the line of sight. All three participant groups (deaf adults, interpreters, and captioners) pointed out that smart glasses would allow deaf patients to maintain eye contact with their healthcare providers. As corroborated by the findings from prior research [22] and would contribute to fewer miscommunications between deaf patients and healthcare providers. Maintaining eye contact may help healthcare providers and deaf patients build rapport and personal connections. However, some participants observed that the healthcare staff may still be unable to see the deaf patient's eyes because of the dark-tinted lenses used by smart glasses, such as Vuzix Blade. Moreover, captioners pointed out that maintaining a line of sight would allow deaf patients to look directly at the healthcare providers' faces for speechreading while following captions. The ability of deaf patients to maintain a line of sight also reduces communication times as healthcare personnel does not have to slow down and allow the deaf patients to look away at the interpreter or handheld screens to follow VRI or captions. Participants also recognized that using smart glasses would help them overcome the limitation of sustained attention because they could view the interpreters or captions while viewing medical reports, demonstrations, or other artifacts simultaneously. Using smart glasses for language access also can improve communication efficiency between deaf patients and healthcare professionals as there will be fewer people in the room that they should pay attention to because of remote access services. Participants noted that AoD would help overcome the limitations of executing activities as it could be helpful while performing certain activities or undergoing medical procedures where viewing the interpreter or VRI and captioning screens would be difficult. Due to the hands-free use of smart glasses, participants thought they could be more mobile instead of carrying a handheld tablet or bringing along the utility cart providing VRI service. Finally, smart glasses-based language access service also shares one of the primary benefits of VRI services: the convenience and flexibility it offers with respect to scheduling, time management, and cost-effectiveness.

On the other hand, participants were concerned about the technical issues hindering the implementation of smart glasses-based language access services, such as Internet connectivity issues and hardware malfunctions. Based on their experiences with VRI or remote captioning services, participants observed that there would be a learning curve to using smart glasses, and often, personnel at healthcare centers are not comfortable troubleshooting technical issues. Another significant barrier to using smart glasses is that, in its current version, two-way communication is not possible. In addition, some participants noted that building rapport with the remote interpreter or captioner would be challenging, depriving them of personal connections and relationships found in in-person contexts. Interpreters and captioners were also concerned that they would have less contextual information about everything happening during the consultation. Therefore, they expect a potential solution where they will have access to a live feed of the whole consultation room.

6   Limitations and Future Work

The sample sizes for the three surveys were relatively small as the sample population was somewhat challenging to reach because the inclusion criteria were limited to stakeholders with prior experience using or providing language access services in biomedical and healthcare settings. This reflects the limited pool of healthcare interpreters and captioners and fewer deaf individuals who have experience using VRI or captioning, which corroborates prior research findings that deaf individuals often avoid healthcare because of recurrent communication barriers [22]. This study also did not obtain feedback from healthcare providers – doctors, nurse practitioners, paramedical professionals, and healthcare administrators, even though they are also another key stakeholder group who would be involved if the proposed smart glasses-based language access service, AoD, is to become commonplace. Future studies will be focused on optimizing the AoD application based on the feedback received from this study, as summarized in Table 3. We will also conduct a technical feasibility study on using smart glasses for language access in live medical settings, where feasible, by involving all key stakeholders, including healthcare professionals.

7   Conclusion

This study explored the perspectives of deaf adults, sign language interpreters, and captioners on using AR smart glasses for language access in biomedical and healthcare settings. All three stakeholder groups who participated in this study emphasized the benefits of how smart glasses would allow deaf adults to overcome the limitations of the line of sight, the limitation of sustained attention, and the limitation of executing actions. Interpreters and deaf adults who primarily use sign language interpreting stated their preference for onsite language access services over remote services in healthcare contexts. However, both these stakeholder groups recognized the benefits of implementing a smart glasses-based application, such as AoD, whenever onsite access services are unavailable or not feasible. Deaf adults who primarily rely on captioning and captioners unanimously agreed that viewing captions through AR smart glasses was significantly better than traditional captioning methods. The research team will apply the findings from this study to further optimize the AoD application and plan a technical feasibility study on the usability of AR smart glasses in live medical settings.

Acknowledgments.

1. This material is based upon work supported by the National Science Foundation under Award No. 1811509. Any opinions, findings and conclusions, or recommendations expressed in this material are of the author(s) and do not necessarily reflect the views of the National Science Foundation.

2. This project was also partially supported by the American Recuse Plan (ARP) and Public Law 117-2.

3. The authors acknowledge Research Computing at the Rochester Institute of Technology for providing computational resources and support that contributed to the research results reported in this publication.

References

1. Zazove, P., Atcherson, S.R., Moreland, C., McKee, M.M.: Hearing loss: diagnosis and evaluation. FP Essent. **434**, 11–17 (2015)
2. Agrawal, Y., Platz, E.A., Niparko, J.K.: Prevalence of hearing loss and differences by demographic characteristics among US adults: data from the national health and nutrition examination survey, 1999–2004. Arch. Intern. Med. **168**, 1522–1530 (2008). https://doi.org/10.1001/archinte.168.14.1522
3. Blackwell, D.L., Lucas, J.W., Clarke, T.C.: Summary health statistics for U.S. adults: national health interview survey, 2012. Vital Health Stat. **10**, 1–161 (2014)
4. Text of H.R. 8070 (93rd): Rehabilitation Act (Passed Congress version). https://www.govtrack.us/congress/bills/93/hr8070/text. Accessed 10 Feb 2023
5. Guide to Disability Rights Laws. https://www.ada.gov/resources/disability-rights-guide/. Accessed 10 Feb 2023
6. Barnett, S., et al.: Community participatory research with deaf sign language users to identify health inequities. Am. J. Public Health. **101**, 2235–2238 (2011). https://doi.org/10.2105/AJPH.2011.300247
7. McKee, M.M., Stransky, M.L., Reichard, A.: Hearing loss and associated medical conditions among individuals 65 years and older. Disabil. Health J. **11**, 122–125 (2018). https://doi.org/10.1016/j.dhjo.2017.05.007
8. Moreland, C., Atcherson, S.R., Zazove, P., McKee, M.M.: Hearing loss: issues in the deaf and hard of hearing communities. FP Essent. **434**, 29–40 (2015)
9. McKee, M.M., Barnett, S.L., Block, R.C., Pearson, T.A.: Impact of communication on preventive services among deaf American Sign Language users. Am. J. Prev. Med. **41**, 75–79 (2011). https://doi.org/10.1016/j.amepre.2011.03.004
10. Preventing Chronic Disease: March 2011: 10_0065. https://www.cdc.gov/pcd/issues/2011/mar/10_0065.htm. Accessed 10 Feb 2023
11. de Graaf, R., Bijl, R.V.: Determinants of mental distress in adults with a severe auditory impairment: differences between prelingual and postlingual deafness. Psychosom. Med. **64**, 61 (2002)
12. Fellinger, J., et al.: Mental distress and quality of life in a deaf population. Soc. Psychiat. Epidemiol. **40**, 737–742 (2005). https://doi.org/10.1007/s00127-005-0936-8
13. Kelly, R.R., Quagliata, A.B., DeMartino, R., Perotti, V.: 21st-century deaf workers: going beyond "Just Employed" to career growth and entrepreneurship. In: Marschark, M., Lampropoulou, V., Skordilis, E.K. (eds.): Diversity in Deaf Education, p. 0. Oxford University Press (2016). https://doi.org/10.1093/acprof:oso/9780190493073.003.0017

14. Richardson, J.T.E., Marschark, M., Sarchet, T., Sapere, P.: Deaf and hard-of-hearing students' experiences in mainstream and separate postsecondary education. J. Deaf Stud. Deaf Educ. **15**, 358–382 (2010). https://doi.org/10.1093/deafed/enq030

15. Qi, S., Mitchell, R.E.: Large-scale academic achievement testing of deaf and hard-of-hearing students: past, present, and future. J. Deaf Stud. Deaf Educ. **17**, 1–18 (2012). https://doi.org/10.1093/deafed/enr028

16. Kurz, K., Hauser, P., Listman, J.: Work-related resilience: deaf professionals' perspectives. JADARA **50**(88), 109 (2016)

17. McKee, M.M., et al.: Deaf adults' health literacy and access to health information: protocol for a multicenter mixed methods study. JMIR Res. Protoc. **8**, e14889 (2019). https://doi.org/10.2196/14889

18. ADA Requirements - Effective Communication. https://www.ada.gov/resources/effective-communication/. Accessed 10 Feb 2023

19. National Association of the Deaf – NAD. https://www.nad.org/resources/health-care-and-mental-health-services/health-care-providers/questions-and-answers-for-health-care-providers/. Accessed 10 Feb 2023

20. James, T.G., et al.: "They're not willing to accommodate deaf patients": communication experiences of deaf American Sign Language users in the emergency department. Qual. Health Res. **32**, 48–63 (2022). https://doi.org/10.1177/10497323211046238

21. Olwal, A., et al.: Wearable subtitles: augmenting spoken communication with lightweight eyewear for all-day captioning. In: Proceedings of the 33rd Annual ACM Symposium on User Interface Software and Technology, pp. 1108–1120. Association for Computing Machinery, New York, NY, USA (2020). https://doi.org/10.1145/3379337.3415817

22. Sheppard, K.: Deaf adults and health care: giving voice to their stories. J. Am. Assoc. Nurse Pract. **26**, 504–510 (2014). https://doi.org/10.1002/2327-6924.12087

23. Rauschnabel, P., Brem, A., Ro, Y.: Augmented Reality Smart Glasses: Definition, Conceptual Insights, and Managerial Importance. Working Paper, The University of Michigan-Dearborn (2015)

24. Vuzix Blade Upgraded Smart Glasses. https://www.vuzix.com/products/vuzix-blade-smart-glasses-upgraded. Accessed 10 Feb 2023

25. Mathew, R., Mak, B., Dannels, W.: Access on demand: real-time, multi-modal accessibility for the deaf and hard-of-hearing based on augmented reality. In: Proceedings of the 24th International ACM SIGACCESS Conference on Computers and Accessibility, pp. 1–6. Association for Computing Machinery, New York, NY, USA (2022). https://doi.org/10.1145/3517428.3551352

26. NTID Research Center on Culture and Language | National Technical Institute for the Deaf | RIT. https://www.rit.edu/ntid/nccl#research-laboratories. Accessed 10 Feb 2023

27. Schniedewind, E., Lindsay, R.P., Snow, S.: Comparison of access to primary care medical and dental appointments between simulated patients who were deaf and patients who could hear. JAMA Netw. Open **4**, e2032207 (2021). https://doi.org/10.1001/jamanetworkopen.2020.32207

28. Hommes, R.E., Borash, A.I., Hartwig, K., DeGracia, D.: American Sign Language interpreters perceptions of barriers to healthcare communication in deaf and hard of hearing patients. J. Commun. Health **43**(5), 956–961 (2018). https://doi.org/10.1007/s10900-018-0511-3

29. Middleton, A., et al.: Preferences for communication in clinic from deaf people: a cross-sectional study. J. Eval. Clin. Pract. **16**, 811–817 (2010). https://doi.org/10.1111/j.1365-2753.2009.01207.x

30. Morisod, K., Malebranche, M., Marti, J., Spycher, J., Grazioli, V.S., Bodenmann, P.: Interventions aimed at improving healthcare and health education equity for adult d/Deaf patients: a systematic review. Eur. J. Pub. Health **32**, 548–556 (2022). https://doi.org/10.1093/eurpub/ckac056

31. Panko, T.L., et al.: Experiences of pregnancy and perinatal healthcare access of women who are deaf: a qualitative study. BJOG (2022). https://doi.org/10.1111/1471-0528.17300
32. Lesch, H., Burcher, K., Wharton, T., Chapple, R., Chapple, K.: Barriers to healthcare services and supports for signing deaf older adults. Rehabil. Psychol. **64**, 237–244 (2019). https://doi.org/10.1037/rep0000252
33. Kushalnagar, P., Paludneviciene, R., Kushalnagar, R.: Video remote interpreting technology in health care: cross-sectional study of deaf patients' experiences. JMIR Rehabil. Assist. Technol. **6**, e13233 (2019). https://doi.org/10.2196/13233
34. Napier, J., Skinner, R., Turner, G.H.: "It's good for them but not so for me": inside the sign language interpreting call centre. Trans. Interpr. **9**, 1–23 (2017)
35. Mussallem, A., et al.: Making virtual health care accessible to the deaf community: findings from the telehealth survey. J. Telemed. Telecare. 1357633X221074863 (2022). https://doi.org/10.1177/1357633X221074863
36. Mitchell, R.E., Young, T.A., Bachelda, B., Karchmer, M.A.: How many people use ASL in the United States?: why estimates need updating. Sign Lang. Stud. **6**, 306–335 (2006)
37. Piper, A.M., Hollan, J.D.: Supporting medical conversations between deaf and hearing individuals with tabletop displays. In: Proceedings of the 2008 ACM Conference on Computer Supported Cooperative Work, pp. 147–156. Association for Computing Machinery, New York, NY, USA (2008). https://doi.org/10.1145/1460563.1460587
38. Findlater, L., Chinh, B., Jain, D., Froehlich, J., Kushalnagar, R., Lin, A.C.: Deaf and hard-of-hearing individuals' preferences for wearable and mobile sound awareness technologies. In: Proceedings of the 2019 CHI Conference on Human Factors in Computing Systems, pp. 1–13. Association for Computing Machinery, New York, NY, USA (2019). https://doi.org/10.1145/3290605.3300276
39. Tu, J., Lin, G., Starner, T.: Conversational greeting detection using captioning on head worn displays versus smartphones. In: Proceedings of the 2020 ACM International Symposium on Wearable Computers, pp. 84–86. Association for Computing Machinery, New York, NY, USA (2020). https://doi.org/10.1145/3410531.3414293
40. Towards an Understanding of Real-time Captioning on Head-worn Displays. In: 22nd International Conference on Human-Computer Interaction with Mobile Devices and Services. https://dl.acm.org/doi/10.1145/3406324.3410543. Accessed 10 Feb 2023
41. Lasecki, W.S., Kushalnagar, R., Bigham, J.P.: Helping students keep up with real-time captions by pausing and highlighting. In: Proceedings of the 11th Web for All Conference, pp. 1–8. Association for Computing Machinery, New York, NY, USA (2014). https://doi.org/10.1145/2596695.2596701
42. Miller, A., Malasig, J., Castro, B., Hanson, V.L., Nicolau, H., Brandão, A.: The use of smart glasses for lecture comprehension by deaf and hard of hearing students. In: Proceedings of the 2017 CHI Conference Extended Abstracts on Human Factors in Computing Systems, pp. 1909–1915. Association for Computing Machinery, New York, NY, USA (2017). https://doi.org/10.1145/3027063.3053117
43. HoloSound: combining speech and sound identification for deaf or hard of hearing users on a head-mounted display. In: Proceedings of the 22nd International ACM SIGACCESS Conference on Computers and Accessibility. https://dl.acm.org/doi/10.1145/3373625.3418031. Accessed 10 Feb 2023
44. Jain, D., Franz, R., Findlater, L., Cannon, J., Kushalnagar, R., Froehlich, J.: Towards accessible conversations in a mobile context for people who are deaf and hard of hearing. In: Proceedings of the 20th International ACM SIGACCESS Conference on Computers and Accessibility, pp. 81–92. Association for Computing Machinery, New York, NY, USA (2018). https://doi.org/10.1145/3234695.3236362

45. Glasser, A., Kushalnagar, K., Kushalnagar, R.: Deaf, hard of hearing, and hearing perspectives on using automatic speech recognition in conversation. In: Proceedings of the 19th International ACM SIGACCESS Conference on Computers and Accessibility, pp. 427–432. Association for Computing Machinery, New York, NY, USA (2017). https://doi.org/10.1145/3132525.3134781

46. Kafle, S., Huenerfauth, M.: Evaluating the usability of automatically generated captions for people who are deaf or hard of hearing. In: Proceedings of the 19th International ACM SIGACCESS Conference on Computers and Accessibility, pp. 165–174. Association for Computing Machinery, New York, NY, USA (2017). https://doi.org/10.1145/3132525.3132542

47. 27 March 2019: WFD and IFHOH Joint Statement: Automatic Speech Recognition in Telephone Relay Services and in Captioning Services. https://wfdeaf.org/news/resources/27-march-2019-wfd-ifhoh-joint-statement-automatic-speech-recognition-telephone-relay-services-captioning-services/. Accessed 10 Feb 2023

48. The C-Print®System | C-Print. https://www.rit.edu/ntid/cprint. Accessed 10 Feb 2023

49. Standard Practice Papers – Registry of Interpreters for the Deaf. https://rid.org/about-rid/about-interpreting/setting-standards/standard-practice-papers/. Accessed 10 Feb 2023

50. Hoza, J.: Team interpreting. In: The Routledge Handbook of Sign Language Translation and Interpreting. Routledge (2022)

51. National Association of the Deaf – NAD. https://www.nad.org/resources/american-sign-language/community-and-culture-frequently-asked-questions/. Accessed 10 Feb 2023

52. Certified Deaf Interpreter – Registry of Interpreters for the Deaf. https://rid.org/rid-certification-overview/available-certification/cdi-certification/. Accessed 10 Feb 2023

53. Health Insurance Portability and Accountability Act of 1996 (HIPAA) | CDC. https://www.cdc.gov/phlp/publications/topic/hipaa.html. Accessed 10 Feb 2023

Virtual Reality System to Experience Grasp of Others' Hands with a Different Range of Motion

Natsuki Miyata[1]([✉]) [iD], Akihide Suga[2], Takuya Nakatsuka[2], Reiko Takahashi[2] [iD], and Yusuke Maeda[2] [iD]

[1] National Institute of Advanced Industrial Science and Technology, Tokyo 135-0064, Japan
n.miyata@aist.go.jp
[2] Yokohama National University, Yokohama 240-8501, Kanagawa, Japan

Abstract. This paper proposes a VR-based system to experience a hand with restricted ROM, which differs from the system user's hand, using visual and vibrational stimuli. In order to cope with ethical difficulty to ask an adequate number and variety of actual users with disabilities for usability test, it would be helpful to train engineers to anticipate how to use products designed for various disability conditions. By considering force closure to determine whether a grasp has been established, the grasps realized during the VR experience became more natural. Preliminary experimental results suggested the effectiveness of the experience through the proposed VR system on the degree of understanding of the behavior of a hand with a different joint ROM.

Keywords: Emulated Experience · Human Hand · ROM Limitation · Force Closure · Graspability

1 Introduction

Inclusive designs to consider the usability of a product for people with different physical functions from those of healthy people owing to aging or diseases have been attracting attention. However, it is ethically difficult to ask an adequate number and variety of actual users with disabilities to come and test mock-ups for product usability. Therefore, it would be helpful to train engineers to anticipate how to use products designed for various disability conditions.

Several physical equipment have been developed to experience a disabled hand [1, 2]. The authors' group has also developed a method involving taping to emulate carpal tunnel syndrome (CTS) patients by taping to build grasp database utilized to estimate posture of the disabled digital hand model [3]. Although physical restrictions such as soft planks [1], gloves [2], and taping [3] are effective for artificially limiting the healthy participants' hand motion, disability patterns to be experienced are rather limited.

Regarding a system to experience a "different" hand from the participant's own, Terabayashi et al. constructed a system to experience size differences by appropriately combining the magnifying power of the optical view and size of the objects that the participants physically touched [4]. The strength of the displayed information compared to somatosensory information was also shown for the system to experience pinching of differently sized cylinders without changing the actual size [5]. Nishida et al. enabled experience of children using special attachment on the hand and cameras to convert and transmit physical and visual differences [6].

These studies indicate the possibility of increasing disability patterns experienced by appropriately controlling the displayed information in a virtual reality (VR) environment. As the thumb plays an important role in grasping and its range of motion (ROM) has been shown to strongly affect feasible grasp postures, the authors have aimed to develop a system to experience a different ROM from that of the participant primarily focusing on the thumb and they have reported the developed prototype system in [7]. Even if we do not restrict the movement of the hand strictly, we expect that the participant's posture is approximately maintained within the assumed narrow range of motion and can feel that they experience the hand with its ROM limited by controlling the displayed information. For smooth and agreeable interaction including grasping of a virtual object by a virtual hand model in VR, the system is expected to judge whether the current hand can grasp the object appropriately and stably. Therefore, the purpose of this paper is to implement the function to judge graspability and then to validate the effectiveness of the system through experiments.

2   VR Experience System

2.1   System Overview

An overview of the system, whose main part was implemented in Unity, is shown in Fig. 1. The participants were asked to grasp a virtual object presented in the VR environment. The participant wore a head-mounted display, Oculus Quest2, and moved their hand within the field of view of the hand tracking device, Leap Motion. When the participant's actual posture goes outside the ROM of the experiencing target hand, the participant will be notified both by visual information displayed in VR space and by the vibration stimulus given to the participant's thumb/fingers by each of the five oscillatory actuators [8]. The actuator was controlled via a module called DhaibaDAQ [9] using the OSC communication protocol.

2.2   Posture Control to Keep a Target Hand Model Within the ROM

As the proposed system aims to educate the system user by constantly providing the experience of the posture within the given ROM that is different from that of the system user, the hand model posture is fixed when the actual posture goes outside the ROM. In 2-degree of freedom (DOF) joints such as metacarpophalangeal joints, the actual hand posture might return from outside the ROM to inside in different postures, as shown in Fig. 2. To cope with such posture discontinuity problems and stabilize the hand model behavior, spherical linear interpolation was performed between the current actual hand posture and the previously fixed posture using Unity's Quaternion Slesrp function.

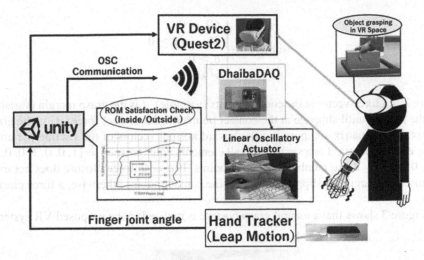

Fig. 1. System Overview

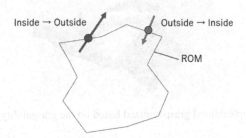

Fig. 2. Postural discontinuity in 2-DOF joint that occurs when returning to the inside from the outside of the ROM

2.3 Judgement of Graspability

The physics calculation function provided by Unity is not adequate to stably realize complex interaction associated with internal force control as grasps. Though several studies such as [10] tried to enable grasping by reproducing actual world dynamics, too heavy processing easily results in the frame rate drops and spoils the quality of the experience. Therefore, our system fixes relative location of the hand to the object once judged to be graspable.

In terms of reducing calculation cost, we employ hard-finger model and judge graspability by considering if the arrangement of the contact points satisfies the force closure. The condition can be checked by solving the following linear programming problem [11]:

$$\underset{d,\lambda}{\text{maximize}} \; d \tag{1}$$

$$\text{subject to} \begin{cases} G\lambda = 0 \\ F\lambda - d\mathbf{1} \geq 0 \\ d \geq 0 \\ e^T \lambda \leq n_c \end{cases} \tag{2}$$

where λ is a force vector at the contact points (variable), d is the grasp margin (variable, i.e. the margin until slippage at the contact points for the contact force), G is the grasp matrix, F is a matrix composed of the inward normal vectors of the friction pyramids at the contact points, $\mathbf{1}$ is a vector with all elements equal to 1, $e^T = [1, 0, 0, 1, 0, 0,\ldots, 1, 0, 0]$, and n_c is the number of contact points. If $d = 0$, force closure does not exist because the margin for slippage is zero at the contact point.; otherwise, a force closure exists.

Figure 3 shows that a natural grasp posture is realized in the proposed VR system.

Fig. 3. Example natural grasp realized based on the graspability judgement

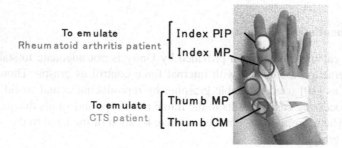

Fig. 4. ROM restriction by taping for the ROM data collection

3 Preparation of an Experiment to Check the Correctness of Understanding Feasible Posture of the Hand with Limited ROM

3.1 Experiment Design

To show the effectiveness of the spontaneous experience in the proposed VR-based system in understanding the characteristics of grasps by different hands, we planned an experiment to investigate whether the correctness of the judgements about posture feasibility in the assumed ROM differs across learning methods. The method of learning through watching videos (video learning method) was prepared for comparison with the developed VR system (VR learning method).

As a target hand to be experienced, we assumed an ROM-limited hand that reflected conditions similar to those of CTS and rheumatoid arthritis. Restriction of palmar abduction movements of the thumb carpometacarpal (CM) joint is a specific symptom of CTS. In most rheumatoid arthritis patients, the metacarpophalangeal (MP) and proximal interphalangeal (PIP) joints are symptomatic. Therefore, we prepared a hand model that is limited in the ROM of the thumb CM and MP joints and the index finger MP and PIP joints. To model the ROM, we artificially limited the motion of the above-mentioned four joints of the actual participant by taping as shown in Fig. 4 and then collected the posture data during 12 types of exercises proposed to cover the entire ROM [3].

3.2 VR Learning Method

To familiarize the participants with the system, they were first asked to experience a healthy hand model without ROM restrictions. The participant moved his/her hand freely for 45 s and then moved on to the trial session of grasping two types of rectangular solids (Object L1 and Object L2 in Table 1) for 45 s. After this one-and-a-half minute experience with the healthy hand, the participant then started to experience the ROM-restricted hand model, which also consisted of 45 s free movement and 45 s object grasping. As shown in Fig. 5, a mirror was set at the back of the VR space, which allowed the user to know what their hand looked like when viewed from the front as this could not be realized from their current viewpoint.

3.3 Video Learning Method

For comparison with the VR learning method focusing on the difference in spontaneity, we used the recorded screen while the experimenter used the VR system. We prepared a video of the hand model without and with ROM restrictions. As in the VR learning method, each video started with free unloaded movement and then moved to the grasping scene. From the viewpoint of learning enhancement, the video for the free movement part was created to cover as much of the range of motion of the hand model as possible, by employing some of the movements while collecting the ROM data. Participants were asked to watch the video once from beginning to end, and they were then allowed to rewind it at will for the remainder of the time. An image of a still from the video is shown in Fig. 6. The entire video-learning process took approximately five minutes.

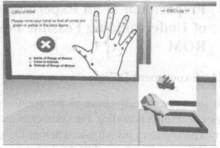

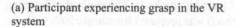

(a) Participant experiencing grasp in the VR system

(b) Example view diplayed on a head-mounted display

Fig. 5. Learning through experience in the VR system

Table 1. Dimensions of virtual objects.

Usage	Object Name	Height × Width × Depth [mm]
Learning	Object L1	200 × 50 × 50
Learning	Object L2	200 × 95 × 95
Comprehension Test	Object T1	250 × 20 × 20
Comprehension Test	Object T2	250 × 40 × 40
Comprehension Test	Object T3	8 × 45 × 45
Comprehension Test	Object T4	8 × 70 × 70
Comprehension Test	Object T5	8 × 100 × 100
Comprehension Test	Object T6	40 × 70 × 70
Comprehension Test	Object T7	65 × 65 × 65

3.4 Comprehension Test

A comprehension test was conducted by showing images of the hand model grasping an object and asking a participant whether they thought the posture could be realized by the learned ROM-restricted hand. As shown in Fig. 7, each question was given by presenting a pair of still images from two directions: one from the system's viewpoint and the other from the mirror location. Posture data for the questions were collected from the experimenter's VR experience to grasp one of the seven objects listed in Table 1 (Objects T1–T7). Each comprehension test set consisted of ten questions selected from the collected posture data. The selection was conducted to maintain the given ratio of the postures within the ROM to those outside the ROM, which was set at 6-4 in this study. The order of the questions in each set was randomly determined, and the questions were given to all participants.

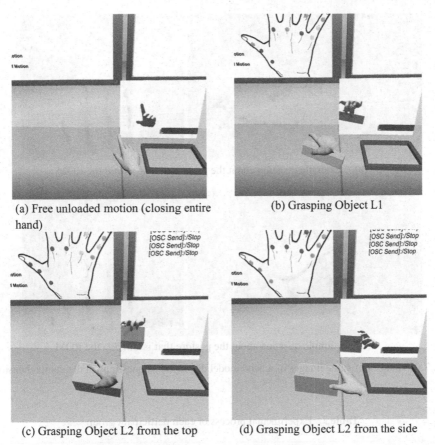

(a) Free unloaded motion (closing entire hand)

(b) Grasping Object L1

(c) Grasping Object L2 from the top

(d) Grasping Object L2 from the side

Fig. 6. Snapshots from the videos for learning.

4 Experimental Results

The experiment was conducted with five healthy participants (four males and one female) in their 20s. This study was reviewed and approved by the Institutional Review Board of the ergonomic research, National Institute of Advanced Industrial Science and Technology (HF2022-1285). Based on the age of the participants, the friction coefficient used in the graspability judgement was set to 0.53, which is the average value for the people in their 20s, as shown in [12].

The participants were divided into two groups (Group A and Group B) that differed in the order of the learning method, as summarized in Table 2.

The average percentage of correct answers on the comprehension test is summarized in Fig. 8. The average correctness in Comprehension Test 1 of Group A, who learned the target hand through VR, was higher than that of Group B, who learned by watching videos. Although statistical differences cannot be discussed due to the small number of participants, the results suggest the effectiveness of the experience in VR on

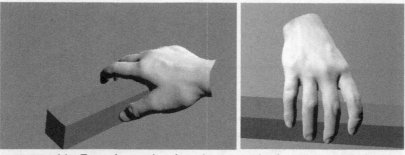

(a)   Example question about the posture that is *within* the ROM

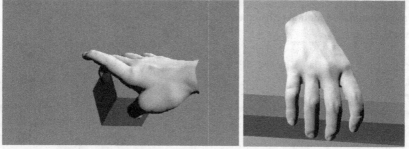

(b)   Example question about the posture that is *outside* the ROM

Fig. 7. Examples of static images of a hand model displayed as questions in the comprehension test

Table 2. Experimental process of each participant group

Step	Group A	Group B
1	VR learning	Video learning
2	Comprehension Test 1	
3	Rest	
4	Video learning	VR learning
5	Comprehension Test 2	

understanding others' hands that differ in ROM. From the comparison between Comprehension Tests 1 and 2, the average correctness increased regardless of the group, that is, the order of the learning method. In addition, free comments from the participants showed that most of them experienced difficulties in controlling the hand model at will, at least at the beginning. This suggest that the participants were not fully familiar with the system control to adequately understand the characteristics of the target hand, so they could answer the question correctly in the first test. Moreover, the correctness ratio was largely different depending on the questions (from 20% to 100%). In addition to the displayed order, the characteristics of the posture itself should be investigated in detail

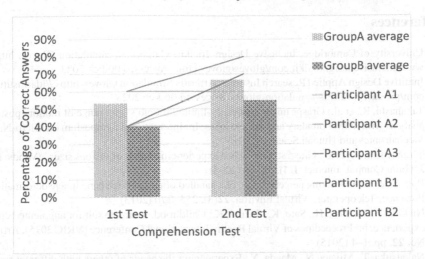

Fig. 8. Average percentage of correct answers in comprehension tests. Participants were grouped according to the learning method. (Group A: VR learning -> Video learning, Group B: Video learning -> VR learning)

with ROM, which will be included in our future work. The participants also referred to the difficulty in controlling the hand motion at will in their free comments particularly when their actual posture was considerably different from that of the temporary fixed hand model owing to ROM violation. We believe that the additional display of a hand model that simply obeys the actual captured posture can help solve this problem. To further validate the system, it is necessary to devise a process to familiarize participants with the system and improve its basic usability.

5   Conclusion

In this study, we developed a VR-based system to experience a hand with restricted ROM, which differs from the system user's hand, using visual and vibrational stimuli. By considering force closure to determine whether a grasp has been established, the grasps realized during the VR experience became more natural. Preliminary experimental results suggested the effectiveness of the experience through the proposed VR system on the degree of understanding of the behavior of a hand with a different joint ROM. As the number of participants was very small in this study, further validation experiments, as well as system improvement based on the feedback from the experiment participants, such as the need for additional cues to help the system user match the actual posture with the displayed model posture, should be conducted.

Acknowledgements. This work was supported by JSPS KAKENHI grant number JP20H04268.

References

1. University of Cambridge, Inclusive Design Toolkit, Cambridge Simulation Gloves. http://www.inclusivedesigntoolkit.com/gloves/gloves.html. Accessed 06 Feb 2023
2. Intuitive Design Applied Research Institute, Arthritis Simulation Gloves. https://idarinstitute.com/products/arthritis-simulation-gloves. Accessed 06 Feb 2023
3. Takahashi, R., et al.: Grasps under artificially-limited thumb's joint range of motion–posture analysis with ROM boundary and muscle loads. In: International Symposium on Micro-Nano Mechatronics and Human Science (2018)
4. Terabayashi, K., et al.: Grasp strategy when experiencing hands of various sizes. eMinds: Int. J. Hum. Comput. Interact. I(4), 55–74 (2008)
5. Ban, Y., et al.: Modifying perceived size of a handled object through hand image deformation. Presence: Teleoperators Virtual Environ. 22(3), 255–270 (2013)
6. Nishida, J., Takatori, H., Sato, K., Suzuki, K.: Childhood: wearable suit for augmented child experience. In: Proceedings of Virtual Reality International Conference (VRIC 2015), Article No. 22, pp. 1–4 (2015)
7. Nakatsuka, T., Miyata, N., Maeda, Y.: Experiencing the hands of others with different range of motion-schematic design and prototype system development. In: Proceedings of 16th Joint Symposium between Sister Universities in Mechanical Engineering (JSSUME2020+1), pp.11–15 (2021)
8. The Linear Oscillatory Actuator [LD14–002] (P-06838), Nidec Copal Corporation. (In Japanese). https://akizukidenshi.com/catalog/faq/goodsfaq.aspx?goods=P-06838. Accessed 06 Feb 2023
9. Tada, M.: Wireless sensor and display modules for on-site motion measurement and intervention. In: Proceedings SI 2018, pp. 418–422 (2018). (in Japanese)
10. Garre, C., et al.: Interactive simulation of a deformable hand for haptic rendering. In: Proceedings of 2011 IEEE World Haptics Conference, pp. 239–244 (2011)
11. Prattichizzo, D., Trinkle, J.C.: Grasping. In: Siciliano, B., Khatib, O. (eds.) Springer Handbook of Robotics, pp. 955–988. Springer, Cham (2016). https://doi.org/10.1007/978-3-319-32552-1_38
12. Mabuchi, K., et al.: Effect of ageing on friction of human fingers. In: Biosurface and Biotribology, vol. 4, no. 4, pp.117–121 (2018)

Learning Labs and Virtual Reality. The Metaverse to Enhance Learning

Stefania Morsanuto(✉) , Elèna Cipollone(✉) , and Francesco Peluso Cassese(✉)

HeracleLab, Niccolò Cusano University, Rome, Italy
stefania.morsanuto@unicusano.com, {elena.cipollone,
francesco.peluso}@unicusano.it

Abstract. Virtual Reality (VR) is one of the scientific and technological frontiers of our era, a new mode of knowledge that puts the person at the center, becoming the highest point of approach of technological interfaces towards a progressive incarnation. This research is based on the prototype construction of a VR laboratory teaching project, in which, through an immersive experience, students will be able to experience simulations of different educational moments in kindergarten. The virtual environment is built with 360°video that allows students to look in all directions, to facilitate the exploration of the environment, observe the individual reactions of the children, decide where to place themselves in the space. We investigate the relationship between experiential teaching through VR and learning and if mnestic skills were implemented through this approach. Exploration of a new environment promotes memory formation through the concept of novelty mediated by hippocampal dopamine and has also shown that new environments not only promote learning in these environments but can also promote long-term enhancement for events occurring before/after exposure to the novelty. In fact, a new episode's memory is formed immediately after the experience and can last a lifetime. The hippocampal network plays a key role in the rapid acquisition of a memory of a once-in-a-lifetime experience, in which the novelty component of the experience promotes the prompt formation of the memory. Furthermore, dopamine has been documented to be the neuromodulator most implicated in novelty signaling [1], and the dopaminergic system is closely related to learning [2].

Keywords: university training · learning environment · design research

1 Virtual Reality and Learning

"Virtual reality (VR) is one of the scientific, philosophical and technological frontiers of our era. It is a means to create a complete illusion of being in a different place that can also be a fantastic, alien environment, with a body far from that of the human being. It is at the same time the most advanced tool to understand what a human being is in terms of cognition and perception" [3]. Virtual reality is a new mode of knowledge that focuses on the person, a new form of communication and experience, which becomes a revolutionary device for scientific research and development of educational projects.

M. Antona and C. Stephanidis (Eds.): HCII 2023, LNCS 14021, pp. 63–80, 2023.
https://doi.org/10.1007/978-3-031-35897-5_5

Unlike any other type of mediated communication, such as photography or cinema, thanks to VR users become protagonists of the proposed experience, passing from the feeling of "being perceiving information" to the feeling of "being in a place of information [4]". "The illusory experience in VR is possible because the main peculiarity of this technology lies in the inclusive relationship that can be created between user and environment" [5].

In VR systems every movement becomes information, modifying the environment and creating new communication scenarios. This is possible thanks to some peculiar elements that characterize VR, namely the level of immersiveness - the objective level of sensory fidelity of a VR system - and the sense of presence - the subjective feeling of really being inside the environment. Immersion is objective and measurable, while presence is the subjective response of the user dependent on the context, related to the psychological experience of being there virtually [6, 7].

VR is an adapted or simulated environment that users can explore and interact with [8]. Today, VR is used in many areas, such as play, psychological treatment, learning and social skills and attracts the attention of many educators as it allows you to simulate the real world for learning [9, 10]. VR emerges as a three-dimensional environment, increases the efficiency of the learning process and allows students to adapt to new conditions that occur as a result of modern technological developments. Thus, real-world objects can be represented visually in a VR environment, settings can be created that users cannot visit in real life due to various limitations, and real-time interaction can be offered to people in these environments [11].

Considering such a multifaceted nature of VR, it's no surprise that the last decade has also seen a surge of interest in immersive technologies in education [12–15]. VR has been, for example, used to develop and inspire communication, collaboration and other soft skills that are at the heart of pedagogy and learning [16].

Research has in fact shown that video and VR can bring numerous benefits to teaching, as it is able to generate new learning contexts that shape and transform mental processes, improve learning processes through the vision of real facts and experiences, processes and professional performance, promoting knowledge and procedural skills also offers schematizations and symbolizations to form concepts, guides reflection and self-reflection to form principles, provides stimuli to feed the imagination and creative thinking, thus being able to represent different points of view and therefore the complexity of situations [17–20]; finally, it simplifies abstract and complex concepts through the visualization of concrete examples, simulations and increases the degree of attention, motivation and participation [21, 22].

Virtual technology gives individuals the freedom to use technology interactively in knowledge acquisition [23] and supports various individual learning styles both audio, visual and kinesthetic. In addition, the interactive learning process about the use of virtual reality technology in knowledge acquisition supports the concept of constructivist learning, i.e., the learning process is carried out actively, interactively and collaboratively [19].

Mayer's cognitive theory [24] of multimedia learning takes place within two distinct systems of information processing: a visual system for processing visual knowledge and a verbal system for processing verbal knowledge. According to this theory, the computer is a system for providing information to learners. The role of the educational designer is to present the information (for example, as words or images, or both) and the role of the learner is to receive the information. The cognitive information processes enunciated by McLaren [25] include: "selecting relevant information, mentally organizing it into a coherent structure and integrating it with other knowledge". Mayer stated that "generative cognitive processing occurs when a learner engages in deep processing of working memory in service of the purpose of learning, such as organizing the material and integrating with previous knowledge." [24].

On the one hand, Cognitive Learning Theory specifically discusses individual cognitive abilities in material processing from the perspective of cognitive learning theory. On the other hand, VR technology explains that the acquisition of knowledge can be carried out interactively. Materials that encourage the process of understanding tend to be more effective in supporting learning media and can improve individual learning outcomes [19].

From a purely technical point of view, it is possible to identify VR systems depending on the level of immersiveness. Three types of VR are identified: immersive virtual reality (I-VR), in which the subject is completely immersed on a sensory level within the three-dimensional environment generated by the computer through "closed" viewers, semi-immersive virtual reality, composed of rooms within which computer-generated environments are projected on the walls (CAVE), and non-immersive virtual reality, where computer-generated environments that exist in 3D but are shown on a 2D display [26].

Dewey [27] suggested and defended the idea that students should learn by doing, experimenting in an authentic learning environment, about a century ago. Today, this topic is likely to come true with I-VR. Therefore, I-VR supports and motivates students to receive education in a safe environment, allowing them to directly experience learning activities or access settings that they cannot physically reach [28]. I-VR technologies offer users the opportunity to control the environment with a wide field of view, comprehensive stereoscopic vision and translational and rotational perspective [29]. Some research reports how I-VR technologies increase students' recall of learned concepts [28, 30], knowledge transfer [30], and positively influence emotional experiences, influencing learning outcomes [31].

Many studies indicate that I-VR is more effective than other VR technologies in terms of learning performance. The adoption of immersive virtual reality (I-VR) as a pedagogical method in education has challenged the conceptual definition of what constitutes a learning environment. High-fidelity graphics and immersive content using head-mounted displays (HMD) allowed students to explore complex topics in a way that traditional teaching methods cannot.

2 Embodied Virtual Reality (EVR) for Learning

One of the main innovations of VR has been to give life to a new form of human-machine interaction, able to convey experience and knowledge [32]. During the evolution in the development of advanced graphical interfaces, it is possible to observe a process of approach towards what has been called an embodied interaction, a progressive embodiment of technology in the user's body in order to make human-computer interaction even more natural [26, 33]. This approach to interaction - called direct manipulation - is based on the idea that people should act on digital objects in the same way as they interact with physical artifacts, without having to learn new commands, but simply adapting their perceptual-motor patterns to the proposed interface [6].

VR is considered the highest point of approach of technological interfaces towards this progressive incarnation [26]. With the aim of supporting an embodied mind - that is able to acquire knowledge not only in direct interaction with the physical world but also by using mediated information - VR has in fact always aspired to a progressive adaptation of interfaces to the body, developing increasingly advanced systems capable of fully involving the perceptual apparatuses, up to a complete sensory immersion [6, 34].

According to the contemporary vision of Embodied Cognition, the body constitutes together with the mind a single complex system, a psychosomatic network [35].In a certain sense, the body represents a primordial device of thought, a sort of "internal mental simulator". In analogy to a VR system, the body represents both a device for collecting and processing information from the surrounding environment, and a communication channel, covering two fundamental functions [36]. Through the body – more or less rationally, verbally and non-verbally – messages are sent and received [37].

Therefore, the human mind is closely linked to the body in which it resides, from which it continuously acquires information about the world [35]. Thought needs bodily mediation to originate, and it is precisely on the body that it is adapted, therefore it is embodied [38]. Therefore, the organization of man's thought can only be understood through the contextualized experience of a body-environment system [38, 39].

According to this conceptualization of Embodied Cognition, which argues that environments are conceptualized in terms of bodily experience, a model of embodied virtual presence has been developed, according to which the perception of the possibilities of interaction in the virtual environment activates in the first place the spatial presence, as they model the mental representation of the user about what bodily actions are possible in the virtual space. Starting from the Embodied theory, in recent decades, the integration of VR in the field of neuroscience has led to the following question: is it possible to experience the same sensations towards a body within a virtual environment as if it were a biological body and, if so, to what extent? [40].

Thanks to VR it is possible to replace the real body of a person with its representation in a virtual body - called avatar - allowing the individual to incarnate in it [40]. This allows you to experimentally manipulate the virtual body, in ways that would be impossible in physical reality [41]. For example, through immersive virtual reality it is possible to manipulate the body representation in terms of structure, shape, size and color [26] and it has emerged how the manipulation of the characteristics of the virtual body can influence the physiological responses of the real body [34, 42], as well as is able to modulate the behavioral responses of individuals [36, 43].

VR allows users to create, explore and interact within environments perceived as close to reality. Typically, users who enter a VR lab feel part of this world and act as if they are in the real world. In particular, although users do not always move their bodies in real space, users have the subjective perception of being "in action". The effect of a virtual action on cognitive processing has been demonstrated by Repetto et al. [32] who found that performing a virtual movement with a limb (i.e. virtual running performed with the legs/feet) accelerates the understanding of verbs that describe actions performed with the same limb (kicking, performed with legs/feet).

For example, it has been shown that when a virtual knife stabs a virtual body embodied in an I-VR environment, participants demonstrate an autonomous response and activation of the motor cortex in preparation to move the hand off the road, just as they would in real life. So, anything that can happen in reality can be programmed to happen in VR and be experienced as a real situation [26, 33].

The embodiment in a virtual body is a complex phenomenon, which can give rise to different subjective illusions [40], linked to both spatial, motor and affective aspects. Among these we find the illusion of ownership of a virtual body, understood as "perceptual illusion that a virtual body coincides in space with the real body of the person" [26]. A consequence of this illusion is the Proteus effect, or that phenomenon whereby "when a person wears an avatar, he becomes that avatar" [44].

This effect can lead to different effects on a cognitive and psychological level such as: 1) empathy: VR is renamed "the empathy machine" because it allows you to easily put yourself in the shoes of the other and perceive the world from a different perspective. 2) Self-confidence: the type of avatar and the environment in which you are inserted influences the increase in self-confidence [45]. 3) problem solving: in a recent experiment, it was shown that individuals embodied in a virtual representation of Albert Einstein showed improvement in problem solving processes [46]. 4) motor behavior: thanks to VR you can also get to the modification of your motor behaviors; for example, the incarnation for a few minutes of the virtual body of the famous musician Jimi Hendrix, led people to play a virtual djembe with more movements than another man [40].

Most existing education VR systems are based on constructivist learning theory, which assumes students build their own understanding of what they study while interacting within VR environments. It is suggested that virtual reality facilitates new types of learning experiences of a highly perceptive nature, which allow students to immerse themselves in a phenomenon of a visual nature. The idea is that students are better able to master, retain and generalize new knowledge when they are actively involved in building knowledge through learning-by-doing [45].

For true embodiment to occur, the individual must integrate different perceptual, sensory and motor characteristics of the environment, through the physical interaction of the whole body with the context in which the experience or learning takes place. Virtual reality offers a great platform to allow this type of experience without the student being physically present in the real environment. The theory of embodied cognition highlights the interaction between perception, action, body and environment. According to the theory, body-specific experiences (e.g., head, hand, or foot) and modality (e.g., auditory, visual, or tactile) help construct bottom-up mental representations by integrating memories of these experiences with relevant conceptual representations. Once integrated as such, representations can activate the perceptual and sensorimotor regions of the brain when they are engaged or retrieved in real time [47]. If virtual environments could base learning on perception and action, students should be more successful and benefit from meaningful and lasting learning [39].

In this regard, some emerging publications on learning embodied in VR have begun to suggest that practical manipulation and bodily interaction could benefit learning in immersive technologies [7].

In particular, it has been argued that the ability to encode and retrieve information is limited by the actions we can perform on it and the limitations/opportunities provided by our bodies [48]. The ontogeny of memory is closely connected with the onset of locomotion during childhood and related to the maturation of the hippocampus [48]. This brain structure, along with the entorhinal cortex, contains different types of cells dedicated to different tasks. Hippocampal place cells encode location. Head-direction cells provide a direction of visualization on remembered content and allow the generation of an egocentrically consistent representation in the medial parietal areas. Grid cells in the entorhinal cortex support the process of updating a viewpoint in relation to self-movement signals. Glenberg and Hayes [48] specifically proposed that aligning hippocampal position cells and grid cells relative to environmental cues triggers the encoding of the space in which personal events are experienced. Embodied navigation and memory are therefore closely connected [49].

Particularly relevant to this study are the initial ideas linking immersion in VR to the virtual learning environment [50], which suggest that being located in simulated environments could help pedagogical outcomes during learning in immersive media by improving spatial knowledge construction, memory, and recall [32].

2.1 Virtual Reality Learning Environment (VRLE)

Virtual realities are used as virtual learning environments (VLE) where students can interact with others while performing a series of tasks [51]. They also have the chance to acquire new skills such as spatial socialization, sharing, data visualization, and even acquiring new language skills. It is a heuristic tool to engage students by exploring ideas in real time and in an experimental environment. VLE provides authentic contexts in which users train and share virtual resources and develop new knowledge and learning that are perceived as more meaningful to contemporary, digitally native learners [51].

There is a growing trend to use virtual reality learning environments (VRLEs) in education to improve student learning process and course learning outcomes [10]. In fact, more recent studies [52] have confirmed that when students use VRLE they are more engaged and more motivated than when using conventional tools, such as slide presentations.

VRLE are powerful and useful tools in the educational field as they can solve some of the typical problems that occur during practical lessons in real labs [52].

Why are VRLE effective for subject learning? First, because they allow experimentation from an egocentric point of view. This feature places VR in an intermediate position between the mere observation of the action (as in a video) and the execution of the real action, with an important bounce on brain activity.

Secondly, VR allows active navigation while the user actively explores the environment, manipulating keyboards, joysticks or controllers. Within a virtual world, the user can choose directions and have the impression of walking or running simply by adjusting the speed of movement. Jebara et al. [53] studied the effect of different types of virtual navigation on episodic memory in young and old. In a virtual environment designed as a city to explore from inside a car, participants were asked to retrieve events that happened with questions about "what", "where" and "when". As expected, there was an improvement in storage.

Third, VR provides environmental enrichment using flexible scenarios. From two-dimensional (2D) to three-dimensional (3D) perspectives, the amount of spatial information can increase the degree of enrichment.

Clemenson and Stark [54] found a beneficial effect of virtuous 3D environments on the hippocampus, in terms of neurogenesis and memory and learning tasks. In their study, the authors trained inexperienced gamers for 2 weeks on two different video games. One was based on simple 2D graphics and one was based on complex 3D graphics. The control group did not receive any training. Visual and memory performance was tested: visual accuracy and visual processing speed in an enumeration task, memory discrimination between highly similar recall elements from repeating elements, and a spatial memory score. Participants trained with the 3D video game outperformed both the 2D players and the control group in the discrimination task and spatial memory task, but not in the visual task. Since the discriminating task is associated with hippocampal activity, the authors inferred that 3D VR presumably also affects hippocampal activity. Taken together, these results support the idea that memory can be improved by means of enriched 3D scenarios, as they can stimulate hippocampal activity [32].

The exploration of a new environment has been shown to promote memory formation in healthy adults, thanks to the concept of novelty mediated by hippocampal dopamine [55] and also found that new environments not only promote learning in these environments, but may also promote long-term potentiation for events that occur before or after exposure to novelty [56]. Studies on animal has also suggested that the effects depend on hippocampal dopamine, which may have two potential sources: one is the ventral tegmental area (VTA) and the other is the locus coeruleus (LC) [57]. Research reports that the concept of novelty is a slow event, to such an extent that it can lead weak memory traces towards persistence in memory [31, 57, 58].

Some studies have reported similar effects on humans. For example, Fenker [59] exposed adult participants to images of new or familiar scenes before performing a word-learning task. The results showed a greater memorization of words after being exposed to new stimuli, rather than familiar, reporting beneficial effects of novelty both on consolidation and on coding. Neuroimaging studies have suggested how co-activation of the hippocampus and dopaminergic midbrain positively influences memorization [60]. A study using new and familiar I-VR 3D environments highlighted how exploring the new environment improved information recall in a memory test, but not recognition [61].

Not only new scenes and spatial novelties have proven to have benefits on memory. A study of elementary school children found that experimenting with a novel but not a science or music class familiar 1 h before or after reading a story improved story memory [62]. Similar beneficial effects of novelty have been found on visual memory in adolescents, suggesting that experiencing novelty may have a generalizable effect on long-term memory [63]. In line with this suggestion, a recent study of young adults suggested that active exploration of new environments may be necessary, since only active exploration, but not passive exposure to novelty improved word recall [56, 64].

A systematic review of several VR studies indicated an increase in student learning outcomes and intrinsic motivation. In addition, learning in a virtual space has been found to have an enhanced learning effect especially when the virtual environment is more closely aligned with that of the physical world, such as allowing students to move around space and touch and interact with objects through more sophisticated devices such as HTC VIVE rather than a gamepad such as a PlayStation 4 [65].

Therefore, educational activities that use VR can go beyond simple observation and exploration: they allow students to have experiential learning, in which learning is realized through direct experiences [65]. VR has also been found to influence student motivation where an immersive head-mounted display (HMD) VR positively influenced students' motivational beliefs by decreasing test anxiety [66]. Finally, realistic 360° scenes projected onto HMD have been found to provide immersive experiences that give students a sense of presence by participating in immersive virtual field trips without having to leave their classroom [67, 68].

3 Emotion, Learning and Virtual Reality

VR, thanks to unique characteristics in terms of immersion and interactivity, can make the user live a digital world "as if it were real" as well as to make its computerized representation (avatar) perceive as their own body (embodiment). The person, in this way, is at the center of the experience and has the opportunity to interact with the proposed content simply through the movements of the body [6].

VR is able to elicit a very intense emotional response in the user [69, 70], so much so that it has been defined as an "affective medium" [6]. If it is true that it is possible to feel emotions - even deep ones - while reading a book or watching a movie, with VR these emotional responses are even more intense, in some cases even comparable to those experienced in real life [6, 70]. There was also an increase in positive emotions [71, 72] when using games in VR greater than in on-screen mode, particularly about happiness and surprise [6].

Positive emotions are fundamental for the subject because they expand the repertoire of actions and thoughts, favoring learning, attention, creativity and the desire to get involved [73]. In addition, they build important lasting resources, such as optimism and resilience, that make us more ready to experience additional pleasurable emotions. Neuroscience has shown how, when we are happy, the brain reacts by activating the reward circuit, through dopamine, highly linked to motivation. This chemical discharge involves the creation or consolidation of synapses and this causes the pleasant experience to be repeated, as it pushes us to search for what has already made us feel good [73].

Emotions play an essential role in rational decision-making, perception, learning, and a variety of other functions that affect both the human physiological and psychological state [74]. Emotions, therefore, also play a crucial role in training and contribute to making learning deeper, more aware and meaningful [73].

In other works, Parket [75] has shown that students with positive emotional states show better learning outcomes. The results indicate a significant effect of positive emotion, in the presence of I-VR, on the acquisition of knowledge. Positive emotion is a very strong modulator for both knowledge acquisition and motivation, and high levels of immersion increase this positive effect, as they increase the overall perception of emotion. In fact, positive emotion stimulates curiosity, increases attention and arouses interest in the topic being learned; the absence of emotions has important consequences for learning and the preservation of knowledge in academic life [72].

VR can induce very intense sensations, including awe [76, 77], which is a complex emotional experience in which wonder, amazement, awe, surprise, admiration and reverence combine. The experiences of awe can lead people to profound changes in the way they perceive their relationship with the world, with beneficial effects on an educational level. Among the emotions experienced by the subjects in the use of I-VR we can find the awe, an emotion known to promote curiosity, which is able to amplify the emotions of students, in learning processes [77].

An experience that arouses amazement is triggered by the encounter with a person or event that is perceived as much greater, more complex or more important than the self. A typical example is the experience of vastness, that is, of open and harsh scenes, or of an extreme level of perceived depth [78]. Events or scenes that inspire awe impact the learner's knowledge about the world, and cause feelings of uncertainty. The gap between current knowledge and those needed to accommodate that unexpected event motivates learning [79].

Inducing awe with the help of immersive virtual reality has been shown to be successful in previous studies [80, 81]. Studies report how students have better short-term information retention when they experience a positive emotion in an I-VR. Awe, satisfaction, curiosity and hope were identified as good emotions that were associated with a higher level of learning [72].

The latest research highlights a significant link between awe, I-VR, reporting how this has a positive impact on learning, enhancing it [72, 80–82].

4 Research Design

4.1 Hypothesis

VR is defined as a set of technologies that enhances the perception of reality by superimposing context-sensitive virtual objects or information on it [3, 6, 83]. VR technology has the ability, therefore, to render in 3D model everything that can hardly be visualized in a classroom, on a computer and in the minds of students. The content, abstract and difficult, in this way becomes visible and interactive and thus promotes a better understanding of the topics of the lesson [84]. According to the DM 378/2018, students in the L-19 degree course are expected to participate in approximately 90 h of in-person Pedagogical Laboratory, useful for the acquisition of practical skills related to the observation of typical and atypical child development and educational design. Despite the specificity of the skills, students are not in direct contact with children and it is therefore often difficult to contextualize observation. Therefore, the prototype construction of an educational laboratory designed under virtual reality conditions is proposed. The research will be proposed to the students of the Degree Course in Education and Training Sciences at the Niccolò Cusano University in Rome, who will participate in the Special Pedagogy Childhood Workshops. Through an immersive experience, it is intended to put the students in the condition of living simulations of different educational moments in a nursery and kindergarten.

In the light of these considerations, the research hypothesis assumes that learning in the 'real world', virtual using the virtual and implemented through strategies of repro-cessing, memorization and fast learning, should enhance the workshop experience and consequently learning.

Through the construction of scenarios of lived educational life in services, the inten-tion is to explore the implications for learning that take place at the frontiers of reality where the virtual and the real are integrated to create new learning scenarios.

4.2 Methodology

Considering the scientific evidence identified, the methodological approach involves applying Kolbe's cycle (experiential learning) to the virtual classroom:

(1) Concrete Experience: living the experience in immersive mode, through visors, within the training lab, emphasizing emotional aspects and intuition. VR places 'students' in a digital world and does not require them to be in one place. It is excellent for training students on activities in situations where specific experience is required, which is incompatible with the classroom and where the cost of 'failure' is high. VR adds digital enhancements to the 'real world'. It provides 'learners' with contextual information [84].
(2) Reflective Observation: observing, reflecting and interpreting feelings and behaviour by focusing on understanding and depth of analysis related to situations. Scientific evidence shows the effectiveness of teaching interactions varies between social con-texts, learning activities and their combination. The construction of the learning experience presented in this project takes place via interactive hyperlinks. The dig-ital lesson plan is accurate and aesthetically pleasing, aiming to engage students, arousing their curiosity and engaging them in a variety of tasks that require the use of technology to create, collaborate, think critically, make connections and solve problems.
(3) Abstract Conceptualization: memorizing keywords that lead to theoretical constructs [56].
(4) Active Experimentation: Testing acquired knowledge and skills in new situations through pop-up tests at the end of the experience. Adults have a need to understand why they are learning something. They may be motivated both intrinsically and extrinsically and want to find a direct, concrete application to the learning experience [85].

The virtual environment was built with 360° Video, in real learning spaces and with the permission of both the teaching staff and parents. The 360° Video allows students to look in all directions. The user can explore the environment, observe the individual reactions of the children, decide where to place himself in the space. The VR classroom is integrated with interactive hyperlinks that the student can select within the application to access other environments. The environments designed in this first sample phase are five: structured motor activity (by the educator), unstructured play activity (free play), mealtime (feeding) and bath time (autonomy). Educational time in the nursery will be resumed thanks to collaboration with a private nursery in the Rome province and a nursery school in the Milan province.

The construction of the educational scenes is based on recently published scientific evidence, which shows that the exploration of novel virtual environments enhances declarative memory skills in young adults through novelty effects. In the construction of the virtual room, a pop-up window will appear with a list of 6 key-words, related to the teaching inputs of the lesson, in order to allow the students two levels of encoding of the environment: a superficial one (exploratory and observational) and a deep one of analysis and correlation of the theoretical bases conveyed by teaching pills provided by a virtual teacher [56].

Before moving on to the next room, a test will measure the level of learning of the 6 keywords. After traversing the entire virtual path, a final test will assess the level of memorization of all the proposed key-words. Results of previous research have shown that in the deep encoding condition subjects remembered more words and the transition from one new environment to another implemented this effect in young subjects [56]. In the 'loading' phases of closing the pop-up window with the word strips, an emoji appeared as positive reinforcement. In fact, the memory of a new episode is formed immediately after the experience and can last a lifetime. It has been shown that the hippocampal network plays a key role in the rapid acquisition of a memory of a once-in-a-lifetime experience, in which the novelty component of the experience favors the prompt formation of the memory. Furthermore, it has been documented that dopamine is the neuromodulator most involved in novelty signaling [1] and the dopaminergic system is closely related to learning [2]. The following table summarizes the construction of the experience (Table 1 and Fig. 1).

The learning experience will be offered to the students of the Special Pedagogy Workshop Childhood pathway of the spring sessions. The sample consists of 100 statistical units, of which 70 will participate not only in the regular classroom activities but also in virtual reality activities, 30 will be part of the control group and will attend only the classical activities. All students will be administered Rey's 15-Word Test (Rey Auditory Verbal Learning test - RAVLT), a clinical protocol for the assessment of learning and long-term verbal memory of new information (also called anterograde).

4.3 Objectives

Given the initial premises, i.e., wanting to test the effectiveness of immersive VR, we wanted to test its capabilities of: transferring theoretical knowledge; transferring practical procedural knowledge; stimulating analytical skills; inducing certain behaviours; influencing interest in the subject. The main objective of the activity is to structure a fast, but lasting learning approach in students by attempting to combine the learning experience with memory tasks. Takeuki et al. [55] show how neuronal activation in the locus coeruleus is particularly sensitive to environmental novelties, which associated with mnestic exercises enhance the learning experience leading to both improved memory and consolidation of synaptic transmission. Thus, neurons in the locus coeruleus may mediate the enhancement of postcoding memory in a manner consistent with the possible release of dopamine in the hippocampus. Related objectives are to improve student engagement and arouse curiosity. To develop an inclusive approach that can also

Table 1. Project Design

Virtual tool	Interaction first level	Educational input	Second level interaction	Verification system
Video 360 degrees allows the student to look in all directions. It allows for an 'immersive' lesson because the student is completely immersed in the projected virtual world, within the environment presented to them	The user can explore the environment, observe the individual reactions of the children and decide where to place himself in the environment	By placing the cursor in strategic areas, a pop-up appears with the teacher guiding the student to reflection and observation **STRIPS OF WORDS:** The pop-up appears on the screen listing 6 key-words related to theoretical constructs	**FAST LEARNING:** You triangulate the proposed experience in virtual reality with the teacher's guidance and keywords	Upon leaving each room, a mnestic test appears on the 6 words learnt during the experience
SCENE 1 STRUCTURED MOTOR ACTIVITY	The virtual reality app can also integrate with interactive hotspots that the learner can select within the app, such as web links, videos or text	**STRIPS OF WORDS:** Motricity [86] Learning Relationship Design In and out-door Symbolism	Pedagogical practice that promotes, accompanies and supports learning processes	Six-word mnestic test
SCENE 2 UNSTRUCTURED PLAYFUL ACTIVITY		**STRIPS OF WORDS:** Creativity [87] Problem Solving [88] Fine motor skills Workshop [20] Environment Play [89]	The 'pop-up teacher' reports on Winnicott's theories, development of creative thinking, play	Six-word mnestic test

(continued)

Table 1. (*continued*)

Virtual tool	Interaction first level	Educational input	Second level interaction	Verification system
SCENE 3 SLEEPING		**STRIPS OF WORDS:** Transitional object [87] Perception [90] Routine [55] Cycladic rhythm Space lullaby	The lecturer approaches the topics from the bio-psycho-social aspects	Six-word mnestic test
SCENE 4 BATHROOM		**STRIPS OF WORDS:** Autonomy Enuresis Enuresis Spannulation Emotional development Alliance	The 'pop-up teacher' offers short interventions on autonomy development and sphincter control starting with the development of emotions	Six-word mnestic test
SCENE 5 LUNCH		Feeding Language development Observation Coordination (oculo/manual) Autonomy		Six-word mnestic test

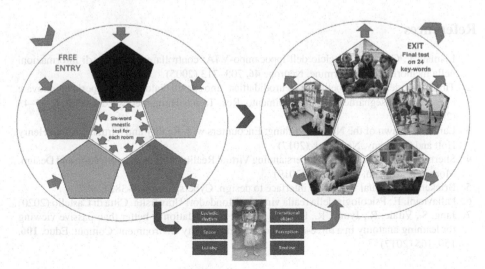

Fig. 1. Functional model

be used by students with Specific Learning Disorders [91]. The aim is the structuring of a VR lesson model, with precise characteristics, which can be replicated and extendable to other teaching contexts.

5 Conclusions

In recent years, marked by the pandemic, attention has been paid to technology and its implications for education. The usability of technology and forced disposition have led to an evolution of digital didactics and the development of strategies due to the crash between technology and experiential learning.

Although virtual simulations were already present in the educational field, they were not used because they were expensive, difficult to find and the frontal mode was familiar and rooted in daily practice. Today, with many advances in technology, VR is easier to access, both because of increased availability (networks, smartphones with high-resolution screens and fast-processing cameras), lower costs and greater readiness to use these tools.

Over the next few years, there will be an increasing need to continue to reinvent learning to keep pace with new challenges. And we will be able to meet these challenges with cheaper and better wearable technology, with data management and even, perhaps, the emergence of powerful quantum computing technologies. With these changes, e-learning experiences will be seamlessly integrated into everyday activities, leading to enhanced learning. In fact, VR gives many and important benefits in didactics, generating new learning contexts that shape and transform mental processes, promote greater understanding of information through the vision of facts and real experiences, increasing the degree of attention, emotion and participation. This project envisages the construction of a didactic experience built, based on the literature related to VR and above the neural correlates of learning. The evolution of the project will be the experimentation, shortly, with a statistically significant sample of subjects and the reproduction of the same on an ever-larger sample. The aim is the structuring of a VR lesson model, with precise characteristics, which can be replicated and extendable to other teaching contexts.

References

1. Lisman, J., Grace, A.: Il ciclo dell'ippocampo-VTA: controllare l'ingresso di informazioni nella memoria a lungo termine. Neurone **46**, 703–713 (2005)
2. Tino, C., Fedeli, M., Mapelli, D.: Neurodidattica: uno spazio dialogico tra saperi per innovare i processi di insegnamento e apprendimento. Res. Trends Humanieties Educ. Phil. **6**, 34–43 (2019)
3. Lanier, J.: Dawn of the New Everything: Encounters with Reality and Virtual Reality. Henry Holt and Company, New York (2017)
4. Sherman, W.R., Craig, A.B.: Understanding Virtual Reality: interface, application and Design. Morgan Kaufmann, Burlington (2019)
5. Bricken, M.: Virtual words: no interface to design. Cyberspace, 363–382 (1992)
6. Pallavicini, F.: Psicologia della reatlà virtuale. Mondadori Università, Città di Castello (2020)
7. Jang, S., Vitale, R., Jyung, R., Black, J.: Direct manipulation is better than passive viewing for learning anatomy in a three-dimensional virtual reality environment. Comput. Educ. **106**, 150–165 (2017)

8. Makransky, N.K., Andreasen, S., Baceviciute, R.E.: Direct manipulation is better than passive viewing for learning anatomy in a three-dimensional virtual reality environment. J. Educ. Psychol. (2020)
9. Coban, M., Bolat, Y.I., Goksu, I.: The potential of immersive virtual reality to enhance learning: a meta-analysis. Educ. Res. Rev. **36**, 100452 (2022)
10. Parong, J., Mayer, R.E.: Learning science in immersive virtual reality. J. Educ. Psychol. **110**(6), 785–797 (2018)
11. Chung, L.: Virtual reality in college english curriculum: case study of integrating second life in freshman english course. In: 26th International Conference on Advanced Information Networking and Applications Workshops, pp. 250–253 (2012)
12. Radianti, J., Maichrzak, T.: A systematic review of immersive virtual reality applications for higher education: design elements, lessons learned, and research agenda. Comput. Educ. **147**, 103778 (2020)
13. Snelson, C., Hsu, Y.-C.: Educational 360-degree videos in virtual reality: a scoping review of the emerging research. TechTrends **64**(3), 404–412 (2019). https://doi.org/10.1007/s11528-019-00474-3
14. Howard, M.: Virtual reality interventions for personal development: a meta-analysis of hardware. Hum.-Comput. Interact. **34**(3), 205–239 (2019)
15. Jensen, L., Konradsen, F.: A review of the use of virtual reality head-mounted displays in education and training. Educ. Inf. Technol. **23**(4), 1515–1529 (2017). https://doi.org/10.1007/s10639-017-9676-0
16. Howard, M., Gutworth, M.B.: A meta-analysis of virtual reality training programs for social skill develpment. Comput. Educ. **144**, 103707 (2020)
17. Demitriadou, E., Stavroulia, K.-E., Lanitis, A.: Comparative evaluation of virtual and augmented reality for teaching mathematics in primary education. Educ. Inf. Technol. **25**(1), 381–401 (2019). https://doi.org/10.1007/s10639-019-09973-5
18. Lee, J.H., Shvetsova, O.A.: The impact of VR application on student's competency development: a comparative study of regular and VR engineering classes with similar competency scopes. Sustainability **11**(8), 2221 (2019)
19. Muhammad, R., Sony, W.: Virtual reality learning media with innovative learning materials to enhance individual learning outcomes based on cognitive load theory. Int. J. Manag. Educ. **20**(3), 100657 (2022)
20. Bonaccini, B.: Atelier aperto. Junior Editore (2018)
21. Yildirim, S.: The effect of educational videos used in History education on academic success. J. Educ. e-Learn. Res. **5**(3), 193–207 (2018)
22. Ganino, G.: Insegnare e apprendere con le tecnologie. PensaMultimedia, Lecce (2022)
23. Zhang, L., Wade, J., Bian, D., Swanson, A., Weitlauf, A.: Cognitive load measurement in a virtual reality-based driving system for autism intervention. IEEE Trans. Affect. Comput. **8**(2), 176–189 (2017)
24. Mayer, R.E.: The Cambridge Handbook of Multimedia Learning. Cambridge University Press, Cambridge (2005)
25. McLaren, B.M.: Polite web-based intelligent tutors: can they improve learning in classrooms? Comput. Educ. **56**, 574–584 (2011)
26. Slater, M., Sanchez-Vives, M.V.: Enhancing our lives with immersive virtual reality. Front. Rob. AI **3**, 74 (2016)
27. Dewey, J.: Nationalizing education. J. Educ. **84**(16), 425–428 (1916)
28. Meyer, O., Omdahl, M., Makransky, G.: Investigating the effect of pre-training when learning through immersive virtual reality and video: a media and methods experiment. Comput. Educ. **140**, 103603 (2019)
29. Calvert, J., Abadia, R.: Impact of immersing university and high school students in educational linear narratives using virtual reality technology. Comput. Educ. **159**, 104005 (2020)

30. Chittaro, L., Corbett, C.: Safety knowledge transfer through mobile virtual reality: a study of aviation life preserver donning. Saf. Sci. **102**, 159–168 (2018)

31. Chen, N., Tai, T., Hsu, K.S.: Novelty and dopaminergic modulation of memory persistence. Molec. Neurobiol. **57**, 3956–3968 (2020)

32. Repetto, C., Serino, S., Macedonia, M.: Virtual reality as an embodied tool to enhance episodic memory in elderly. Front. Psychol. **7**(18), 1–4 (2016)

33. Matamala-Gomez, M., Donegan, T., Bottiroli, S., Sandrini, G., Sanchez-Vives, M., Tassorelli, C.: Immersive virtual reality and virtual embodiment for pain relief. Front. Hum. Neurosci. **13**(279), 1–12 (2019)

34. Bergström, Ilias, Kilteni, Konstantina, Slater, Mel: First-person perspective virtual body posture influences stress: a virtual reality body ownership study. PLOS ONE **11**(2), e0148060 (2016). https://doi.org/10.1371/journal.pone.0148060

35. Damasio, A.: Descartes' Error: Emotion, Reason and Human Brain. Penguin Group, London (1994)

36. Osimo, S., Pizarro, R., Spanlang, B., Slater, M.: Conversation between self and self as Sigmund Freud - a virtual body owenership paradigm for self counseling. Sci. Rep. **5**(1), 13899 (2015)

37. Ekmna, P., Friesen, W.: Unmasking the Face: A Guide to Recognizing Emotions from Facial Clues. Prentice-Hall, Oxford (1975)

38. Cipollone, E., Pilotto, S., Fenso, S., Morsanuto, S.: Learning through theatricality: experimental approach and data analysis. Ital. J. Health Educ. Sports Incl. Didact. **5**(2), 383–396 (2021)

39. Sullivan, J.: Learning and embodied cognition: a review and proposal. Psychol. Learn. Teach. **17**(2), 128–143 (2018)

40. Kilteni, Konstantina, Groten, Raphaela, Slater, Mel: The sense of embodiment in virtual reality. Pres. Teleoper. Virt. Environ. **21**(4), 373–387 (2012). https://doi.org/10.1162/PRES_a_00124

41. Bohill, C., Alicea, B., Biocca, F.: Virtual reality in neuroscience research and therapy. Nat. Rev. Neurosci. **12**(12), 752–762 (2011)

42. Martini, M., Perez-Marcos, D., Sanchez-Vives, M.: What color is my arm? changes in skin color of an embodied virtual arm modulates pain threshold. Front. Hum. Neurosci. **7**, 438 (2013)

43. Seinfwls, S., Arroyo-Palacios, J.: Offenders become the victim in virtual reality: impact of changing perspective in domestic violence. Sci. Rep. **8**(1), 2692 (2018)

44. Bailenson, J.: Experience on Demand: What Virtual Reality is, How it Works, and What it Can Do. Norton & Company, New York (2018)

45. Bertrand, P., Guegan, J., Robieux, L., McCall, C.A.: Learning empathy through virtual reality: multiple strategies for training empathy-related abilities using body ownership illusions in embodied virtual reality. Front. Rob. AI **5**, 26 (2018)

46. Banakou, D., Kishore, S., Slater, M.: Virtually Being Einsterin Results in an improvement in cognitive task perfomance and a decrease in age bias. Front. Psychol. **9**, 917 (2018)

47. Li, P., Legault, J., Klippel, A.: Virtual reality for student learning: understanding individual differences. Human Behav. Brain **1**(1), 28–36 (2020)

48. Glenberg, A., Hayes, J.: Contribution of embodiment to solving the riddle of infantile amnesia. Front. Psychol. **7**, 10 (2016)

49. Buzsaki, G., Mose, E.: Memory, navigation and theta rhythm in the hippocampal-entorhinal system. Nat. Neurosci. **16**, 130–138 (2013)

50. Schott, C., Marshall, S.: Virtual reality and situated experiential education: a conceptualization and exploratory trial. J. Comput. Assist. Learn. **34**(6), 843–852 (2018)

51. Shin, D.: The role of affordance in the experience of virtual reality learning: technological and affective affordances in virtual reality. Telemat. Inf. **34**(8), 1826–1836 (2017)

52. Vergara, D., Tubio, M., Lorenzo, M.: On the design of virtual reality learning environments in engineering. Multimodal Technol. Interact. **1**(2), 11 (2017)
53. Jebara, N., Orriols, E.: Front. Aging Neurosci. **6**(338), 1–16 (2014)
54. Clemenson, G., Stark, C.: Virtual environmental enrichment through video games improves hippocampal-associated memory. Behav. Cogn. **35**(49), 16116–16125 (2015)
55. Takeuchi, T., et al.: Locus coeruleus and dopaminergic consolidation of everyday memory. Nature **547**, 357–362 (2016)
56. Schomaker, J., Baumann, V., Ruitenberg, M.: Effects of exploring a novel environment on memory across the lifespan. Sci. Rep. **12**, 16631 (2022)
57. Duszkiewicz, A.J., McNamara, C.G., Takeuchi, T., Genzel, L.: Novelty and dopaminergic modulation of memory persistence: a tale of two systems. Trends Neurosci. **42**(2), 102–114 (2019). https://doi.org/10.1016/j.tins.2018.10.002
58. Moncada, D.: Evidence of VTA and LC control of protein synthesis required for the behavioral tagging process. Neurobiol. Learn. Memory **138**, 226–237 (2017)
59. Fenker, D.: Novel scenes improve recollection and recall of words. J. Cogn. Neurosci. **20**, 1250–1265 (2008)
60. Jang, A., Nassar, M., Dillon, D., Frank, M.: Positive reward prediction errors during decision-making strengthen memory encoding. Nat. Hum. Behav. **3**(7), 719–732 (2019)
61. Schomaker, J., van Bronjhorst, M.: Exploring a novel environment improves motivation and promotes recall of words. Front. Psychol. **5**, 918 (2014)
62. Ballarini, F., Martínez, M.C., Perez, M.D., Moncada, D., Viola, H.: Memory in elementary school children is improved by an unrelated novel experience. PLoS ONE **8**(6), e66875 (2013). https://doi.org/10.1371/journal.pone.0066875
63. Butavand, D.R.: Novelty improves the formation and persistence of memory in a naturalistic school scenario. Front. Psychol. **11**, 48 (2020)
64. Schomaker, J., Wittmann, B.: Effects of active exploration on novelty-related declarative memory enhancement. Neurobiology, learning, Memory **179**, 107403 (2021)
65. Kwon, C.: Verification of the possibility and effectiveness of experiential learning using HMD-based immersive VR technologies. Virt. Real. **23**(1), 101–118 (2018). https://doi.org/10.1007/s10055-018-0364-1
66. Cheng, K., Tsai, C.: A case study of immersive virtual field trips in an elementary classroom: Students' learning experience and teacher-student interaction behaviors. Comput. Educ. **140**, 103600 (2019)
67. Han, I.: Immersive a case study of immersive virtual field trips in an elementary classroom: students' learning experience and teacher-student interaction behaviors. Brit. J. Educ. Technol. **51**(2), 420–435 (2020)
68. Jang, J., Ko, Y., Shin, W., Han, I.: A case study of immersive virtual field trips in an elementary classroom: students' learning experience and teacher-student interaction behaviors. IEEE Access **9**, 6798–6809 (2021)
69. Gorini, A., Griez, E., Petrova, A., Riva, G.: Assessment of the emotional resposnes produced by exposure to real food, virtual food and photographs of food in patients affected by eating disorders. Ann. General Psychiat. **9**, 1–10 (2010)
70. Villani, D., Riva, G.: Does interactive media enhance the management of stress? suggestion from a controlled study. Cyberpsychol. Behav. Social Netw. **15**(1), 24–30 (2012)
71. Allcoat, D., von Muhlenen, A.: Learning in virtual reality: effects on performance, emotion and engagement. Assoc. Learn. Technol. **26**, 1–13 (2018)
72. Olmos-Raya, E., Ferreira-Cavalcanti, J., Contero, M., Castellanos, C., Giglioli, I., Alcaniz, M.: Mobile virtual reality as an educational platform: a pilot study on the impact of immersion and positive emotion induction in the learning process. J. Math. Sci. Technol. Educ. **14**(6), 2045–2057 (2018)

73. Cipollone, E.: Apprendere con il cuore: come le emozioni influenzano l'apprendimento, Roma: EUR (2021)
74. Marin-Morales, J., Llinares, C., Guixeres, J., Alcaniz, M.: Emotion recognition in immersive virtual reality: from statistics to affective computing. Sensors **20**(18), 5163 (2020)
75. Park, B., Knorzer, L., Plass, J., Brunken, R.: Emotional design and positive emotions in multimedia learning: an eyetracking study on the use of anthropomorphisms. Comput. Educ. **86**, 30–42 (2015)
76. Chirico, A., Ferrie, F., Cordella, L., Gaggioli, A.: Designing awe in virtual reality: an experimental study. Front. Psychol. **8**, 2351 (2018)
77. Quesnel, D., Di Paola, S., Riecke, B.: Deep learning for classification of peakemotions within virtual reality systems. In: Proceedings of the 10th International Workshop on Semantic Ambient Media Experiences (SAME 2017), pp. 6–11 (2017)
78. Klatzky, R., Thompson, W., Stefanucci, J., Gill, D., McGee, D.: The perceptual basis of vast space. Psychon. Bull. Rev. **24**(6), 1870–1878 (2017)
79. Valdesono, P., Shtulman, A., Baron, A.: Science is awe-some: the emotional antecedents of science learning. Emot. Rev. **9**(3), 215–221 (2017)
80. McPhetres, J.: Oh, the things you don't know: awe promotes awareness of knowledge gaps and science interest. Cogn. Emot. **33**(8), 1599–1615 (2019)
81. Stepanova, E., Quesnel, D., Riecke, B.: Space - a virtual frontier: how to design and evaluate a virtual reality experience of the overview effect. Front. Dig. Human. **6**(7) (2019)
82. van Limpt, A., Nilsenova, M., Louwerse, M.: Awe yields learning: a virtual reality study. In: Cognitive Science Society, pp. 488–493 (2020)
83. Makransky, G., Lilleholt, L.: A structural equation modeling investigation of the emotional value of immersive virtual reality in education. Educ. Tech. Res. Dev. **66**(5), 1141–1164 (2018). https://doi.org/10.1007/s11423-018-9581-2
84. Sural, I.: Augmented reality experience: initial perceptions of higher education studentis. Int. J. Instr. **1**, 565–576 (2019)
85. Coryell, J.: Active learning: strategie e tecniche per coinvolgere. Educ. Reflect. Pract. **1** (2020)
86. Vecchiato, M.: Psicomotricità relazionale. Armando Editore (2022)
87. Winnicott, D.W.: Gioco e realtà. Armando Editore, Roma (1971)
88. Gariboldi, A.: Educare alla creatività. Carocci Editore (2020)
89. Donnini, G.: Gioco, narro, disegno. Rivista Internazionale di Pedagogia e didattica della scrittura **1**, 66–75 (2022)
90. Coppi, A.: La ninna nanna e le attività di cura per l'educazione e lo sviluppo dei bambini e delle bambine. MeTis **9**(1), 602–625 (2019)
91. Chiesa, M., Tomatis, C., Romaniello, S.: La realtà virtuale a scuola: le parole dei ragazzi. DigitCult **5**(1), 77–95 (2020)

Visuospatial Ability of Elderly Using Head-Mounted Display with Gaze Measurement Function

Toumi Oohara, Kansuke Kawaguchi, Tomiko Takeuch, and Fumiya Kinoshita(✉)

Toyama Prefectural University, Toyama, Japan
f.kinoshita@pu-toyama.ac.jp

Abstract. The early detection of mild cognitive impairment (MCI) is important for delaying cognitive decline. However, the early detection of MCI is challenging because it is a condition in which some cognitive functions are impaired but are difficult to detect because they do not interfere with daily life. Impaired visuospatial ability, one of the first symptoms of dementia, is a cognitive disorder that causes problems in recognizing the spatial location of objects and spatial–positional relationships of multiple objects. Therefore, a quantitative assessment of impaired visuospatial ability would be useful for early detection of MCI. Our research group has been developing virtual reality (VR) content to quantitatively evaluate a user's depth perception using a head-mounted display (HMD) with a gaze measurement function. In this study, we conducted a preliminary VR content evaluation experiment developed for a healthy elderly group prior to targeting an MCI patient group. Consequently, presbyopia in the elderly did not affect measurement results.

Keywords: mild cognitive impairment (MCI) · head-mounted display (HMD) · VR content · pupillary distance · convergence–divergence motion

1 Introduction

To delay cognitive decline, early detection of mild cognitive impairment (MCI), which lies on the borderline between being healthy and having dementia, is important [1]. However, early detection of MCI is challenging because it is a condition in which some cognitive functions are impaired but are difficult to detect because they do not interfere with daily life. Objective cognitive-function tests are important for the diagnosis of MCI and require the multidimensional assessment of many cognitive domains, including memory, language, executive function, visuospatial cognition, and attention [2]. As a cognitive-function assessment battery for MCI, the Montreal Cognitive Assessment is considered excellent for detecting MCI and is widely used [3]. Although screening tests based on memory loads are effective in detecting amnestic MCI, they are not accurate in detecting nonamnestic MCI. As the annual rate of progression from MCI to dementia is significant (approximately 10%) [4], it is important to establish a testing method for the early detection of nonamnestic MCI.

© The Author(s), under exclusive license to Springer Nature Switzerland AG 2023
M. Antona and C. Stephanidis (Eds.): HCII 2023, LNCS 14021, pp. 81–90, 2023.
https://doi.org/10.1007/978-3-031-35897-5_6

Early symptoms of Alzheimer's dementia, such as difficulty drawing figures, getting lost while driving, and inability to drive in a garage can appear in the absence of visual impairment [5]. These symptoms, known as impaired visuospatial ability, are important clinical manifestations for early diagnosis. There are two pathways for visual information processing in the cerebral cortex [6]. The first is the ventral visual pathway, which processes information to identify an object. The ventral visual pathway originates in the primary visual cortex, passes through the temporal cortex, and ends in the prefrontal cortex. The second is the dorsal visual pathway, which processes information regarding the position and depth of objects. The dorsal visual pathway also originates in the primary visual cortex, a visual pathway that passes through the parietal cortex and connects to the prefrontal cortex. Visual information from these two pathways reconverges in the prefrontal cortex where visual information processing occurs. In Alzheimer's dementia, in addition to parahippocampal damage, blood flow in the parietal-occipital lobe is reduced in the early stages of the disease [7]. Therefore, reduced blood flow in the parietal-occipital lobes in patients with Alzheimer's dementia affects dorsal visual pathway dysfunction. This is believed to be the responsible lesion, causing clinical symptoms such as "I can understand what the object is, but I cannot understand the spatial information, such as exact location and depth."

Impaired visuospatial ability is a clinical symptom observed not only in Alzheimer's dementia but also in MCI [8]. Therefore, a quantitative assessment of impaired visuospatial ability would be useful for early detection of MCI. Our research group has been developing virtual reality (VR) content to quantitatively evaluate a user's depth perception [9, 10]. The VR content was developed using Unity, and the objects placed on the screen could move freely in the depth direction. The VR content was presented through a head-mounted display (HMD) with a gaze-measuring function, and gaze information was obtained while the participants gazed at objects. As a preliminary experiment, we conducted a VR content evaluation experiment developed for a healthy elderly group, before targeting an MCI patient group. The main objective of this investigation was to determine whether any differences in measurement results occurred because of presbyopia in the elderly.

2   Experimental Methods

We conducted a VR content evaluation experiment developed in this study for one young and one elderly group of people. The participants included thirteen healthy young men and women (20.6 ± 1.4 years of age), and eight healthy elderly men and women with no history of dementia (71.5 ± 4.6 years of age). We comprehensively described the experiment to the participants and obtained their written consent beforehand. This experiment was conducted after obtaining approval from the Ethics Committee of Toyama Prefectural University (R4–5).

During this experiment, we used the HTC Vive Pro Eye VR system with a gaze measurement function for the HMD. This HMD is equipped with an eye tracker from Tobii Technology, the world's largest eye-tracking company, and it is capable of acquiring binocular eye-tracking information with a temporal resolution of 119.5 Hz. The gaze information obtained from the Vive Pro Eye system includes gaze vector, eye position, pupil position, pupil diameter, and eye opening/closing [11, 12].

In the VR content, a spherical object was displayed at the center of the screen and periodically moved along the depth direction toward the participant five times every 30 s. The depth movement was set to one to denote the front position and 15 for the distant position, and the size of the spherical object was set to one (Fig. 1). Each participant underwent three measurements.

The experiment was conducted in a relaxed posture, while at rest. The Vive Pro Eye system was calibrated by placing an HMD on the participants, after which we tested the level of comfort when wearing the HMD and the video display. Before conducting the experiment, all participants were instructed to gaze continuously at the spherical object displayed in the center of the screen and not move their head during the gaze measurement. During this experiment, to account for the influence of eyeglasses, we asked participants to remove them.

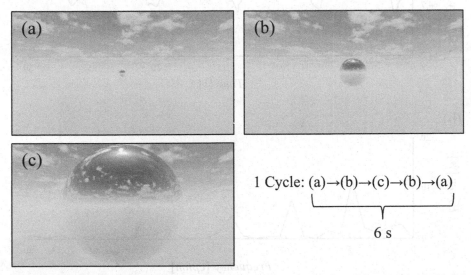

Fig. 1. Examples of VR content with varying depth patterns. Depth positions at (a) 15, (b) 7.5, and (c) 1.

3 Analytical Indices

During the experiment, we used the pupillary distance between the left and right eyes as an index of depth perception while gazing at the object. The pupillary distance fluctuates with the convergence–divergence motion and can be calculated using the Vive Pro Eye system by determining the Euclidean distance from the time-series data at the positions of the left and right eyes. To exclude the influence of blinking eyes in the acquired time-series data of pupillary distance, the intervals where blinks were observed were considered as missing values from 0.05 s before and after the blink, after which linear interpolation was performed.

During this experiment, the position of the peak frequency using the discrete Fourier transform (DFT) and the coefficient of determination between the time-series data of the pupillary distance and sine-wave model were calculated as representative values for each pupillary distance. For the peak frequency obtained using DFT, the number of oscillations per 30 s is denoted as the cycle per half-minute (cphm), which is considered as the peak frequency unit. For the coefficient of determination between the time-series data of the pupillary distance and sine-wave model, an optimal sinusoidal model was

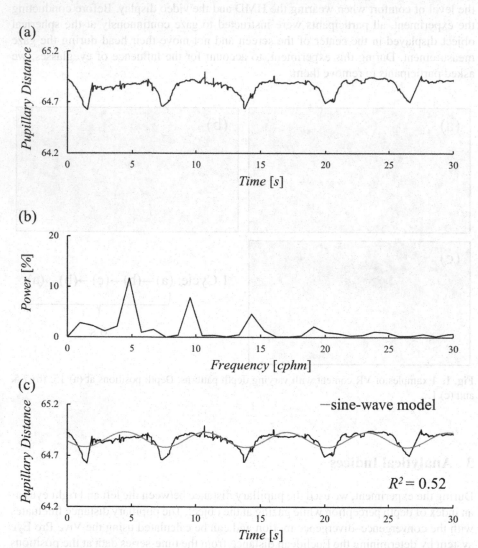

Fig. 2. Example of time-series data when the participant is instructed to gaze at an object (a) Time-series data of pupillary distance averaged by adding three measurements, (b) power spectrum of time-series data, and (c) coefficient of determination between the time-series data of the pupillary distance and the sine-wave model.

created for each time series. This was achieved by searching for the value minimizing the residual sum of squares while changing the amplitude in 0.01 increments for a sinusoidal wave matching the movement period of the spherical object. Figure 2 shows an example of time-series data when the participant was instructed to gaze at an object. As shown in Fig. 2, the pupillary distance tends to decrease as the spherical object approaches the participant (convergent motion). In this example, the peak frequency was detected at 5 cphm, and the coefficient of determination was 0.52. The results of the representative

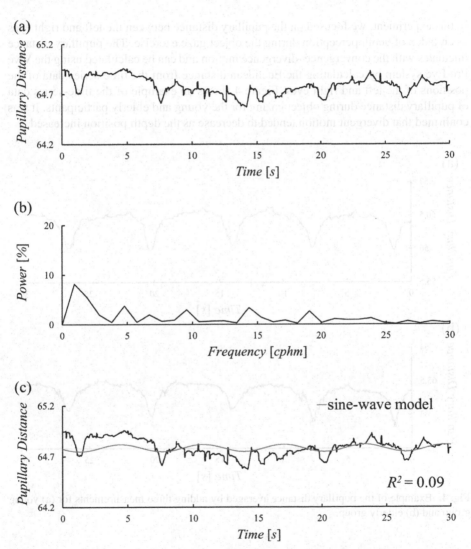

Fig. 3. Example of time-series data when the participant was instructed not to gaze at the object (a) Time-series data of pupillary distance averaged by adding three measurements, (b) power spectrum of time-series data, and (c) coefficient of determination between the time-series data of the pupillary distance and the sine-wave model.

values indicate that a gaze can follow the movement of the object's spatial position. Figure 3 shows an example of time-series data when the participant was instructed not to gaze at the object. In this example, the peak frequency was detected at 1 cphm and the value of the coefficient of determination was 0.09. The results of the representative values indicate that a gaze does not follow the movement of the object's spatial position.

4 Results

In this experiment, we focused on the pupillary distance between the left and right eyes as an index of depth perception during the object gaze exercise. The pupillary distance fluctuates with the convergence–divergence motion and can be calculated using the Vive Pro Eye system by calculating the Euclidean distance from the time-series data of the positions of the left and right eyes. Figure 4 shows an example of the time-series data of pupillary distance during object gazing for the young and elderly participants. It was confirmed that divergent motion tended to decrease as the depth position increased.

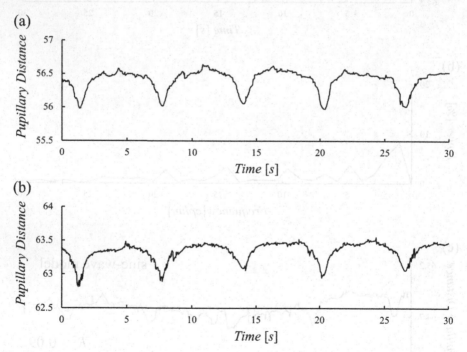

Fig. 4. Example of the pupillary distance averaged by adding three measurements for (a) young group and (b) elderly group.

In this experiment, the position of the peak frequency using DFT and the coefficient of determination between the time-series data of the pupillary distance and sine-wave model was calculated as representative values for each pupillary distance. However, the results for one elderly participant could not be analyzed because of many missing values in the time-series data. Therefore, these data were excluded from the analysis. An example of the peak frequency obtained using DFT is shown in Fig. 5. It can be confirmed that the peak frequency was detected at 5 cphm in both typical time-series datasets. The peak frequency was calculated for all pupillary distance time-series data and the number of false positives was checked (Table 1). Consequently, the number of false positives for peak frequency was not observed in the younger group. However, one false-positive result was observed in the elderly group. An example of the coefficient of determination between the time-series data of the pupillary distance and sine-wave model is shown in Fig. 6. It was confirmed that the coefficient of determination was higher than 0.5 in both typical time-series data. The coefficient of determination was calculated for all pupillary distance time-series data (Fig. 7). Statistical analysis using the Mann–Whitney U test showed no significant differences between the two groups.

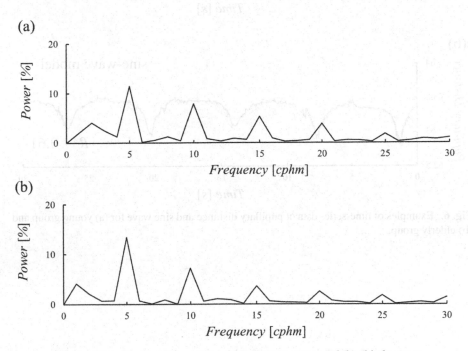

Fig. 5. Example of peak frequency for (a) young group and (b) elderly group.

Table 1. Detection position of peak frequency of pupillary distance.

Depth Position	0 cphm	1 cphm	3 cphm	5 cphm	7 cphm	Total
Young group	0	0	0	**13**	0	**13**
Elderly group	0	**1**	0	**6**	0	**7**

(a)

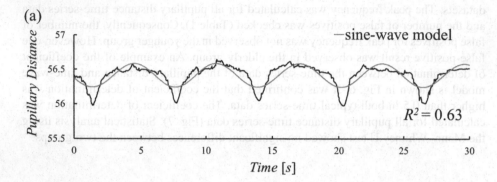

(b)

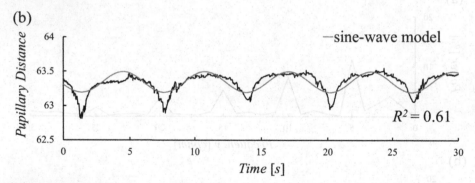

Fig. 6. Examples of time-series data of pupillary distance and sine wave for (a) young group and (b) elderly group.

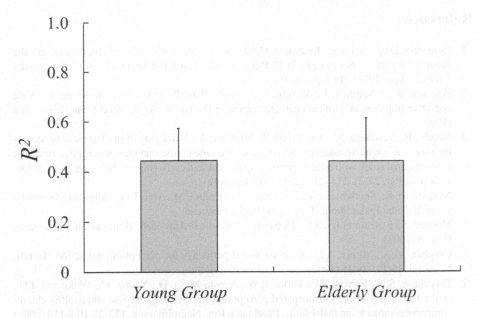

Fig. 7. Coefficient of determination for each group (average ± SD).

5 Discussion

The early detection of MCI is important for delaying cognitive decline. However, early detection of MCI is difficult because it is a condition in which certain cognitive functions are impaired but are difficult to detect because they do not interfere with daily life. Impaired visuospatial ability, one of the first symptoms of dementia, is a cognitive disorder that causes problems in recognizing the spatial location of objects and spatial–positional relationships of multiple objects. Therefore, a quantitative assessment of impaired visuospatial ability would be useful for early detection of MCI. Our research group has been working on the development of VR content that can quantitatively evaluate the depth perception of users. In this study, we conducted a preliminary VR content evaluation experiment developed for an elderly group with no history of dementia prior to targeting the MCI patient group. The main objective of this investigation was to determine whether any differences in measurement results occur depending on presbyopia in the elderly. Consequently, presbyopia in the elderly did not affect measurement results. However, in the case of one elderly participant, false positives occurred at the peak frequency position. Because this may represent a characteristic of MCI, a more detailed study of the data from this participant is required. By conducting measurements on patients with MCI, we will continue to examine whether the VR content developed in this study is effective for the early detection of MCI.

Acknowledgements. This work was supported by JSPS KAKENHI Grant Number 19K20620, Tateisi Science and Technology Foundation, and Hoso Bunka Foundation.

References

1. Dementia Diagnosis and Treatment Guideline Planning Committee (supervised by the Japanese Society of Neurology): 2017 Dementia Diagnosis and Treatment Guidelines, Igaku Shoin, Tokyo (2017). (In Japanese)
2. Petersen, R.C., Smith, G.E., Waring, S.C., Ivnik, R.J., Tangalos, E.G., Kokmen, E.: Mild cognitive impairment: clinical characterization and outcome. Arch. Neurol. **56**(3), 303–308 (1999)
3. Suzuki, H., Yasunaga, M., Naganuma, T., Fujiwara, Y.: Validation of the Japanese version of the montreal cognitive assessment to evaluate the time course changes of cognitive function: a longitudinal study with mild cognitive impairment and early-stage alzheimer's disease. Jpn. J. Geriatr. Psy. **22**(2), 211–218 (2011). (In Japanese)
4. Nakashima, K., Shimohama, T., Tomimoto, H., Mimura, M., Arai, T.: Handbook of Dementia Care, 2nd edn. Igaku Shoin, Tokyo (2021). (In Japanese)
5. Mendez, M.F., Cummings. J.L.: Dementia: A Clinical Approach. Butterworth-Heinemann, Boston (2003)
6. Goodale, M.A., Milner, A.D.: Separate visual pathways for perception and action. Trends. Neurosci. **15**(1), 20–25 (1992)
7. Thiyagesh, S.N., Farrow, T.F., Parks, R.W., Acosta-Mesa, H., Young, C., Wilkinson, I.D., et al.: The neural basis of visuospatial perception in alzheimer's disease and healthy elderly comparison subjects: an fMRI study. Psychiatry. Res. Neuroimaging. **172**(2), 109–116 (2009)
8. Petersen, R.C.: Mild cognitive impairment as a diagnostic entity. J. Intern. Med. **256**(3), 183–194 (2004)
9. Kinoshita, F., Takada, H.: A study on the development of VR content for quantitative evaluation of impaired visuospatial ability. In: HCI International 2022–Late Breaking Papers: HCI for Health, Well-being, Universal Access and Healthy Aging: 24th International Conference on Human-Computer Interaction, HCII 2022, Virtual Event, June 26–July 1, 2022, Proceedings, pp. 440–450. Springer, Cham (2022). https://doi.org/10.1007/978-3-031-17902-0_31
10. Ohara, T., Kinoshita, F.: A study on the development of VR content to evaluate depth perception ability. In: 2022 17th International Conference on Computer Science & Education (ICCSE 2022), pp. 165–168 (2022)
11. Vive Pro Eye Homepage. https://www.vive.com/us/. Accessed 10 Mar 2023
12. Tobii Homepage. https://developer.tobiipro.com/commonconcepts/coordinatesystems.html. Accessed 10 Mar 2023

"Is This Real?": Assessing the Usability and Accessibility of Augmented Reality with People with Intellectual Disabilities

Leandro S. Guedes[1](✉) ⓘD, Irene Zanardi[1] ⓘD, Marilina Mastrogiuseppe[2] ⓘD,
Stefania Span[3] ⓘD, and Monica Landoni[1] ⓘD

[1] Università della Svizzera Italiana (USI), Lugano, Switzerland
{leandro.soares.guedes,irene.zanardi,monica.landoni}@usi.ch
[2] University of Trieste, Trieste, Italy
marilina.mastrogiuseppe@units.it
[3] Cooperativa Sociale Trieste Integrazione a m. Anffas Onlus, Trieste, Italy
http://luxia.inf.usi.ch/

Abstract. This paper assesses the perception of Augmented Reality (AR) by People with Intellectual Disabilities (IDs) when using assistive technologies in preparation for a museum visit. We designed and developed an application to test how AR can provide support and is perceived in this context. We organized a user study with 20 participants with IDs, all members of the same association. Three research visits, including focus groups, enabled us to assess the memorability of the contents before introducing AR technology and collect information about users' habits and preferences. Later, we assessed users' perception of AR individually during a test session and conducted a task-oriented hands-on session. Finally, we went to the museum with our users and gathered information about their preferences and choices when using AR in situ, constantly analyzing verbal and non-verbal feedback. We describe all our findings and discuss their implications in terms of guidelines for future design.

Keywords: augmented reality · accessibility · perception · user studies · people with intellectual disabilities

1 Introduction

Technologies such as Augmented Reality (AR) are becoming more popular as compatible devices are widely available, impacting how we can, for instance, learn new content and have fun. Despite its positive impact on engagement and learning, this technology is still not widely investigated with an accessibility focus, considering its benefits and limitations. Methods to produce inclusive and accessible solutions, such as co-design sessions, are time-consuming and require the involvement of different stakeholders and researchers to play various roles.

The complexity of the design process can impact how people with Intellectual Disabilities (IDs) can interact and benefit from AR.

In this work, we assessed the interaction of people with IDs with an AR application for informal learning. During three research visits, we organized focus groups to assess participants' previous knowledge and familiarity with the app's content. Then, we introduced the technology and collected their preferences. Later, we assessed their perception of AR elements with hands-on individual sessions. Finally, we went to the museum with them to contextualize the app and gather their preferences on the medium to be used during a visit.

Participants provided details about the size, color, and description of each 3D content. Participants did not have a precise preference for the realism of the 3D model, suggesting that incredible detail in the 3D model may not be necessary for the success of the AR application. Audio feedback and self-introduction provided a more immersive experience, while labels were less important but still provided an affordance. Some participants encountered issues with the device itself, highlighting the importance of adapting both the application and the device to ensure that software and hardware are accessible to users. Despite these challenges, participants quickly learned how to use AR technology to explore the model and became more confident in their ability to use the technology.

In this study, we contribute to the field of HCI in several ways. To begin, we provide insights into the preferences of users with IDs interacting with AR, in terms of elements that should be considered during the design. Secondly, the study proved the potential of AR applications in engaging users independently in informal learning experiences, by giving them the possibility to interact and explore independently the learning content. Lastly, the involvement of participants in the iterations of the design process proved the importance of co-design practices and highlight the roles they can take. By involving participants with IDs, designers can have access to their unique experiences and needs, thus allowing the development of more accessible and effective solutions.

This paper is organized as follows: In Sect. 2 we provided a background. Further, Sect. 3 introduces the design of our AR prototype. Section 4 presents the methodology used in this work. Yet, Sect. 5 shows the results we collected. Section 6 presents a discussion focusing on our research questions. Then, Sect. 7 introduces guidelines. Section 8, the limitations and future work. Finally, Sect. 9 concludes this paper.

2   Background

2.1   People with IDs and Informal Learning

ID is a neurodevelopmental disorder characterized by deficits in cognition and adaptive functioning [4]. The severity can vary greatly, with some people experiencing mild challenges and being able to live relatively independently with the right support, while others may need significant and daily assistance [35]. Assistance is needed in the context of formal and informal education, as learning can be difficult for individuals with IDs without accommodations or modifications

[29,48]. This is due in part to limitations in intellectual functions, which may include difficulties with abstract concepts, memory, problem-solving, planning, reasoning and generalization [4,18].

Museums are regarded as informal learning environments [31]. Informal learning is defined as learning in a socially collaborative context where the learner can choose what and how to learn, with activities focused on meaningful tasks that do not require assessment or have a predetermined goal [13]. Museum participation, in fact, is voluntary, since visitors choose based on their interests [31], but also because visitors can plan their tour, creating a personal agenda [20]. This way, the learning process is connected to self-determination, which is critical for achieving positive learning outcomes [51] [24] and ensuring an improved quality of life and life satisfaction for people with IDs [51]. Furthermore, museums can stimulate involvement in cultural life and promote inclusion [36,40]. As a result, accessibility must be considered to let people with disabilities participate in museum experiences and the resulting informal learning [14] [36]. With this goal in mind, technologies can help to achieve accessibility [14,42] through inclusive design that is based on real-world testing and application [42], calling for the involvement of the Human-Computer Interaction community.

2.2   AR for Learning

AR is a rapidly growing field that is changing how people interact with the virtual and real world. It superimposes virtual information onto the real world, creating an immersive and interactive experience [2]. With the increasing availability of devices, AR is quickly gaining popularity [23] and has the potential to revolutionize a wide range of industries, including education [2]. In the field of education, AR has the potential to enhance the learning experience [16,41]. Several studies have explored the benefits of AR in education and the results are positive [22] [2]. AR has been shown to increase motivation [47] and engagement [26] among students, as it presents virtual content in a realistic setting that makes learning more interactive and enjoyable. Because of this, its application has the potential to support individuals with IDs in their learning and development [6]. As previously stated, individuals with IDs may encounter obstacles with traditional learning methods [29,48], and with AR they are able to experience virtual content in a way that is more accessible and engaging [12] [30]. This can increase their motivation and engagement in learning, and reduce their dependence on caregivers [27]. With AR, individuals with IDs are able to independently explore educational material, allowing them to take control of their own learning process and develop new skills [27], making this technology suitable for informal learning contexts. Indeed, AR interventions seem to be the most effective when conducted in informal learning settings as part of informal activities [22].

In recent years, various AR solutions for individuals with disabilities, particularly visually-impaired individuals, have been developed. These can aid in developing important life skills such as ironing, making the bed [10], using ATMs [28], shopping for groceries [52], and even playing games [5]. Additionally, AR has been proven effective in improving literacy [32] [3] and numeracy skills [15] [30,39], as well as in improving learning outcomes in other school subjects, such as scientific knowledge [38]. AR applications can be standalone or enhanced by incorporating other sensory stimuli, such as tactile [33] and olfactory feedback [37].

2.3 Accessible AR in Museums

Accessible AR has been widely adopted in museums because of its *authenticity*, referring to its promise of meaningful experiences, *multisensory affordances*, which refer to its ability to provide multiple sensory modalities, *connectivity*, alluding to its ability to connect quickly with and within an environment, and *exploration* [43]. Some AR applications specifically designed for visually-impaired individuals enhance their museum experience by providing spoken descriptions of artworks [1]. The integration of AR technology not only makes the descriptions more interactive, but also empowers visually-impaired visitors to experience the art independently. In some cases, AR is combined with physical objects to offer a multi-sensory experience, further enhancing the overall experience [33,37]. Hard-of-hearing individuals can also benefit from AR application, which fosters a more direct and authentic interaction with the artwork, promoting independent exploration and enjoyment of cultural heritage [7]. For individuals with IDs, museum AR applications provide assisted navigation [21] and a more interactive approach to cultural heritage, allowing for a more direct experience [49].

2.4 Designing Accessible AR

The development of accessible and inclusive AR is essential for ensuring that everyone, regardless of their abilities, can enjoy the benefits that AR has to offer. One of the key considerations in creating accessible AR content is to follow accessibility guidelines such as the W3C Accessibility Guidelines (WCAG) [50]. These guidelines provide a framework for ensuring that digital content is designed in a way that is usable by as many people as possible, including those with disabilities. Indeed, accessibility features play a crucial role in learning and comprehension, both for individuals with disabilities and for everyone else. Visual accessibility, for example, can be achieved through the use of easy-to-read texts [19], which use simple language and short sentences, or Augmentative and Alternative Communication (AAC) [8] that uses pictograms. Auditory feedback, such as text-to-speech (TTS) technology [11], can also be used to make AR content more accessible. TTS technology is particularly valuable for non-literate individuals with IDs, but further research is needed to fully understand its impact on reading proficiency and comprehension [45].

Aside from following accessibility guidelines, it is critical to include people with disabilities in the design process in order to create truly accessible and inclusive AR content. Ongoing research is exploring methods for working and co-designing with individuals with intellectual disabilities (IDs) through focus groups, co-design, and active support [9,17]. Participatory design helps to ensure that AR technology is designed with the needs of people with disabilities in mind, and that it can be used to improve their learning and development [44]. However, when developing AR applications, the majority of researchers still involve people with IDs as passive subjects [43], posing doubts on those applications efficacy.

3 Designing AIMuseum: The AR Prototype

The development of AIMuseum aimed to provide a solution for people with disabilities to access and interact with cultural environments with ease [25]. In this paper, we are describing how we evaluated the usability of AIMuseum – the AR app – and discussing the implications of our findings.

The application was built using the Unity game engine and the C# programming language, and utilized the Vuforia API. We used QR codes as markers in our application, as they are easily recognizable, even in low light conditions, due to their black and white design. The QR codes were optimized for our needs based on preliminary testing, and the size and quality were adjusted accordingly. Additionally, we integrated a Screen Reader accessibility feature, using a UI Accessibility Plugin for Unity.

We engaged with educators to fit the AIMuseum experience with the learning objectives of the participants and the contents of the local museum. As a result, the application displays natural science content, focusing on dinosaurs, crocodiles, wolves, and deer. Each item was represented by a 3D model, a descriptive label, and audio feedback that provided a self-description (Fig. 1). Except for the dinosaur fossil, all of the selected animals were present in the museum as taxidermied specimens.

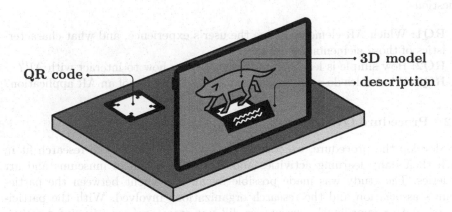

QR code

3D model

description

Fig. 1. Illustration of how the AIMuseum application works: it reads a QR code and generates a 3D model and description of the museum content.

To improve accessibility, the main menu includes a quick tutorial to help participants to use the application, and the possibility to change settings. Users can configure the text-to-speech volume and language, and the descriptive text font size.

When the app is launched, the user simply needs to point their device at a QR code to get information about the animal. The application will scan the code and provide further information, in this case, a brief description of the animal. The user can hear this information if the screen reader is turned on.

We evaluated several characteristics together with the participants in an iterative process for each feature. In particular, we considered the 3D model realism, size, and texture; textual description size, color, and background; voice (text-to-speech) regarding gender, tone, speed, and type.

4   Methodology

4.1   Rationale and Research Questions

This paper assesses the accessibility of AR by people with IDs when using assistive technologies before, during, and after a museum visit - an informal learning domain. While most AR research for IDs has focused on formal education, little is known about its effectiveness in informal settings such as museums.

The research consists of a user study that seeks to understand how people with IDs interact with AR and how they make sense of the information that it provides in the context of informal learning. We conducted three research visits (RV I, RV II, and RV III) to ANFFAS, an association that works with people with IDs in Trieste, Italy. There, we investigated the following research questions:

- **RQ1:** Which AR elements define the user's experience, and what characteristics of those elements are critical?
- **RQ2:** How simple is learning and remembering how to interact with AR?
- **RQ3:** What roles do participants play in the co-design of an AR application?

4.2   Procedure Overview

To develop the procedure, we collaborated with ANFFAS. The research fit in with their daily learning activities and with their visits of museums and art galleries. The study was made possible by an agreement between the participant's association and the research organizations involved. With the participants' and/or guardians' consent, we did not store any sensitive information, only audio and video for data analysis.

Over three visits, lasting a total of nine days, we engaged with individuals with mild to severe IDs to understand their needs and preferences for an AR application. We used a combination of activities and focus groups to gather their feedback and improving the app between visits (Fig. 2).

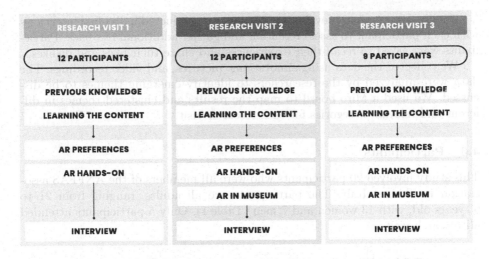

Fig. 2. The procedure of the three research visits presented in this paper.

Our visits started with focus groups to get to know the participants and understand their prior knowledge about the animals we planned to introduce. The group discussed the animals through written responses or drawings, based on the participant's abilities, and we reviewed the key details about each animal with an easy-to-read text. We used easy-to-read guidelines also in the context of interviews and oral communications [34]. During the study, we asked questions to assess their technology habits and preferences.

On each visit we evaluated the AR app with the participants, first introducing AIMuseum at the association. On the first visit, due to COVID-19 restrictions, participants couldn't go to the museum. Without directly interacting with the device, we showed them how AIMuseum worked and we asked them about the size and color of the text, and about the audio feedback parameters, such as the voice's tone, speed, and type (human or synthesized). We also asked about their preferred interaction method. A few participants did a hands-on pilot test. During the second and third visits, all participants directly interacted with the app on a tablet and gave their thoughts on what they saw and heard. On the second visit, we also presented 3D models with different textures, ranging from realistic to minimal, to gather their preferences.

On the second and third visits, participants were given the opportunity to explore AIMuseum in the museum we collaborated with – The Civic Museum of Natural History of Trieste, Italy. Participants were given 10 min to freely use the app, while looking at the full-size animal model provided by the museum. To better understand their preferred method of learning about the animals, we offered three options during the second visit (easy-to-read text, AAC text, and AIMuseum), and five methods during the third visit (easy-to-read text, AAC text, AIMuseum, tablet with ACCESS+, an accessible app for museums [46], and a multisensory experiences box).

Finally, after each user evaluation session, we conducted individual interviews with each participant to assess retention and gather additional feedback. Participants were asked to recall their experiences and share their likes and dislikes.

We collected the data using annotations, pictures, and video recordings. The data were analyzed by the researchers to identify emerging themes to be discussed. We used a Miro board to map the results and clustered themes in different and relevant categories for each research visit.

4.3   Participants

This study involved 20 participants who were all members of the ANFFAS association in Trieste, Italy. The participants are all adults, ranging from 21 to 63 years old, with 13 women and 7 men (Table 1). Only 5 participants attended all research visits.

Table 1. Participants' demographic and diagnostic information.

PID	Gender	Age	Research Visit	Presence	Context	Official Diagnosis
P1	Female	21	I, II and III	In Person	Association and Museum	Moderate Intellectual Disability
P2	Female	44	I, II and III	In Person	Association	Moderate Intellectual Disability
P3	Female	63	I, II and III	In Person	Association and Museum	Mild Intellectual Disability and Down Syndrome
P4	Male	32	I, II and III	In Person	Association and Museum	Moderate Intellectual Disability
P5	Male	49	I, II and III	In Person	Association and Museum	Mild Intellectual Disability
P6	Female	51	I	Hybrid	Association	Moderate Intellectual Disability
P7	Female	34	I	Online	Association	Mild Intellectual Disability
P8	Female	45	I	In Person	Association	Moderate Intellectual Disability and Down Syndrome
P9	Male	63	I	In Person	Association	Mild Intellectual Disability
P10	Male	28	I	In Person	Association	Severe Intellectual Disability
P11	Female	23	I and II	In Person	Association and Museum	Mild Intellectual Disability
P12	Female	55	I and III	Hybrid	Association	Moderate Intellectual Disability
P13	Female	22	II	In Person	Association	Mild Intellectual Disability
P14	Male	21	II	In Person	Association	Severe Intellectual Disability
P15	Female	47	II and III	In Person	Association and Museum	Severe Intellectual Disability
P16	Female	55	II and III	In Person	Association and Museum	Moderate Intellectual Disability
P17	Male	58	II and III	In Person	Association and Museum	Moderate Intellectual Disability and Low Vision
P18	Male	50	II and III	In Person	Association and Museum	Mild Intellectual Disability
P19	Female	53	III	In Person	Association and Museum	Moderate Intellectual Disability and Down Syndrome
P20	Female	55	III	In Person	Association and Museum	Moderate Intellectual Disability

Prior to the in-person visits, the researchers met with the participants via video call to get to know them and make them feel at ease with the research goal and process. Following that, participants and their legal guardians were asked to give permission to take part in the study. During the visits, we emphasized that they could opt-out at any time, and we reiterated the study's goal. The activities were kept short and breaks were included to ensure their comfort. The researchers were able to provide adequate time between sessions thanks to the assistance of educators who knew the participants.

At the first research visit, 12 participants were present. P8 and P9, who had recently recovered from COVID-19, joined online from a separate room. P7 attended fully online and was shown how AR works through a video call. P6, P7, and P11 also contributed with drawings during the first research visit. During the second research visit, 6 new participants joined and 6 participants from the previous visit were not available. Out of the 12 participants present, 9 went to the museum visit. Finally, on the third research visit, 18 participants previously attended one or both of our sessions, while 2 new participants joined. All of the 12 participants also went to the museum with us.

5   Results

5.1   User Evaluation at the Association

Previous Knowledge and Learning the Content. On the first steps of each research visit – previous knowledge and learning the content – we made our participants free to express their ideas in the best suitable way, by writing, drawing, or simply speaking out loud (Fig. 3). Everyone was encouraged to participate. Each correct answer was followed by positive feedback from the educator, stimulating participants to keep engaged.

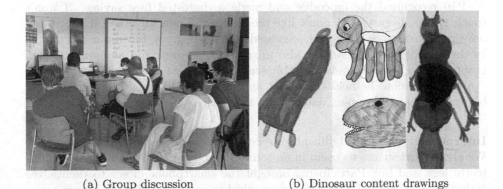

(a) Group discussion   (b) Dinosaur content drawings

Fig. 3. Conducting the previous knowledge and learning the content sessions.

We used the whiteboard to put participants' contributions related to questions such as: What do you remember about the animal?; What characteristics did it have?; Where does it live? The questions slightly changed to adapt to users' needs and museum content. During the activity, the researchers were helping the educator and familiarizing themselves with the participants, including the analysis of their roles and contribution to the group discussion. Personality and abilities played an important role in participants' discussions: verbal and talkative participants always wanted to contribute. The educator managed the participation to achieve everyone's full potential, with collaboration from everyone and scaffolding whenever needed (prompting questions and fading when they achieved the goal).

First Steps. Most participants interacted with AR for the first time and needed help to start the activity. P2 looked at the screen and, when she started touching the tablet, said: "Help, how do I do it?" On the other hand, P1 was so happy and proud of knowing how to complete tasks and interact with the device and the application. She also remembered details of the interface in the following RVs, including the label and its volume icon. Besides, some participants such as P1 demonstrated great independence during our sessions: "And we can start, so I will start now."

Emotions. We noticed several verbal and non-verbal emotional expressions during our work, from surprise to indifference, happiness to fear. The contents, mainly concerning the dinosaur and the crocodile, were not the most helpful in avoiding making some participants afraid. When we asked P2 if she was scared, she said: "A bit. I mean, almost not, because the crocodile is far away." P5 said when the audio played: "Wow, how do you do this?." This magical feedback was met with fun and engagement. On the other hand, some participants were puzzled, confused, or afraid of the content. The more they got comfortable with the application and us, the more they participated.

P16 recognized the crocodile and made a disgusted face saying: "I won't touch it; it's disgusting; I don't like crocodiles." When we asked if she would have preferred to see a dog, she answered: "Yes, a dog yes, but not a crocodile." In the case of P1, the fear was also mixed with surprise and amusement: "Oh gosh, amazing! But it made me a bit scared!" P18 was nervous during our AR evaluation session; he held the tablet and shook his hands. We believe this is because he feared dropping and ruining the device.

Interaction. We noticed difficulties related to dimensions and distances in AR. We asked participants to zoom in on some characteristics of the animal, such as teeth, legs, and tail. Participants brought the smartphone closer to themselves rather than the animal. Likewise, when asked to zoom out, the same issue arose. When using the phone to explore the virtual object, we noted a problem with rotating the device. The difficulty increased for P9, who is in a wheelchair with reduced space for mobility. Another challenge of using the smartphone is related to the position of participants' fingers, as sometimes they unconsciously block the camera and missed the AR experience.

The device's size plays an important role. In the experiment we ran during the second research visit, we used a tablet to provide a bigger screen size and avoid the fingers easily being placed over the cameras. Both devices have pros and cons since a tablet is heavier and harder to hold. It is also essential to have a QR code well positioned to avoid confusion. P17 was, on both research visits, swiping the QR code on the tablet instead of holding the device. Similar to what we do when swiping a card for payment. The QR code was also associated with previous experiences: P3 associated the QR code with a COVID-19 pass and P2 with a photocopy.

Feedback provided by participants on the overall experience proved meaningful too. P7 said, "It's a good idea for someone who can't read" and P3 was surprised, "Let's say it must be screen magic."

Audio: Gender, Speed, Type and Content. During all research visits, we associated each QR code with a 3D model, a label providing its description, and audio feedback with a self-introduction of the content with different parameters, changing the gender to man/woman, the speed to faster/slower, and the type to synthesized/humanized. The dinosaurs said, "Hi, I am a dinosaur" (brown) or "Hi, I am another type of dinosaur" (white), while the crocodiles "Hi, I am the Nile crocodile, and I live in some regions of Africa" (realistic texture) and "Hi, I am another type of crocodile" (light green). We chose to have the animals self-introduce themselves to evaluate the participants' approval of text-to-speech technology and provide an alternative way to understand the text for non-literate participants.

In general, they appreciated having the audio feedback. When we asked, "What would you do if a digital dinosaur/crocodile talked to you?", P2 said, "I would say: Hi, I'm P2"; P4 said, "Oh gosh, no"; P5 said "Makes me a bit scared. If it is a cute animal, ok, but a big one, no"; and P10 said, "It is weird, but I like when it talks." When we tested the voice with different parameters, gender was indifferent to 72% of the participants, while 28% preferred a masculine voice. Most participants could notice when we changed the voice. 28% of the participants preferred a faster, 14% a slower voice, and 58% were indifferent about this aspect. The voice type seems not to get a consensus: 44% preferred a synthesized voice, 28% a humanized voice, and 28% were indifferent. When we asked specifically about the voices, we heard from P3 that "The voices were slow, they were not the clearest, but I could understand the words", and from P15, "The voices were so sweet."

Content: Size, Labels, and Appearance. We asked our participants about the size of the 3D objects, comparing across versions, with one about 25% smaller than the other. Almost all of the participants noticed the first one was bigger. Specifically, P2 said, "Yes, I noticed the difference. That other one was big, and this one was small", and made gestures with her hands to represent the size. When we asked what size they preferred, 28% of the participants were indifferent, while 44% preferred the bigger version and 28% the smaller.

We designed some 3D models with different colors. The dinosaur was available in white or brown, while the crocodile was in light green or with a realistic texture (Fig. 4). Analyzing the results of the first research visit, we found out that 72% preferred the brown dinosaur, while 14% picked the entire white, and 14% did not have any preference. P12 said she saw a plastic dinosaur, referring to the white version.

For the crocodile model, we first introduced the realistic texture (Fig. 4b) and later the light green color (Fig. 4a). After that, we asked if the second crocodile was different and how. 75% of the participants associated the first one with the real one, 17% thought the second was real, and 8% did not have an answer. P10 said "The last one was fake."

5.2 User Evaluation at the Museum

(a) Light green crocodile   (b) Realistically textured crocodile

Fig. 4. Museum visit: participants interacting with the content 3D model.

We focused on participants' preferences when learning about the museum content during the museum visits (Table 1).

On the second research visit, we asked them to choose between AAC text, easy-to-read text, and AIMuseum. AIMuseum was chosen as the first choice by 4 participants. When it was not the first choice, it was the second choice of 4 other participants. It is also important to mention that the AAC text was the primary choice of the other 5 participants. The easy-to-read text was not the first choice of any of the participants. Only P16 didn't choose the tablet between the main choices. She said she had never used a tablet before and disliked technology. This participant often avoided our proposed activities, so we respected her decision to do not proceed with a specific session.

On the third research visit, we asked about their preferences between AAC text, easy-to-read text, AIMuseum, a multisensory experience box, and ACCESS+. All participants chose a high-tech solution as their first choice: 8 chose AR, and 4 chose ACCESS+. AIMuseum was the second choice for 2 participants, third choice for one, and last choice for one. One participant chose a low-tech solution as their first two choices.

5.3 Interviews

We interviewed participants individually after each user evaluation at the association and museum. We applied this method to analyze the retention from each activity, reinforcing what they remembered right after leaving the testing room and expressing their preferences.

On the first research visit to the institution, the educator asked our participants what the researchers showed them, and she provided more specific questions to trigger their memory if needed. Most of the participants could remember details of the dinosaurs. P12 said, "It was a plastic dinosaur", while P1 mentioned she saw "drawings with writings; they look like pictures made on a large white sheet; there was a dinosaur, you could see the body, the legs, the tail." P5 mentioned the dinosaur self-introducing was weird; it reminded him of 3D movies.

On the second research visit, questions were more specific about the crocodile model: What did the researcher show you?; What was the shape and color of the object?; Did the voice change, and what was the voice saying?; Did the text change, and what was written?; Could you interact with the application alone or did you need help?; Have you already seen any other animals with the researcher using the tablet? [to understand if they remembered the previous experience]; What did you like? What did you not like?. All of them could remind a crocodile as the animal they interacted with. Most of them also gave details about the 3D model: size, color, and voice. The label was not perceived as important; some participants could not read it. 7 participants could remember correctly details and order of interaction related to shape and color – surprising information given the complexity of the question. Most could also remember the sentences introduced with the audio.

When we asked if they needed help, most said they needed help to hold or control the tablet. P3 said, "I knew how to do it alone, but sometimes I needed help." We were also interested to know if they had a previous similar experience, and more than half of the participants could remember interacting with AR in our previous session. Most participants mentioned adjectives such as fun and beautiful to describe what they liked about the experience; on the other hand, about what they didn't like, most participants couldn't mention anything specific, while P1 mentioned the woman's voice and P11 the colors.

On the third research visit, we provided more general questions and questioned their level of independence: What did you do?; Did you have to do something by yourself?; Were you able to use the tablet alone?; What animals did you see?; Did you hear any noises?; and What was the experience like?. Ten participants answered the questions related to their experience interacting with the tablet. P1 said, "I had to see the wolf and the big reindeer. You had to move the tablet over the writing on top of the black thing called a QR code." And P18 mentioned, "It is a little scary because seeing it so big made me a bit tense. It was a surprise to see the animal." 4 participants mentioned that the interaction was easy and they could do it alone; 3 said it was difficult, and 2 needed help. P4 and P12 explained it was hard to focus on the QR code, and the content was "disappearing or running away"; they lost track of the tag and asked for help. Most participants were already familiar with the researchers; this time, some of them also mentioned having a lot of fun – highlighting the importance of the connection between researchers and participants.

During the museum visits, they had a follow-up individual interview to elicit extra feedback. We asked the 12 participants about what they experienced and which were their favorites. In particular, they recalled their interaction with the animal displayed by AIMuseum while mentioning the nearby stuffed animal, thus making the connection between virtual and real objects.

6   Discussion

It is important to emphasize the different roles each participant can play. Our 20 participants contributed differently to our co-design sessions; we could associate them as informants, evaluators, or designers. The emotions and contributions of stakeholders play an important role in any research involving people with IDs. This study could have different outcomes for diverse marginalized and under-studied communities.

6.1   3D Models Are the Pivot Point of the Interaction

Most of the participants could provide details about the size, color, and voices of each 3D content. Most participants preferred realistic or colorful textures for the AR interaction. The size of the 3D content is also not a consensus – participants tended to favor the bigger versions, however, a bigger device, such as a tablet, could make them feel scared. This suggests that the interaction with the 3D models is the main touchpoint of the experience, prompting participants to engage with the digital content. However, despite the importance of the model, participants did not have a precise preference for the realism of the 3D model. This implies that incredible detail in the 3D model may not be necessary for the success of the AR application. Instead, the main goal of the AR app should be to provide an enhanced way of looking at the models, as visitors are often unable to freely move around items in the museum. It's also worth noting that the taxidermied animals in the museum can provide the necessary detail, while the AR app can focus on enhancing the experience by enabling visitors to interact with the models in new ways.

By providing audio feedback and self-introduction by the models, the AR app can provide a more immersive experience, catering to visitors who are non-literate or prefer audio feedback. Gender is not essential for audio content inside an AR application; the regular pace is preferred rather than a faster or slower speech speed; and audio type is not a consensus – we could go either with a human or synthesized voice. Lastly, the labels did not appear as important; participants were more interested in the 3D model characteristics. However, while the audio feedback was the preferred method of receiving information about the models, the label still provided an affordance that showed there was additional content beyond just the 3D model. Even though it was not as preferred as the audio feedback, having the label as a visual cue likely helped participants fully engage with the experience.

6.2   Interacting with AR Is Easy to Learn and Easy to Remember

The study involved participants interacting with AR technology in three separate sessions over the course of a year. While not all participants were involved in every session, the majority participated in at least two sessions. The sessions were conducted months apart, allowing researchers to observe how well participants retained their ability to interact with the AR application.

The most common difficulty encountered by participants was related to movement around the model. Specifically, participants needed to move the tablet closer to the QR code to make the model appear larger on the screen. However, many participants believed they needed to move the tablet closer to their face to better see the model. This counterintuitive perception, which differs from their prior experiences of looking at images, is probably caused by the novelty of the encounter. In addition, some participants had issues with the device itself. For some, the smartphone was too small, making it easy to accidentally block the camera with their fingers. Conversely, the tablet was sometimes too heavy, requiring two hands to use. This shows the importance of adapting both the application and the device to ensure that software and hardware are accessible to users.

Despite these challenges, participants quickly learned how to use AR technology to explore the model. Over time, they required less help and became more confident in their ability to use the technology. Participants remembered how the QR code and the device interacted, allowing them to recall how to use the technology easily. Although some participants required a brief recap on how to explore the model (P3: "I knew how to do it alone, but sometimes I needed help"), it did not negatively impact their experience. AR technology is a usable and friendly tool for providing content in a new way. It does not need prolonged use too; it has the potential to be a powerful tool for engaging users and enhancing their learning experience.

6.3   Participants Can Act as Informants, Evaluators and Designers

Collaboration and participation are critical components in developing usable and effective solutions, especially when designing for marginalized and understudied communities. Inclusive design practices aim to involve all stakeholders in the design process to ensure that the resulting solutions are usable and meet the needs of all users.

The value of the participation of people with IDs is significant. As demonstrated by the results of the co-design sessions undertaken in this study, these individuals have unique insights into their experiences and needs, which can inform the design of solutions that are more accessible and effective. Additionally, the active participation of users with intellectual disabilities in the design process can help break down stereotypes and misconceptions about this community and empower them to shape their own experiences actively.

In the context of usability, during the co-design of this study, participants took on spontaneously different roles, such as informants, evaluators, and designers. As informants, participants provided valuable insights and feedback that can inform the design process. As evaluators, participants assessed the usability and effectiveness of the solution, identifying potential issues and areas for improvement. As designers, they were involved in the actual design process, providing input and ideas that shaped the solution through its iterations.

7   Guidelines

From the analysis and discussion of our data, we can extract a few guidelines to address the usability of AR-inclusive applications (G1 to G4) and guide their co-design (G5 to G8) with people with IDs. In order to enhance the usability of inclusive AR applications:

- **G1**: Prepare QR-codes with different colors and sizes
- **G2**: Provide devices with different weights and screen sizes to accommodate participant's needs
- **G3**: Include AAC, text-to-speech, and easy-to-read texts or other strategies to facilitate participant's comprehension and involvement (e.g. Task Analysis)
- **G4**: Give choice to express the participants' creativity in their own way

When designing AR-inclusive applications for and with ID participants:

- **G5**: Encourage different forms of expression and respect the pace and time for each participant to contribute and feel part of the process.
- **G6**: Prepare different questions and materials to adapt to participants' needs
- **G7**: Provide open questions to avoid the yes/no answer
- **G8**: Get to know your participants; they need to be comfortable before they can fully collaborate with you

This is not meant to be a complete list but just an initial step toward defining a flexible framework for designing inclusive applications.

8   Limitations and Future Work

The limitations of this work are primarily related to the context. At the association, we did not have a specific room to conduct the assessments, and we had to consider the influence of museums not being familiar places for the participants. Most participants could read and write, but not all of them. This impacted the interaction with labels and their preference for easy-to-read or AAC texts. Also, familiarity with technology was decisive in evaluating individual experiences. In future works, we plan to combine gamification with AR technology, helping participants to discover new content.

9   Conclusions

Our participants' rich feedback and insights were essential to co-design more inclusive and accessible technologies. We extracted guidelines based on our findings to be shared with other researchers.

This research opens the possibility of designing new AR applications for museums and suggests different factors influencing how people with IDs use AR. Working with individuals who have IDs is both incredibly gratifying and demanding. To ensure their comfort at all times, we concentrated on their needs and adjusted the study as necessary.

Finally, it is essential to recall that the participants have different diagnoses on the spectrum of IDs and can also have other conditions, some not even mentioned because it was out of the scope of this work. Thus, we need to learn with and from them, respecting and understanding their contribution.

Acknowledgements. We would like to thank SNSF for funding this research, ANFFAS and The Civic Museum of Natural History of Trieste for collaborating with this research, and our amazing co-designers for making this work possible.

References

1. Ahmetovic, D., Bernareggi, C., Keller, K., Mascetti, S.: Musa: Artwork accessibility through augmented reality for people with low vision. In: Proceedings of the 18th International Web for All Conference. W4A '21, Association for Computing Machinery, New York, NY, USA (2021). https://doi.org/10.1145/3430263.3452441, https://doi.org/10.1145/3430263.3452441

2. Akçayır, M., Akçayır, G.: Advantages and challenges associated with augmented reality for education: a systematic review of the literature. Educ. Res. Rev. **20**, 1–11 (2017)

3. Al-Megren, S., Almutairi, A.: Assessing the effectiveness of an augmented reality application for the literacy development of arabic children with hearing impairments. In: Rau, P.-L.P. (ed.) CCD 2018. LNCS, vol. 10912, pp. 3–18. Springer, Cham (2018). https://doi.org/10.1007/978-3-319-92252-2_1

4. American Psychiatric Association, A., Association, A.P., et al.: Diagnostic and statistical manual of mental disorders: DSM-5, vol. 10. Washington, DC: American psychiatric association (2013)

5. Bai, Z., Blackwell, A.F., Coulouris, G.: Using augmented reality to elicit pretend play for children with autism. IEEE Trans. Visual Comput. Graphics **21**(5), 598–610 (2014)

6. Baragash, R.S., Al-Samarraie, H., Alzahrani, A.I., Alfarraj, O.: Augmented reality in special education: a meta-analysis of single-subject design studies. Eur. J. Spec. Needs Educ. **35**(3), 382–397 (2020)

7. Barbosa, P., Amorim, P., Leal Ferreira, S.B.: Augmented reality and museum accessibility: A case study to support hard of hearing people. Association for Computing Machinery, New York, NY, USA (2019), https://doi.org/10.1145/3357155.3358434

8. Beukelman, D.R., Mirenda, P., et al.: Augmentative and Alternative Communication. Paul H, Brookes Baltimore (1998)

9. Bircanin, F., Brereton, M., Sitbon, L., Ploderer, B., Azaabanye Bayor, A., Koplick, S.: Including adults with severe intellectual disabilities in co-design through active support. Association for Computing Machinery, New York, NY, USA (2021), https://doi.org/10.1145/3411764.3445057

10. Bridges, S.A., Robinson, O.P., Stewart, E.W., Kwon, D., Mutua, K.: Augmented reality: teaching daily living skills to adults with intellectual disabilities. J. Spec. Educ. Technol. **35**(1), 3–14 (2020)

11. Bruno, L.P., Lewis, A.M., Kaldenberg, E.R., Bahr, P.A., Immerfall, J.: Direct instruction of text-to-speech software for students with intellectual disability. Educ. Train. Autism Develop. Disabilities **55**(4), 424–437 (2020)

12. Cakir, R., Korkmaz, O.: The effectiveness of augmented reality environments on individuals with special education needs. Educ. Inf. Technol. **24**, 1631–1659 (2019)

13. Callanan, M., Cervantes, C., Loomis, M.: Informal learning. Wiley Interdiscip. Rev.: Cogn. Sci. **2**(6), 646–655 (2011)

14. Carrizosa, H.G., Sheehy, K., Rix, J., Seale, J., Hayhoe, S.: Designing technologies for museums: accessibility and participation issues. J. Enabl. Technol. **14**(1), 31–39 (2020)

15. Cascales-Martínez, A., Martínez-Segura, M.J., Pérez-López, D., Contero, M.: Using an augmented reality enhanced tabletop system to promote learning of mathematics: a case study with students with special educational needs. Eurasia J. Math., Sci. Technol. Educ. **13**(2), 355–380 (2016)

16. Chang, Y.L., Hou, H.T., Pan, C.Y., Sung, Y.T., Chang, K.E.: Apply an augmented reality in a mobile guidance to increase sense of place for heritage places. J. Educ. Technol. Society **18**(2), 166–178 (2015)

17. Colin Gibson, R., D. Dunlop, M., Bouamrane, M.M.: Lessons from expert focus groups on how to better support adults with mild intellectual disabilities to engage in co-design. Association for Computing Machinery, New York, NY, USA (2020), https://doi.org/10.1145/3373625.3417008

18. Dermitzaki, I., Stavroussi, P., Bandi, M., Nisiotou, I.: Investigating ongoing strategic behaviour of students with mild mental retardation: implementation and relations to performance in a problem-solving situation. Eval. Res. Educ. **21**(2), 96–110 (2008)

19. Fajardo, I., Ávila, V., Ferrer, A., Tavares, G., Gómez, M., Hernández, A.: Easy-to-read texts for students with intellectual disability: linguistic factors affecting comprehension. J. Appl. Res. Intellect. Disabil. **27**(3), 212–225 (2014)

20. Falk, J.H., Moussouri, T., Coulson, D.: The effect of visitors 'agendas on museum learning. Curator: Museum J. **41**(2), 107–120 (1998)

21. Franchi, F., Graziosi, F., Rinaldi, C., Tarquini, F.: Aal solutions toward cultural heritage enjoyment. In: 2016 IEEE 27th Annual International Symposium On Personal, Indoor, And Mobile Radio Communications (PIMRC), pp. 1–6. IEEE (2016)

22. Garzón, J., Baldiris, S., Gutiérrez, J., Pavón, J., et al.: How do pedagogical approaches affect the impact of augmented reality on education? a meta-analysis and research synthesis. Educ. Res. Rev. **31**, 100334 (2020)

23. Garzón, J., Pavón, J., Baldiris, S.: Systematic review and meta-analysis of augmented reality in educational settings. Virtual Real. **23**(4), 447–459 (2019). https://doi.org/10.1007/s10055-019-00379-9

24. Guay, F., Ratelle, C.F., Chanal, J.: Optimal learning in optimal contexts: the role of self-determination in education. Can. Psychol. **49**(3), 233 (2008)

25. Guedes, L.S., Marques, L.A., Vitório, G.: Enhancing interaction and accessibility in museums and exhibitions with augmented reality and screen readers. In: Miesenberger, K., Manduchi, R., Covarrubias Rodriguez, M., Peňáz, P. (eds.) Computers Helping People with Special Needs, pp. 157–163. Springer International Publishing, Cham (2020)
26. Ibáñez, M.B., Di Serio, Á., Villarán, D., Kloos, C.D.: Experimenting with electromagnetism using augmented reality: impact on flow student experience and educational effectiveness. Comput. Educ. **71**, 1–13 (2014)
27. Jdaitawi, M.T., Kan'an, A.F.: A decade of research on the effectiveness of augmented reality on students with special disability in higher education. Contemp. Educ. Technol. **14**(1) (2022)
28. Kang, Y.S., Chang, Y.J.: Using an augmented reality game to teach three junior high school students with intellectual disabilities to improve atm use. J. Appl. Res. Intellect. Disabil. **33**(3), 409–419 (2020)
29. Kauffman, J.M., Hallahan, D.P., Pullen, P.C., Badar, J.: Special education: What it is and why we need it. Routledge (2018)
30. Kellems, R.O., Cacciatore, G., Osborne, K.: Using an augmented reality-based teaching strategy to teach mathematics to secondary students with disabilities. Career Dev. Transit. Except. Individ. **42**(4), 253–258 (2019)
31. King, B., Lord, B.: The manual of museum learning. Rowman & Littlefield (2015)
32. McMahon, D.D., Cihak, D.F., Wright, R.E., Bell, S.M.: Augmented reality for teaching science vocabulary to postsecondary education students with intellectual disabilities and autism. J. Res. Technol. Educ. **48**(1), 38–56 (2016)
33. Navarro Delgado, I., Fonseca, D.: Implementation of methodological processes of users experience with 3d and augmented reality. case study with students of architecture and users with disablities (2011)
34. Nomura, M., Skat Nielsen, G., Tronbacke, B.: Guidelines for easy-to-read materials. International Federation of Library Associations and Institutions (IFLA) (2010)
35. Patel, D.R., Apple, R., Kanungo, S., Akkal, A.: Intellectual disability: definitions, evaluation and principles of treatment. Pediatric Med. **1**(11), 10–21037 (2018)
36. Rappolt-Schlichtmann, G., Daley, S.G.: Providing access to engagement in learning: The potential of universal design for learning in museum design. Curator: The Museum J. **56**(3), 307–321 (2013)
37. Reichinger, A., Fuhrmann, A., Maierhofer, S., Purgathofer, W.: A concept for reuseable interactive tactile reliefs. In: Miesenberger, K., Bühler, C., Penaz, P. (eds.) ICCHP 2016. LNCS, vol. 9759, pp. 108–115. Springer, Cham (2016). https://doi.org/10.1007/978-3-319-41267-2_15
38. Richard, E., Billaudeau, V., Richard, P., Gaudin, G.: Augmented reality for rehabilitation of cognitive disabled children: A preliminary study. In: 2007 virtual rehabilitation, pp. 102–108. IEEE (2007)
39. Salah, J., Abdennadher, S., Atef, S.: Galaxy shop: projection-based numeracy game for teenagers with down syndrome. In: Alcañiz, M., Göbel, S., Ma, M., Fradinho Oliveira, M., Baalsrud Hauge, J., Marsh, T. (eds.) JCSG 2017. LNCS, vol. 10622, pp. 109–120. Springer, Cham (2017). https://doi.org/10.1007/978-3-319-70111-0_10
40. Sandell, R.: Museums as agents of social inclusion. Museum Manage. Curatorship **17**(4), 401–418 (1998)
41. Sayed, N., Zayed, H.H., Sharawy, M.I.: Arsc: augmented reality student card an augmented reality solution for the education field. Comput. Educ. **56**(4), 1045–1061 (2011)

42. Seale, J., Chadwick, D.: How does risk mediate the ability of adolescents and adults with intellectual and developmental disabilities to live a normal life by using the internet? Cyberpsychology: J. Psychosoc. Res. Cyberspace **11**(1) (2017)
43. Sheehy, K., Garcia Carrizosa, H., Rix, J., Seale, J., Hayhoe, S.: Inclusive museums and augmented reality. affordances, participation, ethics and fun. Int. J. Inclusive Museum **12**(4), 67–85 (2019)
44. Sitbon, L., Farhin, S.: Co-designing interactive applications with adults with intellectual disability: A case study. Association for Computing Machinery, New York, NY, USA (2017). https://doi.org/10.1145/3152771.3156163
45. Soares Guedes, L.: Designing multisensory experiences for users with different reading abilities visiting a museum (129) (2021). https://doi.org/10.1145/3458055.3458058
46. Soares Guedes, L., Ferrari, V., Mastrogiuseppe, M., Span, S., Landoni, M.: Access+: designing a museum application for people with intellectual disabilities. In: Miesenberger, K., Kouroupetroglou, G., Mavrou, K., Manduchi, R., Covarrubias Rodriguez, M., Penáz, P. (eds.) Computers Helping People with Special Needs, pp. 425–431. Springer International Publishing, Cham (2022)
47. Sotiriou, S., Bogner, F.X.: Visualizing the invisible: augmented reality as an innovative science education scheme. Adv. Sci. Lett. **1**(1), 114–122 (2008)
48. Spaulding, L.S., Pratt, S.M.: A review and analysis of the history of special education and disability advocacy in the united states. Am. Educ. History J. **42**(1/2), 91 (2015)
49. Stanco, F., Tanasi, D., Allegra, D., Milotta, F.L.M., Lamagna, G., Monterosso, G.: Virtual anastylosis of greek sculpture as museum policy for public outreach and cognitive accessibility. J. Electron. Imaging **26**(1), 011025–011025 (2017)
50. W3C: Web content accessibility guidelines (2023), https://www.w3.org/WAI/standards-guidelines/wcag/ = "February 5, 2023"
51. Wehmeyer, M.L., Shogren, K.A.: Self-determination and choice. Handbook Of Evidence-based Practices in Intellectual And Developmental Disabilities, pp. 561–584 (2016)
52. Zhao, Y., Szpiro, S., Knighten, J., Azenkot, S.: Cuesee: exploring visual cues for people with low vision to facilitate a visual search task. In: Proceedings of the 2016 ACM International Joint Conference on Pervasive and Ubiquitous Computing, pp. 73–84 (2016)

MetaWelt: Embodied in Which Body? Simplex Didactics to Live the Web 3.0

Maurizio Sibilio[1]([✉]) [iD], Stefano Di Tore[1] [iD], Michele Domenico Todino[1] [iD], Amelia Lecce[2] [iD], Ilaria Viola[1] [iD], and Lucia Campitiello[1] [iD]

[1] Department of Humanities, Philosophy and Education, University of Salerno, Salerno, Italy
sditore@unisa.it

[2] Department of Science and Technology, University of Sannio, Benevento, Italy

Abstract. Nowadays, the increasing use of technologies such as cloud computing, the Internet of Things (IoT), and virtual and augmented reality is blurring the line between real and virtual contexts, leading to the concept of an "on-life" reality. Facebook's recent rebranding to Meta underscores the company's commitment to building a metaverse, a decentralized hybrid ecosystem that combines digital and physical elements. As VR technology becomes more mainstream, it is being incorporated into educational platforms, leading to questions about how teaching will adapt to a new virtual environment where the body's role in learning is different. This study aims to demonstrate how the theories of simplexity and simple didactics can serve as a foundational framework for exploring the potential of virtual reality (VR) in the field of education.

Keywords: Simplex Didactics · Metaverse · Embodied Internet · Virtual Reality · Educational Technologies

1 Introduction

Eric Schmidt (CEO at Google) opens his presentation at The Future of the Digital Economy of the World Economic Forum, in 2015, stating that Internet is destined to disappear soon because there would be so many IPv4 addresses due to IPv6, so many devices, wearable technologies, artefacts to interact with that we will not even perceive and that will be part of our lives all the time. At this point a spontaneous question follows: if we are all online 24 h a day 7 days a week, if the technologies that surround us become completely invisible, what does the term "reality" mean? Not even ten years later, Schmidt's statement seems to have materialised in a different way of living the web compared to the past decade, characterised by an increasing use of devices capable of communicating with each other and with the network.

In the last 10 years, technologies such as ubiquitus, cloud computing, Internet of Things (IoT), Non Fungible Token (NFT), Blockchain, cryptocurrencies etc., seem to have provided a powerful improvement to the hybridisation of digital and real contexts, pushing people to wonder if the real Vs virtual dichotomy still makes sense. The philosopher, Luciano Floridi, synthesises this drive for hybridisation with the concept

M. Antona and C. Stephanidis (Eds.): HCII 2023, LNCS 14021, pp. 111–119, 2023.
https://doi.org/10.1007/978-3-031-35897-5_8

of on-life, offering a perspective that goes beyond dichotomies and recognises virtuality as a space for a social, political, legal, educational construction of reality. This gradual realisation of a Mangrove Society [1] seems to have met a sort of litmus test effect. In fact, even Facebook Inc. Has moved in this direction; it changed its name to Meta Inc. in 2021, making clear its ambition to speed up the change process and to take a pivotal role in the web 3.0 where Virtual reality should be one of the focus business areas. As stated by Zuckerberg, his company will seek to lay the foundations for an interconnected set of experiences in a 3D space, an "embodied Internet", a new decentralised and hybrid ecosystem, both digital and physical, synthesised for some time through metaverse expression. The expression embodied internet is very significant as it leads in an almost natural way to ask "embodied in which body?". Indeed, it seems clear that the main media through which the web of the future appears destined to be enjoyed is made up of extended reality (a set of immersive, mixed and augmented virtual reality) and one of the main characteristics of this media is a high degree of bodily involvement in forms of human-machine interaction. However, the involvement of the body does not imply that a virtual avatar, personified by the user, must necessarily replicate the same properties of the human body (avatars can take on non-humanoid forms). Thus, if we analyse the etymology of the term 'virtual' we understand how the true potential of this media is not in the simulation but in the creation of new forms of reality. The term virtual derives from the Latin word virtus which means "strength" or "power", from which late medieval translators, having to render the Aristotelian term «dynamis» into Latin, coined the neologism "virtualis" understood as "potential". In this sense, the original dimension of virtual reality is not simulation, as is usually assumed, but potential. It is what can come to be, the latent power of a thing (or a body). It is not the illusory nature of the simulated copy, but the dimension of possibility inherent in all of reality [2]. The spread of these technologies might seem far from the world of teaching, yet on 10/10/2022 Microsoft announced a joint venture with Meta aimed at the creation and dissemination of Microsoft Teams Mesh (a version of Teams for VR). Similarly, different versions of MOODLE VR have been released, the development of ZOOM VR has been announced, the Google VR/AR division is working on the VR expansions of Workspace and, in general, all the platforms mostly used in teaching appear to be moving in this direction. If on the one hand, therefore, teaching applications seem to have already reached a good level of development, on the other hand there is a difficulty in imagining what it can mean to teach in an environment in which space and time can take on a different meaning from that to which we are used to and in which the body, the main machine for the construction of meanings, becomes a random variable. In this sense, it is necessary to start a reflection aimed at creating a theoretical framework to analyse and understand the potential of the phenomenon. In this context, simplexity [3], as a theory that studies the way in which all living organisms, regardless of the structure of their body, adapt and learn through common principles and properties, and simple didactics [4], which aims to capitalise on the teaching/learning level these principles and properties, appear as a completely natural starting point to lay the foundations for a reflection aimed at investigating the ways in which users with "variable" bodies will be able to learn in virtual places. In this context, a first pilot experiment has been launched, aimed at analysing the inclusive potential of VR in the didactic/educational field.

2 Real and Virtual: Assonances and Dissonances for a Semplex Didactics

Technologies play an increasingly pervasive role in our lives, influencing the way we act in and on the world and consequently being-there, understood as Heidegger's Da-sein. Digital technology redefines norms, rules of conduct, interpersonal relationships and, at the same time, political decision-makers outline - in an ever clearer way - guidelines for the competent use of digital tools [5]. The current reality seems to be determined by access to the virtual [6], in fact, through technologies the possibility opens up to experiment and create new worlds through the vicarious senses [7]. Such a vision would make digital tools potential vectors and accelerators of social inclusion.

The substantial dichotomy between real and virtual is still an object of interest on an epistemological level, in fact, the real (from the Latin res which means thing and material good) is interpreted as a tangible element, contrary to the virtual which is often referred to as the imaginary, as opposed to "what is". Parmenides recited: "Being is and cannot not be. Non-being is not and cannot be", after millennia, on the other hand, the paradigm turns upside down into "virtual is real" [8]. The virtual, therefore, simultaneously contemplates existence and non-existence, allowing prosumers [9] to continuously build unusual paths, making dialogue "what does not exist, with what, instead, exists" [10, 11]. In this regard, Derrick de Kerckhove [12] states that the brainframe is the synthesis of a cognitive/sensory experience between reality, between the way we use technologies and the way we process the information that comes to us from the surrounding world.

According to Jenkins, "literacy skills for the 21st century (…) enable participation in newly emerging communities within a networked society, enable children and students to exploit new simulation tools - such as video games - i new communication and training media, and social networks; facilitate the exchange of information between different media platforms and social networks" [13].

Technology has pervasive characteristics and, in this sense, virtual reality, understood as a three-dimensional environment in which computers and users interact with each other by simulating real environments [14], is a candidate to become a privileged means to promote meaningful learning. According to Lévy, "the minimal ability to navigate in cyberspace is probably acquired in a shorter time than that necessary to learn to read and, like literacy, will be associated with far more social, economic and cultural benefits than the mere exercise of the right to citizenship" [15].

Virtual learning environments are therefore configured as alternative spaces to promote learning through participation. In fact, an effective virtual environment should be equipped with adequate communication channels [16].

For Steven Ellis, virtual reality must be characterized by three elements:

1. "the shape and kinematics of the actors and objects;
2. Their interactions among themselves and with the environment according to such rules for behavior as Newtonian laws of motion;
3. The extent and character of the enveloping environment" [16].

Therefore, developing virtual reality means enriching environments with an infinity of information that allows users to experiment with new forms of interaction [14].

In this sense, man-machine interaction, which takes the form of virtual reality environments, could represent a possible path to follow to reflect on participatory good practices that influence significant learning. Therefore, this contribution accords with a complex and prothean vision of didactic interaction that interprets semplex as a possible epistemological framework for a theory of didactic action [4].

3 Exploring the Link Between Experience, Education, and Virtual Reality

For a deeper analysis of the connections between experience, education and virtual reality, it may be useful to revisit John Dewey's 1938 book Experience and Education. In this work, the American educator asserts that, despite uncertainties, there exists an organic link between education and personal experience, but this does not mean that "experience = education" as a logical syllogism. John Dewey asserts that the belief that authentic education stems from experience does not automatically mean that all experiences are equally or genuinely educative. His reasoning becomes crucial in formulating two working hypotheses. The first hypothesis is that there is a connection between experience, education, and video games, and that the latter often do not provide educational elements. The second hypothesis, which is a reflection of the first, is that some video games, which meet certain parameters, can become educational experiences. Through the study of Dewey quickly demonstrates the first hypothesis through the following propositions: experience and education cannot be equated. There are, in fact, experiences that are counter-educative. Any experience that appears to halt or mislead further experience is counter-educative. An experience can cause hardening; it can decrease sensitivity and the ability to react. In these cases, the possibilities of having a richer experience in the future are limited. Furthermore, a given experience can increase a person's automatic ability in a certain dimension, yet tend to restrict their freedom of movement: the effect is again to limit the field of future experience. John Dewey cautions against experiences that promote "laziness and neglect" and can limit an individual's potential for growth and development from their experiences. Therefore, Dewey outlines a first educational principle: the experiences a learner must undertake must be well-organized, sequential, progressive and fruitful. How can this be achieved through video games, particularly virtual reality? Continuing to draw a parallel with Dewey's studies, he cautions against the existence of a "universal" principle for determining positive experiences that lead to "growth". This should not come as a surprise given the theoretical approach based on a plurality of learning styles, even in terms of experience, and multiple intelligences. This approach has shown that each person has a preference for certain learning channels over others, and it could be argued that this preference could also extend to the sequence of experiences and their type. The differentiation in learning thus highlights that virtual reality cannot be an appropriate tool for every learner, and their use must be targeted.

4 Virtual Reality as Transformative Technology

"Experience is central in and to learning," a basic assumption confirmed by the pioneers of pedagogy and neuroscience [17–19], who, thanks to the contribution of a complex view of human evolution, add to this principle an adversative conjunction "but," since without an adequate context that responds to the differences and talents of the person [4, 20] the latter can be an obstacle to learning. And it is in this perspective that virtual reality intervenes by configuring itself as a transformative technology that, by reducing the presence of barrier elements, promotes successful experiential learning. As noted by Riva et al., "using VR, subjects can experience the synthetic environment as if it was 'their surrounding world' (incarnation: the physical body is within a virtual environment) or can experience their synthetic avatars as if they were 'their own body' (embodiment: the physical body is replaced by the virtual one). In other words, VR is able to fool the predictive coding mechanisms used by the brain generating the feeling of presence in a virtual body and in the digital space around it" [21]. In this sense, we can talk about experience in the context of simulative technology on the premise that is the involvement of the body stimulates a 'sense of presence' [22, 21] and ownership [23]. Presence refers to the degree to which a person perceives himself physically and mentally present in a simulation [22], this degree of perception depends on the narrative content and the flow state of the experience related to the level of cognitive and emotional involvement in the narrative. Instead, Sense of Ownership-SoO "describes the feeling of mineness that we experience toward our body parts, feelings or thoughts. It is the feeling that is described in statements such as "This is 'my' hand," "It is 'me' who is thinking this thought" or "'I' am the one who is having this feeling." As such, although often experienced at the fringe of consciousness, Sense of ownership has a complex and non-unitary phenomenal structure [24]. In fact, the degrees of freedom in which interaction with virtual reality can act are such to the point that the brain's predictive coding can be fooled by producing a sense of presence and ownership of one's body in a virtual one and in the digital space in which the person is immersed [14]. In the field of neuroscience, it has been widely demonstrated, that an immersive reality experience via a virtual body worn by an individual, induces an alteration in Sense of ownership that results in perceptual, attitudinal and behavioral changes, including cognitive processing [25, 26]. If one considers, from an analogical point of view, learning as a form of adaptation, and considers living things as simplistic systems that learn consistently with principles determined by the way their bodies operate in the world with the world, the metaverse, by offering the possibility of modifying both of these elements, de facto opens the way for a new gnoseology. In other words, the possibility of designing a new aesthetic and creating environments, or settings, in which everything, even the very laws of physics, can be determined by the designer, opens up new horizons for development in constructivist and semiotic fields [27]. What we want to analyze is the kind of impact that the control of a non-humanoid avatar can have on the user, the use of an avatar with certain characteristics can change the behavior and self-perceptions of the individual (a phenomenon called the "Proteus effect"). Starting from the 'embodied cognition perspective, in the area of social cognition, it has been shown that having a Sense of ownership that differs from the virtual body in terms of social role [28], skin [29, 30], sexual gender [31], and cognitive skills [25] results in people fluctuating in the Sense of ownership, and in fact, there are prosocial behaviors and a tendency to reduce discriminatory behaviors and thoughts. In agreement with Berthoz [3], interaction with an avatar promotes inhibition of one's own point of view in favor of the other. While simulative technology fosters the correlates of empathy, on the other hand in a study by Scattolini, Panasiti, Villa & Aglioti [32] it was shown that perspective taking of an avatar who is asked to have dishonest behaviors followed by monetary reinforcement led to a reduction in Sense of Ownership and an increase in dishonesty. In this regard, simplexity theory [3], which studies the way all living organisms, regardless of their body structure, adapt and learn through common principles and properties, and simplex didactics [4], which aims to capitalize on these principles and properties in teaching-learning processes, seem to be an entirely natural starting point for laying the groundwork for reflection to investigate the ways in which teaching and learning can take place in a no-place with a variable body.

5   The Inclusive Potential of the Virtual Museum in the Educational Context

Nowadays we are witnessing the frequent use of intelligent machines that interact with users in an increasingly natural way, in order to make human-machine interaction more similar to that of the real world [33], not only in reference to the size production of society but also to the sphere of social relations. The innovative technologies, which come closest to this type of interaction, are virtual reality systems, which consist of a new form of communication and experience capable of "teleporting" the user to a parallel world where he can live an immersive experience that could change his life. Virtual reality (VR) emerges as a leading technology for the metaverse, capable of creating personalized and meaningful user experiences through greater embodiment between the physical and digital worlds [34]. Specifically, virtual reality systems are wearable technologies through the use of head-mounted displays that offer the opportunity to immerse themselves in the virtual world (which can be the reconstruction of a real or fantasy place) in which the user can live a multi-sensory experience and interact with the elements present in the 3D space. Virtual reality is also defined as a "spatial technology" as physical and digital reality mix and the user can move simultaneously in the physical space and interact with the digital one. The VR interface feels very natural, almost as if it doesn't exist; in fact, the user can explore the digital space by moving in the real environment, without resorting to using the mouse or the computer keyboard. In particular, what differentiates virtual reality from common video games is the *level of immersion* (understood as the sensory fidelity of VR) and the *sense of presence* [14] in which the user experiences the sensation of being really present in that "place of information" [35] becoming the protagonist of his own experience. Initially virtual reality was used mainly in the clinical setting as a tool to help patients with Post Traumatic Stress Disorder (PTSD), as it has a very strong placebo effect in individuals that helps them change their behavior and take on new perspectives different from the own. In other words, we can say that virtual reality is a technology capable of changing human beings. In recent years this technology is also spreading in the educational context, some studies [36, 37] have demonstrated how virtual reality systems can promote the learning process in students through a constructionist model aimed at creating greater emotional engagement through the exploration of the 3D environment. From the point of view of simplex didactics, the digital environment becomes a non-linear choice that takes into account the principle of meaning and the principle of deviation [4, 38] in which through the immersive experience one aims to promote meaningful learning in students. Generally, in these contexts virtual reality is associated with Gamification and Edugames to make a video game stimulating and fun in an educational context, in order to help students understand abstract and complex concepts through concrete experiences. In fact, in the educational context, virtual reality can be used to enhance the phases of the experiential learning process, simulating a real-life situation in an interactive and controlled environment [33]. Furthermore, the sense of presence and embodiment that is experienced in the virtual environment offers the opportunity to those who cannot be available in a certain place (think of people with physical disabilities) to explore and get to know a new reality that adapts to the individual people's needs. Taking advantage of the potential of virtual reality systems, a project was developed at the Laboratory H of the DISUFF Department at the University of Salerno, aimed at promoting cultural accessibility through the creation of an inclusive 3D environment in which to make communication dynamic through different forms of interaction. In detail, the project concerns the creation of a virtual museum designed taking into account the principles of *Universal Design for All*, to create a 3D space accessible to all, especially students with Special Educational Needs. The virtual museum was developed using the *Unity 3D* graphics engine, in which the digital assets of the archaeological finds scanned inside the National Archaeological Museum of Sannio Caudino in Benevento and the Archaeological Museum of Carife were inserted. The virtual museum features a room that can be explored through the *Oculus Quest 2* VR device, or using the computer mouse or keyboard for those who do not have VR devices. This virtual environment can be adapted to the different needs of users, in fact, it is possible to customize the environment by making remote changes in terms of brightness, avatar height and color intensity [27]. The height of the avatar can be adjusted to make it easier for a person with a physical disability to move around in 3D space, while the "vignette" effect could reduce the feeling of nausea that often occurs when people use the avatar for the first time in virtual reality. Furthermore, in order to maximize the accessibility of the virtual museum, different fonts (Arial, OpenDislexic and Times New Roman) have been used and which ones can be changed to facilitate the reading process in dyslexic students. An initial experiment was conducted to understand how much the avatar's properties and the different ways of perception influenced the sense of presence and "agency" in users through the use of tasks with different ways of interacting which involve new forms of interaction and, consequently, learning. However, the experimentation of the virtual museum is still ongoing and the collected data will be presented in the next work.

6 Conclusions and Perspectives

The arguments presented open to a complex and heterogeneous (meta)universe of possibilities in the field of education. In other words, the contribution wants to present itself as a *positio questionis*, which starting from the opportunities and risks, presented and argued in the previous paragraphs, offered to the field of education by the metaverse, highlights how an adequate scientific language does not seem to be available at the moment to deal with the subject. In this sense, the theory of simplicity can represent a guide for the development of a scientific lexicon suitable for this purpose. However, the development of adequate epistemological tools for the analysis and prediction of the implications in the pedagogical.

References

1. Floridi, L.: Luciano Floridi—commentary on the onlife manifesto. In: The Onlife Manifesto, pp. 21–23. Springer, Cham (2015)
2. Accoto, C.: Il mondo in sintesi: Cinque brevi lezioni di filosofia della simulazione. Milano: EGEA spa.pp.35 (2022)
3. Berthoz, A.: La semplessità. Codice, Torino (2011)
4. Sibilio, M.: La didattica semplessa. Liguori, Napoli (2014)
5. Bocconi, S., Earp, J., Panesi, S.: digCompedu. il quadro di riferimento europeo sulle competenze digitali dei docenti. istituto per le Tecnologie didattiche, Consiglio nazionale delle ricerche (Cnr) (2017). https://doi.org/10.17471/54008 Link alla sperimentazione italia- na digCompeduSaT: https://tiny.cc/digCompedu_italia
6. Kelly, K., Locca, A.: L'inevitabile. Le tendenze tecnologiche che rivoluzioneranno il nostro futuro. Italia: Il Saggiatore (2017)
7. Berthoz, A.: La vicarianza. Il nostro cervello creatore di mondi. Codice, Italia (2015)
8. Grandi, G.: Virtuale è reale. Aver cura delle parole per aver cura delle persone. Paoline Editoriale Libri, Italia (2021)
9. Toffler, A.: Powershift: Knowledge, Wealth, and Power at the Edge of the 21st Century. Random House Publishing Group, Regno Unito (1991)
10. Pfeffer, A., Gerosa, M.: Mondi virtuali: benvenuti nel futuro dell'umanità. Castelvecchi, Italia (2006)
11. Coiffet, P., Burdea, G.C.: Virtual Reality Technology. Stati Uniti, Wiley (2017)
12. de Kerckhove, D.: Communication arts for a new spatial sensibility. Leonardo 24(2), 131–135 (1991)
13. Jenkins, H.: Confronting the Challenges of Participatory Culture: Media Education for the 21st Century, p. 69. The MIT Press, Cambridge (2009)
14. Riva, G., Gaggioli, A.: Realtà Virtuali, Giunti, Firenze (2019)
15. Lévy, P.: Qu'est-ce que le virtuel?. La Découverte. tr.it. Il virtuale, Raffaello Cortina, Milano, p. 76 (1995)
16. Ellis, S.R.: What are virtual environments? IEEE Comput. Graph. Appl. 14(1), 18 (1994). https://doi.org/10.1109/38.250914
17. Dewey, J.: Esperienza ed educazione. Raffaello Cortina Editore, Milano (2014)
18. Kolb, D.A.: Experiential Learning Experience as the Source of Learning and Development. Prentice Hall, Englewoods Cliffs (1984)
19. Pellerey, M.: L'apprendimento esperienziale come risultato e come processo. Roma, Note di Pastorale Giovanile (2010)
20. Dehaene, S.: Imparare: Il talento del cervello, la sfida delle macchine. Raffaello Cortina Editore (2020)
21. Riva, G., Wiederhold, B.K., Mantovani, F.: Neuroscience of virtual reality: from virtual exposure to embodied medicine. Cyberpsychol. Behav. Social Netw. 22(1), 82–96, 89 (2019)
22. Coelho, C., Tichon, J., Hine, T.J., Wallis, G., Riva, G.: Media presence and inner presence: the sense of presence in virtual reality technologies. From Commun. Pres. Cogn. Emot. Cult. Towards Ultim. Commun. Exp. 11, 25–45 (2006)
23. Gallagher, S.: Ambiguity in the sense of agency. In: Kiverstein, J., Vierkant, T. (eds.) Decomposing the Will, pp. 1–17. Oxford University Press, Oxford (2010)
24. Braun, N., et al.: The senses of agency and ownership: a review. Front. Psychol. 9, 535 (2018). https://doi.org/10.3389/fpsyg.2018.00535
25. Banakou, D., et al.: Virtually being einstein results in an improvement in cognitive task performance and a decrease in age bias. Front. Psychol. 9, 917 (2018)

26. Riva, G., Marchetti, A. (eds.): Humane robotics. A multidisciplinary approach towards the development of humane-centered technologies. Università Cattolica del Sacro Cuore, Milano (2022)
27. Di Tore, S.: Dal metaverso alla stampa 3D. Prospettive semplesse della didattica innovativa. Studium (2022)
28. Yoon, G., Vargas, P.T.: Know thy avatar: the unintended effect of virtual-self representation on behavior. Psychol. Sci. **25**, 1043–1045 (2014)
29. Maister, L., Slater, M., Sanchez-Vives, M.V., Tsakiris, M.: Changing bodies changes minds: owning another body affects social cognition. Trends Cogn. Sci. **19**, 6–12 (2015). https://doi.org/10.1016/j.tics.2014.11.001
30. Peck, T.C., Seinfeld, S., Aglioti, S.M., Slater, M.: Putting yourself in the skin of a black avatar reduces implicit racial bias. Conscious. Cogn. **22**, 779–787 (2013). https://doi.org/10.1016/j.concog.2013.04.016
31. Gonzalez-Liencres, C., et al.: Being the victim of intimate partner violence in virtual reality: first versus third-person perspective. Front. Psychol. (2020)
32. Scattolin, M., Panasiti, M.S., Villa, R., Aglioti, S.M.: Reduced ownership over a virtual body modulates dishonesty. Iscience **25**(5), 104320 (2022)
33. De Giorgis, G.: Unity. Guida pratica per sviluppare applicazioni di realtà virtuale e aumentata. Apogeo, Milano (2021)
34. Moon, J., Jeong, M., Oh, S., Laine, T.H., Seo, J.: Data collection framework for context-aware virtual reality application development in unity: case of avatar embodiment. Sensors **22**(12), 4623 (2022)
35. Bricken, M.: Virtual Worlds: No Interface to Design. MIT Press, Cambridge (1994)
36. Kalyvioti, K., Mikropoulos, T.A.: Memory performance of dyslexic adults in virtual environments. Procedia Comput. Sci. **14**, 410–418 (2012)
37. Kast, M., Meyer, M., Vögeli, C., Gross, M., Jäncke, L.: Computer-based multisensory learning in children with developmental dyslexia. Restor. Neurol. Neurosci. **25**(3–4), 355–369 (2007)
38. Aiello, P., Pace, E.M., Sibilio, M.: A simplex approach in Italian teacher education programmes to promote inclusive practices. Int. J. Incl. Educ., 1–14 (2021)

Impact of Multisensory XR Technologies
on Museum Exhibition Visits

Elena Spadoni(✉) ⓘ, Marina Carulli ⓘ, Francesco Ferrise ⓘ, and Monica Bordegoni ⓘ

Politecnico di Milano, 20158 Milan, Italy
elena.spadoni@polimi.it

Abstract. The use of digital technologies in museums is becoming increasingly popular, with a growing trend towards using multisensory eXtended Reality (XR) technologies to enhance visitor engagement and involvement. XR technologies like Virtual Reality (VR), Augmented Reality (AR), and Mixed Reality (MR) have the potential to bring numerous advantages to museums, including increased accessibility and inclusivity. By allowing visitors to experience a sense of immersion and actively engage with cultural artifacts, XR technologies can improve emotional engagement and learning activities. However, the integration of these technologies is often related to temporary exhibitions, and there are concerns about the costs associated with implementation and the potential for technology to negatively impact the visitor experience. Despite these challenges, evaluating the impact of multisensory XR technologies on visitor experience is difficult. This paper outlines a laboratory-based research activity that compares the impact of traditional exhibitions and XR technologies on visitor experience and learning performance. The study simulates a museum exhibition and allows the user to interact with different paintings using different XR technologies in a controlled environment.

Keywords: Cultural Heritage · Multisensory XR technologies · Museum exhibitions

1 Introduction

Museums are fundamental Cultural Institutions of modern society, being places of reference, research, and dissemination of knowledge related to many disciplines. In museums exhibitions, tangible Cultural Heritage, which refers to physical artefacts and sites, and intangible Cultural Heritage, which includes practices, representations, expressions, knowledge, and skills [1], are preserved and presented to the visitor as traces that witness the culture and reveal its deep meanings.

To keep up to date with emerging social needs, museums use different approaches to communicate and exhibit Cultural Heritage. Among different approaches, digital technologies are commonly adopted to engage visitors in memorable and amusing experiences. Furthermore, museums integrate digital technologies to pursue their objectives of education, entertainment, accessibility, and exploration [2].

© The Author(s), under exclusive license to Springer Nature Switzerland AG 2023
M. Antona and C. Stephanidis (Eds.): HCII 2023, LNCS 14021, pp. 120–132, 2023.
https://doi.org/10.1007/978-3-031-35897-5_9

Among the digital technologies adopted, there seems to be a growing trend related to the enhancement of traditional museum exhibitions through the use of multisensory eXtended Reality technologies (XR) – which include Virtual Reality (VR), Augmented Reality (AR), and Mixed Reality (MR) - to blur the line between the physical and virtual worlds and allow visitors to experience an engaging sense of immersion [3]. Indeed, multisensory XR technologies can greatly impact the realm of Cultural Heritage, bringing numerous advantages to museums such as increased visitor engagement and involvement. Furthermore, XR technologies enable the digital restoration of Cultural Heritage sites that have been lost or are inaccessible, or even the partial reconstruction of ancient artifacts to bring back their original form. The digital recreations of the artifacts are displayed to visitors as interactive and immersive experiences. The visitor is actively involved in a journey of discovery where the artifact serves as a tool for communicating cultural significance. Additionally, XR technologies can enable tangible and intangible interactions between visitors and the artifacts, allowing for exploration of pieces that may be too delicate to handle in real life. Finally, XR technologies may be crucial in increasing accessibility and inclusivity. Many studies in museums and art galleries also point out the integration of multisensory XR technologies to stimulate multiple human senses [4, 5], enhance emotional engagement and improve learning activities.

Although museums seem to recognize the substantial benefits of XR technologies, these experiences are frequently only temporarily incorporated into museum exhibitions [6]. The integration of these technologies is often related to extemporaneous attempts that make it difficult to assess the actual effect of multisensory XR technologies on visitors' perception, learning experiences and engagement.

In addition, some researchers have highlighted several problems that may arise from incorporating technology in museum exhibitions, such as the costs associated with implementation, adoption, and maintenance of the technologies and the potential risks in their use related to the limited visitor experience [7, 8]. Indeed, some museum professionals are cautious in adopting new technologies to avoid "disturbing" the intimate relational experience created between the visitor and the artefacts [9], or to prevent the risks of favouring entertainment over educational purposes in a "Disneyfication" of the museum's offerings [10].

However, despite the existence of a limited number of comparative studies, such as [11, 12], it appears challenging to assess the impact of multisensory XR technologies on museums and exhibitions visitors experience. Indeed, to perform a comprehensive assessment, various factors must be taken into consideration and compared. These include the use of different multisensory XR technologies, and the consequent different levels of interactivity and immersion, the levels of satisfaction and enjoyment of the experiences, and if the integration of technology is more effective for learning and engagement compared to traditional exhibitions. However, evaluating all these elements in a real-world setting is a complex task.

The paper presents a comparative evaluation by conducting a laboratory-based research activity based on a framework to compare different experiences of the same museum exhibition using a traditional approach and various XR technologies. Furthermore, the framework compares the impact of adopting multisensory approaches and different degrees of immersion on visitors' experience and learning performances.

The study outlines experimental activities that simulate a museum exhibition, allowing the user to interact with different paintings using different XR technologies within a laboratory environment.

2   Multisensory Immersive Technologies in Museum Exhibitions

Museums and other Cultural Institutions often incorporate digital technologies alongside traditional methods, either before or after the exhibit, to provide additional exploration or recall of content. However, some museums choose to enhance and supplement the viewing and comprehension of artifacts during the actual exhibition visit [13, 14].

Regarding museum exhibitions, traditional methods such as panels and audio guides may not be seen as effective by visitors in terms of user engagement and content learning and may be perceived as limiting. More often, museums include 3D reconstructions and digital heritage representations and integrate immersive multisensory technologies, such as eXtended Reality (XR), by offering Virtual Reality (AR), Augmented Reality (VR), and Mixed Reality (MR) experiences.

XR technologies have the advantage of making content more engaging for the visitor, who is often called to interact first-hand with museum artifacts, becoming an active participant in the experience. In addition, XR technologies also allow the creation of amazing and stunning experiences for the user. Thanks to the reproduction of virtual environments, they can find themselves immersed in another world estranged from the surrounding real one. This aspect can be crucial to allow visitors to focus on the proposed content, resulting in higher engagement and positively impacting learning activities. Additionally, XR technologies enable the combination of various digital media to provide multisensory stimuli, frequently engaging multiple senses such as hearing, sight, and touch at the same time. This feature is regarded as crucial to enhance content learning, as research has shown that multisensory engagement leads to better retention of information in the user's memory [15].

Many researchers explored the integration of XR technologies in museum exhibitions. Li et al. stated that the digital museum should not replace the traditional museum, but the digital contents should complement the physical ones by also considering the role that museums have for the visitor [16]. This aspect can be easily assessed by using AR to complement physical artifacts exhibited inside museums and by using VR to recreate a virtual representation of the museum or of the artifacts exposed. Geroimenko [17] investigates the potential of AR as a new artistic medium, and underlines some advantages compared to other more traditional media, stating that AR is spatially not limited, not expensive to produce and exhibit, and easy for making interactive and multimedia content.

Numerous examples can be found in literature that demonstrate the positive impact of XR technologies on enhancing the visitor experience in museum exhibitions. Weiquan et al. developed AR Muse, an iPad application where users can view the AR animated versions of six paintings after framing the original ones, showing a higher time spent looking at the artwork and better long-term identification when AR is used [18]. Ararat is an iPhone application designed by Kei et al. where it is possible to see real-time animated versions of different paintings, including those of Van Gogh and Da Vinci

[19]. Baradaran used AR to display an animation on the Mona Lisa painting, adding a political and patriotic message to the original artwork [20].

Concerning VR, some Institutions have integrated this technology to provide visitors with historical content about the artist and his paintings, as in the case of "The Modigliani VR: The Ochre Atelier" experience that was developed as part of the Modigliani exhibition at the Tate Modern Museum in London and was integrated into the collection made of paintings, sculptures, and drawings [21]. Others instead adopt VR to revive the paintings themselves, such as "Mona Lisa: Beyond the Glass", which is the Louvre's first VR project that consists of a journey back in time to meet the real woman that da Vinci painted [22]. Also, the Salvator Dalì Museum created "Dreams of Dalì", an immersive VR experience in which it is possible to explore Dali's painting *Archaeological Reminiscence of Millet's Angelus* [23]. And yet, in other cases, VR is used to create fully virtual displays, such as "The Kremer Museum" launched in 2017, which consists of a virtual museum where Dutch and Flemish Old Master paintings from the Kremer Collection are exposed [24].

It appears that the use of immersive, multisensory technologies is more prevalent in science and technology museums, where the focus is on enhancing the user's interactive experience. In these museums, audience engagement is typically achieved through hands-on exploration. As stated by Dalsgaard, Dindler, and Eriksson [25], science and technology Institutions build their processes by providing means to explore cultural heritage in a participative and active way. Instead, in art museums, there seems to prevail a contemplative paradigm in which the adoption of traditional technologies is preferred.

In the realm of museums, determining the effects of XR technologies on the visitor experience can be challenging, especially in the context of art museums. Measuring the impact that these technologies have on the museum visit is also difficult to define. To explore the hypothesis that XR technologies can enhance the museum experience, the authors created a framework and used it as a guide for conducting various experimental case studies to evaluate the impact of multisensory XR technologies on the museum visitors' experience.

3 A Framework for Investigating the Factors that Influence the Visitor Experience at Museums

In this Section, we present a framework for creating and evaluating museum experiences that takes into account various elements such as the *museum objectives*, *target audience*, *technological tools*, *digital resources*, and *experience modalities* (Fig. 1).

The purpose of the framework is to bring together various aspects for designing and evaluating museum visits. It is intended to be adaptable to any type of museum, including science and technology museums and art museums and galleries.

The framework serves as the foundation for conducting case studies to explore and compare different museum visit experiences. These case studies will be evaluated to determine which factors and combinations are most successful in fulfilling the *museum objectives* and meeting the needs of the *target audience*. The studies will be conducted in a laboratory setting as this environment offers a better control and allows for a clearer understanding of the correlation between variables, as opposed to in a real-life museum exhibit.

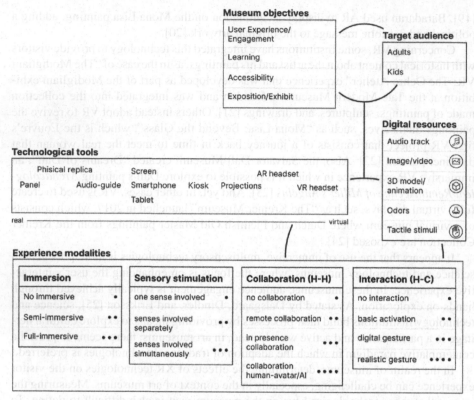

Fig. 1. Framework including various elements for creating museum experiences.

3.1 Framework Description

At the top level, the framework includes two dimensions: the *museum objectives* and the *target audience*, that are interconnected. These two dimensions are then linked to another dimension, related to the *technological tools* used within the museum exhibitions, the *digital resources*, which provide the means for content delivery, and the *experience modalities*, including elements such as *immersion*, *sensory stimulation*, *collaboration*, and *interaction*.

The *museum objectives* have been limited to *User Experience (UX) and engagement*, *learning*, *accessibility*, *exposition*, and *exhibit*. This allows us to focus on specific aspects of the visitor experience during a museum exhibition and exclude objectives such as the preservation of cultural heritage that are not related to the visitor experience. The *target audience* is adults or kids.

At the bottom level of the framework, the three other dimensions are included.

The *technological tools*, which are used by the museum to enhance the visitor experience, are categorized on a scale ranging from real to virtual. These technologies include more traditional tools, such as panels and audio-guides, and more forefront ones, such as AR and VR headsets.

Digital resources concern the modalities of conveying content through technological tools. They include representations of different sensorial stimuli, such as *audio tracks, images and video, 3D models and animation, odors* and *tactile stimuli*. Connected to these two dimensions, are the *experience modalities*, which include *immersion, sensory stimuli, collaboration*, and *interaction*. Each category is presented with different levels, ranging from no immersion to full immersion, with dots indicating an increase in the level.

3.2 From the Framework to the Experimental Case Studies

Among the proposed combinations, the comparison will initially focus on traditional technologies versus cutting-edge ones (see Fig. 2). Experimental case studies have been designed to compare four types of experiences, with a focus on the UX and engagement and learning museum goals and an adult target audience.

The content proposed in the four experiences is the same, enabling a comparison of the experiences from a learning perspective. In the chosen experiment, the dimensions of sensory stimuli, collaboration, and interaction have been considered null for all four experiences. Concerning the immersion aspect, the AR experience is considered not-immersive as it is delivered through a smartphone application, whereas the VR experience is considered semi-immersive.

Moreover, two of the selected experiences use more conventional methods (panel and audio-guide) with little or partial integration of digital resources.

The authors posit that XR technologies are more effective in terms of engagement and content learning for museum visits rather to more traditional approaches.

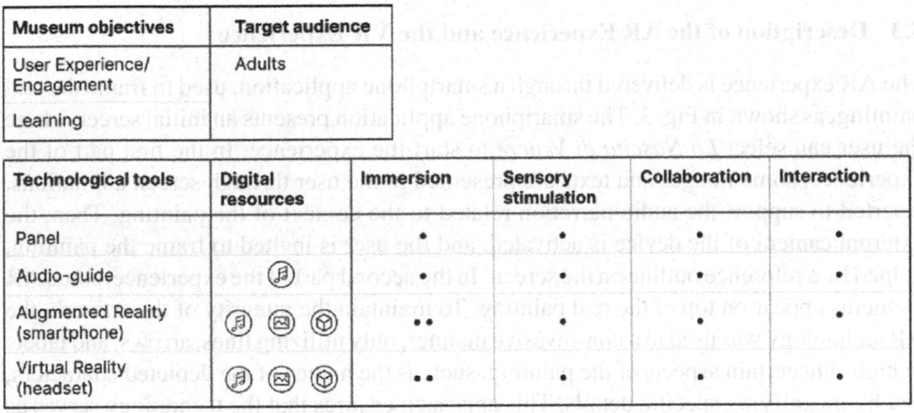

Museum objectives	Target audience
User Experience/ Engagement	Adults
Learning	

Technological tools	Digital resources	Immersion	Sensory stimulation	Collaboration	Interaction
Panel		•	•	•	•
Audio-guide	(♫)	•	•	•	•
Augmented Reality (smartphone)	(♫) (▣) (◉)	••	•	•	•
Virtual Reality (headset)	(♫) (▣) (◉)	••	•	•	•

Fig. 2. Framework dimensions adopted for developing the first experimental case studies.

4 Case Studies

The first comparison of experiences will be based on a visit to an art museum exhibit. A traditional piece of art (a painting) has been selected as the basis for the design, development, and testing of the experimental case studies.

4.1 Content Selected for the Experiment

The painting used for the experimental case studies is Sandro Botticelli's *La Nascita di Venere*, located in the Uffizi Galleries in Florence, Italy. This painting was selected because it is a classic artistic representation displayed in an art museum, where the use of XR technologies may be seen as riskier. While multisensory XR technologies are more frequently utilized in scientific or interactive museums where visitors can experience the content by interacting with it, they may not be as widely accepted in art museums where technology may be seen as an obstacle between the visitor and the artifact. However, this technology has the potential to enhance the visitor experience.

The content for the experimental case studies has been chosen and separated into three primary areas: background information about the painting, general knowledge about the elements depicted, and an in-depth analysis of each character.

4.2 Description of the Panel Experience and the Audio-Guide Experience

The contents related to the painting have been collected in a document and used as a reference for the four experiences. During the panel experience, the user can stand in front of the real painting and read the information presented as text written on a small panel near the painting. This way, he/she can observe the painting and read some details about it. The same textual information has been used to produce an audio track, adopted for the audio-guide experience. In this experience, the user can listen to the audio delivered through a smartphone while observing the painting. The same audio track has also been used in AR and VR experiences.

4.3 Description of the AR Experience and the VR Experience

The AR experience is delivered through a smartphone application, used to frame the real painting, as shown in Fig. 3. The smartphone application presents an initial screen where the user can select *La Nascita di Venere* to start the experience. In the first part of the experience, some images and texts are presented to the user through screen animations, inserted to support the audio narration related to the context of the painting. Then, the external camera of the device is activated, and the user is invited to frame the painting, helped by a reference outline on the screen. In the second part of the experience, some AR elements appear on top of the real painting. To maintain the integrity of the artwork, the AR technology was used in a non-invasive manner, only utilizing lines, arrows, and labels to highlight certain aspects of the painting, such as the names of the depicted characters, and by magnifying specific details. This approach ensures that the technology serves as a supplement to the physical painting, highlighting its features and not replacing it with augmented reality content. The user can adjust the volume of the background music and the voice narration through a menu accessible through a burger menu at any point during the experience.

In the VR experience, the participants find themself inside a virtual recreation of a museum. The real painting is reproduced virtually and presented on a white wall. The experience is delivered using an Oculus Quest headset, as shown in Fig. 3. The VR experience starts automatically and presents the same sequence of images, animations, and texts used for the AR experience. Indeed, the user can view the elements superimposed on the virtual replica of the painting.

Fig. 3. Participants during the AR and VR experiences.

4.4 Development of the AR and VR Applications

The AR and VR experience applications have been developed using the Unity3D game engine [26]. The first step of the development regarded preparing the images presented during the experiences as layers on top of the painting. These images were extracted from the original painting using Adobe Photoshop [27] and then imported into Unity. In Unity, images and audio tracks were incorporated, and all animations were produced. Moreover, magnifying visual effects (similar to small stars) have been used to better highlight the characters of the painting described in the last part of the explanation. The AR application was created using the Unity Mars tool [28] and the real painting was utilized as the image marker to trigger the AR content, as shown in Fig. 4.

Regarding the design of the AR application's Graphical User Interface, neutral colors (black, sand, and cream) and rounded shapes were chosen not to distract the use from the information being presented. For the VR experience, the virtual environment and the painting were created. The environment was designed as a simple room with the painting displayed on one of the white walls. As the last step, both applications were optimised and exported for use on a smartphone and the Meta Quest device.

Fig. 4. Screenshot of the AR application

5 Testing

The experiment was conducted in a laboratory setting, where a 60x90cm reproduction of the painting *"La Nascita di Venere"* was used to simulate a real museum visit during the testing experience.

5.1 Participants and Questionnaires

The study involved 40 participants (21 female) aged between 19 and 58, (M = 28; SD = 5,58) who voluntarily participated in the experiment. They were divided into groups of 10 people to test the four experiences equally. All the participants considered were Italian native speakers since the proposed experiences were in Italian.

The participants' educational levels varied from high school to PhD. They indicated a technological level comprising the use of PC, tablets, smartwatches, and smart TVs, but no one mentioned using VR headsets. Demographic information and technology proficiency were gathered through a pre-experience survey questionnaire administered to the participants. The questionnaire also investigated familiarity with the painting and reported that 26 out of 40 visited the Uffizi Galleries. Only 10% of the participants considered themselves to be highly knowledgeable about the painting's details. Furthermore, their familiarity with the painting's content was evaluated through a second questionnaire that consisted of specific questions related to the painting. The questionnaire was given to the participants prior to the experience, and it included open-ended questions, such as asking for the names of the characters depicted.

After the experience, the participants were asked to compile two more questionnaires related to UX and engagement and learning performances.

The first questionnaire, previously utilized by the researchers to assess UX and engagement in other studies [29, 30], was developed using similar works found in the literature [31–33] and incorporated elements of the Davis's variation Technology Acceptance Model (TAM) model [34] Regarding the technology and the modalities assessed during the experiment, the questions that aimed to explore the interactivity aspects with the content were removed since, as stated, the experiences did not include any interactive elements. The questionnaire comprises seven sections, mainly regarding quality and engagement of the overall experience, playfulness, self-efficacy, information quality, perceived usefulness, attitude toward use, and behavioral intention. The questionnaire is structured using a 7-point Likert scale, and the overall experience was also evaluated through the use of semantic differential.

The second questionnaire focused on measuring the participants' learning outcomes. Participants were asked to provide closed responses on the information presented during the experience. There were six questions in total, covering the three aforementioned content topics. The questionnaires were delivered using Google Forms.

5.2 Analysis of the Collected Data

Regarding the questionnaire that assessed UX and engagement during the experience (as depicted in Fig. 5), the AR experience was rated as the most engaging, with an average score of 6.5 out of 7. Meanwhile, the panel experience was rated as the least engaging, with an average score of 4.6 out of 7.

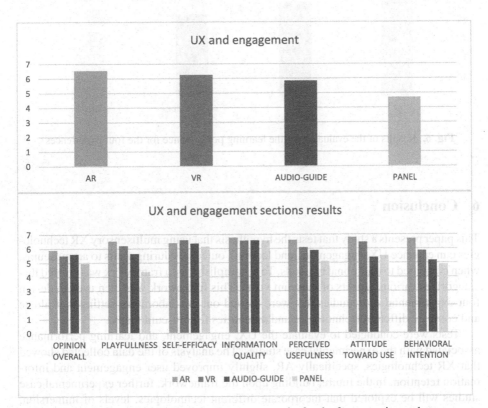

Fig. 5. Graph showing the UX and engagement results for the four experimental groups.

The VR experience has been considered most satisfying in terms of self-efficacy, with an average score of 6.6 out of 7, and making the subjects feel more "safe in using the application autonomously." The quality of the information was perceived as consistent across the VR, audio-guide, and panel experiences, while the AR experience received an average score of 6.7 out of 7 for information quality.

With regards to the questionnaire evaluating learning performance, the comparison analysis showed that the group of participants who underwent the AR experience acquired more knowledge compared to the other groups. Unlike engagement, the panel experience appeared to have a greater impact on learning performance as opposed to the audio-guide. The results have been obtained considering the delta between the pre-experience and the post-experience knowledge. The results indicate that the participants retained 53.6% of the content from the AR experience and 49% of the content from the VR experience (as shown in Fig. 6).

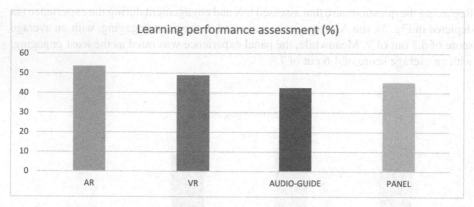

Fig. 6. Results of the evaluation of the learning performance for the four experiences.

6   Conclusion

This paper presents a study that tests the hypothesis that using multisensory XR technologies can enhance UX, engagement, and learning outcomes during visits to art museums, when compared to traditional methods. To accomplish this, a framework was created that categorizes various aspects of museum visits. This framework was then used to design four experimental case studies that were carried out in a laboratory setting to evaluate and compare different technologies and modalities for museum visits.

Tests were conducted to evaluate the UX, engagement, and learning performance associated with the experimental case studies. The analysis of the data collected showed that XR technologies, specifically AR, slightly improved user engagement and information retention. In the future, building upon the framework, further experimental case studies will be explored that incorporate different technologies, levels of immersion, sensory stimuli, and interactions.

References

1. Kurin, R.: Safeguarding Intangible Cultural Heritage in the 2003 UNESCO Convention: a critical appraisal. Museum Int. **56**(1–2), 66–77 (2004)
2. Bekele, M.K., et al. A survey of augmented, virtual, and mixed reality for cultural heritage. J. Comput. Cult. Herit. (JOCCH) **11**(2), 1–36 (2018)
3. Suh, A., Prophet, J.: The state of immersive technology research: a literature analysis. Comput. Hum. Behav. **86**, 77–90 (2018)
4. Obrist, M., et al.: Multisensory experiences in HCI. IEEE Multimedia **24**(2), 9–13 (2017)
5. Marto, A., et al.: A survey of multisensory VR and AR applications for cultural heritage. Comput. Graph. **102**, 426–440 (2022)
6. Sheade, M., Stylianou-Lambert, T.: Virtual reality in museums: exploring the experiences of museum professionals. Appl. Sci. **10**(11), 4031 (2020)
7. Cerquetti, M.: The importance of being earnest: enhancing the authentic experience of cultural heritage through the experience-based approach. In: The Experience Logic as a New Perspective for Marketing Management: From Theory to Practical Applications in Different Sectors, pp. 149–168 (2018)
8. Menegaki, A.N.: New technologies in hotels and museums: supply-side perceptions with education implications for managers and curators. J. Knowl. Econ. **13**(4), 2935–2956 (2021). https://doi.org/10.1007/s13132-021-00849-z
9. Leoni, L., et al.: Technology adoption in small Italian museums: an empirical investigation. Il Capitale Culturale **23**, 57–87 (2021)
10. Cerquetti, M.: More is better! current issues and challenges for museum audience development: a literature review. J. Cult. Manag. Policy **6**(1) (2016)
11. Leopardi, A., et al.: X-reality technologies for museums: a comparative evaluation based on presence and visitors experience through user studies. J. Cult. Herit. **47**, 188–198 (2021)
12. Rzayev, R., et al.: The effect of presence and appearance of guides in virtual reality exhibitions. In: Proceedings of Mensch Und Computer 2019, pp. 11–20 (2019)
13. Kuflik, T., Wecker, A.J., Lanir, J., Stock, O.: An integrative framework for extending the boundaries of the museum visit experience: linking the pre, during and post visit phases. Inf. Technol. Tourism **15**(1), 17–47 (2014). https://doi.org/10.1007/s40558-014-0018-4
14. Marty, P.F.: Museum websites and museum visitors: before and after the museum visit. Museum Manag. Curatorship **22**(4), 337–360 (2007)
15. Brunye, T.T., Taylor, H.A., Rapp, D.N.: Repetition and dual coding in procedural multimedia presentations. Appl. Cogn. Psychol. **22**, 877–895 (2008)
16. Li, Y.C., Liew, A.W.C., Su, W.P.: The digital museum: challenges and solution. In: 2012 8th International Conference on Information Science and Digital Content Technology (ICIDT 2012), vol. 3, pp. 646–649. IEEE (2012)
17. Geroimenko, V.: Augmented reality technology and art: the analysis and visualization of evolving conceptual models. In 2012 16th International Conference on Information Visualisation, pp. 445–453. IEEE (2012)
18. Lu, W., Nguyen, L.C., Chuah, T.L., Do, Y.L.: Effects of mobile AR-enabled interactions on retention and transfer for learning in art museum contexts. In: 2014 IEEE International Symposium on Mixed and Augmented Reality – Media, Art, Social Science, Humanities and Design (ISMAR-MASH'D), Munich, pp. 3–11 (2014)
19. https://www.designboom.com/technology/arart-augmented-reality-app-brings-paintings-to-life/. Accessed 09 Feb 2023
20. https://amirbaradaran.com/2019/works-pages/fml.html. Accessed 09 Feb 2023
21. Modigliani, V.R.: The Ochre Atelier. https://www.tate.org.uk/whats-on/tate-modern/modigliani/modiglianivr-ochre-atelier. Accessed 09 Feb 2023

22. https://www.louvre.fr/en/what-s-on/life-at-the-museum/the-mona-lisa-in-virtual-reality-in-your-own-home. Accessed 09 Feb 2023
23. https://thedali.org/dreams-of-dali-2/. Accessed 09 Feb 2023
24. The Kremer Museum. https://www.thekremercollection.com/the-kremer-museum/. Accessed 09 Feb 2023
25. Dalsgaard, P., Dindler, C., Eriksson, E.: Designing for participation in public knowledge institutions. In: Proceedings of the 5th Nordic Conference on Human-Computer Interaction: Building Bridges, pp. 93–102 (2008)
26. https://unity.com/. Accessed 09 Feb 2023
27. https://www.adobe.com/it/products/photoshop.html. Accessed 09 Feb 2023
28. https://unity.com/products/unity-mars. Accessed 09 Feb 2023
29. Spadoni, E., Porro, S., Bordegoni, M., Arosio, I., Barbalini, L., Carulli, M.: Augmented reality to engage visitors of science museums through interactive experiences. Heritage 5(3), 1370–1394 (2022)
30. Porro, S., Spadoni, E., Bordegoni, M., Carulli, M.: Design of an intrinsically motivating AR experience for environmental awareness. Proc. Des. Soc. 2, 1679–1688 (2022)
31. Mumtaz, K., Iqbal, M.M., Khalid, S., Rafiq, T., Owais, S.M., Al Achhab, M.: An e-assessment framework for blended learning with augmented reality to enhance the student learning. Eurasia J. Math. Sci. T 13 (2017). https://doi.org/10.12973/eurasia.2017.00938a
32. Rese, A., Baier, D., Geyer-Schulz, A., Schreiber, S.: How augmented reality apps are accepted by consumers: a comparative analysis using scales and opinions. Technol. Forecast. Soc. Chang. 124, 306–319 (2017)
33. Salloum, S.A., Alhamad, A.Q.M., Al-Emran, M., Monem, A.A., Shaalan, K.: Exploring students' acceptance of e-learning through the development of a comprehensive technology acceptance model. IEEE Access 7, 128445–128462 (2019)
34. Davis, F.D.: Perceived usefulness, perceived ease of use, and user acceptance of information technology. MIS Q. 13(3), 319 (1989)

Empowering Virtual Humans' Emotional Expression in the Metaverse

Elena Spadoni[1] , Marina Carulli[1]([✉]) , Maura Mengoni[2] , Marco Luciani[2] ,
and Monica Bordegoni[1]

[1] Politecnico di Milano, 20154 Milan, Italy
marina.carulli@polimi.it
[2] Università Politecnica delle Marche, 60126 Ancona, Italy

Abstract. The Metaverse is defined as an interconnected network of 3D environments that enable multisensory interactions with virtual environments, digital objects, and people. A central component of a Metaverse is the realism of human interaction with the environment and each other, which is achieved through emotional expression. However, there are limitations in realistically representing human emotions and facial expressions in real time through virtual avatars. In this paper, the authors present a research project called Meta-EmoVis aimed at improving the realism of the Metaverse by detecting human facial expressions and translating them into emotional feedback that influences aspects of the virtual avatar and environment. The Emoj tool is used to collect data and map facial expressions to basic emotions, as well as detect the human engagement level. The goal is to create a world of real social interaction and emotional sharing in virtual spaces that are sensitive and adaptive to human emotional and mental states. Preliminary user tests to evaluate the effectiveness of the application are presented.

Keywords: Metaverse · Emotion · Virtual Reality

1 Introduction

The Metaverse is defined as an interconnected network of immersive 3D environments integrated into persistent multi-user platforms, and it is based on technologies that enable multisensory interactions with virtual environments, digital objects, and people [1].

Since human beings express their emotions in everyday interactions with the environment and with others, one of the central components of a Metaverse is considered the realism through which human beings interact with the environment and each other. Emotions are often expressed through facial expressions, hand and body movements, and vocal inflections. As such, these elements play a crucial role in creating the illusion of liveliness, which enhances the sense of being fully immersed in the Metaverse [2]. An approach to enhance the virtual experience is to equip virtual humans with the capability to display their emotions and connect with others through gestures and expressions [3–5]. However, currently, there appear to be limitations in realistically representing human emotions and facial expressions in real-time through virtual avatars. Therefore,

M. Antona and C. Stephanidis (Eds.): HCII 2023, LNCS 14021, pp. 133–143, 2023.
https://doi.org/10.1007/978-3-031-35897-5_10

it is necessary to explore alternative methods for representing emotions and improving the realism of the Metaverse.

In this paper, the authors present an experimental research project called Meta-EmoVis (recalling the emotions visibility in the Metaverse), with the aim of filling this gap and trying to connect reality and virtuality more deeply, influencing aspects of the appearance of the virtual avatar based on the real emotions of human beings in real-time. Since facial expressions are crucial in expressing and communicating emotions [6, 7], in this study human facial expressions are detected and translated into emotional feedback that influences some aspects related to virtual avatars and the appearance of the virtual environment.

Different virtual effects to increase avatars' realism and emotional expressions in Metaverse have been designed using data collected through Emoj, a tool that allows detecting faces and recognizing emotions through the device webcam [8]. The Emoj tool maps facial expressions to six basic emotions, i.e., surprise, happiness, sadness, anger, disgust, and fear, plus a neutral one. Furthermore, the humans' engagement level is detected and integrated with the emotions.

The inclusion of emotions in a Metaverse environment aims at contributing to the creation of a world of real social interaction and emotions sharing in which also virtual spaces become sensible, adaptive, and empathic to humans emotional and mental state.

Preliminary user tests have been performed to evaluate the effectiveness of the application. The analysis of the data collected in the tests will be presented in the paper.

2   Related Works

The term "Metaverse" refers to an increasingly popular form of socialising and collaboration within a virtual world, a shared virtual space where users can interact with each other and with virtual objects and environments. The concept of a Metaverse has been popularised in science fiction and technology circles as a vision of a global, unified digital space where people can engage in immersive experiences, participate in virtual communities, and access vast amounts of information and data. The Metaverse is often seen as a convergence of Virtual Reality, Augmented Reality, and the internet, providing an environment that is both real and virtual simultaneously [9]. Such environments allow users to enter virtual worlds that simulate real-life experiences through different social activities. The development of the Metaverse is still in its early stages, and many technical, ethical, and societal challenges need to be addressed before it can become a reality [10].

Realism in the metaverse refers to the degree to which the virtual environment accurately represents the real world and provides a convincing user experience. The goal of creating a realistic metaverse is to create an immersive virtual environment that feels as real and natural as possible, allowing users to interact with it in a way that feels intuitive and lifelike. The level of realism in the metaverse is a key factor in determining its success and usability. Ongoing research and development efforts are focused on improving the realism of virtual environments to create more engaging and immersive experiences for users [11].

In order to achieve realism, various aspects of the metaverse need to be considered, such as the representation of physical objects and environments, the behaviour of virtual characters, and the quality and responsiveness of user interactions. Other factors contributing to realism include the accuracy of lighting and shadows, realistic sounds and textures, and the ability to convey emotions and social cues naturally and believably.

Emotion is a powerful feeling that arises from one's circumstances, mood, or interactions with others, and in daily life, we instinctively interpret others' emotions through their facial expressions [7].

However, in remote communication settings such as social media and Metaverse environments, it can be difficult to grasp other people's emotions, which can hinder remote socialisation.

On social media, posts can be interpreted differently by different people, and the lack of nonverbal cues, such as body language and tone of voice, can make it difficult to understand the emotions behind a message fully. Despite these limitations, emotions are an essential part of social media interactions, as they allow people to connect and engage with one another on a deeper level. They also contribute to the overall atmosphere and mood of social media platforms and can influence how people interact and behave online.

So, to convey emotions in a concise and easily recognisable way, people usually use emoticons, emojis, and other symbols.

In the Metaverse environments design and development, the representation of emotions is used to create a more realistic and immersive experience for users by allowing them to interact with other users and respond to events in the virtual world in a way that mirrors real life. In these environments, one way that emotions are represented is through the use of nonverbal cues, such as body language and facial expressions. Avatars can be programmed to display specific emotions through changes in posture, gestures, and facial expressions, allowing users to communicate how they are feeling in real time.

Another way that emotions are represented in the Metaverse is through the use of virtual objects and environments. For example, the color, shape, and texture of virtual environments can be used to evoke different emotions and moods, such as happiness, sadness, or excitement.

Finally, emotions can also be represented through the use of sound and music. In virtual environments, background music, sound effects, and other audio cues can be used to create a specific emotional atmosphere and to enhance the overall user experience.

The emotions depicted in the Metaverse can either stem from the user's deliberate inputs and they can be identified automatically.

In particular, the detection of facial expressions is a field of study that focuses on recognising the emotional states of individuals by analysing their facial movements and associating them with their emotions. This technology generally uses deep learning algorithms. Many of these algorithms are based on the results of research works as [12] and [13]. This technology is used in a variety of applications, including human-computer interaction, emotion recognition in virtual environments, and psychological research.

Facial expression detection is usually performed using computer vision techniques that analyse images or video streams to identify specific facial landmarks and track changes in facial movements over time. Deep learning algorithms can then be used to classify facial expressions into specific emotions based on the patterns of movement that have been identified.

The accuracy of facial expression detection technology varies depending on the specific method used and the level of sophistication of the algorithms involved. However, despite the limitations of current technology, the use of facial expression detection is growing in popularity and is expected to play an increasingly important role in the development of more immersive and realistic virtual environments.

2.1 Emoj: A Tool for Analyzing Emotions

The development of emotions and mutual interfacing in moments of conviviality and sociability turn out to be the basis of human being's ability to create human relationships. Over the past decades, different studies have revealed the relevance of performing emotion analysis through face analysis and its applications.

Founded in 2017 as a spin-off of the Polytechnic University of Marche, Emoj is an Italian startup that has developed a proprietary tool for emotional analysis.

Based on research by Paul Ekman [14] this tool uses simple RGB cameras to estimate a person's emotional state, engagement values, valence, and arousal, in line with the levels of attention and research conducted by Russell [15].

The main challenge faced by Emoj is to ensure real-time operation of their system. This approach ensures compliance with the privacy regulations established by GDPR 2016/679 since the images are immediately processed and discarded, with no association between the individual's identity or name and their face. Additionally, the technology used by Emoj is capable of detecting people's emotional responses to specific elements they interact with in real-time, providing insight into user emotions throughout their journey.

3 Main Idea

In this paper, the authors present a research project called Meta-EmoVis, which aims to bridge the gap between reality and virtuality by connecting real-time human emotions to the appearance of virtual avatars in the Metaverse.

In this study, human facial expressions, which play a vital role in emotional communication, are detected and used to provide emotional feedback that affects aspects of the virtual avatar's appearance and the virtual environment. Specifically, virtual effects aimed at enhancing the realism and emotional expressions of avatars in the Metaverse have been developed using data collected from Emoj. The integration of emotions into a Metaverse environment aims to foster the creation of a world where real social interaction and emotional sharing occur, making virtual spaces responsive, adaptable, and attuned to humans' emotional and mental states. The Emoj tool associates facial expressions with six basic emotions (surprise, happiness, sadness, anger, disgust, and fear) and a neutral emotion. Additionally, it detects the level of human engagement and valence and incorporates it with emotions.

In the Meta-EmoVis project, the authors used various elements to depict emotions detected by Emoj and influence the appearance of the virtual avatar and the environment in the Metaverse.

Specifically, a colour has been associated with each emotion, represented by a coloured halo that appears on the head of the virtual avatar. According to the detected user emotion, the colour changes in real time. The colour-emotion association is created according to studies reported in the literature [16–18].

In addition, facial expressions have been designed and developed. In fact, it is well known that the most expressive way in which human beings show their emotions is through facial expressions. Therefore, by renouncing anonymity and privacy, the user can decide to show their emotions by activating the camera directly. The user's real face is displayed in a circle at the top of the virtual avatar's head.

Another option is expressing emotions through emojis, which are graphic symbols representing facial expressions, appearing in real-time and spreading around from the avatar body, as shown in Fig. 1. Emojis have been used because they are widely used means for online communication and are increasingly adopted, especially on social media with a well-known shared meaning [19].

Fig. 1. Screenshot showing virtual emotional effects in the Meta-EmoVis project.

While experiencing the environment, some visual features, such as the colour of some elements, may change according to the detected emotions. In addition, specific avatar motion animations and clothes have been designed and associated with the emotions and are triggered by the detected facial expressions of the users. These effects strengthen the social interaction and the empathic perception occurring among virtual humans.

To test the effectiveness of the application, two virtual scenarios have been designed, one referred to a formal context of use and the other to an informal context. The formal scenario consists of a conference room, where avatars can sit around a table to watch presentations, discuss, and share opinions. The informal scenario concerns a natural environment in which the avatars experience a moment of social life, interacting with each other at a virtual party.

Emotional virtual elements have been integrated into the two scenarios, depending on their purpose and level of formality. For example, emoji symbols and changes to the avatar's motion animations and looks were only integrated into the second scenario. In fact, these elements can be considered too gaudy and distracting when applied in a more serious context.

4   Development of the Application

The Meta-EmoVis project has been implemented by using Unity3D (unity.com) for the creation of the Metaverse virtual experience.

Initially, three main categories composed of all the elements necessary for constructing the Metaverse environments have been identified (see Fig. 2). The first group focuses on the creation of scenes, including both the environments and the avatars. The second group encompasses the Emoj tool integrated with Unity, including its ability to detect emotions and display them in the Metaverse. The third group deals with the Graphical User Interface (GUI), which includes an on-screen menu and various virtual elements.

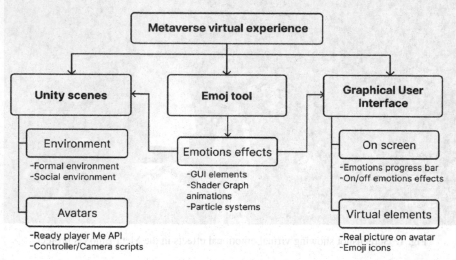

Fig. 2. Schematic representation of the constituent elements of the Metaverse virtual experience.

Virtual Environments and Avatars. Two main scenes have been developed, corresponding to the formal environment and to the natural environment. Both virtual environments presented in the two scenes have been created by importing some assets freely available on the Unity Assets Store (https://assetstore.unity.com/) to facilitate the development process. The formal environment scene presents a futuristic conference room, in which a big table is positioned at the centre of the room, and a big screen is presented on a white wall. The natural environment consists of a forest presented during the night. A bonfire has been added as the central element of the scene to stimulate social behaviours between avatars. The avatars selected for the project present a humanoid figure with the aim of fostering the users' virtual presence and embodiment. The Ready Play Me API, an avatar interoperability layer that improves performance and avatar integration flexibility for the Metaverse, has been used to generate avatars based on photos. Each avatar presents an asset that can be customised to reflect the user's personal style or mood, adding details such as glasses or clothes that can be personalised in the Metaverse. Moreover, the user can control the avatar by using the keyboard to move inside the space and interact with other avatars and digital objects. The user can move in any direction by using the WASD command, increase the speed by pressing shift, and jump by using the spacebar. This uncomplicated and user-friendly interaction that recalls the videogame one has been integrated by using three scripts to control the character and the camera within the Unity scenes.

Emoj Tool Integration with Unity. This section describes how the Emoj tool has been integrated with Unity. Ad hoc interfaces were employed to establish a communication model between Unity and Emoj, which was created and developed in the form of a Dynamic Link Library (DLL). The Emoj tool consists of 4 modules, as shown in Fig. 3.

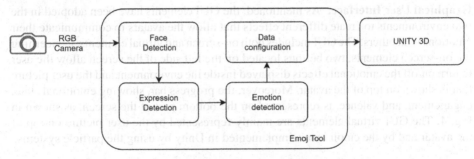

Fig. 3. The Emoj architecture.

The first module discerns the individual positioned in front of an RGB camera, whereas the second module identifies the structure and facial features of the person. The third module processes the emotional information, while the fourth module takes care of correctly preparing the response toward Unity3D. The Emoj module generates an output in the form of a percentage value linked to the magnitude of the primary Ekman emotions, namely joy, sadness, anger, fear, disgust, surprise, and neutral [20]. Furthermore, it provides measurements for engagement, which gauges the degree of involvement of the subject, and valence, which provides a quantification of the emotional state's positivity or negativity.

The tool uses images from standard RGB cameras, in real-time, without saving sensitive information of the person being analysed, in accordance with GDPR 2016/679. The Emoj model manages the interfacing and acquisition of frames from the camera, operating independently of the Unity3D model. By adopting this approach, the authors were able to address concerns regarding the application of computer vision libraries, such as the OpenCV library, with Unity3D.

Emotions Effects in the Virtual Environment. The authors decided to depict the six emotional states and also two conditions, engagement and valence, using some visual effects in the virtual environment. The neutrality emotion has not been reported. Different colours have been used to impact the avatars and surroundings to represent emotions.

The effects have been implemented in Unity by using GUI elements, shader graph animations, and particle systems. The GUI is adapted to exhibit emotions, utilizing a small component that appears on the avatar's head and displays the real-time image captured by the camera device. This feature enables the user to establish a connection between themselves and their representation in the Metaverse. This feature also takes the colour of the user's emotion in order to show it in real time. To demonstrate engagement and valence, which are essential for conveying the participant's status and degree of attentiveness during both formal and social occasions, the authors incorporated a GUI progress bar that employs colors and percentages to indicate the dominant emotion. Shader graph animations have been used in both settings to impact certain components of the environment itself. For example, in the formal scene, the tabletop light has been animated, while in the social scene, the sky's aura has been modified. Additionally, within the social context, emoji icons are conveyed through particle systems that materialize on the avatar, signifying the corresponding emotion.

Graphical User Interface. As mentioned, the GUI elements have been adopted in the two environments to create different effects that allow the avatars to communicate their emotions with others. The GUI includes both on-screen and virtual elements. Concerning the on-screen elements, two buttons located on the left side of the screen allow the user to turn on/off the emotional effects displayed inside the environment and the user picture that is shown on top of the avatar. Moreover, the progress bar, showing emotional state, engagement, and valence, is represented on the bottom part of the screen, as shown in Fig. 4. The GUI virtual elements are mainly represented by the user picture on top of the avatar and by the emoji icons, implemented in Unity by using the particle systems.

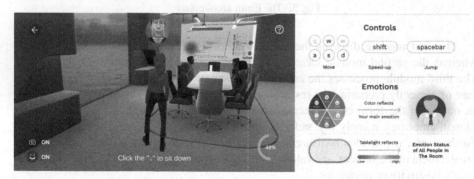

Fig. 4. Image of the formal environment and scheme showing controls and emotions.

5 User Testing

Preliminary testing was conducted with a targeted group of individuals. The objective of these tests was to:

- Confirm the viability of the application's concept by verifying that its design functions are as intended.
- Assess the application's usability to determine if users can effectively use it.
- Evaluate the users' experiences with a focus on the use of emotion representations in the Metaverse.

The authors obtained preliminary feedback from users who tested the applications (refer to Fig. 5). They expressed a high level of satisfaction with the applications and reported a positive experience while engaging with them. In particular, they remarked that the scenes were highly realistic and that they felt fully immersed in the experience.

Regarding the visual aspect of the Metaverse environments, the users found that interacting with other avatars was both engaging and inspiring, prompting them to continue socializing. Furthermore, they reported that Emoj accurately identified their emotions, and the depiction of those emotions within the Metaverse environment was both impactful and straightforward to comprehend.

Finally, a few suggestions for enhancement were gathered. Some users requested clarification about potential tasks and sought recommendations. To address this issue, the authors suggest incorporating audio guidance to provide information and assist users throughout their Metaverse experience. Furthermore, improvements to the User Interface and the visual representation of the data collected by Emoj will also be considered.

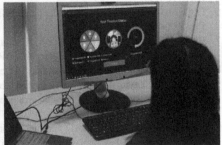

Fig. 5. Users testing the application.

6 Conclusions

The paper describes the Meta-EmoVis research project, which aims to enhance the Metaverse's realism and emotional expressions by connecting real time human emotions to the appearance of virtual avatars and environments. The system uses data collected from Emoj to integrate emotions into a Metaverse environment, fostering a world where real social interaction and emotional sharing occur. The study presents various elements to depict emotions detected by Emoj and influence the appearance of the virtual avatar and the environment in the Metaverse, such as the association of emotions with colours, facial expressions, emojis, and avatar motion animations. The initial testing with users revealed high satisfaction with the application's concept and usability, with some suggestions for improvement, including adding audio guidance and improving the user interface and visual representation of the data collected by Emoj.

Acknowledgement. the authors want to thank Siyu Hu and Weiyu Li, student of the Virtual and Physical Prototyping course, School of Design, Academic Year 2020/2021, for their contribution to the project.

References

1. Mystakidis, S.: Metaverse. Encyclopedia **2**(1), 486–497 (2022)
2. Dionisio, J.D.N., Burn, W.G., Gilbert, R.: 3D virtual worlds and the metaverse: current status and future possibilities. ACM Comput. Surv. (CSUR) **45**(3), 1–38 (2013)
3. McCquiggan, S.W., et al.: Modeling parallel and reactive empathy in virtual agents: an inductive approach. In: Proceedings of the 7th International Joint Conference on Autonomous Agents and Multiagent Systems, vol. 1, pp. 167–174 (2008)
4. Ochs, M., Pelachaud, C., Sadek, D.: An empathic virtual dialog agent to improve human-machine interaction. In: Proceedings of the 7th International Joint Conference on Autonomous Agents and Multiagent Systems, vol. 1, pp. 89–96 (2008)
5. Boukricha, H., Wachsmuth, I.: Mechanism, modulation, and expression of empathy in a virtual human. In: 2011 IEEE Workshop on Affective Computational Intelligence (WACI), pp. 1–8. IEEE (2011)
6. Darwin, C.: The Expression of the Emotions in Man and Animals. The University of Chicago Press (1969)
7. Ekman, P., Friesen, W.V., Ellsworth, P.: Emotion in the Human Face: Guidelines for Research and an Integration of Findings. Pergamon Press Inc. (1972)
8. https://www.emojlab.com/. Accessed 15 Feb 2023
9. Dincelli, E., Yayla, A.: Immersive virtual reality in the age of the Metaverse: a hybrid-narrative review based on the technology affordance perspective. J. Strateg. Inf. Syst. **31**(2), 101717 (2022)
10. Baker-Brunnauer, J.: Ethical Challenges for the Metaverse Development (2022)
11. Slater, M., et al.: Visual realism enhances realistic response in an immersive virtual environment. IEEE Comput. Graphics Appl. **29**(3), 76–84 (2009)
12. Bailenson, J.N., et al.: Real-time classification of evoked emotions using facial feature tracking and physiological responses. Int. J. Hum Comput Stud. **66**(5), 303–317 (2008)
13. Borth, D., et al.: Large-scale visual sentiment ontology and detectors using adjective noun pairs. In: Proceedings of the 21st ACM international conference on Multimedia, pp. 223–232 (2013)
14. Ekman, P., et al.: Basic Emotions. Handbook of Cognition and Emotion, vol. 98(45–60), p. 16 (1999)
15. Russell, J.A.: Core affect and the psychological construction of emotion. Psychol. Rev. **110**(1), 145 (2003)
16. Hanada, M.: Correspondence analysis of color–emotion associations. Color. Res. Appl. **43**(2), 224–237 (2018)

17. Naz, K.A.Y.A., Helen, H.: Color-emotion associations: past experience and personal preference. In: AIC 2004 Color and Paints, Interim Meeting of the International Color Association, Proceedings, Jose Luis Caivano, vol. 31 (2004)
18. Takahshi, F., Kawabata, Y.: The association between colors and emotions for emotional words and facial expressions. Color. Res. Appl. **43**(2), 247–257 (2018)
19. Kralj Novak, P., et al.: Sentiment of emojis. PloS One **10**(12), e0144296 (2015)
20. Ekmann, P.: Universal facial expressions in emotion. Stud. Psychol. **15**(2), 140 (1973)

eXtended Reality is Not What It Seems: Instil 360° Topsy-Turvy Society to Perceive Real World Reality[†]

Robert E. Wendrich[(✉)] (iD)

Rawshaping Technology RBSO, 2402 AB Nieuwkoop, ZH, The Netherlands
info@rawshaping.com

Abstract. "eXtended Reality" technologies (XRTs) are advanced interactive systems and/or synthetic environments that incorporate continuums, such as; virtual reality (VR), mixed reality (MR) and augmented reality (AR) tools, devices, systems and services. XRTs have emerged in various domains, ranging from manufacturing, entertainment, cultural heritage, anthropogenic climate awareness, to training and mission critical applications. Global Society (GS) requires enhanced connection of people, time, place, context and/or technology to provide coherent and trustworthy multisensory, multidimensional, multimodal, multidisciplinary interactions to create hyper-mediated- and hyper-realistic experiences to enhance knowledge, amplify communication, gain insight, change relationships and foster understanding. Within this context XRTs, could be seen as *'just another adaptive toolbox of multi-mediated realities,'* and as such an enabler for current and ongoing digital transformation, digitization, and virtualization in GS to escape from the 'illusionary cave' and discover there are 'whole new perspectives and other worlds' outside of that what people were previously unaware of, thought possible or not capable to expose themselves to as of yet.

Keywords: extended reality · artificial · synthetic · natural reality · global society

1 Introduction

Our identities are shaped by culture as much as birth, and categories like race, division of labour, class (e.g., *transnational class*) and gender depend on the complicated interaction between how we see and present ourselves and how others see us. Still, our perception of risk and/or security is dominated by our emotional brain. It favors proximity, draws on personal experience, and deals with images and stories (e.g., narratives, ideologies) that speak to existing values and attributes [1]. Yet, our perception of risk and/or security is formed socially, hence showing the power of society.

What one thinks does not matter; what counts is, that people think it together. In this way, the masses come to accept even the most absurd ideas as true, or at least to act as if

---

[†]Society in context, here used alternatively as in global society (GS); people; humans; human kind; humanity.

© The Author(s), under exclusive license to Springer Nature Switzerland AG 2023
M. Antona and C. Stephanidis (Eds.): HCII 2023, LNCS 14021, pp. 144–160, 2023.
https://doi.org/10.1007/978-3-031-35897-5_11

they were true. Mass formation is the highest form of collectivism, a sense of mythical belonging that those fascinated by groups rather than individuals have routinely labeled "society," "solidarity" or "democracy" [2].

The recent pandemic has accelerated the incorporation of digital technologies into the interactions and strategies of mediators. As a result, an innovate hybrid model of mediation has started to emerge (see Fig. 1). It combines digital interactions with physical meetings, organized at critical times and under specific risk mitigation protocols[1].

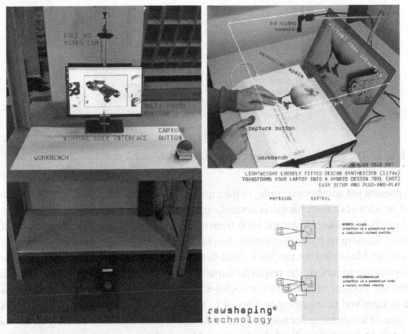

Fig. 1. Various hybrid XRT embodiments inter- & intra-actions, stochastic configurations and diverse transformations of XRXs [12].

The promise of XRTs as enabler for current and ongoing digital transformation, digitization, and virtualization in GS, could assist to help us escape from the metaphoric 'cave boundaries' and instil discovery (e.g., novelty, realities) that there exist 'whole new and other worlds' outside that of what people were previously unaware (or ignored) of or not capable or willing to expose themselves to.

To wit, people in general (i.e., humans), consider the anthropogenic climate change[2] (i.e., planetary crisis) as something that '...*clearly seems to exceed present cognitive and emotional abilities of the species...*' [3, 4]. This holds true, even when one argues, '*that climate breakdown shatters the deepest bonds that hold us together: our families,*

---

[1] See: https://peacemaker.un.org/digitaltoolkit.

[2] According to the international legal definition: 'attributed directly or indirectly to human activity that alters the composition of global atmosphere and which is in addition to natural climate variability observed over comparable time periods.'

our health and our communities.' The real story nonetheless, is about our fear, denial, uncertainty and struggle to accept our own responsibility and accountability. Blakemore [5] stated the following, '...climate change is not the elephant in the room; it is the elephant we are all inside of...' Hence, real objects are not seen from a perspective-they are within that perspective! To have a habitable planet earth, for humans, non-humans and nature alike, necessitates the comprehensive decarbonization of all realms of social life [6] (see Fig. 2). Later in this article we will see that the right hemisphere tends to confront "us" what is "really out there."

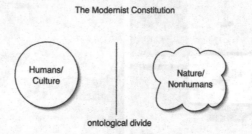

Fig. 2. The great divides: delegated, mediated, distributed, mandated, uttered [24].

To present yet another example; in the current meta-crisis of education [7] (i.e., teachers and academics), the change is actually in transforming what teaching and research should really be about. However, such transition(s) (i.e., radical change) seems difficult by devise, constraint by conservatism (*crises in the minds and souls*), idiosyncrasies, ostracism and bounded by the basic idea that societies require each new generation to be in a position to inherit the requisite capabilities, legitimacy, and meaning-making to continue the project of cooperative social-industrial life. Biosemiotics is the idea that all life is involved in *meaning making* [8]. Today's GS (i.e., children) who will be the workforce of the coming decades will need decision-making and creativity as key skills. Skills such as analysis, critical thinking, problem-solving, and creativity require abilities to understand abstract concepts and visualize those concepts in real-time scenarios. Science, technology, engineering, the arts, and mathematics (STEAM) education is now more critical than ever. Hence, critical thinking and problem-solving skills are necessary to solve complex challenges and problems, such as, migratory crisis, land grabbing, deforestation, heat bulbs, erosion, resource depletion, pollution, habitat destruction and freshwater sources.

XRTs therefore could provide different insights and understanding in multiverse continuums. In addition, XRTs could provide realistic (i.e., extended natural reality, intuitive, tacit, expertise) XR experiences (XRXs) and interactive multi-modalities that actively engage users (connectivity of human, non-human, more-than-human) with immersive and semi-immersive systems (i.e., intra-actions) and processes, whilst fully exercising their full autonomy and agency based on informed choice (politics). To use semi-immersive and/or immersive technologies, users contact or "dive" into a virtual realm or interact with an extended virtual world/sphere. The added virtual content layer(s) could be perceived as ultra- or very realistic. The degree of immersion depends mostly on the possibility or affordances of interaction build in. Besides, we need to watch out for excessive hype, after peak hype (e.g., virtual reality, google glass, meta-verse, singularity, autonomous cars) these experiences and technologies will enter the trough of disillusionment (see Fig. 3). Keeping the tacit-tangible closely is of utmost importance and essential to keep grounded and physically realistic.

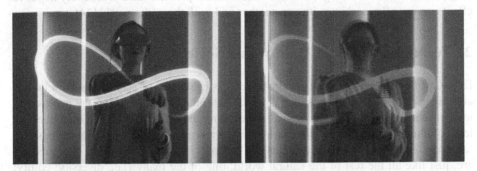

Fig. 3. Virtualization and immersion: depicting right-hand left hemisphere dominance.

1.1 Global Society and Nature: Interactions and Intra-actions

Still today, GS (*humankind*) is being surrounded by walls [9] (e.g., boundaries, borders), "*us and them*" are metaphorically hidden in the depth of a cave, chained by ignorance, bounded by bespoke ideological culture, preconceived ideas and beliefs, and blinded by *their* prejudices, whilst, at the same time GS feeble senses unveil only shadows cast upon a wall (projections) by a fire behind them [10]. We admire and belief in these fancy illusionary projections and interpret them as viable, true and realistic. However, projections are habitual and behavioural, new habits are therefore hard to develop. As such, we follow the projections, as in, the cognitive process that takes place both inside and outside the minds of people and by which humans attribute to others what is in their own minds [11]. GS requires enhanced connection of humans, species, entities, time, place, context and technology to provide coherent and trustworthy multisensory, multidimensional, multimodal, multidisciplinary interactions to create hyper-mediated- and hyper-realistic experiences to enhance knowledge, amplify communication, gain insight, cultivate relationships and foster understanding. For example, perceived benefits of *virtual nature* experiences point to feelings of 'calm,' 'relaxed' or 'refreshed' after immersion. Next to our natural experiences (e.g., walk in nature), the former points to intrinsic advantages of virtual-stimuli for restoration and reconnection with nature.

For instance, the prevalent human idea of nature is, for example, intensive farming that severely threatens human health, as well as the health of the living world. However, research knowledge tells us, the more land that can be spared for nature, without disturbance by farming or any other extractive industry, the fewer species are likely to become extinct. Farming[3] is actually the GS's greatest cause of habitat destruction, the greatest

---

[3] Regenerative farming is a holistic approach prioritizing regeneration of resources, improvement of the environment and biodiversity, and honest (no "greenwash") sustainable business practices.

cause of GS wildlife, and the greatest cause of the GS extinction crisis. In addition, it is responsible for around 80% of the deforestation in this century [13]. In fact, everything GS use, GS take from someone or some-*thing* else. Be it human and/or non-human. GS become more and more like 'the machines-systems-networks' (or more-than-human; *singularity*) that GS envisage, in ways which, in the present, have profoundly negative effects on our relationships with one another and with the wider world [14].

2 Technology, Science, Culture and Society

Exposing the current narrative within 'mechanistic science,' [2] where human beings are reduced to 'biological organisms,' whilst, simultaneously ignoring the psychological, emotional, symbolic, and ethical dimensions, instigate devastating effects at the level of human relationships and communities, subsequently turning human beings into 'atomized subjects.' There is no finality, no purpose, in this endless dance of atoms. GS are, just like all the rest of the natural world, one of the many (i.e., diversity; equity; variety) products (*things*) of this infinite dance. GS have successively become oppressed to an account of *things* dominated by the brain's left hemisphere, one that blinds us to a formidable 'real-world reality' that is all around us, had we but eyes to see (see Fig. 4). The essence of things is not rationally knowable, and reality cannot be reduced to mechanistic frameworks [2].

Fig. 4. 'Turning the Tables': Hemispherical conflict in perception (Taken from: Shepard, R. N.: Mind sights: Original visual illusions, ambiguities, and other anomalies, with a commentary on the play of mind in perception and art. WH Freeman/Times Books/Henry Holt & Co. (1990).).

The perception of Shepard's tabletop illustration shows us the 'inverse perspective illusion' of an orthographic perspective; although the oblique receding lines for the two sides are parallel, they appear to diverge into the distance, giving the impression that the tabletops are getting wider as they recede in depth. Things appear different to our minds than what we belief we see and how things actually are in reality. Moreover, three apparent paradoxes are present as well; paradoxical slant of the two tabletops, paradoxical lack of perceived depth and paradoxical distortion of the length of the rear legs [15]. People often cannot see-or even sense- what they do not know. This also helps in the realization and adaptation that it is 'normal' and human to be wrong or flawed. In fact, GS need to be more transparent about 'our' knowledge thereby showing others what "we" know and what "we" do not know. Uncertainty underpins "the wish to know" (predict) in order to be able to influence present and future. In the long run anti-fragility gains from prediction errors, complexity and asymmetry lead to explosive errors. Our current world is getting less and less predictable, have more-and-more nonlinearities-asymmetries which are increasingly error-prone [16].

2.1 Physical and Agential Realism: XRXs as eXtensions

At present (now), 'the real thing' to actually understand ourselves and GS around us, it would need both science and "gut-feelings"; thinking and feeling; intellect and intuition; objective analysis and subjective insight, not just one or two; that they are in any case far from being in conflict; and that the brain's right hemisphere (*the world is upside down*) plays the most important part in each [17, 18]. The left hemisphere in our thinking accrues as dominant factor in current decision- and prediction making, that actually bring disaster and perturbation in their wake (*brains make things up*). In fact, we know (as in *gut-feeling*), that we thrive on diversity, that we need more accountability and prosper through actuated responsibility. Wilson[4] observed that GS are '...simulation machines [that] become decision machines," combining inputs with objectives, knowledge, beliefs, relations, contexts, constraints, and whatnot, all in order to act (action-intent). Unlike "our" machines and models, GS [sometimes] mistake "our" immediate perceptions for the world-as-it-is...'.

What it comes down to is, that "post-/hypermodern" GS discriminate against the right hemisphere [19]. Actually, there are two parallel 'ways of knowing.' GS are in dire need to discover, explore and apply solutions to the aforementioned, increasingly difficult problems, issues and challenges.

In the final analysis, it is the logical consequence of *mechanistic ideology* (science) and the delusional belief in the omnipotence of human rationality, that stagnates progress and upholds transformative change [2]. In fact, people do not specifically like too much novelty. Most new things that are accepted, is a bringing together of received wisdom and some fresh combination of existing technologies (innovation). The theory of perception depends on the claim that *eidôla*[5] or images, thin layers of atoms shrink and expand; only those that shrink sufficiently can enter the eye. It is the impact of these on our sense organs that enables us to perceive. Basically, the immediate objects of the perception of our senses are merely particular states induced in the nerves [20].

2.2 360° Topsy-Turvy Society to Perceive Real World Reality

The possibility of XRTs to facilitate, generate and represent alternate realities through a topsy-turvy 360° experience for GS to instil, transform existing perceived realities and (re-) formulate novel perspectives and/or provide extensions for outlooks is our premise.

Consequently, XRTs possess the ability to create contrasting narratives, signal possible variations, bestow imaginative experiences, transformed by, for example, storytelling and visualization in order to open 'the myopic eyes' (translates to: willful- or inattentional

---

[4] Wilson, E. O.: Biophilia. Harvard university press (1986).

[5] Democritus' theory of perception depends on the claim that eidôla or images, thin layers of atoms, are constantly sloughed off from the surfaces of macroscopic bodies and carried through the air. See also: Berryman, S., Democritus (2004).

blindness) onto a vaster, diverse, varied, equitable and more inclusive world than GS had as yet been able to perceive or conceive it. Therefore, good tools, systems and technologies have the capability to empower and engage human beings. "Noise" is always already part of the signal; blindness (*blindspots*) inescapably accompanies vision. Noise is productive and creative: noise through its presence and absence, the intermittence of the signal, produces the new system. All that is not information, not redundancy, not form, not restraints-is noise, the only possible source of new patterns [21]. GS is hemmed in by stories ('noise') that prevent "us" from seeing, or believing in, or acting on the possibilities for change. Change is, however, constant. The physical world, as "us" knows, experience and sees it, is in a continual state of flux. A stream of ever-mutating, emergent patterns. "Noise" the event, constantly forces temporarily homeostatic systems of interaction/intra-action to reconstitute and reorganize themselves.

Barad [22] states there are not *things* that interact, but rather through and within intra-actions there is a differentiating-entangling, so that an agential cut is enacted that cuts things together-apart (one move) such that differences exist not as absolute separations but in their inseparability (i.e., agential separability). Important here is, that this view of knowledge provides a framework for thinking about how culture and habits of thought can make some *things* visible and other *things* easier to ignore or to never see.

3   Hybrid Mixed Reality: Humans, Non-humans, More-Than Humans

The idea of forming new relationships with non-human intelligences (i.e., other than artificial intelligences (AIs)) should be a central theme in conjunction with XRTs to represent and present XRXs that recognize various levels of complexity in four quadrants (see Fig. 5).

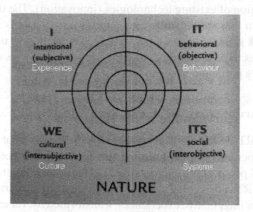

Fig. 5. Simplified levels of complexity in four quadrants.

GS needs to become more conscious and progressively aware of the increasingly evident, pervasive technology push and pressing 'unreal reality' of our utter entanglement with the more-than-human world. Next, reconcile GS technological prowess and restore the sense of GS uniqueness with an earthy (i.e., ecology, ecosystems, mycorrhizal networks, environments, ecology of technology) sensibility and an attentiveness to the interconnectedness of all things (some things are more connected than others) [23]. Additionally, in these mediated experiences more comprehensive patterns arise in all four quadrants- (a) experience (subjective), (b) behaviour (objective), (c) culture (inter-subjective), and (d) systems (interobjective). In essence GS must learn to live with the world surrounding "us," rather than to dominate from failed hubris centricity. The endless striving of "modern GS" for world domination, clearly shows "humanity" became an animal seeking power and security, the rational ego wanting to rise above nature[6] and its own bodily impulses (see Fig. 6) [24].

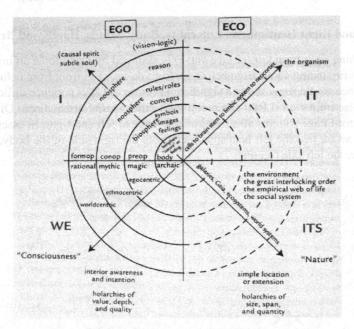

Fig. 6. The GS ego and Natural eco before the collapse.

3.1   Topsy-Turvy: The 360° Enhanced Networked World

Now, if there is no planet, no earth, no soil, no territory to house the GS of globalization toward which all these countries claim to be headed, then there is no longer an assured "*homeland*," as it were, for anyone [24]. The proposed upside-down 360° XR visualization and representation is envisioned as an enabler for humanity to deliver

---

[6] We can distinguish three definitions of "nature," for purpose of clarity, '*nature*' as in the whole cosmos (*intergalactic universe*) in all its dimensions (interior and exterior), '*nature*' as studied by natural- and social sciences and '*nature*' as the empirical-sensory world (outer- and inner worlds) [20].

eye-mind-body opening experiences on a range of themes—algorithmic, socio-political, economic, environment, ecological and cultural—to explore the impact, consequences, thereby changing their conceptual world, shifting consciousness, increase awareness, entice receptiveness, while navigating between their two-brain hemisphere modes.

Do GS continue to nourish *'dreams of escaping,'* or do GS start seeking a territory that GS and the children (*future generations*) can inhabit? [24] As stated, situations change, but stories have not, GS follows old versions, explore outdated maps, patterns and stagnant beliefs (i.e., migratory crisis, land grabbing, deforestation, heat bulbs, erosion, resource depletion, pollution, habitat destruction). Furthermore, *"our"* psyche are not just temporary feelings, but distinct ways of being, which come with their own "sets of beliefs, agendas, and roles in the overall ecology of GS lives [25].

3.2 Left and Right Hemisphere: Laterality, Body, Minds, Hands and Brains

Distinguishing right from left (or vice versa) is assumed by many to be an innate skill, such as discriminating above from below, up from down, or in front from behind. However, evidence would suggest that a significant portion of GS experience difficulty with left-right discrimination (LRD) compared with other spatial orientations. Discrimination of mirror-image patterns also requires reference to left and right. In essence, most people are aware that the left hemisphere controls the right side of the body, the right hemisphere, the left side (see Fig. 7).

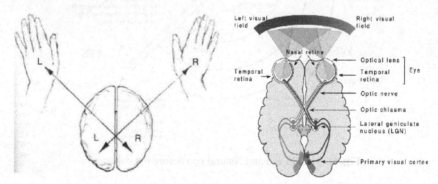

Fig. 7. Left and right hemisphere crossover connections.

People tend to find it easier to judge, if an image shows a left or right hand, by imagining their own hand or body rotating. Besides, the idea of mentally rotating an object adds an extra degree of complexity. The 360° capability of XRTs could be useful in assisting the laterality, the interplay between symmetry and asymmetry (bilateral symmetry adaptation). Handedness, footedness, or eyedness is in any case a poor proxy for cerebral asymmetry; it is only weakly related to cerebral asymmetry for language and not related at all to asymmetry for spatial attention [26]. Research suggests that the more asymmetrical someone's body is (in terms of writing hand preference, for example) the easier they find it to tell left and right apart. If one side of your brain is slightly larger than the other, you tend to have a better right-left discrimination [27]. The limbs are innately programmed to operate in mirrored fashion. Walking (e.g., nature walk, biophilia[7]) running, swimming and flying all involve mirrored movements, whether in succession or simultaneously. Even skills learned with one hand may be reversed with the other, providing further evidence for interhemispheric mirror-image reversal. Up to 90% of human communication occurs in the non-verbal, right-hemisphere part of the brain, which also processes spatial relations [25]. Our physical environment directly affects our physical sensations and begins to shape our nervous system and our model of the world. Much research revealed the many cognitive (e.g., associationistic and divergent thought), personality (e.g., an open orientation, perseverance, risk-taking), developmental (e.g., education, early trauma), economic (e.g., high-status parental background), political (e.g., political turbulence, war), and social factors (e.g., mentor availability, collaborators) that characterize the creative genius across culture, time, and geography [27].

3.3 Two Ways of Parallel Knowing and Duality in Hemispherical Changes

Worldwide there seems to exist numerous words, phrases and language that implies that people have a sense that there is a difference between left hemisphere and right handedness (dexter) and right hemisphere and left handedness (sinister). These language semiotic's, that explain the crossover connections, seems to speak more of hands, handedness, than of brain-halves and control of hands issues [28, 29]. The importance of bi-manual tangible and tactile inter- and intra-actions relies on inbred (innate) skill sets and experiential dexterity of humans. For example, hands-on experiences (multi-sensorial) adaptive environments with a plethora in tools, applications, modalities and testbeds engrained with narratives and story-telling capabilities enhance and engage the users/end-users to be or become aware of their surroundings/actions.

Merges (blended realities) with the intuitive, spontaneous and imaginative qualities of analogue craftsmanship and inseparably aligned with current technological digital-virtual advances, tools and means (e.g., AI) provided by cyber-technology systems and/or networks will foster and hone these skills, experiences and abilities [16]. Words, phrases, signs and symbols that refer to left and right hands indicate not just bodily location, but deep differences in fundamental traits and/or qualities as well [28]. Openness to experience is considered a trait, next to mental ability that leads certain individuals to see the world with a 'fresh' perspective. Main divisions are between thinking and feeling, intellect and intuition, and objective analysis and subjective insight (*gut-feeling*).

Research [30] identifies two systems of the mind in people, expressed as System 1 and System 2. Computational assistive systems (e.g., HDTs) could be programmed and working in concurrence, for example, as System 1-fuzzy mode (FM) [right hand-left hemisphere] and System 2-logic mode (LM) [left hand-right hemisphere] [31]. System 1 operates automatically and quickly, with little or no effort and no sense of voluntary control. System 2 allocates attention to the effortful mental activities that demand it, inclusive of complex computations. The automatic operations of the FM could generate surprisingly complex patterns of ideas (iteratively), but only the slower LM could construct thought in orderly series of iterative steps and/or sequences (see Fig. 8) [32].

---

[7] A strong attraction for or emotional attachment to the living world.

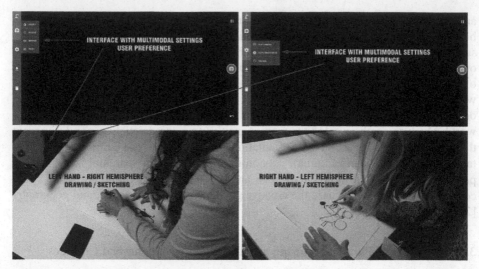

Fig. 8. Concurrent handedness and cross-sectional iterative ideation processes with HDTs.

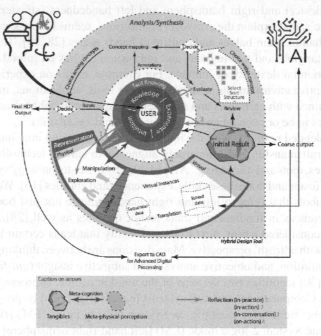

Fig. 9. Flow diagram of the design process with an XRT (i.e., cyber-physical HDT system) including assisted reflective AI. The blue arrow represents the meta-cognitive interaction between tangibles and the meta-physical perception of the user. The green arrows represent different types of reflection that can occur during the iterative ideation process. (Color figure online)

Working bi-manually and cross-sectional (shifting from left-to-right hemispheres) in conjunction with the 'machine' could lead to increased and enhanced awareness, creativity and foster insight thereby increasing subconscious and consciousness knowledge and understanding [28, 30] (see Fig. 9). XRTs are shaping the reality around the user to integrate motion in real-time, adapt the content, and apply information (data) such as route, pathway, process and duration, while transition and transforming everything. The left hemisphere - right hand dominance (i.e., verbalizes, analyzes, abstracts, counts, etc.) rationalizes and includes past experiences to approach 'new' problems. A second way of knowing, lies in the right hemisphere-left hand modality (i.e., metaphorical, images, spatial, etc.) the visual-reality seeing mode: coined as 'mind's eye,' when something is too complex to describe in words, whereby gestures, symbols or signs are used to communicate meaning (see Fig. 10).

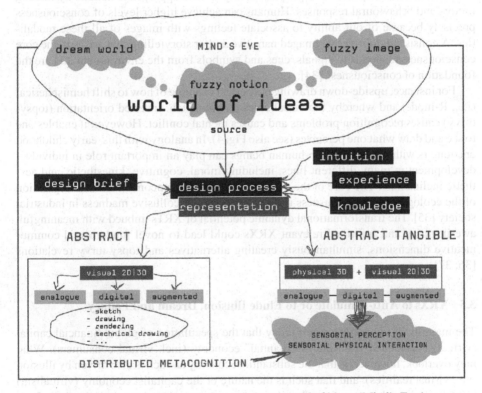

Fig. 10. Framework inner-, outer- and shared world of ideas: 'Mind's Eye.'

Knowledge is based on reciprocally compared and corroborated representations of the world, that we perceive somewhere outside ourselves, but that is duplicated inside us in words and images. In fact, human ex-centricity inevitably leads to a division into inner-, outer- and shared world.

Followed by three primary laws of the ex-centric life-form: mediated immediacy, artificiality by nature, and the utopian standpoint. Boundaries between inner- and outer are not fixed and depend on the negotiations between people and their mediatory instances. As such, XRTs could have impact, affect-change and influence on the self and will undergo drastic changes in the quotidian physical reality and mediated realities based on XRXs [16].

3.4 XRTs for Enhanced Cognition, Creativity, Emotion and Sudden Intuition

The human experience of the physical world through the eight senses is inherently multi-modal. XRTs (e.g., hybrid design tools (HDTs)) could provide accurate simulated experiences (XRXs) in the entire multisensorial spectrum; visual, acoustic, tactile, olfactory, and gustatory realms including the engagement of vestibular, interoceptive and proprioceptive systems [33]. There exists a critical connection between the multi-sensorial of inner- and outer-spheres and people's ability to take appropriate actions by making motor- and behavioural responses. Humans can achieve higher levels of consciousness precisely because of our ability to associate feelings with images of all these modalities. A consistent, non-verbal imaged narrative and/or storytelling that arises in the core consciousness responds to signals, cues and symbols from the environment and are the foundation of consciousness [34].

For instance, upside-down drawing is a perfect example of how to shift hemispherical (i.e., R-mode) and whereby the visual clues do not match. Inverted orientation (topsy-turvy) causes recognition problems and causes mental conflict. However, it enables one to see and draw what one perceives (see also Fig. 4). In analogy with this, early childhood encounters with nature and non-human beings can play an important role in individual development in many different lines, including moral, cognitive, kinesthetic, and aesthetic inclinations. The core of the mind is the ecological unconsciousness. Repression of the ecological unconsciousness is the deepest root of collusive madness in industrial society [35]. The transformational dynamic potential of XRTs imbued with meaningful, awe-inspiring and informed relevant XRXs could lead to novel fundamental communicative dimensions, simultaneously creating alternatives and topsy-turvy revelations [36, 37].

3.5 XRXs to Anti-stimulate or to Elude Illusion, Dream and Fallacy

The majority of economists warn today that the speculation of global financial capital (virtual) is detached from the "substantial" economy (incl. virtual consumers). What they overlook, however, is that the substantial economy as such is also driven by illusion (i.e., virtual realities), and that such is the nature of the capitalist economy (virtualism) [38, 39]. Hence, the reasoning of mainstream economics that abstracts its analysis from its social context and constructs a virtual reality of so-called rational individuals and the belief that economic analysis can exist as some kind of disembodied study [38]. In terms of the dream, it is fundamentally nothing more than a special form of our thinking, which is made possible by the conditions of the sleeping state. It is the dream-work which produces this form, and it alone is the essence of dreaming-the explanation of its singularity [40].

The question arises, 'why is GS so hopelessly seduced by the mechanistic ideology?' Is it perhaps, because of a naïve belief (*fallacy*) that a flawless, humanoid being and an utopian society can be produced by scientific knowledge? [2, 41].

3.6 Conferring Non-human Intelligence on XRTs and Assist XRXs

The current XRTs and 'content greedy' XRXs could substantially be improved and ameliorated in experiences and effectiveness by inclusion of AI. Metamorphic AI as a set of technological approaches that depend on, for example, animal-machine communications, industrial infrastructures, supply chains, social-democratic (habeas corpus) cohesion, human labour (physical-mental work), political agency for human, non-human and more-than-human entities as intertwined ecologies and entangled networks.

Next to the high-end virtual visualizations, dynamic representations and advanced interactivity, AI could possibly help to effectively (unbiased) communicate, intra- and interact with users (see also Fig. 9). Of course, there seems to be a persistent difference between "natural" and "synthetic/artificial" things or products. Whenever GS produce or dream-up an artificially reproduce of a natural phenomenon from a rational analysis and reasoning, GS realizes that the reproduction (the artificial) is not identical to the original [2]. Complex ubiquitous cyber-physical systems (CPS) (i.e., Internet-of-Things (IoT)) integrates various devices and/or tools equipped with sensing, identification, processing, communication, and networking capabilities.

GS can clearly witness this in the heavily mediated and increasing digitalization of human interactions in recent times. Face-to-face and "natural" human interactions are being replaced by digital-virtual ones, a transition and rethink to curb, to question and re-harmonize this cyber-digital process is actually needed. The increasing effect and affect on GS subsequently lead to, for example, digital depression, solitude, post-traumatic stress disorder (PTSD), cognitive inhibition and anxiety. Digitalization dehumanizes conversation, embodiment and 'natural' communication on multiple emotive-sensorial-cognitive-psychological-empathic-physiological levels.

Our relationships human, non-human, the nature of our minds (mind and bodies) is fundamentally physical-embodied-mentally contracted and extended, connected and stochastically communicating with the life of animals, plants, natural systems, planet earth and space (animated reality).

Human conversation actually is full of ambiguities, irrationality, misunderstandings, bias and doubts. Ethical and trustworthy AI could provide a solution to support and assist users in their digital relationships (e.g., connections between knowledge and action), user intentions in communications and better (ameliorate) decision-making and analysis (informed) based on 'true' observations. AI could be considered and configured as a tool to support and/or assist as reflective AI, intentional AI, context-aware AI, affective AI or domain-adaptive AI. New arrangements and configurations of human-machine symbiosis carry undoubtedly substantial promise to the benefit of GS. Symbiosis is the notion of the tacit dimension (human skills and ingenuity) and the objective (computational capacity of the machine) working playfully together (interplay).

4 Discussion

We can work to change our culture(s). Technological processes and progressions (e.g., AI, XR, autonomous vehicles) will not build a better world by themselves, it tells us nothing useful about our own general human intelligence. What these *things* can do is, to lay bare the real workings of the moral, ethical, and more-than-human landscape we find and immersed ourselves in, consequently inspire and direct us to create better worlds together [14]. As humans we could benefit from the extension of political-, legal-, handing ecological rights and autonomy to non-humans, just as human society benefit from all our encounters with the more-than-human world. Integral ecology…increase randomness and diversity…basically, for true randomness we must leave the domain of abstract computation, human-created anthropocentric laws and programs and re-engage with the world-around-us. Randomness increases intra-actions. The more-than-human world, AI for that matter, reveals that GS is meekly indebted to non-human-minds (e.g., plants, animals, bugs); the entangled complexity of fungal networks is reproduced as "our" internet; gene sequencing expose and resemble the origins of "our" biology; trail the random trends or intuitively follow non-perceptible variable patterns, provide the best pathway(s) through unknowable complexity towards meaningful understanding [14]. Whitehead[8] stated: 'The continuity of nature arises from extensions. Every event extends over other events, and every event is extended over by other events.' If the former seems plausible, are we then able to recreate associations of 'our' minds with nature, through natural observations (e.g., and XRXs in perception) through our senses and understand our place in nature anew?

5 Conclusion

What is our place in nature? All things small and all things large are connected, everything is part of an overarching, complex, and dynamic system. We have to reflect and contemplate GS and observe the principles of nature. We will never know or understand what our place is or necessarily be determined in a pure rational way. The control of reality is not an end goal in itself, the essence lies in the final acceptance that there are limits to human rationality, that knowledge (e.g., intelligence) is not owned by GS alone, it is situated in wider contexts and connectivity to other elements of which GS forms a part. The fragility of future making all of GS is engaged in, goes far beyond the idea that GS, individually or collectively, are to be held responsible and/or accountable for the future consequences of their actions. GS rely on huge machinery for predicting, managing, accessing, exploiting, and assuring against everything that stands between "our" plans, "our" anticipation and imaginaries of the future, and what actually happens [24, 42]. The hiatus in between them is risk, uncertainty and volatility, which are central categories in "hyper-modern" GS. Nature from GS became blurred. The current crisis shows "us" clearly, that GS cannot any longer *ignore* the tragic negligence of the damage to the natural environment. GS now needs to be aware or become aware that Nature needs protection from GS. XRTs could provide a spectacular echo and awe-inducing XRXs to become attached and engaged again to the non-human and natural-systems-world.

---

[8] Whitehead, A. N.: *The concept of nature.* Courier Corporation (1919/2013).

References

1. Slovic, P.: Perception of risk. Science **236**(4799), 280–285 (1987)
2. Desmet, M.: The Psychology of Totalitarianism. Chelsea Green Publishing (2022)
3. Metzinger, T.: Spirituality and Intellectual Honesty (2013)
4. Marshall, G.: Don't Even Think About It: Why Our Brains are Wired to Ignore Climate Change. Bloomsbury Publishing USA (2015)
5. ABCNews, The Elephant We're All Inside. http://abcnews.go.com/blogs/technology/2012/09/the-elephant-were-all-inside/. Accessed 23 Jan 2023
6. Pörtner, H.O., et al.: Climate change 2022: impacts, adaptation and vulnerability. In: IPCC Sixth Assessment Report, pp. 37–118 (2022)
7. Stein, Z.: Education is the Metacrisis: Why it's Time to see Planetary Crises as a Species-Wide Learning Opportunity (2019). Perspectiva, https://systems-souls-society.com/education-is-the-metacrisis/. Accessed 23 Jan 2023
8. Calvo, P., Lawrence, N.: Planta Sapiens: Unmasking Plant Intelligence. Hachette UK (2022)
9. Linebarger, C., Braithwaite, A.: Why do leaders build walls? Domestic politics, leader survival, and the fortification of borders. J. Conflict Resolut. **66**(4–5), 704–728 (2022)
10. Rovelli, C.: Reality is Not What It Seems: The Journey to Quantum Gravity. Penguin (2018)
11. Hutchins, E.: Cognition in the Wild. MIT Press (1995)
12. Wendrich, R.E.: Multiple modalities, sensoriums, experiences in blended spaces with toolness and tools for conceptual design engineering. In: International Design Engineering Technical Conferences and Computers and Information in Engineering Conference, vol. 51739, p. V01BT02A046. American Society of Mechanical Engineers (2018)
13. Monbiot, G.: Regenesis: Feeding the World Without Devouring the Planet. Penguin UK (2022)
14. Bridle, J.: Ways of Being: Beyond Human Intelligence. Penguin UK (2022)
15. Tyler, C.W.: Paradoxical perception of surfaces in the Shepard tabletop illusion. i-Perception **2**(2), 137–141 (2011)
16. Wendrich, R.E.: Anti-fragility in design engineering procedures embedded in hybrid multiple realms and blended environments: the physical real of reality. In: Manufacturing in the Era of 4th Industrial Revolution A World Scientific Reference: Volume 3: Augmented, Virtual and Mixed Reality Applications in Advanced Manufacturing, pp. 239–270). World Scientific (2021)
17. Sachse, P., Beermann, U., Martini, M., Maran, T., Domeier, M., Furtner, M.R.: "The world is upside down"–the Innsbruck goggle experiments of Theodor Erismann (1883–1961) and Ivo Kohler (1915–1985) (2017)
18. McGilchrist, I.: The matter with things: our brains, our delusions, and the unmaking of the world (2021)
19. Sperry, R.W.: Lateral Specialization of Cerebral Function in the Surgically Separated Hemispheres (1974)
20. Mather, G.: Foundations of Sensation and Perception. Psychology Press (2016)
21. Serres, M.: The Parasite, vol. 1. U of Minnesota Press (2013)
22. Barad, K.: Meeting the Universe Halfway: Quantum Physics and the Entanglement of Matter and Meaning. Duke University Press (2007)
23. Esbjorn-Hargens, S., Zimmerman, M.E.: Integral Ecology: Uniting Multiple Perspectives on the Natural World. Shambhala Publications (2011)
24. Latour, B.: Down to Earth: Politics in the New Climatic Regime. Wiley (2018)
25. Van der Kolk, B.: The body keeps the score: brain, mind, and body in the healing of trauma, New York (2014)
26. Badzakova-Trajkov, G., Häberling, I.S., Roberts, R.P., Corballis, M.C.: Cerebral asymmetries: complementary and independent processes. PLoS ONE **5**(3), e9682 (2010)

27. Parsons, L.M.: Imagined spatial transformation of one's body. J. Exp. Psychol. Gen. **116**(2), 172–191 (1987). https://doi.org/10.1037/0096-3445.116.2.172
28. Edwards, B.: Drawing on the Artist Within. Simon and Schuster (2008)
29. Edwards, B.: Drawing on the right side of the brain. In: CHI 1997 Extended Abstracts on Human Factors in Computing Systems, pp. 188–189 (1997)
30. Kahneman, D.: Thinking, Fast and Slow. Macmillan (2011)
31. Wendrich, R.E.: Hybrid design tools for design and engineering processing. Adv. Comput. Inf. Eng. Res. 215–238 (2014)
32. Wendrich, R.E.: Blended spaces: collaborative work and computer supported learning and tools. In: International Design Engineering Technical Conferences and Computers and Information in Engineering Conference, vol. 51739, p. V01BT02A027. American Society of Mechanical Engineers, August 2018
33. Wendrich, R.E., et al.: Hybrid design tools in a social virtual reality using networked oculus rift: a feasibility study in remote real-time interaction. In: International Design Engineering Technical Conferences and Computers and Information in Engineering Conference, vol. 50084, p. V01BT02A042. American Society of Mechanical Engineers, August 2016
34. Damasio, A. R.: The Feeling of What Happens: Body and Emotion in the Making of Consciousness. Houghton Mifflin Harcourt (1999)
35. Roszak, T.: Awakening the ecological unconscious. Exploring Our Interconnectedness **34**(48), 108–115 (1993)
36. Wendrich, R.E.: Design tools, hybridization exploring intuitive interaction. In: Proceedings of the 16th Eurographics Conference on Virtual Environments & Second Joint Virtual Reality (EGVE - JVRC 2010). Eurographics Association, Goslar, DEU, pp. 37–41 (2010)
37. Wendrich, R.E.: On how to add SALT: 'PLAYGORA'—a real-world case study and experimentation (Out of the Lab). In: Chakrabarti, A., Poovaiah, R., Bokil, P., Kant, V. (eds.) Design for Tomorrow—Volume 3. SIST, vol. 223, pp. 761–773. Springer, Singapore (2021). https://doi.org/10.1007/978-981-16-0084-5_62
38. Zizek, S.: The Parallax View. MIT Press (2009)
39. Carrier, J.G., Miller, D. (eds.): Virtualism: a New Political Economy. Routledge (2020)
40. Freud, S., Strachey, J.: The Interpretation of Dreams, vol. 4, p. 5. Allen & Unwin (1900–1977)
41. Voegelin, E.: The origins of scientism. Soc. Res. 462–494 (1948). Cited in Arendt, The Origins of Totalitarianism: 453 (1973)
42. Nowotny, H.: The Cunning of Uncertainty. Wiley (2015)

Participation Through Innovation – Mixed Reality in Vocational Rehabilitation Training to Prepare for the Labour Market 4.0 (Project EdAL MR 4.0)

Laura Wuttke(✉) ⓘ, Christian Bühler ⓘ, Linda Dziarstek ⓘ, and Yvonne Söffgen ⓘ

Department of Rehabilitation Sciences, Research Unit of Rehabilitation Technology, TU Dortmund University, Emil-Figge-Str. 50, 44227 Dortmund, Germany
laura.wuttke@tu-dortmund.de

Abstract. This paper deals with mixed reality in vocational training settings. The main focus of this paper is a state-of-the-art analysis conducted in April 2022. Trainers from three vocational sites in Germany were questioned and interviewed on the state of digitization in their facilities as well as expectations and worries concerning the work with mixed reality (MR). The results give valuable insights on current digital learning standards in vocational training and help to formulate recommendations. This will be used for MR development in the project EdAL MR 4.0. But gives also hints beyond the project. Three training programs with a certain distance from digital skills have been examined: hairdressing, warehouse/logistics and kitchen specialist. Through learning offers that run via mixed reality glasses, people are directly supported at work and can do interactive exercises that are intended to prepare them for entering the labour market and increase their ability to work on the first labour market.

Keywords: Mixed Reality · Vocational Training · Digital Media

1 Mixed Reality in Vocational Education

The digitalization of work is becoming increasingly present and dominates the development of work and work structures under the name "Industry 4.0" [1]. While this offers many possibilities it can also challenge workers, especially workers with disabilities. Implementing digital products as early as in vocational training can help to build digital competencies and thus offers opportunities of participation in working life. An important requirement for this is individual adaption to the needs and resources of the people as well as targeting digital learning to the work process [2]. Mixed reality technologies (MR) offer novel options for visualisation and acoustic instruction, such as interactive 3D-holograms for teaching theoretical learning content [3]. The project EdAL MR 4.0 researches, develops and tests MR technologies in three vocational training facilities that offer various trainings in Germany. Three different occupational fields, warehouse/logistics specialist, kitchen specialist, and hairdresser, are identified as suitable and challenging for the implementation of MR solutions in these facilities. These occupational fields represent a wide range of activities and also have been little digitized to date. Furthermore, an association for rolling out the project activities as well as scientific, economic and IT partners are supporting the project. The project aims to offer attractive learning opportunities tailored to the needs and pace of people with disabilities during their rehabilitation training, helping them transition into the general labour market. By focusing not only on the visual possibilities of MR but also acoustic instructions, learning processes can be prepared for different needs and minimise barriers. MR offers a playful engagement with learning content and the possibility to learn practically yet risk free. Furthermore, the working environment is to be integrated holistically, so that stimuli from the real environment (such as smells, sounds or taste) are taken into account in addition to the digital information. This way, a transfer between digitally supported learning and everyday work can be ensured.

2   State-of-the-Art Analysis

In a first step a state-of-the-art analysis of the three occupational fields is carried out. The goal is to determine which digital potentials already exist in the fields, which future potentials can be unlocked and an evaluation of the technical infrastructure.

In total nine trainers (N = 9) from three facilities participate in the analysis. The selection of the vocational training fields is based on a declaration of intent to participate in the project.

Trainers of each training facility and field are questioned by an online group discussion, which is preceded by an initial survey via the online tool "Mentimeter". Mentimeter is an online survey application that can be used to obtain responses in real time [4]. The answers given by the trainers are then discussed and therefore form the basis for the group discussion.

The online survey consists of closed questions (items) that can be answered on a Likert-scale with 6 choices. In addition the trainers are asked open questions that are answered in the form of keywords. To cover all areas of interest, questions are developed on the following topics (Table 1).

After answering the questions in the online tool, the interviewers show the results to the participants and discuss the results for every question asking for details and explanations concerning the chosen answers. The discussions are recorded and transcribed. Using transcriptions from the interviews a Qualitative Content Analysis according to Mayring is performed [5]. The categorisation is carried out inductively.

Table 1. Questions and answer options in the state-of-the-art-analysis.

Questions	Response Options
1. Assessment of the state of digitization	Likert-scale
2. Evaluation of the digital equipment	Likert-scale
3. Assessment of the technical infrastructure	Likert-scale
4. Necessity for digitization	Likert-scale
5. Positive expectations concerning digitization	Open
6. Where to use digital media	Open
7. Concerns about digitization	Open
8. Where digital media can't be used	Open
9. Previous use of analog and digital teaching/learning offerings	Open
10. Experience in creating own digital teaching/learning content	Yes or No
11. Assessment of own digital competencies	Likert-scale
12. Assessment of the learners digital competencies	Likert-scale

3   Results

3.1   Results of the Questionnaire

The first three questions concern the state of digitization, the availability of digital devices as well as the technical infrastructure. The categories of the Likert-scale are called after ratings in the German grading system (*very good, good, satisfactory, sufficient, poor* and *insufficient*).

The results of the Mentimeter questionnaire show that the status of digitization is perceived heterogeneous by the trainers. The majority choses category 3 *satisfactory* (4) to describe their institution. However, the option *very good* and *good* is not chosen at all for this question, whereas three participants see the digitization in their institution as *poor* (category 4). One participant even choses the worst category *insufficient* (compare Fig. 1).

When asked to evaluate the digital equipment provided at their institution the results are equally heterogeneous ranging from *good* to *insufficient* with no one choosing very good. The most selected category is *poor* with three votes.

Also, the participants are asked about the technical infrastructure primarily concerning the availability of WLAN in their institution. The results show, that the trainers evaluate the infrastructure very negatively as the two worst categories are chosen most with three votes each and the two best categories receive no votes.

After the low ratings in the perceived digitization in the facilities the partners were asked about the necessity for digitization. Figure 2 shows that the necessity of digitization is given importance by the trainers.

Four of the questioned trainees assess digitization as *very important*, three *as important* and two as *rather important* whereas lower categories are not chosen at all.

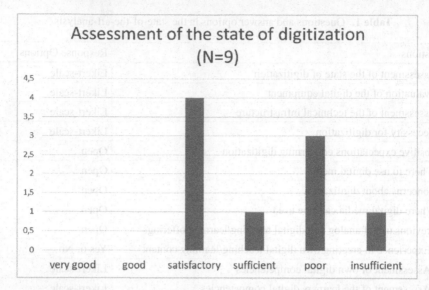

Fig. 1. Assessment of the state of digitization by the partners.

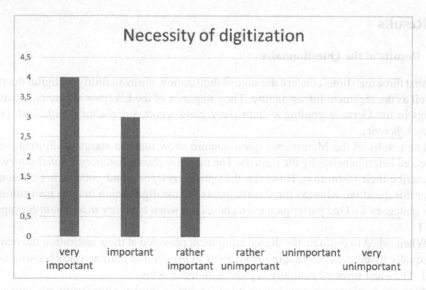

Fig. 2. Necessity of digitization as seen by the partners.

Concerning the experience in creating own digital learning content five participants state that they have no experience. In their assessment of their own digital skills, only two rate themselves as *good*, five as *satisfactory* and two as *sufficient*. A similar picture emerges in the assessments that the trainers make of their trainees' digital skills. Here, too, the categories chosen are mainly *satisfactory* and *sufficient*. Therefore, one can say that the digital skills of the trainers as well as the trainees are heterogeneous but there is still room for improvement in both target groups.

The respondents mainly have positive expectations of digitization, like greater independence, flexibility, motivation, new teaching methods and better learning opportunities. Only few reservations are expressed such as the fear of being overwhelmed or that a large effort is not matched by enough practical benefit. In addition, the respondents express various expectations and wishes regarding the use of digital media, such as faster learning, visualization, additional repetition, support, monitoring of learning progress, differentiation and individualization. The findings from the open questions are discussed in more detail in the following.

3.2 Results of the Interviews

For more qualitative information an inductive qualitative content analysis according to Mayring [5] is performed. Five different main thematic categories can be extracted from the interviews: *Digitization, Expectations, Media, Competencies* and *Implementation*.

As seen in the results of the questionnaire the partners assess the state of digitization in their institution mainly from *satisfactory* to *insufficient*, but never *good* or *very good*. From the interviews one can see the reasons for these answers.

The subcategory *insufficient digitization* (D1) is voiced by all three project partners, six times in total throughout all interviews. For example a hairdressing trainer states:

"Digitization has simply not yet arrived in the hairdressing craft, I would say. It's a handicraft, and that's why many people don't have the creativity to think about it, or to imagine that it might be something that could be supportive in training." (Quote from a trainer, 2022)

A quote from another participant sums up the insufficient technical infrastructure in the vocational training facilities:

"We have neither comprehensive WLAN, nor are our participants equipped with the appropriate technology, especially in the training area." (Quote from a trainer, 2022)

The subcategory *missing devices* (D2) is voiced by all three partners. This mainly refers to devices for the trainees, while the trainers are usually provided with equipment (subcategory D3). However trainers of two facilities state that the digital infrastructure as well as the availability of digital devices are planned to be expanded in the future (Fig. 3).

The expectations of the partners concerning the use of MR and digital media are gathered using a question with open answers. The content analysis shows that the partners have very different expectations. For example trainers from the facility offering training for hairdressers voice expectations concerning sustainability and more precise working that the other partners don't mention at all. This example suggests that, when asked about their expectations, trainers think strongly in terms of the training program they offer. In the hairdressing program puppet heads are used for haircut training which is necessary but produces much waste, so a digital alternative would be much more sustainable.

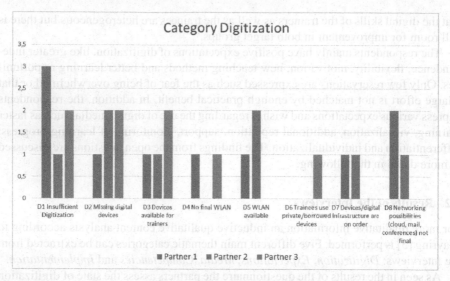

Fig. 3. Category Digitization.

The subcategory with the most mentions (five) from at least two of the partners is E7 *Additional support/repetition* (Fig. 4).

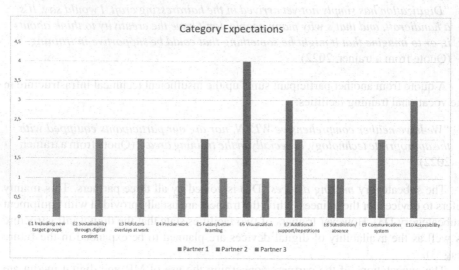

Fig. 4. Category Expectations.

Like the expectations also the digital competencies of the participants vary. For example, not all respondents have experience in creating their own digital learning content. In the interviews trainers from all partners express that they have *No experience in content creation* (subcategory K5) and express the *Need for support* (subcategory K6). All partners use existing learning (YouTube) videos. YouTube videos in particular, however, are often described as too general and unsuitable because they do not reflect company-specific conditions. In addition, the language level in the videos is described as too difficult for the trainees.

3.3 Consequences and Recommendations

Based on the results of the state-of-the-art analysis, key action and transition points are identified. In addition to the technical equipment and the handling of the technology, these relate to the design of the learning offering and the development of digital skills among trainers and trainees.

With regard to digitization and the handling of technical equipment, it has become clear that the facilities have to catch up to meet the standards necessary for the project. This must be ensured before further steps can be taken. Therefor it is considered relevant that clear contact persons and responsibilities are defined at an early stage. Furthermore WLAN must be made available in the work and training areas so future project goals can be achieved.

Also the analysis shows that when working with partners with diverse approaches also different project expectations arise. Therefor it is necessary to find a general consensus on how the digital learning offerings will be integrated in the vocational training and what form they will have (e.g.: 3D holograms, short videos, playful elements, etc.).

The insights gained in the course of the state-of-the-art analysis will also be taken into account in the conception of media competence-promoting offers. Since the professionals do not yet have extensive experience in teaching and developing digital learning offerings, especially with regard to MR content, training on these topics will be necessary. However, it must be clarified that the trainers cannot create their own MR content, as this requires programming skills that only IT staff can provide. The training courses therefore aim rather to provide competencies in teaching with MR and to support the creation of accompanying digital materials (learning videos, online courses, etc.).

This can be done with in-house-trainings, with the benefit of mutual support and resolving problems on site, as well as making learning content digitally available on a learning platform. A precise survey of the media competence of the participants can provide clarity about what content these courses should offer.

On the other hand it can be assumed that the trainees also do not yet have enough experience in digital learning, especially with MR technologies. That is why an introduction to the hardware as well as the mixed reality learning environment is crucial. The trainees should be involved in the project from the beginning, testing and evaluating the app at multiple stages of the project.

4 Development of Learning Scenarios and Prototyping EDAL MR 4.0

Considering the different expectations of the project partners discovered through the state-of-the-art analysis it is important to first find a general consensus on how the mixed reality learning app should look like and what options are possible regarding the form of the learning content. Therefore, in addition to the three specific learning scenarios (one per partner) that will be developed in the project, it is decided that a fourth overarching scenario is generated first. For this scenario the topic "Work safety" is chosen, because different safety instructions occur in all three occupational fields and are therefore part of the vocational training. This first overarching learning scenario can be seen as a prototype that can be evaluated and monitored by trainers and trainees from all institutions before working on individual content.

As a first form of mixed reality content, a challenge is implemented for the HoloLens in form of an interactive quiz on safety signs. Therefore, safety signs of different categories are distributed in the room and can be collected following a specific instruction (e.g.: "Collect all fire safety signs."). This way the real environment is integrated into the game. The workplace becomes the place of learning [6]. There are different levels of difficulty, which require more general or more specific knowledge. Figure 5 shows a prototypical visualization of the challenge as seen through the HoloLens.

Fig. 5. Visualization of the MR learning scenario "Safety signs".

To create a learning scenario, an overall structure of the MR application is defined. Each learning scenario is split into three forms of learning content: information, challenge and 3D hologram. The category information offers pure contextual information on the chosen topic, which can be retrieved via a 2D display panel shown in MR. The challenge offers gamified elements similar to the quiz on safety signs shown in Fig. 5. The hologram shows 3D objects relevant to the learning scenario (e.g.: equipment, theoretical models, etc.) that allow interaction.

Alongside the development of the first learning scenario a catalogue of criteria is developed as an instrument for selecting the partners' concrete learning scenarios. The catalogue helps to identify which content is suitable for presentation in MR and what exactly should be shown digitally, opposed to what input comes from the real environment. The selection of scenarios happens during on-site meetings at the partners and in close exchange with the trainers to help identify learning scenarios tailored to the facilities' trainings.

5 Future Work/Conclusions

Future project milestones include methodological approaches for building a trans-modal technical infrastructure, the design of the hybrid learning arrangements and development of concrete learning content for each partnering occupational field. These will be evaluated, tested and adapted with the involvement of trainers and learners alike.

To accomplish the primary goal of EdAL MR 4.0, the improvement of participation in an increasingly digitized labour market for people with disabilities, it is important to make full use of what mixed reality has to offer and integrating it purposefully in vocational tasks. Therefor the technology development will be performed in the sense of a user-centred design to make the offer accessible for a heterogeneous group of learners.

All relevant stakeholders will participate in the research and development process of mixed reality arrangements. This way, aspects of usability and acceptance are taken into account as well as finding learning scenarios tailored to the partner's needs.

To ensure that the mixed reality learning arrangements can also be used competently in the future, the training of the digital competences of the vocational trainers is a further goal, which is to be achieved through a survey of media competence as well as training courses on teaching with mixed reality technologies.

Acknowledgements. EdAL MR 4.0 is funded by the "Ausgleichsfonds für überregionale Vorhaben zur Teilhabe schwerbehinderter Menschen am Arbeitsleben" ("Compensation Fund for Supra-regional Projects for the Participation of Severely Disabled People in Working Life") of the German Federal Ministry of Labour and Social Affairs (BMAS).

References

1. Dehnbostel, P., Richter, G., Schröder, T., Tisch, A.: Kompetenzentwicklung in der digitalen Arbeitswelt, 1st edn. Schäffer-Poeschel Verlag, Stuttgart (2021)
2. Materna, D., Söffgen, Y., Wuttke, L.: Einsatz digitaler Medien für Menschen mit Lernschwierigkeiten in hauswirtschaftlichen Ausbildungsberufen. Ansätze und Ziele im Projekt LernBAR. BWP Berufsbildung in Wissenschaft und Praxis **48**, 53–54 (2019)
3. Fehling, C.D.: Erweiterte Lernwelten für die berufliche Bildung. Augmented Reality als Perspektive. In: Thissen, F. (eds.) Lernen in virtuellen Räumen: Perspektiven des mobilen Lernens, pp. 125–142. De Gruyter, Berlin, Boston (2017)
4. Mentimeter Homepage. https://www.mentimeter.com/de-DE/features/live-polling. Accessed 24 Feb 2023

5. Mayring, P.: Einführung in die qualitative Sozialforschung, 6th edn. Beltz, Weinheim (2026)
6. Dehnbostel, P.: Die Digitalisierung verändert den Lernort betrieb. In: Baron, S., Dick, P., Zitzelsberger, R. (eds.) weiterbilden#weiterdenken. Den Strukturwandel in der Metall- und Elektroindustrie durch berufliche Weiterbildung gestalten, pp. 119–141. wbv Publikation, Bielefeld (2021)

Universal Access to Learning and Education

Shifting from the Discrete to the Continuum: How Are Italian Universities Facing the Challenge?

Paola Aiello[✉] [iD], Diana Carmela Di Gennaro [iD], Erika Marie Pace [iD], Emanuela Zappalà [iD], and Flavia Capodanno [iD]

Department of Humanities, Philosophy and Education, University of Salerno, Fisciano, Italy
{paiello,ddigennaro}@unisa.it

Abstract. The latest innovation in technology, its pervasive influence in the field of education and the recent experience of emergency remote teaching in higher education institutions during the Pandemic have stimulated the need to rethink Faculty Development (FD). In addition, the even more recent forms of human-computer interaction, such as extended reality, seem to blur the distinction between in presence and online modes of teaching and learning completely, giving rise to unprecedented approaches of teacher-student-environment interaction. Prior experience has taught us that unless faculty members are adequately prepared to take on the challenge posed in this new era of digitalization, the risk is that the affordances of these digital artefacts remain unexplored and unexploited. In light of these considerations and drawing on the lessons learned especially during the Pandemic, the paper proposes a reflection on possible future scenarios for the adoption of innovative methodological approaches apt to promote holistic change through systematic FD processes to facilitate this shift from the discrete to the continuum.

Keywords: Digital Education Hubs · Faculty Development · Teaching Learning Centers

1 Introduction

Over time, the widespread diffusion of technology in all educational and training contexts has produced a gradual evolution of the teaching-learning dynamics and a progressive reduction of the boundary between physical and virtual environments. This process turned out to be even more rapid and pervasive during the Covid-19 Pandemic which involved a radical and global transformation of university systems, called to quickly identify methods and tools capable of ensuring the continuity of students' training and development (Mishra et al. 2020; García-Morales et al. 2021). Initially, this led to mainly focus the attention on the organisational and technical aspects of distance learning, primarily linked to the use of Learning Management Systems (LMS). However, with the persistence of the Pandemic, a reflection on the opportunities deriving from this transformation became increasingly necessary and urgent.

© The Author(s), under exclusive license to Springer Nature Switzerland AG 2023
M. Antona and C. Stephanidis (Eds.): HCII 2023, LNCS 14021, pp. 173–189, 2023.
https://doi.org/10.1007/978-3-031-35897-5_13

This implies the need to overcome a *discrete* approach based on the tendency to make choices between diametrically opposed alternatives, such as 'in presence' versus 'online' teaching-learning processes (Anderson, 2021), by embracing a *continuum* perspective which envisages more nuanced and integrative choices. The assumption is that the potential of distance learning, especially in the synchronous mode, lies in the creation of new teaching and learning spaces, of interactive digital ecologies (Riva et al. 2009) in which the technological artefact is made invisible thanks to the high level of interaction between physical and virtual reality while also preserving participation; a key factor for promoting inclusive processes (Ainscow, 2020). Indeed, the sense of presence and the level of participation seem to be the two main vectors capable of implementing teaching and learning in their *onlife* dimension (Floridi, 2017) by redefining the embodied entanglements and the system of underlying interactions (Gourlay, 2021; Sibilio, 2022).

The term *presence* was diffused among the scientific community in 1992 when Sheridan and Furness used it as the title of a new journal dedicated to the study of virtual reality and teleoperation systems: Presence, Teleoperators and Virtual Environments. In the first issue, Sheridan describes the presence starting from the experiences of teleoperator users who, after a few minutes of use, stopped feeling they were in their workplace but instead felt present in the teleoperator's remote space. But how can the feeling of presence be explained? According to the point of view expressed by each discipline that studies it, there are three main operational definitions of presence, each characterized by a specific focus: technological, cognitive or communicative.

The technological definition of presence is characterized by the way in which the relationship between reality and virtuality, objective space and simulated space is conceived: reality is understood as a set of objects placed outside the mind and endowed with spatial characteristics, whereas the virtual environment is intended as a simulation of real objects. In this context, the concept of presence plays a functional role: the higher the level of presence, the greater the ease with which the individual is able to operate in the virtual environment. Therefore, the basic idea is to reduce the complexity of technology, allowing the human operator to interact with the remote environment as if he were present in it. Starting from this point of view, Lombard and Ditton (1997) have elaborated the definition of presence that today is mostly shared within the world of technologies: the illusion of not experiencing a mediation of technology. In practice, according to this approach, being present within a medium means having an experience in which the individual is not aware of the role of technology in supporting his/her action and/or communication. This means that the less the subject is aware of the mediation operated by the medium during the action, the greater the level of presence will be.

Cognitive sciences have recently begun to describe presence as a selective and adaptive mechanism, which allows the self to define the boundary of action by distinguishing between inside and outside in a sensory flow. In practice, presence can be considered as the sensation of *being* within a real or virtual environment, the result of the ability to implement one's intentions in the environment through the opportunities (affordances) that it offers (Riva, 2008). In other words, the cognitive vision of presence focuses on the individual's intention and his/her ability to implement it in action, including communicative action. However, the effectiveness of communication also requires the social presence, the feeling of *being with other selves* within a real or virtual environment; the result of the ability to recognize the intentions of others in the environment (Riva et al. 2009). This means that regardless of the physical or virtual presence of the interlocutor, the *other self* is present in the communication act only when one is able to recognize his/her intentions.

Short, Williams, and Christie (1976) originally developed the theory of social presence to explain the effect telecommunications media can have on communication. They defined social presence as the degree of salience (i.e., quality or state of being there) between two communicators using a communication medium. They posited that communication media differ in their degree of social presence and that these differences play an important role in how people interact (p. 65). They conceptualized social presence primarily as a quality of a communication medium that can define the way people interact and communicate. In their opinion, people perceive some media as having a higher degree of social presence (e.g., video) and other media as having a lower degree of social presence (e.g., audio) (Lowenthal, 2010).

The Pandemic period, thanks to and albeit the differences in remote teaching approaches used, proved timely to collect data, on an international level, on the impact of this new form of presence (Ashour et al. 2021; Jandrić et al. 2020; Peters et al. 2020). The choices made in a state of emergency, which were based on the technological resources and online learning experience available at the time, have generated unprecedented methods of teacher-student-environment interaction overnight that lacked careful planning and may have unconsciously or consciously ignored the faculty members and the students' ability of *being and being with other selves* in virtual spaces.

In light of these considerations and drawing on the lessons learned especially during the Pandemic, the paper proposes a reflection on possible future scenarios for the adoption of innovative methodological approaches apt to promote holistic change through systematic Faculty Development (FD) processes and facilitate this shift from the discrete to the continuum. It is argued that, although digital competence is fundamental for this new era of immersive technological experiences, it is definitely not enough to guarantee inclusive quality education opportunities for all. The socio-emotional aspects and issues related to presence from a cognitive perspective not only influence the agency of faculty members but also of the students.

2 The Downfalls and Upturns of Teaching Online: Lessons Learned

Although the discourse and the perspectives for the future of higher education are different and sometimes contrasting, there is a growing consensus that "nothing could be worse than a return to normality" (Roy, 2020, p. 3). Notwithstanding the difficulties faced by faculty members, students and institutions, now the focus should be on the opportunities deriving from the Pandemic and on the process of innovation it has stimulated.

Before analyzing these opportunities, it seems necessary to distinguish the so-called emergency remote teaching (Hodges et al. 2020; Xie and Rice, 2021) linked to the Pandemic from the online learning and teaching and even from the Internet-based distance education (Rapanta, 2021). Although they share one common feature, which is teaching with digital technologies, they differ in terms of goal, design process, instructional delivery mode or ways to integrate technology (Xie & Rice, 2021). On the one hand, emergency remote teaching refers to a shift due to crisis circumstances (Hodges et al. 2020). Its goal is to provide "a reliable, temporary, fast, and durable access" to instruction and its affordances (Mohmmed et al. 2020, p. 2). In this case, the lack of support and resources resulted in mostly synchronous class meetings (Manfuso, 2020) and often the strategies adopted, mainly aimed at providing access to education rather than redefining the educational framework (Hodges et al., 2020; Lowenthal et al., 2020). On the other hand, online teaching and learning is a subset of distance education using digital media within designed learning environments (Keengwe & Kidd 2010). It provides a learning ecosystem (Manfuso, 2020) aimed at increased flexibility and better access to learning opportunities through the careful design of courses that appropriately combine synchronous, asynchronous and independent study activities (Anderson, 2008). Internet-based distance education refers to "an institution-based, formal education where the learning group is separated, and where interactive telecommunications systems are used to connect learners, resources and instructors" (Schlosser & Simonson, 2009, p. 1).

This slight distinction between online teaching and emergency remote teaching is necessary because the implementation of the latter is often misconceived as the transferal of traditional teaching strategies from in-person classroom environments to online teaching (Corsi et al., 2019). As a result, online lectures are limited to expository rather than interactive teaching and learning (Moorhouse & Kohnke, 2021).

As Rapanta et al. (2021) point out, other aspects of technology-based teaching, which to a higher or lower degree were also present in traditional university practices, were underemphasized probably because they were not as integrated in existing in-presence teaching as they could, or should, have been. These include aspects of blended learning and flipped classroom activities, in which the in-class time is combined with productive learning outside the classroom: "Such aspects can easily be incorporated into exclusively online interactive instruction, replacing the 'in-class' time by dynamic synchronous activities (including small-group discussions) and the 'outside-class' time by group asynchronous activities and individual activities" (Rapanta et al., 2021, p. 717). Nonetheless, the pre-Covid-19 level of digitalization of higher education systems and the underdevelopment of teaching strategies made the shift from face-to-face to emergency remote learning disruptive (Wyatt-Smith et al., 2021), aggressive (Watermeyer et al., 2021), disastrous (Dhawan, 2020) and unwelcome (Watermeyer et al., 2021).

In the last two years, a copious number of publications has drawn the attention on how teachers reacted to the urgent shift from face-to-face to online teaching and whether this transition has brought about positive changes in their implicit and explicit teaching models and strategies (Aiello et al., 2023; Jandrić et al., 2020; Peters et al., 2020; Sangra et al., 2020). For example, from the study carried out by Damşa et al. in 2021 three profiles emerged according to whether teachers showed a low (Profile 1), medium (Profile 2) or high (Profile 3) use of new online teaching methods, software and support from others they found useful. Faculty members pertaining to Profile 1 showed a tendency towards iterative, non-transformative agency where activity in emerging contexts replicated existing practices. Those grouped in Profile 2 were more prompt to show a practical-evaluative type of agency in which teachers acknowledge the use(fulness) of technologies as alternatives to their ordinary practice, but not their potential as triggers for new practices. Finally, Profile 3 teachers (only 8% of the participants) showed evidence of future-projective, transformative agency.

The survey conducted by Scherer et al. (2021), aimed at identifying the pedagogical and content-related aspects of faculty members' online teaching readiness, identified three profiles describing faculty members' readiness for online teaching, namely (a) a low readiness profile, with teachers rating low on both personal and contextual readiness indicators; (b) an inconsistent readiness profile, with low ratings of pedagogical content knowledge self-efficacy and perceived online presence, but high ratings on perceived institutional support; and (c) a high readiness profile with consistently high ratings on all readiness indicators.

In contrast to the previous research, where the large majority of participants did not have any previous experience with online teaching, a great part of the sample involved in the Marek et al. (2021) study had used online technologies in their classes before the Pandemic and this prior experience, when present, predicted the ease and comfort with which the participants shifted to online teaching during the pandemic. Furthermore, research also highlighted that teachers gained awareness regarding both the use of technologies and distance education resources to improve students' learning and productivity, and to improve the accessibility of students with different difficulties (Crawford, 2020; Aiello et al., 2023). Another important positive aspect concerns the great interest shown by faculty members in being able to implement blended learning formats and their intention to continue to use technological resources to enhance interaction in face-to-face teaching contexts (Trevisan et al., 2020).

3 Teaching-Learning Approaches in Higher Education in Italy Prior to, During and After the Pandemic

The issue regarding the feelings of *being* and *being with other selves* during this sudden experience of emergency remote teaching from the faculty members' perspective leads to wonder what the students' perception was, especially for those who had completed their high school during lockdown and enrolled at university but could not set foot on campus.

In normal circumstances, university life marks the starting point for the transition from adolescence to adulthood, independence, the creation of new social networks, the ability to adapt to new demands and responsibilities that is already critical in its own right (Auerbach et al., 2018; Saleh et al., 2017; Zivin et al., 2009). Indeed, most first-year students frequently experience high level of stress due to academic reasons, feelings of loneliness, job hunting, family issues, life goals, and social pressure (Karman et al., 2019; Saleh, Camart & Romo, 2017; Zurlo, Cattaneo Della Volta, & Vallone, 2020, 2022) In this regard, the containment mechanisms put in place during COVID-19 Pandemic and the perception of health-related risk made the situation worse (David et al., 2022; Islam et al. 2020; Koffman et al., 2020; Plakhotnik et al., 2021). Before delving further into this reflection, a brief description of the Italian developments in Internet-based teaching and the academic scenario during the Pandemic will provide the context.

3.1 The Italian Approach to Emergency Remote Teaching

Before March 2020, Internet-based teaching in higher education was already diffused and implemented (Garrison & Vaughan, 2008; Limone, 2013; Gaebel et al., 2014; Bonaiuti et al., 2017; Rivoltella, 2017, 2020), yet it still represented a niche mode of delivery (Perla, Agrati & Vinci, 2019). A number of online universities had already been established and MOOCs had also gained popularity. On the other hand, the use of technology at on-campus universities was mainly restricted to the communication for administrative and organizational purposes, which was strictly via online management systems and emails. As for lecturing and assessment, traditional pedagogical approaches and oral or written exams was the norm in most faculties. Students were used to visiting faculty members in classrooms or their offices for one-to-one tutoring and to enquire about any service related to their studies and academic experience.

The Ministerial Decree dated 9th March 2020 hit the whole education system by storm. Naturally, the goal was to safeguard public health and safety while guaranteeing the right to education. Co-responsibility between central and territorial institutions ensured a systematic approach in the reorganization of all the activities. In a few weeks, universities identified the most suitable virtual learning platforms, and provided initial guidance and support in order to facilitate remote teaching in both synchronous and asynchronous methods. This was possible since e-learning was already present and adopted by other universities or other education and training institutions. Such an approach was in line with what was happening in the rest of the world. As reported by Aristovnik et al. (2020), who carried out an investigation involving five continents, there was autonomy and a variety of choice on how universities decided to resume learning. Real-time video conferencing and lectures on platforms such as Zoom or Teams were the most popular. Other less common interaction included presentations sent to students and written communication through online fora and chats. In Italy, other approaches included posting videos on e-learning platforms, having faculty members set up their own webpage, the activation of YouTube channels and the creation of virtual classrooms.

Considering the emergency situation, it must be said that the solutions did meet the characteristics mentioned earlier. The systematic approaches used were fast, temporary and durable (Mohmmed et al. 2020), yet not completely reliable. Although they ensured continuity, the high price to pay was the quality of interaction. The fact that, as months passed by, the choice of using asynchronous forms of lecturing prevailed over synchronous interaction is evidence of this. The complexity characterizing the organizational component (Weick & Sutcliffe, 2010) of distance learning required all actors involved to have and use specific skills needed to manage the unexpected, to adapt to the peculiarities of this new context, and to adopt effective teaching strategies for online learning. Obviously, this was more complex than expected for faculty members who had never worked at on-line universities and also for students who found themselves facing a new experience and interacting in a *third space* (Potter & McDougall, 2017). The inherent complexity brought about by these abrupt changes, highlight the central role of faculty members to increase the likelihood that the affordances of these digital artefacts are further explored and capitalized (Perla, Agrati & Vinci, 2019).

3.2   The Students' Perspective on *Being and Being with Other Selves* in a Virtual Space

Several studies explored daily experiences and opinions of students during the Pandemic and other stressful situations and worries emerged. In fact, as claimed both by UNESCO (2020) and in an array of studies (Cao et al., 2020; Commodari et al., 2021; Di Nuovo, Moschetto, & Narzisi, 2021; Commodari & La Rosa, 2022; Leal Filho et al. 2021; Zurlo, Cattaneo Della Volta, & Vallone, 2020, 2022), they perceived high level of stress due to their isolation and to the significant changes that took place on a relational level. According to Vallone et al. (2020), the lockdown "affected all relationships, either restricting or, conversely, strengthening them, including those with peers, family members, and lovers as well as those with professors and university colleagues in the academic field" [author trad.] (p. 3). The lockdown forced the students to reduce their freedom to interact within multiple contexts and to have face-to-face contacts with colleagues and friends (Rosenberg et al., 2021). Several students away from their homes were obliged to return. This meant (re)negotiating the boundaries, spaces and time to ensure intimacy, especially in the case of students belonging to families with disadvantaged socio-economic backgrounds (Lee, 2020).

Italian university students were the first in Europe to experience lockdown. All academic activities, including classes, assessment, studying with peers, and graduation days shifted to the online world (D'Addio & Endrizzi, 2020; Aristovnik, 2020). Students 'simply' had to adopt feasible methods to study online (Sandhu & de Wolf, 2020; Sharma & Ogle, 2020).

A longitudinal study conducted by Commodari et al. (2021, 2022) among 655 Italian university students revealed that the experience of quarantine proved to have a substantial psychological influence on the students interviewed. About 40% of the students reported feeling sadder, more anxious, angrier and ruminating more than usual. Sleep and attention problems were also very common. More than 50% of the students studied less than normal and 47.5% of them were worried that this incident might have a negative impact on their academic careers. On a positive note, 55.9% had no significant issues in organizing their time nor their study environment (64.4%) (Commodari et al., 2021). In another study (Di Nuovo, Smeriglio, 2021), the university students perceived that their overall status had worsened, they were afraid of taking online exams, found it more difficult to make decisions about their academic careers and perceived the study load as heavier. Meanwhile, Jones et al. (2021) found that economic problems and financial instability were the factors that mostly affected students' academic performance.

One year after the start of the Pandemic, and all activities were still offered remotely, the results of the investigation by Di Nuovo et al. (2021) revealed that only some students were able to adequately respond to the discomfort deriving from social restrictions and the new teaching methods. Irritability, difficulties in concentrating, enjoying their free time and relaxing were all symptoms of stress that negatively impacted academic performance and their perception of student status. The students also felt that different activities and behavioral and relational habits had changed after the lockdown. These included negative eating habits, tendency to use the Internet, social networks and play online for longer hours online.

Similar results were also reported in international studies. Social interaction was identified as one of the factors for which face-to-face lectures are usually preferred because it is perceived as a support to motivation and interest (Baym, Zhang, Ling, 2004; Monteduro, 2021; Kemp & Grieve, 2014). Thanks to the potential of non-verbal communication that was not always possible to observe in the distance learning, in some circumstances, reduced the educational value of immediacy mentioned by Baker (2010). Moreover, the students often affirmed they missed the opportunity to live the university experience, made up of studying in the classroom with their colleagues and professors and greater face-to-face interactions.

These results are also consistent with other studies that involved students with special needs (Siletti et al., 2021). The recent ANVUR Report on students with disability and Specific Learning Disorders in Italian universities (Borgonovi et al., 2022) and other investigations (Borgonovi et al., 2022; Gin et al., 2022; Hanjarwati & Suprihatiningrum, 2020; Siletti et al., 2021) outlined that the challenges faced were strictly connected to:

– the specific way of functioning or to particular disabilities, such as sensory and motor;
– absence or limited forms of mentoring and tutoring support, even if several universities shared initiatives to monitor their appreciation about teaching activities and assessment methods and detect any problems in order to promptly act to solve them;
– problems related to assessment, especially when this envisaged an oral examination that took place in online public sessions;
– problems of a psychological nature: feelings of loss, uncertainty, disorientation, lack of concentration, tiredness due to prolonged screentime, disorganized study; anxiety and rumination related to the health emergency, fear of being forced to separate from caregivers due to potential quarantines, loss of relationships built over the years and social isolation.

Nevertheless, for some students with special needs, the closure of the university had paradoxically turned out to be a positive experience. Some students reported that both the synchronous and asynchronous modes had been more accessible and easier to attend, and some had really positive experiences with tutoring supports (Borgonovi et al., 2022, p. 78; Di Vita, 2021). According to prior research (Biancalana, 2020), students with special needs enrolled at the university of Bari sustained to have more positive relationships and feelings of calmness, less tension, and less embarrassment while asking questions during distance learning (Silletti et al., 2021).

With regards to the whole student population irrespective of ability, as reported by Loscalzo et al. (2021), after the lockdown some claimed that they had had the opportunity to focus on studying and that it was considered as a suitable activity to kill time during quarantine. They also affirmed that the quarantine also gave them the opportunity to have more free time. Lastly, according to the students, participating in remote lectures was useful and gave them the advantage of saving time and energy since they did not have to commute.

4   The Italian Proposal: A Multi-level Approach to Faculty Capacity Development

As we move on to the last part of our reflection and draw to a close, a summary of the main points emerged so far deems useful. At this point, we can claim that hybrid modes of teaching and learning in on-campus universities have become the present and future trend. The period of emergency remote teaching has left a significant impact on faculty members and students' lives. As a result, three main issues were brought to the fore, although in all cases the literature prior to 2020 is evidence that these concerns had been amply anticipated. The first concern regards the lack of digital competencies among faculty members. The second challenge is how to overcome the reluctance among faculty members to capitalize the affordances technology has to offer to promote learning for all rather than considering Internet-based teaching as a static virtual classroom where the only difference is that the actors are not physically in the same room. Lastly, and of major concern, regards the cognitive perspective of the concept of *presence* in virtual environments and the underestimation of the importance of *being* and of *being with other selves* in the absence of physical interaction and non-verbal communication.

This leads to the conclusion that FD has never been as much a priority as it is today and a multi-level approach that takes into account a wide spectrum of competencies is a must. The investment in digital competence cannot be overstated but can neither be considered sufficient. As we approach a new world where more recent forms of human-computer interaction, such as extended reality, seem to completely blur the distinction between in presence and online modes of teaching and learning, we will witness unprecedented forms of interactions among the faculty member, the student and the environment.

Nevertheless, even in terms of FD, history has much to teach us. Since the 1970s, terms such as academic, professional, faculty and educational have often been collo-cated with words like training, upgrading, development or renewal to refer to some form of planned activity apt to facilitate knowledge and skill acquisition in an area or areas considered indispensable to change or improve the performance of a faculty member (Brawer, 1990). Although agreement hasn't yet been reached with regards to its name and the field of research is relatively new, FD has, to date, garnered a lot of attention internationally (Sorcinelli, 2020). The aforementioned challenges encountered by aca-demic staff and students during the Covid-19 Pandemic have definitely given impetus. Notwithstanding this, reviews of literature in the field prior to 2020 provide evidence of the plethora of publications (Phuong, Foster & Reio, 2020) that focused on various characteristics ranging among FD design (outcomes and processes), FD activity formats (formal programs and self-directed activities), FD cooperation (introspective and inter-active), learning theories, and FD levels of development (individual and organizational). Steinert (2011) summarizes how FD activities have, so far, moved along two specific dimensions: from a formal to an informal approach and from an individual to a group context for learning. At the heart of the cross-section of these two axes is mentorship since "any strategy for self-improvement can benefit from the support and challenge that an effective mentor can provide" (p. 410).

Sorcinelli (2020) argues that the Age of the Network has oriented FD for the past two decades of the 21st Century. Despite the "unprecedented changes in faculty appointments and responsibilities, student demographics, and the nature of teaching and scholarship"

(p. 21), expectations with regards to accountability and guaranteeing quality education opportunities for all throughout life have increased. Contrary to what one would expect, the ubiquitous presence of instructional technology may have been perceived by faculty members as an added complexity in meeting these demands: its unlimited potential in facilitating communication and providing captivating ways of teaching and learning, on the one hand, has heightened students' expectations and, on the other hand, has brought to light their lack of competence to master it. Indeed, what the studies related to the effectiveness of remote learning during the Pandemic brought to the fore was not much the vulnerabilities and uncertainties in using technology but the degree of seriousness finding ill-prepared faculty members has been in terms of student performance irrespective of the investment in training. Despite these difficulties, it was also clear that the teachers' dedication, commitment, and tenacity have been central to holistic student development (Aiello et al, 2023).

What is worrisome is that two years on not much seems to have been learnt. Digital competence is not being given its due relevance and lecturing seems to have gone back to the traditional ways of teaching (Roy, 2020). If more than twenty years had passed since the introduction of e-learning and the use of the first LMS, and digital competence in 2020 was still the power in the hands of the few, what will happen in the very near future when the new digital era will take education and our everyday lives to a whole new level? How well-prepared are we to guarantee inclusive practices, facilitate the acquisition of global and transformative competencies, manage student-faculty member relationships, plan and assess learning, design curricula to meet unforeseeable needs in the labor market, and support students to face this complex world? Before we know it, there will be no shift from the physical to the virtual world. Dichotomies such as online/offline and virtual/real will soon become obsolete (Di Tore, 2022) as the two worlds will merge into the metaverse defined as:

"a massively scaled and interoperable network of real-time rendered 3D virtual worlds and environments which can be experienced synchronously and persistently by an effectively unlimited number of users with an individual sense of presence, and with continuity of data, such as identity, history, entitlements, objects, communications, and payments" (Ball, 2021).

What can be done so as to ride the waves of this evolution and capitalize what the metaverse has to offer to higher education? Definitely, focusing exclusively on digital competence is not enough and neither is it effective to concentrate solely on faculty members. Indeed, the Pandemic has represented an opportunity to rethink not only education but also faculty members' scholarship as a core strategy to be able to deal with this change and improve the system.

Boyer's proposal in the early 90s to overcome the "teaching versus research" (1990, p. 16) debate is still valid today in this regard. He suggests four categories on which to focus the attention. The scholarship *of discovery* is not only inherent to the faculty members' research outcomes that can be measured quantitatively on the basis of grants and peer-reviewed publications. It also refers to the process, the passion, that provide meaning to the effort. The second category is scholarship *of integration* which refers to the ability in viewing one's own discipline from an interdisciplinary and transdisciplinary perspective, thus making connections across fields of research by searching for the meaning of the findings within a broader picture. The third category is the scholarship *of teaching*. This regards the pedagogical and didactic approaches used to convey one's knowledge and skills that is highly impacted by one's professional and personal beliefs and opinions (Sharma et al., 2017; Aiello et al., 2017). It is a process that educates and transforms both the student and the scholar; it requires careful planning, constant reflection in action and upon action, observation and assessment for evaluation and continuous improvement. The fourth category, often disregarded, is the scholarship *of application* that is the faculty members' ability to bridge theory to practice. In this sense,

> new intellectual understandings can arise out of the very act of application – whether in medical diagnosis, serving clients in psychotherapy, shaping public policy, creating an architectural design, or working with the public schools. [...] Such a view of scholarly service – one that both applies and contributes to human knowledge is particularly needed in a world in which huge, almost intractable problems call for the skills and insights only the academy can provide. As Oscar Handlin observed, our troubled planet "can no longer afford the luxury of pursuits confined to an ivory tower.... [S]cholarship has to prove its worth not on its own terms but by service to the nation and the world (Boyer, 1990, p. 23).

Obviously, these four categories are inextricably linked as they dynamically bring together the various forms of work required to improve the quality of the experience from both the faculty members and the students' perspective. Underpinning values include a major sense of ownership, motivation, mutual support, mentorship, self-directed and collective transformative learning processes for self and group development and mean-ing making. In light of these considerations, a reflection on possible future scenarios of FD is necessary for the adoption of innovative methodological approaches able to promote a systemic change through multi-level FD processes. In Italy, in response to the economic and social disadvantage caused as a result of the pandemic crisis, an innova-tive framework was proposed within the six-year National Recovery and Resilience Plan (Ministry of Economy and Finance, 2021). The Plan is developed around three strate-gic axes shared at a European level. These are: digitization and innovation, ecological transition, and social inclusion. Among its six policy areas is 'Education and Research' and the strategic actions proposed include: the strengthening of the education system, digital and technical scientific skills, research, and technology transfer. The objectives envisaged in Action 3.4 of the Plan include:

- the creation of 3 Teaching and Learning Centers to improve teaching skills (including digital skills) of university lecturers and schoolteachers, in all disciplines, including those less traditionally oriented towards the use of ICT. The Centre will therefore organize courses on pedagogy and didactics to promote inclusive teaching practices and strategies, while acting as a support center for FD;
- the creation of 3 Digital Education Hubs (DEHs) to improve Higher Education Sys-tems and offer ICT training for university students and staff that is not limited to technical aspects but will improve teaching skills for hybrid learning environments,

reduce the digital divide and, thus, aim to promote quality inclusive education at all levels.

These TLCs and the DEHs will be instituted in the North, Centre, and South of Italy. Whereas the Digital Education Hubs will be set up and managed by three universities, the TLCs will be separate foundations annexed to universities. These two institutions will collaborate for the collection, analysis, and dissemination of results to provide inclusive evidence-based practices in education on a national level. This organizational structure will create the necessary conditions for a teacher education system in which, on a local level, universities, through the Higher Teacher Education Schools and the Departments of Education will be responsible for pre-service teaching whereas, on a regional level, the TLCs will be the main proponents of high-quality in-service training for schoolteachers, school principals, and faculty members. The DEHs will concentrate on equipping university staff and faculty with the digital skills required to enhance the students' learning experience and the FD levels of individual and organizational development. In conclusion, the innovative aspect of this proposal is the creation of a systematic multi-level network, a system that aims to reduce the gaps in terms of digital infrastructure and digital competence of all administrative staff and faculty members responsible for educating current and future generations to work towards reducing the disparities for all.

5   Conclusions

In higher education, the shift from the discrete to the continuum requires to rethink practices that move towards a more harmonious integration of physical and digital tools and methods for the sake of more active, flexible and meaningful learning (Rapanta et al., 2021). The need to "manage the unexpected" (Weick & Sutcliffe, 2010) should stimulate universities to reflect on the possibility of assuming a broader approach to higher education by envisaging and providing different kinds of teacher-student-environment interactions. Of course, such a hybrid scenario implies the need of developing a new and broader set of competencies for faculty members, by focusing not only on the acquisition of digital competencies but also, and especially, on pedagogical competencies aimed at favoring higher levels of participation and inclusion.

This transformative process has to take into account how such transformation will occur for all the faculty members in order to make the above-mentioned shift from the discrete to the continuum possible. In this sense, the discrete is represented by the individual or groups of individuals' professional development, while the continuum refers to FD with the aim of creating universities that cultivate connected, participatory personal and professional development, and which takes equity, social justice and differences into consideration, thus promoting agency (Macdonald et al., 2019; Sibilio & Aiello, 2018).

Indeed, the concept of agency provides insight in terms of FD to promote inclusion. Within an ecological perspective, agency is seen as an emerging phenomenon that results from the interrelationship between the individual's capability, the resources available and the environmental affordances and barriers: as an "interplay of individual efforts, available resources and contextual and structural factors as they come together in particular and, in a sense, always unique situations (Biesta & Tedder 2007, p. 137). Hence, the focus is on the importance of both the individual ability and the contextual dimensions in shaping agency, thus overcoming the longstanding cultural orientations which considered action and structure as two separate and autonomous entities and attributing to either one or the other conceptual category diverse levels of responsibility in modeling social reality.

References

Aiello, P., et al.: Identifying teachers' strengths to face COVID-19: narratives from across the globe. Cambridge J. Educ. 1–18 (2023). https://doi.org/10.1080/0305764X.2022.2159013

Aiello, P., et al.: A study on Italian teachers' sentiments, attitudes and concerns towards inclusive education. Formazione, Lavoro, Persona, Anno VII **20**, 10–24 (2017)

Ainscow, M.: Promoting inclusion and equity in education: lessons from international experiences. Nordic J. Stud. Educ. Policy **6**(1), 7–16 (2020)

Anderson, W.: The model crisis, or how to have critical promiscuity in the time of Covid-19. Soc. Stud. Sci. (2021). https://doi.org/10.1177/0306312721996053

Anderson, T. (ed.): The Theory and Practice of Online Learning, 2nd edn. Athabasca University Press, Edmonton (2008)

Aristovnik, A., Keržič, D., Ravšelj, D., Tomaževič, N., Umek, L.: Impacts of the COVID-19 pandemic on life of higher education students: a global perspective. Sustainability **12**(20), 8438 (2020)

Ashour, S., El-Refae, G.A., Zaitoun, E.A.: Post-pandemic higher education: perspectives from university leaders and educational experts in the United Arab Emirates. Higher Educ. Future (2021). https://doi.org/10.1177/23476311211007261

Auerbach, R.P., et al.: WHO world mental health surveys international college student project: prevalence and distribution of mental disorders. J. Abnorm. Psychol. **127**(7), 623 (2018)

Baker, C.: The impact of instructor immediacy and presence for online student affective learning, cognition, and motivation. J. Educators Online **7**(1), 1 (2010)

Ball, M.: Framework for the metaverse (2021). https://www.matthewball.vc/all/forwardtothemet averseprimer. Retrieved 30 Jan 2023

Baym, N.K., Zhang, Y.B., Lin, M.C.: Social interactions across media: interpersonal communication on the internet, telephone and face-to-face. New Media Soc. **6**(3), 299–318 (2004)

Biesta, G., Tedder, M.: Agency and learning in the lifecourse: towards an ecological perspective. Stud. Educ. Adults **39**(2), 132–149 (2007)

Bonaiuti, G., Calvani, A., Menichetti, L., Vivanet, G.: Le tecnologie educative. Carocci, Roma (2017)

Borgonovi, E., et al.: Rapporto ANVUR. Gli studenti con disabilità e DSA nelle università italiane. Una risorsa da valorizzare (2022). https://www.anvur.it/wp-content/uploads/2022/06/ANVUR-Rapporto-disabilita_WEB.pdf. Retrieved 29 Jan 2023

Boyer, E.L.: A Special Report. Scholarship Reconsidered: Priorities of the Professoriate. The Carnegie Foundation for the Advancement of Teaching, Stanford (1990)

Brawer, F.B.: Faculty development: the literature. An ERIC review. Commun. Coll. Rev. **18**(1), 50–56 (1990). https://doi.org/10.1177/009155219001800107

Cao, W., et al.: The psychological impact of the COVID-19 epidemic on college students in China. Psychiatry Res. **287**, 112934 (2020)

Commodari, E., La Rosa, V.L.: Riflessioni sull'impatto della pandemia di COVID-19 sul benessere psicologico degli studenti universitari: una rassegna della letteratura. Annali della facoltà di Scienze della formazione Università degli studi di Catania **21**, 17 (2022)

Commodari, E., La Rosa, V.L., Carnemolla, G., Parisi, J.: The psychological impact of the lockdown on Italian university students during the first wave of COVID-19 pandemic: psychological experiences, health risk perceptions, distance learning, and future perspectives. Mediterr. J. Clin. Psychol. **9**(2) (2021)

Corsi, M., Giannandrea, L., Rossi, P.G., Pons, J.D.P.: Innovating didactics at university. Educ. Sci. Soc.-Open Access J. **9**(2), 1–7 (2019). https://doi.org/10.3280/ess2-2018oa7331

Crawford, J., et al.: COVID-19: 20 countries' higher education intra-period digital pedagogy responses. J. Appl. Learn. Teach. **3**(1), 9–28 (2020). https://doi.org/10.37074/jalt.2020.3.1.7

D'Addio, A.C., Endrizzi, F.: Covid-19: how is Italy coping with school closure? (2020). https://gemreportunesco.wordpress.com/2020/04/02/covid-19-how-is-italy-coping-with-school-closure/. Retrieved 30 Jan 2023

Damşa, C., Langford, M., Uehara, D., Scherer, R.: Teachers' agency and online education in times of crisis. Comput. Hum. Behav. **121**, 106793 (2021). https://doi.org/10.1016/j.chb.2021.106793

David, M.C.M.M., et al.: Predictors of stress in college students during the COVID-19 pandemic. J. Affect. Disord. Rep. **10**, 100377 (2022)

Dhawan, S.: Online learning: a Panacea in the time of COVID-19 crisis. J. Educ. Technol. Syst. **49**(1), 5–22 (2020). https://doi.org/10.1177/0047239520934018

Di Nuovo, S., Moschetto, C., Narzisi, V.: Lo studente universitario in tempi di covid, pp. 1–21 (2021). https://doi.org/10.13140/RG.2.2.12715.98085

Di Tore, S., et al.: Education in the metaverse: amidst the virtual and reality. Giornale Italiano di Educazione alla Salute, Sport e Didattica Inclusiva, pp. 1–14 (2022)

Di Vita, A.: Tutoraggio didattico tra pari a distanza: una ricerca-intervento svolta con gli studenti universitari. Excellence Innov. Learn. Teach.-Open Access **6**(2) (2021)

Floridi, L.: La quarta rivoluzione: come l'infosfera sta trasformando il mondo. Raffaello Cortina Editore, Milano (2017)

Fusco, P., Zappalà, E., Lecce, A., Barra, V., Todino, M.D.: Sense of presence alteration while using learning management systems at university during the lock down alterazione del senso di presenza con l'utilizzo dei learning management systems all'università durante il lock down. Giornale Italiano di Educazione alla Salute, Sport e Didattica Inclusiva/Italian J. Health Educ. Sports Inclusive Didactics **5**(3 Supplemento), 33–43 (2021). ISSN 2532-3296. ISBN 978-88-6022-423-1

Gaebel, M., Kupriyanova, V., Morais, R., Colucci, E.: E-Learning in European Higher Education Institutions. European University Association (EUA), Brussels (2014)

García-Morales, V.J., Garrido-Moreno, A., Martín-Rojas, R.: The transformation of higher education after the COVID disruption: emerging challenges in an online learning scenario. Front. Psychol. **12**, 196 (2021)

Garrison, D.R., Vaughan, N.D.: Blended Learning in Higher Education: Framework, Principles, and Guidelines. Wiley, San Francisco (2008)

Gin, L.E., Pais, D.C., Parrish, K.D., Brownell, S.E., Cooper, K.M.: New online accommodations are not enough: the mismatch between student needs and supports given for students with disabilities during the COVID-19 pandemic. J. Microbiol. Biol. Educ. **23**(1), e00280-21 (2022)

Gourlay, L.: There is no'virtual learning': the materiality of digital education. J. New Approach. Educ. Res. **10**(1), 57–66 (2021)

Hanjarwati, A., Suprihatiningrum, J.: Is online learning accessible during COVID-19 pandemic? Voices and experiences of UIN Sunan Kalijaga students with disabilities. Nadwa **14**(1), 1–38 (2020)

Hodge, S.C., Moore, S., Lockee, T., Bond, A.: The difference between emergency remote teaching and online learning. Educausereview, 27 March 2020. https://er.educause.edu/articles/2020/3/the-difference-between-emergency-remote-teaching-and-online-learning

Islam, M.A., Barna, S.D., Raihan, H., Khan, M.N.A., Hossain, M.T.: Depression and anxiety among university students during the COVID-19 pandemic in Bangladesh: a web-based cross-sectional survey. PLoS ONE **15**, e0238162 (2020)

Jandrić, P., et al.: Teaching in the age of Covid-19. Postdigital Sci. Educ. **2**(3), 1069–1230 (2020). https://doi.org/10.1007/s42438-020-00169-6

Jones, H.E., Manze, M., Ngo, V., Lamberson, P., Freudenberg, N.: The impact of the COVID-19 pandemic on college students' health and financial stability in New York City: findings from a population-based sample of City University of New York (CUNY) students. J. Urban Health **98**(2), 187–196 (2021). https://doi.org/10.1007/s11524-020-00506-x

Karaman, M.A., Lerma, E., Vela, J.C., Watson, J.C.: Predictors of academic stress among college students. J. Coll. Couns. **22**(1), 41–55 (2019)

Keengwe, J., Kidd, T.T.: Towards best practices in online learning and teaching in higher education. MERLOT J. Online Learn. Teach. **6**(2), 533–541 (2010)

Kemp, N., Grieve, R.: Face-to-face or face-to-screen? Undergraduates' opinions and test performance in classroom vs. online learning. Front. Psychol. **5**, 1278 (2014)

Koffman, J., Gross, J., Etkind, S.N., Selman, L.: Uncertainty and COVID-19: how are we to respond? J. R. Soc. Med. **113**(6), 211–216 (2020). https://doi.org/10.1177/0141076820930665

Leal Filho, W., et al.: Impacts of COVID-19 and social isolation on academic staff and students at universities: a cross-sectional study. BMC Public Health **21**(1), 1–19 (2021)

Lee, J.: Mental health effects of school closures during COVID-19. Lancet Child Adolesc. Health **4**(6), 421 (2020)

Limone, P.: Ambienti di apprendimento e progettazione didattica. Proposte per un sistema educativo transmediale. Carocci, Roma (2013)

Lombard, M., Ditton, T.: At the heart of it all: The concept of presence. J. Comput. Mediated-Commun. **3**(2) (1997)

Loscalzo, Y., Ramazzotti, C., Giannini, M.: Studyholism e Study Engagement in relazione alle conseguenze sullo studio dovute alla pandemia da Covid-19: Uno studio pilota quali-quantitativo su studenti universitari (Studyholism and Study Engagement in relation to the consequences on study due to the Covid-19 pandemic: a qualitative quantitative pilot study on university students). Counseling **14**(2), 79–91 (2021)

Lowenthal, P.R.: The evolution and influence of social presence theory on online learning. In: Social Computing: Concepts, Methodologies, Tools, and Applications, pp. 113–128. IGI Global (2010)

Macdonald, R.H., et al.: Accelerating change: the power of faculty change agents to promote diversity and inclusive teaching practices. J. Geosci. Educ. **67**(4), 330–339 (2019)

Manfuso, L.G.: From emergency remote teaching to rigorous online learning. Ed Tech, 7 May 2020. https://edtechmagazine.com/higher/article/2020/05emergency-remote-teaching-rigorousonlinelearning-perfcon. Retrieved 25 Jan 2023

Marek, M.W., Chiou, S.C., Wu, W.C.V.: Teacher experiences in converting classes to distance learning in the COVID-19 pandemic. Int. J. Distance Educ. Technol. **19**(1), 40–60 (2021). https://doi.org/10.4018/ijdet.20210101.oa3

Ministero dell'Economia e della Finanza. Italia Domani Piano Nazionale di Ripresa e Resilienza (2021). https://www.italiadomani.gov.it/content/sogei-ng/it/it/home.html. Retrieved 30 Jan 2023

Mishra, L., Gupta, T., Shree, A.: Online teaching-learning in higher education during lockdown period of COVID-19 pandemic. Int. J. Educ. Res. **1**, 100012 (2020)

Monteduro, G.: La vita degli studenti universitari al tempo del COVID-19. Erikson, Trento (2021)

Mohmmed, A.O., Khidhir, B.A., Nazeer, A., Vijayan, V.J.: Emergency remote teaching during Coronavirus pandemic: the current trend and future directive at Middle East College Oman. Innov. Infrastruct. Solutions **5**(3), 1–11 (2020). https://doi.org/10.1007/s41062-020-00326-7

Moore, M.G.: Theory of Transactional Distance. In: Keegan, D. (ed.) Theoretical Principles of Distance Education, pp. 22–38. Routledge, Londra (1997)

Perla, L., Agrati, L.S., Vinci, V.: The 'Sophisticated' knowledge of eTeacher. Re-shape digital resources for online courses. In: Burgos, D. et al. (eds.) HELMeTO 2019. Communications in Computer and Information Science, vol. 1091, pp. 3–17. Springer, Cham (2019). https://doi.org/10.1007/978-3-030-31284-8_1

Perla, L., Felisatti, E., Grion, V.: Oltre l'era Covid-19: dall'emergenza alle prospettive di sviluppo professionale. Oltre l'era Covid-19: dall'emergenza alle prospettive di sviluppo professionale, pp. 18–37 (2020)

Peters, M.A., et al.: Reimagining the new pedagogical possibilities for universities post-Covid-19. Educ. Philos. Theory (2020). https://doi.org/10.1080/00131857.2020.1777655

Phuong, T.T., Foster, M.J., Reio, T.G.: Faculty development: a systematic review of review studies. New Horizons Adult Educ. Hum. Resour. Dev. 32(4), 17–36 (2020). https://doi.org/10.1002/nha3.20294

Potter, J., McDougall, J.: Digital Media, Culture and Education: Theorizing Third Space Literacies. Palgrave MacMillan, London (2017)

Rapanta, C., Botturi, L., Goodyear, P., Guàrdia, L., Koole, M.: Balancing technology, pedagogy and the new normal: Post-pandemic challenges for higher education. Postdigital Sci. Educ. 3(3), 715–742 (2021)

Riva, G.: Psicologia dei Nuovi Media. Il Mulino, Bologna (2008)

Riva, G., Valataro, L., Zaffiro, G.: Tecnologie della presenza. Concetti e applicazioni. Mondo Digitale 3, 32–45 (2009)

Rivoltella, P.C.: Media Education. La Scuola, Brescia (2017)

Rivoltella, P.C.: Nuovi Alfabeti. Educazione e culture nella società postmediale. Morcelliana, Brescia (2020)

Rosenberg, M., Luetke, M., Hensel, D., Kianersi, S., Fu, T.C., e Herbenick, D.: Depression and loneliness during April 2020 COVID-19 restrictions in the United States, and their associations with frequency of social and sexual connections. Soc. Psychiatry Psychiatric Epidemiol. 1–12 (2021)

Roy, A.: The pandemic is a portal. Financial Times, 3 April 2020. https://www.ft.com/content/10d8f5e8-74eb-11ea-95fe-fcd274e920ca. Retrieved 25 Jan 2023

Saleh, D., Camart, N., Romo, L.: Predictors of stress in college students. Front. Psychol. 8, 19 (2017)

Sandhu, P., de Wolf, M.: The impact of COVID-19 on the undergraduate medical curriculum. Med. Educ. Online 25(1), 1764740 (2020)

Sharma, R., Ogle, H.L.: Students should allow the COVID-19 Pandemic to influence their training programme choices. MedEdPublish 9 (2020)

Sharma, U., Aiello, P., Pace, E.M., Round, P., Subban, P.: In-service teachers' attitudes, concerns, efficacy and intentions to teach in inclusive classrooms: an international comparison of Australian and Italian teachers. Eur. J. Special Needs Educ. (2017)

Scherer, R., Howard, S.K., Tondeur, J., Siddiq, F.: Profiling teachers' readiness for online teaching and learning in higher education: who's ready? Comput. Hum. Behav. 118, 106675 (2021). https://doi.org/10.1016/j.chb.2020.106675

Schlosser, L.A., Simonson, M.: Distance Education: Definition and Glossary of Terms, 3rd edn. Information Age Publishing, Charlotte (2009)

Short, J., Williams, E., Christie, B.: The Social Psychology of Telecommunications. Wiley, London (1976)

Sibilio, M.: L'interconnessione tra natura e cultura: implicazioni pedagogiche in tempo di pandemia. In: Stramaglia, M. (ed.) Abitare il futuro. Politiche per la formazione. Atti del Seminario di Studi del Centro di Documentazione, Ricerca e Didattica nel Campo delle Professioni Educative e Formative (CIRDIFOR) dell'Università degli Studi di Macerata Lecce-Rovato: Pensa Multimedia (2022)

Sibilio, M.: Le criticità dell'autonomia scolastica e universitaria e la funzione strategica dell'educazione al tempo del COVID-19. Nuova Secondaria **10**, 282–287 (2020)

Sibilio, M., Aiello, P.: Lo sviluppo professioanle dei docent. Ragionare di Agentività per una Scuola Inclusiva. Edises, Naples (2018)

Silletti, F., et al.: Distance learning in Higher Education during the first pandemic lockdown: the point of view of students with special educational needs. Qwerty **16**(2), 30–46 (2021). https://doi.org/10.30557/QW000042

Sorcinelli, M.D.: Fostering 21st Century teaching and learning: new models for faculty professional development. In: Lotti, A., Lampugnani, P.A. (eds.) Faculty Development in Italia. Valorizzazione delle competenze didattiche dei docenti universitari, pp. 19–25 (2020)

Steinert, Y.: Commentary: faculty development: the road less traveled. Acad. Med. **86**(4), 409–411 (2011). https://doi.org/10.1097/acm.0b013e31820c6fd3

Trevisan, O., De Rossi, M., Grion, V.: The positive in the tragic: Covid pandemic as an impetus for change in teaching and assessment in higher education. Res. Educ. Media **12**(1), 69–76 (2020)

United Nations Educational, Scientific and Cultural Organization [UNESCO]. Education: From Disruption to Recovery (2020). https://en.unesco.org/covid19/educationresponse. Retrieved 27 Jan 2023

Vallone, F., Nieves Mordente, N., Cattaneo Della Volta, M.F.: Stress e condizioni di salute psicologica negli studenti universitari durante la pandemia da COVID-19: fattori di rischio e fattori protettivi. TOPIC-Temi di Psicologia dell'Ordine degli Psicologi della Campania **1**(1), 1–16 (2022). https://doi.org/10.53240/topic001.11

Xie, J., Rice, M.F.: Instructional designers' roles in emergency remote teaching during COVID-19. Distance Educ. **42**(1), 70–87 (2021). https://doi.org/10.1080/01587919.2020.1869526

Watermeyer, R., Crick, T., Knight, C., Goodall, J.: COVID-19 and digital disruption in UK universities: afflictions and affordances of emergency online migration. High. Educ. **81**(3), 623–641 (2020). https://doi.org/10.1007/s10734-020-00561-y

Weick, K.E., Sutcliffe, K.M.: Governare l'inatteso. Organizzazioni capaci di affrontare le crisi con successo. Raffaello Cortina Editore, Milano (2010)

Wyatt-Smith, C., Lingard, B., Heck, E.: "Lenses on Covid-19": provocations. In: Wyatt-Smith, C., Lingard, B., Heck, E. (eds.) Digital Disruption in Teaching and Testing. Routledge, New York (2021). https://doi.org/10.4324/9781003045793

Zivin, K., Gollust, S.E., Golberstein, E.: Persistence of mental health problems and needs in a college student population. J. Affect. Disord. **117**(3), 180–185 (2009)

Zurlo, M.C., Cattaneo Della Volta, M.F., Vallone, F.: COVID-19 student stress questionnaire: development and validation of a questionnaire to evaluate students' stressors related to the coronavirus pandemic lockdown. Front. Psychol. **11**, 576758 (2020)

Computational Technology as a Tool for Integration of the Different Intellectual Capabilities in the Classroom with Children

Francisco Javier Álvarez Rodriguez(✉) ⓘ, Arturo Barajas Saavedra, and Ana Cecilia Oviedo de Luna

Universidad Autónoma de Aguascalientes, Avenida Aguascalientes 940, Ciudad Universitaria, 20210 Aguascalientes, México
fjalvar@correo.uaa.mx, {arturo.barajas,ana.oviedo}@edu.uaa.mx

Abstract. The use of technology in education is a tool that has gained much strength today, especially due to the changes in the paradigms of education that seek to provide attention to the needs and learning styles of the individuals who make up the community. Educational; a wide variety of applications, with various styles of use, are available for teachers to download and integrate into their daily practice. As there are so many modalities, applications and multimedia content available, it is of great importance to have a selection process for these resources that involves taking into account the needs of the students, the context, and even YOUR tastes of the students, so that, the use of digital resources has a positive impact on teaching-learning methods. This article proposes a methodology that supports teachers in the incorporation of technological resources in their daily practice, taking into account the diversity of the members of the community, accompanying them from the planning phase to the selection of content, all of the above through instruments that allow you to assess technical feasibility, the relationship with the content addressed, visual aspects, agreement with the interests and context of the group, the closure and evaluation of the appropriation of knowledge. The case study presented reflects the positive results obtained with students from the city of Aguascalientes, Mexico, during their training in the fourth grade of basic education (corresponding to the age of 9 years), culminating in the preparation and attendance at the National Competition of Robotics RoboMath Challenge.

Keywords: Education · Cooperative Learning Environments · Inclusive Education · Technology appropriation · ICT · Robotics · STEM

1 Introduction

1.1 ICT in Education and Its Applications

Education is constantly changing, adapting to the needs of the new generations and their ways of learning, one of the most important changes has been education focused on the individual as part of a community. Understanding that in the classroom there are individuals with different ways of learning and perceiving their environment, however, the detection and evaluation of multiple intelligences is a complex issue and without an accessible evaluation for teachers (Garmen, 2019). Another important change in education is the integration of ICT in search of the construction of competences that allow it to be part of the knowledge society; Hence, UNESCO (UNESCO, 2008) has exposed the importance of developing digital skills in teachers necessary for the use of technologies and transmitting knowledge to their students in solving everyday problems. Studies carried out on the teacher's perception of ICTs highlight the importance of training teachers to include technology in their classroom activities as a means that allows students to build complex cognitive processes (Mundy, 2012).

As citizens of the 21st century, the ways of learning have been changing, the skills that must be acquired have been changing in response to the needs of an interconnected world, the appropriation of digital skills has an important role to be part of the knowledge society (Fernandez Morales, 2015). Likewise, it is an inherent quality to this is the development of collaborative work, being part of an interconnected society that contributes more and more to the construction of individual and group knowledge; In response to this, a study was carried out by the Junta de Castillo y León in which the contributions of ICTs in the development of collaborative work strategies are evaluated, observing a positive influence on their use (García-Valcárcel A. B., 2014).

In 1986, the article by D. H. Clements "Effects of Logo and CAI environments on cognition and creativity" explained in its conclusions that boys and girls who used Logo in Early Childhood Education demonstrated greater attention span, more autonomy, and showed greater pleasure. For the discovery of new concepts.

The impact of the use of ICT at different educational levels is an important study topic. The Benemérita Universidad Autónoma de Puebla, for example, through a study indicates that the population between 25 and 38 years of age is more willing to use the ICT in their teaching strategies, being the main tools email, multimedia presentations and web pages (Tapia, 2017). The use of serious video games contributes to the appropriation of skills, since it is attractive, fun and requires activating skills in the student to meet the objectives (Barajas, 2016).

Gamification consists of a system of games and rewards as motivation to obtain significant learning; In a study carried out by the Tecnológico Nacional de México and the Instituto Tecnológico de Culiacán, they were able to observe that the motivators used by gamification contribute to a better acceptance of knowledge, since they take into account their affective emotional states (Zatarín, 2018). In the article Process for modeling competencies for developing serious games proposed by Barajas and Álvarez, the creation of short serious video games is considered as a gamification tool (Barajas, 2016).

The use of mobile devices is a very common practice today, hence Mobile Learning (M-learning) is a concept that allows the generation of knowledge through the use of mobile devices to become a novel and attractive tool for education; The Tecnológico de Monterrey carried out an M-learning project to evaluate the benefits of these learning environments, obtaining positive results as they are supported by educational strategies (Ramos, 2010).

Educational or pedagogical robotics is a trend that has gained great strength for various reasons, it contributes substantially to the acquisition of computational thinking and digital skills, it is also considered an important current for the development of STEM projects (Science, Technology, Engineering and Maths). According to García and Caballero, it has been shown to obtain positive results in the development of computational thinking through robotics in preschoolers using the TangibleK program (Marina Umaschi Bers, 2014), evaluating aspects such as: the development of algorithms; that is to say; the ability to solve problems through the automation or use of educational robots, the correspondence of instruction-action; that the robot fulfills the missions determined by the student for the solution and debugging, that is, to improve and correct the operation of the robot (García-Valcárcel A. &.-G., 2019). The TangibleK program in curricular activities that guide the student in the process of construction, programming and implementation of robotics. Working in the classroom on projects for competition purposes such as the Robomath challenge (Jalisco Ministry of Education, 2018), science fairs, among others, are an application of what gamification is and STEM projects that allow students to be motivated in compliance goals, knowledge acquisition, challenges, etc.

According to Shuchi Grover and Roy Pea, the term STEM proposed by Jeannette Wing's (Wing, 2006) has arrived with great force to be introduced into the education curriculum from an early age, leading to a series of studies that seek to define what is computational thinking (Shuchi & Roy, 2013).

Educational inclusion not only refers to the integration of children with disabilities, but also to the fact of minimizing or eliminating the barriers that may represent a limitation for learning, that is, contemplating the social and cultural diversities that influence the acquisition of knowledge. When talking about inclusion, reference is made to the process through which the school seeks and generates the supports that are required to ensure the educational achievement of all students who attend the school.

The different definitions (Ainscow, 2005; Barton, 1998; Corbett, 1999; D'Alessio, 2011; Iron, 1985; Fostes, 1994; Nirje, 1980; Rodriguez, 1986) social, political and educational aspects stand out and their common denominator is the consideration of integration as a dynamic and complex process by means of which it is possible to gather all the students with or without needs special educational programs in a common educational context.

2 Technology-Assited Intervention Model

Educational trends point every day to a more personalized intervention, where particular characteristics such as learning styles, interests, moods, classroom environments, inclusion are taken into account; gamification proposals are incentives for the achievement of objectives.

Next, the ICT implementation strategy model in preschool education (Oviedo de Luna & Álvarez Rodriguez, 2017) is described, as well as its different phases to assist teachers in the integration of technologies in their school activities, this model is accompanied by instruments that guide each phase of the process. The model is designed in such a way that, together with the pedagogical practices of teachers, it is possible to select applications that will reflect an impact on the use of available digital resources (Table 1).

Table 1. Technology-assisted intervention model.

Stage	About the stage	Instruments
Evaluation	This stage is seeking to know the ways of working, the degree of knowledge acquired, learning styles, interests, motivations, etc. Managers, educational advisors and teachers should be involved in the execution, they can use multiple intelligence tests, diagnostic evaluations, learning styles as support	In this section, diagnostic evaluations, multiple intelligence tests, learning styles, psycho-pedagogical evaluation are recommended, to know the particular needs of each member
Content Selection	Once the teacher has obtained the information from the group, he raises the knowledge that he wishes to develop in the group, he must dose the contents that he wishes to cover in the time designated for compliance with the contents established by the Ministry of Education	Plans and study programs, curricular adaptations for students with high abilities School Planning Forms
Pedagogical Planning	Once the contents that you want to work on have been established, the elaboration of the pedagogical planning begins to establish the times, strategies, activities, evaluation methods, among others. It is important to consider aspects such as collaborative work, the integration of working members, the skills to be developed and the indicators that allow measuring the degree of appropriation. Suggested formats for the elaboration of the pedagogical planning are attached	School Planning Forms

(*continued*)

Table 1. (*continued*)

Stage	About the stage	Instruments
App Select	Once the pedagogical planning has been prepared, taking into account the topics that are to be addressed, we can select the applications that contribute to the development of said competences, according to the dosage established in the planning, the necessary applications that satisfactorily fulfill the contents are sought. The use of the selection instrument proposed in this model is suggested, it presents considerations such as technical feasibility, attention to the interests and context of the working group, correspondence with the contents	Application Selection Tool
Integration of ICT in pedagogical planning	It is important to readjust and capture the activities that will be integrated into the didactic planning, determining the objectives that are sought with the use of each application, the moments of learning, as well as the evaluation activities	School Planning Forms
Sequence Development	The introduction of the teacher to the activities, as well as strategies adapted to the interests and needs of the group will be important factors for obtaining better results, creating a favorable environment for students to acquire the desired skills	We can consider handling observation formats in class that help us record the successes and areas of opportunity in the selected strategies
Evidence and Results	Once the session is over, it is important to see the progress made in the appropriation of content through an evaluation activity, thus giving us elements to have evidence of evaluation progress	Evidence portfolios, checklists, etc.

The previous table shows the phases that make up the model, in addition to the instruments that accompany it. It is a progressive and flexible model that allows adapting the contents to the particular needs of each center. As it is a progressive model, each instrument used will be a resource for the fulfillment of each proposed phase.

3   Analisis of Results

Our case study describes the experiences obtained in the preparation and participation in the RoboMath Challenge contest (Secretaría de Educación Jalisco, 2018) held in Guadalajara Jalisco within the Talentland event (Talent Land, 2019) in its 2018 edition. Said contest consisted of 3 categories according to the school level, these being: primary, secondary and upper secondary. In events like this we see the principles of gamification and STEM clearly embodied, since concepts of mathematics, technology, science and engineering are put into practice, as well as rewards as a motivator for the fulfillment of objectives or challenges.

The primary competition consisted of the elaboration of one or more robots that will carry out three different missions or competition phases, in each phase or mission the robot had to meet characteristics of dimensions, construction and operation. Below is a brief description of each of them:

1. Gladiators in motion: It is a test that consists of a revolving platform, it has gradual increases in its angular velocity (time it takes to complete a turn of the platform). Sand is a rough, non-flat surface. The goal of the test is to knock the opponent out of the arena. Some of the conditions to be met are the dimensions of the robot 10 * 10 * 10 cm, the pieces must not damage the arena or the opposing robots, each round lasts 3:00 min. The robots can be elaborated in any platform of construction and free programming.
2. Mice in search of cheese: From an open platform or commercial robotics platform, develop an autonomous robot (called defender mouse) whose objective will be to detect objects (called robber mice) at a constant distance and knock them down without leaving its track and without falling. The dimensions of the robot must not exceed 10 * 10 * 10 cm, it can use any sensor, but it cannot use signals that interfere with the operation of the robots.
3. Dogs on the run: From an open platform or commercial robotics platform, develop an autonomous robot (called a dog on the run) whose objective will be to travel a race track (escape path) through a black line on a white background, dodging cans (canine obstacles) in the course of this tour. The dimensions of the robot must not exceed 10 * 12 * 14 cm, it can use any sensor, but it cannot use signals that interfere with the operation of the robots.

3.1   How Do We Apply the Model?

We start by evaluating the knowledge of each team in terms of programming, problem solving, algorithm creation as well as teamwork, to decide the best strategy to meet the objectives and see its feasibility.

Considering the skills of the team members, the use of Lego Mindstorms was chosen for its intuitive and flexible interface, allowing to focus efforts on prototyping and problem solving (Fig. 1).

Fig. 1. Construction of prototypes. Through Lego construction sets they were able to experiment and create prototypes for what they considered a robot and solve challenges.

A work scheme was elaborated that doses the pertinent activities to conclude the challenges of the competition:

Preparation of a work log, this must be kept to record the different activities that the work team carries out; elaboration of prototypes that comply with the regulatory dimensions; study the issues related to each challenge, that is, what factors influence the performance of the robot, such as angular speed, how the robot's motors work, among others; competition strategies through flowcharts that will be reflected in the robot's programming; finally, the team poster (Fig. 2).

In a very short period of time, considering the complexity of the challenge, the activities were prepared in days of 5 to 8 h per day, each day they had to record the activities they carried out as well as the evidence.

Assigned the activities required for participation, and considering the required materials, we began with prototyping, having a base robot we were able to study the properties of the motors and some of the factors related to each challenge, several sessions were dedicated to this activity, in parallel, a robot was made that complied with the regulatory dimensions.

Once the construction phase of the robot was finished, the objectives of the tournament were announced, which challenges the robot should meet, and from there generate the related concepts, that is, the skills that must be acquired are selected in order to meet the challenges in their different stages. Physics consultancies were used to understand the effects of the arena, in this case a three-dimensional simulator was selected to make

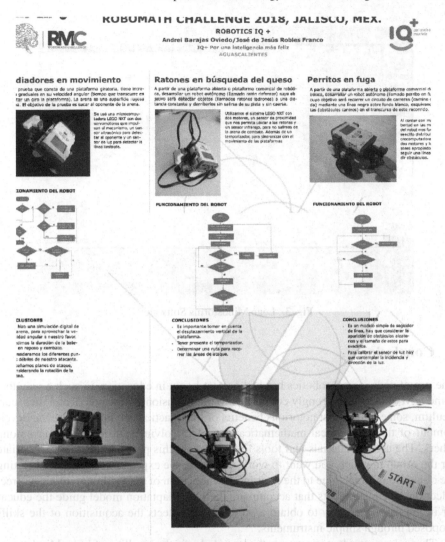

Fig. 2. Poster prepared by the team to present in the competition.

it easier for them to visualize the competition arena, based on this representation they could then draw the course of action to meet different challenges (Fig. 3).

The experience acquired by the competitors was of great importance in their training, they managed to appropriate advanced knowledge of physics and mathematics in a short period, all this thanks to the use of the appropriate tools for the time, age and experience of each one of the participants members.

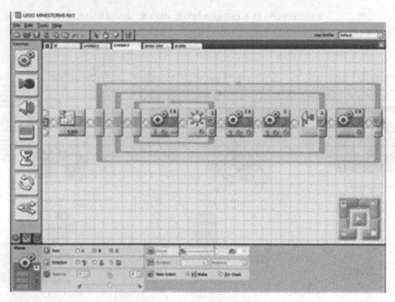

Fig. 3. Lego Mindstorms Software.

4 Conclusions

The use of pedagogical robotics has had a great boom in education, in such a way that some governments are strongly committed to the inclusion of this practice in their curriculum, some of the most notorious benefits of this practice in education are the development of thinking logical-mathematical, problem solving, abstract thinking among others. The use of materials and tools to be used for this practice must be appropriate for the group in which you want to work, obtaining the expected learning and meeting the objective is largely due to the appropriate mediation of the facilitator and its correct selection. The instruments that accompany the ICT adaptation model guide the educator in the tasks necessary to obtain a product that reflects the acquisition of the skills proposed through simple instruments.

Through an introductory course, the knowledge in the handling of Lego Mindstorms technology of the Robomath Challenge participants was evaluated, allowing the selection of relevant contents for the handling of the robot, to select which robotics equipment would be used, indicators of the model of adaptation of ICT to preschool, such as the work platform, ease of use, user interface, and intuitive handling.

From the experience, a favorable attitude to the use of technologies for the appropriation of competences is observed, there was an adequate understanding of the terms and conditions of the competition, the members adapted to collaborative work and the use of the capacities that each member was capable of. to contribute to the team. There is a good acceptance of the approach of particular objectives that contribute to a general objective in this case the participation in the contest; We can also observe that project-based work benefits the acquisition of transversal skills, that is, different skills are addressed to achieve a final product. The methodology manages to integrate different capacities of the team members, since the instruments are oriented to unite the pedagogical practices of the applicator's success with the digital resources accepted by the members of the group.

Regarding programming, the most important challenges were given in terms of sensor calibration, learning to handle the different degrees of illumination, the values that the microcomputer receives for its performance.

References

Barajas, A.Á.: Process for modeling competencies for developing serious games. Revista Electrónica de Investigación Educativa **18**(3), 146–160 (2016). http://redie.uabc.mx/redie/article/view/1071

Fernández Morales, K.V.: APROPIACIÓN TECNOLÓGICA: UNA VISIÓN DESDE LOS MODELOS Y LAS TEORÍAS QUE LA EXPLICAN. Perspectiva Educacional, Formación de Profesores **54**, 109–125 (2015). http://www.redalyc.org/articulo.oa?id=333339872008

García-Valcárcel, A.: Robotics to develop computational thinking in early Childhood Education. [Robótica para desarrollar el pensamiento computacional en Educación Infantil]. Comunicar (59), 63–72 (2019). https://doi.org/10.3916/C59-2019-06

García-Valcárcel, A.B.: ICT in Collaborative Learning in the Classrooms of Primary and Secondary Education. [Las TIC en el aprendizaje colaborativo en el aula de Primaria y Secundaria]. Comunicar, 65–74 (2014). https://doi.org/10.3916/C42-2014-06

Garmen, P.: Inteligencias múltiples y videojuegos: Evaluación e intervención con softwareTOI. Comunicar (58), 95–104 (2019). https://doi.org/10.3916/C58-2019-09

Marina Umaschi Bers, L.F.: Computational thinking and tinkering: exploration of an early childhood robotics curriculum **72**, 145–157 (2014). http://www.elsevier.com/locate/compedu

Mundy, M.A.: Teacher's perceptions of technology use in the schools. SAGE Open 1(2) (2012)

Oviedo de Luna, A.C., Álvarez Rodriguez, F.: Estrategia de implementacion de tic's en la educación preescolar. Intersaberes **12**(26), 241–262 (2017)

Ramos, A.H.-M.: Developing cognitive skills with mobile learning: a case study. [Desarrollo de habilidades cognitivas con aprendizaje móvil: un estudio de casos]. Comunicar (34), 201–209 (2010). https://doi.org/10.3916/C34-2010-03-20

Secretaría de Educación Jalisco: Robomath Challenge (2018). http://robomath.se.jalisco.gob.mx/robomath-challenge-2018/

Secretaria de Educación Pública: Programa de estudios 2011/ guia para la educadora-básica. Portal de la Educación Básica en México (2011). www.reformapreescolar.sep.gob.mx/actualizacion/programa/Preescolar2011.pdf. Accessed 03 Oct 2014

Shuchi, G., Roy, P.: Computational thinking in K–12: a review of the state of the field. Educ. Res. **42**(1), 38–43 (2013). https://doi.org/10.3102/0013189X1246305

Talent Land (2019). https://www.talent-land.mx/

Tapia, C.N.: El uso de las TIC en las prácticas académicas de los profesores de la Benemérita Universidad Autónoma de Puebla. Revista Electrónica de Investigación Educativa **19**(3), 115–125 (2017). https://doi.org/10.24320/redie.2017.19.3.1270

UNESCO: Estándares de competencias en TIC para docentes (2008). www.oei.es/historico/tic/UNESCOEstandaresDocentes.pdf

Wing, J.M.: Computional Thinking. Commun. ACM **49**(3), 33–35 (2006)

Zatarín, R.: Reconocimiento afectivo y gamificación aplicados al aprendizaje. Revista Electrónica de Investigación Educativa **20**(3), 115–125 (2018). https://doi.org/10.24320/redie.2018.20.3.1636

Children's Literature and Technology to Promote Motivation and Inclusion in Nursery Schools. The Case Study of Babalibri's Storie da Ascoltare

Anna Ascenzi and Elena Girotti[(⊠)]

Department of Education, Cultural Heritage and Tourism, University of Macerata, Macerata, Italy
{anna.ascenzi,e.girotti1}@unimc.it

Abstract. Considering the contemporary debate on children's literature, technology and accessibility, the paper investigates the use in the school context of a specific editorial product to understand its potentialities in terms of inclusion, motivation and modifications of the reading experience. A preliminary interview with the publishing house Babalibri has been carried out to gather background information on its project and to understand how the illustrated picture books were translated, thanks also to the use of technology, into audio format, and to figure out the impact it already had, for example on the reading experience of blind people and in the promotion of access to reading during the COVID-19 pandemic. Secondly, an exploratory experiment and investigation have been conducted with preschool children. Results suggest that the project impacted children's motivation and changed their consumption of the reading experience. Controversial outcomes have been produced in terms of inclusion and further experimentation is needed in this field.

Keywords: Audiobooks · Children's Literature · Inclusion · Literacy Development · Visual Impairment

1 Introduction

In recent years, the importance of reading and telling stories to children has emerged both for the capacity of storytelling to give voice to the world of feelings and emotions [1] and for the contribution of children's literature to the development of literacy [2]. In particular, the central role of reading aloud and dialogic reading has proven adequate for [2–4] promoting the processes of recognizing and naming emotions and of developing literacy through storytelling. Furthermore, the benefits of accessing to and experiencing children's literature has been also recognized by the UN Convention on the Rights of the Child and Adolescent [5] which encourages, in Article 17, the production and dissemination of children's books. In addition to that, the UN Convention on the Rights of People with Disabilities emphasizes that people with disabilities should be guaranteed "the full realization of all human rights and fundamental freedoms without discrimination of any kind on the basis of disability" [6]. Therefore, several studies focus on the need to make the reading experience inclusive and accessible [7, 8] by promoting, for instance, Augmentative and Alternative Communication interventions [9–11]. High-tech aided Augmentative and Alternative Communication systems show how technology can contribute to make reading accessible [7]; more in general, technology can be considered as an environmental factor that gives support in promoting the Quality of Life [12–14] and so, it can play a role in eliminating discriminations and fostering the right to read, as well as the pleasures and benefits derived from reading listed above. Moreover, technology can make reading accessible to reluctant readers through e-books and audiobooks [15] or can contribute to social inclusion among children from minorities and difficult backgrounds [16]. With specific reference to audiobooks, research has also focused on their impact on learners' language competence [17] and their attitude towards listening [18]. Together with promoting access to reading, technology has also changed the experience of reading itself [19, 20]: the production and spreading of e-books, audiobooks, online literature, and apps contribute to a change in literacy practices, in the consumption of books and in their production [21]. As Aliagas & Margallo write quoting Kress [22]: "Nowadays, e-reading devices are widening access to these forms of literature for children through a particular process of experimentation with multimodality and interactivity that is changing the nature of children's literature itself" [21].

In this context, this paper describes a research study conducted in the period from November 2022 to January 2023; the study focused on the Italian publishing house Babalibri and its editorial project Storie da ascoltare - Stories to listen – which "combines the importance of reading aloud with listening to music" [23] and which is composed of "stories accessible to all and everyone, even those with a visual impairment" [24]. Taking all of this into consideration the study has two main objectives. The first one is to analyze how the literary texts were translated by Babalibri into audio format, thanks to the use of technology too. The second objective of the research is to investigate how the Storie d'ascoltare format can be used by teachers in classrooms and how they can foster motivation in students and the inclusion of children of different backgrounds and with different needs.

2 A Pilot Case: Babalibri and Its Storie d'ascoltare

The publishing house Babalibri was founded in 1999 in Milano by Francesca Archinto; since its foundation, it has worked in the field of children's literature to make accessible to the Italian public the best and most famous books for children published abroad. In addition, it works in strict contact with schools, libraries, and bookshops with the aim to promote reading and organize creative activities and laboratories so that children can encounter the pleasure of reading and the adventures it involves [25]. In 2020, to celebrate its anniversary, Babalibri decided to create on their website the section Storie da ascoltare: it offers twenty books from the Babalibri catalogue read by an actress and accompanied by classical music. Thanks to technology, this project "combines the importance of reading aloud with listening to music" [23] and everyone could listen to them provided that they have an Internet connection. These stories were also made available – and still are - from the MLOL Digital Library, an online platform with the largest collection of content for all Italian libraries [24] providing free access to books and magazines. In the MLOL Digital Library, Babalibri's Storie da ascoltare are described as "stories accessible to all and everyone, even those with a visual impairment" [24].

An online semi-structured interview [26] was conducted with the editor and the curator of the project so to understand how the project was born, what the Storie da Ascoltare represent, and which definition and experiences of accessibility they contribute to create. Moreover, questions were asked regarding the modalities used for the books translation into vocally narrated stories accompanied by music.

As for the genesis of the project, the creator and the editor of the project explained that the Storie da Ascoltare have an antecedent; in the previous years, Babalibri has published the children's books Piccolo blu e piccolo giallo [27] and Pezzettino [28] by Leo Lionni in the special edition of Fiabe musicali - musical fairy tales. By scanning the QR code at the end of each book, it is possible to access a webpage from the Babalibri website; here, it is possible to listen to the story read by a professional actor and accompanied by classical music pieces performed by professional musicians. In this way, narrative and musical language intertwine in what scholar Rita Valentino Merletti has described - in the in-depth parts of one of the volumes - as an "extraordinary path of discovery of music and reading together" [27]. Consequently, the visual and tactile perception of the images and the paper book are intertwined with listening to the story and music. Due to this, according to Babalibri, the Fiabe musicali cannot be considered audiobooks but as a complex editorial product that combines the illustrated book with the musical album.

In 2020, to celebrate the publishing house's twentieth anniversary at the Bologna Children's Book Fair, Babalibri decided to take up the idea behind the Fiabe Musicali - musical fairy tales, focusing however only on the listening dimension. Given the centrality of listening and the absence of images and physical visual support, the writing had to be able to well narrate, describe and evoke the illustrations: this was one of the criteria used to select twenty stories for this project from the publishing house's catalogue of illustrated books. According to the creator and the curator of the project, in the Stories da Ascoltare format, the illustrations are indeed present, but in a different form: it is the voice that makes them possible and alive. If in the Fiabe musicali experiment, attention was already given to a fluid and light reading, in the Storie da Ascoltare project, the voice and the reading were also supposed to help the listener understand and imagine the illustrations. Therefore, the actress chosen for the reading of the Stories focused heavily on the different tones and expressiveness of the voice. Moreover, an additional element was used to encourage the encounter between the illustrations and the listeners' imagination: music. Thus, as with the Fiabe musicali, pieces of classical music that were well suited to the peculiarities and atmospheres of the chosen books were selected. They were performed by professional musicians who worked to foster absolute harmony between the musical pieces and the reading of the texts.

Due to the first lockdown of the COVID-19 pandemic in spring 2020, it was not possible to launch the Storie da Ascoltare project during the Bologna Children's Book Fair. However, the publishing house did not abandon the project and shared it on its website in a section called Radiobaba; so, some opportunities for accessibility and inclusion arose. Indeed, everyone could have access to the Stories provided that they had an internet connection. At the same time, the collaboration with the Unione Italiana dei Ciechi e degli Ipovedenti UICI - Italian Union of the Blind and Visually Impaired also began. The creator of the Storie da Ascoltare was volunteering for the distribution of braille books from the Italian Library for the blind Regina Margherita among blind people belonging to her local community. This gave her the idea to propose the Stories to the UICI section in Varese and to the blind and visually impaired people who turn to it. The Storie da Ascoltare were thus 'tested' by these listeners with visual impairment, and, in a way, they also confirmed what Best and Clark claimed, namely that, during the lockdown, "audiobooks were a lifeline for many children and young people, particularly those for whom access to print books was limited" [15]. The collaboration extended to other local UICIs and resulted in the Storie da Ascoltare being included in the national MLOL catalogue [24].

After the lockdown, to support this project that aims to be strongly accessible by including children and adults, the publishing house proposed the Storie da Ascoltare during in-person listening workshops with people with visual impairment and during training courses for educators revealing all the potential of the online audio format as an effective tool vehiculating impressions, information, and feelings.

Finally, the project also aims to vehiculate the pleasure derived from the contact with music in general and classical music in particular, by attempting to make it more accessible and usable.

In this context, it seems relevant to try to verify if and to what extent the Storie da Ascoltare can be used in a school context as an enabling technology to avoid students' isolation and improve inclusive teaching practice.

The following sections will describe the experimentation conducted in a local Nursery School and will illustrate the context, the methodology used and the outcomes.

3   Storie da Ascoltare at School: Research Context and Methodology

The experimentation was conducted on a sample consisting of preschool children from a local Nursery School spread over two different locations. Normally, there are 140 children, but about 20 of them were absent on the days of the activity. Three of them have a disability: one child has high-functioning autism; another child has a motor disability; one child suffers from a severe cognitive disability; the latter was absent. A quarter of the children involved are either second-generation migrants or from disadvantaged social backgrounds. Most of the children are born in Italy; some of them have one or both parents of foreign origins. Different areas of the world are present with countries such as China, Moldavia, Poland, Kosovo, Macedonia, Albania, Romania, Morocco, Guinea Bissau, Senegal, Iran, Cuba, and China. Some children come from Ukraine. Many of them show language difficulties. Attention problems, listening and comprehension difficulties, struggle with autonomous work are reported in almost all the classes.

Seven teachers were involved in the project: two of them are undergoing specialized training in literacy education and children's literature reading; in addition, three of the teachers involved are support teachers.

Three stories - of the twenty available - were indicated to the school, each relating to each age group (3, 4, 5 years). The selected stories were chosen following the publisher's advice and taking into account their length, their potential to generate interest and the themes addressed such as shyness, living with different animals and different emotions. However, the teachers were allowed to choose a different story from the three suggested. Furthermore, they were given complete freedom in the modality through which the activity was introduced and carried out, as the research also aimed at understanding if and how different approaches could contribute to making the Storie da Ascoltare truly enabling technologies.

Inspired by study cases on the use of technology in school [16], on educational planning [29] and on cultural accessibility [30], a semi-structured questionnaire was used for the survey. The questionnaire was disseminated via Google Forms and it consisted of four sections, composed of closed and open items [31] and organized as follow:

• The first section consists of ten items concerning the composition of the class, age of the children and their social and geographical origin, the possible presence of disabilities and problematic situations. It had to be filled in after the first time the activity was conducted.
• The second section was composed of nine items concerning teachers' practices, the modalities through which they usually propose children's literature in the classroom, the way they carried out the Stories da Ascoltare activity, their impressions, and any difficulties they encountered. It had to be filled in after the first time the activity was conducted.
• The third section was composed of eleven items concerning the children's reactions, their understanding of the story, the interest shown and future applications. It had to be filled in after the first time the activity was conducted.
• The fourth section had to be filled in after the repetition of the listening activity, and it was composed of twelve items concerning how many times they had already used the Storie da Ascoltare, the story they listened to, the effects in terms of children's interest and their ability to understand and articulate language.

A descriptive analysis of the answers [29] was carried out in order to figure out the emergent attitudes towards the Storie da Ascoltare and their potential and effectiveness in promoting inclusion in the classrooms.

4 Data Analysis

It can be noticed that classroom reading emerges as a shared and often implemented practice: daily for some teachers, weekly for others, but still very present. Various techniques are used, such as dramatized reading through puppets or reading during circle time. The tools are different, too: not only paper books, but also videos and kamishibai. All the teachers sometimes use the interactive whiteboard for telling stories and make children dance or listen to music; one of them underlines that recently, they have decreased its use because contemporary children are very used to watching videos and using electronic devices, so they propose listening often and watching less frequently. In one case, the weekly reading appointment is introduced and concluded by a mediating character, a mouse with glasses. In general, there emerges an awareness of the capacity of storytelling to capture the attention and draw out the emotions and experiences of the children, to increase their knowledge by leveraging their imagination, to create opportunities to discuss the sequentiality of events, to reason about cause-and-effect, and to make hypotheses. All teachers also believe reading improves listening skills, memorization, and attention and stimulate language and vocabulary. Finally, for three months, from February to April, a book loan is activated every year to provide families with a moment to share with their children, to get to know each other better and strengthen the parent-child relationship.

Regarding the activity with the Storie da Ascoltare, it was introduced in different ways: one teacher used the mediating character utilized also in the case of the 'normal' reading moment, dividing the class into two smaller groups.

In another case, the class was divided into two groups to encourage attention, and one group at a time listened to the story. The children were arranged in a circle, sitting on benches next to each other. Listening was presented in a whisper to create curiosity and interest.

Another teacher invited her students to create a comfortable corner, closed the curtains and turned the light off.

In two other cases, listening was announced by a conversation about books and the possibility of enjoying them differently than usual; a teacher then read the title and asked what they imagined. Again, listening was presented as something exceptional, an activity that had never yet been proposed and linked to a new instrument: a large loudspeaker.

After listening, five teachers out of seven proposed activities to be carried out, such as dramatizing the story, collective re-elaboration and storytelling in circle time. In some cases, children were also invited to choose a character to color and to draw either a picture of the story or their favorite part.

Regarding the difficulties encountered, four out of seven teachers reported problems with attention and bewilderment of the children who, in one case, could not follow all the characters, while, in another, they found the story too long. It is worth mentioning that maintaining attention and listening time was one of the main difficulties often encountered also in 'classic' reading activities, without the use of the Storie da Ascoltare.

We asked the teachers' opinions on this extended, virtual, technology-mediated type of 'book' and its use in the classroom. The results that emerged seem somewhat mixed. For half of them, the Storie da Ascoltare are an excellent tool to train the children to listen and to stimulate concentration and imagination. One teacher expresses a positive opinion, but highlights the difficulty for the youngest children, aged three, to imagine the characters; another teacher thinks the idea is interesting but has difficulty in rendering with words and music alone the close interaction between illustrations, narration and graphic code that is instead the main characteristic of picture books. Finally, a final teacher points out how difficult it is to capture and maintain the children's attention without the support of the pictures and feels that the stories are perhaps too long. It can be observed that these last three less enthusiastic opinions concern activities carried out with three different stories and implemented in different age groups. The class where the greatest difficulty was reported consisted of fifteen pupils aged four/five, all Italian and without any disability or certified disorder. The other teacher who highlighted some attention problems proposed the story in a class of twenty-five four-year-olds, with four Ukrainian children and three of non-European origin. In these latter two classes, distraction replaced the initial amazement.

As for the remaining classes, the children showed curiosity and were engrossed in the music, which, according to one teacher, was in one case crucial in maintaining attention even though it produced a lot of movement in the children (aged 3).

All the children reacted differently, imagining the characters aloud, laughing, communicating their feelings or remaining silent. In general, children with speech difficulties, little knowledge of the Italian language (e.g., Ukrainian children) and few skills in personal autonomy and emotional regulation during the Story tended to become distracted, as did those who usually have limited communication skills and are unresponsive to any proposal that requires listening and dialogue. These children had more difficulties in the comprehension, but when circle time activities and joint reworking were carried out, they managed to put the pieces together and collectively reconstruct the whole story. In all cases, the children highlighted the lack of images as the main difference with the paper medium and, at times, the consequent difficulty in following along. In one class in particular - where the music was particularly appreciated - the children were highly involved emotionally and by the novelty of the medium proposed.

All the teachers, except one, believe that if repeated over a long period of time the activity with the Storie da Ascoltare might first and foremost foster the children's emotional skills and also language acquisition, especially with regard to phonological competence (i.e., the ability to perceive and recognize sounds), listening skills and vocabulary expansion. Only one teacher considers this tool to be cold and detached.

Moreover, all the teachers, except one, believe that, given the possibility of accessing these stories also from home, it might be a good idea to implement and promote a joint listening project in the classroom and at home to favour children's literacy development, foster communication between families and the school, and promote trust between parents and teachers.

As for the repetition of the activity with the Storie da Ascoltare, it was repeated on successive days, for three or four times, by listening to the same story. In two cases, another story was also added. A verbal introduction was almost always proposed before the activity; in one case, the teachers summarized the story. The mediating character was not re-proposed; in half of the cases, a repeated and shared rituality was recreated, which is considered important in dialogic reading practices [3]: in the three cases indicated, the children recognized the prepared instruments, the use of the loudspeaker and the soft setting by associating them with this type of reading activity. In one case, the children seemed more attentive and able to listen and understand.

These results suggest the important role of the teachers have in the organization of the activities realized with the Storie da Ascoltare. In addition to this and concerning an expected difference in terms of children's motivation and inclusion between reading a traditional book and listening to it in the online version of the Storie, the data analyzed partially confirm the ability of the Storie and the music that accompanies them to create emotional involvement in children but do not give significant indications on the inclusion of students with language and communication difficulties, including the child with the autistic disorder. Despite the fact that previous research has shown that "audiobooks have many benefits such as especially developing vocabulary skills in students, getting accustomed to literary language, anticipating unfolding events in the content they listen to, facilitating the interpretation process of the text, and raising language awareness" [18], these effects were not concretely observed in the experiment carried out, where, on the contrary, faced with the dematerialization of the book object and the physical disappearance of the illustrations, teachers reported increasing difficulty for children with language, communication and attention issues. It is true, however, that the processes of literacy development are extremely complex, especially in preschool children [2] and more careful and prolonged observation should be made.

5 Discussion and Conclusion

This paper focused on the editorial project Storie da Ascoltare realized by the Italian publishing house Babalibri and investigates its use in the school context to understand its potentialities in terms of inclusion, motivation and modifications of the reading experience. The literature review conducted in planning this research made it possible to assume that the audio format of the editorial project analyzed and the technological and multimodal features characterizing it should have widened the access to children's literature by changing its nature [21] and should have contributed to social inclusion among people from minorities and difficult back-grounds [16].

The investigation conducted was an exploratory study, which therefore has all the limitations of research of this kind. Given the brevity of the experience, we were not able to demonstrate the effects on inclusion and literacy development and we did not show consistent results in terms of impact on listening and attention skills, especially in children with difficulties; this path is still open, especially given to the success that the publishing house has had with people with visual impairments, and which is a symptom of the inclusive potential of this technology-mediated publishing product. Probably, in order to have more significant results in this respect, longer, more structured and participatory research should be conducted; furthermore, we believe that it could be useful to work on promoting greater synergy between the publishing house, the university and teachers, perhaps through specific training courses, designed and implemented taking into account the peculiarities of individual contexts, as happened in the case of the collaboration between Babalibri and the UICI.

However, the experience conducted in the Nursery School has shown how the Storie da Ascoltare have an impact on the modalities through which the reading experience is enjoyed, modifying it [21]; furthermore, due to their being easily accessible and usable, they could be used to strengthen relations with families and reinforce the community gathered around the school. Future studies should be also conducted to investigate the latter hypothesis.

References

1. Ascenzi, A.: La letteratura per l'infanzia oggi. Vita e Pensiero, Milano (2003)
2. Arnold, D.H., Lonigan, C.J., Whitehurst, G.J., Epstein, J.N.: Accelerating language development through picture book reading: replication and extension to a videotape training format. J. Educ. Psychol. 86(2), 235–243 (1994)

3. Panza, C.: Born to read and dialogic reading: for whom and how. Quaderni ACP **22**(2), 95–101 (2015)
4. De Rossi, M.: Narrazione e nuovi orizzonti metodologici. In: De Rossi, M., Petrucco, C. (eds.) Le narrazioni digitali per l'educazione e la formazione, pp. 17–18. Carocci editore, Roma (2013)
5. UN: Convenzione sui diritti dell'infanzia e adolescenza, Gazzetta Ufficiale 11 giugno 1991. https://www.datocms-assets.com/30196/1607611722-convenzionedirittiinfanzia.pdf. Accessed 17 Oct 2022
6. UN Convenzione sui diritti delle persone con disabilità (2009). https://www.esteri.it/mae/res ource/doc/2016/07/c_01_convenzione_onu_ita.pdf. Accessed 17 Oct 2022
7. Costantino, M.A.: Costruire libri e storie con la CAA: gli IN-book per l'intervento precoce e l'inclusione, Edizioni Erickson, Trento (2011)
8. Malaguti, E.: Inclusive early childhood education and right of literacy even for children with disabilities. Form@re - Open J. per la Formazione Rete **17**(2), 101–112 (2017). ISSN 1825-7321. https://doi.org/10.13128/formare-20564
9. Cafiero, J.M.: Comunicazione aumentativa e alternativa. Strumenti e strategie per l'autismo e i deficit di comunicazione. Edizioni Erickson, Trento (2009)
10. Nicoli, C., Re, L.G., Bezze, E.: Caratteristiche ed efficacia degli interventi di Comunicazione Aumentativa Alternativa in bambini affetti da Disturbi dello Spettro Autistico. Children's Nurses–Italian J. Pediatr. Nurs. Sci. **8**(1), 27–34 (2016)
11. Fontani, S.: La Comunicazione Aumentativa Alternativa per l'inclusione sociale del giovane adulto con Disturbi dello Spettro Autistico. Uno studio randomizzato. Italian J. Spec. Educ. Incl **5**(1), 73–88 (2017)
12. Verdugo, M.A., Navas, P., Gómez, L.E., Schalock, R.L.: The concept of quality of life and its role in enhancing human rights in the field of intellectual disability. J. 4 4 Intellect. Disabil. Res. JIDR **56**(11), 1036–1045 (2012). https://doi.org/10.1111/j.1365-2788.2012.01585.x
13. Giaconi, C.: Qualità della Vita e adulti con disabilità. Percorsi di ricerca e prospettive inclusive. Franco Angeli, Milano (2015)
14. Giaconi, C., Capellini, S.A., Del Bianco, N., Taddei, A., D'Angelo, I.: Study Empowerment per l'inclusione. Educ. Sci. Soc. **2**, 166–183 (2018)
15. Best, E., Clark, C.: National Literacy Trust (United Kingdom): The Role of Audiobooks to Engage Reluctant Readers and Underrepresented Children and Young People. A National Literacy Trust Research Report. In National Literacy Trust (2021)
16. Zacharová, J.: Digital support of developing narrative competence among children from excluded rural communities in Slovakia. In: 15th International Scientific Conference eLearning and Software for Education, Bucharest (2019). https://doi.org/10.12753/2066-026X-19-080
17. Alcantud-Díaz, M., Gregori-Signes, C.: Audiobooks: improving fluency and instilling literary skills and education for development. Tejuelo **20**, 111–125 (2014)
18. Çarkit, C.: Evaluation of audiobook listening experiences of 8th grade students: an action research. Educ. Policy Anal. Strateg. Res. **15**(4) (2020). https://doi.org/10.29329/epasr.2020.323.8
19. Campagnaro, M.: International Conference "The Child and the Book 2013": Children's Literature, Technology and Imagination. Research, Problems and Perspectives. Libri Liberi, 151–152 (2013)
20. Araújo, M.D.V., Moro, R.G.: Mediação de leitura literária digital com crianças. Perspectiva **39**(1), 1–23 (2021) https://doi.org/10.5007/2175-795X.2021.e72463
21. Aliagas, C., Margallo, A.M.: Children's responses to the interactivity of storybook apps in family shared reading events involving the iPad. Literacy **51**(1), 44–52 (2017). https://doi.org/10.1111/lit.12089

22. Kress, G.: Literacy in the New Media Age. Routledge, London (2003)
23. Babalibri, Storie da Ascoltare. https://www.babalibri.it/categorie-ascolti/storie-da-ascoltare/. Accessed 27 Oct 2022
24. MLOL Media Library Online. https://www.medialibrary.it/home/index.aspx. Accessed 27 Oct 2022
25. Babalibri, Chi siamo. https://www.babalibri.it/chi-siamo/. Accessed 09 Feb 2023
26. Lucidi, F., Alivernini, F., Pedon, A.: Metodologia della ricerca qualitativa. Il Mulino, Bologna (2008)
27. Lionni, L.: Piccolo blu e piccolo giallo. Ed. Speciale Fiaba musicale. Babalibri, Milano (2015)
28. Lionni, L.: Pezzettino. Ed. Speciale Fiaba musicale. Babalibri, Milano (2019)
29. Amatori, G., Del Bianco, N., Aparecida Capellini, S., Giaconi, C.: Training of specialized teachers and individualized educational planning: a research on perceptions. Form@re - Open J. per la Formazione in rete **21**(1), 24–37 (2021). https://doi.org/10.13128/form-10435
30. Giaconi C., Ascenzi A., Del Bianco N., D'Angelo I., Aparecida Capellini S.: Virtual and augmented reality for the cultural accessibility of people with autism spectrum disorders, a pilot study. Int. J. Inclusive Museum **14**(1), 95–106 (2021). https://doi.org/10.18848/1835-2014/CGP/v14i01/95-106
31. Trinchero, R.: I metodi della ricerca educativa. Editori Laterza, Lecce (2004)

Cowork: Gamified, Virtual Coworking Web Application to Support Remote Learning for Students

Isaac Blake and Tania Roy(✉)

New College of Florida, Sarasota, FL 34243, USA
{isaac.blake18,troy}@ncf.edu

Abstract. Coworking spaces allow students focused on different tasks to work in the same environment, support productivity and self-efficacy, and promote social interactions and peer support. These spaces, physically, can include coffee shops, libraries, dedicated coworking spaces, and·other locations. Since the onset of the COVID-19 pandemic, many of these spaces have been shuttered to potential visitors or are simply unsafe. Extended online learning periods during COVID-19 have led to social isolation and decreased student productivity and motivation. Some online applications begin to address the void left by the closure of these physical spaces. However, they all suffer from a lack of real-time interaction, productivity tools or focus, major accessibility issues, or a combination of those mentioned above. Cowork is a new interactive system that supports online coworking for students in a comfortable, virtual environment, built with accessibility features like keyboard navigation and screen-reader support.

Keywords: Education/Learning · Prototyping/Implementation · Accessibility

1 Introduction

Cowork is a virtual, accessible online web application designed to emulate a coworking environment. It is in the form of a two-paneled website. Cowork was developed during the pandemic to support student-led study groups that abruptly switched to Zoom. Cowork consists of two panels; the left-side panel includes an open tab, like a list of tasks, a chat, a timer, or productivity statistics. The right-side panel is a top-down view of a virtual workspace, with avatars representing online members of the space. Users can chat with each other, set timers to work simultaneously, share their tasks, and generally work in the same online environment. The application is designed to be accessible, focusing on keyboard-only navigation and screen-reader use. This paper describes the development of Cowork and its features that were designed from a student-centric view keeping the needs of an online learning modality in mind.

2 Background

Coworking spaces in the physical world have been widespread, especially in workspace design and building architecture. Coworking space is defined as a space that "professionals opt to work in for the opportunity of social interaction" [1] to dimmish the feeling of isolation that many people struggle with working alone. Bilandzic et al. describe a coworking space as a place that provides information on what others are working on and provides an opportunity for ice-breaker conversations and networking [2]. Several coworking spaces around the globe support flexible workspaces, and a leading example of this is WeWork [1], which provides physical spaces to facilitate coworking. Several technology companies, such as Google and Facebook, also offer these to incentivize their team members to work from any global location [3].

Coworking in the digital world has also promoted the creation of several tools such as Slack [4] and Discord [5] for communication, Trello and JIRA [6, 7] to support task prioritization, and Google Calendar-like applications [8, 9] to track productivity. Software like Habitica [15] provides a social version of traditional productivity software with asynchronous interactions between users. Gather [13] provides users with shared virtual spaces to decorate and interact with participants in the space. In conjunction with the workforce, education, significantly higher education, is another domain where coworking is promoted and encouraged to engage students in social conversation and promote growth.

Most educational institutions have libraries or coffee shops to help foster collaborative learning environments. Digital or physical coworking spaces foster collaboration and give users a sense of belonging. The COVID-19 pandemic resulted in the closure of most physical spaces for collaboration. The tools for coworking, such as Slack and Discord, support communication, but the sense of social space still needs to be replicated. Habitica adds social and coworking elements to productivity software, but all interactions are asynchronous, so the benefits of coworking may be diminished. Gather provides live interactions between users but lacks in-depth productivity features or a way to share what users are working on with others. The pandemic also made it difficult for students who had to quickly switch to remote learning environments to adapt and create healthy study habits. A study conducted by Campbell and Kelly in 2021 discussed how virtual homework sessions on video conferencing platforms like Zoom helped keep students engaged and promoted healthy work habits [10]. The primary motivation behind the development of the software artifact Cowork was to create a space for students to work together and get a sense of social gathering when it was impossible to meet people in study halls safely. The features of Cowork support collaborative learning, self-reflection, social commitment, peer support, and accountability to help alleviate the stress of learning online in an isolated space [11, 12]. A software artifact must be usable and accessible to be an accurate digital coworking tool. A software artifact must be usable by everyone who wishes to work with others; it thus must be broadly accessible.

2.1 Web Accessibility

Web Content Accessibility Guidelines (WCAG) by the W3C [13, 14] have provided several guidelines for creating accessible web pages and software artifacts. However, many websites are inaccessible despite these guidelines' pervasiveness [15]. As the goal and motivation of this project are to foster collaboration and a sense of belonging, developing a software artifact accessible to different user groups was of utmost importance [16]. The necessity of building technology that is universal accessibly has become extremely urgent, primarily due to the pandemic.

The design and development of Cowork kept in mind the requirements of the primary target audience (students) and accessibility principles by incorporating features these other services lack: it incorporates real-time user-to-user interactions, features of traditional productivity tools, and added capabilities of coworking, like chatting, seeing what others are working on, and running focus sessions with others.

3 System Architecture Diagram

The system architecture (Fig. 1) is split into a server and a client. The server is built in Python to host a WebSocket server. When the client, a static Angular application [5], loads, it connects to the remote WebSocket server, allowing the client and server to maintain a continuous connection. Both the server and client are organized mainly through features. The server has handlers for each significant feature, where a handler is responsible for reading and responding to messages sent from clients and executing the server-side logic relating to one feature; for example, the server routes all tasks-related messages to the Tasks Handler, which then reads that message, executes logic and replies to the client if necessary. All communication between the server and client is based on messages formatted in JSON, which are serialized and sent back and forth. Every message has channel and type attributes. When the server receives such messages, the server uses the specified channel to route the message to the interested handler; then, the handler uses the type to route the message to a specific function responsible for that message. On the client side, a subscription pattern is used instead. Each component interested in processing messages received from the server provides the Socket service with a callback function to be executed when messages with a specific channel are received. That callback function then routes the message to the logic within the interested component responsible for handling the type of message received. This architecture was used across all iterations of the software.

4 Software Artifact Design

4.1 Target Audience

The target audience for this application is students across educational institutions, and the design of the application keeps in mind the various aspects of learning and learning styles and abilities that students have. Students can organize and tag their tasks as they see fit. This application aims to reach students who feel isolated due to the pandemic and recreate social and co-working spaces that have had to be replaced due to pandemic necessities.

4.2 Feature Description

We used an iterative development paradigm to develop Cowork. This paper only describes the final iteration. Cowork has been developed using Kontra.js [17] and Angular [18] to support accessibility needs and design features.

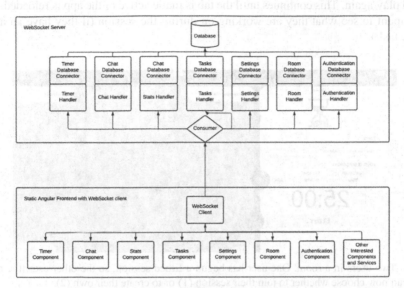

Fig. 1. Illustrates the system architecture of Cowork that was followed across all iterations.

4.3 Collaboration Rooms

The virtual workspace was made 2D with the home page compromising of 'room' (Fig. 2). Figure 2 also contains a timer that allows the user to start a task. Using the Pomodoro technique of [19, 20] breaking down tasks into achievable units increases motivation, and the propensity to complete the task increases. The room is a grass texture area that allows the user to interact with other participants. A virtual avatar represents the user in a 'room' shared with another member. Anywhere a display name appears, a user can select their name to view this information Fig. 3 shows a step-by-step task creation/deletion process. The collaboration feature, as shown below, also has various information about each session displayed with it, including the list of participants and the expected end time. The session ends early if all participants leave; otherwise, it ends at the expected end time.

5 Chat and Communication

The synchronous chat feature (Fig. 4) allows for collaboration during co-work sessions; however, a chat notification system was also developed along with other notifications such as a new chat message (Fig. 5), a timer is started or ends, an achievement is earned, or a new update note is released, a white one surrounded by a red circle appears next to the corresponding menu icon and a sound chirp if that tab is not active or the browser tab is not in view. If more such notifications are created, the number increments, and the sound play again. This continues until the tab is made not active or the browser tab is not in view. If more such notifications are created, the number increments, and the sound play again. This continues until the tab is made active or the app is reloaded. Any participant to see what they are working on during the session (if they have an active public task).

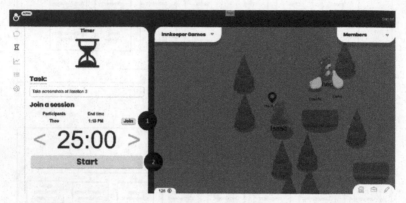

Fig. 2. Two users in a room. One user has begun a timed session, so the other user (the active user) can now choose whether to join their session (1) or to create their own (2).

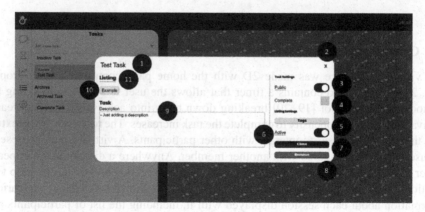

Fig. 3. Feature illustrated to show the ability to mark tasks as complete, add tags to tasks for better organization, and remove tasks.

Figure 8 shows a new achievement system (2) implemented to motivate the continued use of the software. Each achievement has a title, a description, and a currency reward displayed in its foreground. Behind the achievement is a yellow-orange progress bar indicating the user's progress toward completing that achievement. For example, if the user needs to use the timer tool for five hours to earn an achievement and has used it for four hours, 80% of the bar will be a yellow-orange color from left to right. If the achievement is 100% or more complete, the progress bar in the background will be green. When the user earns an achievement, it will flash from dark to light green until they view it, and the coins associated with the achievement will be added to the user's account. Completing a timer session awards all participants with coins equal to the number of minutes the session was active. The number of coins a user has is visible in the lower-left-hand corner of the room, visible at (1) in Fig. 6.

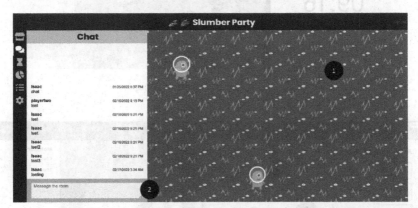

Fig. 4. Cowork developed using Kontra.js and Angular. The room area now is in the form of a grass texture, the user avatar is in the form of pink 2D aliens, and the chat area is expandable.

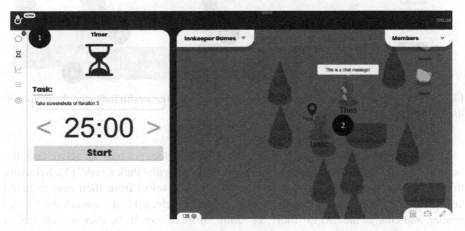

Fig. 5. A chat notification

Users can spend coins in the shop, which they can open in any room they have permission to edit via the three icons in the lower right-hand corner of Fig. 7: This opens a popup that can be repositioned by clicking and dragging. The shop includes a grid of items on display for purchase; each item (5) is listed with an image representing the item, a price, and an associated button labeled "Buy." Selecting the "Buy" button reduces the user's coin count by price and adds the item to their inventory.

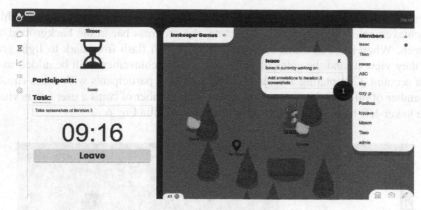

Fig. 6. A user information popup

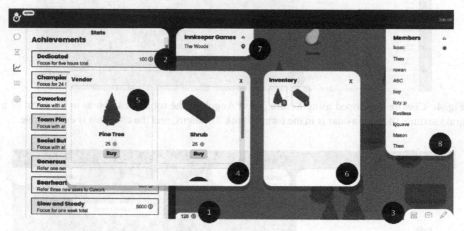

Fig. 7. The store and inventory windows, the editing toolbar, the wealth indicator, the members' list, the checkpoints list, and the achievements.

In the current iteration, as seen in Fig. 10, if the user does not have an active task, the buttons to start or join a session have their text replaced with "Pick a task" (1). Selecting this button opens a popup window prompting users to select from their non-archived tasks. Selecting a task will close the popup, place the selected task beneath the "Task" header, and change the text to "Start" or "Join," respectively. If the user already has an active task, they can select the task from the Timer tab to expand the popup at (2) and exchange it for another.

On the Stats tab is a stacked bar graph (Fig. 9) displaying the time the user spent on each tag in the selected duration, organized by day. In the task editor popup shown in Fig. 9, users can add the Tags and close it via an "X" in the upper right-hand corner of it (1). This is to improve the usability of the popup, as before this update, it was unclear whether users could close the popup by selecting the "Tags" button again.

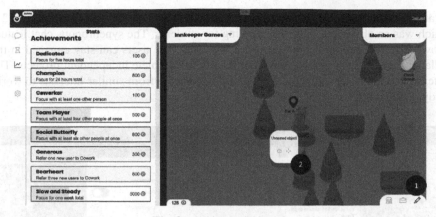

Fig. 8. Achievement board

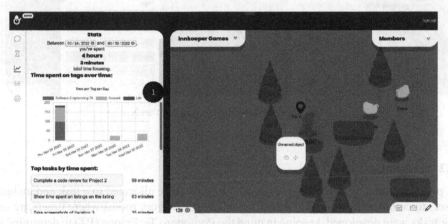

Fig. 9. The new Stats tab.

6   Supporting the Transition to Online Classes and Future Potential

6.1   The Feeling of Togetherness and Communication

All the features described in the section above support online learning communities beyond the pandemic classroom phase. During the pandemic when classes had to switch to online learning spaces, students and faculty struggled to replicate the pedagogical approaches that make learning collaborative and inclusive and the feeling of community and belonging. A common phenomenon for all institutions was students and faculty gathering for discussions, and whiteboard problem solving gathered in space. This helped build community and a sense of togetherness. This is also impactful in terms of building a cohort and encouraging collaboration. Cowork's features such as the 'room', virtual avatars, synchronous chat, and task list are an alternative to physical coworking spaces. Although the users would not get to see each other, having a 2D avatar walk around the space intends to promote a sense of belonging. We also decided against a video or audio chat feature like the ones supported by Discord due to zoom fatigue [21] which was an obstacle to effective learning for students. The synchronous chat feature allows communication without cognitive overload. The users can stay engaged in the collaborative space or just use the timer feature to complete independent projects. The potential use-case scenarios for these groups can range from similar interests to work-study groups etc.

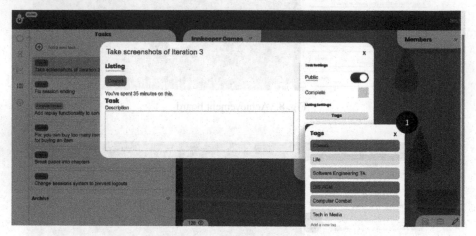

Fig. 10. The new Tags popup with an X.

6.2 Accountability

A predetermined timer allows a set amount of time to be allocated to a task and nudges users to complete it within that time. The collaborative work rooms where timers are set for tasks were developed, keeping in mind the Pomodoro Technique (PT) to determine if the student will improve their academic tasks [22]. The Pomodoro technique is a popular time management method that focuses on breaking down tasks into small achievable goals and setting timers to complete them. Cowork's timer feature draws inspiration from other timer applications that use this technique. In addition to the timer, Cowork's task creation, labeling, and list features help with accountability and reflection. Users can create tasks and add labels to them to cluster groups of tasks together. Custom labels are supported in the application to promote customization based on user needs. The cumulative time and achievement boards (Fig. 8) are also part of the accountability and reflection process. Sometimes we get so focused on a particular problem that we ignore the other things we need to achieve. These features can provide a snapshot of the week and let the user know what tasks they spend their time on. Self-reflection often leads to increased accountability and self-efficacy leading to better time-management skills.

6.3 Reduce Cognitive Overload

Cowork is designed and has features to reduce cognitive overload. Online learning during a pandemic is stressful, so we were determined to avoid adding stress or distractions.

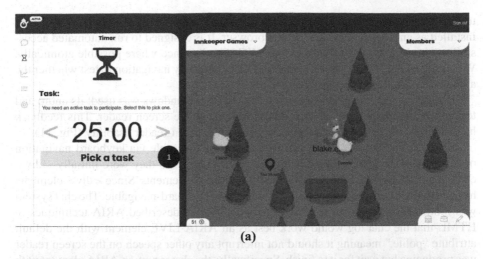

(a)

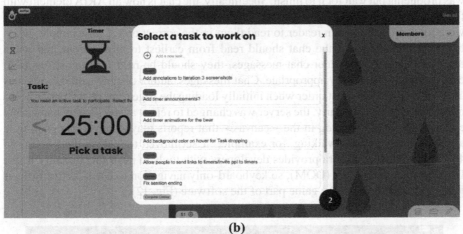

(b)

Fig. 11. a. Adapted Workflow to support communication. b. The new workflow for selecting an active task.

The gamification features of the virtual space are built-in 2D and have limited features to avoid this space evolving into a simulator gaming world. Notifications are text-based, and an audio signifier ('chirp' sound) alerts the user. The gamification of this Coworking space is also done to reduce the boredom generated by online learning spaces. A 2D environment also supports users with different abilities. In particular, many users need help with 3D environments and navigation.

6.4 Accessibility Automated Testing

Cowork aims to support students/users with different abilities, including low-vision users. We used the Kontra.js framework to incorporate accessibility features that supported ease of use and universal access. We used two different accessibility checkers to evaluate the application. We used Siteimprove [23], which is proprietary software installed as an extension for the Firefox browser. It is designed to run automated accessibility checks and explicitly checks for WCAG adherence where possible atomically. We also used the NVDA screen reader and keyboard-only navigation to test whether the application could support these features.

During the test, the NVDA screen reader [24] on Windows was used; its audio and text-log feature kept track of everything available to the screen reader. This feedback helped adjust the application's features to improve screen-reader usability (Fig. 11).

Firstly, some buttons in the software were not focusable via keyboard navigation or read out as navigation elements by the screen reader, as they were initially <div> elements instead of the semantically correct <button> elements. Since <div> elements have no defined purpose, they are not automatically keyboard-navigable. The chat system was modified based on the talk "Accessibility," which described ARIA techniques in HTML-that the chat log would work best as an ARIA-LIVE element with the default attribute "polite," meaning it should not interrupt any other speech on the screen reader was producing but wait for it to finish. Specifically, the chat is now an ARIA element with the role "log," suitable for chat updates. We made a change to the order chat messages were loaded for the screen reader to read them in the correct order; for example, when the page initially loads, the chat should read from earliest to most recent, but when the user wants to load older chat messages, they should be read from most recent to earliest to be contextually appropriate. Chat messages, author display names, and dates are now read in the correct order when initially loading the page (though the parsing also needs more work). Similarly, the server was changed to report avatar display names and created a second ARIA log in the <canvas> that reports player movement each time a player avatar finishes walking, for example, "User moved to 324 on the x-axis and 432 on the y-axis." Kontra provides developers with tools to push functionality to the Document Object Model (DOM), so keyboard-only navigation to users' active tasks is fully supported, even in the game part of the software (Fig. 12).

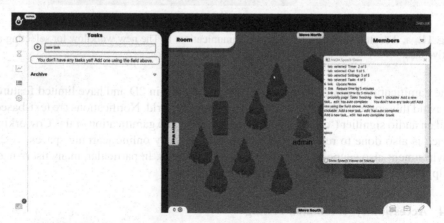

Fig. 12. The process of adding a new task with output from the screen reader.

7 Extendibility

We envision Cowork being used in various academic institutional settings and the web framework and architecture have been designed with modularity and the potential to expand. To scale, we believe that a template or Canvas LMS system-like approach would be ideal. The institution would receive this framework and integrate it into their IT infrastructure to support data storage and authentication. The virtual rooms and avatars can also be customized to match institutional themes and iconography. Although we are nearing the end of the pandemic in-person classes have resumed in most cases, however, the new normal is vastly different from the pre-pandemic educational landscape. Regular COVID clusters have become prevalent on campuses and the need for a hybrid or more flexible learning approach is necessary. We envision Cowork supporting that hybrid learning sphere outside of traditional classrooms.

8 Future Work and Limitations

Next, a keyboard-navigable movement system for the game part of the application will be implemented via keyboard-navigable buttons that move users an arbitrary distance in a cardinal direction. Additionally, context is provided to screen readers about a user's surroundings, as currently, only the position of each user is reported. Existing software artifacts in this space, like Habitica and Gather, should be evaluated with screen reader software like NVDA [29], as Cowork has been for benchmarking purposes. Our current work focused disproportionately on working toward use cases involving screen readers and keyboard navigation. It generally does not address many other accessibility challenges (ex., Color contrast issues). For future work, we continue to investigate other accessibility challenges and iteratively work on creating robust software. Cowork in its current form has yet to be user-tested; hence the primary limitation of this work is the lack of user feedback. Although some load testing on the server was conducted with mock users and multiple connections, we would like to investigate the server's robustness further. We plan to conduct user tests with target user groups and iteratively align our features to match the goals of the target demographic.

9 Conclusion

Overall, this paper describes the design and development process of Cowork that allows students to work online in a collaborative space, promotes a sense of belonging, and allows users to self-reflect. Through an iterative approach, a prototype was developed, followed by an accessibility review which necessitated a change in framework and collation of features. Although the pandemic is nearing its end, student learning and coworking have changed significantly. While we struggle to find our way back to *normal*, the need for accessible digital tools in the higher education space has never been more, and the design of Cowork explicitly supports that need. The COVID-19 pandemic has dramatically, perhaps permanently, changed how students work. The need for digital tools in higher education has never been greater in an increasingly digitally augmented world. As an accessible, virtual coworking tool, Cowork aims to fill that gap.

References

1. WeWork: WeWork | Office Space and Workspace Solutions. https://www.wework.com/. Accessed 18 Feb 2022
2. Bilandzic, M., Foth, M.: Libraries as coworking spaces: understanding user motivations and perceived barriers to social learning. Library Hi Tech. (2013)
3. What we can Learn from the Offices of Amazon, Facebook, and Google. https://loopphonebooths.com/what-we-can-learn-from-the-offices-of-amazon-facebook-and-google/. Accessed 18 Feb 2022
4. Slack is where the future works. https://slack.com/. Accessed 18 Feb 2022
5. Discord | Your Place to Talk and Hang Out. https://discord.com/. Accessed 18 Feb 2022
6. Atlassian: Jira | Issue & Project Tracking Software. https://www.atlassian.com/software/jira. Accessed 18 Feb 2022
7. What is Trello? - Trello Help. https://help.trello.com/article/708-what-is-trello. Accessed 18 Feb 2022
8. Li, A.: Google Calendar rolling out "Time Insights" that show how much time you spend in meetings. https://9to5google.com/2021/08/30/google-calendar-time-insights/. Accessed 18 Feb 2022
9. Google Calendar (2022). https://en.wikipedia.org/w/index.php?title=Google_Calendar&oldid=1070985098
10. Campbell, R., Kelly, K.: Conducting guided, virtual homework sessions to support student success during COVID campus closures (2021)
11. Chiong, R., Jovanovic, J.: Collaborative learning in online study groups: an evolutionary game theory perspective. J. Inf. Technol. Educ. Res. 11, 81–101 (2012)
12. Herrera-Pavo, M.Á.: Collaborative learning for virtual higher education. Learn. Cult. Soc. Interact. 28, 100437 (2021). https://doi.org/10.1016/j.lcsi.2020.100437
13. Caldwell, B., et al.: Web content accessibility guidelines (WCAG) 2.0. WWW Consortium (W3C) 290, 1–34 (2008)
14. WWW Consortium: Web content accessibility guidelines (WCAG) 2.0. (2008)
15. Pelzetter, J.: A declarative model for accessibility requirements. In: Proceedings of the 17th International Web for All Conference. https://doi.org/10.1145/3371300.3383339. Accessed 18 Feb 2022
16. Lazar, J.: Managing digital accessibility at universities during the COVID-19 pandemic. Univ. Access Inf.Soc. (2021). https://doi.org/10.1007/s10209-021-00792-5
17. Kontra.js – What is Kontra.js? https://straker.github.io/kontra/. Accessed 18 Feb 2022
18. Angular. https://angular.io/. Accessed 18 Feb 2022
19. Costales, J., Abellana, J., Gracia, J., Devaraj, M.: A Learning assessment applying pomodoro technique as a productivity tool for online learning. In: 2021 13th International Conference on Education Technology and Computers, pp. 164–167. ACM, Wuhan, China (2021). https://doi.org/10.1145/3498765.3498844
20. The Pomodoro Technique—Why It Works & How to Do It. https://todoist.com/productivity-methods/pomodoro-technique. Accessed 3 July 2022
21. Shoshan, H.N., Wehrt, W.: Understanding "Zoom fatigue": a mixed-method approach. Appl. Psychol. 71, 827–852 (2022). https://doi.org/10.1111/apps.12360
22. Browne, R., Raeside, L., Gray, G.: Gamification in education: productivity and motivation through gamified time management software. In: European Conference on Games Based Learning, pp. 867–871. Academic Conferences International Limited (2018)
23. Browser extensions. http://prod.siteimprove.com/integrations/browser-extensions/. Accessed 5 May 2022
24. NV Access. https://www.nvaccess.org/. Accessed 5 May 2022

A Greed(y) Training Strategy to Attract High School Girls to Undertake Studies in ICT

Tiziana Catarci[1]([✉])[iD], Barbara Polidori[2], Daniel Raffini[1][iD], and Paola Velardi[2][iD]

[1] Dipartimento di Ingegneria Informatica, Automatica e Gestionale Antonio Ruberti,
Sapienza University, Roma, Italy
catarci@diag.uniroma1.it

[2] Dipartimento di Informatica, Sapienza University, Roma, Italy

Abstract. It has been observed in many studies that female students in general are unwilling to undertake a course of study in ICT [1]. Recent literature has also pointed out that undermining the prejudices of girls with respect to these disciplines is very difficult in adolescence, suggesting that, to be effective, awareness programs on computer disciplines should be offered in pre-school or lower school age [2]. On the other hand, even assuming that large-scale computer literacy programs can be immediately activated in lower schools and kindergartens, we can't wait for >15–20 years before we can appreciate the effectiveness of these programs. The scarcity of women in ICT has a tangible negative impact on countries' technological innovation, which requires immediate action.

In this paper, we describe a strategy, and the details of a number of programs coordinated by the Engineering and Computer Science Departments at Sapienza University, to make high school girl students aware of the importance of new technologies and ICT. We call our proposed training strategy "greed(y)", because it has been conceived as a *grid* of vertical (hard) and horizontal (soft) skills, intertwining topics to which girls are traditionally sensitive, such as environmental sustainability, health, etc., with digital skills and soft skills that the public education system more rarely considers - such as team-working, public speaking, social networking, and competition - with visible consequences more for girls than for boys [3]. In fact, outside school life, boys can acquire a greater aptitude for teamwork, competition, and leadership, by practicing more markedly masculine sports, and they also have a better chance of approaching information technology, through video games.

Greedy is also a term used in Computer Science to denote sub-optimal strategies, as in our case, since we acknowledge that, in order to achieve a higher impact, similar programs should be proposed much earlier in a student's career.

In addition to describing the theoretical approach, the paper offers some project examples.

Keywords: gender gap · greedy · soft skills · high-school

1 Introduction

In recent years, many studies pointed out the presence of a significant and long-lasting gender gap in the field of Computer Science [1]. The gender gap exists at all levels: university students, researchers, professors, public administration, and industry. Among

M. Antona and C. Stephanidis (Eds.): HCII 2023, LNCS 14021, pp. 223–233, 2023.
https://doi.org/10.1007/978-3-031-35897-5_17

STEM disciplines, Computer Science is the one with the highest gender unbalance, with the percentage of women enrolled in ICT graduate programs usually ranging between 10 and 20 percent depending on the country.

The shortage of female ICT professionals also affects the job market and the sustainable development of our society. Digital transformation is currently predominantly guided by men, and this does not guarantee the diversity of positions and ways of thinking that would be indispensable in such an important field. The lack of women also contributes to the severe shortage of skilled digital workers that is retarding many countries' development.

Next Generation EU (also known as the Recovery Fund) includes digitization, innovation, competitiveness, culture, green revolution, and ecological transformation among the most funded objectives of national plans. However, the risk is that those benefiting from the funds made available by the European Community are mainly male-dominated sectors (such are indeed digital, construction, agriculture, and transport), although the pandemic has had devastating effects on female employment in particular. Therefore, the need for actions to reduce the gender gap in these areas is extremely urgent.

In order to face this problem, since 2014 the European Commission has been monitoring the digital progress in the Member States by means of the Digital Economy and Society Index (DESI[1]), which analyzes four key areas: Human capital, Connectivity, Integration of digital technology, and Digital public services. The European Commission also launched the Digital Skills and Jobs Platform. The lack of digital skills affects companies and public administrations at different levels: there are no experts who can develop cutting-edge technology and there are not enough employees which are able to use existing technology to improve efficiency. The DESI also focus attention on the gender gap, considered one of the causes of the lack of digital workers: from the 2022 DESI Report [14] emerges that only 19 percent of ICT specialists are female.

Despite the fact that Computer Science is the area where there are the most job offerings and the highest salaries, girls still do not enroll in ICT degree programs and do not pursue careers in Computer Science. To understand the reasons why girls are not enrolling in ICT degree programs, we do not have to focus on the job market. In fact, the factor that drives girls away from Computer Science disciplines is the persistence of gender stereotypes and biases, which lead people to consider computer science-related jobs inappropriate for women. Unlike other types of prejudices, the one relating to women's limited aptitude for information technology appears rooted and more difficult to weaken, because it tends to condition girls' interests and inclinations from an early age, leading to a rejection of information technology disciplines which is very difficult to break down in adolescence or adulthood.

While boys, when choosing a course of study, are particularly attracted by the possibilities of career and economic progression, for girls social and innovation impact are a very relevant factor [13]. Studies conducted at UCLA show that for boys the main attractor in choosing to study Computer Science is a passion for videogames, while girls like computer games less [4,5,18]. Furthermore, recent studies demonstrate how a strong deterrent for girls is the stereotype of "nerd", as an antisocial individual with poor communication skills, thus antithetical to their aspirations [6]. Many researchers have

---

[1] https://digital-strategy.ec.europa.eu/en/policies/desi.

also suggested that the media is largely responsible for this kind of stereotyping [7]. It is no coincidence that Artificial Intelligence, whose fascinating applications have been widely covered by the media in more recent times, attracts girls instead [17]. In corroboration, the bachelor's degree program in Applied Computer Science and Artificial Intelligence started in 2020/2021 by the Department of Computer Science at Sapienza University of Rome has already reached 35 percent of girls' enrollment.

We may conclude that the gender gap in ICT is not the consequence of difficulty for women in accessing job positions (although some obstacles remain to reach the top positions), but rather a cultural resistance of the girls themselves when choosing their course of study. Compared to other fields, where women face objective difficulties in advancing their careers, in the case of Computer Science it is the discipline itself that does not attract school-age girls, as a consequence of deeply rooted stereotypes at the societal level.

To mitigate this problem and redirect girls into the Computer Science field, many initiatives have been launched at the European and national levels. For example, in Italy a portal to collect and connect the numerous national initiatives has been recently created[2], while at European level is to mention the EUGAIN Project[3]. Most initiatives have been aimed at female high school students. Some of these projects achieved some results on a small scale but failed to reverse the general trend. Recent studies have pointed out that undermining the prejudices of girls with respect to Computer Science is very difficult in adolescence, suggesting that, to be effective, awareness programs on computer disciplines should be offered in pre-school or lower school age, that is the moment when gender biases take root in girls' mind [2]. Even if these studies show that the most effective way to proceed is to intervene at a younger age, the ongoing digital transformation and the absence of workers with adequate skills in Computer Science requires fast action. There is a need to keep acting on the high school age range, even if the bias is already deep-rooted in girls, by looking for effective compensatory measures to show girls the potential of the Computer Science field. The "greedy" strategy proposed in this paper is built on this extremely urgent problem.

2   Methodology

The term greedy refers to two aspects of the methods shaped in this paper:

1. A sub-optimal strategy, since we acknowledge that, in order to achieve a higher impact, similar programs should be proposed much earlier in a student's career. It refers to an approach to solving a problem by selecting the best option currently available, similar to greedy algorithms.
2. A strategy conceived as a *grid* of vertical (hard) and horizontal (soft) skills, intertwining topics to which girls are traditionally sensitive - such as environmental sustainability, health, and creativity - with digital skills and soft skills that the public education system more rarely considers - such as team-working, public speaking, social networking, and competition - with visible consequences more for girls than for boys [3].

---

[2] https://www.gict.it/.
[3] https://eugain.eu/.

As we discussed in Sect. 1, misconceptions concerning ICT-related professions, such as the "nerd" stereotype and the belief that ICT consists only in programming or fixing computers, affect more females than males [16]. ICT curricula in schools are, depending on the country, absent, deficient, or late, in the sense that they are introduced when these prejudices are well-established.

Likewise, education systems often lack programs aimed at cultivating horizontal or "soft" skills, which are known to be very important in career development [20]. The progress of women in any career is hampered not only by a male-dominated organization of society but also by the fact that girls' education in families and schools does not favor the learning of essential soft skills, such as the ability to compete, public speaking, teamwork, and networking. Outside of school life, boys have the opportunity to acquire some of these skills by practicing more masculine sports, which could justify the results of a recent study in which a substantial gap was observed between the performance of men and women in teamwork and team competition [19].

In conclusion, girls have fewer opportunities to develop both soft and hard skills. To mitigate these deficiencies, our method is based on two principles:

1. To attract girls' interest in ICTs at a later stage of education, it is necessary to make them understand that Computer Science has significantly contributed to the advancement of other disciplines or subjects in which women traditionally show great passion and aptitude, such as medicine [8], environment and sustainability [9], art, and social sciences.
2. Furthermore, it is necessary to integrate technical skills with horizontal skills, essential for progressing in the professional career, especially in male-dominated sectors such as ICT.

For these reasons, we have conceived a grid-shaped approach in which Computer Science is one of the vertical (hard) skills that are taught and intersected with other vertical and horizontal (soft) skills, such as those previously listed. We believe that empowering women is a complex process that requires not only upgrading their skills in strategic and traditionally male-dominated sectors, such as ICT, but also acquiring soft skills that provide them with the right tools to progress in their careers. This can help girls understand that computational skills nowadays are very important in different careers, and are becoming an increasingly required competence to access all levels and fields of the job market. It is also important to make girls understand that ICT disciplines open up many professions that are not limited to being programmers but can offer a very strong bond with society, culture, economy, and business.

3   Examples

The context in which the 'Greedy' strategy proved to be most effective in raising awareness of equal opportunities concerned two academic projects:

1. The first one, WomENcourage 2019 [10], brought together women in the computing profession and related technical fields to exchange knowledge and experience, and to provide special support for young women who were pursuing their academic degrees

or starting their careers in computing. Through a program packed with insightful interdisciplinary topics and engaging educational and networking activities, WomENcourage provided a unique experience of the collective energy, leadership, and excellence that professional women must share to support each other;

2. The other program is G4GRETA (Girls for Green Technology Applications) [11], which involves third and fourth-year students from high schools in and around Rome. This two-year project - which started in 2022 and is still ongoing - combines the development of hard and soft Computer Science skills with the theme of Environmental Sustainability. The participants learn to design apps with an eco-sustainable theme, with the help of tutors and university lecturers. G4Greta proposes lessons, exercises, and training courses that foster the self-determination of young female students in technical-scientific career paths with a holistic approach, interconnected to environmental sustainability, encouraging female students to develop digital applications and solutions that embrace innovation.

In what follows we provide additional details on these projects.

3.1 The Womencourage 2019 Conference

The ACM Celebration of Women in Computing (WomENcourage) is an annual conference whose aim is to bring together women in the computing profession and related technical fields to exchange knowledge and experience and provide special support for women who are pursuing their academic degrees and starting their careers in computing. This conference has reached in 2023 its tenth edition and has a well-assessed program including a hackathon, a career fair, workshops, and keynotes. The 2019 edition [10], although starting from this initial program, has been enriched with activities and events according to the grid scheme previously described.

Description. As regards the objective of strengthening vertical (hard) skills, we have combined workshops on traditional IT topics such as gaming, cybersecurity, data science, and more, with several events concerning interdisciplinary topics that notoriously attract women, such as artificial intelligence and health, smart cities, sustainability, architecture and technology for a conscious city, art and digital. Interdisciplinary topics were given higher visibility, organizing them in the main Auditorium, in the form of Mini-conferences, keynotes, and Panels, with a focus on the scientific quality of all the invited speakers, who were selected to inspire the young attendees.

The major innovation was in the number and quality of activities aimed at strengthening vertical (soft) skills, among which the hackathon, the poster presentations, and the poster karaoke. The latter was a rather challenging activity in which girls were asked to present each other's poster, assigned by drawing among the 10 best posters selected at the end of the standard poster sessions. This activity aimed at fostering mutual listening, the ability to improvise, and to face challenges even when one feels unprepared.

Results. The sixth edition of ACM Celebration of Women in Computing took place in Rome, at Museum MAXXI, from September 16th to 19th, 2019. More than 350 participants took part in the event, 55% of whom were young: 62% of them graduates, and

38% still university students. WomENcourage also showed a good presence of male participants, who represented 15% of all participants (although they were all involved in the organization of some events as speakers, company representatives during the career fair, etc.). The participants came from 32 countries and covered 4 different continents (Europe, Asia, Africa, and America). The rich program included the hackathon, the career fair, one laboratory, 9 workshops, 2 mini-conferences, 2 panels, 3 poster sessions, the poster karaoke, two scientific and four technical keynotes, and a number of recreational events. A designer created and projected the infographics of all the main events in real-time, as shown for example in Fig. 1.

To date, Womencourage 2019 remains the conference edition with the largest number of participants, and the largest number of sponsoring and/or supporting partners[4] (both national and international) to demonstrate the great interest not only of the girls involved but also of companies, public bodies, and non-profit organizations.

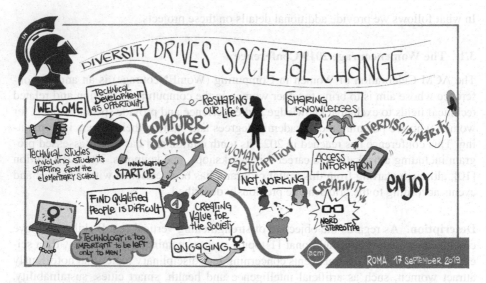

Fig. 1. One amongst the many infographics generated in real-time during the Womencourage 2019 event

3.2 The G4GRETA Project

The G4GRETA project intercepts many elements of the Next generation EU [12] programme: digitization and innovation, the green revolution, and the gender gap, albeit on a small scale, such as the proposal of a pilot program on digital and environmental culture, aimed at female students of high schools in Lazio, Italy.

The objectives of this initiative were manifold. The most obvious is to encourage greater access for women to leadership roles, including technological ones, which today

---

[4] https://womencourage.acm.org/2019/supporters/.

are almost exclusively male-dominated. In turn, this could increase the push towards a green evolution of the current consumer society, in which it is usually women who demonstrate greater sensitivity towards social and environmental problems. In this regard, an article published in December 2017 by Scientific America titled "Men Resist Green Behavior as Unmanly" states the following:*"Women have long surpassed men in the arena of environmental action; Across all age groups and in all countries, women tend to lead a greener lifestyle. Compared to men, women throw less waste, recycle more and leave a smaller carbon footprint. Some researchers have suggested that personality differences, such as women's altruism priority, may help explain this gender gap in ecological behavior."* Whatever the explanation, it seems clear that greater involvement of women in technology choices can only advance the green economy more rapidly.

Description. The project (see [11] for a detailed description of the program) is organized into 10 afternoons, 8 of which are repeated twice to be able to include a greater number of girls. The meetings are dedicated to the following activities: teambuilding, design thinking, environmental sustainability and use of technologies for sustainability, app coding (4 meetings), videomeking and social networking, pitching, final awards and party. During two months the girls independently develop their own projects (with the remote support of tutors) and submit them to a jury. In designing the coding lessons, we assumed no previous knowledge of coding, an assumption that turned out to be correct for 80% of the participants.

The G4GRETA project started in November 2022 and is currently ongoing. Overall, the project will span over a period of 7 months, followed by a period (currently scheduled for one year) during which we will follow the cohort of female students involved in the program, to evaluate its impact. For its entire duration, the project also includes a community building and management program, through social media, some of which (such as Linkedin) aimed at putting girls in contact with professionals and role models, others (Tiktok, Instagram) more suitable for networking among participants.

The proposed initiative has involved a large number of beneficiaries:

- School teachers: they will be made aware of ICT and green issues, and then independently - or with advice from the University - design similar educational projects for their students[5];
- High school students: they will acquire technical (horizontal) skills in the field of software design and green technologies, as well as vertical skills such as:
  - team building: creating groups and learn to work collaboratively;
  - communication skills: presenting their projects effectively;
  - competition: learning to face the difficulties of competition, and accept its rules and outcomes;
  - problem solving: familiarizing themselves with the Design Thinking methodology[6];
  - networking: actively participating in the online network created during and after the initiative has taken place.

---

[5] All the teaching material is made available on the project web site.
[6] https://www.ideou.com/pages/design-thinking.

- Students, doctoral students, and young researchers of the University: they have been involved in the tutoring of school students participants, increasing their awareness of gender issues, being encouraged to network with each other and with the participating students, strengthening their sense of community, and reducing the discomfort of working in predominantly male contexts;
- University professors: they are involved in the design and implementation of the initiative, acting as lecturers, role models, and mentors, thus contributing to an important goal such as that of gender equality in ICT. They also have the opportunity to strengthen relationships with the schools, companies, and bodies participating in the initiative;
- Companies, institutions, and local bodies: the project also aimed to involve public and private institutions. We obtained the active participation of IBM Italy, the Foundation Mondo Digitale (FMD), and the Lazio Region (which co-financed the initiative). All of these organizations are already engaged on the issues of gender equality and the green transition. Participation in the G4GRETA project will therefore make it possible to develop priority issues for these organizations and consolidate relations with schools and universities.

Initial Results. As we said, the project is still ongoing, although, in terms of feedback and participation, the results have been very encouraging. 24 schools have joined the project, of which 15 are in the city of Rome and 9 are in the Lazio Region. More than 600 candidates applied, but only 216 were eventually selected due to limitations of space and resources. 30 school teachers are actively following the initiative. Figure 2 shows one of the G4GRETA classrooms, during a teambuilding lesson, while Figure 3 shows a pitch during the Design Thinking meeting.

The comments - in terms of lessons learned - that we can make at this stage are purely qualitative and will need to be further explored when the follow-up program will be concluded. During the first meetings (teambuilding, design thinking, sustainability lesson and first two coding lessons) the attention of the girls has always remained high, likely as a consequence of the great effort made by the organizers to keep it high, promoting interactivity, minimizing the time dedicated to teaching lessons, and challenging them with fun but not simple tasks. We observed with surprise that, after an initial phase of stress, the girls reacted very effectively to our requests to get out of their comfort zone, answering questions in public, engaging in activities never performed before (coding, pitching), and working in a team with girls they've never met before rather than, as they would have preferred, with their schoolmates. This demonstrates, if proof were needed, that disinterest in information technology, or resistance to public exposure and competition, are certainly not female characteristics, but only a limitation of the educational system, which does not engage them sufficiently in these activities.

4 Ongoing Work: Designing Follow-Up Strategies

With a view to evaluating the impact of these projects, we consider very important to design follow-up actions, in order to identify the real effect of the programs on female students when choosing to enroll in a university degree.

Fig. 2. One of the classrooms of the G4GRETA project during the team-building session (courtesy of Mindsharing.tech)

A follow-up has been planned for the G4GRETA project and it is in the process of being defined. The challenge is the lack, in the current literature, of follow-up studies that constitute examples for this type of orientation projects. Based on classroom experience, we have identified some instruments that could be useful in view of the follow-up. We plan at the end of the project to deliver a survey to understand how girls' perceptions have changed in relation to the world of Computer Science, as a result of the greedy strategy. The ultimate goal is to monitor how many girls will choose a university program in Computer Science. This is done by tracking a study cohort consisting of girls who participated in the project and comparing it with a control cohort consisting of girls with similar characteristics but who did not attend the program, in addition to designing a social engagement strategy to keep all the project participants connected and active. Since the choice of a university program is expected, in the case of the G4GRETA girls, in two years, it is necessary to maintain contact and team up with the girls until that time. This will be done by maintaining a community through social and in-person events.

The follow-up strategy will help identify best practices that need to be implemented on large scale, and similar projects to actually impact enrollment numbers in Computer Science degree programs. This leads us to a second theme of great importance, which is the necessity to identify effective strategies and, subsequently, to apply them at the national and European levels.

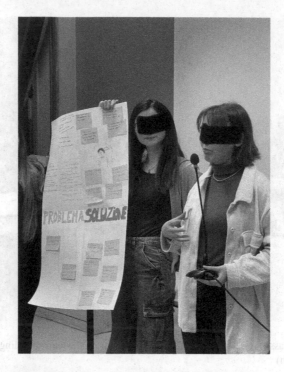

Fig. 3. A pitch during the Design Thinking meeting

5 Concluding Remarks

The scarcity of women in ICT-related professions not only has a detrimental effect on women's career progression but also affects the lack of experts in the digital sector, with a negative impact on society. In this article, we have presented a mitigation strategy for the problem, building on the evidence offered by several studies on the motivations that determine the low interest of women in these disciplines.

We believe that it is necessary for the best practices identified in the projects described in this paper, and other similar projects undertaken worldwide, to converge to the definition of an intervention model, which, applied on a large scale, will be actually effective in reversing the negative trend of girls' enrollment percentages in Computer Science programs. We also believe it is very important to design initiatives for sharing similar experiences with other universities, public bodies, and private organizations. To encourage this exchange of experiences and best practices, we have undertaken another national networking initiative on this issue, supported by the @GICT (Atlas of Italian gender Initiatives in ICT) portal, as mentioned in Sect. 1.

References

1. Saxa, L., et al.: Anatomy of an enduring gender gap: the evolution of women's participation in computer science. J. Higher Educ. **88**(2), 258–293 (2017)

2. Master, A., Meltzoff, A., Cheryan, S.: Gender stereotypes about interests start early and cause gender disparities in computer science and engineering. PNAS **118**(48), e2100030118 (2021)
3. Varava, I.P., Bohinska, A.P., Vakaliuk, T.A., Mintii, I.S.: Soft skills in software engineering technicians education. J. Phys: Conf. Ser. **1946**, 012012 (2021)
4. Collain, M., Tryttenva, D., : "You don't have to be a white male that was learning how to program since he was five:" Computer Use and Interest From Childhood to a Computing Degree SIGCSE '19, February 27-March 2,: Minneapolis. MN, USA (2019)
5. Smith, S., Sobolewska, E., Bhardwaj, J., Fabian, K.: Exploring women's motivations to study computer science. IEEE Front. Educ. Conf. (FIE) **2018**, 1–7 (2018)
6. Berg, T., Sharpe, A. and Aitkin, E.: Females in computing: Understanding stereotypes through collaborative picturing. Comput. Educ. **126**,105–114 (2018). https://doi.org/10.1016/j.compedu.2018.07.007
7. Cheryan, S., Plaut, V., Handron, C., Hudson, L.: The stereotypical computer scientist: gendered media representations as a barrier to inclusion for women. Sex Roles **69**, 58–71 (2013)
8. Fridsma, D.B.: Health informatics: a required skill for 21st century clinicians. In: BMJ: British Medical Journal, vol. 362 (2018)
9. Mondejar, M.E.: at Alii, Digitalization to achieve sustainable development goals: Steps towards a Smart Green Planet, Science of The Total Environment, Vol. 794, p. 148539 (2021)
10. WomENcourage Homepage, https://womencourage.acm.org/2019/. Last Accessed 10 Nov (2022)
11. G4GRETA Homepage. https://g4greta.di.uniroma1.it/home. Last Accessed 10 Nov 2022
12. Next Generation EU - A European instrument to counter the impact of the coronavirus pandemic, https://www.europarl.europa.eu/RegData/etudes/BRIE/2020/652000/EPRS_BRI(2020)652000_EN.pdf. Last accessed 1 Feb 2023
13. Cracking the code: why aren't more women in majoring in Computer Science https://newsroom.ucla.edu/stories/cracking-the-code:-why-aren-t-more-women-majoring-in-computer-science Last accessed 1 Feb 2023
14. Digital Economy and Society Index (DESI) 2022 - Thematic chapters. https://ec.europa.eu/newsroom/dae/redirection/document/88764 Last Accessed 1 Feb 2023
15. European Network For Gender Balance in Informatics, COST ACTION CA19122. https://eugain.eu/ Last Accessed 1 Feb 2023
16. Kindsiko, E., Trk, K.: Detecting Major Misconceptions about Employment in ICT: A Study of the Myths about ICT Work among Females. In: International Journal of Social, Behavioral, Educational, Economic, Business and Industrial Engineering, pp. 107–114 (2017)
17. Vachovsky, M.E., Wu, G., Chaturapruek, S., Russakovsky, O., Sommer, R., Fei-Fei, L: Towards More Gender Diversity in CS through an Artificial Intelligence Summer Program for High School Girls. In: Proceedings of the 47th ACM Technical Symposium on Computing Science Education, pp. 303–308 (2016)
18. Leonhardt, M., Overå, S.: Are There Differences in Video Gaming and Use of Social Media among Boys and Girls?-A Mixed Methods Approach. In: Int. J. Environ. Res. Public Health **18**, 6085 (2021)
19. Ivanova-Stenzel, R., Kübler, D.: Gender differences in team work and team competition. J ECON PSYCH. **32** 797–808 (2011)
20. Mitashree, T.: Significance of Soft Skills in Career Development. In: Career Development and Job Satisfaction, chapter 3, IntechOpen, Editor Josiane Fahed-Sreih (2020)

Promoting Inclusion in Pre-schools Between Pedagogical Competences and Technological Supports. The Role of a WebApp in the Early Detection of Developmental Difficulties for Children Aged 06 Years

Luigi d'Alonzo(✉), Elena Zanfroni(✉), Silvia Maggiolini(✉), and Paola Molteni

Università Cattolica del Sacro Cuore, Milan, Italy
{luigi.dalonzo,elena.zanfroni,silvia.maggiolini,
paola.molteni}@unicatt.it

Abstract. The promotion of a quality pedagogical culture to support pre-school education has long been a priority within European educational policies. Guaranteeing all children equal starting conditions, reducing forms of disadvantage and social inequality (2030 European Agenda), is the horizon within which the EU Project, MOEC - More Opportunities for Every Child has developed.

The aim of the project was to support the training and skills development of pre-school teachers. During the three years of research, toolkits were developed and tested, along with innovative ways of working and collaborating. The main goal is the promotion of a professional outlook as a *modus operandi* oriented towards recognizing diversities, in order to build an inclusive school, based on the values of equity and personalization. Specifically, the fourth intellectual output of the project has been the realization of a WebApp, conceived and designed as a possible tool to support the professionalism of teachers and educators.

The project's results underline the importance to broaden research paths to continue to support and guarantee, beyond the mere use of digital tools, however significant they may be, quality planning in pre-school realities, capable of effectively guiding that process of systematic observation, beyond the risk of excessive medicalization.

Keywords: Inclusion · Early detection · WebApp · Preschool system · Teachers

This contribution is the result of the joint work of the research group of the Research Centre on Disability and Marginality (CeDisMa) of the Università Cattolica del Sacro Cuore. In addition to the authors, Luigi d'Alonzo, Paola Molteni and Roberta Sala contributed to the re-search. Paragraphs 3. and 4. of this article are attributable to Elena Zanfroni and paragraphs 1. and 2. to Silvia Maggiolini.

1 Pre-schools Integrated System in Italy: The State of the Art

The dimension of care and the educational relationship in the pre-school context has always played a very important role in the tradition of studies and pedagogical literature. In recent years, in particular, interest in this specific age group, especially in the early years, has been renewed and strengthened. This is due to the evidence offered by neuroscientific studies, but also because of the new and complex demands arising from ongoing social, cultural and legislative transformations. Indeed, numerous studies have highlighted and continue to highlight the enormous potential contained, in particular, in the first years of life of every human being and, consequently, the inestimable value of educational and care actions.

As a recent research report stated *"investments in early childhood education services, pre-schools and support for parents' skills should be considered in their own right as investments in education, because they are the solid foundation on which girls and boys are guaranteed the opportunity to fully develop their capacities, combating inequalities and educational poverty. This is why they are strategic both socially and economically. A large body of international literature shows, in fact, that access to quality education and education services from the earliest years of life and parental support has positive effects on three dimensions:*

1. *the well-being and skills of children, with long-term effects on their entire personal growth pathway;*
2. *the well-being of their families, favouring both fertility choices for those who work and work participation for those who have children (currently low, especially for women), with positive effects on curbing child poverty;*
3. *social cohesion and the economic development of communities and society as a whole, by strengthening the knowledge and skills of the new generations, with a consequent reduction in vulnerability (with associated social costs) and a strengthening of employment prospects (i.e. a positive contribution to the country's growth)"*[1].

Of relevance for a pedagogical reading of the contents of the regulations and for the scientific foundations referred to -necessary for an understanding of the child's learning methods at the age of 0–6 years- is the contribution of one of Italy's leading experts in early childhood education- repeatedly quoted in this work- Anna Bondioli, Professor of General and Social Pedagogy at the University of Pavia. In it she states that: *"the diversity between institutions for children 0–3 and those for children 3–6 is more organisational, due to differences in history and tradition, than strictly pedagogical [...]It is now taken for granted by the reference literature and research that childhood is a period of life that has its own peculiarity, and that children 0–6 therefore require specific educational attention, pedagogical backgrounds different from those that mark the following school periods"*[2]. For these reasons, it goes on, it is fundamental to affirm the uniqueness of

---

[1] Alleanza per l'Infanzia, *Investire nell'infanzia: prendersi cura del futuro a partire dal presente*, Report 2020 in https://www.savethechildren.it/cosa-facciamo/pubblicazioni/investire-nell-inf anzia-prendersi-cura-del-futuro-a-partire-dal-presente (Alleanza per l'Infanzia, 2023).

[2] Bondioli A., *How to form educators for children from 0–6 years old*, in Pedagogia Oggi, anno XV, n.2, 2017, Pensa Multimedia, Lecce –Brescia, p.66 (Bondioli 2017).

that educational and growth pathway between the ages of 0 and 6, thereby recognizing its role and peculiarities, and thus fully implementing the idea that *"care and education, in this age group, cannot be analyzed and considered in isolation"*. It is therefore clear that the importance and responsibility of such a delicate and fundamental task cannot be entrusted to personnel without adequate and solid pedagogical training, in the name of an alleged natural inclination towards the world of childhood and education in general.

Specifically, in Italy, after a long period characterized by political and cultural debates with Law no. 107 of 13 July 2015, the Integrated System of Education and Instruction from birth to six years of age was established, later implemented by Legislative Decree no. 65 of 13 April 2017. Through these legislative interventions, the two educational realities aimed at welcoming and taking charge of pre-school children, the crèche and the kindergarten, which in Italy have had different histories and approaches, meet at the regulatory level, giving rise to a new path that requires a new pedagogical orientation, capable of drawing on the experience gained to date on both fronts (Silva, 2018). As established by Legislative Decree 65/2017, the integrated system guarantees all children, from birth to six years of age, equal opportunities to develop their potential, promoting their learning and integral development and overcoming inequalities and barriers. More specifically, the key points of the integrated system are: the promotion of participation by children and their families in childcare services, so that social, cultural and relational disadvantages can be reduced; the activation of an educational continuity; the enhancement of accessibility, diffusion and above all of the quality of services; the importance of in-service training and the role of pedagogical coordination. More recently, with the aim of defining pedagogical guidelines and identifying clear lines of action on the subject, the Ministry of Education has drafted two documents: Pedagogical guidelines for the integrated 0–6 system (2021) and the National guidelines for 0–3 (2022). In line with the policies and interventions that have guided international actions in the field of ECEC (Early Childhood Education and Care) and with what is promoted by the working groups and the specifically established European Commissions (ECEC Thematic Working Group: see European Commission, Proposal for key principles of a Quality Framework for Early Childhood Education and Care. Report of the Working Group on Early Childhood Education and Care under the auspices of the European Commission), these documents aim to define in a clear, unitary and a national pedagogical and organizational framework in which some key principles in the construction of the educational network are structured with a shared and participatory perspective. What key principles? Curriculum and planning, organizational choices, monitoring and evaluation, governance, accessibility, all with a view necessarily aimed at a more sustainable and child-friendly future. Both documents therefore address particularly topical and significant issues in the field of child education and care. Alongside the construction of a unitary curriculum and the promotion of continuity (of observational postures, of educational proposals, of co-responsibility actions) we can consider, for instance, the need for targeted and systematic training for all staff in the services, the role of observation, documentation, evaluation, as pivotal points in the planning process, the importance of organizational aspects, the formative relevance of space and time.

Worthy of relevance, as a structural component and overall design of the macro- and micro-planning processes, is the issue of accessibility and inclusion, central to any reflection on the role, functions and purposes of educational and training systems capable of welcoming, but above all of offering quality responses to the complex, diverse and specific needs of people, starting with the youngest children. Today, more than ever, it seems unquestionable to consider every educational process within an inclusive horizon understood as a global, systemic vision and, as such, transversal to every programmatic action that should have as its goal the construction of processes of participation in community life by all and for all.

For these reasons, the need to guarantee and monitor high levels of effectiveness and quality in educational services for pre-school children requires the possibility of building environments that are attentive, skilled and open to forms of experimentation and innovation, capable of guaranteeing equal opportunities of access and success (in terms of participation and training) for each individual child.

These issues are therefore not only important, but fundamental and a priority for defining the actions needed to meet the challenges of a future that, in a sense, is already here, as the title of Save the Children's recent Atlas indicates. As we know, with the Agenda 2030's sustainable development goal *"to provide quality, equitable and inclusive education and learning opportunities for all"*, target 4.2 reads: *"By 2020, ensure that all girls and boys have access to quality early childhood development, care and access to pre-school, so that they are ready for primary education"*. In light of the above, it is clear that the inclusive dimension of an educational service such as pre-school can no longer be assumed as a corollary of the pedagogical project, but must be understood as a structural element at the level of management.

2 Children in Kindergarden and Disability Between Conceptual Framework and Some Data

In recent years, the presence of pupils with disabilities and with different types of difficulties has been a constant, if not constantly growing, element. This has contributed to making the management of educational realities more and more complex, since pre-school age. Alongside this phenomenon, it is necessary to consider some relevant aspects especially if analyzed in relation to possible applications in the educational field:

– recent studies in Neuroscience have promoted a better understanding of the development of brain structures and have emphasized the role of early educational intervention for the cognitive, linguistic, emotional, and relational development of children. The ways in which adults care for a child, thanks to a wide range of stimuli (verbal and non-verbal communication), have a significant influence on the child development's process, not only in terms of skills, but also in the construction of a strong and well-structured personality (Conkbayir 2017; Center on the Developing Child at Harvard University, Applying the Science of Child Development in Child Welfare Systems, October 2016);
– the need to ensure high-quality preschool education services as a priority goal in European educational policies and welfare (ECEC). To promote the development and enhancement of these agencies, it is important to guarantee not only the achievement of quantitative parameters, but also - and mainly - of qualitative improvement.

Regarding this, a very important aspect is represented by the possibility of promptly identifying signs of difficulties from the first years of a child's life.

In Italy, the attendance of children in pre-schools, although declining in recent years, and in particular since the 2012/2013 school year, has always been characterized, as in other European countries such as France, Denmark, Belgium, Sweden, by high participation rates, above 90% as required by the objectives of the 2002 Barcelona Council. In particular, with regard to the number of children attending pre-schools in the school year 2021/2022 (latest available statistics), there were 846,775 children in public schools, of whom 18269 had a disability certificate. In fact, although there has been a reduction in preschool attendance, as mentioned above, there has been a steady increase in the percentages of certified disabled children (from 1.5% in the 2015–2016 school year, to 2.4% in 2018–2019, to 2.4% in 2020–2021). We can therefore understand how the pre-school system, despite the fact that it is not compulsory, represents a crucial role that it plays, also given the high percentage of children that it receives, especially, as the data show, with a condition of fragility, and cannot miss the opportunity to offer its fundamental contribution not only by favouring the growth pathway of those who are experiencing difficulties but also, at the same time, by allowing for the early recognition of any signs of developmental disharmonies. What is not secondary, in this sense, is also the support that preschool teachers could give to families who have just been diagnosed in order to orientate, from the first years, the life project of their child. It seems worth remembering then that "[…] *transition to early childhood education and care [can] help all children, and not just those who have won the birth lottery, get a good start in life. This could help reduce the educational, developmental and behavioural problems that disadvantaged children and the societies in which they live often face*"[3]. Indeed, several authors emphasize the role that high-quality pre-school programmes can play, especially for those considered disadvantaged children, in fostering greater opportunities for participation in social life.

In short, it could be said that the time is ripe for the development of a culture, perhaps implicitly already in place, but now more than ever shared and supported by scientific evidence, according to which man's education, in the deepest meaning that the expression brings with it, does not begin, as has already been pointed out, only with access to formal learning opportunities, but from the child's earliest years of life. And this is even more true for children who present a condition of greater fragility, as in the case of a more or less complex disability.

---

[3] UNICEF, *Come cambia la cura dell'infanzia. Un quadro comparativo dei servizi educativi e della cura per la prima infanzia nei paesi economicamente avanzati*, Report Card 8, 2008 (UNICEF 2008).

3   "More Opportunites for Every Child". The European MOEC Project

The More Opportunities for Every Child (MOEC) project focused on the domain of "early detection of difficulties" in the early childhood education of pupils in kindergarten in Italy, France, Spain, and Poland, with the overall objectives to:

1. research and review current early detection of child difficulties in kindergarden schools policies in each country;
2. share educational practices, experiences, and knowledge in early detection of child difficulties in kindergartens schools;
3. design a training suite for kindergarten teachers in order to develop speciic pedagogical competencies for allow them to early detect difficulties in children;
4. develop an educational toolkit to support observation of teachers to properly detect difficulties and the further communication to parents and specialists;
5. create a website with Open Educational Resources developed from the project to support both the education of children with disability and difficulties and teachers daily activities internationally.

Funded by the European Commission through Erasmus Plus Key Action 2, Strategic Partnerships scheme, the project involved a range of Italian, French, Polish and Spanish partners.

While the requirements of each country were distinct, and so necessitated careful adaptations of the original materials developed by the CeDisMa (Research Center for Disability and Marginality) team to their specific needs, what united all aspects of the project was a desire to improve the educational support for children and teachers in kindergarten, as well as their general experiences in school and their outcomes.

Starting in 2019 and running over three years, the MOEC project has traversed several stages, such as the underpinning research, piloting of training materials and the launch of the website and the WebApp, and it has included a number of international meetings in Spain, Italy, France and Poland. These incorporated a range of academic and practical activities, including conferences during which information about the project was shared with teachers, researchers and parents.

"More opportunities for Every Child" used communities of practice theory and a participatory methodology to inform the collaborative and participatory working practices of the project.

The partners developed all materials in partnership with kindergarten teachers, expert reference groups, regional authority staff and teachers. Through an iterative developmental approach involving feedback from training deliverers and other stakeholders throughout the creation of the observation tools and webapp, the project team ensured that all content was clear and accessible, and relevant to the local educational context and practitioners in partner countries. Nearly 250 school staff in all the four countries received this training.

Evaluations indicate that the training and the webapp materials show sensitivity to the local and national delivery context and provide the basis for further organic development. The project has impacted on the team members themselves, on school and therapeutic staff in all four involved countries, and it has led to practitioners enhancing their practice in meeting the needs of better observe the child's needs in kindergarten. The work has resulted in a sustainable model of good early childhood education practice in partner countries and has made a contribution to local, national and international knowledge, skills and experience. The project has therefore had positive effects on the participant organisations and policy systems as well as on the individuals directly or indirectly involved in the project. Project results have been disseminated widely through social media, publications, reports, conferences and workshops.

The MOEC project therefore started from these needs with the aim of supporting the skills of pre-school teachers in a complex task: to balance the need for early recognition of possible developmental disharmonies in children, in the one hand, and the risk of giving in to excessive medicalisation of possible developmental fragilities, which instead require attention with the right pedagogical expertise, on the other. These statements are of particular importance especially when certain difficulties or delays in the child's development are detected that require attention without necessarily having to assume a medical or sanitary perspective.

The realisation of pedagogical tools for the observation and detection of possible developmental difficulties of pre-school children aimed to respond, through different project actions, to these emerging needs.

This project has as main object the promotion of good practices towards early detection of possible difficulties of the child in age 3–6 years, defining educational instruments shared internationally by the partner institutions. The more detailed objectives of the MOEC project have been:

1. Develop, through specific training courses, the observational skills of teachers of the schools involved;
2. To raise awareness on the importance of an adequate observation and on the acquisition of responsibilities in educational-related terms;
3. Promote a unity of aims in the educational and didactic team: the goal is a thorough management of the child from every perspective;
4. Reach, between the partner bodies (universities and schools involved), a shared definition of a tool for the early detection of possible difficulties in children and a protocol of its application which takes into account the specificities of the context;
5. Experiment the use of the tool in different contexts;
6. Outline good working practices;
7. Promote the relationship with the families, in a co-responsibility orientation of education.

All these original objectives of the project were met. MOEC partnership consisted of 11 partners, including Universities and public and private kindergartens and school districts. Partners worked together through planned regular communications and activities such as project meetings; seminars, conferences, workshops and expert reference groups, and with policy makers and practitioners in each partner country, to jointly develop and deliver a range of training resources.

Many activities have been promoted. First of all, the actual training needs of the preschool teachers participating in the project were identified. The analysis of educational needs represents a fundamental subject, particularly at a time when the professional offer is wide and varied, both in presence and in blended mode.

The analysis of educational needs lies within a research program adopting a structured methodology, consistent with the twofold requirement of the survey itself: to obtain qualitative answers, which would make sense of the real needs of the school and its professionals, and at the same time, to obtain, through as many participants as possible, quantitatively significant data.

More specifically, the objectives of this research can be summarized as follows:

- to carry out an early identification of the knowhow possessed by teachers, in terms of investigating their previous educational experience;
- to identify the needs of teachers with respect to a particular subject – e.g. the early detection of difficulties – which is considered significantly important, not so much in terms of contents, as in relation to the methodologies of the educational intervention they consider as qualitatively more effective.

Subsequently, a training course was delivered, which, due to the outbreak of the pandemic, was delivered almost entirely online, through live meetings that were also video-recorded to allow the greatest possible dissemination of the training content even for teachers not directly involved in the project.

The topics covered were as follows: "Let's start with us: the educational team as the first resource at school"; "The developmental stages of the pre-school child for a correct reading of any disorders and difficulties"; "Metacognition: strategies, activities and tools for everyone"; "How and when to observe the child: towards the construction of an operational tool". For the realisation of this training course, professionals from various disciplinary backgrounds were involved in or- der to meaningfully reach the training needs of teachers (pedagogists, teachers, neuropsychiatrist, psychometrist). The activities in which the project is structured were oriented to achieve the general aims and the objectives in which it is divided. Specifically, the key MOEC outputs were:

1. The State of the Art report (O1) on childhood education and care in pre- school years in all four countries and EU overview (written in EN and translated in each national language).
2. The training on Early childhood education and detection of child difficulties in kindergarten (O2), delivered timely in all four Countries in presence and online despite to the pandemic upcoming.
3. The reports on quality assurance (O3 - O5), fundamental overview on how the training and implementation of the project was conducted in a coordinated and efficient manner (written in EN and translated in each national language).
4. Observation Toolkit development (O4), core output of all the MOEC project activities. The toolkit was firstly developed for "pen-and-paper" use then is was digitalized into a webapp application more accessible and usable for teachers and school professional.
5. The website development (O6), a digital Open-Source repository of information, resources and materials in languages in use in the MOEC project, including the Observation webapp tool.

6. The final report and dissemination (O7), including a detailed description of what has been done, for dissemination and sustainability use (written in EN and translated in each national language).

The project drew on the experience and expertise developed through the creation of the Italian FISM training and observation tool programme, which has been developed in 2015–2017 by the CeDisMa team (Research Center on Disability and Marginality) from Università Cattolica del Sacro Cuore (UCSC). The UCSC programme was developed through an innovative partnership model, in which a number of schools worked together to develop a shared ethos and a vision for autism education, which linked the public, private and voluntary sector together. It received excellent evaluation, with clear evidence of enhancing the knowledge, understanding and practice of autism practitioners. A publication was made by the CeDisMa team in 2017 and it was the guide to start and implement the whole MOEC project internationally. The methods for reaching the objectives of the MOEC project were based on adapting and translating the materials created in Italy, as well as the lessons learnt State of the Art report conducted nationally by each university team, and by developing close team work in translating the Italian observation materials to Poland, Spanish and French, with IT team members advising on the process. Materials were developed and reviewed through an iterative process of team members working together and eliciting feedback from the expert reference groups in each country, and in particular by consulting with school professionals and child development specialists (such as paediatricians, speech therapist, neuropsychiatric doctors) in the creation of training and observation tool materials. After a process of review, the training materials were delivered in each country and were used by local teams. Feedback from this stage informed the further development of the observation materials. Having concluded the deliver of the training materials, the teams began the development of coherent observation tools, with school teachers actively participating in each review session and team members improving the tools accordingly. With the upcoming of the Covid-19 pandemic followed by massive school closure, the MOEC team deeply agreed to develop an online resource (WebApp) that allows to used the observation tool in digital and shared way, instead of only "pen and paper" mode.

Feedbacks from teachers indicated that the training educational programme and the digital observation tool was worthwhile, of high standard, with an appropriate balance of theoretical information and practical advice and resources. Teachers reported that they were now more able to observe children in the classroom and detect difficulties timely, and that the training and the webapp use affected their everyday practice. As a result of the MOEC project, schools and practitioners have requested further collaboration with the partner organizations and a sustainable model for continuing to develop the training and the observation WebApp has been developed in all four countries.

4   The MOEC WebAPP: A Pedagogical Opportunity for Inclusion in Pre-school System

The Observation Toolkit development is the core output of all the MOEC project activities. The toolkit is firstly developed for "pen-and-paper" use then is was digitalized into a WebAPP application more accessible and usable for teachers and school professional (For more details, see the website https://www.moecproject.eu).

The theoretical frame of reference is the ICF, International Classification of Functioning, promoted by the World Health Organisation (2001). From this perspective, the person's development process is seen as dynamic, in continuous evolution, adopting a bio-psycho-social approach. In fact, a child's growth takes place within a physical and environmental, but also relational and psychological context, which strongly influences its development.

The pedagogical tool created can represent the starting point for teachers to reflect on their own educational strategies, on the way they approach children, and on the meaning of the practices adopted. Within the project, grids were created that could be used in each of the countries involved, thus translating them into Italian, French, Spanish and Polish. In addition to the linguistic focus, a very fruitful comparison was carried out between the realities present in the different countries, in order to arrive at transferable tools that can be applied in the various international contexts.

Given the peculiarities that characterize early childhood, such as the rapid change that involves the whole child from all points of view, the partnership deemed it appropriate to structure different variants of the grids according to age. In particular, for the Italian context, four versions of the grid were created, which present differences due to age-specific acquisitions:

- "Anticipatari" for children between 2 and 3 years old, who attend pre-school a few months earlier than their peers.
- Toddlers, for 3-year-old children.
- Mezzani, for 4-year-old children.
- Large, for 5-year-old children.

The final observation tool was included in a WebApp that can be consulted from any type of device (phone, computer, tablet, etc.), so as to facilitate easy compilation by teachers. In this way, it is also possible to share the observations within the educational team, since everyone can access the forms inserted within the platform.

The areas of development analyzed within the Italian context are:

- Reception and insertion.
- Autonomy area.
- Motricity.
- Communication.
- Interpersonal relations and emotional aspects.
- Learning and application of knowledge.

The teacher has a choice of four response options per item (always, often, sometimes, never). This number is the result of careful consideration: in fact, it was decided to avoid leaving five options, because in that case there would have been a risk of the medium option being chosen (Fig. 1).

Based on the answers selected by the teacher, at the end of each area, the algorithm "switches on" a light bulb whose colour indicates the teacher's degree of concern (red bulb for "I am very worried"; orange bulb for "I am worried; yellow bulb for "I think it is better to check the child development with great attention"; green bulb for "I think it is better to check the child development without as usually") (Fig. 1).

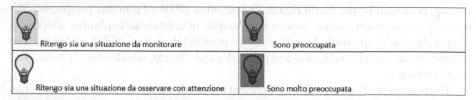

Ritengo sia una situazione da monitorare   Sono preoccupata

Ritengo sia una situazione da osservare con attenzione   Sono molto preoccupata

Fig. 1. Light bulb in MOEC WebApp

This initial automatic 'switch-on' can, however, be modified in such a way as to leave ample room for change for the teacher, who has an overview capable of grasping elements beyond the items on the observation sheet. During the internal discussions that took place during the design of the WebApp, this aspect was given special attention. Indeed, it was decided to avoid following an overly deterministic approach, relying exclusively on the programme algorithm.

The observational tool designed within the MOEC project thus represents a stimulus for the teacher's reflexivity, a means through which to refine one's view of individual children and to engage in discussion with colleagues.

In addition, the teachers involved in the experimentation of the WebApp and the whole work process stated that this tool can also become a starting point through which they can share their concerns with the children's parents. In fact, the moment when the teacher finds herself communicating to the parents that their child has some aspect that would be better investigated or some particular difficulty, is a very delicate passage. If the teacher has an objective support for their concerns, such as a table in which is marked how many times the child has performed a certain behaviour and at what times, it may be easier to stimulate parents to listen.

The WebApp, therefore, was conceived, designed and implemented as a tool to support the professionalism of teachers and educators. They, in fact, have very high and complex educational and care tasks; therefore, they deserve adequate support from pedagogues and researchers, so that they can base their interventions on solid scientific foundations. Furthermore, the fundamental importance of a complementary training course to the construction of the observation grid was highlighted, so as to encourage teachers' reflection and the adoption of an attentive and sensitive gaze towards the children in their classrooms. This kind of support for the professional growth of early childhood practitioners is in line with the demands that have emerged within the European documentation explored in depth within the first chapters of the paper (to name a few: Council of Europe, 2016; European Agency for Special Needs and Inclusive Education, 2017; European Commission Network of Independent Experts on Social Inclusion, 2014).

A strength of the designed tool is the fact that it is the result of an ongoing collaboration between research teams and teachers, who were able to test the first draft version within their own sections and were later invited to share feedback and impressions. In this way, the observation grid was modified and adapted according to the perceived needs of the first teachers who made use of it and were able to detect critical points and weaknesses. In addition, this feedback was also shared among the partners in the countries involved, through a highly collaborative working methodology (Fig. 2).

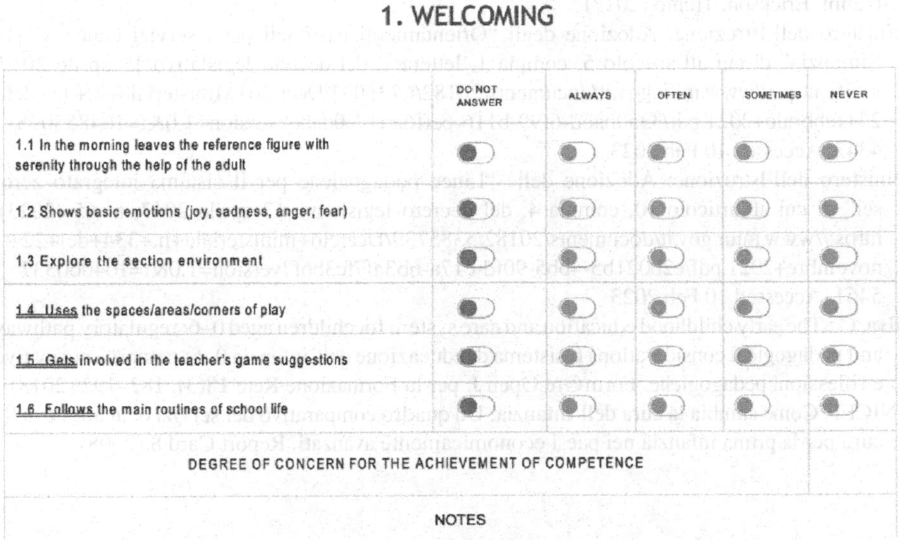

1. WELCOMING

	DO NOT ANSWER	ALWAYS	OFTEN	SOMETIMES	NEVER
1.1 In the morning leaves the reference figure with serenity through the help of the adult	●	●	●	●	●
1.2 Shows basic emotions (joy, sadness, anger, fear)	●	●	●	●	●
1.3 Explore the section environment	●	●	●	●	●
1.4 Uses the spaces/areas/corners of play	●	●	●	●	●
1.5 Gets involved in the teacher's game suggestions	●	●	●	●	●
1.6 Follows the main routines of school life	●	●	●	●	●

DEGREE OF CONCERN FOR THE ACHIEVEMENT OF COMPETENCE

NOTES

Fig. 2. An example of observational sheet of MOEC WebApp

In order to summarize and to conclude, the WebApp is a valuable support for the competent preschool teacher and for professionals in educational services. It is not intended to diagnose, nor to emphasize certain characteristics typical of the growth stages in the child's development. Rather, the tool is a kind of repository of observations. It makes it possible to keep track of any emerging criticalities in development and offers elements for making inclusive educational action more incisive.

References

Alleanza per l'Infanzia: Investire nell'infanzia: prendersi cura del futuro a partire dal presente, Report 2020 (2020). https://www.savethechildren.it/cosa-facciamo/pubblicazioni/invest ire-nell-infanzia-prendersi-cura-del-futuro-a-partire-dal-presente. Accessed 10 Feb 2023

Barger, B., Rice, C., Wolf, R., Roach, A.: Better together: developmental screening and monitoring best identify children who need early intervention. Disabil. Health J. 11(3), 420–426 (2018)

Bondioli, A.: How to form educators for children from 0–6 years old. Pedagogia Oggi, XV, 2 (2017)

Boh, A., Johnson, L.: Universal screening to promote early identification of developmental delays: exploring childcare providers' beliefs and practices. Early Child Dev. Care **188**(12), 1696–1710 (2018)

Chödrön, G., Pizur-Barnekow, K., Viehweg, S., Puk-Ament, A., Barger, B.: Childcare providers' attitudes, knowledge, and practice related to developmental monitoring to promote early identification and referral. Early Child Dev. Care **191**(4), 520–534 (2021)

Conkbayir, M.: Early Childhood and Neuroscience: Theory, Research and Implications for Practice. Bloomsbury Academic Publishing, New York (2017)

d'Alonzo, L. (ed.): La rilevazione precoce delle difficoltà. Una ricerca-azione su bambini da 0 a 6 anni, Erickson, Trento (2017)

Ministero dell'Istruzione: Adozione degli "Orientamenti nazionali per i servizi educativi per l'infanzia" di cui all'articolo 5, comma 1, lettera f, del decreto legislativo 13 aprile 2017, n. 65. https://www.miur.gov.it/documents/20182/6735034/Decreto+Ministeriale+n.+43+del+24+febbraio+2021.pdf/33a0ba6d-6f99-b116-6eff6a417e0dabe?version=1.0&t=164855095 4343. Accessed 10 Feb 2023

Ministero dell'Istruzione: Adozione delle "Linee pedagogiche per il sistema integrato zero-sei" di cui all'articolo 10, comma 4, del decreto legislativo 13 aprile 2017, n. 65 (2023). https://www.miur.gov.it/documents/20182/5385739/Decreto+ministeriale+n.+334+del+22+novembre+2021.pdf/e2b021b5-4bb5-90fd-e17a-6b3af7fc3b6f?version=1.0&t=164060337 5461. Accessed 10 Feb 2023

Silva, C.: The early childhood education and care system for children aged 0–6: regulatory pathway and pedagogical considerations Il sistema di educazione dell'infanzia 0–6: percorso normativo e riflessioni pedagogiche. Form@re Open J. per la Formazione Rete **18**(3), 182–192 (2018)

UNICEF, Come cambia la cura dell'infanzia. Un quadro comparativo dei servizi educativi e della cura per la prima infanzia nei paesi economicamente avanzati, Report Card 8 (2008)

VeeMo: An Universal Exergame
for Kindergarten

Sandyara Beatriz Doro Peres(✉) [ID] and Julio Cesar dos Reis [ID]

Institute of Computing and NIED, UNICAMP, Campinas, SP, Brazil
s184368@dac.unicamp.br, jreis@ic.unicamp.br

Abstract. There are few studies addressing technological solutions to be applicable in physical education in an online learning context. We observe that games proposed in literature use expensive devices such as motion sensors, requiring players' physical presence. This context requires games be accessible and affordable considering the participation of students with disability. This article proposes the design and development of a mobile exergaming, named VeeMo. Our solution is based on Universal Design principles and Accessibility Design Guidelines. We characterize participants' experiences, focusing on viability, usability and accessibility from the perspective of kindergarten children in the context of online physical education learning. Our design methodology considered how promoting physical activity and inclusiveness among kindergarten students. In particular, our design explored wearable artifacts to address vibrational feedbacks. Our results contribute to the development of inclusive technology for young children. Our findings present relevant implications for the promotion of physical activity and social inclusion in early childhood education. The application has potential to be a useful technological tool for physical education, suggesting that the application is accessible, universal and reliable to distinct learning contexts.

Keywords: Exergames · Inclusive Design · Universal Design · Accessibility

1 Introduction

Nowadays, the term "serious games" refers to all games that have a purpose other than enjoyment. Although the term is new, the fundamental principle is not: it was coined by Clark in 1970 to describe a particular style of game [1]. Aside from providing amusement, these games can be categorized based on their purpose: knowledge, behavior, mental coaching [2].

Exergames promote Physical Activity from the player through game mechanics, such as bending down and standing up to move an avatar or shaking his arms to perform an action. Pokémon GO and Just Dance are well-known examples of exergames. Exergames enable how to determine a user's level of physical activity and open up a realm of possibilities [4]. These games became an important ally for several health and education professionals, such as physical education instructors [3].

Papastergiou [5] holds the view that exergames are a complement to the traditional P.E. (Physical Education) and offer the possibility to exercise oneself: exergames are

M. Antona and C. Stephanidis (Eds.): HCII 2023, LNCS 14021, pp. 247–262, 2023.
https://doi.org/10.1007/978-3-031-35897-5_19

a successful approach in P.E. classes when associated with the traditional curriculum because the students can become more physically active.

In this article, we investigate how to develop an accessible, affordable, and replicable exergame for physical education to promote its already known benefits. This study proposes the design and development of a mobile exergaming, named VeeMo. Our solution aims to digitize a practical activity that is already applied in physical education classes: the chosen activity is the Brazilian play "*Vivo ou Morto*".

The game consists of a leader dictating commands in which other participants must obey, when he says "Vivo", everyone must stand up and "Morto", everyone crouches. As time passes, the leader alternates the ordering speed, whoever makes a mistake leaves the game. The last one to stand is the winner.

VeeMo supports players based only on the need to use their smartphone and support it somewhere so that the front camera can capture their body. VeeMo was constructed based on WCAG 2.1 A and AA success criteria for providing screen reader and any assistive technologies compatibility. Our solution proposes the building of a wearable for enhancing players sensorial experience: the VeeMo Watch stands for a wearable that announces the given command through an braille display and provides the feedback through vibration. Deafblinded players could use their braille displays only for navigation and the Veemo Watch for a portable experience during gameplay, allowing major movements.

The remaining of this article is structured as follows: Sect. 2 synthesis the state-of-the art; Sect. 3 details our designed and developed solution; Sect. 4 presents the discussion of our findings; Sect. 5 concludes the paper.

2 Related Work

In June 2022, we conducted a literature search in IEEExplore and ACM Digital Library that returned 17 results for the search terms "exergames" AND "physical education". Limitations of this review so far include the fact that, as this is a multidisciplinary subject, the small number of results from only one search engine was to be expected. Our main inclusion criteria were (1) primary studies on exergaming in the context of school physical education; (2) thematizes the use of exergames as pedagogical tools; and (3) does not use exergames in students' rehabilitation. Researches that did not meet the above three conditions was excluded from our exploratory literature review. Our literature review selected three articles based on the inclusion criteria adopted.

Finco *et al.* [6] conducted a qualitative approach with 24 students aged 8–14 years. They had one regular PE lesson each week and the second lesson in the Exergames Lab: the activities consisted of the games Kinect Sports and Kinect Adventures, both of which included a variety of sports and physical tasks. The results of observations collected over a 5-month period showed that students were more confident in playing sports and other physical activities taught through the use of Exergames. This shows motivation and interest in interacting with their classmates. In addition, they observed that the students were more open-minded and willing to participate in P.E. class, being interested in learning sport rules, new movements and how to maintain a healthy lifestyle through physical activity.

Reategui *et al.* [7] used the Your Shape Fitness Evolved 2012, Kinect Adventures and Kinect Sports games as activities once a week over a 20-week period with 28 students from primary to high school. The aspect of enjoyment in relation to the curriculum was rated particularly positively by the students. Some of the students stated in the interviews that they found the activities very interesting because they combined the use of video games with the actual practice of sports, which made it fun. The questionnaire attempted to assess the perceived usefulness indicating positive results, such as health improvements.

Lindberg *et al.* [8] developed Running Othello 2 (RO2), a mobile exergame that uses near-field communication (NFC) tags and wearable sensors to transform the board game Othello into a stimulating exergame that requires players to think tactically as well as perform physical exercises and solve educational challenges. The study used a mixed method to evaluate RO2 with 61 South Korean primary school students. Responses to the fun game were positive among 32 third grade students and their teacher in South Korea. The learning effect was stronger with the game than with the traditional learning method, but the long-term learning effects of the game still need to be verified.

Most of the studies investigated used Xbox360 as its main resource as an intervention tool, presenting games as Kinect Adventures and Just Dance, which are games that promote social, achievement and action motivation. Since they are collaboration games, they work on agility, coordination, balance, speed and reaction time fitness skills.

We observed that all of the selected studies focused on games limited to four players per turn and utilized video games, which can be costly for schools to provide. While the use of video games in physical education classes can be engaging and effective, it is important to consider the financial impact it may place on educational institutions. Moreover, the restriction to only four players per turn may limit the potential for social interaction and teamwork, which are key components of physical education.

Whereas existing studies have explored video games, our study employed the use of a mobile device integrated with other components. It is worth noting that this device is not commercially available, and as such, schools would need to construct it themselves. This can be a significant challenge, as it requires specialized knowledge and expertise in both technology and physical education. Moreover, the cost of materials and labor involved in constructing such a device may be prohibitive for some educational institutions. Despite these challenges, the potential benefits of incorporating technology in physical education cannot be ignored. Therefore, it is essential to explore alternative approaches that are both feasible and effective in promoting physical activity and healthy habits among students.

Overall, most games proposed in literature demand the use of expansive devices. All of them required players' physical presence. Our literature results showed that none of them mention the participation of students with disabilities. The design and ideation of our exergame considered these aspects.

In general, the studies reviewed did not mention the participation of students with disabilities. Furthermore, those which involve the creation of an artifact do not delve into the design process in a comprehensive manner, and do not adopt inclusive premises. This is a significant issue, as students with disabilities often face unique challenges in physical education classes and may require specialized accommodations to fully participate. Additionally, inclusive design principles are essential for ensuring that all students can access and benefit from technology-based approaches in physical education. Therefore, it is necessary to prioritize the inclusion of students with disabilities in both research and practice in the field of physical education. By doing so, educators can ensure that all students have access to high-quality physical education that promotes their health and well-being.

Our proposal stands out from other studies in the field of physical education technology, as it aims to utilize a resource that is accessible to both students and teachers - the mobile phone. Moreover, our design process is documented using the principles of Accessible, Inclusive and Universal Design, which prioritize the needs and perspectives of diverse users. By adopting this approach, our goal is to ensure that our technology-based approach to physical education is accessible and beneficial to all students, regardless of their abilities or backgrounds. This represents a significant step towards promoting inclusive and equitable physical education practices; and can serve as a model for other educators and researchers in the field.

3   Game Concept and Development

The double diamond design process is a relatively new and well-known methodology. It was developed by the Design Council in 2005. An in-depth study of eleven global brands and the methods they use was conducted in 2007. The double diamond method was produced as "a simple graphical way of describing the design process" [3]. This model (Fig. 1) was used to guide our design process which has four phases resulting in a high-fidelity prototype, providing the user interface for an assertive instrument development.

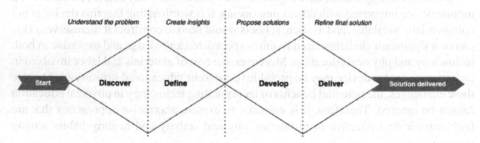

Fig. 1. Double Diamond Diagram by the Author.

1. Discover: Problems are explored, insights and user needs gathered and ideas generated by extracting from literature;
2. Define: Problems are defined and refined, providing insights;
3. Develop: Solutions are created and explored;
4. Deliver: The product is tested and evaluated.

3.1 Discover

During the pandemic, many changes were necessary in the educational field, and physical education was not left out. With social distancing restrictions in place, in-person physical activity became unviable, leading many physical educators to adapt their classes for remote learning. Therefore, selecting studies in physical education during the pandemic became relevant to understand the challenges and opportunities of remote teaching in the field. Through these studies, it was possible to analyze the different strategies used by physical educators to keep their students active and engaged during the period of social isolation, as well as identifying possible limitations and suggestions to improve remote teaching in physical education.

All studies selected through our exploratory literature review contributed on identifying potential user needs from the perspective of teachers and kindergarten students. They resulted in key requirements that the game must have. To this end, we conducted a thorough and exploratory literature review by searching scientific databases (such as Google Scholar).

The studies selected during our literature analysis phase contributed to characterizing a user persona and potential game requirements, such as investigations by Alencar *et al.* [4], Barbosa [9], Coelho *et al.* [10], Godoi *et al.* [11], Silvia *et al.* [12] and Skowronski [13]. From literature, we extracted the following challenges for the development of a mobile exergaming application from the obstacles faced by P.E. professionals and primary students:

- One of the problems identified by educators in the new educational setting altered by the epidemic was adjusting to online classrooms and mastering technology tools. In terms of obstacles, the teachers emphasized the students' hesitation or unwillingness to turn on the camera during online sessions or participating actively.
- Teachers believe that this makes it harder to assess pupils and raises concerns about whether or not students are following the class.
- P.E Educators miss physical touch with students and fear that physical education is losing its character, as a result of their lack of physical presence in class. Furthermore, the setting in which they reside may be unsuitable for learning, with noise and others interfering.
- P.E. classes are basically communal in person; a group of students meets with the teacher to learn about bodily practices that are mostly collective in nature. During the pandemic, students and teachers meet in a virtual environment in remote teaching, but there is no body connection as in face-to-face sessions. As a result, teachers must devise educational activities that children can complete independently or, at most, while engaging with a family member
- One of the biggest challenges during the pandemic was tolerating network instabilities or quality internet access. Teacher had to think on online or offline activities, thus everyone can engage into. In addition, those activities needed to be viable considering the available resources that the student have at home: not everyone could have a ball or a videogame, for example.

3.2 Define

We explored the "How Might We" (HMW) method to define what are solved with our exergame. The HMW method describes a technique that generates novel approaches by formulating questions with the identical beginning "How might we…". The prompt works as a source of inspiration for idea generation that broadens perspectives, discovers connections, and generates unexpected ideas [14].

The answers to the questions are hypotheses raised by the authors to create a base version of the product solution, if they are valid or not, they will be validated during the research with professionals and students. By doing brainstorming, the authors aimed to come up with ideas for each of those HMWs stated in Define. This helped us (the authors in the role of designers) come up with fresh ideas, such as:

- **HMW1. How might we improve online P.E. lessons experience?**

  o Exergames as a pedagogical tool with gamification resources.

- **HMW2. How might we help students to participate in online P.E. lessons using low-cost tools?**

  o Using their smartphone as tool instead of a videogame.
  o Allowing offline gameplay to deal with any Internet instability.

- **HMW3. How might we help students to participate in P.E. lessons regardless on their characteristics such as disability?**

  o Any Design Rational must follow Universal, Inclusive and Accessibility Design Principles and its development must be following the WCAG 2.1 A and AA criteria for ensuring minimum digital accessibility and assistive technology compatibility.

- **HMW4. How might we help students to create bonds with classmates?**

  o Students must be able to see and perceive each other, seeing them as individuals with their own characteristics and needs.

- **HMW5. How might we help teachers on using this solution as a P.E. lesson?**

  o The solution can be based on the National Common Curricular Base (BNCC), making it easier to implement in classrooms. By aligning our project with the BNCC, we ensure that it meets the requirements and expectations of the curriculum, making it easier for educators to integrate it into their lesson plans.

We designed the concept of a possible solution based on features and requirements for the game. We built an overview of the main journeys available in-app for users.

3.3 Develop

With the purpose of developing a game that can be approached in classrooms, we proposed to digitalize a practical activity that is already applied in physical education classes: the chosen activity is the Brazilian play *"Vivo ou Morto"*. Similar to "Simon says", it is a game suggested based on the BNCC. As a lesson plan curriculum activity, the game

"*Vivo ou Morto*" is recommended for young children - from 4 to 5 years and 11 months of age. It focuses on working agility, physical conditioning, motor coordination, attention, concentration, body expression [15].

The game consists of a leader dictating commands in which the other participants must obey: when (s)he (the leader) says "*Vivo*", everyone must stand up and "*Morto*", everyone crouches. As time passes, the leader alternates the ordering speed. Whoever makes a mistake leaves the game. The last one to stand is the winner.

For VeeMo, the player only needs to use their smartphone and support it somewhere so that the front camera can capture their body. When the host starts the game, the player with the highest preparation time – time for get ready for doing the movements, custom per player - uses as the countdown, reaching 0, the game starts (cf. Fig. 2).

Fig. 2. Gameplay and score points by the Author.

The player makes the previously calibrated move consistent with the displayed command. The feedback of your movement is given through words and symbols, and the more you get it right, the more points you earn and other messages of encouragement are presented. This type of gamified real-time feedback strategy with motivating messages and allowing even the player who lost to continue playing was a way to make the process challenging at the same time as fun. For each mistake, 1 chance is lost and, when 3 chances are lost, the player loses the chance to be on the podium, but it can continue playing to not feel excluded from the group, however, its points will no longer be counted. (cf. Fig. 3).

The last one remaining is the winner, receiving a bonus score as reward and the podium is shown, allowing the players to play again (cf. Fig. 4).

The game recognizes the right movement through a previous calibration (cf. Figure) done by the players. At this stage, they decide the pattern for the "*Vivo*" and "*Morto*" movement, any movement is acceptable: the user can set as only lifting up and down its

Fig. 3. Gameplay and score points by the Author.

Fig. 4. End-game by the Author.

arms or setting a standing/crouch position, thus, any user in any physical situation can play VeeMo (Fig. 5).

In VeeMo, you can go through the following journeys according to the VeeMo's information architecture diagram in Fig. 6:

1. **Onboarding:** Step of registration of permissions and calibration of movements for the game;
2. **Create lobby:** Step of creating a room to play alone or with more people. For security reasons, given that the target audience is children, it was not chosen to create an online multiplayer lobby, so that the player can play with people close to them, they must pass the room code directly to that person, either face-to-face or online through their parents with communication apps such as *WhatsApp*.
3. **Join game:** Step to join a room created by someone, having the option of entering the code formed by a sequence of illustrations or scanning a QR Code face-to-face.

Fig. 5. Movement setup by the Author.

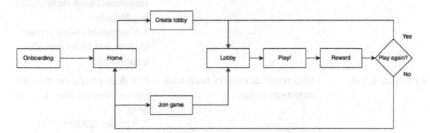

Fig. 6. VeeMo's Information Architecture Diagram by the Author.

4. **Gameplay Loop:** Main gameplay where the players are gathered in lobby and can start playing until the winner is announced.
5. **Settings:** Step to adjust information established in Onboarding, such as nickname, preparation time and calibration.

All VeeMo design decisions were taken based on universal design principles to promote an enjoyable experience to students with permanent, temporary or situational disabilities according to Table 1. This process resulted in a high-fidelity prototype, providing a user interface which may answer to any users' needs.

VeeMo's follows WCAG 2.1 A and AA success criteria, as achieving this level is recommended by the W3C for a solution to be minimally accessible for providing provide screen reader and any assistive technologies compatibility [16]. An accessibility annotation was done to document the screen reader behaviors. In this sense, it is possible to provide visual and hearing feedbacks. An accessibility annotation was created to guide the development expected behaviors on assistive technology such as screen readers. The following set of annotated components represent a small sampling of annotations focused on accessibility properties and roles (cf. Fig. 7).

We proposed the building of a wearable for enhancing players experience: the VeeMo Watch (cf. Fig. 7); an watch that announces the given command through an braille display and provides the feedback through vibration. Thus, deafblinded players could use their braille displays only for navigating through the app for a portable experience during gameplay, allowing major movements. Veemo Watch was designed to be worn in any

Table 1. Universal Design and VeeMo features.

Principle	Description	Design Rationale
Equitative Use	Design is appealing and provides the same means of use to all individuals	1. Larger touch areas and typography are default, there is need for customization for each user 2. All action components are centralized and occupied the whole width area, accommodating right or left handed use 3. Compatible with screen readers and other assistive technologies
Low Physical Effort	Effectively & easility used with minimum effort	1. It doesn't require multiple interactions such as drag and drop 2. The default timer for preparation is 10 s, but it is customizable upon 30 s 3. There is no need for crouch, any up/down movements counts for playing
Tolerance for Error	Consider and minimize hazards and the adverse consequences of accidental or unintended actions	1. Every finish action such as give up on gameplay comes up with an confirmation modal 2. The player has 3 chances until defeat, not only 1 as in the original game 3. Players can calibrate their movements any time
Perceivable Information	Ambient conditions do not affect use and consider individual's sensory abilities	1. Adoption of high contrast colors recommended by WCAG 2.1 2. All components are standardized and weighted for easy recognition recommended by WCAG 2.1

(continued)

Table 1. (*continued*)

Principle	Description	Design Rationale
Simple and Intuitive	Use of the design is easy to understand	1. Use of universal icons and colors such as "X" and red for closing actions 2. Every main textual informations has a visual representation composed by icons & colors
Flexible in Use	There is choice in methods of use	1. The player can set up their movements for gameplay
Size and Space	Appropriate size & space is provided for approach, reach, manipulate and use for all body sizes, postures, or mobility	1. Touch areas are, at least, 48dp recommended by WCAG 2.1 2. The player set up its camera according to their needs and calibrated movement

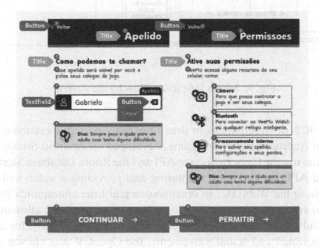

Fig. 7. VeeMo's accessibility annotation sample by the Author.

form with less movements as possible; the user can wear it as a necklace, wristband or even a pin given that the watch is coupled to nodes and its closure is through magnets.

Through VeeMo Watch, the player can feel the actual command through a Braille display ("*Vivo*" or "*Morto*") with vibrational feedback, consisting on 1-fast vibration meaning success; and 2 fast-vibrations meaning failure. If the player loses all their chances, a 1 fast plus a 1 long vibration is player. At the end of the match, a single long vibration is played. All of this is connected by Bluetooth, no Wi-Fi connection is needed. VeeMo Watch enhances players experience, but it is no required for playing VeeMo according to Fig. 8.

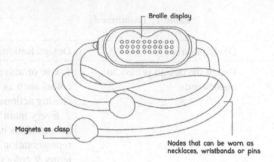

Fig. 8. VeemoWatch Concept Art by the Author.

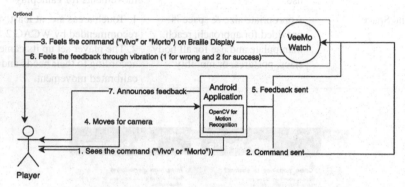

Player

Fig. 9. Macro Interaction Flow by the Author.

Given that 90% of smartphones in Brazil use the Android operational system [17], we provided an Android smartphone game, developed on Android Studio using Kotlin language. We can use the Camera Service API and the Room Database Storage provided by the Android API. For the image capturing and providing a video call up to 4 participants, we chose the WebRTC, an open-source real-time communication tool which supports video, voice, and generic data to be sent between peers, allowing developers to build powerful voice and video-communication solutions. Finally, for image matching from the expected and actual movements, the OpenCV was chosen since it is an open-source image processing library.

Because authentication is not required to play, all data such as movement calibration as well as the player's name and points are saved on the local device through Shared-Preference API[1]. As for the VeeMo Watch, an accessory for promoting a sensorial experience, the chosen components were chosen for its construction:

- Arduino Mini: The microcontroller that uses ATmega 328p mini chip. It has 2 KB RAM, 32 KB EPROM, 64 KB FLASH;
- Braille Display: Metec P20. Metec is a well-known company specialized in Braille displays, being able to purchase the cell individually, the braille display informs the command "*Vivo*" or "*Morto*";

---

[1] https://developer.android.com/reference/android/content/SharedPreferences.

- Bluetooth Module: A Bluetooth Serial Transceiver HC06 is used. The HC06 Bluetooth module is the most widely used module with an Arduino project. It has low power consumption so that it can be powered by a small rechargeable battery;
- Vibration Motor: LR50 Piezo LEGS Rotary 50. The LR50 motor is a Piezo motor in a rotary configuration. The main purpose of the motor is to feedback if the done movement was right (one-long vibration) or wrong (two short-vibration);
- Battery - 3.7 v 100 mah Lithium-ion. Batteries with charging modules are used. Powering the whole system is a battery which can last up to 12 h with 2 h of charging.

3.4 Deliver

The game is tested and evaluated by P.E. professionals through a focus group dynamic, rejecting parts that do not work and improving on those that do. Then, an exploratory study must be conducted with kindergarten children to observe the players' behavior and to obtain initial feedback on their satisfaction and first impressions.

A demo version of the game must be available in a workshop, mediated by the researcher along with the teachers, for 4 participants (players) at a time over a period, at least, of 30 min. Then we ask the candidates to play the current version of our solution. The whole activity is video-recorded to be further analyzed. Due to the fact that it has already been established a trusting relationship with the participants, the mediator applies an interviewer-administered questionnaire.

The questionnaire is an important tool for gathering data in our research with children. While children can provide valuable information, it is important to remember that they may have limitations in their ability to understand and respond to complex questions. To ensure that addressing how to gather accurate and meaningful information, it was necessary to grab data from teachers who work with children on a daily basis. This helps us anticipating the diversity of children and ensure that the questionnaire is appropriate for their level of understanding. By including both children and teachers' perspectives, we gain a comprehensive understanding of the topic and make more informed conclusions.

The target audience consists of kindergarten students, which consists of children from 4 to 5 years and 11 months of age. Both the unit of analysis and observation are the respondent as an individual, that is, the student itself. The search unit for the study is the Children Living Center (CeCI – Portuguese acronym of *Centro de Convivência Infantil*). Located on the campus of the University of Campinas, it is a space that gives access to the education of infants and children from six months to six years old.

The collected data are digitalized for further manipulation. The questionnaire is composed of a series of individual questions. In this sense, data analysis is based on Single Likert-type items.

4 Discussion

Inclusive exergames can help to promote social inclusion and reduce the stigma and barriers that students with disabilities may face in traditional physical education settings. However, creating inclusive exergames requires careful attention to the needs and perspectives of diverse users, including those with physical, sensory, and cognitive impairments. Enriching a game experience with wearables such as VeemoWatch is becoming increasingly popular. This promotes a multisensory experience for the player. Neverthe-less, creating a wearable from scratch can be a challenging task, requiring significant time and efforts in designing and building the device. Additionally, the availability of parts outside the country can also be a hindrance. If an accessible wearable product already existed in the market, it could simplify the development process and expedite the implementation of the product in the game.

Many of the principles and practices that support inclusivity can also lead to more effective and user-friendly solutions overall, although it may require some extra effort and attention to details. Similarly, involving diverse stakeholders in the design process can help to identify and address a wide range of user needs and perspectives, leading to solutions that are more effective and relevant to a broader range of users.

By focusing on the difficulties identified in research, such as the lack of engagement and participation from students and taking into consideration accessibility needs for students with disabilities, inclusive design can be a powerful tool in developing solu-tions that address the specific needs of remote teaching. With an inclusive approach, as we developed, technology can be harnessed to make education more accessible for all students, regardless of their individual needs and circumstances.

Despite not having involved end-users in the design process due to time constraints and solely basing the solution decisions on existing literature, we were able to develop an initial version of the solution to be validated and receive feedback. By following inclusive design guidelines and leveraging existing knowledge about the target audi-ence's challenges, the solution was able to address key issues faced by remote teachers. The iterative design process must allow continuous refinement and improvements of the solution based on feedback from end-users, ensuring that it meets their needs and remains accessible and inclusive.

User feedback is critical in ensuring that a product meets the needs of its intended audience. Accessibility and inclusive design guidelines provide a framework for creating products that are usable by as many people as possible, but the ultimate test is in the hands of the users. Through user feedback, designers and developers can learn what works well, what doesn't, and what needs to be improved.

We considered a probabilistic sample for the number of children enrolled in CeCi. This sampling plan may change depending on the actual population size. Since we aim to obtain generalizations from a larger population, we must use a simple random sampling to promote an equal chance that any of the samples in the subset are chosen.

One of the limitations of researching with children is the potential for bias. Children may not be fully aware of their own abilities and may not be able to accurately report their experiences. Additionally, their responses may be influenced by their caregivers, the researchers or even the teachers involved in the study. As a result, it is important for researchers to take extra care when conducting research with children, and to consider these potential biases when interpreting their findings.

Collecting the opinions of children in research can be challenging as it is important to avoid bias and ensure that their voices are heard authentically. One approach is to use age-appropriate language and methods that allow children to express their thoughts freely. Involving teachers in the construction of a research evaluation method with children in their classroom is crucial for several reasons. First, teachers have a deeper understanding of their students' individual and collective learning processes and can provide valuable insights into what types of research methods and evaluation techniques would be most effective. Second, by involving teachers in the process, they become invested in the research project and can provide additional support and encouragement to their students to participate fully. Third, teachers can help to ensure that the research process is conducted ethically, with appropriate measures taken to protect the privacy and rights of the children involved. Overall, involving teachers in the development and implementation of research projects with children can lead to more meaningful and effective outcomes.

One of the possible limitations of our study is the inability to test the application with children with disabilities if they are not present in the school. Despite our efforts to create an inclusive solution, it is essential to include the perspectives and needs of children with different disabilities to ensure that the application meets their requirements. However, if there are no children with disabilities in the school, it may not be possible to test the application with this population.

5 Conclusion

The development of an inclusive exergame requires attention to diverse needs and abilities of players, as well as an understanding of how to make physical activity enjoyable and engaging. Our solution demonstrated that by following inclusive design guidelines from literature, plus involving players and educators in an evaluation process, it is possible to create a game in an agile manner that promotes physical activity and is accessible to a wider range of players.

Our proposed research has the potential to reveal a field of possibilities for new studies to solve a societal problem in an educational context through innovative and financially accessible technologies: exergames contribute positively to the teaching-learning process, emerging as a new possibility for the educational field. VeeMo has the potential to expand the Exergames' point of view due to gap found about universal design and proposing to develop a body movement game considering its diversity.

There is still room for improvements and future work to expand our game to address players' specific disability needs by incorporating more feedback from players and educators. We can study ways to integrate the game into existing physical education curriculums. Additionally, it would be valuable to conduct studies concerning how to promote inclusive and accessible multisensorial experiences on exergames.

References

1. Clark, C.: Serious Games. University Press of America (1970)
2. Michael, D.R., Chen, S.L.: Serious Games: Games that Educate, Train, and Inform. Cengage Learning (2005)
3. Lindberg, R., Seo, J., Laine, T.H.: Enhancing physical education with exergames and wearable technology. IEEE Trans. Learn. Technol. 9(4), 328–341 (2016)
4. Silveira, I.F.: O papel da aprendizagem ativa no ensino híbrido em um mundo pós-pandemia: reflexões e perspectivas. Revista Paulista de Pediatria 35, 464–471 (2017)
5. Papastergiou, M.: Exploring the potential of computer and video games for health and physical education: a literature review. Comput. Educ. 53, 603–622 (2009)

6. Finco, M.D., Bittencourt, M.Z., Reategui, E.B., Zaro, M.A.: Collaboration and social interaction in physical education classes: experience with the use of exergames. In: IEEE International Games Innovation Conference (IGIC), pp. 50–56. IEEE, Vancouver (2013)
7. Reategui, E., Bittencourt, M.Z., Mossmann, J.B.: Students' attitudes in relation to exergame practices in physical education. In: 8th International Conference on Games and Virtual Worlds for Serious Applications (VS-GAMES), pp. 1–4. IEEE, Barcelona (2016)
8. Design Council. The Design Process: What is the Double Diamond? (2018). https://www.designcouncil.org.uk/news-opinion/design-process-what-double-diamond. Accessed 20 Aug 2022
9. Barbosa, H.: Aulas de educação física em meio a uma pandemia: dificuldades e superação. Educação em Foco 1(1) (2021)
10. Coelho, C.G., da Fonseca Xavier, F.V., Marques, A.C.G.: Educação física escolar em tempos de pandemia da covid-19: a participação dos alunos de ensino médio no ensino remoto. Int. J. Phys. Educ. 2(2) (2020)
11. Godoi, M., Kawashima, L.B., de Almeida Gomes, L.: "temos que nos reinventar": os professores e o ensino da educação física durante a pandemia de covid-19. Dialogia 36, 86–101 (2020)
12. da Silva, A.J.F., Pereira, B.K.M., de Oliveira, J.A.M., Surdi, A.C., de Araújo, A.C.: A adesão dos alunos às atividades remotas durante a pandemia: realidades da educação física escolar. Corpoconsciência 24(2), 57–90 (2020)
13. Skowronski, M.: Educação física escolar no ensino fundamental e médio: atuação docente frente às dificuldades do cenário de pandemia. In: IV Congresso Internacional de Educação Inclusiva (2021)
14. da Educação, M.: Base nacional curricular comum (2018). Accessed 16 May 2022
15. Siemon, D., Becker, F., Robra-Bissantz, S.: How might we? From design challenges to business innovation 4, 96–110 (2018)
16. Web Content Accessibility Guidelines 2.0, W3C World Wide Web Consortium Recommendation XX Month Year. http://www.w3.org/TR/200X/REC-WCAG20-20081211/. Latest version at http://www.w3.org/TR/WCAG20/. Accessed 20 Aug 2022
17. Moura, L., Camargo, G.: Impacto econômico e social do android no Brasil (2020). Accessed 16 May 2022

Towards a Smart Learning Application for Visual Impaired People

Abdalah Amadou Gueye[1]([✉]), Swati Chandna[1], Markus Lang[2], and Frank Laemers[1]

[1] SRH University of Heidelberg, 69123 Heidelberg, Germany
AbdalahAmadou.Gueye@stud.hochschule-heidelberg.de,
swati.chandna@srh.de, laemers@ph-heidelberg.de
[2] Pädogogische Hochschule, 69120 Heidelberg, Germany
lang@ph-heidelberg.de

Abstract. Education is the key to the success of the development of a country. Worldwide we have many people with low-vision issues when we look at the statistic globally, especially in Germany. Low-vision people face a big challenge interacting with visual information, which impacts their learning process. That is why a device like Braille, a tactile code used by blind and visually impaired people, is created. It is a non-vision way of reading and writing texts system composed of dots which Blind people can feel by touching and can read it as well. Being able to read Braille for low-vision people will significantly impact them, as they will have the same access as sighted people. However, a lot of time, training, and assistance is required to read and understand it. It takes about four months to learn the uncontracted version and up to two years for the contracted. In addition, there need to be more resources and expensive costs for the resources available, which can vary between 500 - 2000 dollars [6]. With all these obstacles combined, it will be difficult for new learners, adults or child to master it very well. Therefore, effective training is required. In our century, new technologies made things to be accessible easily.

In this case, screen readers, braille displays, and speech recognition help the low-vision interact with the smartphones like any other person. Applications like Braille Tutor [3], mBraille [5], E-Braille [1], and others support visually impaired people using Braille without difficulties. But most of them are limited to teaching only how to read and write letters. For instance, Braille Tutor teaches basic alphabets and how to read numbers. This application was developed by Anjana Joshi [3]. Suppose we take the example of mBraille [5], which helps low vision people write letters and practice them simultaneously by playing some game. In addition, the application was developed to learn other kinds of letters, like Bangla. We do have many of them, as we listed above, and they have existed for years. However, we need a generic platform that starts from the basic until the most challenging part, where the school children will learn from A to Z everything he needs to know about Braille by feeling it on their fingertips. So after analyzing that, we are discussing in this paper smart learning application which is an extension of our previous work done on D-Braille [2]. This effective and user-friendly mobile application will help visually impaired people read or write braille characters. But not only letters, we assist the low-vision in understanding how Braille works with the dots, then teach him to read letters, words, and numbers. A complete

© The Author(s), under exclusive license to Springer Nature Switzerland AG 2023
M. Antona and C. Stephanidis (Eds.): HCII 2023, LNCS 14021, pp. 263–274, 2023.
https://doi.org/10.1007/978-3-031-35897-5_20

application like this is the first to our knowledge, so it is done by connecting the Braille keyboard with the mobile and starting from the lowest to the highest. We are first making the user familiar with dots on the Braille, recognizing them in their forms and patterns. This is done in a gaming format, making it more interesting and making them love it, as our target is mostly children. Then we move on with the letters. The low-vision must know how each letter is represented in Braille. With the help of the voice-over and an effective User Interface, the application will be easy for them. After learning the letters, a practice session is provided to them so that they can manage them well before moving on to the numbers, where knowing the letters will make it easier for them. Because as we know, numbers are a combination of dot 6 and one letter in computer braille system that is common is Germany in the context of assistive technologies, so knowing the letters and training them with the game of getting familiar with the dots will make it much easier for them. After every learning session, we have a practice session to ensure that they master it, so the same goes for the numbers and words, which they will practice after learning. In the end, the result we will get is that the User will know everything he needs to know about Braille and will promote more features compared to existing applications like the one mentioned above.

Keywords: Braille · Visually Impaired · Mobile Application · User Interface Design

1 Introduction

Low-vision people use Braille to read and write, but it can affect their learning growth due to difficulties in understanding and interaction, lack of resources, and time consumption. In addition, the resources out there are quite costly, making it more difficult for them to access and learn. Knowing the technology has grown, this is a specific case requiring specific training and assistance. Therefore, this research focused on finding a solution by working on a mobile application interface called "D-Braille" [2] for people with low vision, which is extended in this paper. This application has been designed specifically for people new to Braille who want to learn Braille from the beginning. This application helps them to learn and feel simultaneously. Braille is a tactile system that allows people with blindness and low vision to read and write, granting them access to literacy but teaching them how to use and understand Braille is also essential. Braille is a system that consists of touch reading and writing for blind and low-vision people. Braille consists of 6 dots, two horizontal and three vertical dots. It's read from left to right, and both hands are used in the process. It also contains punctuation equivalents and provides symbols to indicate the grouping of characters. The reading, on average, is 100 words per minute and can go up to 200 words per minute in some cases. Therefore, all the printed words can be read and enjoyed by blind and visually impaired people just like everyone else. But over the year, technology has developed, and touch-based applications are trending as everyone uses smartphones in their daily lives. The smartphone now comes with voice-over technology to help low-vision people access smartphones. And so, some applications were developed to help them learn to use Braille. However, the features are limited. Therefore during our research, we developed the first part of our application which, with many features, teach low-vision people how to read and write numbers, letter, and words and practice them by connecting their smartphone with the Braille device.

2 Related Work

In the past, such applications have been developed and gained popularity. Anjana Joshi and Ajit Samasgikar developed the "Braille Tutor [3], a Gift for the Blind". It is an automatic device capable of making blind people learn the Alphabet in Braille without anybody's help. The basic idea is to use solenoid actuators which use electromagnetism to convert electrical energy into mechanical motion. To give a feel of Braille script to the blind children. An Arduino board [3] controls the actuators. The device uses ten solenoid actuators for basic alphabets and numbers. In addition, the device has Bluetooth connectivity which can connect to a Computer far at 300 m that the professors can use to monitor what the students are learning. In Fig. 1, we can see how students use the Braille Tutor with the monitors included.

Fig. 1. Braille tutor [3]

E-Braille [1] is a solution as well for Braille learners. The idea was to create a self-learning kit that would behave like a teacher teaching the low-vision to learn Braille. The design is such that they use a keypad as input and a microphone as output for the learner. So basically, we have an Audio Input like the microphone and a Braille keypad as another input. Which will be then processed by the main processor according to the operation entered, then give output on the speaker and Braille cell. The system is composed of Hardware and Software, as mentioned in [1], which helps achieve the final result.

mBraille [5] application mobile app was designed for Visual Impaired Students (VIS-focused) elementary education, as shown in Fig. 2. It helps low-vision people by being able to write letters and practice them simultaneously by watching tutorials. This app contains all characters and words in Bengali and English. The tutorial aims to help the students verify the spelling of letters and practice well in Braille. Unfortunately, the application works only on low-cost Android phones, which, during this time, only a few uses or are no longer used. Regarding how the application works: the screen contains six dots (as we know, most about Braille is on those six dots) which the student can press. It has all the letters to learn in the" learn letter" sub-function and practice the letter in the sub-function"practice letters." However, as mentioned above, it works only on Android devices as we need a generic platform that starts from the basic to the most challenging part, where the user will learn from A to Z and be able to use it in our age as technology has improved a lot. The student will get everything he needs to know about Braille by feeling it on their fingertips.

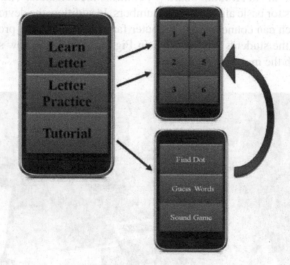

Fig. 2. mBraille user interface [2]

From the research mentioned above, many applications were implemented to help the VIS learn Braille as easily as possible. However, no generic educational mobile application exists for people with visual impairment to learn and practice letters, words, and sentences at a low cost. Furthermore, most importantly, most of them still need to adapt to the new world of technology we live in, which grows very fast. Therefore, in this paper, we first design and implement a generic mobile application to learn and practice Braille. Also, we evaluate this application with professors that teach the VIS in the first place before doing it with six low-sighted people to check the application's usability.

3 Research Methodology

To develop an effective design for the digital braille application, we first tested usability with two professors at the University of Education in Heidelberg [7]. They have been working in the domain of low- vision for more than ten years and are in contact with other schools for low vision. Through this testing, basic needs were identified, and all necessary features were identified. The students were using the Braille display to learn Braille.

3.1 Software Architecture

The application has many features which are the following:

- Learning and practicing letters,
- Learning and practicing numbers,
- Learning and practicing words,
- Different platform for the professors.

The first feature, learning and practicing reading letters, enables the students to learn the alphabet and practice them with the voice-over assistant, indicating what is being represented on the screen. The second feature is about the words, so of course, before knowing them, you have to know the letters, which is why we started with it. On the other hand, those words to be learned are chosen by the teacher or professor, who will be the application user, to check the student's progress and see what is to be done for it. The third feature is about the numbers, a combination of letters and dots, but we have built them in such a way that it will be easy for the student to learn. Last but not least is that the professor will have different login credentials to follow the student's progress and add words he should learn and the practice section that should be done. With that, the learning process becomes easier for the students.

The system employs a Braille terminal to provide input and receive output. The application uses Bluetooth and voice-over features to connect to the Braille display. It is required to enable the voice-over function in the IOS device to use the app since this allows the app to provide audio feedback. We are using computer braille [8], which is different from the international one, as we also consider the German language here. The application teaches letters from A to Z, numbers from 1 to 10, and a few simple words for the student to start.

On the other hand, there is a second user, not the student but the teacher, who will enter the words that the student should learn to make it easy for him. Also, the teacher can check the progress of each of their students to know where they struggle most, as they sometimes need help. In Fig. 3, we will find the architecture flow of the application.

Application Flow: The main features of the application are designed in the German language. When users launch the application, they have six alternatives to choose from. On the screen, there are six buttons:

1. Learn Reading Letters
2. Practice Reading Letters
3. Learn Reading Words
4. Practice Reading Words
5. Learn Reading Numbers
6. Practice Reading Numbers

Since the application is for visually impaired people, while navigating through the options, the voice feedback will help the users know which button they are on; to guide,

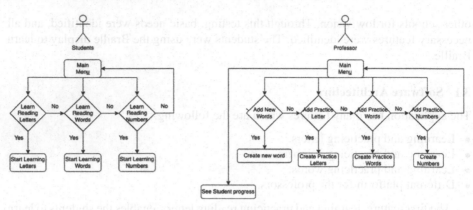

Fig. 3. Architecture

they must use the Braille display. Once they know which mode to learn, they must press okay from the Braille keyboard. Learn Reading Letters, Words, and Numbers.

In this mode, the user navigates through the numbers 1 to 6 using a mobile application while the audio feedback tells them which digits are dotted and what is clicked on the screen. Every letter or dot touched will be felt on the braille.

- To check which letter is dotted, the user presses the "NACHSTE" (NEXT) button."
- In the new screen, voice feedback displays which letter, word, or number it was.
- The user now has three alternatives to select from:

- Either they can go back and recheck the numbers if they are confused by clicking the "WIEDERHOLEN"(REPEAT) button.
- Or they can go to learn the following letter by pressing the button "NACHSTE"."
- Or they can go to the main menu to change their learning mode by pressing the "STARSEITE"(STARTING PAGE) button.
- The same process is done when they choose to learn to read words or learn to read numbers.

Application Design and Implementation: To build this application, we used Swift [9] as a programming language and Realm [10] as the database. Since the braille device works on iOS devices, building it with Swift will be more efficient. As for the design of the application Figma [11] was used. Swift is a fantastic way to write software, whether it's for phones, desktops, servers, or anything else that runs code. It is a safe, fast, and interactive programming language that combines the best in modern language thinking with wisdom from the wider Apple engineering culture and the diverse contributions from its open-source community. But before that, the designing was done using Figma, the best tool suitable for this application. The application's home page design, seen in Fig. 4, is the first screen visually impaired users encounter when they open the app. The home screen has been designed to make it more noticeable to them. After doing the usability testing we have decided to go with the colors blue and yellow chosen for the design because they are more visible to visually impaired individuals. On the main screen, users have six options to choose from: learn reading letters, practice reading letters, learn reading words, practice reading words, and learn reading numbers by practicing reading numbers. Then the next screen to it is the one that displays after he has chosen one option. That second screen represents the six dots of the Braille keyboard that students will fill on the keyboard once it is touched. Once he feels a dot, Fig. 4 is shown.

Figure 5 displays a standard screen, the first screen of all three learning modes of the application. It consists of seven buttons, of which the first six are numbers from 1 to 6. Some are colored in blue to show that the button is clicked. For example, it is dot one and the button"NEXT" to see the result on the second screen. For example, in here, the result is"Dot 1 is shown and represents the letter a". On the other hand, voice feedback will always mention what is on the screen and what is clicked to guide the user. Then the user can click"nächste" for the following letter or"wiederholen" to repeat the letter, Or click the"HOME ICON" to go to the main screen.

Figure 8 displays a screen which is the second part of the application, and it is learning words. It consists of learning short-form words by starting with the words beginning with the letter A. Firstly, simple words like "aber," "bei," "das", are simple German words that the student can learn. Then, according to what he will select, "aber" in this scenario, he will feel dot 1 on the braille representing the short form of "aber." Then that explanation will be given at the final screen when he clicks "nächste." However, the student does not choose the words he should learn, that is where the teacher, who is the second user of the applications, comes in to enter the terms the student should learn and assign it to him to make it more efficient. As we see in Fig. 6, the Professor has his own account where he should log in first. Once that is done his homepage will have four different option the first "Übung vorbeiten" which is to prepare an exercise for the student. With this, when the student goes to "Buchstabe üben" for example, on Fig. 4 he will be able to practice the letter the Professor has assigned to him. So for the words, the Professor will click on "Wort hinzufügen" for him to add comments. Once that is done, it will redirect him to the page where the list of words he already has are there in Fig. 7. Here he has the option to edit, which is "Wörter bearbeiten", to add a new one, "hinzufügen," or to go back "vorherige."

Fig. 4. Home screen of the application

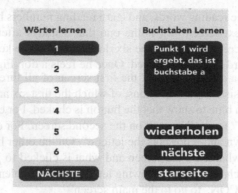

Fig. 5. Letter 'a' dots

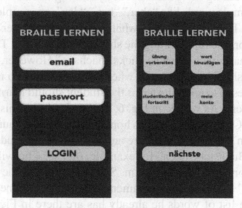

Fig. 6. Professor Account

Fig. 7. Word List

Figure 9 displays the screen of the third part of the application, and it is learning numbers. It consists of learning numbers where first an explanation of how number works is given. It is different from other learning concepts here since it is a combination. Users must first know to read the letter before learning numbers.

Figure 10 shows the result user has clicked dot 1, which is letter a, and is asked to add a number sign which he was thought in Fig. 9. Then after adding the number sign on the second screen, the third screen shows the result and explains how the process was done.

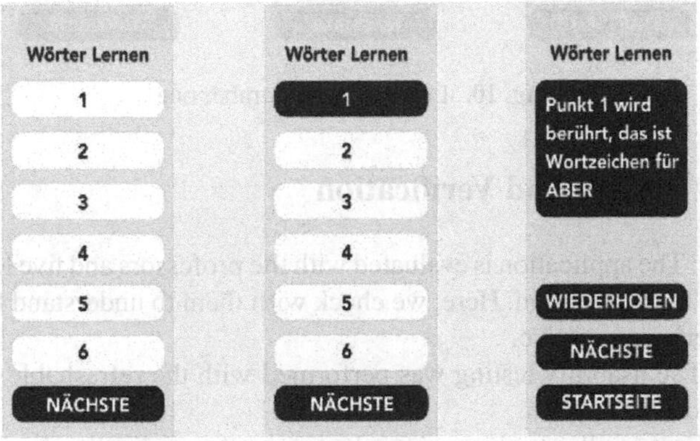

Fig. 8. Learn word Starting with A

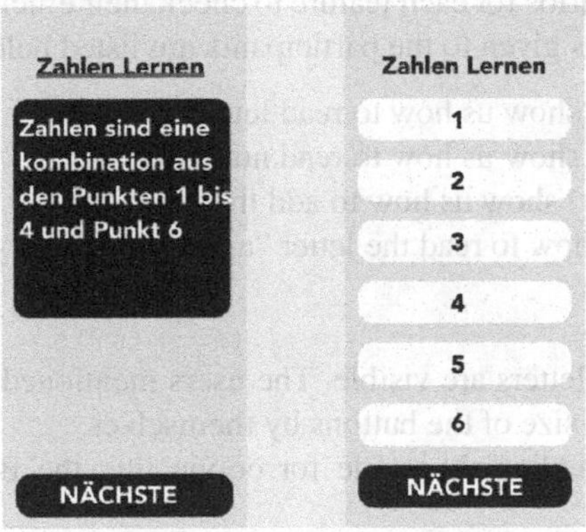

Fig. 9. Learning numbers

Fig. 10. Learn reading number one

4 Usability Testing and Verification

- *Participants*: The application is evaluated with the professors and five low-vision people who test the application. Here, we check with them to understand the application from the user's perspective.
- *Apparatus*: The usability testing was performed with the refreshable braille display Focus 40 and iPad devices.
- *Procedure*: First of all, we give an introduction to the application by explaining how it works and showing different scenarios. After that, we gave them 15 min so that they get familiar with the application. The we gave a few tasks to the students by giving different scenarios for each feature to check their efficiency, effectiveness, and satisfaction. The tasks given to the participants are listed below:

  1. Would you please show us how to read letter "G"?
  2. Would you please show us how to read numbers "4"?
  3. Can you(professor) show us how to add the word "ab"
  4. Can you show us how to read the letter "apfel" added by your lecturer

- *Results*

  1. The numbers and letters are visible. The users mentioned it would benice if they could increase the size of the buttons by themselves.
  2. Users suggested adding the guide for connecting the Braille display with the smartphone

- Discussions

  - **Target Audience**: Visually impaired and blind people are the primary audience for the application. Although, the application can be used for learning Braille by ordinary people as well.
  - **Opportunities**: The application is unique such that all the features of the application are merging to provide a stage for visually impaired people to learn how to read in a faster way at their own pace. The most astonishing thing about the

application is that it is integrated with a Braille keyboard that helps users learn and feel simultaneously.

– **Future Scope**: The current application helps the users to learn how to read Braille letters. They can even feel the dots by their fingertips using the Braille display. The application consists of three functionalities, of which the first functionality has been developed. The scope for the future of this project consists of building an intelligence in such a way that the application will be clever enough to read what the user touches on the Braille, basically it will be the other way around, which means instead of reading on the mobile or table and feeling it on braille they will be able to touch the Braille and display it on the mobile with the assistant of Voice Over.

5 Conclusion

To conclude, the developed application has provided a platform for visually impaired and blind people to read the letters from 'a to z' and feel the braille dots in the braille keyboard. The application helps them to grow their knowledge and allows them to learn at their own pace. As discussed in the long term, the application will develop further and have more advanced features. It will stand out from other applications as it is integrated with the Braille keyboard, unique. The application is built with Swift UI to build the user interface for the application on the Apple Platform. Realm Database open-source object database Since the Braille Focus 40 keyboard integrates the application and can be only connected to IOS devices. Therefore we use them for our development to be more efficient.

References

1. Wagh, P., et al.: E-Braille-a self-learning Braille device. In: 2016 Twenty Second National Conference on Communication (NCC). IEEE (2016)
2. Gueye, A.A., Chandna, S.: D-Braille: a digital learning application for people with low vision. In: International Conference on Human-Computer Interaction, pp. 455–465. Springer, Cham (2022)
3. Joshi, A., Ajit, S.: Braille tutor. In: Advances in Signal Processing and Intelligent Recognition Systems, pp. 237–244. Springer, Cham (2016). https://doi.org/10.1007/978-3-319-04960-1
4. Cahya, R.A.D., Handayani, A.N., Wibawa, A.P.: Mobile braille touch applicationfor visually impaired people using double diamond approach. In: MATEC Web of Conferences. vol. 197, p. 15007. EDP Sciences (2018)
5. Nahar, L., Jaafar, A., Sulaiman, R.: Usability evaluation of a mobile phone basedbraille learning application "mbraille". Malaysian J. Comput. Sci., 108–117 (2019)
6. Brailletec pricelist page. https://en.brailletec.de/price-list/
7. Pädogogische Hochschule Homepage. https://www.ph-heidelberg.de/
8. Computer braille. https://de.wikipedia.org/wiki/ComputerbrailleApple
9. Apple developer Swift UI Page. https://developer.apple.com/xcode/swiftui/
10. Real Database, by mongo DB. https://realm.io/
11. Figma homepage. https://www.figma.com

12. Chandna, S., Singhal, A.: Towards outdoor navigation system for visually impaired people using YOLOv5. In: 2022 12th International Conference on Cloud Computing, Data Science & Engineering (Confluence). IEEE (2022)
13. Hamilton, R.H., Pascual-Leone, A.: Cortical plasticity associated with Braille learning. Trends Cogn. Sci. **2**(5), 168–174 (1998)
14. Guerreiro, J., et al.: The today and tomorrow of Braille learning. In: Proceedings of the 15th International ACM SIGACCESS Conference on Computers and Accessibility. (2013)
15. Lopez, R.M.: MASc "Matuto, Magbasa, Maglaro: Learning to read braille through play." Assistive Technology (2019)
16. Li, T., Zeng, X., Xu, S.: A deep learning method for Braille recognition. In: 2014 International Conference on Computational Intelligence and Communication Networks. IEEE (2014)
17. Jawasreh, Z.H.M., Ashaari, N.S., Dahnil, D.P.: Braille tutorial model using braille fingers puller. In: 2017 6th International Conference on Electrical Engineering and Informatics (ICEEI). IEEE (2017)
18. Hall, A.D., Newman, S.E.: Braille learning: Relative importance of seven variables. Appl. Cogn. Psychol. **1**(2), 133–141 (1987)
19. Keil, S.: Teaching braille to children. Br. J. Vis. Impair. **22**(1), 13–16 (2004)
20. Gadiraju, V., Muehlbradt, A., Kane, S.K.: Brailleblocks: computational braille toys for collaborative learning. In: Proceedings of the 2020 CHI Conference on Human Factors in Computing Systems (2020)

Promoting Independence Through a Novel e-Learning Solution to Practice Online Purchasing

Sara Kjellstrand(✉), Susanna Laurin, and Lisa Engström

Funka Nu AB, Stockholm, Sweden

{sara.kjellstrand,susanna.laurin,lisa.engstrom}@funka.com

Abstract. This paper presents the development and testing of an innovative e-learning solution where persons who find it challenging to understand e-commerce and digital payment services can learn about and practice online shopping in a safe environment without stress and fear of errors. The core of the solution is a series of exercises that break down the online purchasing experience into small steps where the user can practice specific steps in the process at their own leisure. User tests conducted with persons with cognitive impairments and older adults confirmed that the solution was perceived as useful for improving ability and confidence to use online shopping services. The main difficulties encountered by the users in the tests concerned the understanding of concepts and vocabulary involved in online shopping. Further to the user feedback, the solution was adapted to provide further support in terms of explanations of difficult terms and illustrations of words. Nevertheless, the results of the user testing raise questions on the importance of reading level and vocabulary support as part of the accessibility of e-commerce websites in general. More research is needed to investigate the impact of understandable text on the inclusion of users of all abilities in the expansion of e-commerce across the EU and beyond.

Keywords: Cognitive accessibility · e-learning · e-commerce

1 Introduction

Although convenient for many, online shopping and payment services can present accessibility challenges in terms of understanding and handling the interfaces involved. These services include several different features that can present barriers of accessibility: the handling of passwords can be challenging in terms of memorization or spelling [1], the amount of information and choices can be daunting, and there are often time-limits that are stressful [2]. All of these barriers and more pertain to issues of cognitive processes, that is, the way in which people take in and process information. Surveys have shown that e-commerce websites can be particularly difficult to use for persons with cognitive disabilities, with users describing the payment process as confusing and not safe [3].

Persons in need of more support when it comes to cognitive accessibility include a wide variety of users with different strengths and challenges. The broad category of persons with cognitive impairments includes a wide range of conditions from learning disabilities to neuropsychiatric conditions. In addition, older adults may also encounter cognitive challenges as well as persons with temporary or situation-based impairments (for example due to stress) [4]. There is therefore a lot of variation between individuals and between sub-sections of the target groups when it comes to needs and preferences.

Regardless, there are also many commonalities, especially when outcomes are concerned. Whereas some will find it difficult with choices, others struggle with the meaning of words, but the overarching problem is the same: the online shopping experience becomes a stressful experience when you are confused and uncertain of how it works. In addition, there is also the added stress factor when stakes are involved, for example when the user needs to complete a task within a certain timeframe [2]. Altogether, these barriers and stress may lead to abandoning the online errand, or to putting it off until help is at hand. In both cases, the independence of the users is hampered.

The objective of the present study was to develop and test a solution that helps users overcome the factor of uncertainty and stress by learning and practicing the different steps in online shopping and payments in a safe environment. The underlying concept of the solution is that breaking down, explaining and providing a way to practice the key steps involved in online shopping in your own pace will help the user get familiarized with key concepts and procedures of online shopping. This will, in turn, make it easier for the user the next time they need to make errands online as they will have developed a basic understanding of online shopping interfaces, and do not need to add the stress of learning on the spot while completing the tasks as intended.

The e-learning was developed as a web-based solution open to the public without the need for registration. The core of the solution is a series of exercises that take the user through the whole online purchasing experience from finding items to finalizing the payment. The process has been broken down into 7 small steps where the user can go back to each step at any time and progress in their own leisure. It offers gamified exercises in three different degrees of difficulty. The exercises are supplemented by multimodal support material, including illustrations, videos and easy-to-read text explaining key concepts and processes involved in online purchasing.

2 Method for Developing and Testing the Training Solution

The development and testing of the training solution followed an iterative method developed by Funka based on the framework for user-centred design. The method involves a stepwise development where users are involved in every stage to provide input based on their needs, and to validate the training solution as it evolves.

In this project, the development took place in 3 main phases: Requirements gathering, Iterative development of the solution including sketches and prototypes, Finalisation of the solution and demonstration. Each of the steps is described in Sects. 3, 4, 5, and 6 below, with Sect. 5 dedicated to providing details on the user testing, as part of the iterative development.

Representatives of the target groups of the training were involved in usability testing in all stages of the project. The target groups included older adults, persons with learning disabilities, persons with autism spectrum disorder or ADHD, persons with language disorders and persons with stress syndrome. All participants were Swedish nationals, and all tests were conducted in Swedish.

The project was run in close collaboration with the County Administrative Board of Skåne (the Board), to leverage their knowledge and outreach. The Board is leading a national multiple-year government assignment on ensuring that all users can use payment services no matter where they live, their socio-economic situation, age, living conditions, physical or mental abilities [5]. As part of this assignment, the Board has collected extensive knowledge about the challenges these target groups experience when it comes to payments. They have also developed a network consisting of users with varying reasons for experiencing problems with payments, as well as banks and financial intermediaries, who are interested in new ideas and innovations to achieve a more inclusive payment system.

3 Requirements Gathering

The first step of the development process was to collect information about the user needs. At this early stage, the user research focused on three aspects:

- Types of difficulties faced by persons with cognitive disabilities, and older adults in the context of online shopping and payments, and possible solutions to deal with these difficulties.
- Specific needs related to the content of the training, that is, what types of information should be included in the learning material and what are the skills the potential users need to learn.
- Initial feedback on the concept of a training solution for learning and practicing online shopping and payments.

3.1 Method

Two series of interviews were conducted in the requirements gathering phase. In the first series, eight people were interviewed over the phone to better understand how and why older persons and persons with cognitive impairments used or did not use online shopping services. The interviews covered the topics of devices, motivation, economy and the possibility to receive support. The objective was to identify barriers and possible solutions. The next round of interviews involved six people from the target groups and focused on the use case for a training solution, both in terms of self-studies, and group studies. Respondents were asked how, when and where they could imagine themselves (or a friend) using a training solution, if they had ever tried something similar before and what it would take for them to give it a try.

To support the development of the content, the user research was supplemented by an inventory of major online shopping websites and a collection of data on the different payment services used in online shopping in the Swedish context. This included both services connected to credit cards and other types of payment based on mobile solutions or direct debit. A scoping review of grey literature was also conducted to find information about existing educational and informational material.

3.2 Results

The answers from the first interviews showed that a major reason for avoiding online shopping was uncertainty and fear of committing errors or something going wrong in the process. A common response among interviewed users, especially older adults, who claimed not to shop online, was that someone (often a younger relative, but also information from society via TV etc.) had warned them so much about the risks, that they did not feel comfortable trying. Another common response was that the respondent was unsure whether the effort needed for doing online shopping was worth it. For these users it seemed too difficult to deal with the complex e-commerce platforms and therefore it was hard for them to imagine any benefits from online shopping.

In terms of the concept of the training solution, the most common feedback was that it was important that the solution had a format that enabled repetition. Several respondents also replied that they would need to be able to take their time in doing the exercises. It was also clear from the responses that it would take recommendation, guidance or handholding from a peer, relative or friend to nudge the non-tech-savvy users into trying even the simplest of training solutions on online shopping. Two older adults interviewed had experienced younger relatives trying to convince them during the pandemic of how easy it was to do online shopping and they had found it extremely complicated and never tried it on their own. But they understood the potential, and were willing to continue testing together with us.

When it comes to the content required in the training, the interviewees mentioned many different aspects that did not only concern the e-commerce interfaces as such but also issues related to the more general aspect regarding the handling of funds online. One recurring item was security, and another was the pros and cons of different ways of getting orders delivered.

Other common themes that were mentioned in the interviews include:

- The importance of being motivated and enjoying the experience to be able to learn new things related to the web.
- That online shopping websites have a lot of text that is difficult to understand with many unusual words and concepts.
- That online shopping websites are very different from one another, something which causes confusion.

From the inventory of online shopping websites and information from the Board it transpired that there is no standardized way of conducting selection, payment and delivery of items. The steps needed to carry out online shopping from start to end vary a lot and the different steps can appear in different order. Both terminology and icons used differ a lot even within the same category of items. This information is coherent with the perception of the users interviewed that online shopping websites are very different from one another, adding to the uncertainty and reluctance among certain users to try out online shopping.

Table 1 summarizes the analysis of the key needs of the user groups and the ensuing requirements of the training solution that were taken forward to the design and development stages.

Table 1. User needs and requirements.

Target group	Need	Solution
Persons with cognitive disabilities	To become more independent. Common difficulties include data unfamiliarity, uncertainty, difficulty understanding context and concepts	Being able to practice in a simple interface with stepwise instructions Having unknown words and concepts explained
Older adults	To get the motivation to learn how to do errands online Varying degrees of computer knowledge, uncertainty, fear of doing something wrong or getting tricked Difficulty understanding concepts	Being able to try out shopping in an interface where it is possible to practice by repetition. Having unknown words and concepts explained
Persons with temporary cognitive impairments	This target group often have difficulties with memory. They need to be able to practice by repetition, and to choose the progression	Being able to repeat in their own pace. Stepwise training and reminders

As a result of the desk research and interviews, it was decided to add gamification features to the solution to make the training more enjoyable and provide motivation. In view of the long wish list of content for the training from the interviews, it was decided to add a library of resources outside the actual training part of the solution, where users can learn more about key concepts in online shopping by reading a text or listening to the information being read out loud.

4 Iterative Development of the Solution

The results of the requirements gathering were brought forward to the design and development of a first concept of the training solution. The development started with a workshop together with the County Administrative Board Skåne to develop a specification for the solution. On the basis of the specifications, a first simple Miro sketch was prepared, showing how all the steps of the various exercises, including tasks, questions, answer options and rewards would work and interact in a pedagogical way. After this, the iterative user testing began based on the sketches. This led to the continued development of the sketches into prototypes that were iteratively improved and refined based on the test results.

Two main methods were used to gather feedback on the training solution in the development process: focus groups and one-on-one online user testing. The method and results from the user tests are detailed in Sect. 5. The results from the focus groups are detailed below.

4.1 Focus Groups

Focus group participants included:

- 18 persons with learning disabilities participating in activities at three day-care centres in the Stockholm area.
- 24 older adults active in the organisation SeniorNet, a network where older adults are teaching and supporting each other in matters related to internet use and digital services.

Day-Care Centers. Three day-care centres participated throughout the whole project. Each of the day-care centres involved 6 persons in the focus groups. Their participation was facilitated by a coordinator at the day-care centres working together with the researchers. In the first phase, the day-care coordinators facilitators collected user experiences and needs via group discussions, and in the iterative development phase they tested prototypes and terminology on paper and later online. At the end of the project, they played the training game in the groups, using a smartboard so everyone could participate actively.

The key result from the focus group discussions and testing was that the participants struggled mostly with the terminology and understanding the abstract parts of the actual game. Many of the concepts involved in online shopping in general and the training in particular were perceived as abstract. For example, participants had difficulties understanding the ideas of a virtual cart and check-out. However, with a little help from the coordinators, the participants were able to complete the tasks and did enjoy using the training. As a result of these focus groups, a section with material for facilitators was added to the solution. The material includes questions and guidance to use the training solution as part of group exercises, either at day-care centres or in special needs education.

SeniorNet Groups. Three groups, each including 8 older adults tested the training solution as part of their SeniorNet mentoring program where seniors are teaching seniors practical skills in ICT. The groups met to discuss the training together, but each of the participants used their own smart phone or tablet for the actual testing.

All of the participants in the SeniorNet groups were positive to the concept of gamified training on online shopping, especially for persons with little experience of online shopping. As a result of the pilot tests conducted by the focus groups, the training solution became a part of the staple training programs, that are spread throughout the country.

Main aspects to improve as pointed out by the participants in the SeniorNet group discussions was that the concept of the game and the instructions around the exercises needed to be clarified. In the first phases of development the game was conceptualized as a simulation where the person playing the game was sent out on a quest to complete certain tasks. In these early tests some of the SeniorNet participants were confused about the purpose of the exercises. It was unclear to them whether the training solution was an online test to check the person's level of skills or whether it was a game. This feedback was coherent with feedback from the individual user tests and influenced the subsequent decision of the design and development team to reconstruct the training as a game where the user helps a fictive character to complete the tasks.

5 Online User Testing on Sketches and the Prototypes

In addition to the focus groups, 17 persons participated in three usability tests in the design and development of the training interface. One pilot test was conducted on the initial sketches and two more extensive tests, one on general usability and the other on understandability and terminology, were conducted on the basis of the clickable prototypes.

Due to the pandemic, the user tests were held online, using Miro for creative workshops on content, structure and UX, and XD for object placement, layout logic and graphical design. User tests were conducted via Teams or Zoom where the participant received a link to the session and logged-in from their own device. A mix of talk out loud and observational methods were used in the sessions. The participant was assigned a limited number of tasks to complete in the training. The participant then described their experience at the same time as the researcher observed the actions of the participant as they clicked through the prototype.

5.1 Pilot Tests on the First Sketches

4 users participated in the first pilot test: 2 older adults and 2 persons with autism syndrome disorder (ASD). The participants were recruited to represent different degrees of familiarity with online shopping websites: 1 person had no experience; 2 persons had some experience, and 1 person had a lot of experience.

The purpose of the pilot test was to gather information on the:

– Understandability of the concept of the gamified training
– Understandability of the training instructions
– Ease of use in terms of navigation

At this stage of the test, three out of four users participating struggled with understanding the concept of the gamified training. The typical response to the task "You would like to buy socks, where on the website would you expect to find out more about socks?" was variants of "I don't want/need to buy socks//I don't like that colour//that is not my size …" This led to confusion about the purpose of the individual exercises.

Half of the participants in the test had difficulties finding the instructions. The first sketches had the instructions to the left of the screen and the actual game on the right side of the screen. One of the participants expressed difficulties in understanding the vocabulary used in the instruction and the exercises. With a little help, all of the participants were able to complete the assignments. Despite these difficulties, all of the participants reported that the overall idea of the online training was useful, and they thought it would be of value for themselves or others to become more familiar with online shopping.

5.2 Usability Tests on the Prototypes

In the next phase of the study, the first sketches were improved based on the feedback from the user testing and were developed into clickable XD prototypes. These prototypes were the basis of the next round of user testing where both separate functions and objects, and entire flows were tested. The participants in the second round of testing included 4 persons with autism spectrum disorder (ASD) and 4 older adults. 2 of the participants reported they had no experience of using online shopping, 4 had some experience and 2 had a lot of experience.

The participants evaluated the solution regarding:

- Usefulness of the content in terms of learning about online shopping
- Understandability of the game concept
- Understandability of text and instructions
- Ease of use, in particular navigation and layout

Between the sketches and the clickable prototype, the visual layout had been improved by adding separating elements and changing the formatting. These actions helped to clarify which parts of the interface were part of the game and which parts belonged to the instructions. Nevertheless, the first two users who tested the prototypes still had problems with the level of abstraction in the game part. The concept was therefore changed from "Buy socks for yourself" into "You can help Milo to buy socks" instead – and like magic, the issue was solved and all participants who subsequently tested the training solution understood the concept. One possible interpretation of why this worked well with users is that the obstacle was not only about the abstraction level but also about psychological factors. The testers might have felt that they themselves were being tested, despite reassurances from the test leaders that this was not the case. It feels better to support someone in need of help, than to ask for help (and possibly fail) yourself.

Similar to the participants in the focus groups, participants in the second round of testing also encountered difficulties regarding the information. Half of the participants requested more explanations as they struggled with grasping key words and concepts involved in online shopping. Concepts that were perceived as difficult included ways to verify your identity online, through electronic IDs, payment options (for example invoice), and delivery options (for example post representative). On the other hand, two of the participants got stuck in or skipped instructions perceived as too long. This contradictory feedback raised the issue of how to strike a balance between providing enough information to improve understanding and avoiding information overload. As described under Sect. 4.1, part of the solution to this issue was to implement a library feature with more in-depth explanations and additional material, outside the actual game.

Overall, the feedback of the participants on the training were positive. All users found the training content relevant and the gamified training useful for themselves or others. Some of the remarks from participants included:

"It is good that the training website simulates an actual shopping experience where you can click around on the site, not only look at a video of how it is done".

"It is good that the interface is simple with not too many graphic elements or choices".

5.3 Terminology

The language level of the vocabulary used in the training solution was tested in an iterative way as the prototypes evolved. In this part 7 people participated, 2 with learning disabilities, 2 with ASD, 2 older adults and 1 with language disability. The tests on vocabulary were conducted in a stepwise approach. As a first step, one word was showed and/or read out loud and the participant was asked about the meaning. If the participant was unable to respond, the word was put in context, or a synonym was provided. At the last stage, the word was showed (and read out loud) together with a symbol or icon.

Key findings from the terminology tests include:

- Concepts should be described as concretely as possible.
- Terms need to be presented with synonyms. Some users understand the word "product" better while others are more familiar with the words "item" or "article".
- Vague words such as "often" should be avoided.
- Picture support worked well for enhancing understanding. For example, a picture of a basket was shown next to the word basket.

The level of understanding and (vocabulary) differed a lot between the participants which made it hard to find the "perfect" level, but after series of iterations, it was concluded that using short and simple words were beneficial for most users – even though some of the more linguistically advanced initially claimed it to be "far too easy". A dictionary was also created for each section of the game with explanations of possibly difficult or unknown words in the "tips" part of each section. The instructions and the game themselves were not relying on the users knowledge of these terms. This made it possible for users with very limited knowledge of specific terms to play the game and learn by relying more on the illustrations.

6 Final Prototype with In-Depth Material, Final Tests

Based on the feedback from the user tests on the clickable prototypes, the following improvements were made to the online training interface:

1. The game was changed from "I want to buy X" to "help Milo to buy X".
2. The on-boarding was improved to provide more explanations.
3. Visual pointers were included to make it easier to find exercises without scrolling.
4. A checklist was implemented, detailing the progress of the user and the different exercises.
5. Vocabulary support was added.
6. Language and style of the instructions were adapted in accordance with the results of the terminology tests.
7. More in-depth explanations were included in a library feature outside the game part of the training solution.

After this, the technical development of the prototype was finalized, and the online training solution moved to its final domain. Once all the material was migrated, additional technical testing was performed, as well as 4 final user tests of all material and flows to make sure that everything was working correctly. These final user tests did not unveil any new insights beyond confirming that the issues raised in earlier user tests had been adequately dealt with.

7 Discussion

The positive feedback from the participants on the overall concept of learning by doing on the online training solution indicates that there is a good potential for similar types of training services with step-by-step exercises for improving ability and confidence to use digital services. The study participants in particular highlighted the usefulness of practical exercises in comparison with manuals or video-based training.

Results are mixed regarding the use of the training solution for self-study. For some of the target groups with cognitive impairments, the training solution was too difficult to handle despite simplifications in language and navigation. However, the feedback from the focus groups at the day-care centres was that the participants found it both meaningful and interesting to try out the exercises when the training was facilitated by staff at the day-care centres. One lesson learned for the future is therefore that similar e-learning solutions are conceived to be possible to use on your own or with the help of facilitators. Another one was to include a section with information for facilitators. Along these lines, Funkabutiken has recently also been included in a list of recommended course material for special needs education provided by the Swedish National Agency for Special Needs Education and Schools [6].

The findings from the first phase of requirements gathering, concerning the variety and complexity of e-commerce interfaces and the difficulties with vocabulary and concepts, were also reflected in the user testing throughout the study. One recurring issue concerned how much information to provide without running the risk of overwhelming the user. One possible solution offered in this case was to provide more options by including additional information and in-depth material as an extra feature outside the main training exercises. Another recurring issue was the handling of unusual vocabulary. The study team found that support for difficult words could often be better placed in context, to avoid that users need to look for information elsewhere. Several participants requested image support for words in direct connection with the exercise, and these were added. More tests are needed to investigate more systematically the different ways in which textual information can best be adapted to enhance accessibility to users in different situations – whether as further instructions, vocabulary support or in-depth material.

In a broader perspective, the results from the study raise the issue of the importance of understandable information and instructions when it comes to designing and developing e-commerce services in general. In particular, the study results bring to attention the roles of reading level and support for understanding the concepts and vocabulary involved in online shopping. Support for understanding instructions and terms on e-commerce websites is important not only because of the eventual complexity of the individual e-commerce service, but also because as the study showed, the services are so different from one another, adding to a feeling of complexity and confusion.

With the implementation of the European Accessibility Act (EAA), e-commerce will be covered by European accessibility legislation [7]. Current European legislation on web accessibility points to the requirements in the European accessibility standard EN 301549. While it is yet to be decided what exact accessibility requirements the EAA will point to, it can be noted that the standard WCAG 2.1 which is the basis for the web accessibility requirements of EN 301549 has received criticism for not sufficiently covering cognition [2, 8]. In this context, further research would be useful to better understand the potential of requirements related to understandable text and vocabulary, to improve accessibility for users with cognitive disabilities.

References

1. Renaud, K., Johnson, G., Ophoff, J.: Dyslexia and password usage: accessibility in authentication design. In: Clarke, N., Furnell, S. (eds.) HAISA 2020. IAICT, vol. 593, pp. 259–268. Springer, Cham (2020). https://doi.org/10.1007/978-3-030-57404-8_20
2. Kjellstrand, S. Laurin, S., Mohamed, S., Chowdhury, N.: Inclusive web-accessibility for persons with cognitive disabilities pilot project study: Final report. In: European Commission. Directorate General for Communications Networks, Content and Technology. European Commission, Brussels (2022)
3. Begripsam. Swedes with disability and the internet 2019 (In Swedish: Svenskarna med funktionsnedsättning och internet 2019"). Begripsam. https://www.begripsam.se/forskning/internet/2019-rapporter-och-resultat. Accessed 14 Feb 2023
4. W3C. Making content usable for people with cognitive and learning disabilities. W3C (2023). https://www.w3.org/TR/coga-usable/. Accessed 14 Feb 2023
5. Länsstyrelserna. Coverage of basic payment services (In Swedish; Bevakning av grundläggande betaltjänster). Rapport 2022:13. Länsstyrelsen i Dalarna (2022)
6. Swedish National Agency for Special Needs Education and Schools: List of resources on domestic science. SPSM. https://hittalaromedel.spsm.se/inspiration/sarvux/hem--och-konsum entkunskap/. Accessed 14 Feb 2023
7. Directive 2019/882/EU on the accessibility requirements for products and services. OJL **151**, 70–115 (2019)
8. Gartland, F., Flynn, P., et al.: The state of web accessibility for people with cognitive disabilities: A rapid evidence assessment. Behav. Sci. J. **12**(2), **2**(5), 26 (2022)

Better Balance in Informatics: An Honest Discussion with Students

Elisavet Kozyri[1(✉)], Mariel Evelyn Markussen Ellingsen[2],
Ragnhild Abel Grape[1], and Letizia Jaccheri[3]

[1] UiT The Arctic University of Norway, Tromsø, Norway
elisavet.kozyri@uit.no
[2] Woid AS, Oslo, Norway
[3] Norwegian University of Science and Technology, Trondheim, Norway

Abstract. In recent years, there has been considerable effort to promote gender balance in the academic environment of Computer Science (CS). However, there is still a gender gap at all CS academic levels: from students, to PhD candidates, to faculty members. This general trend is followed by the Department of Computer Science at UiT The Arctic University of Norway. To combat this trend within the CS environment at UiT, we embarked on structured discussions with students of our department. After analyzing the data collected from these discussions, we were able to identify action items that could mitigate the existing gender gap at our department. In particular, these discussions elucidated ways to achieve (i) a balanced flow of students into CS undergraduate program, (ii) a balanced CS study environment, and (iii) a balanced flow of graduates into higher levels of the CS academia (e.g., PhD program). This paper presents the results of the discussions and the subsequent recommendations that we made to the administration of the department. We also provide a road-map that other institutions could follow to organize similar events as part of their gender-balance action plan.

Keywords: Gender balance · computer science · diversity · inclusion · student study

1 Introduction

Innovations in Computer Science shape the lives of everyone in our society. To create innovative solutions tailored to everyone, it is important that all groups of society are represented in the creation of these solutions. However, this is still not the case in the field of Computer Science (CS). Having an awareness of the lack of representation and the different barriers people face in CS are fundamental in helping the field target those challenges and becoming more equitable and inclusive [8].

Statistics from Europe show that women are still highly underrepresented in CS. According to Eurostat [4], the percentage of female specialists in Information and Communications Technology has evolved from 17% in 2012 to 19,1% in 2021.

Mariel's contribution was made while she was a Master's student at UiT.

At university level in STEM, the percentage of female Bachelor, Master, and PhD students is 20%, while the percentage of female professors is 15%.

Specifically for the Department of Computer Science at UiT The Arctic University of Norway, only 13% of students, 14% of PhD candidates and 21% of faculty members are female.

Better Balance in Informatics (BBI), a program led by the CS department at UiT and funded by the Research Council of Norway, aims to rectify this imbalance and create a more diverse learning environment for Computer Science. BBI is connected and builds upon an ecosystem of national and international projects which address gender balance in CS acting on different levels: school ([7,13]), university ([2,6,16]), industry ([3,5,17]), and the interplay of these levels ([1]).

BBI aimed to identify some of the reasons that led to the current gender dynamics in our CS department, and then propose measurements that could address those reasons. Hearing directly from the CS students (Bachelor, Master) seemed to be a sensible way for us to identify those reasons. So, BBI organized structured discussion sessions, where we invited CS students (Bachelor, Master) to share their thoughts about:

1. the reasons they picked CS for their studies,
2. their current experience with the CS studies,
3. their intention to pursue an academic career in CS, and
4. ways to make the CS community more diverse and inclusive.

The answers of the students illuminated points of intervention, which could lead to a balanced flow of students into CS undergraduate program, a study environment that embraces diversity, and a balanced flow of students into higher levels of the CS academia.

This paper presents the methodology (Sect. 2) we employed to organize the discussion sessions, to collect responses, and to report the results. We then present the specific questions we asked the students and the analysis of their answers (Sect. 3). Finally, we list the recommendations (Sect. 4) submitted to the CS department for achieving a gender-balanced environment, we discuss related work (Sect. 5), and we conclude (Sect. 6) with reflections about the discussion sessions.

2   Methodology

The end goal of the discussion sessions was to identify points of interventions that could increase the gender balance among the incoming CS students, the current CS students, and the CS graduates that are interested in entering the CS academia. To identify those points, we were aiming for a high number of participants in the discussion sessions: the more participants, the greater the plurality of experiences, and thus, the higher the chances to find opportunities for improvement. Deciding which questions to ask was crucial to ensure that experiences from different aspects of the CS studies are captured and then analyzed. But, we also had to create a trusting discussion environment for the students to honestly share those experiences with us. This section describes the methodology we followed to prepare and organize the discussion sessions such that all these targets are met.

2.1   Outreach

Attracting the attention of students and persuading them to participate in the discussion sessions was not trivial. Unless there is an immediate academic or employment gain, motivating students to devote part of their busy schedules to a university-led event is indeed challenging. Our strategy to address this challenge comprised the following steps:

Hiring Students as Project Assistants. We hired two talented and enthusiastic female students as assistants for the project. They were our bridge to the student community in our CS department. And this bridge was functioning in both ways. Their thoughts, insights, and experience informed all aspects of the BBI project, including the questions we asked during the discussions. At the same time, they knew best how to reach their fellow-students and promote the agenda of BBI (e.g., what advertisement means to employ and what to say in these means).

Website. The BBI website (https://uit.no/project/bbi) is the main official space where the mission of BBI is communicated to the world. So, we redesigned this website to include a clear and short motivation for the BBI mission, and describe the upcoming BBI events, in particular the discussion sessions.

Advertisement. To reach a wider set of students and persuade them to participate in the BBI discussion sessions, we employed a variety of means. We posted advertisements on the monitors of the Department, the social networks of the Department, on Canvas, the UiT calendar, and the local student organization forum, which is a Discord server that is maintained by the student organization TD. The student assistants also gave 5-minutes talk about BBI and the discussion sessions to courses with high enrollment, they created and distributed flyers, and they organized a stand with coffee and cookies, where students could casually socialize and talk about BBI. In terms of registrations to the BBI discussion sessions, Canvas and TD seemed to have been the most effective, since we observed a high correlation between the time a post about the BBI event was created and the time students were registered.

Open to Everyone. The invitation to participate in the BBI discussion sessions was open to all students of the CS department, independently of their gender (female, male, non-binary). This is because the gender imbalance is a problem that owes to concern everyone—not only a part of the community. And because any further actions that the Department will take to address the problem might effect every student, there needs to be a wider understanding that these actions are worthwhile. Leaving specific groups of students outside the discussion, would not have increased this understanding.

2.2   Discussion Sessions

The discussion sessions were held at Árdna, UiT. Árdna is an iconic place in the university, ideal for secluded discussions. Its central fire place and the surrounding wooden benches invites people to open up and discuss honestly.

In the BBI discussion sessions participated around 20 participants.[1] Comparing to events organized in the past by BBI, this number of participants was a very welcoming surprise. From those participants, around 50% were female or non-binary students, and around 50% were male students. The vast majority of the students participated physically, but there were some that participated remotely. There were around three participants per discussion session. Each discussion session was moderated by two BBI members: one member was asking the questions, and the other member was typing the answers (we used no video or sound recording). At least one of the moderators was always one of the BBI student assistants; having participants talking to their peers led to frank discussions. To preserve anonymity, each participant was assigned a number, so the recorded answers were associated with these numbers—not with the identity of the student. For the discussion sessions, we gave the option to the student to select either Norwegian or English as the speaking language. All participants, apart from those that participated remotely, were offered a full meal and a free cinema ticket.

2.3   Selection of Questions

The selection of questions was inspired by questionnaires developed by other gender-balance projects, such as EUGAIN [1], Prestige in UiT [2], and Balanse-Hub [6]. However, the questions were tailored for the needs of the CS department in UiT. And, in particular, the questions were intended to cover a wide range of students' experience: from the point they considered applying for CS, to their current studies and their future plans.

2.4   Reporting of Results

For most of the questions asked during the BBI discussion sessions, we compiled the answers into graphs. Each graph depicts how answers are correlated with different genders. This information help us guide our selection of action items for improving the gender balance. We protect the anonymity of the participants, so we do not give specific numbers at graphs. Also, we do not have a separate category for non-binary participants, because the number of non-binary participants was not high enough to protect their anonymity. Instead, we group female and non-binary participants together, and we explore the dynamics between majority (males) and minorities (female, non-binary).

---

[1] We do not give specific numbers to preserve the anonymity of the participants.

I started to study CS because...

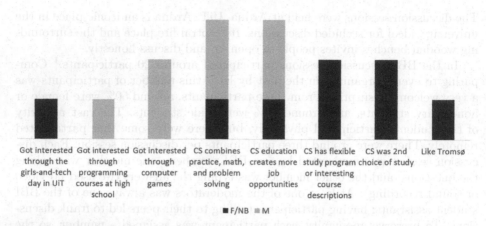

Got interested through the girls-and-tech day in UiT | Got interested through programming courses at high school | Got interested through computer games | CS combines practice, math, and problem solving | CS education creates more job opportunities | CS has flexible study program or interesting course descriptions | CS was 2nd choice of study | Like Tromsø

■ F/NB ■ M

Fig. 1. Reasons for choosing to study CS. Each column corresponds to a different reason. The height of a column represents the number of participants that submitted the corresponding reason. Dark blue represents female or non-binary participants (F/NB); yellow represents male participants (M). (Color figure online)

3   Results

This section presents the questions we asked the participants and their answers concerning:

1. the reasons they picked CS for their studies,
2. their current experience with the CS studies,
3. their intention to pursue an academic career in CS, and
4. ways to make the CS community more diverse and inclusive.

Correlating their answers with their gender, we identified action items that could lead to a balanced flow of students into CS undergraduate program, a study environment that embraces diversity, and a balanced flow of students into higher levels of the CS academia.

3.1   Intention to Study CS

To increase the balance in Computer Science, one first needs to increase the balance in the new-coming students. So, when advertising CS to younger students, one could also include aspects that attract minorities. We tried to identify those aspects by asking the participants the reason they decided to study CS in the first place. Figure 1 shows the different answers we received. The higher the column, the more students gave that answer. The graph also shows how the answers are split between the minority (F/NB) and majority (M). There is a correlation between the gender and the reason for selecting CS studies.

Action Items. Observing Fig. 1, we can identify the reasons the minority chose CS studies: the problem solving aspect of CS, the flexibility of the CS studies, the job opportunities that CS graduates enjoy. To increase the diversity of incoming students, we can then emphasize those reasons when advertising CS. Also, as a possible means of advertisement Fig. 1 indicates the UiT girls-and-tech day.

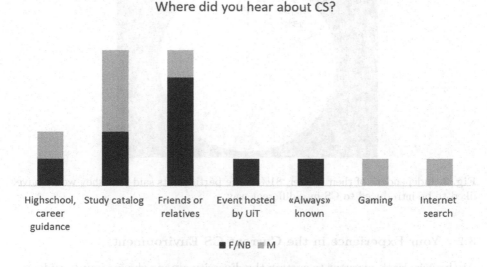

Where did you hear about CS?

Highschool, Study catalog Friends or Event hosted «Always» Gaming Internet
career   relatives   by UiT   known   search
guidance

■ F/NB ■ M

Fig. 2. Ways for becoming familiar with CS.

Apart from the UiT girls-and-tech day, we wanted to understand what would be other effective means of advertisement for attracting minorities to CS studies. So, we asked the participants where did they hear about CS. Figure 2 plots the answers, which are again correlated with the gender.

Action Items. Figure 2 indicates that one could use the highschool and the university's study catalog to better promote CS to minorities. Interestingly, friends and relatives have a high impact on the decision of minorities to study CS. So, one can make tech employees ambassadors of CS to young female and non-binary members of their families.

In general, the vast majority of the participants, independently of their gender, would have liked CS to have been introduced differently to them, as Fig. 3 indicates. Participants indicated that CS should be introduced as something that everyone can do and something that offers a plausible path to a regular job.

Action Item. When advertising to high-school students, we need to break stereotypes on who can study CS.

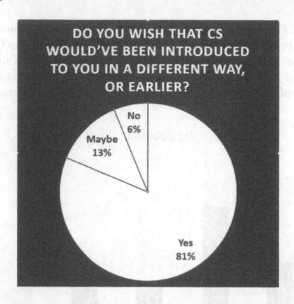

Fig. 3. Independent of their gender, 81% of the participants said that they would have liked to be introduced to CS in a different way.

3.2 Your Experience in the Current CS Environment

At the very least, we want to sustain the diversity among the incoming students, while these students progress to more senior years; we aim to decrease the number of drop-outs, with an emphasis on the minority group. To achieve this, we need to assess the student's experience within the CS department and identify aspects that can be improved to accommodate gender diversity.

We start by asking the participants whether the CS studies met their initial expectations. Their answers are depicted in Fig. 4. Almost all minority participants gave a negative answer: they found their studies either more difficult or more practical than expected. In particular, they found the learning curve of programming to be particularly steep, something that might drive some of the minority students to drop-out. We believe addressing this concern is important for maintaining a diverse environment in the department.

Action Item. We propose the adoption of a smoother introduction to programming, which will be appropriate for students with no prior programming experience.

Returning to Fig. 4, one also notices that, for most of the male participants, their experience in the CS studies met or even exceeded their initial expectations. So, this question highlights a striking difference between the minorities and the male students in terms of how they view their studies. This difference might be a cause of the current gender imbalance in the department.

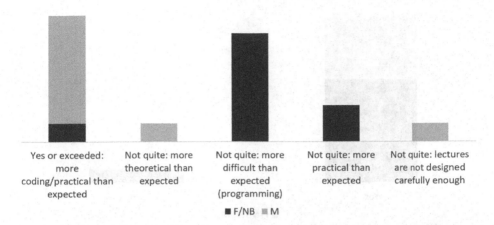

Do your CS studies meet your initial expectations? If not, why?

Fig. 4. The first column corresponds to the answer that the CS studies met or exceeded the expectations of the participant. The remaining four columns correspond to the answer that the CS studies did not quite meet the expectations of the participant, and they also represent different reasons why. The height of a column represents the number of participants that submitted the corresponding answer. Dark blue represents female or non-binary participants (F/NB); yellow represents male participants (M). (Color figure online)

All the participants agreed, though, that the social environment built around their studies exceeded their initial expectations. This is a great achievement of the department that needs to be preserved for the future, too.

Participants were then explicitly asked whether they have thought to drop-out of their study program. As Fig. 5 shows, most of the participants answered affirmatively. Notice that this is a concern across all genders, opposing the misconception that the minorities are more likely to have such thoughts. Notice also that even though most of the male students thought to drop-out of the program, they still had an overall positive assessment of their study experience, according to Fig. 4.

As reasons for thinking to drop-out, the participants cited the difficulty of some courses, the time-consuming assignments with overlapping deadlines, the demanding task of writing thesis (a task for which they did not feel prepared), and the complications that the COVID-19 pandemic brought. For a student to be thinking to drop-out, it means that the student's self esteem might be low at that point. Figure 6 validates this claim, showing that most of the participants felt "useless" or "not-deserving" being in the CS program. Again, the answers do not seem to be correlated with the gender. However there is an underlying difference: many of the males had this feeling once, related to a specific assignment or for short period of time, whereas the minority students had this feeling for a long period of time (i.e, months or even years).

Have you ever thought of dropping out of your study program?

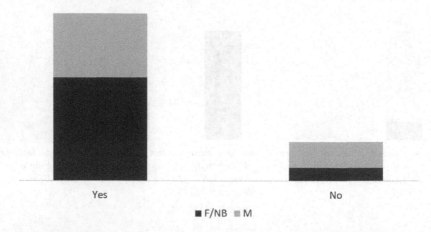

Yes   No

■ F/NB ■ M

Fig. 5. The majority of the participants replied that they have thought of dropping out of their CS study program.

Have you ever felt "useless" or "not-deserving being here"
(i.e., imposter syndrome) during your studies?

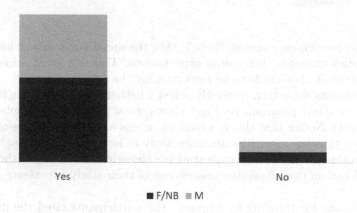

Yes   No

■ F/NB ■ M

Fig. 6. The majority of the participants replied that they have have felt "useless" or "not-deserving to be here" during their CS study program.

When asked about the reasons they instead decided to stay in the program and not drop out, the participants mentioned:

- the robust social network that they have built within and outside UiT, where they could talk about their struggles,
- the senior student advisor Jan Fuglesteg,
- their self-determination and discipline,
- taking time to relax.

Action Items. Given the stimulating power that the social groups exercised on the students, we should further support actions and groups that promote social networking in the department. Also, we will organize events where senior students can offer tips and tricks from their experiences to the junior students, where the main message will be "if we have made it, so can you".

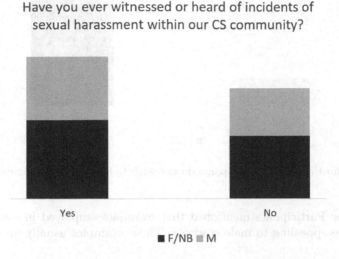

Have you ever witnessed or heard of incidents of sexual harassment within our CS community?

Fig. 7. More than half of the participants said that they have witnessed or heard of sexual harassment incidents within our CS community.

Concentrating on minority students, one of the reasons they might feel uncomfortable in an environment (and ultimately drop-out of the program) is when they have experienced sexual harassment. So, we asked the participants whether they have ever witnessed or heard of sexual harassment incidents within the CS community. Figure 7 depicts their answers. More than half of the participants answered positively.

Action Item. The "Yes" column in Figure 7 should not exist. So, we will propose to the department to devise videos and examples of unacceptable behavior, so the student can recognize and dissociate from these phenomena.

The experience that a student gets from their CS program is a collection of many educational aspects, such as lectures, colloquiums, and assignments. For the CS program to be inclusive and diverse, all these aspects should promote inclusiveness and diversity. We asked the participants if they feel that the educational aspects below promote only a particular way of thinking.

Do you wish to have an academic career in CS?

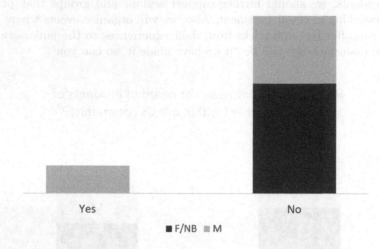

Yes   No

■ F/NB   ▪ M

Fig. 8. Almost all of the participants do not wish to have an academic career in CS.

- Lectures: Participants mentioned that examples employed in some lectures are more appealing to male students. These examples usually involve games or cars.
- Colloquiums:[2] Participants, from all genders, mentioned that a colloquium can quickly get a "boys-club" atmosphere if the TA is not attentive enough. The participants also express the wish for more female TAs.
- Assignments: Some assignment are very focused on gaming or promote competitiveness, which might be uncomfortable for some students.

Action Items. We will advise the faculty members to ensure that lectures and assignments accommodate a variety of interests. The department should organize a seminar for TAs in which they become sensitized on not allowing colloquiums to become "boys-clubs" and accommodating different interests and needs. We also need to brainstorm on how to hire more female TAs.

3.3   Intention to Enter Higher Levels in CS Academia

We are striving to achieve balance at all levels of the CS academia, from students to professors. At this section, we focus our attention to higher levels in CS academia (from PhD candidates and above), and we want to understand the intention of the current students to enter that level. According to Fig. 8, the vast majority, and in particular all female and non-binary participants, do not wish to have an academic career in CS. Here are some reasons why:

---

[2] A colloquium is associated with a course and it is often led by a TA, who answers student's questions about the course material and assignments.

- The academic career seems difficult or exhausting.
- No interest in research or writing or teaching.
- Preference for work-life balance offered by the industry (pay, social, use tools, practical).
- The description of an academic career is not clearly communicated.

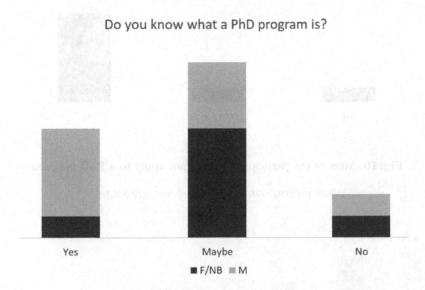

Do you know what a PhD program is?

Fig. 9. Most of the participants are either unsure about or do not know what the CS PhD program.

In fact, as indicated by Fig. 9, there is uncertainty between the students, and in particular the minority students (i.e., female and non-binary), about what a PhD program is—the first stepping stone towards building an academic career. Given this uncertainty, it is expected that many students will not apply to a PhD program, something that is affirmed by Fig. 10. Notice, though, that comparing Figs. 8 and 10, the participants are less negative towards pursuing a PhD program than ultimately following an academic career. This is because, after obtaining a PhD degree, there is always the possibility to follow a career in the industry. And some of the participants that replied "no" to the prospective of applying to a PhD program now, they contemplate the possibility of applying after working in the industry.

And if a participant does not want to apply to a PhD program, what are their immediate plans after graduation? Fig. 11 answers this question. Notice that participants from the minority group explore a wider variety of options.

Also, for the participants that are not considering to apply to the CS PhD program, Fig. 12 gives the main reasons behind this disposition. Figure 12 informs how we can intervene and address some of these reasons, possibly leading to more students applying to our PhD program.

Would you apply to a PhD program?

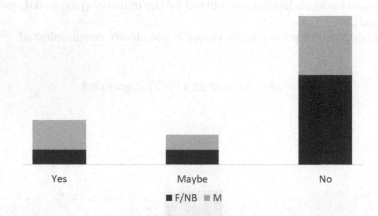

Fig. 10. Most of the participants would not apply to a PhD program.

What do you want to do when you graduate?

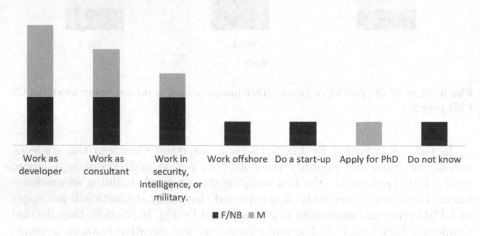

Fig. 11. Columns correspond to different options the participants consider to follow after graduation.

Action Items. According to Fig. 12, some participants said that the PhD program "sounds too heavy", and they described PhD students as being "alone" and "depressed". While this description might portray one aspect of the PhD experience, it is definitely not the entire truth. So, we are going to hold events that clearly describe the characteristics of a PhD program, emphasizing the positive aspects of being a PhD student. These events will also address the uncertainty that was surfaced in Fig. 9 about what is a PhD program.

Why would you **not** apply to a PhD program?

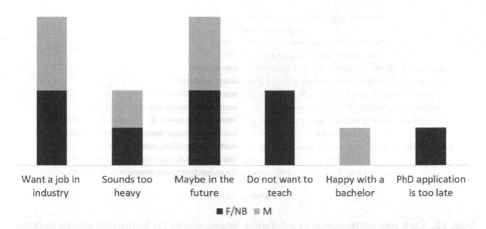

Fig. 12. Columns correspond to different reasons why the participants are not considering to apply to a PhD program.

The late deadline for applying to a PhD, which is not synchronized with the job-search period of senior students, is another reason why current students do not select a PhD program. To remedy this, we will advise the faculty members of the CS department to consider moving the PhD application earlier in in the academic year (i.e., fall semester).

Finally, given that many participants said that they might consider applying to a PhD program in the future (i.e., after acquiring some experience in the industry), we advocate to advertise new PhD positions explicitly to CS alumni. For some of these alumni, these positions might seem attractive.

3.4 The Gender Gap and Possible Measurements to Close It

In previous sections, we attempted to understand the reasons why a gender imbalance exists in the CS department, and concluded with action items that could address those reasons. In this section, we explicitly discuss gender balance with the students and record their opinions and proposals on the subject.

To begin with, the vast majority of the participants said that the current gender-imbalance in the department is a problem. They actually see that gender-balance has advantages: promotes innovation, enables plurality of perspectives, and leads to a better study and work environment. Many of the participants said that there are no disadvantages with gender balance, although some expressed the concern that gender-balance efforts, such as gender quotas, might "lead to people being hired for the wrong reasons".

The participants were then presented with different measurements that could be employed to improve the gender balance within the department and asked to say whether they are in favor or not of each presented measurement. Figure 13

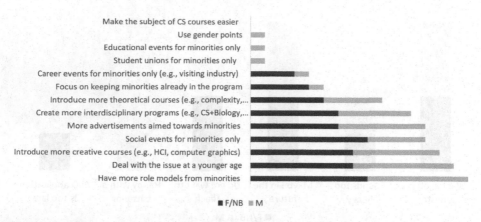

Which of the following measurements are you in favor of?

Fig. 13. Each row corresponds to a different measurement for improving gender balance in CS. The length of each row represents the number of participants that agree with the corresponding measurement. Dark blue represents female or non-binary participants (F/NB); yellow represents male participants (M). (Color figure online)

depicts their answers. Notice that measurements that blatantly favor minorities in the education or in the career were among the least popular (for both minority and male participants). We aim to focus on the most popular measurements.

Participants also proposed two additional measurements that did not appear in our pre-selected list:

- Share success stories from minorities.
- Have a few preparatory weeks for programming before starting the first semester in CS.

4   BBI Recommendations for the Near Future

Throughout this report we presented a variety of action items for improving gender balance in our CS department. We have motivated these action items using the findings from the discussions with the participants. We now summarize those actions that BBI recommends for the near future. These actions aim to achieve a balanced flow of students into CS studies, a balanced environment within the CS department, and a balanced flow towards CS academia. Figure 14 gives a schematic representation of these three categories of actions, which are listed below.

Action items for a balanced flow of students into CS.
- Student-ambassadors of all genders to present CS to high school and middle high school students.
- Highlight problem solving aspect of CS, flexible and interesting program, job opportunities. CS is something that everyone can do.

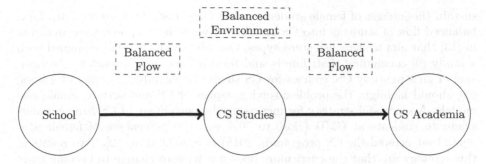

Fig. 14. We propose action items for (i) a gender-balanced flow of students from the school to CS studies, (ii) a gender-balanced student environment in our department, and (iii) a gender-balanced flow of graduates from the CS studies to the CS Phd program, and eventually CS academia.

Action items for a balanced CS study environment.
- Organize social events where senior students offer tips and share experiences and success stories with junior students.
- Have mandatory videos with examples of unaccepted behaviors (e.g., inappropriate jokes, stalking, etc).
- Advise faculty members to ensure that lectures and assignments accommodate a variety of interests.
- Advise faculty members to ensure that colloquiums are not transformed into boys-clubs.
- Increase the number of female TAs.
- Explore the opportunity to have a few preparatory weeks for programming before starting the first semester in CS.

Action items for a balanced flow of candidates into CS academia.
- Hold events that clearly describe the academic career and the PhD program in CS.
- Advise faculty members to move PhD applications earlier at the academic year.

5 Related Work

The discussion sessions with the students helped us identify action items to achieve (i) a balanced flow of students into CS studies, (ii) a balanced environment within the CS department, and (iii) a balanced flow towards CS academia (i.e., PhD and beyond). This section discusses how prior work tackles these three aspects separately. For an extensive overview of initiatives for improving gender balance in CS, we refer the reader to Jaccheri et al. [14].

Our discussion participants highlighted in Fig. 13 that we need to "deal with the issue [of gender balance] at a younger age". A recent aggregated study [13] collects 22 measures and strategies for CS educators in secondary education to sustain the interest of female students in the CS classes. Our action items for a balanced flow of students into CS are aligned with the proposed measurements in [13] that aim to demolish stereotypes. Our observations are also aligned with a study [9] concluding that: family and friends have high impact to the decision of girls to study CS, courses for CS should be introduced earlier at school, one should highlight the problem-solving aspect of CS and surface female role models. A successful strategy for increasing the percentage of CS female undergraduate students at CMU (close to 50% was the percentage of female students that entered the CS program in 2018) is presented in [12]. Two points of this strategy are that the curriculum does not have to change to become more "female-friendly", and that it is important to promote cultural changes within the institution (e.g., create entry level courses for students with no prior programming experience, increase the visibility of women, break stereotypes). These points address two main reasons [23] for the low enrollment of female students in CS programs: "bias in early socialization" and "anxiety towards technology". A more recent paper [22] refines those reasons into three categories: social (e.g., stereotypes), educational (e.g., unattractive CS learning environment), and labor market (e.g., unattractive jobs). Then the authors present ways to address those reasons, by communicating different perspectives of CS and engaging female students to various CS experiences.

Understanding the culture within the study environment of a CS department is a prerequisite for decreasing the gender gap. CMU employed student interviews [11] to inform its strategy for better gender balance. Margolis et al. [18] investigate how the interest of female students about their CS studies might decline and eventually lead to drop-out. Rosenstein et al. [21] report that, within a sample of 200 students, "57% were found to exhibit frequent feelings of the Impostor Phenomenon with a larger fraction of women (71%) experiencing frequent feelings of the Imposter Phenomenon than men (52%)". Miller et al. [19] focus on students with minoritized identities of sexuality and/or gender (MIoSG) in STEM, and concludes that these students are enduring a "dude culture" that fosters hypermasculinity and suppresses discourses related to sexual orientations other than heterosexuality. On the positive side, interviewing STEM students, Rainey et al. [20] conclude that active teaching may improve the sense of belonging for underrepresented students. Finally, Lagesen [15] interviews Malaysian female students, which form around 50% of the student body, to see how their perception about CS differs from the western culture.

A more limited number of studies have been devoted to fostering a gender-balanced flow of students towards PhD and beyond. For example, Moreno et al. [10] interview doctoral CS students on the reasons that led them to apply to a PhD program. The authors identified five mean reasons: academic career goal, professional development, career change, employment opportunity and personal fulfillment. Personal fulfillment was the most popular reason given.

Fig. 15. A discussion session at Árdna, UiT.

6   Conclusion

To understand how the gender balance in our CS department can be improved, we organized discussion sessions among CS undergraduate students, who shared their thoughts about: the reasons they picked CS for their studies, their current experience with the CS studies, their intention to pursue an academic career in CS, and ways to make the CS community more diverse and inclusive. From their answers we identified action items for achieving a balanced flow of students into CS undergraduate program, a study environment that embraces diversity, and a balanced flow of students into higher levels of the CS academia. After the completion of the discussion sessions, the students were able to submit their feedback. We were pleased to see that they enjoyed the discussion and thought that the questions we asked were important. The participants also appreciated our effort to use neutral and not-offensive language for the questions and the discussion that they triggered.

Acknowledgements. We would like to thank Lilli Mittner for recommending Árdna for holding the discussion sessions and for giving inspiration for the discussion questions. Lynn Nygaard gave us inspiration for these questions, too. We also thank Melina Duarte for providing network support for BBI within UiT, and Ingeborg Owesen for providing network support for BBI within BalanseHub. Finally, we are grateful to the administration of the CS department and the members of BBI for their help in organizing the discussion sessions. This work has been partially supported by the COST Action CA19122, from the European Network for Gender Balance in Informatics, and by the NFR grant 321075 for BBI.

References

1. European network for gender balance in informatics. https://eugain.eu/
2. Gender balance in research leadership. https://uit.no/research/prestige
3. Google 2022 diversity annual report (2022). https://about.google/belonging/diversity-annual-report/2022/
4. ICT specialists in employment. https://ec.europa.eu/eurostat/
5. Microsoft diversity & inclusion report. https://www.microsoft.com/en-us/diversity/default.aspx
6. Network support to promote gender balance in norwegian research. https://www.forskningsradet.no/utlysninger/2021/balansehub/
7. Booklet: Best practices from school to university. https://eugain.eu (2022)
8. Albusays, K., Bjorn, P., Dabbish, L., Ford, D., Murphy-Hill, E., Serebrenik, A., Storey, M.A.: The diversity crisis in software development. IEEE Softw. **38**(2), 19–25 (2021)
9. Alshahrani, A., Ross, I., Wood, M.I.: Using social cognitive career theory to understand why students choose to study computer science. In: Proceedings of the 2018 ACM Conference on International Computing Education Research, pp. 205–214. Association for Computing Machinery, New York, NY, USA (2018)
10. del Carmen Calatrava Moreno, M., Kollanus, S.: On the motivations to enroll in doctoral studies in computer science - a comparison of phd program models. In: 2013 12th International Conference on Information Technology Based Higher Education and Training (ITHET), pp. 1–8 (2013)
11. Fisher, A., Margolis, J., Miller, F.: Undergraduate women in computer science: Experience, motivation and culture. In: Proceedings of the Twenty-Eighth SIGCSE Technical Symposium on Computer Science Education, pp. 106–110. SIGCSE '97, Association for Computing Machinery, New York, NY, USA (1997)
12. Frieze, C., Quesenberry, J.L.: How computer science at CMU is attracting and retaining women. Commun. ACM **62**(2), 23–26 (2019)
13. Happe, L., Buhnova, B., Koziolek, A., Wagner, I.: Effective measures to foster girls' interest in secondary computer science education. Educ. Inform. Technol. **26**(3), 2811–2829 (2020). https://doi.org/10.1007/s10639-020-10379-x
14. Jaccheri, L., Pereira, C., Fast, S.: Gender issues in computer science: Lessons learnt and reflections for the future. In: 2020 22nd International Symposium on Symbolic and Numeric Algorithms for Scientific Computing (SYNASC), pp. 9–16 (2020)
15. Lagesen, V.: A cyberfeminist utopia?: Perceptions of gender and computer science among malaysian women computer science students and faculty. Sci. Technol. Human Values **33**, 5–27 (2008)
16. Letizia, J., et. al.: Where are the female professors in STEM? (12 2022). https://doi.org/10.36227/techrxiv.21760532.v1

17. Lewin, A., Sathianathan, D., Lenhard, J., Britton, A.O., Warnock, E., Bavey, N.: The state of diversity in european tech. https://eic.ec.europa.eu/system/files/2022-05/EIC%20report%20presentation.pdf
18. Margolis, J., Fisher, A., Miller, F.: The anatomy of interest: women in undergraduate computer science. Women's Stud. Q. **28**(1/2), 104–127 (2000)
19. Miller, R.A., Vaccaro, A., Kimball, E.W., Forester, R.: "It's dude culture": Students with minoritized identities of sexuality and/or gender navigating stem majors. J. Diversity Higher Educ. **14**, 340–352 (2021)
20. Rainey, K., Dancy, M., Mickelson, R., Stearns, E., Moller, S.: A descriptive study of race and gender differences in how instructional style and perceived professor care influence decisions to major in STEM. Int. J. STEM Educ. **6**(1), 1–13 (2019). https://doi.org/10.1186/s40594-019-0159-2
21. Rosenstein, A., Raghu, A., Porter, L.: Identifying the prevalence of the impostor phenomenon among computer science students. In: Proceedings of the 51st ACM Technical Symposium on Computer Science Education, pp. 30–36. Association for Computing Machinery, New York, NY, USA (2020)
22. Szlávi, A., Bernát, P.: Young women's barriers to choose it and methods to overcome them - a case study from Hungary. Teach. Math. Comput. Sci. **19**(1), 77–101 (2021)
23. Varma, R.: Why so few women enroll in computing? gender and ethnic differences in students' perception. Comput. Sci. Educ. **20**(4), 301–316 (2010)

Designing AI Writing Workflow UX for Reduced Cognitive Loads

Brian Packer(✉) ⓘ and Simeon Keates ⓘ

University of Chichester, Chichester, Bognor Regis PO21 1HR, UK
b.packer@chi.ac.uk

Abstract. This paper explores how Large-Language Model Artificial Intelligences (LLM-AIs) can be used to support people with Attention Deficit Hyperactivity Disorder (ADHD), Autism Spectrum Disorder (ASD), and other learning differences which effect cognition and self-regulation. It examines the cognitive load associated with complex writing tasks and how it affects users who have trouble with high-order thinking and planning. OpenAI's GPT-3 API is used to analyze how AI can help with complex language-based tasks. The paper first reflects on how GPT-3 uses natural language processing to generate text, translate, summarize, answer questions, and caption images, as well as how it adapts to respond to different situations and tasks to accurately classify them.

Bloom's Taxonomy and SOLO Taxonomy are highlighted as language-driven methods of assessing learner understanding and to design activities and assessments that encourage high-order thinking. Literature is reviewed which suggests that students with disorders which effect executive functions need extra help with their writing skills to do well in school, and that early and accessible interventions such as digital self-management tools already help these learners.

A model of executive-cognitive capacity is proposed to assess how best to manage the cognition of tasks and workloads, and to support a design matrix for assistive tools and processes. Finally, the Social Cognitive Theory (SCT) model for writing is evaluated for use as a procedural high-order writing process by which the tools can be designed and against which their efficacy can be validated.

This review illustrates a universal design method for the development and evaluation of future AI writing tools for all users, with specific consideration towards users with atypical cognitive and sensory processing needs.

Keywords: Human-centered design · cognitive load · artificial intelligence · user experience · accessibility · high-order writing · AI pedagogy

1 Introduction

The recent deployment of natural language "AI" transformer models such as GPT-3 may offer an unprecedented acceleration in technological interventions for some common communication challenges shared between users with Autism, ADHD, NVLD, Dysgroup disorders, and other cognitive and sensory processing disorders. These learning differences tend to initially effect language, cognition, comprehension, and literacy;

M. Antona and C. Stephanidis (Eds.): HCII 2023, LNCS 14021, pp. 306–325, 2023.
https://doi.org/10.1007/978-3-031-35897-5_23

which, in turn, has implications on executive function, coordination, organization, and emotional regulation. These factors have repeatedly been demonstrated as predictors for poorer quality outcomes in many aspects of life [1], resulting in (or perhaps exacerbated by) reduced access to special educational needs, assistive technologies, and opportunities to access further and higher education and career options.

Cognitive load is the amount of mental effort required to understand and complete a task and is broadly applicable to all areas of human-centered design as well as facets of behavioral and educational psychology [2]. It can refer to the total amount of information presented at once, how difficult it is to process and remember, or how long it takes for a user to become familiar with a process or system. Within the domain of human-computer interaction, cognitive load represents a constraint on processes and user interface design, including considerations towards how much information is presented by the interfaces (visual or otherwise), the simplicity of navigation paths and menus, the clarity and conciseness of how instructions or feedback is processed, and the amount of customization is possible to accommodate user needs.

This article seeks to review the available literature regarding cognitive load in both the context of HCI and psychopathology for neurodivergent (ND) learners. Executive dysfunction is a comorbidity of many cognitive processing disorders but learners with ADHD will be the focus for this paper due to the breadth of literature available surrounding ADHD and cognitive and/or executive functions (Fig. 1), though other ND characteristics are commonly listed as secondary throughout that literature.

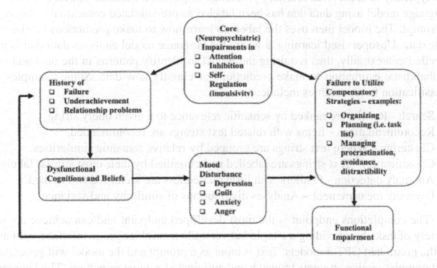

Fig. 1. A cognitive-behavioral model of challenges experienced by adults with ADHD. [3]

Recent advances in machine learning for large language models has resulted in some impressive demonstrations of human-like transcription that are already passing the benchmark of human detection. Tools like OpenAI's GPT-3 offer natural-language prompts which can be processed by several functionality endpoints to achieve emulation of specific cognitive and human-language tasks. AI language tools have developed to provide natural language interfaces that are complex in capability and accessible with minimal barriers to accessibility in terms of technical requirements or prior learning for use. Large-language models such as GPT-3 may be able to mitigate these challenges by automating linguistic processes to bridge the disparity in traditional approaches and requirements to access higher education and the diverse range of cognitive and communicative capabilities of people living with these conditions.

1.1 Current State of Large-Language Model Machine-Learning Tools

GPT-3 is a natural language processing (NLP) model developed by OpenAI, first released in June 2020 following the on-going development of a pre-trained natural language model [4] which uses transfer learning [5] to infer instructional prompting using natural language [6] which can be refined with limited (few-shot) examples of the intended language patterns desired from the task prompt [6]. This allows users to provide natural language instructions to the GPT-3 API, optionally accompanied by contextual samples of language patterns sought from the instructional language or data, to transform or process language against a corpus of pretrained data models.

GPT-3 offers 2 main groups of API 'end-points' used for different high-level processing of text: Text classification or text completion. Classification is used for task where the model is given an input and must return a label or category that best describes it. Classification tasks are typically supervised learning problems, while generation tasks are typically unsupervised learning problems. Supervised machine learning trains the language model using data that has been labeled as pre-validated contextual answers to a prompt. The model then uses the labels to learn how to make predictions or classify new data. Unsupervised learning is where the language model analyses data that is not labelled contextually, thus requiring the model to identify patterns in the data and use probabilistic estimation to make predictions or classify new data. Some examples of classification functionalities include:

- Search - Results are ranked by semantic relevance to a given query string.
- Recommendations - Items with related text strings are recommended.
- Clustering - Where text strings are grouped by relative semantic similarities.
- Classification - Text strings are labelled and classified by their most similar labels.
- Anomaly detection - Outliers with little relatedness are identified and ranked.
- Diversity measurement – Analyses distributions of similarity and variance.

The completions endpoint is the most developed endpoint and can achieve a wide variety of tasks by providing a simple but versatile natural language interface with any of the pretrained GPT-3 models. Text is input as a prompt and the model will generate a text completion that attempts to match and anticipated context or pattern. The language model can distinguish between instructive and demonstrative language within prompts, which can be used to delineate between the functional semantics and the (often more nuanced) emotional sentiment within the prompt. Unlike classification, which inherently uses and produces reductive functions and outputs, generative functions are expansive, making it harder to define the discrete types of functionality possible. As such, the generative functionality examples provided here should not be considered exhaustive, but nonetheless may include:

- Context-based completion: Suggestions of possible completions based on the context from a sentence or phrase are made by an algorithm interpreting the context.
- Multi-token completion: Completions which fit the pattern are looked for in multiple tokens (words) by this more advanced type of completion.
- Completion with constraints: Completions that adhere to user specified parameters such as language, topic, length, etc. are suggested by this type of completion.
- Text generation: Coherent and grammatically correct text is generated using natural language processing techniques and a given set of inputs.
- Translation/Transformation: Text is translated from one language (or style of language, i.e. formal to informal) to another without needing any additional training data or labels from GPT-3.
- Summarization: Complex texts are summarized into more concise versions while maintaining their original meaning through algorithmic identification of key points.
- Question answering: The model's knowledge of context and ability to extract relevant information from the training data (or few-shot sample data) is used to attempt to factually answer questions.
- Image captioning: Captions for images are automatically generated based on what is identified in the image, plus any associated metadata and contextual information about the image's content or scene as provided.
- Natural language understanding: Natural language input is understood by GPT-3 breaking it down into its component parts (e.g., nouns, verbs, adjectives) and then using this analysis to infer the user's intent to provide an appropriate response.

When combined, these completion end-points may be utilized in a large number of language-based tasks limited only by the creativity and specificity of the prompt and the competence and breadth of the training data on which the model was trained. However, as with human attempts at using language to communicate, successful outcomes are never guaranteed and often bound by interpretations within undefined fuzzy logic.

1.2 Limitations of LLM-AI Tools

The success of a prompt depends on the complexity of the task asserted and the quality of the prompt. OpenAI recommends prompt engineers design a prompt as a word problem to be solved by a human with moderately developed language skills but undeveloped higher-order and abstract thinking skills. NLP prompts should provide information for the model to understand the functionality desired and format to be output. By default, OpenAI's API is non-deterministic, such that a given prompt may not result in the same completion each time despite the use of identical prompts. There are some variables, such as "temperature", which can be used to control probabilistic selection of outputs. A temperature of zero will make outputs mostly deterministic, but some variability may remain. Plain language is preferable for describing the instructions and specifying outputs, with the types of input being named as simply and broadly as possible, for example, "Survey response:", and the expected output being made explicit, such as "Sentiment:". This helps to mitigate variability within the prompt and analysis of any few-shot training within it. The API can also return aggregate or multiple results from one prompt, however additional consideration is required of the probability settings to avoid multiplicative statistical drift throughout analysis.

The API must also be given demonstrations of how to respond to many (or all) given use-cases, including an allowance for neutral sentiment analyses. Neutral classifications are essential as there will often be subjective data which even human verification would struggle to ascribe positive or negative sentiment, or, situations will arise whereby classification is not mutually exclusive. If a classifier is being built for something with which the API might not be familiar, such as abstract or fictionally-derived categories, then more examples will be necessary and the intention of the fine-tuning may undesirably drift towards the statistical normal of the model's wider text corpus of training data.

2 Cognitive Load Modelling for High-Order Writing

Specific neurological and biological mechanisms, particularly evident in ADHD and ASD, result in tangible disparities in the learner's ability to engage in higher-order learning functions. Whilst these effects tend not to be profound at a young age, with atypical rates of various measures of early years development being reliable predictors for the conditions in early learning, they gradually lead to challenges with learning engagement and interrelated behavioral and emotional impacts. Without the benefits of early recognition and intervention, these effects tend to become systematic and grow to have a significant impact on standardized learning throughout adolescence which results in reduced access to continuous professional development and higher education. One of the most common systemic impacts is on executive functions, the ability for a learner to plan, prepare, coordinate, and initiate activities and behaviors which they recognize to be necessary and constructive. This has a particularly notable impact on the formulation of long-form writing. [7].

Words are the basis of academic communication, and this applies to the development of academic learning and its assessment at all levels. Without deferring too deeply into greater pedagogical or epistemic theory, it is given by governance throughout education (in the United Kingdom, at least) that two formative pillars uphold Further and Higher Education: SOLO [8] and Bloom's Taxonomy [9].

Bloom's Taxonomy is a classification system used to organize the different levels of thinking and understanding required for academic assessment. It is divided into six categories: knowledge, comprehension, application, analysis, synthesis, and evaluation. Each category is further broken down into various skills and objectives. Knowledge involves remembering facts, comprehension involves understanding concepts, application involves using knowledge in a practical way, analysis involves breaking down complex ideas into simpler parts, synthesis involves combining ideas to form new ones, and evaluation involves making judgments based on criteria. This is a useful tool for developing higher-order thinking skills. By breaking down the different levels of understanding and thinking, educators can create assessments that measure students' abilities to think critically and apply knowledge in a practical way. This can help them identify areas where students need more support and help them target instruction to meet their needs. Additionally, Bloom's Taxonomy can be used to create lesson plans that focus on higher-order thinking skills, such as analysis, synthesis, and evaluation. This can help students develop their problem-solving and critical thinking skills.

Conversely, SOLO Taxonomy stands for Structure of Observed Learning Outcome. It is a model for assessing students' understanding of a concept or topic. It is divided into five levels: prestructural, unistructural, multistructural, relational, and extended abstract. At each level, students are asked to demonstrate their understanding in different ways. For example, at the prestructural level, students may be asked to recall facts, while at the extended abstract level, they may be asked to make predictions or draw conclusions. SOLO taxonomy can be used to help teachers design activities and assessments that promote higher-order thinking. This emphasizes the use of vocabulary intended to evokes methods of analysis, investigation, discovery or reflection (Fig. 2).

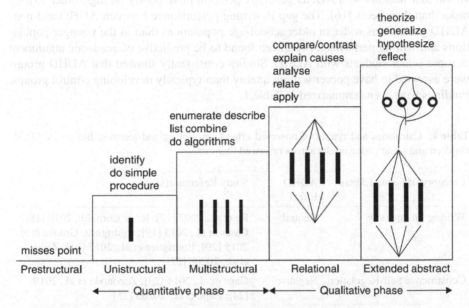

Fig. 2. A hierarchy of verbs that may be used to form intended learning outcomes. [8]

2.1 Cognitive and Executive Functions vs. Higher Thinking and Writing

As most typically developing children reach adolescence, their cognitive load increases as they are presented with more complex information and tasks. This increased cognitive load can lead to increased stress and anxiety, as well as difficulty in understanding and processing the information.

[10] found that adults with ADHD had difficulty paying attention and controlling their reactions when presented with visual-response tasks. They had lowered amplitudes in their brain activity compared to control group individuals, which provided neurophysical evidence that ADHD results either in or from consistent neurological difference. The

results showed that adults with ADHD had difficulty with response control and effortful engagement, with performance unaffected by either mood or anxiety. This has been observed to correlate with secondary characteristics which act as predictors for difficulties with behavioral and emotional regulation, resulting in further impact on learning and attainment. These findings appeared to be mostly consistent in a similar study of adolescents aged between 12–21 with ASD [11] and is further supported by the findings of [12–14] and [15] which each isolate characteristics of various cognitive processing disorders by executive function. Thus, it can be presumed that those factors are not exclusive to non-ADHD conditions.

[1] undertook a comprehensive survey of literature reviewing the interactions between ADHD learners, writing construction, and many other factors of learning in ADHD populations. Their findings across the literature supported the common observation that students with ADHD generally perform more poorly on high-order writing tasks than their peers [16]. The gap in writing performance between ADHD and non-ADHD groups was wider in older school-age populations than in the younger populations and writing performance has been found to be predictive of academic attainment in more senior students with ADHD. Studies consistently showed that ADHD groups were assessed to have poorer writing quality than typically developing control groups. Findings have been summarized in Table 1.

Table 1. Categories and typing of observed effects on writing and learning factors in ADHD children and some young adults across reviewed literature.

Category of Found Effects	ADHD Effect	Study Reference(s)
Writing Productivity	Neutral	Re et al., 2007 [17]; Re & Cornoldi, 2010 [18]; Casas et al., 2013 [19]; Rodríguez, Grünke et al., 2015 [20]; Rodríguez et al., 2017 [21]; Zajic et al., 2020b [22]
Constructive Self-Regulation	Negative	Gage et al., 2014 [23]; Zendarski et al., 2019 [24]; Zajic et al., 2020a [25]
Writing Quality	Negative	Re et al., 2007; Re & Cornoldi, 2010; Casas et al., 2013; Rodríguez, Grünke et al., 2015; Rodríguez et al., 2017;
Emotional Regulation	Inconclusive	Gage et al., 2014; Zendarski et al., 2019
Cognition and Language	Positive	DeBono et al., 2012 [26]; Gage et al., 2014; Rodríguez et al., 2017; Eckrich et al., 2019 [27]; Berninger & Abbott, 2010 [28]; Mehta et al., 2005 [29]

Notably, negative relationships between writing productivity in both ADHD and non-ADHD groups was inconclusive and positive relationships between language systems (receptive and expressive oral language, reading, and written expression) and ADHD groups was supported but not conclusive. This suggests that the inhibiting effect on writing is actually the ability to construct writing and engage in review and reflection as applies to redrafting, as the evidence affirmed the learner's non-written communication abilities and cognitive capabilities. Teacher-reported ratings of inattention were identified as a significant predictor of writing performance, as opposed to teachers' reported hyperactivity or teacher/parent-reported inattention/hyperactivity symptoms [21, 26]. This suggests that inattention, a manifestation of broader executive dysfunction, is the formative predictor of learning disassociation. Cognitive factors and language skills, including phonological short-term memory, sustained attention, working memory, reading abilities, as well as receptive and expressive oral language skills, were identified as significant predictors of writing performance in ADHD samples [21, 23, 26–27]. Discussion throughout the literature suggested that high-order writing performance is strongly linked to overall academic achievement in adolescent students with ADHD and that a higher proportion of students with ADHD, across a wide range of age groups, failed to demonstrate the minimum writing skills needed for their grade level. Recurrent observations were made of the relationships between language development, writing skills, attainment predictors, and factors of cognition which included:

- Working memory
- Processing speed
- Fine motor abilities
- Receptive language
- Reading efficiency (Reprocessing)
- Phonological short-term memory
- Expressive oral language
- Contextual language and conventions
- Grammar and sentence construction
- Selective use of vocabulary range
- Reading comprehension
- Sustained attention

Four studies examined the relationships between cognitive factors and writing performance in ADHD samples [26] employed correlative and simultaneous regression analyses to examine how different cognitive processing measures (e.g., working memory, processing speed, language, fine motor ability, and reading efficiency) related to writing performance in both ADHD and sub-threshold ADHD learners. Findings suggested that receptive language and reading efficiency were significant predictors of contextual conventions (e.g., accurate capitalization, spelling, and punctuation) and expressive oral language was a significant predictor of contextual language (e.g., grammar, sentence construction, and richness of vocabulary [27] combined parallel and serial multiple-mediation models to identify that phonological short-term memory and expressive oral language collectively mediated ADHD-related written expression difficulties with moderate effects [23] found that reading performance has a partial but significant mediation effect on writing for individuals with both ADHD and emotional disturbances [21] found that working memory and sustained attention explained a significant amount of the variance in writing performance after controlling for IQ, age-within-year, and ADHD diagnosis using multiple hierarchical regression.

Finally, there was evidence that individuals displaying ADHD symptoms, but whom did not meet a full clinical diagnosis of ADHD, who also demonstrated writing difficulties [1] concluded that students with ADHD, and possibly the other sub-threshold learners with symptoms characteristic of ADHD, required early intervention to make adequate progress in their schooling; otherwise internal and external psychosocial effects were observed to become detrimental and self-fulfilling. Early identification and interventions for learning and writing were recommended for any students displaying features of ADHD and that these interventions should focus on developing procedural skills in planning and self-regulation during the writing process.

2.2 Summary of Impacts of ADHD on Development Through Writing

Successful high-order writing requires sustained attention and strategies to help students stay on task during the writing process. Conduct and disruptive behaviors may be related to writing performance in students with ADHD, though attentional factors reported in the education setting are more strongly related to high-order writing performance than parents' reported inattention and parents/teachers' reported hyperactive-impulsive. Interventions should therefore focus on developing procedural skills in planning and self-monitoring during the writing process and enhancing meta-cognitive knowledge of writing may help structure academic development.

Similar strengths of correlation between similar cognitive or behavioral factors were demonstrated throughout these reviews, with behavioral predictors becoming stronger in older age groups. This may suggest that the strongest effects in studies of the younger cohorts may be observing the causal factors of the weaker effects observed in maturing cohorts. Based on this, it was possible to categorize cognitive, learning, and behavioral factors into primary (causal) and secondary (correlative) impacts common in learners with ADHD (Table 2).

Table 2. Summary of primary and secondary effects observed by meta-analysis of impacts of ADHD on higher-order writing, including frequency observed.

Primary Effects		Secondary Effects	
Cognitive Resources/Impairments	6	Behavioral Problems	2
Attentional Factors	4	Meta-cognitive Knowledge	2
Reading Skills	3		
Oral Language Skills	3		

The most common observations being that cognitive load, or factors relating to it, were consistent throughout all cohorts. This supports the notion that designing writing tools that provide interventions, which must be accessible from a young age, to alleviate cognitive demand of complex learning tasks, particularly development through writing, may mitigate the detrimental effects predicted for in later learning and development.

3   Experience Design for Cognitive Processes

In human-computer interaction, cognitive load specifically relates to the amount of mental effort required to understand and complete a task using a digital interface. As best practice, cognitive load should be minimized for users to have an enjoyable and successful experience with a tool, product, or service [30] and this is particularly important for users with cognitive impairments [31].

Technological interventions are already widely used to assist with the management of attention and executive function disorders [32–33]. The difficulties encountered by these users can be offset by using responsive tools that reduce the cognitive load of executive tasks, such as task management apps, reminders, and timers. These tools can also help the users stay organized and on track with their tasks, whilst utilizing multisensory cues to help grab control user attention or sustain focus on a given by reduce distractions. Finally, these tools can also provide feedback and incentives to engage the reward mechanisms within the brain and thus help motivate individuals to stay focused and complete their tasks [34–36].

By cross-referencing inhibited functional processes with intervention success rates, it was possible to derive a matrix of design to guide the development of AI applications to assist with complex writing tasks for learning. Cognitive and executive impacts of ADHD throughout the literature were extracted and classified to derive a model of high-order writing task cognitive constraints (Fig. 3) and functional domains.

Any given examples observed as specific challenges were then modelled as tasks and attributed to dysfunctions within the criteria (Table 3).

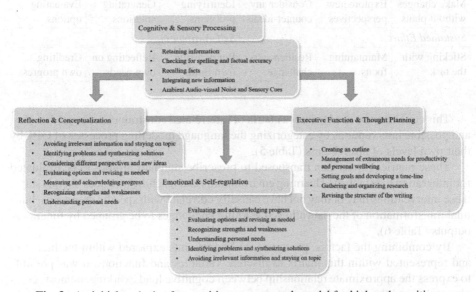

Fig. 3. An initial analysis of a cognitive-resource task-model for high-order writing.

3.1   Modelling Literacy-Cognition Differences as a Design Matrix

By reviewing the models of literacy and high-order writing from [37–39] it was possible to derive a hierarchy of literacy tasks by abstractness (Table 4) which correlated with the language abstraction utilized in large-language models like GPT.

Table 3. Non-weighted survey of identified challenges of essay writing from library/learning support service literature about cognitive processing or executive function disorders.

Attentional Control			*Planning*		
Focusing on the task	Maintaining concentration	Ignoring any distractions	Creating an outline	Developing a timeline	Setting goals and outcomes
Self-Monitoring			*Inhibition*		
Checking for accuracy	Evaluating progress	Revising as needed	Ignore new irrelevant info	Staying on topic	Resist any distractions
Emotional Control			*Initiation*		
Managing stress	Regulate emotions	Stay and get motivated	Starting the task	Undertake any research	Drafting a plan
Organization			*Working Memory*		
Survey research	Structuring the essay	Creating a logical flow	Retain prior information	Recall facts and details	Process new information
Flexibility			*Problem Solving*		
Make changes without plans	Explore new perspectives	Consider any counter-ideals	Identifying problems	Generating solutions	Evaluating options
Sustained Effort			*Self-Awareness*		
Sticking with the task	Maintaining focus	Resilience to challenge	Recognising own limits	Reflecting on own needs	Crediting own progress

This could then be used to infer a matrix of interrelated constraints, associated causes, and possible interventions by categorizing the language modelling processes of GPT by their own levels of abstractness (Table 5).

These matrices were then transposed to prescribe standard utilities to be evaluated for integration to established learning environments and teaching practices. At this stage, these interventions may or may not have causally correlate with specific user needs, but a final transformation of the data allowed learning challenges to be grouped by functional outputs (Table 6).

By combining the factors, processes, and constraints explored within the literature and represented within this matrix as discrete variables and functions, it was possible to express the approximate relationship between cognitive load, working memory, complex tasks, and the onset of executive dysfunction as a function of combined cognitive-executive capacity (Eq. 1). This model is intended to be illustrative rather than comprehensive and attempts to convey the combined dynamics observed by [40–41] and [10] as summarized by [40] in Fig. 4.

Table 4. Examples of how language-level abstraction applies to cognitive processes.

Cognitive-Literacy Skill Categories		Examples				
Level 1	Low-Level Transcription	*Spelling*	*Word Recognition*	*Handwriting*	*Typing*	...
Level 2	Sentence Formation	*Grammar*	*Sentence Structuring*	*Comprehension*		...
Level 3	Higher-order Writing	*Structured Planning*	*Writing Prose*	*Review*	*Abstract Learning*	...
Level 4	Internalized Learning	*Research Synthesis*	*Critical Evaluation*	*Thematic Interrelation*	*Revision*	...

Table 5. Examples of how GPT-3 language abstraction applies to procedurally generated text.

LLM-AI Abstraction		Examples				
Level 1	Classification	*Sentiment Analysis*	*Complex Searching*	*Recognizing Relatedness*	*Simple Translation*	...
Level 2	Clustering	*Fuzzy Searching*	*Semantic Relatedness*	*Language Processing*	*Linear Text Regression*	...
Level 3	Insert-editing	*Connected Topics*	*Prose Generation*	*K-Nearest Matching*	*Transform Language*	...
Level 4	Summation	*Connecting Themes*	*Thematic Regression*	*Linguistic Synthesis*	*Domain Limits*	...

'*P(Dys)*' models a probability function of the onset of executive dysfunction and the increased cognitive demand over time from cognitive processing, working memory, and self-regulation over extrinsic factors such as task complexity or sensory loads.

$$P(Dys) = 1 - ecc \vdots ecc = Q - C(i_n)$$
$$ecc = Q - (A + W)$$
$$ecc = Q - \left(\frac{y}{G} \cdot \left(\frac{1}{LTC} \right) + \left(\frac{wmu}{wmc} \cdot \frac{1}{LTC} \right) \right)$$
$$ecc = Q - \left(\frac{\left(\frac{S}{N \cdot D} \right)}{G} \cdot \left(\frac{1}{LTC} \right) + \left(\frac{\left(D \cdot \frac{S}{N} \right) + \left(\frac{DG}{B} \right)}{(wmc_k \cdot wmc_d)} \cdot \frac{1}{LTC} \right) \right) \quad (1)$$
$$G = \sum_{i_n} [g] \vdots D = \sum_{i_n} [d] \vdots S = \sum_{i_n} [s] \vdots g_i = \left(\frac{d_i}{s_i} \cdot \frac{1}{r} \right)$$

Equation 1. Probability function which models the inverse relationship between the onset of executive dysfunction and executive-cognitive load over a set of a tasks i_n.

Table 6. Disorganized matrix of interrelated writing constraints resulting from challenges of different processing disorders and possible LLM functions for automated intervention.

Intervention	Executive Functions	Cognitive Functions	High-Order Processes
Translation and Transformation	Self-discipline and Sustaining Effort	Contextual language and conventions	Thematic Interrelation
Natural language understanding	Scheduling and Task Planning	Grammar & sentence construction	Connecting Theories
Completion with constraints	Attentional Control	Selective use of vocabulary range	Critical Evaluation
Context-based completion	Emotional Control	Reading efficiency (Reprocessing)	Research Synthesis
Multi-token completion	Impulse Inhibition	Phonological short-term memory	Sentence Structuring
Diversity measurement	Self-Monitoring	Expressive oral language	Word Recognition
Anomaly Detection	Problem Solving	Reader comprehension	Structured Planning
Question answering	Self-Awareness	Fine-motor abilities	Revision & Review
Recommendations	Task Initiation	Sustained attention	Abstract Learning
Text generation	Organization	Receptive language	Comprehension
Summarization	Flexibility	Working memory	Writing Prose
Classification	-	Processing speed	Typing
Clustering	-	-	Spelling
Search	-	-	Grammar

As executive-cognitive capacity 'ecc' is reduced, the chance that executive dysfunction 'dys' will occur increases, whereby:

- Q is the cognitive quotient, the apparent mutual cognitive resource pool which moderates an individual's initial capacity for executive and cognitive demands.
- C is an estimate of the total cognitive load, which is the amount of mental effort required to complete a set of complex tasks 'i_n'.
- A represents interference control, a measure of attention self-regulation, capacitated by the ability to process sensory loads 'y', and mediated by cognitive flexibility 'B'.
- W is the working-memory load, a function of the amount of information being stored against the individual's short and long-term memory capacity, notably deregulated by reduced ability to iteratively compare against long-term memory [42].
- L is the working-memory demand, which is the amount of information being stored in working memory within the given time span (estimated to be 7 ± 2 s).
- S is the total sensory load, which is the combined sensory inputs which must be processed at any given time during the tasks or prompts within that duration.

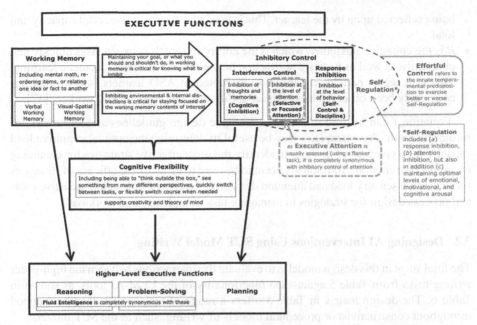

Fig. 4. Diamond's review of composite factors which influence executive function and control.

- *G* is the average task complexity, based on the sensory and working memory demand of all tasks, and mediated by cognitive flexibility and working-memory capacity.
- *D* is the average task duration, which is the average amount of time it takes to complete a task in seconds and *N* is the total number of concurrent tasks being evaluated.
- *g* is the average sensory input of tasks, which is the average amount of sensory input shared between all concurrent tasks being processed.

'*ecc*' approximates executive-cognitive capacity, which will vary based on the user or learner who is being evaluated. It combines several intrinsic and likely non-static cognitive or neurological traits of individual differences, including:

- *y* which is the sensory processing capacity, which appears to be a function of emotional and cognitive regulation over time throughout exposure to on-going rates of different types of sensory load.
- *r* is the attention regulation, which is the ability to regulate one's attention in order to complete a task and *y* is the sensory capacity, which is the amount of sensory input that can be processed at any given time. These factors are both often affected by processing disorders from across the spectrum. [43–44]
- *wmc* is the working-memory capacity which has been observed to be a combination of an individual's ability to chunk sensory data (wmc_k) and hold it in a limited memory store for a duration (wmc_d). [41]
- *LTC* is the long-term memory capacity, which is the amount of information that can be stored in the long-term memory and *ltm* is the current long-term memory utilization, which is the amount of information in long-term memory that is actively

being reflected upon by the learner. This is used to estimate active recall capacity and load.

• *B* is the cognitive flexibility, which is the ability to switch between tasks quickly and efficiently, as well as perceive abstraction between tasks to invoke memetic learning. This trait seems particularly absent or disrupted in ASD learners [45–46], but has conversely been observed as a high capability trait amongst ADHD workers [47].

Equation 1 can be used to provide actionable design guidelines and takeaways for further research. For example, it may be useful to determine the optimal cognitive load capacity for a given set of tasks, or to identify the most effective strategies for managing executive dysfunction. Additionally, it could be used to measure the efficacy of strategies for managing sensory load and attention demand, as well as the design of assistive tools and process design for strategies to managing task complexity and workload.

3.2 Designing AI Interventions Using SCT Model Writing

The final stage in this design model is to evaluate the interactions between the high-order writing tasks from Table 5 against the functionality of the LLM-AI tools, as shown in Table 6. The design matrix in Table 5 offers a range of tasks which may be mapped throughout constructivist or procedural models of writing, such as the SCT model.

According to Social Cognitive Theory (SCT), learning occurs through a reciprocal interaction between the individual, their behavior, and the environment [37]. In the context of higher-order writing, this means that a writer's behavior and writing skills are shaped by their environment (e.g., classroom, peers, feedback), and that the individual writer also has agency in their selection and utilization of writing tools or reflective and adaptive strategies to support their own needs and writing process. The model is generally divided into 3 stages: 1) prewriting, 2) drafting, and 3) revision & review.

As examples, in the 'prewriting stage, a writer using the SCT model might begin by setting goals for their writing task and selecting appropriate writing strategies and tools based on their prior experiences and feedback. The writer might use a mind map or outline to organize their ideas, or they might consult online resources or guides to help them develop their understanding of their task's requirements. In the drafting stage, the writer must engage in the act of writing construction, while also drawing on their self-efficacy beliefs and utilizing the writing strategies and tools selected in the prior stage. In the revision and editing stage, the writer should seek feedback from others, either peers or instructors, to refine their writing and improve their overall writing skills.

Overall, the SCT model suggests that the writing process is shaped by the individual writer's self-efficacy beliefs, their prior experiences, and their learning infrastructure, which emphasizes the use of their writing tools. Effective use of AI writing tools, therefore, requires an understanding of the writing process and the individual writer's goals, needs, and abilities. This is concurrent with the previously developed findings of [1] and further supported by [48, 36]. Combining these hypotheses, we can attest that AI tools should not only improve the quality of writing in users with cognitive processing disorders, but that they can empower these users with a greater sense of self-efficacy

[49]. Some examples of how LLM-AI tools can be applied at each stage of the SCT model of writing may include:

1. **Prewriting**: AI writing tools can be helpful in this stage by providing writing prompts, generating topic ideas, or suggesting relevant sources for research.
2. **Drafting**: This might involve using an AI writing tool to generate alternative phrasing or to check for grammatical errors.
3. **Revision and review**: LLM-AI tools can provide suggestions to improve clarity and coherence and also review structure or redundancy, or check for language errors.

However, these are just a few examples of possible applications of AI writing tools. The full extent of possible interventions is likely to emerge in the coming months. It is likely that a prompt could be designed for every permutation of writing skill against a functional cognitive process. By determining prerequisite inputs, it is possible to rearrange the tasks into a corresponding input and LLM-AI function (Table 7), leaving only the task of designing the correct natural language to invoke the task functions required.

Table 7. Possible interventions for high-order writing and language skill or tasks as assigned to their corresponding LLM-AI functions, per the OpenAI GPT-3 API.

Writing Skill	Ideal LLM-AI Interventions		
Typing	Search	Recommendations	Clustering
Spelling	Search	Recommendations	Clustering
Word Recognition	Search	Recommendations	Clustering
Grammar	Classification	Anomaly Detection	Diversity Measurement
Sentence Structuring	Context-based Completion	Multi-token Completion	Completion with Constraints
Comprehension	Text Generation	Translation and Transformation	Summarization
Structured Planning	Question Answering	Natural Language Understanding	Text Generation
Writing Prose	Text Generation	Translation and Transformation	Summarization
Revision & Review	Search	Recommendations	Clustering
Connecting Theories	Text Generation	Translation and Transformation	Summarization
Critical Evaluation	Classification	Anomaly Detection	Diversity Measurement
Research Synthesis	Text Generation	Translation and Transformation	Summarization
Thematic Interrelation	Text Generation	Translation and Transformation	Summarization

For now, priority should be placed on exploring and evaluating the measurable effects of deploying these tools for individual tasks to mitigate the largest effects of ADHD and other executive-cognitive disorders. This should especially emphasize the utilization of such tools in the context of self-regulated strategies for writing development [50–52] and might include task fulfillment in areas such as:

- Difficulties with task initiation due to insufficient formative incentive resulting in poor executive function, whereby LLM-AI may be used for idea generation or exploratory questioning to identify research questions.
- Recontextualizing task descriptors to remodel proactive processes as reactive processes, whereby the use of LLM-AI text transformation can formalize summaries and sentiments for reflection over forcing learners to engage in mechanically slow typing and cognitive exhausting language construction.
- Emphasis should be placed on emotional contexts rather than detail-oriented classification, whereby summarization of research abstracts can be used to expedite the generation to contextualize findings.
- The use of self-summarization to redraft and classify, where post-process classification to generate structured or chronological lists can be used to avoid topical drift or challenges of perceived sameness.

4 Conclusions

LLM-AI tools such as those developed using OpenAI's GPT-3 API can be used to create custom models for specific tasks such as summarization, question answering, and translation. This allows users to explore different concepts in a more efficient and effective way. Prefix and suffix prompting can be combined to bridge prompts or text samples, and this can help summarize the main points of each sample and then connect them in a meaningful way, as well as generating questions or further discussion points based on the recessive and successive context. This can be further extended to revise and improve human writing by providing alternative wordings, sentence structures, and phrases that may better fit the context of the writing. It can also suggest additional ideas or topics to include in the writing in order to make it more complete. Finally, GPT-3 can help detect and contextual or complex errors in grammar and spelling, which can mitigate human editing beyond existing technologies which assist in this process.

By combining these utilities and applying them through a procedural model of high-order writing, it is possible to identify targeted intervention for tasks which may be inhibiting the participation of students with executive-cognitive disorders from accessing the same opportunities to develop their higher-order thinking within education settings. Critically, these interventions must occur early within the learner's development and continue to scale with task complexity as they grow older.

Modelling for cognitive load and other factors of language and working cognition will allow the evaluation of these interventions which may then be validated against established methods of measuring successful interventions for such learners in an academic setting in the later years of their studies.

References

1. Cheng, S., Coghill, D., Zendarski, N.: A rapid systematic review of attention-deficit/hyperactivity disorder (ADHD) and high order writing: Current findings and implications for intervention. Res, Developm. Disabilities **123** (2022)
2. Card, S., Moran, T., Newell, A.: Cognitive Skill. In: Card, S. (ed.) The Psychology of Human-Computer Interaction, 1st edn., p. 45. CRC Press, Boca Raton, USA (1983)
3. Safren, S., Sprich, S., Chulvick, S., Otto, M.: Psychosocial treatments for adults with attention-deficit/hyperactivity disorder. Psychiatric Clinics North America **27**(2) (2004)
4. Radford, A., Narasimhan, K., Salimans, T., Sutskever, I.: Improving Language Understanding by Generative Pre-Training. Tech. rep. (2019)
5. Raffel, C., et al.: Exploring the limits of transfer learning with a unified text-to-text transformer. J. Mach. Learn. Res. **21**, 1–67 (2020)
6. Radford, A., Wu, J., Child, R., Luan, D., Amodei, D., Sutskever, I.: Language Models are Unsupervised Multitask Learners. Tech. rep. (2018)
7. Soto, E., Irwin, L., Chan, E., Spiegel, J., Kofler, M.: Executive functions and writing skills in children with and without ADHD. Neuropsychology **35**(8), 792–808 (2021)
8. Biggs, J.: Contexts for effective teaching and learning. In Biggs, J., Tang, C., eds. : Teaching for Quality Learning at University 4th edn., p. 58. McGraw Hill (January 2011)
9. Bloom, B., Krathwohl, D.: Taxonomy of educational objectives: the classification of educational goals. In : Handbook I: Cognitive Domain (1956)
10. Grane, V., et al.: ERP correlates of proactive and reactive cognitive control in treatment-naïve adult adhd. PLoS ONE **11**(7) (2016)
11. Høyland, A., et al.: Event-related potentials in a cued Go-NoGo task associated with executive functions in adolescents with autism spectrum disorder; A case-control study. Front. Neurosci. **11** (2017)
12. Cools, R.: The cost of dopamine for dynamic cognitive control. Curr. Opin. Behav. Sci. **4**, 152–159 (2015)
13. Mattsson, T., et al.: Electrophysiological characteristics in children with listening difficulties, with or without auditory processing disorder. Int. J. Audiol. **58**(11), 704–716 (2019)
14. Nieoullon, A.: Dopamine and the regulation of cognition and attention (2002)
15. Diamond, A.: Chapter 18 - Biological and social influences on cognitive control processes dependent on prefrontal cortex. In Braddick, O., Atkinson, J., Innocenti, G., (eds.) : Gene Expression to Neurobiology and Behavior: Human Brain Development and Developmental Disorders, vol. 189, pp. 319–339. Elsevier (2011)
16. Molitor, S., Langberg, J., Evans, S.: The written expression abilities of adolescents with Attention-Deficit/Hyperactivity Disorder. Res. Dev. Disabil. **51–52**, 49–59 (2016)
17. Re, A., Pedron, M., Cornoldi, C.: Expressive writing difficulties in children described as exhibiting ADHD symptoms. J. Learn, Disabilities **40**(3) (2007)
18. Re, A., Cornoldi, C.: ADHD expressive writing difficulties of ADHD children: When good declarative knowledge is not sufficient. Europ. J. Psychol. Educ. **25**(3) (2010)
19. Casas, A., Ferrer, M., Fortea, I.: Written composition performance of students with attention-deficit/ hyperactivity disorder. Appli. Psycholinguistics **34**(3) (2013)
20. Rodríguez, C., Grünke, M., González-Castro, P., García, T., Álvarez-García, D.: How do students with attention-deficit/ hyperactivity disorders and writing learning disabilities differ from their nonlabeled peers in the ability to compose texts? Learn. Disabilities: A Contemporary Journal **13**(2), 157–175 (2015)
21. Rodríguez, C., Torrance, M., Betts, L., Cerezo, R., García, T.: Effects of ADHD on writing composition product and process in school-age students. J. Atten. Disord. **24**(12), 1735–1745 (2017)

22. Zajic, M., Solari, E., McIntyre, N., Lerro, L., Mundy, P.: Task engagement during narrative writing in school-age children with autism spectrum disorder compared to peers with and without attentional difficulties. Res. Autism Spectrum Disorders **76** (2020)
23. Gage, N., Wilson, J., MacSuga-Gage, A.: Writing performance of students with emotional and/or behavioral disabilities. Behav. Disorders **40**(1) (2014)
24. Zendarski, N., Mensah, F., Hiscock, H., Sciberras, E.: Trajectories of emotional and conduct problems and their association with early high school achievement and engagement for adolescents with ADHD. J. Attention Disorders 25(5) (2021)
25. Zajic, M., Solari, E., McIntyre, N., Lerro, L., Mundy, P.: Overt planning behaviors during writing in school-age children with autism spectrum disorder and attention-deficit/hyperactivity disorder. Res. Developm. Disabilities **100** (2020)
26. DeBono, T., Hosseini, A., Cairo, C., Ghelani, K., Tannock, R., Toplak, M.: Written expression performance in adolescents with attention-deficit/hyperactivity disorder (ADHD). Reading and Writing **25**(6) (2012)
27. Eckrich, S., Rapport, M., Calub, C., Friedman, L.: Written expression in boys with ADHD: The mediating roles of working memory and oral expression. Child Neuropsychol. **25**(6) (2019)
28. Berninger, V., Abbott, R.: Listening comprehension, oral expression, reading comprehension, and written expression: related yet unique language systems in grades 1, 3, 5, and 7. J. Educ. Psychol. **102**(3) (2010)
29. Mehta, P., Foorman, B., Branum-Martin, L., Taylor, W.: Literacy as a unidimensional multi-level construct: Validation, sources of influence, and implications in a longitudinal study in grades 1 to 4. Scient. Stud. Reading **9**(2) (2005)
30. Stephanidis, C.: The universal access handbook (2009)
31. Keates, S., Kozloski, J., Varker, P.: Cognitive impairments, HCI and daily living. In: Stephanidis, C. (ed.) UAHCI 2009. LNCS, vol. 5614, pp. 366–374. Springer, Heidelberg (2009). https://doi.org/10.1007/978-3-642-02707-9_42
32. Hariyanto, D., Triyono, M., Koehler, T.: Usability evaluation of personalized adaptive e-learning system using USE questionnaire. Knowl. Manag. E-Learn. **12**, 85–105 (2020)
33. Smet, M., Brand-, S., Leijten, M., Kirschner, P.: Electronic outlining as a writing strategy: Effects on students' writing products, mental effort and writing process. Comput. Educ. **78**, 352–366 (2014)
34. Oliveira, W., et al.: Does gamification affect flow experience? A systematic literature review. **2883**, 110–119 (2021)
35. Lightbown, D.: The User-Centered Design Process. In : Designing the User Experience of Game Development Tools (2020)
36. Oudeyer, P.-Y., Gottlieb, J., Lopes, M.: Intrinsic motivation, curiosity and learning: theory and applications in educational technologies. Prog. Brain Res. **229**, 257–284 (2016)
37. Flower, L., Hayes, J.: A cognitive process theory of writing. College Compos. Commun. **32**(4) (1981)
38. Graham, S., Harris, K.: Writing better: Effective strategies for teaching students with learning difficulties. Brookes Publishing (2005)
39. Berninger, V., Winn, W.: Implications of Advancements in Brain Research and Technology for Writing Development, Writing Instruction, and Educational Evolution (2006)
40. Diamond, A.: Executive functions. Annu. Rev. Psychol. **64**(1), 135–168 (2013)
41. Baddeley, A.: Exploring Working Memory, 1st edn. Routledge, London, UK (2017)
42. Capodieci, A., Re, A., Fracca, A., Borella, E., Carretti, B.: The efficacy of a training that combines activities on working memory and metacognition: Transfer and maintenance effects in children with ADHD and typical development. J. Clin. Exp. Neuropsychol. **41**(10), 1074–1087 (2019)

43. Lincoln, A., Bloom, D., Katz, M., Boksenbaum, N.: Neuropsychological and neurophysiological indices of auditory processing impairment in children with multiple complex developmental disorder. J. Am. Acad. Child Adolesc. Psychiatry **37**, 100–112 (1998)
44. Hitoglou, M., Ververi, A., Antoniadis, A., Zafeiriou, D.: Childhood autism and auditory system abnormalities. Pediatr. Neurol. **42**(5), 309–314 (2010)
45. Ullman, M., Earle, F., Walenski, M., Janacsek, K.: The Neurocognition of Developmental Disorders of Language (2019)
46. Marocchini, E.: Impairment or difference? The case of Theory of Mind abilities and pragmatic competence in the Autism Spectrum. Appli. Psycholing., 1–19 (2023)
47. Lauder, K.: A critical examination of the evidence for effective reasonable adjustments for adults with attention deficit hyperactivity disorder in the workplace (October 2020)
48. Glynis, C.: Strategies for Researching Learning in Higher Education (2009)
49. Lauder, K., McDowall, A., Tenenbaum, H.: A systematic review of interventions to support adults with ADHD at work—Implications from the paucity of context-specific research for theory and practice. Front. Psychol. **13** (2022)
50. Sexton, M., Harris, K., Graham, S.: Self-Regulated strategy development and the writing process: effects on essay writing and attributions. Except. Child. **64**(3), 295–311 (1998)
51. Scrivani, A.: Effects of Self-Regulated Strategy Development on the persuasive Effects of Self-Regulated Strategy Development on the persuasive essay writing of seventh grade students with disabilities essay writing of seventh grade students with disabilities (2017)
52. Latif, M.: Remodeling writers' composing processes: Implications for writing assessment. Assessing Writing **50** (2021)

Introducing Computer Science and Arts for All (CSA4ALL): Developing an Inclusive Curriculum and Portal for K5 Children

Prashamsa Pandey[✉], Fatemeh Jamshidi, and Daniela Marghitu

Auburn University, Auburn, AL, USA
{pzp0052,fzj0007,marghda}@auburn.edu

Abstract. The difficulty of acquiring computer programming skills is a plausible cause for the elevated attrition rates in Computer Science (CS). Music and robotics integrated with computer programming are approaches to engage students in CS by prioritizing personal expression, creativity, and aesthetics. This paper conducts a systematic review of using music and robotics to teach CS concepts to elementary school students. The authors aim to identify the existing problem in the literature to make CS more interactive, accessible, and engaging for students to improve their motivation in enhancing CS concepts and develop creative interpersonal skills. This paper also identifies a mixed-methods study to determine ways to promote CS among elementary school students. The mixed methods describe an adaptation of Blockly, Xylophone, and Dash robots for use in an introductory elementary school-level programming course that will be implemented in an open-access camp at Auburn University where American grades 3–5 will participate in pre-, post-, and follow-up surveys while attending the CS camp. The authors want to demonstrate how music and robotics programming can contribute to STEAM (Science, Technology, Engineering, Arts, and Mathematics) education regarding technology and engineering integration and include existing research studies resulting from the search and review processes. These studies were synthesized according to some common characteristics, including their use of educational robotics, preliminary results, subjects, and potential contributions to STEAM education. A few educational implications of educational robotics are also discussed as possible contributions to technology and engineering education. As a result of this systematic review, using robotics and music in early childhood STEAM education is a promising tool and application for integrating technology and engineering. The study concludes with a summary of the findings on the effectiveness of this approach.

Keywords: Computational thinking · Music · Robotics · Programming · Computer science education · Elementary school

1 Introduction

The challenge of learning computer programming is a possible explanation for the high dropout rates in CS. Several studies have shown that students struggle to remain motivated, engage in programming, and learn the subject [1–3]. Traditional methods of learning programming may not be appealing to students as they are more interested in meaningful and relevant projects [4]. Researchers propose that alternative approaches are necessary to keep students engaged in the learning process [5]. However, it is a complex task, as programming involves writing code and developing the ability to think computationally to solve problems in any field. Thus, computational thinking (CT), a problem-solving method that combines logical thinking and CS concepts, is used as a viable solution for many students [6].

The importance of this concept stems largely from Papert's work on the LOGO programming language, where the author envisioned that children manipulating the computer through programming could help them develop their procedural thinking skills [7, 8]. The students need to consider the design and problem-solving steps before they jump into coding, which makes learning programming simpler [9]. It requires a deep understanding of CT to describe a problem and propose a solution before converting it into code [3]. Thus, CT is becoming increasingly crucial in K-5 education in CS as it helps students develop critical thinking and problem-solving skills, understand how computers work, and create simple programs [10].

Robotics and music activities embedded with CS concepts are another approach to overcoming the difficulties in understanding CS topics for young children [11]. Computer programming shares substantial structural similarities with robotics and music. Moreover, music is a universal language, and working with music and robots is exciting. A formal language used in music and a computer program code share the same control structures -- sequences, selections, and repetitions -- and can describe any computation. Research has shown that combining CS with music and robotics in elementary education can make learning more engaging and effective. These subjects can make CS concepts more interactive and help to improve students' understanding and retention of the material. Additionally, incorporating music and robotics into the curriculum can make CS more approachable for a diverse range of students [12].

A web-based CS curriculum using HCI principles, interactive and visual programming languages, games, simulations, interactive activities, web-based tools and resources, problem-based learning, storytelling, animation, interactive media, virtual reality, and collaborative environments can also be engaging and interactive for students. A full-fledged responsive, usable, and accessible online web platform will benefit a broader range of students and teachers and make the material easier to understand and retain [13].

This paper includes an overview of the literature focused on the effectiveness of introducing elementary school students to the fundamental music vocabulary using CS and robotics concepts and how it enhances students' intellectual abilities and creativity, improves their performance and interpersonal communication, and spurs interest in STEAM courses and a career in that sector. The following research questions guide this review:

- Can a curriculum incorporating music and robotics improve students' motivation and understanding of CS concepts?
- Does participating in activities that combine CS, music, and robotics enhance students' creative and interpersonal skills?

- What are the usability and accessibility features of current web-based learning applications for K-5 students, and what impact do they have on the learning experience?

In this paper, the second and third section describes the literature review and methodology used for the review, including the search strategy and criterion used to select the studies; the fourth section provides a detailed analysis of the studies reviewed. The fifth section concludes the study with a summary of the findings.

2 Methodology

The authors have meticulously developed a K-5 student programming curriculum based on a three-stage model encompassing the phases of introduction, examination, and implementation [14]. The curriculum is designed to impart an understanding of music and robotics in CS education by teaching students fundamental music vocabulary and programming principles through utilizing the Blockly, Xylophone and Dash robots. Hands-on and unplugged activities for composing music and programming robots to perform and dance to rhythm patterns are incorporated into the curriculum to enhance student engagement and learning. This paper also identifies a mixed-methods study to determine ways to promote CS among elementary school students and for use in an introductory elementary school-level programming course that will be implemented in an open-access camp at Auburn University where American grades 3–5 will participate in pre-, post-, and follow-up surveys while attending the CS camp. Furthermore, the curriculum aims to foster comprehension of CS fundamentals by linking concepts and highlighting progression. Before the curriculum's development, a comprehensive literature review was conducted to understand the impact of integrating music and robotics in CS education on students of varying ages and backgrounds. The insights gained from the literature review were then incorporated into the development of the curriculum.

2.1 Search Strategy

This study aims to showcase the latest advancements and tendencies in the field by analyzing and summarizing the research on teaching and learning programming to k-5 children. This study was conducted according to the PRISMA (Preferred Reporting Items for Systematic Reviews and Meta-Analyses) statement's systematic review procedure to ensure a thorough examination of the literature [15, 16]. Following the PRISMA guidelines, a flow diagram illustrating the various stages of the review process, such as identification, screening, eligibility assessment, and article selection process, is presented in Fig. 1. A comprehensive search for all pertinent publications from different sources is essential in a literature review. This study searched candidate publications in four online databases: ERIC, EBSCO, Web of Science, and Science Direct.

The research for this review, which centers on programming in elementary school education, involved using keywords such as "computational thinking" and "computer science education", as programming plays a crucial role in developing these concepts. An analysis of studies on CT also revealed that many articles were directly related to programming, CS, and the methods and tools used to teach and develop these skills [17].

The study utilized a combination of search terms to scour various databases and search engines, such as "computational thinking", "music", "robotics", "programming", "computer science education", "computer science curriculum", "k-5" and "web portal", and "HCI". The initial search yielded 1762 articles from the first four databases, 571 from ERIC, 123 from EBSCO, 1051 from Web of Science, and 17 from Science Direct.

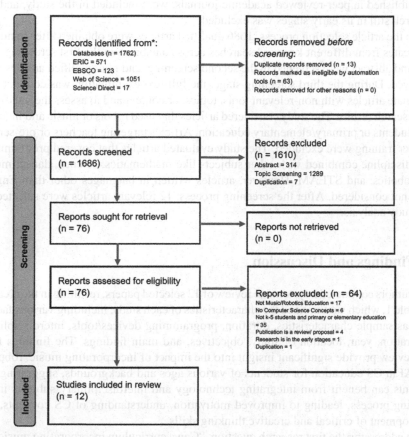

Fig. 1. The systematic review process. *Source:* Adopted from the Prisma.**Group, 2009.**

2.2 Eligibility Criteria

Inclusion Criteria. The criteria for selecting relevant studies included the publication year, content and language, and publication type. Since there were relatively few studies on programming for k-5 or elementary kids before 2013, the publication period was limited to 2014–2022 [17–19]. There was a significant increase in programming and CT papers after 2016 [17, 20]. Moreover, all included articles addressed either music or robotics education using CS concepts and were published in English. The search criteria included k-5 students and primary or elementary education, either from the database or as a keyword.

Exclusion Criteria. The study excluded specific articles such as surveys, reports, concept papers, literature reviews, opinion papers, thesis, summaries, newsletters, meeting and conference papers, and proceedings. Only primary sources, such as empirical studies published in peer-reviewed academic journals, were included in the study, and any research still in its early stages was excluded.

In the article selection process, 1686 qualified articles were obtained after removing duplicates from different keyword searches across databases in the first screening. The title and abstract were screened in the second screening, and non-qualified articles were removed. During the third screening stage, the full-text examination was conducted to eliminate articles with non-relevant tools, topics, or content and to assess the validity of the research results. The study considered articles that used robots or music and involved k-5 students or primary/elementary education. Articles targeting teachers or pre-service teacher training were excluded. The study evaluated articles that covered programming as a discipline combined with other subjects like mathematics, science, dance, music, art, robotics, and STEAM. However, articles written in languages other than English were not considered. After the screening process, 12 relevant articles were selected for the study analysis.

3   Findings and Discussion

The authors conducted a systematic review of 12 selected papers, resulting in the creation of Table 1, which summarized the characteristics of each study, including various factors such as sample characteristics, duration, programming devices/tools, interdisciplinary integration, year, location of study, objectives, and main findings. The findings from this review provide significant insight into the impact of incorporating music, robotics, and AI in CS education for students of various ages and backgrounds, suggesting that students can benefit from integrating technology and interdisciplinary subjects in the learning process, leading to improved motivation, understanding of CS concepts, and development of critical and creative thinking skills.

In addressing the first research question, "Can a curriculum incorporating music and robotics improve students' motivation and understanding of CS concepts?" the results indicate a positive impact, demonstrating that teachers can effectively integrate coding and CT into their regular curricula by linking it to subjects such as art, music, and social studies, resulting in increased student engagement and mastery of both coding and CT.

The second research question, "Does participating in activities that combine CS, music, and robotics enhance students' creative and interpersonal skills?" was also addressed, revealing that the use of educational robots as tangible cognitive tools can positively impact mental rotation and spatial vocabulary skills, and foster communication, collaboration, and creativity among students.

Regarding the third research question, "What are the usability and accessibility features of current web-based learning applications for K-5 students, and what impact do they have on the learning experience?" the study found that students can effectively learn

Table 1. List of Articles in Included Study

Author; Year; Place of Study	Objective of the Study	Sample Characteristics (Age Group, Number of Participants, Grade levels)	Integration with other subjects	Tools	Duration of Intervention	Main Findings
Marina U. Bersa et al.; 2019; Spain [21]	The study assesses the effectiveness of the KIBO robotics kit in teaching coding and interpersonal skills such as communication, collaboration, community building, content creation, creativity, and choices of conduct to young children within a PTD-based educational program	Preschool children; Aged 3–5 years old (N = 172)	Robotics	KIBO robot	Three to five sessions (45- min sessions, while the other two planned sessions lasting 1 h 15 min)	The study shows that it is possible to teach coding and CT to 3-year-olds. This approach successfully integrates coding into various subjects, promoting communication, collaboration, creativity, and teacher empowerment, with positive implications for expanding this learning environment
Einat Brainin et al.; 2022; Israel [22]	To assess the impact of robot programming on improving spatial language skills (vocabulary) and spatial abilities (such as mental rotation and visual-spatial memory) in preschool children who are at risk of developing a Specific Learning Disability (SLD)	84 kindergarten children; Aged five to 7 (M = 5.80; SD = .49 in years); 56 were boys (66.7%) and 28 girls (33.3%)	Robotics	Bee-Bot programmable robot	10 half-hour sessions	The study suggests that using a child-controlled robot as a tangible tool can enhance mental rotation and spatial vocabulary skills and recommends incorporating educational robots into preschool education to support cognitive and learning development

(*continued*)

Table 1. (*continued*)

Author; Year; Place of Study	Objective of the Study	Sample Characteristics (Age Group, Number of Participants, Grade levels)	Integration with other subjects	Tools	Duration of Intervention	Main Findings
J. Elizabeth Casey et al.; 2017; U.S.-Mexico border (southern United States) [23]	The study aimed to identify efficient metacognitive strategies and support for English Language Learners (ELLs) in upper-elementary science classes by providing research-based strategy instruction, opportunities for hands-on experience programming a floor robot, and critical engagement with support	Fourth and fifth grade students	Robotics	Floor-robots	2016 – 2017 school year	This study shows the positive impact of exposing students, especially ELLs and those from underserved populations, to educational robots, coding, and programming, with increased engagement, critical thinking, and problem-solving skills, emphasizing the importance of providing 21st-century programming skills and allocating resources for floor robots and teacher training, explicitly benefiting Hispanic students on the US-Mexico border

(*continued*)

Table 1. (*continued*)

Author; Year; Place of Study	Objective of the Study	Sample Characteristics (Age Group, Number of Participants, Grade levels)	Integration with other subjects	Tools	Duration of Intervention	Main Findings
Salomi Evripidou et al.; 2021; Greece [24]	The study presents a learning framework for introducing algorithmic thinking and sequencing to elementary or intermediate learners using tangible robots, gamification, interactive feedback, and researched educational methods to improve their algorithmic thinking and sequencing skills and reinforce their interest in programming	30 students, with 9 girls and 21 boys, primarily from grades 1 and 2	Robotics	Bee-Bot robot	Six sessions; Each session took place and lasted up to three teaching periods of 45 min each, without an intermediate break	The study suggests that combining educational robots, a gamification environment, a fuzzy-rule-based feedback system, and computer vision enhances programming education for young students and results in improved learning outcomes

(*continued*)

Table 1. (*continued*)

Author; Year; Place of Study	Objective of the Study	Sample Characteristics (Age Group, Number of Participants, Grade levels)	Integration with other subjects	Tools	Duration of Intervention	Main Findings
Danielle Herroa et al.; 2022; USA [25]	The study aims to examine strategies for encouraging student participation in STEAM challenges in elementary classrooms guided by constructionism theory, focusing on the design and implementation of instructional practices that promote CT during STEAM problem-solving and understanding student perspectives on CT learning activities	Grades 3–8	Science, English Language Arts (ELA) and Music	Scratch, Hummingbirds, Sphero Robots, littleBits (programable electronic circuits) Lego Robotics and 3-D modeling software	N/A	The study found that students demonstrated CT while problem-solving in STEAM subjects, using prior knowledge and experience, dividing tasks based on strengths and interests, and seeing failure as a learning opportunity, with teachers recognizing CT opportunities and helping students make connections

(*continued*)

Table 1. (*continued*)

Author; Year; Place of Study	Objective of the Study	Sample Characteristics (Age Group, Number of Participants, Grade levels)	Integration with other subjects	Tools	Duration of Intervention	Main Findings
Ting-Chia Hsu a et al.; 2021; Taiwan [26]	The study aimed to develop an AI education tool for young students and analyze their learning behavior using learning analytics through a program combining learning MIT App Inventor and Personal Image Classifier followed by a CT board game and robot car project in pairs	Fifth grade of a public elementary school	Robotics	AI 2 Robot City	9 weeks	The study found that an interdisciplinary AI and STEM course using the PIC web tool effectively taught machine learning through hands-on activities, leading to improved learning outcomes when students participated in cooperative learning by expressing personal opinions and predicting results, and suggested that teachers should include these elements in hands-on, interdisciplinary courses

(*continued*)

Table 1. (*continued*)

Author; Year; Place of Study	Objective of the Study	Sample Characteristics (Age Group, Number of Participants, Grade levels)	Integration with other subjects	Tools	Duration of Intervention	Main Findings
Gesu India et al.; 2019; India [27]	To present Torino Tangible Programming as a tool for promoting creativity and play while introducing CT concepts to children in India through stories, songs, and music	12 children (8 boys and 4 girls); Age group 7 to 13, either blind or partially sighted participated in the study	Music	Torino (Tangible Programming Environment)	12 play sessions (45–60 min)	The study found that children using Torino Tangible Programming demonstrated an understanding of CT and programming concepts through their created programs while maintaining a balance between learning objectives and play and creative exploration
Jiyae Noh et al.; 2016; Korea [28]	To assess the impact of a robotics programming course on the growth of CT and creativity among elementary school students, considering the influence of prior skills and gender and reviewing relevant teaching and learning strategies	155 Korean elementary school students in the fifth and sixth grades	Robotics	Scratch and MakeyMakey instrument, Entry and the Hamster robot	11 weeks	The study found that incorporating robots in programming courses improved students' understanding of CS concepts and their CT and creativity, emphasizing the importance of including robotics programming in elementary education and considering students' prior skills and gender differences

(*continued*)

Table 1. (*continued*)

Author; Year; Place of Study	Objective of the Study	Sample Characteristics (Age Group, Number of Participants, Grade levels)	Integration with other subjects	Tools	Duration of Intervention	Main Findings
Alex Pugnali et al.; 2017; New England region [29]	To investigate the impact of tangible and graphical interfaces on children's positive technological development and their gain in CT skills	Group of children ages 4–7	Robotics	KIBO Robotics Kit	3 weeks	The study showed that young children aged 4–7 could learn CT skills through appropriate tools and instruction, using the tangible KIBO Robotics kit or the graphical ScratchJr iPad app, which encourage positive socio-emotional development while teaching abilities like sequencing, repeating, conditionals, and debugging
Ceylan Sen et al.; 2021; Turkey [30]	To identify the CT skills that gifted and talented students utilize during robotics activities within STEM activities based on the Engineering Design Process (EDP)	Seven gifted and talented students diagnosed by the Guidance and Research Center (GRC) and pursuing their support education programs at the Science and Art Centre (SAC); 2nd and 5th grades	Robotics	Building robots using Lego Mindstorms and modeling robots with a 3D modeling software tool and producing robots with a 3D printer	Ten weeks; 3h per subject once or twice weekly	The study found that gifted and talented students who participate in STEM activities using the Engineering Design Process demonstrate active use of critical thinking skills, including critical problem-solving, creativity, and problem-solving skills like defining problems, generating solutions and evaluating solution effectiveness

(*continued*)

Table 1. (*continued*)

Author; Year; Place of Study	Objective of the Study	Sample Characteristics (Age Group, Number of Participants, Grade levels)	Integration with other subjects	Tools	Duration of Intervention	Main Findings
Kellie Taylor et al.; 2019; USA [31]	It aims to determine the impact of grouping students by gender and assigned role on their performance in robotics, CT skills, motivation for learning computer programming, and any interaction effects between gender and role grouping	One hundred ninety-one students in fourth and fifth grade; Age range 8–11	Robotics, Music	LEGO Mindstorms EV3 robotics	Fourteen weeks for 1h each week	The study found that implementing group roles in collaborative robotics projects improved students' performance and CT skills with no significant impact on the gender composition of the group. Still, group roles did impact students' motivation to learn computer programming
Leyla Uşengül et al.; 2018–2019; Turkey [32]	The study aimed to compare the impact of LEGO WeDo 2.0 robotics education on academic achievement, attitude towards science, and CT skills between the Experimental group and the Control group and assess if students in the Experimental group have higher science achievement, positive attitudes towards the science course and improved CT skills	36 students studying at 5th grade	Robotics	LEGO Wedo 2.0 Robotics set	Eleven weeks	Results showed that the experimental group students who received the robotics education showed significant differences in attitudes, academic achievements, and CT skills towards the science course compared to the control group

CT skills through appropriate tools and instruction, using either tangible robotics kits or graphical programming apps, but that the choice of technology interface can impact the learning experience, thus requiring educators and parents to carefully consider which one is best for their students/children.

The results also highlight the positive impact of robotics education on underrepresented groups, particularly ELLs and students from underserved populations, revealing that exposure to floor robots can increase student engagement, critical thinking, and problem-solving skills, with a specific positive impact observed on Hispanic students, including many ELLs, on the US-Mexico border. Moreover, incorporating group roles in collaborative robotics projects impacted student performance and CT skills. The results indicated that group roles influence students' motivation for learning computer programming. Still, gender composition does not have a significant impact. Additionally, gifted and talented students who participated in STEM activities using the Engineering Design Process demonstrated active use of critical thinking skills, including necessary problem-solving and creativity skills.

In conclusion, this systematic review results provide valuable insight into the impact of incorporating music, robotics, and AI in CS education, suggesting that students of all ages can benefit from integrating technology and interdisciplinary subjects in the learning process, leading to improved motivation, understanding of CS concepts, and development of critical and creative thinking skills. The results underscore the importance of providing students with 21st-century programming skills and the need for districts to allocate resources for acquiring educational robots and providing teacher training and emphasize the importance of considering students' prior programming skills, gender differences, and the choice of technology interface in designing classes to achieve optimal learning results.

4 Conclusions

The study analyzed 12 studies between 2016 and 2022 that integrated CS with arts and an inclusive curriculum to improve CT and understanding of CS concepts. Researchers have been exploring alternative approaches to addressing the high dropout rate in computer programming courses, such as integrating CT into the curriculum and utilizing web-based CS curricula emphasizing HCI principles, interactive programming languages, visual programming languages, games, simulations, and collaborative environments. The study's authors developed a K-5 student programming curriculum using Xylophone and Dash robots to teach music vocabulary and programming principles. Furthermore, the authors reviewed the literature to understand the benefits of incorporating music and robotics into CS education. Thus, this systematic review evaluated the impact of teaching elementary school students' music vocabulary and CS and robotics concepts on intellectual abilities, creativity, performance, and communication skills.

The findings suggest that incorporating music and robotics can enhance students' motivation and understanding of CS concepts. Additionally, students' creative and interpersonal skills have been enhanced by participating in activities combining CS, music, and robotics. Web-based learning applications for K-5 students were also found to be accessible and usable. This systematic review, therefore, supports integrating music and robotics into the CS curriculum to improve engagement and learning. The authors' K-5 student programming curriculum, which incorporates music and robotics, provides a novel approach to address the challenges of learning computer programming and enables students to gain a deeper comprehension of CS fundamentals. Further research is needed to develop developmentally appropriate programs, while instructional technologies and teacher training programs are essential to implementing programming in early childhood education.

References

1. Beaubouef, T., Mason, J.: Why the high attrition rate for computer science students: some thoughts and observations. ACM SIGCSE Bulletin 37(2), 103–106 (2005)
2. Kinnunen, P., L. Malmi.: Why students drop out CS1 course? In: Proceedings of the Second International Workshop on Computing Education Research (2006)
3. Fletcher, G.H., Lu, J.J.: Education human computing skills: rethinking the K-12 experience. Commun. ACM 52(2), 23–25 (2009)
4. Fincher, S., Petre, M.: Computer science education research. 2004: CRC Press
5. Ali, A.: A Conceptual Model for Learning to Program in Introductory Programming Courses. Issues Inform. Sci. Inform. Technol. 6 (2009)
6. Wing, J.M.: Computational thinking. Commun. ACM 49(3), 33–35 (2006)
7. Papert, S.: Children, computers, and powerful ideas. Harvester (1980)
8. Papert, S., Harel, I.: Situating Constructionism [Internet]. Constructionism. Ablex Publishing Corporation. www. papert. org/articles/SituatingConstructionism. html (1991)
9. Rajaravivarma, R.: A games-based approach for teaching the introductory programming course. ACM SIGCSE Bulletin 37(4), 98–102 (2005)
10. Williams, H.: No fear coding: Computational thinking across the k-5 curriculum. 2022: International Society for Technology in Education
11. Rodger, S.H., et al.: Enhancing K-12 education with alice programming adventures. In: Proceedings of the Fifteenth Annual Conference on Innovation And Technology in Computer Science Education (2010)
12. Chung, C.C.J., Cartwright, C.,Chung, C.: Robot music camp 2013: An experiment to promote STEM and computer science. In: 2014 IEEE Integrated STEM Education Conference. IEEE (2014)
13. Obrenović, Ž., Rethinking HCI education: teaching interactive computing concepts based on the experiential learning paradigm. Interactions. 19(3), 66–70 (2012)
14. Touretzky, D.S., et al.: Accelerating K-12 computational thinking using scaffolding, staging, and abstraction. In: Proceeding of the 44th ACM Technical Symposium on Computer Science Education (2013)
15. Page, M.J., et al.: Updating guidance for reporting systematic reviews: development of the PRISMA 2020 statement. J. Clin. Epidemiol. 134, 103–112 (2021)
16. Moher, D., et al.: Reprint—preferred reporting items for systematic reviews and meta-analyses: the PRISMA statement. Phys. Ther. 89(9), 873–880 (2009)
17. Kalelioğlu, F.: Characteristics of studies conducted on computational thinking: A content analysis. In: Khine, M.S. (ed.) Computational Thinking in the STEM Disciplines, pp. 11–29. Springer, Cham (2018). https://doi.org/10.1007/978-3-319-93566-9_2
18. Jung, S.E., Won, E.-S.: Systematic review of research trends in robotics education for young children. Sustainability 10(4), 905 (2018)

19. Lye, S.Y., Koh, J.H.L.: Review on teaching and learning of computational thinking through programming: What is next for K-12? Comput. Hum. Behav. **41**, 51–61 (2014)
20. Zhang, L., Nouri, J.: A systematic review of learning computational thinking through Scratch in K-9. Comput. Educ. **141**, 103607 (2019)
21. Bers, M.U., Carina, G.G.-//-Armas–Torres, Mª. B.: Coding as a playground: Promoting positive learning experiences in childhood classrooms. Comput. Educ. **138**: 130–145 (2019)
22. Brainin, E., Shamir, A., Eden, S.: Promoting spatial language and ability among sld children: can robot programming make a difference? J. Educ. Comput. Res. **60**(7), 1742–1762 (2022)
23. Elizabeth Casey, J., Gill, P., Pennington, L.,Mireles, S.V.: Lines, Roamers, and Squares: Oh My! Using Floor Robots to Enhance Hispanic Students' Understanding of Programming. Educ. Inform. Technol. **23**(4), 1531–1546 (2018)
24. Evripidou, S., Amanatiadis, A., Christodoulou, K., Chatzichristofis, S.A.: Introducing algorithmic thinking and sequencing using tangible robots. **14**(1), 93–105 (2021)
25. Herro, D., Quigley, C., Plank, H., Abimbade, O., Owens, A.: Instructional practices promoting computational thinking in STEAM elementary classrooms. J. Digital Learn. Teacher Educ. **38**(4), 158–172 (2022)
26. Hsu, T.C., Abelson, H., Lao, N., Tseng, Y.H., Lin, Y.T.: Behavioral-pattern exploration and development of an instructional tool for young children to learn AI. Comput. Educ.: Artif. Intell. **2** 100012 (2021)
27. India, G., Ramakrishna, G., Bisht, J., Swaminathan, M.: Assoc Comp, Machinery, Computational Thinking as Play: Experiences of Children who are Blind or Low Vision in India. In: Assets'19: The 21st International Acm Sigaccess Conference on Computers and Accessibility, pp. 519–522 (2019)
28. Noh, J., Lee, J.: Effects of robotics programming on the computational Think. Creativity Elementary School Stud. **68**(1), 463–484 (2020)
29. Pugnali, A., Sullivan, A., Bers, M.U.: The Impact of User Interface on Young Children's Computational Thinking. J. Inform. Technol. Educ. **16**, 171–193 (2017)
30. Sen, C., Ay, Z.S., Kiray, S.A.: Computational thinking skills of gifted and talented students in integrated STEM activities based on the engineering design process: the case of robotics and 3D robot modeling. Thinking Skills Creativity **42**, 100931 (2021)
31. Taylor, K., Baek, Y.: Grouping matters in computational robotic activities. Comput. Human Behav. **93**, 99–105 (2019)
32. Usengül, L., Bahçeci, F.: The Effect of LEGO WeDo 2.0 Education on Academic Achievement and Attitudes and Computational Thinking Skills of Learners toward Science. World J. Educ. **10**(4), 83–93 (2020)

Technologies, Sports and Motor Activities for an Inclusive School

Loredana Perla[1] , Ilenia Amati[1]([✉]) , Laura Sara Agrati[2] ,
and Antonio Ascione[1]

[1] University of Bari Aldo Moro, Bari, Italy
{loredana.perla,ilenia.amati,antonio.ascione}@uniba.it
[2] University of Bergamo, Bergamo, Italy
laurasara.agrati@unibg.it

Abstract. The relationships between sport, motor activities, new technologies and disabilities within the educational environment is to be considered a relatively unexplored area of research. Movement activities combined with technologies provide an original area of pupil enhancement, as they guarantee opportunities and participation also for pupils with psychophysical and sensory difficulties. Primary school, in particular, has worked a really inclusive-didactic laboratory in recent decades; due to its educational specificity, it has experimented with itineraries of inclusion that have capitalized on the bodily-kinesthetic dimension of students. Inclusive didactics that use the resources of motor activity and technology is able to enhance and enrich the entire teaching-learning process, thanks to the methodology based mainly on cooperation and socialisation. Specifically, didactics, cooperation and socialization interface and generate an inclusive knowledge which, through multidisciplinary and multilateral motor games and through technology, defines the so-called motor-techno-games. The work helps to build an interdisciplinary epistemological framework of the educational side of motor and sports activity which, by investigating the relationship between body, movement and learning processes, highlights the bodily-kinesthetic dimension within the processes of knowledge construction. Furthermore, it detects the educational, training and integrative potential of teaching practice aimed at enhancing motor and sporting activities also in their adapted form. Reference is made to a fact-finding investigation, realized within a research-training experience at the ForPsiCom Department of the University of Bari. The study, started in 2022 and still in progress, focuses on the perception of disability and on the use of two technological systems integrated in teaching practice. The first results are presented.

Keywords: Motor Activity · Digital Technology · Inclusion

1 Introduction

Sensory disabilities are closely linked to new didactics as innovative languages, teaching methods and strategies can improve the learning experience. Primary school, in particular, has worked a really inclusive-didactic laboratory in recent decades; due to its educational specificity, it has experimented with itineraries of inclusion that have capitalized on the bodily-kinesthetic dimension of students (Salerno et al., 2022; Farina, 2020; Caione, 2021; Giaconi & Del Bianco, 2019). Inclusive didactics (Perla, 2013; Agrati, 2018; Amati, 2022) that use the resources of motor activity and technology is able to enhance and enrich the entire teaching-learning process, thanks to the methodology based mainly on cooperation and socialisation. Specifically, didactics, cooperation and socialization interface and generate an inclusive knowledge which, through multidisciplinary and multilateral motor games and through technology, defines the so-called motor-techno-games (Barnett & Baranowski, 2011). The relational dynamics of visually and hearing-impaired students improves with physical activity, increasing communication, socialization and relationship methods, enhancing knowledge and access to knowledge (Rusyani et al, 2021). Thus, the presence of children with disabilities in the classroom stimulates considerations about inclusion, methods and strategies (Fabiano, 2022; Perla, 2013; Votta, 2022; Reddy, 2000; Knight et al., 2009; Armitage, 2006; Amati, 2022), to support learning. This leads to overcoming the clinical and bio-medical paradigm, to embrace the inclusive logic, in favor of the context and the class group, to support the educational training process for all (Perla, 2013; Valijonovna, 2022). The current problem is to consider in the inclusive school a teaching practice which concretely uses movement sciences as the main discipline in the teaching-learning processes. As Boeris & Gozzelino (2022) argue, inclusive didactics cannot fail to be global, the pedagogical observation axis must be oriented towards the educational conditions of the classroom, the welcoming environment for all, and the activity aimed at differentiated learning, individualized and personalized (Perla, 2013; Amati, 2022). The teaching of motor and sports sciences, in the specificity of its languages and techniques, falls within the context of the educational and training action of all schools and in particular of primary school, thus providing an important contribution to the growth of the person and of the citizen. This discipline has formative purposes, such as: the awareness of corporeity, the efficient psycho-motor dynamism in the framework of the full development of the personality; the valorisation of formative experiences of personal and group life (Bertucci et al., 2015). The didactic process is supported by teaching technologies and multisensory aids whose function is vicarious (Belfiore, 2022), these are able to guarantee better access to information, enhance the child's autonomy. Information and Communication Technologies are powerful mediators of the man-knowledge combination, replacing or integrating the sensorimotor process and adapting to the context. In fact, in reference with sensory disabilities there are many software, technological tools for Augmentative and Alternative Communication, apps and technologies that satisfy the need for accessibility in favor of inclusion and interaction. Some accessible didactics (Mangiatordi, 2017) is necessary for autonomy and inclusive planning, capable of considering the plurality of individual needs, vicariance, multimodality and multisensoriality, using all the technological resources available. Educational services teachers, families, specialized operators and health rehabilitation professionals, communication assistants, class peers, local associations (Perla, Agrati, Scalera, 2019), have a role in the education of children with sensory disabilities inside and outside the classrooms, represent the resource for concretely structuring the inclusive teaching setting in the presence of students with sensory disabilities. The practice of motor activity is therefore a path towards knowledge, control of one's emotions and the autonomy of the pupils, as playful activity and playing sports represent the way to test oneself and with others. Through the motor experience the interested dimensions of the person concern the cognitive, biological, expressive, relational and emotional area.

1.1 Inclusion and Disability Through Sport

The United Nations Organization uses the term 'disability' to refer to all those people who have long-term physical, mental, intellectual or sensory impairments and in relation to architectural barriers that can prevent their full and effective active participation in society, in compliance with the equality and the rights of all (Baratella, 2009; Perla, 2013). The idea of sport for all has as its background that of uniting the specific characteristics of the individual skills of overview, of global perception, of the ability to read situations in a broader way, which allow the vision of different perspectives, with different approaches and methods (Benzing & Schmidt, 2018). Thus, sporting activity for pupils with and without disabilities becomes a tool for educating in autonomy, for strengthening existing skills, for enhancing self-esteem. For these reasons, the practice of physical activities is a privileged means of individual development, re-education and social integration (Canevaro, 2007). Motor activity gives rise to the desire tophysically detach from the family nucleus and thus to relate to the outside world, integrating diversity with the discovery of new possibilities that guarantee self-acceptance. The educational capacity of sport is evident, which gives individuals with disabilities a unique opportunity to compensate for training absences and development problems due to specific deficits. Practicing physical activity means acquiring general and specific motor skills, enhancing and differentiating the development of one's skills, improving movement, competitiveness and group life (Moliterni, 2013). Through sport, growth is stimulated, individual potential and integration in life contexts rich in meaningful relationships are developed (Rosa & Madonna, 2019). In addition to the improvement of physical fitness, the cognitive development resulting from motor learning, the socialization resulting from integration into the sports world, there is an improvement in self-esteem and all fundamental experiences for personal growth in its relational dimension (Sgambelluri & Vinci, 2020). For this reason, in recent years, awareness has grown that sport and even before that motor activity are promoters of the psychosocial and motor development of people with disabilities. In this regard, Hutzler introduces the meaning of empowerment in sport for pupils with disabilities, placing awareness of one's own skills and the perception of self-efficacy at the basis of empowerment (Hutzler, 1990).The focus of the motor and sports experience, on which the study is conducted, is to increase new personal resources, to be exploited within the environment in which we live. Hutzler (2004), argues through his model that sporting activity combined with disability determines a sequence of psycho-pedagogical and social benefits (see Table 1):

This brings to light that sport influences the psychophysical dimension of the person, since through motor experience, the body improves the perception of individual physical skills, and increasing autonomy and self-confidence (Di Palma, 2022). The main reason for developing motor and sports activity in children with intellectual and/or sensory disabilities is to improve the predominantly sedentary attributes, thus improving other aspects such as: cognitive, affective processes, social integration. Continuous

Table 1. Sequence of psycho-pedagogical and social benefits.

Growth in skill level leads to better social acceptance

Motor performance drives functional efficiency

Mood and affective disorders become lighter

Successful experiences improve self-efficacy

Improved body confidence improves physical self-concept and self-esteem

motor practice over time is effective and supportive of psychophysical therapies (Zhang et al., 2022). In fact, even medium-intensity motor activity can improve joint flexibility, increase cardiovascular endurance, reduce weight and fat mass index (Scurt et al., 2022). Furthermore, thanks to sport, improving the independence of the self also enhances intellectual abilities (Dias & Braganza, 2022).

1.2 The Motion Capture System and the Dynamometric Platform for the Assessment of Didactic Achievement and Movement

The studies of kinematics have offered useful concepts to analyze motion in its forms: displacement, velocity and acceleration. The Motion Capture, specifically, analyzes and studies the movement since it is able to capture the movements. It is a recording system that processes human movement data so that it can be used in 3D on a computer. Therefore, the mathematical realization of the movement of a subject is possible, by interpreting a movement in a digital model, to be used for further studies and specific applications. The sectors in which the use of Motion Capture is consolidated concerns clinical and sports analysis. In the clinical field, it is useful for the reconstruction of the movement by favoring the understanding of the locomotor difficulties of the patients, in the sport field instead, the motion capture allows to record the sporting activity for the purpose of improving the performance of the athletes (Mündermann et al., 2006; Moeslund et al., 2006; Knight et al., 2009; Menolotto et al., 2020). Dynamometric platforms, on the other hand, have had little application over time in the school context for research purposes. On the other hand, experimentation in the sports and clinical fields is different, both for the purpose of developing performance and, in the clinical sector, above all for post-injury rehabilitation purposes. A study by Manno (2008) illustrates the importance of muscle strength in the developmental age, of evaluation and training in motor and sports activities. In fact, it is above all in the developmental age that the main motor skills necessary for social life, the relationship with the environment and for sporting performance are learned and structured. Many motor skills require a sufficient level of strength to achieve them, and vertical jumping, throwing, sprinting and accelerations and decelerations are a good foundation for development. Furthermore, good levels of strength can positively influence psychological aspects such as self-esteem, body schema, particularly in boys and in their social life, positively influence the initiation of sports activities and their result in the competitive phase (Simonetti, 2016). For these reasons, the functional assessment of strength through the dynamometric platform is a necessity for good teaching planning. The dynamometric system used in this work is of the mechanical type, formed by a rubbery but conductive material, suitably shaped to vary the resistance with the load (Bieć & Kuczyński, 2010).

2 Research-Training

The research-training presented aims to investigate pupils' perception of the presence of different abilities in their classroom context and the use of integrated technologies in teaching practice useful for promoting compensation in some areas of development with disabled and non-disabled pupils. The investigation started from the reflection on teachers' beliefs, on the *study on action* (Perla, 2012; 2016, 2018; Theureau, 2006, Durand, Filliettaz, 2009), on the organizers' analysis of teacher practice and regularities observable in the profession (Bru 2002; Pastré 2011; Vinatier, Altet, 2008). It referred to the *collaborative* research-training paradigm, based on the partnership between researchers and teachers, equally implicated, even if with different postures, in front of the same object of study (Perla, 2010, 2011, 2012), in order to guarantee the school-university relationship which is increasingly rethought through the recovery of training models through research (Beillerot, 1991; Calidoni, 2000; Perla 2011). This represents a great opportunity in order to be able to grasp the strengths and weaknesses of a methodology starting from the experiences in the field that the teachers report (Edwards, Mercer, 1987; Bednarz, Rinaudo & Roditi, 2015; Vinatier & Morrissette, 2015). The investigation pursues two main objectives:

1. detect how much school-leaders and in-service teachers in primary school and pupils know technologies integrated in teaching practice
2. know how much and in what way they actually put these tools into practice in their teaching activity.

   The research-training used a self-study phenomenological protocol (Loughran et al., 2019; Perla, 2010) based on the analysis of practices (Altet, 2003; Vinatier, Altet, 2008; Laneve 2005; Perla, 2010; Damiano, 2006; Vinatier & Morrissette 2015). The collaborative research-training (Perla, 2010; 2011; Bednarz, 2015) lends effectively to the exchange between the experience of practical teachers and that of us researchers. The procedure began with a joint reflection between school-leaders and teachers of some schools in Campania and Basilicata and researchers from the For.Psi.Com. Department of the University of Bari Aldo Moro regarding the opportunity to build protocols to plan interventions with students with sensory disabilities through the use of technologies combined with motor skills and sport. The long-term goal is, in fact, to promote awareness in teachers not only about the theoretical aspects but also about the concrete actions that must be implemented in order to face the pupil's needs thanks to 'professional gestures' act with awareness. Any didactic intervention for pupils with disabilities passes both through didactic planning and through the daily educational dialogue of "doing school" (Perla, Riva, 2016). The dialogue between teachers and students and between the teachers themselves have brought out the needs and actions necessary for the change of postures, of 'being in the world' in a conscious, active, altruistic way. The research protocol was divided in four actions:

1. Exploration of pupils' perception of the presence of different abilities in their class-room context by the CAWI questionnaire to a random sample of primary school teachers from two regions of Italy.
2. Activation of a theoretical-practical training course with teachers and school-leaders.
3. Classroom laboratories by researchers and administration of an implicit test (Implicit Association Test, Nosek, Greenwald, Banaji, 2007) aimed at pupils of some primary schools in the Campania and Basilicata regions. Integration in teaching practice of two different types of technological systems: motion capture and dynamometric platforms in order to verify the relationship with disciplinary knowledge, postures of motor gestures, motor sequences and coordination models of pupils with disabilities.
4. Administration of a second post-action questionnaire to the participants in the training, evaluation and feedback.

During the first action, a CAWI questionnaire was administered to a random sample of primary school teachers from Campania and Basilicata regions. At present (the survey is still ongoing) 12 school-leaders and 90 teachers (curricular n. 65 and specialized n. 25) replied to the questionnaire;

The second action provided a 20-h theoretical-practical training course in telematic mode in which 102 teachers took part (divided into two groups).

The third action was divided into two sub-actions: in the first, technology-motor laboratories were activated in school classes (6 in Campania, 6 in Basilicata) involving students; in the second, implicit test (Implicit Association Test, Nosek, Greenwald, Banaji, 2007) was administered to pupils of III, IV and V classes of primary school. About 110 students have responded to date. The last phase is still in progress.

2.1 Data Analysis

Data analysis has been made at two levels: descriptive and inferential statistical analysis of the questionnaires and grounded analysis of the textual transcripts. The triangulation of the first available data reveals that:

- the perception of pupils regarding the recognition of disability is lower than the formal data (Fig. 1);
- the adaptive and compensatory potential of movement is considered possible for educability aimed at the use and construction of different skills (Fig. 2);
- the ways in which technologies are used in teaching practice are aimed at facilitating access to training courses, including educational-motor-sports ones (Fig. 3).

Checking the data reveals that the really inclusive and integrated didactics reduces the perception of disability and/or diversity in pupils (Fig. 1). Such consideration arises through the fact-finding investigation still in progress, and started in the 2022/23 school year and conducted in collaboration with the For.Psi.Com. Department of the University of Bari, focused on perception of disability and the use of two integrated technological systems in teaching practice. The descriptive investigation on the basis of the mixed method design aimed at obtaining useful information to verify the following previously clarified questions:

- pupils' perception of different abilities in the classroom context;
- the use of integrated technologies in teaching practice useful for promoting compensation in some areas of development.

A further investigation has been started on the same sample of students, the analysis of which at the moment allows to know the integration in the teaching practice of two different types of technological systems, Motion Capture and dynamometric platforms. The purpose of such investigation is to verify:

- relations with disciplinary knowledge;
- the postures of motor gestures;
- the motor sequences;
- the coordination skills.

A score between 1 (low) to 5 (high) was assigned, considering that:

- in the first question, 1 refers to a perception of absence of disability within the class, while 5 to a very high presence of disability;
- in the second question, 1 refers to a perception of little use of integrated technologies in teaching practice, instead, 5 refers to a perception of a strong use of integrated technologies in teaching practice.

Data reading shows at the moment that for school-leaders the perception score of disabled students is low, since perception is based on documentary data. Instead, for teachers who have direct contact with pupils, the documentary data of the disability may not correspond to the perception and therefore have a lower perception of the pupil's disability. Instead, for both school leaders and teachers, the use of technologies manages to compensate for the demand. As regards the analysis begun and still in progress, based on currently available data (see averages and dv/st, Fig. 4), the integration in teaching practice of two different types of technological systems, Motion Capture and dynamometric platforms, is evaluated positively by the pupils.

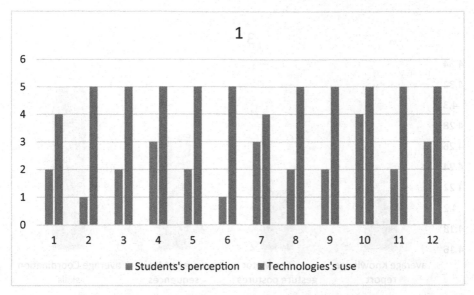

Fig. 1. The perception of pupils regarding the recognition of disability.

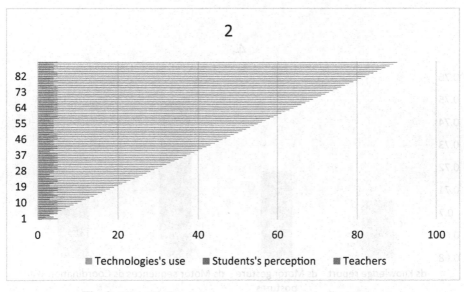

Fig. 2. The adaptive and compensatory potential of movement

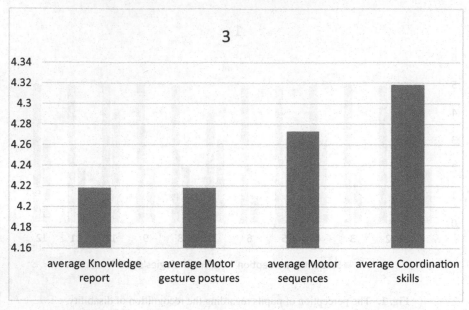

Fig. 3. The ways in which technologies are used in teaching practice

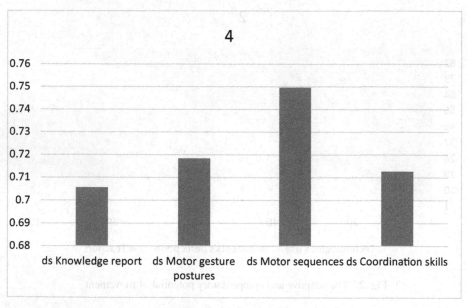

Fig. 4. Standard Deviation

3 Conclusions

The Web 2.0 and social networks, the evolution of media platforms, the considerable commercialization of portable multitasking tools equipped with touch screens, the creation of increasingly complex video games, such as online home games equipped with movement and speech recognition, can offer us an example of change in the training and learning sector (Drigas et al., 2022). In fact, the new technologies and learning (Mustaeva et al., 2022), are to all effects, relational devices, through which new ways of orientation, interaction, research, information processing and memory are structured. Such new interconnection transforms our mental landscapes and our thinking and doing (reading, playing, searching, socializing, travelling, buying, sharing, looking for information, exchanging messages, cultivating friendships etc.). For many authors (Bates, 2005; Kern, 2006; Foley & Maddison, 2010; Pennazio, 2015; Monacis & Colella, 2019; Munafò, 2020; Piccolo et al., 2020; Krouska et al., 2023), new technologies guide students to discuss, study and experiment with solutions, stimulate research and their imagination, study and implement innovative solutions. In this regard, the analysis by Zappalà (2022), demonstrates the effectiveness of educational technologies in promoting full development and inclusion, both for students with Autism Spectrum Disorder (ASD), and for the entire educational community. Therefore, the need to integrate the use of these devices in all contexts of life of the students is highlighted, but also to adopt them both in presence and at a distance while maintaining the same levels of efficiency (Bocci et al., 2022). Furthermore, in reference with such studies, educational technologies, if annexed to inclusive and hybrid learning spaces, are an advanced proposal to favor shared and individualized planning according to an ecological perspective (Knight et al., 2009). Motor activity combined with the habit of multitasking and the combination of languages (text, image, video, audio) can have multiple functions and, above all, has an undisputed value for the purposes of learning and the intellectual well-being of learning (Mittelstädt et al., 2022). Functions such as memory, attention, concentration, reasoning, problem-solving and decision-making are exercised through movement (Moliterni, 2013).The scientific theories of play (Coco, 2014; Mezzetti, 2012; Vecchiato, 2007) and of motor and sports activities (Altavilla, 2021; Guicciardi, 2000; Lipoma, 2022), in the feasible relationship between movement and playful experience in an educational environment, allow for a significant correlation with educational values and training processes. The playful dimension plays a fundamental role in the psychophysical development of students, on a par with new technologies, which use the body as the main means of accessing knowledge. This study confirms the important combination of motor activity and technological innovation in school contexts and above all for the purposes of inclusion for pupils with disabilities. In particular, the socio-relational, emotional and cognitive aspect is highlighted, the analysis of the benefits that users with different abilities can obtain from the use of specific software and aids in relation to the type of sensory and psychophysical deficit. The search is still ongoing.

References

Agrati, L.: Per una didattica inclusiva attraverso il movimento. Premesse teoriche, spunti operativi. Pensa Editore, Lecce (2018)

Altavilla, G.: Indicazioni metodologiche per l'educazione all'attività motoria, fisica e sportiva nella formazione docente. FORMAZIONE & INSEGNAMENTO. Rivista internazionale di Scienze dell'educazione e della formazione **19**(3), 96–106 (2021)

Altet, M.: Une démarche de recherche sur la pratique enseignante: l'analyse plurielle. Revue Française de Pédagogie **138**, 85–93 (2003)

Amati, I.: Personalizzare l'intervento didattico per gli alunni con DSA. In: Guerini, I. (a cura di). Scuola e inclusione. Riflessioni teoriche ed esperienze di didattica. Edizioni Conoscenza, Roma (2022)

Armitage, M., Woolley, H.: Inclusion of disabled children in primary school playgrounds. Jessica Kingsley Publishers (2006)

Baratella, P.: I diritti della persona con disabilità. Dalla convenzione internazionale ONU alle buone pratiche. Edizioni Erickson (2009)

Barnett, A., Cerin, E., Baranowski, T.: Active video games for youth: A systematic review. J. Phys. Act. Health **8**, 724–737 (2011)

Bates, A.T.: Technology, e-Learning and Distance Education. Routledge (2005)

Beillerot, J.: La "recherché", essai d'analyse. Recherche et Formation **9**, 17–31 (1991)

Belfiore, P.: La pedagogia nell'era digitale: il ruolo dei social media nella promozione dell'attività motoria. FORMAZIONE & INSEGNAMENTO. Rivista internazionale di Scienze dell'educazione e della formazione **20**(1), 35–47 (2022)

Bednarz, N., Rinaudo J.L., Roditi É.: La recherche collaborative. Carrefours de l'éducation **39**(1), 171–184 (2015)

Benzing, V., Schmidt, M.: Exergaming for children and adolescents: Strengths, weaknesses, opportunities and threats. J. Clin. Med. **7**(11), 422 (2018)

Bertucci, A., Meloni, C., Johnson, D.W., Johnson, R.T.: Cooperative learning: Effetto dell'utilizzo dell'interdipendenza degli obiettivi e del compito con bambini frequentanti la scuola primaria. G. Ital. Psicol. **42**(3), 549–570 (2015)

Bieć, E., Kuczyński, M.: Postural control in 13-year-old soccer players. Eur. J. Appl. (2010). https://doi.org/10.1007/s00421-010-1551-2

Bocci, F., Gaggioli, C., Giannoumis, A., Ranieri, M.: Editoriale Un numero speciale per riflettere su Media Education e Inclusione. Media Educ. **13**(1), 3–5 (2022)

Boeris, C., Gozzelino, G.: Educare alla cittadinanza nella prospettiva della competenza globale. In: Educare alla cittadinanza nella prospettiva della competenza globale, pp. 125–139 (2022)

Brymer, E., Lacaze, A.: An overview of sustainable development goal 3. In: The Routledge Handbook of Sport and Sustainable Development, p. 8 (2022)

Caione, G.: Bes e attività motorie inclusive: Proposte didattiche operative. Soares Editore (2021)

Canevaro, A.: L'integrazione scolastica degli alunni con disabilità. Trent'anni di inclusione nella scuola italiana. Erikson, Trento (2007)

Calidoni, P.: Didattica Come Sapere Professionale. La Scuola, Brescia (2000)

Coco, D.: Pedagogia del corpo ludico-motorio e sviluppo morale, vol. 2014, pp. 1–224. Anicia (2014)

Damiano, E.: La Nuova Alleanza, temi, problemi e prospettive della Nuova Ricerca. Didattica. La Scuola, Brescia (2006)

Dias, M.V., Braganza, S.J.: Motivation: A key factor impelling student participation in sports. J. Positive School Psychol. 10172–10177 (2022)

Di Palma, D.: Design and experiment new formative and evaluation protocols for motor and sports sciences from a didactic-pedagogical point of view. Giornale Italiano di Educazione alla Salute, Sport e Didattica Inclusiva **6**(1) (2022)

Drigas, A., Mitsea, E., Skianis, C.: Virtual reality and metacognition training techniques for learning disabilities. Sustainability **14**(16), 10170 (2022)

Durand, M., Filliettaz, L.: Travail et Formation des Adultes. Presses universitaires de France, Paris (2009)

Edwards, D., Mercer, N.: Common Knowledge. The Development of Understanding in the Classroom. Methuen Publishing Ltd, London (1987)

Fabiano, A.: Ipotesi per una migliore giustizia sociale: La scuola inclusiva tra didattica digitale e Intelligenza Artificiale. Formazione & insegnamento 20(1 Tome I), 116–126 (2022)

Farina, T.: La crisi dei valori simbolici, rituali e mimetici del gioco infantile durante la pandemia di COVID-19. Educ. Sci. Soc. Open Access 11(1) (2020)

Foley, L., Maddison, R.: Use of active video games to jncrease physical activity in children: A (virtual) reality? Pediatric Exer. Sci. 22, 7–20 (2010)

Giaconi, C., Del Bianco, N.: Inclusione 3.0. FrancoAngeli (2019)

Guicciardi, M.: La psicologia in movimento. G. Ital. Psicol. 27(4), 661–678 (2000)

Hutzler, Y.: The concept of empowerment in rehabilitative sports. In: Adapted Physical Activity, pp. 43–51. Springer, Berlin (1990)

Mangiatordi, A. (2017). Didattica senza barriere. Universal Design, Tecnologie e Risorse Sostenibili

Hutzler, F., Ziegler, J.C., Perry, C., Wimmer, H., Zorzi, M.: Do current connectionist learning models account for reading development in different languages? Cognition 91(3), 273–296 (2004)

Kern, R.: Perspectives on technology in learning and teaching languages. TESOL Q. 40(1), 183–210 (2006)

Knight, A., Petrie, P., Zuurmond, M., Potts, P.: 'Mingling together': Promoting the social inclusion of disabled children and young people during the school holidays. Child Fam. Soc. Work 14(1), 15–24 (2009)

Krouska, A., Troussas, C., Sgouropoulou, C.: Extended technology acceptance models for digital learning: review of external factors. In: Novel & Intelligent Digital Systems Conferences, pp. 52–63. Springer, Cham (2023). https://doi.org/10.1007/978-3-031-17601-2_6

Laneve, C.: Analisi della pratica educativa. Metodologie e risultanze della ricerca. La Scuola, Brescia (2005)

Lipoma, M.: XVIII. Educazione Motoria e Sportiva. Prospettive di cambiamento. Società Italiana di Pedagogia, p. 193 (2022)

Loughran, J.J., et al.: International Handbook of Self-Study of Teaching and Teacher Education Practices. Springer (2019)

Manno, R.: Muscle strength development in children and adolescents: training and physical conditioning. Med. Sport 61, 273–297 (2008)

Menolotto, M., Komaris, D.S., Tedesco, S., O'Flynn, B., Walsh, M.: Motion capture technology in industrial applications: A systematic review. Sensors 20(19), 5687 (2020)

Mezzetti, R. (2012). Corporeità e gioco. Edizioni Nuova Cultura

Mittelstädt, V., Mackenzie, I.G., Leuthold, H., Miller, J.: Electrophysiological evidence against parallel motor processing during multitasking. Psychophysiology 59(1), e13951 (2022)

Moeslund, T.B., Hilton, A., Krüger, V.: A survey of advances in vision-based human motion capture and analysis. Comput. Vis. Image Underst. 104(2–3), 90–126 (2006)

Moliterni, P.: Didattica e scienze motorie: tra mediatori e integrazione. Didattica e scienze motorie, pp. 1–320 (2013)

Monacis, D., Colella, D.: Il contributo delle tecnologie per l'apprendimento e lo sviluppo di competenze motorie in età evolutiva. Italian J. Educ. Res. 22, 31–52 (2019)

Munafò, C.: Le tecnologie dell'informazione in Educazione fisica. Edicare. it 20(1), 5–11 (2020)

Mündermann, L., Corazza, S., Andriacchi, T.P.: The evolution of methods for the capture of human movement leading to markerless motion capture for biomechanical applications. J. Neuroeng. Rehabil. 3(1), 1–11 (2006)

Mustaeva, G., Kurbanova, M., Mamajanova, G.: The place and role of using pedagogical technologies in learning English. Uzbek Scholar Journal 9, 191–193 (2022)

Nosek, B.A., Greenwald, A.G., Banaji, M.R.: The Implicit Association Test at age 7: A methodological and conceptual review (2007)

Nunes, A.R., Lee, K., O'Riordan, T.: The importance of an integrating framework for achieving the sustainable development goals: The example of health and well-being. BMJ Glob. Health 1(3), e000068 (2016)

ONU: Convenzione sui diritti delle persone con disabilità. Organizzazione delle Nazioni Unite, New York (2006)

Pastré, P.: La didactique professionnelle. Educ. Sci. Soc. 1, 83–96 (2011)

Pennazio, V.: Disability, play and robotics in kindergartens. Italian J. Educ. Technol. 23(3), 155–163 (2015)

Perla, L.: Didattica dell'implicito. Ciò che l'insegnante non sa. La Scuola, Brescia (2010)

Perla, L.: Giovani insegnanti e "scrittura-compagna. In: Corsi, M., Spadafora, G. (eds.) Progetto generazioni. I giovani, il mondo, l'educazione, pp. 221–230. Tecnodid, Napoli (2011)

Perla, L.: Scritture professionali. Metodi per la formazione. Progedit, Bari (2012)

Perla, L.: Per una didattica dell'inclusione. Prove di formalizzazione. Lecce, Pensa Multimedia (2013)

Perla, L., Riva, M.G.: L'agire Educativo. Manuale per educatori e operatori socio- assistenziali. La Scuola, Brescia (2016)

Perla, L., Agrati, L.: L'agentività dell'insegnante inclusivo. Uno studio esplorativo sul Coordinatore per l'inclusione. In: Sibilio, M., Aiello, P. (Eds.). Lo sviluppo professionale dei docenti. Ragionare di agentività per una scuola inclusiva, pp. 239–258. EdiSES, Napoli (2018)

Perla, L., Agrati, L.S., Scalera, E.: Una 'traccia' di modello inclusivo scuola-territorio. L'esperienza del progetto 'LabInclusion'. In: Lucisano, P. (ed.). Alla ricerca di una Scuola per tutti e per ciascuno. Impianto istituzionale e modelli educativi, pp. 405–419. Atti del Convegno Internazionale SIRD, Roma 13-giugno 2018. PensaMultimedia, Lecce (2019)

Piccolo, A.L., Mingrino, M., Passaniti, V.M.: La scuola italiana ai tempi del Covid-19. Fra innovazione tecnologica e recupero delle individualità e della socialità. Giornale Italiano di Educazione alla Salute, Sport e Didattica Inclusiva, 4(4_si) (2020)

Reddy, L.A.: Inclusion of disabled children and school reform: A historical perspective. Spec. Serv. Schools 15(1–2), 3–24 (2000)

Regazzoni, C.S., Marcenaro, L., Campo, D., Rinner, B.: Multisensorial generative and descriptive self-awareness models for autonomous systems. Proc. IEEE 108(7), 987–1010 (2020)

Rosa, R., Madonna, G.: Strategie educative per l'Inclusione Sociale: Biodanza SRT e Baskin. Giornale italiano di educazione alla salute, sport e didattica inclusiva, 3(1_Sup) (2019)

Rusyani, E.N.D.A.N.G., Maryanti, R.I.N.A., Utami, Y.T., Pratama, T.Y.: Teaching science in plant structure for student with hearing impairments. J. Eng. Sci. Technol. 16(2), 1577–1587 (2021)

Salerno, V., Marcelli, A., Casasola, G.: Orientamento degli adolescenti svantaggiati nei contesti socioeducativi: Soluzioni dal Friuli Venezia Giulia. STUDIUM EDUCATIONIS-Rivista semestrale per le professioni educative 2, 054–063 (2022)

Scurt, M.D., Balint, L., Mijaică, R.: Improving body mass index in students with excess weight through a physical activity programme. Children 9(11), 1638 (2022)

Sgambelluri, R., Vinci, V.: Corporeità e inclusione. Una ricerca con i futuri insegnanti specializzati. Formazione & Insegnamento XVIII – 1 – (2020)

Simonetti, C.: Educazione motoria e sport tra scuola e realtà sociale. Riflessioni Pedagogiche. Pensa Multimedia (2016)

Theureau, J.: Le cours d'action: méthode développée. Octarès, Toulouse (2006)

Valijonovna, X.I.: Improving of motivation for studying in primary school. Eur. Multidiscip. J. Mod. Sci. 6, 131–137 (2022)

Vecchiato, M.: Il gioco psicomotorio. Psicomotricità psicodinamica. Armando Editore (2007)

Vinatier, I., Altet, M.: Analyser et comprendre les pratiques enseignantes. PUR, Rennes (2008)

Vinatier, I., Morrissette, J.: Les recherches collaboratives: enjeux et perspectives. Carrefours de l'éducation **39**(1), 137–170 (2015)

Votta, M.: Le parole dell'inclusione e la didattica inclusiva. Ali Ribelli Edizioni (2022)

Zappalà, E.: Ambienti di apprendimento ibridi per l'inclusione degli allievi con ASD. Verso una progettazione ecologica. J. Inclusive Methodol. Technol. Learn. Teach. **1**(1) (2022)

Zhang, Y., Li, R., Miao, X., Cheng, L.J., Lau, Y.: Virtual motor training to improve the activities of daily living, hand grip, and gross motor function among children with cerebral palsy: Meta-regression analysis. Gait Posture **91**, 297–305 (2022)

Surmounting Obstacles for Academic Resilience: A Dynamic Portal for Supporting an Alliance of Students with Disabilities

Alexis N. Petri[1,2(✉)] ⓘ, Duy H. Ho[1,3] ⓘ, Ye Wang[1,3,4] ⓘ, and Yugyung Lee[1,3] ⓘ

[1] University of Missouri-Kansas City, Kansas City, MO, USA
[2] NSF's Eddie Bernice Johnson INCLUDES Initiative TAPDINTO-STEM Alliance, Auburn University, Auburn, AL, USA
petria@umkc.edu
[3] UMKC School of Science and Engineering, Kansas City, MO, USA
[4] UMKC School of Humanities and Social Sciences, Kansas City, MO, USA
https://www.tapdintostem,https://www.soar-ai.com

Abstract. Description of the development and use of a dynamic portal for supporting an alliance of colleges and universities focused on supporting students with disabilities and transitioning to careers in science and technology. Called SOAR, the portal is designed to support separate institutes achieve collective impact through shared measures. Significant aspects of SOAR are the user-driven design with three different communication roles, dynamic generation of survey forms, the ability to schedule surveys, collecting data through the surveys, and data presentation through dynamic chart generation. SOAR utilizes and advances the best practices of Universal Access and is central to the alliance's ability to empower individuals with disabilities to live their best lives. One of the most interesting features is the ability for different institutes to customize their forms and collect campus-relevant data that can be changed and the application of machine learning to produce the dynamic chart generation. SOAR allows the alliance to meet individual campus needs and the reporting and evaluation needs of the National Science Foundation.

Keywords: User-friendly Survey App · Inclusive User Experience · Tailored User Interface · Interactive Data Visualization

1 Introduction

In a knowledge-based, technology-driven economy, earning a college degree is requisite for many people, whether for career or personal achievement, and benefits both the individual and society [9]. People with disabilities also have career

This material is based upon work supported by the National Science Foundation under Grant No. 2119902.

Authors would like to acknowledge Ahmed Alanazi for his contribution to the mobile app development and Nichole Stahly for her work on form design and as NSF INCLUDES backbone associate.

or personal achievement goals that require college. According to the U.S. Bureau of Labor Statistics, 27.7% of individuals with disabilities have a bachelor's degree and are employed, compared with 73.2% of those without disabilities. Additionally, individuals with disabilities were more likely to work part-time (29.0%), work in service occupations (18.2%), or work in transportation and material moving occupations (14.6%), compared with those without a disability (16%) [12]. Success for individuals and for communities requires trajectories of opportunity [6]. In the U.S., we are failing to make available trajectories of opportunity for people with disabilities.

Education, at all levels, strives to be evidence-based. In the U.S., what institutions of higher education, and associated scholarship, know the least about are students with disabilities. One reason may be because reporting outcomes data for students with disabilities is not typically required. Achievement gaps must be closed, but it is difficult to ascertain the achievement gaps for students with disabilities. Students with disabilities often face barriers that hinder their persistence [19]. Increasing numbers of researchers are focused on broadening participation [7], especially since the National Science Foundation launched the Eddie Bernice Johnson INCLUDES Initiative, and yet, disability is rarely a data point for making evidence-based decisions about student outcomes.

Working to achieve collective impact for one of the most significantly underrepresented groups in STEM education and employment, researchers at the University of Missouri-Kansas City have designed a dynamic data portal to support efforts to better understand the successes and barriers of students with disabilities. Named Surmounting Obstacles for Academic Resilience, and referred to as SOAR, this accessible portal was developed as the shared measurement system for the Eddie Bernice Johnson INCLUDES Initiative: The Alliance of Persons with Disabilities for Inclusion, Networking, and Transition Opportunities in STEM (TAPDINTO-STEM), which seeks to increase the number of postsecondary degrees completed by students with disabilities. Shared measurement is one of the five core elements to achieving a powerful collective impact, the commitment of a group of important actors from different sectors to a common agenda for solving a specific social problem, in addition to having a common agenda, mutually reinforcing activities, continuous communication, and a backbone that oversees the work of the collective group [17]. In this nationally collaborative alliance composed of 31 higher education institutions, UMKC serves as one of six regional hubs and the backbone for TAPDINTO-STEM, while SOAR collects individual and institutional data alliance-wide and brings it together in a way that faculty and advocates can use and understand.

While the first step is to develop a functional data collection system that utilizes and advances the best practices of Universal Access, the researchers also understand that the eventual research must tackle the whole system. This research converges around systematic data collection, student policies and practices, and the current societal understanding of empowering individuals with disabilities to realize their best lives. SOAR engages with students, faculty, and institutional data at four points: connection, entry, progress, and completion. Having specific evidence will allow institutions, faculty, and researchers to better consider how their structures, systems, policies, and personnel support or impede student success. If institutions can identify, understand, and help students successfully navigate these points, then they have an increased opportunity to promote protective factors for momentum outcomes and work to remove or lessen the occurrence and the severity of their impact to avoid losses.

In this paper, we explore how the portal supports programming focused on students with disabilities through architectures and tools for universal access, design for all best practices, and interaction personalization. Through the design of SOAR, researchers strive to achieve the following aspirations:

- To make the human-computer interface intelligent instead of static.
- Incorporate an individual workflow based on role, dissemination of data collection, and backed by an integrated database.
- Use an integrated database to connect different sources of data.
- Dynamically generates forms with an autofill option that knows where the user left off.
- Dynamically generates charts that can be automated with machine-learning-led identification of important parameters.
- Data schema design can be part of the research.
- Part of the interaction personalization minimizes questions and maximizes program personnel's understanding of learning outcomes based on the data collection.
- Try to minimize questions and maximize learning outcomes from data collection.

2   Related Work

There is an urgent need to introduce more flexible data management systems into higher education, which are traditionally dominated by relational databases (RDBMS) [16]. The urgency comes from a few sources. First, there has been plenty of research on warehoused data for enterprise solutions, but studies on data warehouses for higher education have lagged behind [16]. Data warehouse research is often bounded by the specific usage setting, for example, telecommunication business [14], agriculture [20], supply chain [24], and academic research [3]. There are largely two streams of data warehouse research in higher education. Tria, Lefons, and Tangorra [11] were among the earlier studies that introduced enterprise data warehouse solutions to higher education. Additionally, e-learning has motivated the design and implementation of data dashboards that collect heterogeneous data and visual analytics for quality assurance [15]. In general, there has not been sufficient research on the use of data warehouses in higher education settings, even though data-driven decision-making is urgently needed for institutes to implement changes to better serve all students.

Second, one of the needed transformational changes is to address the lack of diversity in STEM education and the tech industry [2,18]. These changes require a systematic approach that involves multiple institutions and recognizes various perspectives of stakeholders. In terms of data warehouse design, the decision-making and strategies in such a setting cannot become data-driven without a DW [16]. Existing relational databases used by organizations may have different data schemas. Integrating these existing relational databases into one "data warehouse" must address the complexity of the global and local perspectives of stakeholders. "A schema is a description of a piece of the information system" [4]. Data schema integration for local and global queries is a challenging task due to the various perspectives of the stakeholders [5].

In multi-institutional settings, there is very limited research on satisfying the needs of stakeholders from multiple institutions/organizations. Specifically, to what extent and to whom should be involved in the designing process of a data warehouse is a complicated question to answer. Additionally, given the different hierarchies within organizations, how do we create various management roles and access levels that can serve the needs of cross-institution and single-institution planning? Current research on ontology matching investigates element-level and structure-level semantic and syntactic matchings, by employing language-based, string-based, and graph-based techniques, to name a few [21]. With so many questions remaining unanswered, research is needed to find the best methods for integrating data schema from multiple higher educational institutions.

The third challenge is automation. The growing volume and complexity of data have posed challenges to the traditional approach to constructing data warehouses [23]. The tech industry (e.g. Google, Facebook, Twitter, Amazon, etc.) plays the leading role in "big data" solutions, motivated by large amounts of data from Web platforms [23]. As a result, "Not only SQL" (NoSQL) data management systems have attracted a lot of attention due to their flexibility of handling data [23]. NoSQL treats data as key-value dictionary pairs, and each record does not have a prior schema [8]. Due to their scalability and flexibility, NoSQL databases have become the mainstream of big data technologies [13].

In the educational setting, large amounts of data are accumulated from multiple relational databases year after year. Accordingly, implementing "big data" solutions to higher education requires automation. Phipps and Davis [1,22], as one of the earlier studies, presented a user-driven approach to automating the conceptual schema design and evaluation for data warehouses. They pointed out that the initial determination of measures, facts, or events was the most difficult and often needed to be done manually. The automation could help designers to conceptualize data warehouse schema, and users should be consulted on their querying needs. In recent years, the potential for utilizing word embedding and machine learning in automatic ontology matching has also attracted attention [21]. With the rising popularity of NoSQL databases, Bouaziz, Babli, and Gargouri [8] proposed an algorithm to extract data schema from NoSQL records, to assist designers in data warehouse schema design.

Accordingly, three research questions guide this study:

- RQ1: What is the process of designing data warehouse solutions to reflect stakeholders' perspectives from multiple higher ed institutions?

- RQ2: What are the best strategies for automating data warehouse design in such a setting?
- RQ3: How can the data warehouse be designed to support decision-making in such a setting?

3 The SOAR Portal

3.1 User-Driven Design

How to implement user-driven design has been a challenge in data warehouse design due to the huge communication gaps between users and system designers [5]. In this project, communicating with participating stakeholders was crucial to the success of the data warehouse design. Thus, the user-driven design was mandatory. To ensure success, three different communication roles were defined. The first role involved human-to-human communication, directly communicating with the stakeholders. This person was familiar with higher education management. The responsibility of this role was to listen to the stakeholders, collect information on existing relational databases, and seek clarification for the data warehouse design team. The second role handled content-to-content communication. The person was an interaction expert [10] who understood the human and the machine sides of data warehouse design. The responsibilities were to manually examine and compare the data schemas of the existing relational databases by consulting stakeholders' inputs, and to create an integrated data dictionary and a data schema that could be parsed by machines. The third role dealt with content-to-machine communication. This person was an expert in computer science. The responsibilities were to implement the automation of data warehouse design.

3.2 Design of SOAR Portal

The SOAR portal provides an easy-to-use human and machine interface that makes it simple for students, student mentors, teachers, staff, hub lead/campus lead, and hub lead administrators to communicate and share data. Their responsibilities and authority would be explained in terms of SOAR's two main parts: 1) collecting data through a series of surveys and 2) analyzing and showing the data in the form of a dashboard with several charts.

The customized interfaces contain various features and services based on the individual's tasks and responsibilities. The most interesting aspect of this system is that tasks (survey forms) are always being made and sent to users as online or mobile applications, depending on their responsibilities. Through the individualized interfaces of Web and mobile applications, data is collected and stored in serverless distributed databases for dynamic analysis and visualizations shared through intelligent dashboards. The frontend will dynamically link to the backend, including real-time data storage and machine learning, using a cloud-based Jupyter notebook. Thus, this is an end-to-end system that includes data collection via online or mobile applications, data analysis, and analytics via populating real-time databases with data. User interfaces are always being changed by adding new forms, changing forms that are already there, and moving forms around. Users can be deleted from or added to our systems via our applications.

Dynamic Generation for Survey Form Application. SOAR's forms look like Google Forms, which are designed to support inquiry by giving users different ways to ask questions. The dynamic form generation application is made so that a survey form can be used to make a mobile or web application automatically. Automatic application generation will be generated dynamically with multiple capabilities, such as a speech interface, encrypting sensitive information (e.g., student names, GPAs, etc.), survey scheduling and publication, anonymous nickname generation, and automatic validation. This allows the alliance to meet the needs of individual campuses and programs and their students and faculty, while still meeting the reporting and evaluation needs of the National Science Foundation.

A form is composed of a set of different question types:

- Multiple Choice: One answer per question can be selected from an available set of items.
- Check-boxes: Multiple answers can be selected from an available set of items, including "other" for short answers.
- Drop-Down Menu: The respondent selects the appropriate response from a drop-down menu. With this option, the respondent can upload a file from Google Drive in the form of an answer sheet to answer a question.
- Scale Ranging: Respondents answer the question using a scale from 0 to 10.
- Multiple Choice Grid: The system gives the respondent choices from which to choose one answer per row. This option allows individuals to select one or more replies per row.
- Start Date: This is set to determine when a particular survey is available.
- End Date: This is set to determine when a particular survey is closed.

Survey Forms. The SOAR portal has a number of different survey forms that are made and sent to users based on their roles and requirements for NSF's Eddie Bernice Johnson INCLUDES Initiative data collection. Survey questionnaires are designed for the following users:

- Hub or Campus Lead: This group is administrators. They are given the highest level of accessibility. This form collects institutional data, such as resources, disability services, etc.
- Faculty or Staff: This group includes all faculty and staff who have participated in the project. This form collects faculty/staff's activities and interactions with students.
- Student Mentor: This group includes participating students, who, meanwhile, serve as mentors for other students. This form collects the demographics, academic performances, participation, and mentoring status.

– Student: This group includes all student participants. This form collects demographics, academic performances, and participation.

Survey Scheduling. The survey forms will be arranged based on the beginning and end dates. Before the start date, the form will not be posted, and after the end date, the form will no longer be accessible. In addition, form prerequisites are defined. For instance, the demographic form is a prerequisite for the performance form. So, it will be decided that the student performance form will be filled out after the demographics form.

Data Collection Through Survey Generation. The SOAR portal supports specific users as follows:

– Admin can design, generate, and deploy survey forms with minimal effort.
– Hub or Campus Lead can design, create, and schedule survey forms. The Admin reviews and publishes the forms.
– Faculty and staff are required to complete surveys in the order they are sent to them.
– Student mentors are required to respond to the surveys in the order they are deployed. Student mentors are required to fill out 10 forms. The sole distinction between students and student mentors is that student mentors also act as mentors for students. Thus, the forms for students and student mentors are nearly identical.
– Students have to fill out the surveys in the order that they are given to them. Students are responsible for completing 10 surveys.

Data Presentation Through Dynamic Chart Generation. The dashboard for the SOAR portal is innovative because the charts that are shown are made automatically by (1) figuring out which parameters in the data are most important and putting them in order of importance using machine learning (ML) algorithms; (2) finding a link between parameters; (3) computing the links as a correlation coefficient matrix by using ML; and (4) making individual charts based on the characteristics that are strongly linked. The goal of the intelligent dashboard is to make the work of domain experts easier. Of course, domain experts can also build charts by hand to find connections in the data that were not known before. This automation will be set up as soon as there are sufficient data points from which meaningful information can be elicited.

We also look at the charts suggested by domain experts to get around the limitations of the data-driven dashboard system. If domain experts' charts were suggested instead of machine learning's automated charts, the missing charts would be added to the dashboard. Consequently, the intelligent dashboard system relies on human and computer cooperation.

3.3   The SOAR Portal's Frontend Component

Front-end design considerations for SOAR include (1) User friendliness and accessibility; (2) Customized interfaces; (3) Task completion with minimal effort and time; and (4) Assistance for users with disabilities.

User friendliness: As an example of being user-friendly, scheduled surveys are well-organized based on what users need to do first and when each survey begins and ends. SOAR divides the forms into two categories - completed and unfinished - so the user can easily figure out what comes next. It's easy for Lead Hub Administrators to create, update, copy, and send surveys to all roles or institutions, or just to some of them.

Customized interfaces: The user interface will differ depending on the user's identification. For instance, if the user is a student who has already finished three forms and has two more to do, the user interface will change. This interface will show unfinished forms in the order they need to be finished, along with start and end dates and requirements. In addition, the user can update completed forms using the auto-fill options of prior responses.

User efficiency: Users can update completed forms using the auto-fill options from prior responses so that they are not answering the same questions multiple times.

Supporting people with disabilities: Users with disabilities are supported throughout SOAR. Each form is reviewed for universal design for evaluation so that the questions are clear for a broad array of respondents. Users have multiple ways to interact with SOAR. Users may complete the forms in various ways: They may complete forms using speech-to-text where SOAR reads aloud the forms and the respondents speak the answers, or SOAR reads aloud the forms, and the respondent types the answers, or the respondent reads the forms and types the answers. The determination is fluid, so respondents do not need to decide that their forms will always be presented and answered in one way.

The interfaces for the personalized services for various individuals are illustrated with screenshots.

Student Interface: The student interface of the SOAR mobile app, shown in Fig. 1, includes five forms that require completion. When users access the login screen (Fig. 1(a)), those who haven't registered can proceed to the registration screen (Fig. 1(b)). After successfully logging in, the main screen is displayed (Fig. 1(c)). By selecting the "Forms" button, a list of available forms is presented (Fig. 1(d)), allowing the user to choose a specific form to complete (Fig. 1(e)). The form can be completed by typing or using voice commands, which can be activated by holding down the microphone icon. The list of voice commands includes:

Selecting options, e.g., saying "My gender is male" to select the male option Typing text, e.g., saying "My first name is John" to type "John" into the text field. Resetting a field, e.g., saying "reset my first name" to empty the first name text field. Turning on/off the speak out feature by pressing its corresponding button. This feature speaks outs the selected part of the application, but only if the user's phone is not in silent mode. Finally, the user can submit the form by pressing the submit button. After submission, the user can view the remaining forms or applications to be submitted.

When it is turned on, the app will announce which part of the application the user has selected, for example, the first name field. When it is turned off, the user will no longer hear the speech from the app. Note that to use this feature, the user's smartphone must not be in silent mode. Once the form is complete, the user can submit it by pressing the submit button. After submitting the form, the user can see a list of the remaining forms or applications that need to be submitted.

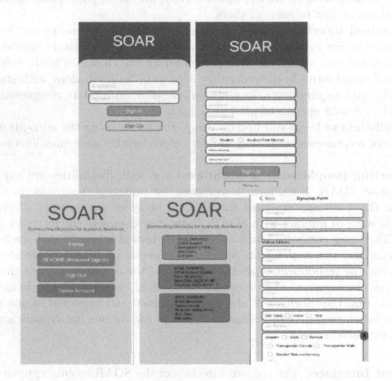

Fig. 1. SOAR Student's Mobile App: (a) login screen (top left) (b) registration screen (top right) (c) main screen (bottom left) (d) list of available forms (bottom middle) (e) filling out the form by typing or using voice command (bottom right)

Student Peer Mentor and Faculty/Staff Interface: Since student peer mentors and faculty/staff have equivalent system rights compared to students (meaning they can only complete assigned surveys), the interfaces are similar in terms of layout and design, except for the individual sequence of forms specified by Hub Lead Admins that need to be completed by each role respectively.

Hub Lead/Campus Lead Interface: Hub Lead/Campus Leads have the ability to create, edit, clone, and delete surveys. However, they cannot publish

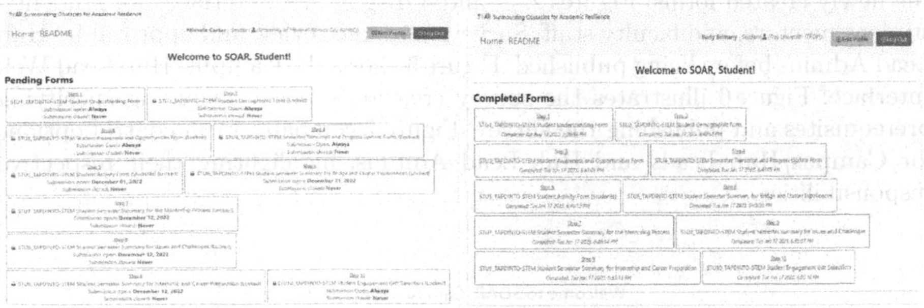

Fig. 2. Student Web Interface Dashboard: (a) Initial State (left) (b) All Surveys Completed (right)

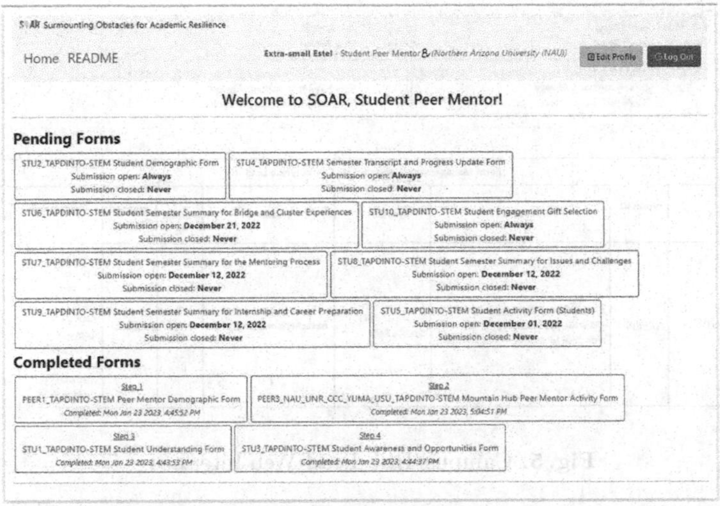

Fig. 3. Student Peer Mentor Web Interface

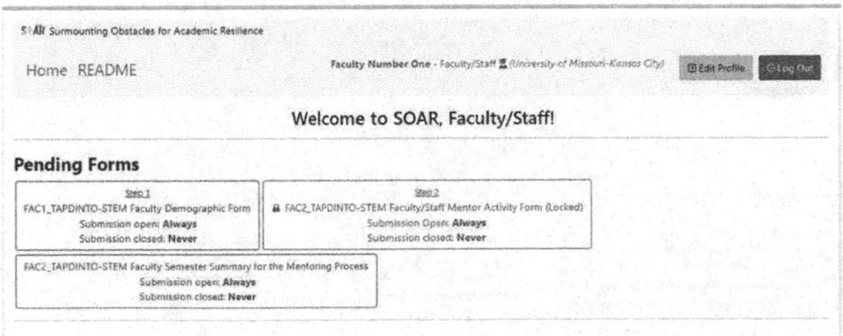

Fig. 4. Faculty/Staff Interface

the newly created forms. Figures 2, 3, and 4 display web interfaces for students, student mentors, and faculty staff. Surveys undergo review and approval by Hub Lead Admins before being published. Figure 5 shows the Campus/Hub Lead Web Interface. Figure 6 illustrates the survey creation process, including specifying prerequisites and publishing the survey. Figure 7 compares form control options for Campus/Hub Leads and Hub Lead Admins, highlighting their respective responsibilities.

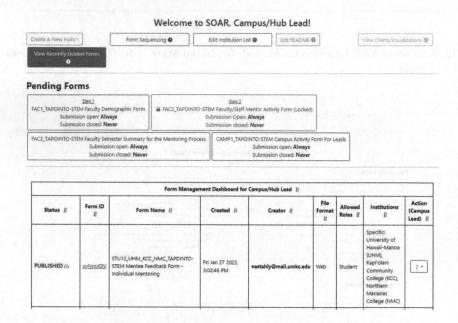

Fig. 5. Campus/Hub Lead Web Interface

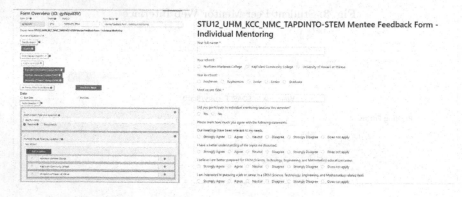

Fig. 6. Survey creation process (a) Specify all prerequisite requirements, access restrictions, and questions. (b) Publish and Render Survey

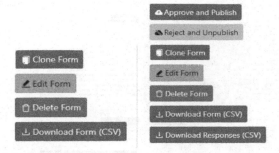

Fig. 7. Campus/Hub Lead vs Hub Lead Admin's form control options. Campus/Hub Leads can create, edit, and delete forms, while survey status is managed by Hub Lead Admins only. Hub Lead Admins can also download form responses in CSV format.

Hub Lead Admin Interface: Hub Lead Admins possess higher authority and access additional options compared to other roles. This includes Fig. 8 for the Established Form Sequence for Students, Student Peer Mentors, and Faculty/Staff. Figure 9 shows additional rights that Campus/Hub Leads and Hub Lead Admins share, such as updating institutions, editing README pages, recovering deleted surveys, and modifying account type. Figure 10 depicts the pending form workflow, Fig. 11 is the Hub Lead Admin interface, and Fig. 12 displays a sample user roster exclusively for Hub Lead Admins, containing name, email, institution, and account type.

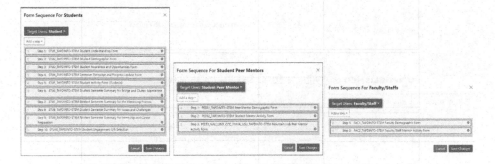

Fig. 8. Established Form Sequence for Individual Roles: (a) Students (b) Student Peer Mentors (c) Faculty/Staff

SOAR Frontend Implementation: The frontend of SOAR was created using the two frameworks listed below. First, the Web application is the main SOAR frontend, and all user roles can use all of its features. The frontend provides each of the five main types of users (i.e. student, student peer mentor, faculty/staff, hub lead/campus lead, and hub lead administrator) a dedicated interface. We build the SOAR web application via React (a component-based Javascript frontend library) and deployed to the public domain through Firebase Hosting and Vercel via a private GitHub repository. The established development and deployment workflow through GitHub branches is seamless because stable and nightly

Fig. 9. Additional rights shared by Campus/Hub Leads and Hub Lead Admins. (a) Update list of institutions (top left) (b) Edit individual README pages for each account type (top right) (c) Recover recently deleted surveys (bottom left) (d) Modify account type and role (bottom right).

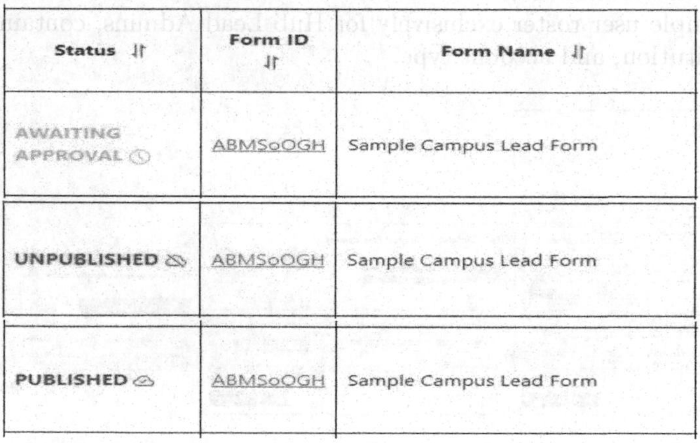

Status ↕	Form ID ↕	Form Name ↕
AWAITING APPROVAL ⏲	ABMSoOGH	Sample Campus Lead Form
UNPUBLISHED ⬚	ABMSoOGH	Sample Campus Lead Form
PUBLISHED ☁	ABMSoOGH	Sample Campus Lead Form

Fig. 10. Pending Form Workflow after Creation: Awaiting Approval from Hub Lead Admin (top), Rejected by Hub Lead Admin and Unpublished (middle), Accepted and Published to Users (bottom).

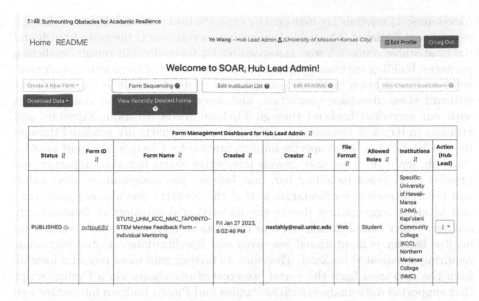

Fig. 11. Hub Lead Admin Interface

FirstName	LastName	email	Institution	Role
			San Diego State University (SDSU)	student-mentor
			Northern Arizona University (NAU)	student-mentor
			University of Hawaii at Manoa	student
			University of Missouri-Kansas City (UMKC)	hub-lead-admin
			University of Wisconsin-Milwaukee (UWM)	student
			University of San Diego (USD)	student
			Northern Arizona University (NAU)	student-mentor
			University of Missouri-Kansas City (UMKC)	student
			Columbus State University (CSU)	faculty
			Troy University (TROY)	student
			Coconino Community College (CCC)	student-mentor
			Auburn University (AU)	faculty
			Auburn University (AU)	faculty
			Northern Arizona University (NAU)	student
			University of Missouri-Kansas City (UMKC)	hub-lead-admin
			Wichita State University (WSU)	student
			Northern Marianas College (NMC)	faculty
			Purdue University (PURDUE)	student
			University of Missouri-Kansas City	student
			Purdue University (PURDUE)	student
			University of Wisconsin-Milwaukee	administrator
			University of San Diego (USD)	student
			Northern Arizona University (NAU)	campus-lead
			Point Loma Nazarene University (LOMA)	student
			University of Hawaii-Manoa (UHM)	faculty

Fig. 12. Sample exported user roster from the Google Cloud Build backend, accessible to Hub Lead Admins only. Information includes name, display email, institution, and account type.

(development) versions are managed by separate branches and deployed through separate subdomains. The publicly available soar-ai.com is the main branch and the most stable version. Vercel is responsible for managing Git pushes, gathering packages, building environments, and ultimately ensuring the continuous deployment and integration of the project into our custom domain is successful. For authentication, database connection, and storage, the frontend communicates with our serverless backend through Firebase Authentication, Firestore, and Storage. In terms of visualizations, the data-driven charts are rendered through React ChartJS 2, a React-specific implementation for Chart.js, the most popular chart library. It does not only provide interactive charts but also supports many popular chart types including bar, line, bubble, pie, doughnut, scatter, radar, and polar. However, its limitation is that these charts provide only univariate and bivariate aggregations due to the underlying constraints of frontend-only renders. Other complex tasks such as correlation, regression, and classification involve heavier computational resources and specific data-oriented platforms, requiring a dedicated backend. Therefore, to further gain more powerful insights from the responses from the portal, we created our charts via a Python script that supported data analysis such as Pandas and Plotly, built an interactive web application through Flask, and deployed it through our secure private endpoint services via JupyterDash and Ngrok (more details in Sect. 3.4).

Second, the mobile application is developed from React Native, a software development framework with React principles with native functionalities enabled. The mobile application is tailored for students or student peer mentors who prefer a convenient way to fill out the surveys without having to type a lot of answers. The mobile application shares real-time access to the same Firestore database and, therefore all user and survey information is always up-to-date and in sync with the React web application. Moreover, to leverage the power of speech recognition, we developed our cross-platform mobile application with high compatibility for both Android devices along with iOS phones and tablets (Fig. 1).

3.4   The SOAR System's Backend Component

As illustrated in Fig. 15, the SOAR architecture consists of 3 main components: Serverless backend and database, Python backend with dedicated domain, and multi-platform frontend, in which each component is composed of several smaller modules and services. The functions and communication are also clearly defined within and between each component.

Serverless Backend. The serverless backend is structured on top of Google's Firebase ecosystem, which provides powerful services to create a secure application in terms of scalability, reliability, and maintainability. The Firebase authentication service provides a ready-to-use and secure system to create and manage our users via multiple options such as email, phone number, and social media accounts. The database was built using Firestore, a well-known real-time NoSQL

Fig. 13. Visualization Dashboard (Frontend Render) (a) Bar Chart (top left) (b) Pie Chart (top middle) (c) Radar Chart (top right) (d) Line Chart (bottom left) (e) Geographic Map Chart (bottom right).

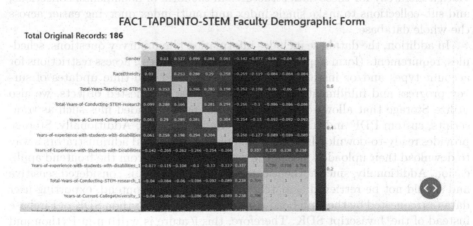

Fig. 14. Advanced Visualization: correlation matrix. These types of advanced visualizations were created from a dedicated Python script, deployed through JupyterDash, and hosted via Ngrok.

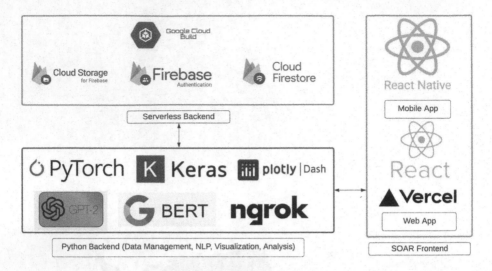

Fig. 15. SOAR Architecture

database, not only because of its flexibility in structuring data and automatic scaling, but also its integration with other Google and third-party services like Authentication, Cloud Messaging, Google Cloud Console, Storage, and Google Analytics written across multiple native SDKs and programming languages such as Javascript, C#, Python, Java, and more. Thus, the information stored in our database can be fetched from multiple platforms and elevated even further with numerous powerful backend tools. Even though the database is designed to work with all kinds of structured, semi-structured, and unstructured data, it also provides a hierarchy for these data structures in the form of documents, collections, and sub-collections to make single-index and multi-index querying easier across the whole database.

In addition, the database includes information about survey questions, schedules, requirements (form sequence, deadline, prerequisites), access restrictions for account types and/or institutions (universities), and real-time updates of survey progress and fulfillment. Aside from primitive and nested objects, we also utilize Storage that allows developers to store user-uploaded files such as transcripts, custom PDF and text documents, and audio files. Additionally, Storage provides ready-to-download URLs, which provide users and administrators a way to download their uploaded files in the database directly from the frontend application. Additionally, since authenticated user information is considered sensitive and should not be retrieved as batches from the React frontend, exporting user data (as requested by the Hub Lead Admin) requires the Python SDK of Firebase instead of the Javascript SDK. Therefore, this feature is written in Python and deployed as an API endpoint through the Google Cloud Build (which containerized the script, the Firebase Admin SDK, and the remaining packages required in the environment in a Docker file) that is available 24/7 as a standalone URL embedded in a button on the web application. Once clicked, the API will invoke a method that fetches, constructs, and aggregates the latest user data, and finally download a file directly to the user's computer in the CSV format.

Python Backend. Even though Firebase provides a well-integrated system to establish, store, and manage data, its ability to perform complex data-related tasks is still limited, whereas data comprehension and analysis tasks are vital to understanding what users would like to convey and improving the quality of the service. Since the SOAR database and authentication system are hosted on the cloud that is seamlessly integrated with various native libraries, we had an opportunity to expand the application further with the second component in the architecture, our dedicated backend that carries out extensive analysis, efficient querying, data insight, interactive visualization, in-depth interpretation, and prediction using powerful state-of-the-art techniques such as natural language processing (NLP), machine learning (ML), and deep learning (DL).

The backend is based on the JupyterLab environment written in Python. For data comprehension, we utilized GPT-2 and Bert models (built on top of PyTorch and Keras). Each model is trained on specialized tasks suitable to their architecture and design. Our chatbot, besides being able to follow the strict order of questions established by the Hub Lead Admin in the survey, is also enhanced by OpenAI's GPT-2 with the ability to generate sentences based on user inputs and engage in a natural conversation with the users. GPT-2, an autoregressive decoder, is extremely good with text generation. On the other hand, tasks regarding understanding the data, such as sentiment analysis and question answering, are performed with Google's BERT model, a deep learning model that aims at learning the words and the surrounding context.

For comprehensive data analysis and analytics, we utilized Firestore data export and constructed tables to facilitate various statistical methods such as filtering, dimensionality reduction, correlation, regression, classification, topic modeling, and clustering. These techniques enabled us to identify significant variables, uncover data relationships, and derive valuable insights. Interactive charts visualizing these connections were created using Plotly. To make these visualizations accessible, we deployed them locally as a web application through JupyterDash and made them publicly available using Ngrok. JupyterDash, built on Flask, serves as a development server, while Ngrok enables secure deployment of the Flask-based JupyterDash web application with HTTPS, requiring minimal code modification. Refer to Figs. 13 and 14 for illustrations. These technologies provide an excellent opportunity to incorporate complex interactive visualizations into the web application to accommodate the evolving backend features. By leveraging their computational power and resources, we achieve decoupling of complexity while seamlessly integrating our data-driven backend with the React frontend. Finalized charts, designed and implemented by administrators, will be containerized using Docker. Depending on their frequency and computational workload, these containerized charts will be either pushed to the cloud using Google Cloud Build or deployed on our dedicated server.

SOAR Mobile Apps Support Speech Interface: SOAR delivers speech recognition, synthesis, and message translation utilizing robust APIs such as Google Translation API and Speech-To-Text to encourage diversity and inclusion. SOAR does audio transcription by using the Speech-To-Text API, which is one of the most advanced voice recognition services, to turn audio communications from moderators and participants into state-of-the-art captions. This enables multi-modality and privacy protection. The domain-specific deep learning model used in this study was trained with a large dataset and advanced techniques to give the most accurate captions regarding meaning and grammar. Each temporary audio file added to our database is then sent to our cloud-based speech recognition engine, which makes real-time captions for participants and moderators. We provide students and student mentors via SOAR's mobile applications (iOS and Android).

4   Discussion and Future Work

In this paper, we discussed the design and development of a data portal to support a large multi-institution alliance that supports college students with disabilities who are majoring in and transitioning to careers in STEM. SOAR is designed to support shared measures and evidence-based decision making. It connects operations, internal evaluation, external evaluation, and embedded research. Through use, the application will become more focused on the specific project. In the future, we would like to encourage the use of this system for other large collaborations. Having real-time access to data can help large collaborations stay focused and adapt to student needs as they emerge. Additionally, a system such as SOAR provides users with an advanced interface that is accessible, and intelligent, connects data systems from multiple sources, aids implementation, and advances discovery.

References

1. Abai, N.H.Z., Yahaya, J.H., Deraman, A.: User requirement analysis in data warehouse design: a review. Procedia Technol. **11**, 801–806 (2013)
2. Alfred, M.V., Ray, S.M., Johnson, M.A.: Advancing women of color in stem: an imperative for us global competitiveness. Adv. Dev. Hum. Resour. **21**(1), 114–132 (2019)
3. Amorim, R.C., Castro, J.A., Rocha da Silva, J., Ribeiro, C.: A comparison of research data management platforms: architecture, flexible metadata and interoperability. Universal Access Inform. Soc. **16**(4), 851–862 (2017)
4. Batini, C., Di Battista, G., Santucci, G.: Structuring primitives for a dictionary of entity relationship data schemas. IEEE Trans. Software Eng. **19**(4), 344–365 (1993)
5. Batini, C., Lenzerini, M., Navathe, S.B.: A comparative analysis of methodologies for database schema integration. ACM Comput. Surv. (CSUR) **18**(4), 323–364 (1986)

6. Bierbaum, A.H., Vincent, J.M., Katz, J.P.: Planning for opportunity: linking smart growth to public education and workforce development. In: Handbook on Smart Growth, pp. 207–227. Edward Elgar Publishing (2022)
7. Blaser, B., Ladner, R.E.: Why is data on disability so hard to collect and understand? In: 2020 Research on Equity and Sustained Participation in Engineering, Computing, and Technology (RESPECT), vol. 1, pp. 1–8. IEEE (2020)
8. Bouaziz, S., Nabli, A., Gargouri, F.: Design a data warehouse schema from document-oriented database. Proc. Comput. Sci. **159**, 221–230 (2019)
9. Cimera, R.E., Thoma, C.A., Whittenburg, H.N., Ruhl, A.N.: Is getting a postsecondary education a good investment for supported employees with intellectual disability and taxpayers? Inclusion **6**(2), 97–109 (2018)
10. Collins, H.M., Evans, R.: The third wave of science studies: Studies of expertise and experience. Soc. Stud. Sci. **32**(2), 235–296 (2002)
11. Di Tria, F., Lefons, E., Tangorra, F.: Research data mart in an academic system. In: 2012 Spring Congress on Engineering and Technology, pp. 1–5. IEEE (2012)
12. DOL: Table 1. employment status of the civilian noninstitutional population by disability status and selected characteristics, 2021 annual averages. In: U.S. Bureau of Labor Statistics Economic News Release (2022). https://www.bls.gov/news.release/disabl.t01.htm
13. Emani, C.K., Cullot, N., Nicolle, C.: Understandable big data: a survey. Comput. Sci. Rev. **17**, 70–81 (2015)
14. Garani, G., Chernov, A., Savvas, I., Butakova, M.: A data warehouse approach for business intelligence. In: 2019 IEEE 28th International Conference on Enabling Technologies: Infrastructure for Collaborative Enterprises (WETICE), pp. 70–75. IEEE (2019)
15. Guitart Hormigo, I., Rodríguez, M.E., Baró, X.: Design and implementation of dashboards to support teachers decision-making process in e-assessment systems. In: Baneres, D., Rodríguez, M.E., Guerrero-Roldán, A.E. (eds.) Engineering Data-Driven Adaptive Trust-based e-Assessment Systems. LNDECT, vol. 34, pp. 109–132. Springer, Cham (2020). https://doi.org/10.1007/978-3-030-29326-0_6
16. Hamoud, A.K., Marwah, K.H., Alhilfi, Z., Sabr, R.H.: Implementing data-driven decision support system based on independent educational data mart. Int. J. Elect. Comput. Eng. **11**(6), 5301 (2021)
17. Kania, J., Kramer, M.: Collective impact. Stanford Soc. Innovat. Rev. **9**, 36–41 (2011). https://doi.org/10.48558/5900-KN19
18. McGee, E.O.: Interrogating structural racism in stem higher education. Educ. Res. **49**(9), 633–644 (2020)
19. Moriña, A., Sandoval, M., Carnerero, F.: Higher education inclusivity: When the disability enriches the university. Higher Educ. Res. Developm. **39**(6), 1202–1216 (2020)
20. Ngo, V.M., Le-Khac, N.A., Kechadi, M.T.: Data warehouse and decision support on integrated crop big data. Int. J. Bus. Process. Integr. Manag. **10**(1), 17–28 (2020)
21. Otero-Cerdeira, L., Rodríguez-Martínez, F.J., Gómez-Rodríguez, A.: Ontology matching: A literature review. Expert Syst. Appl. **42**(2), 949–971 (2015)
22. Phipps, C., Davis, K.C.: Automating data warehouse conceptual schema design and evaluation. In: DMDW, vol. 2, pp. 23–32. Citeseer (2002)
23. Sellami, A., Nabli, A., Gargouri, F.: Transformation of data warehouse schema to NoSQL graph data base. In: Abraham, A., Cherukuri, A.K., Melin, P., Gandhi, N. (eds.) ISDA 2018 2018. AISC, vol. 941, pp. 410–420. Springer, Cham (2020). https://doi.org/10.1007/978-3-030-16660-1_41

24. Vieira, A.A.C., Pedro, L., Santos, M.Y., Fernandes, J.M., Dias, L.S.: Data requirements elicitation in big data warehousing. In: Themistocleous, M., Rupino da Cunha, P. (eds.) EMCIS 2018. LNBIP, vol. 341, pp. 106–113. Springer, Cham (2019). https://doi.org/10.1007/978-3-030-11395-7_10

Effective Strategies for Encouraging Girls in Informatics

Zeynep Şahin Timar[1]([✉])[iD] and Özge Mısırlı[2][iD]

[1] Karadeniz Technical University, Trabzon, Turkey
zeynep.sahin@ktu.edu.tr
[2] Eskişehir Osmangazi University, Eskişehir, Turkey

Abstract. Although the increasing availability of technology and its widespread use by people of all genders, women continue to be underrepresented in academic and industry careers related to Informatics. Research has consistently shown that a gender gap exists in computer science education, with a lower participation rate of female students than their male counterparts. Despite changes in technology and accessibility, similar obstacles persist, which necessitates a reexamination of the need to acknowledge these barriers and emphasize the development of strategies to eliminate them. To emphasize this, the aim of this study is to identify effective strategies for encouraging pre-university girls to pursue study informatics by gathering and analyzing the existing initiatives' points of view. To reach this aim, we conducted phenomenological research with twelve initiatives from twelve different countries. We conducted semi-structured interviews to gather enriched information about the participants' experiences. We analyzed the data inductively. As a result, we found mentorship programs, role models, aware teachers, collaboration with parents, early contact with computing, creating interest by challenges, broader knowledge about informatics, educating boys, and multidisciplinary approach in teaching as effective strategies.

Keywords: Gender inequality · Barriers · Strategies · informatics

1 Introduction

Despite notable progress in recent years, gender inequality remains a pervasive and significant issue across multiple domains, spanning education, health, social life, business, and politics. The field of Informatics is no exception to this trend. Despite the increasing availability of technology and its widespread use by people of all genders, women continue to be underrepresented in academic and industry careers related to Informatics. Recent statistical data from a report by Statista [1–3] reveal that major technology companies such as e-Bay, Twitter, and Google have a predominantly male workforce in their technology departments, with percentages ranging from 67.1% to 75% male employees. This highlights the

This work has been partially supported by the EUGAIN COST Action CA19122 - European Network for Gender Balance in Informatics.

persistent gender gap in the field of Informatics and the need for further action to address this issue and promote gender equality in this and other fields.

Certainly, the phenomenon of under-representation is not unique to the business world and does not arise in isolation. Rather, it is a complex issue that is rooted in a variety of societal, cultural, and historical factors that have contributed to the unequal distribution of resources, power, and opportunities across different demographic groups. In this sense, the lack of diversity in the workplace is not simply a business problem but reflects deeper structural inequalities in the broader society. Addressing this issue requires a multi-faceted approach that goes beyond simply increasing representation and involves addressing underlying biases and promoting more inclusive practices and policies at all levels of society.

This statement highlights the correlation between the underrepresentation of women in the business world and the lack of female participation in computer science. It is important to note that gender disparities exist in both fields, and addressing one issue may help to mitigate the other. Therefore, it is crucial to recognize that efforts to increase the participation of girls in computer science can have positive effects on the representation of women in the business world.

To effectively address the issue of the underrepresentation of girls in computer science, it is essential to first identify the specific barriers that hinder their participation. Once these barriers have been identified, strategies can be developed to overcome them. This approach requires a comprehensive understanding of the factors that discourage girls from pursuing computer science, such as cultural and social biases such as families' and teachers' attitudes and behaviors, lack of role models, and educational barriers such as school environment and personal characteristics. By taking into account these obstacles and developing tailored strategies to address them, we can create a more inclusive and equitable environment that promotes greater participation of girls in computer science.

1.1   Barriers on Girls' to Study Informatics

There is a notable correspondence between the limited presence of women in the informatics field and the relatively low enrollment of female students in computer science (CS) courses, particularly in the later stages of education. This association suggests that gender disparities may play a significant role in the underrepresentation of women in informatics and related disciplines. The connection between the two phenomena highlights the importance of addressing issues of gender diversity and equity within the field of CS education and in STEM fields more broadly. Such efforts may be critical to reducing gender-based barriers to participation and enhancing opportunities for women to pursue and succeed in informatics and other tech-related fields.

It would be inaccurate to assert that the barriers described in the literature are entirely separate and distinct from one another. In reality, these barriers exhibit varying degrees of interrelatedness and mutually influence one another, either directly or indirectly. This interconnectedness among the barriers implies that addressing one barrier may impact other related barriers and that a comprehensive approach is necessary to effectively overcome them. Therefore, it is crucial to consider the interdependence of the various barriers when devising strategies and interventions to tackle them.

The under-representation of women in the field of informatics can be attributed to various factors, including social, personal, and economic reasons, all of which affect the participation of girls in any sub-field of informatics. Some primary reasons include stereotypes, a lack of awareness, a shortage of role models, misunderstandings and misconceptions about the field, and biases regarding girls' abilities [4]. All of these factors can negatively impact girls' confidence, which is a crucial personal factor.

Families. Families' behaviors, attitudes, and perspectives on gender stereotypes are crucial indicators of their children's participation in any activity [5,6]. It is possible to say that the different support or attitudes of families between genders will have an effective impact on their children's education and even their careers. Even though the financial opportunities offered to children of different genders are the same, and technology is similarly available to adults and children of all genders, still, Eccles [7] states that parents spend more time with their sons than with their daughters engaging in technology-related situations. In addition, boys are more likely than girls to receive encouragement from their parents to improve their knowledge about ICT [6]. There is no doubt about how these situations will affect the tendency and attitudes of girls.

Even if there are real differences in the relationship between family and children compared to the past, it is possible to say that when stereotypes are concerned, these relationships are like a difficult cycle to break. Within this cycle, the easiest way is to behave like your previous one, and that could be one of the reasons why this cycle always ends with more positive beliefs about the appropriateness and value of informatics. According to Eccles' expectancy-value theory, parents have an effect on children's self-perceptions about their abilities [8]. As Eccles [8] stated, girls give more importance to their parents' views on making occupational decisions, and this gives another idea about why parents' support is important for girls in attending CS classes and choosing informatics as a career.

Schools. Schools are secondary places where all students spend a great deal of time. Although those are the secondary ones, when it comes to the time that children spend in, it can be said that children spend most of their daily time at school. In other words, what is valid for the effect of parents' attitudes is also valid for schools. Some teachers' thoughts that gender difference is a factor in informatics, and based on this idea, the differences in their approach to girls and boys affect girls' achievements and attitudes. According to Vekiri's [9] research, there is a significant relationship between student perceptions of teacher expectations and their motivational beliefs toward information and communication technology (ICT). This suggests that the attitudes of teachers towards ICT can have a substantial impact on student motivation and engagement with this technology. Consequently, it can be argued that the influence of teachers on student ICT engagement is as crucial as the impact on families.

One significant barrier that impedes girls' participation in the field of computer science is their experiences and attitudes toward computer science classes during their schooling. Research has shown that girls often have negative experiences in computer science classes, including feeling excluded and undervalued, receiving less encouragement and feedback from teachers, and facing greater scrutiny from their male peers. These experiences can shape their attitudes toward the subject and deter them from pursuing further studies or careers in the field. Furthermore, societal expectations and stereotypes regarding gender roles and abilities can also influence girls' attitudes and beliefs toward computer science. These stereotypes can lead to a lack of confidence and self-efficacy in the subject, which further reinforces the gender gap in computer science. Literature suggests that female students often harbor negative attitudes towards informatics, with many assuming they are less competent and experienced than their male peers. This negative perception can lead to a lack of interest in the field and a reluctance to pursue further studies or careers in informatics. Research findings suggest that male and female students have different attitudes toward computer use and programming. They show that male students generally exhibit a greater level of comfort in computer science classes compared to their female counterparts, and also, female students show less interest in computer science [10,11]. In addition to these, research that was conducted by Yates and Plagnol [12] has shown that classes that are predominantly attended by males can have a significant impact on the technological self-efficacy of female students. This means that when girls are surrounded by boys who are more dominant in the class, they may begin to perceive themselves as less competent in technology-related fields, even if their actual abilities are comparable to those of their male peers. This phenomenon can be particularly pronounced in subjects such as computer science, where male students are often overrepresented and may contribute to the underrepresentation of women in technology fields.

Addressing this gender disparity in computer science requires a multi-faceted approach, including creating a more inclusive learning environment that values the participation of all students, providing female role models and representation in the field, and challenging gender stereotypes and biases. By doing so, we can promote greater participation and success among female students in computer science and bridge the gender gap in the field. Starting to work on girls' attitudes toward technology and triggering their curiosity and passion for Informatics from early education is a way to foster changes leading to a better gender balance in Informatics. The number of women in the informatics field will increase naturally if female students in the first stage of formal education (primary and secondary school) are better supported and actively encouraged to consider Informatics as a rewarding and satisfactory future career.

Lack of Role Models. Research has shown that female role models are more effective than male role models in inspiring girls and women. Additionally, it is widely believed that having female role models can enhance women's confidence in their ability to succeed in STEM fields [13]. According to van der Molen [14], studies conducted worldwide indicate that girls' interest in STEM typically begins to decline at the age of 15. However, one key factor that can help reignite their interest in STEM is the presence of engaging and motivational female role models. However, seeing same-sex professionals for a long time increases girls' self-efficacy and encourages them to choose STEM fields as a career [15].

Working as an expert in a male-dominated field, or being a minority in the classes usually taken by boys, can feel like doing something inappropriate because being a minority may come across as a situation that needs to be struggled with. To address this issue, steps can be taken to promote gender diversity in computer science classrooms by normalizing the presence of female students. For changing girls' minds about this issue, introducing girls to positive but relatable role models [16] and exposing them to successful female role models is important [15]. Meeting with the female experts allows girls to feel similar to them and identify with them [17] This approach can help to enhance girls' comfort level with selecting a career in informatics, thereby encouraging their participation in this field in the future.

Self Confidence. Another reason for women being underrepresented in the field of informatics is their lack of confidence. In fact, it can be argued that the foundation of women's confidence when starting their professional careers is shaped by factors that have been previously discussed, such as the influence of family and schools on the confidence of girls.

In terms of confidence, Beyer et al. [18] found that female CS majors who were experts in the field actually had less computer confidence than male non-majors. This suggests that confidence in the field may be independent of expertise. This also supports the idea that social factors could affect confidence, which is influenced by past experiences with computers (cited in Beyer et al. [18]). Therefore, it is clear that past experiences with technology-related situations, in which families tend to spend more time with their sons, could have an impact on the confidence of girls compared to boys.

Confidence also affects the willingness to take action on that subject. For example, in Compeau and Higgins's [19] model, computer self-efficacy affects the usage of computers and anxiety. In addition to this, it also affects the intention to take CS [20] and Information Science [21] courses. A considerable number of high school girls exhibit reluctance to register for computer science courses, and if they do, they often find themselves in a classroom dominated by males. Due to the low enrollment of females in high school computer classes, it is no surprise that there is a notable shortage of women pursuing computer science as a major in the college [22]. Given the circumstance, it is possible to provide yet another example in which the deficiency in self-assurance impedes the impetus to undertake action.

The literature has noted various barriers to girls' participation in informatics, in line with the advancement of technology in different years. Despite changes in technology and accessibility, similar obstacles persist, which necessitates a reexamination of the need to not only acknowledge these barriers but also to emphasize the development of strategies to eliminate them.

1.2 Purpose of the Study

Existing research on effective strategies to encourage girls to pursue informatics is limited. Despite the presence of various initiatives aimed at promoting informatics education among girls, their experiences and perspectives have not been extensively explored in the literature. Hence, the purpose of this study is to identify effective strategies for encouraging pre-university girls to pursue informatics by gathering and analyzing the existing initiatives' points of view.

2 Method

2.1 Research Design

The study was designed as phenomenological research. Phenomenological research aims to reduce individual experiences through a phenomenon for describing the universal essence [23]. In this study, we aimed to identify effective strategies to encourage girls in informatics by capturing the participants' lived experiences on the effective strategies to overcome the barriers for girls to study informatics. In this way, we can gather enriched information about the participants' experiences and get an insight into the overall essence of the experiences.

2.2 Participants

The participants of the study were the participants of "EUGAIN Existing Initiatives Meet-ups". EUGAIN is a COST action that aims to explore ways towards gender balance in Informatics. The Existing Initiatives subgroup, inside working group 1: from School to University, aims to investigate whether and how existing initiatives successfully encourage girls to choose Informatics in their higher education. To reach this aim, we organized two meet-ups with the initiatives that help girls in informatics. These initiatives were invited to the meet-ups. We interviewed 12 different initiative representatives from 11 different countries in total. There were eight representatives from eight different countries at the first meet-up. And there were four representatives from four different countries at the second meet-up. All the initiative presenters had an experience with pre-university girls in coding classes.

2.3 Data Collection and Analysis

We collected data through focus group interviews to get a deeper understanding of the effective strategies to overcome the barriers through their lived experiences. In the interviews, we asked questions about their experiences with effective strategies to overcome the barriers. Focus group interview is a good way to gain insights from the participants about their beliefs, behaviors, and attitudes about the related subject [24]. Focus group interviews are also an effective way to encourage the participants to talk on a topic more thoughtfully [25].

The procedure was carried out on the Zoom Platform during EUGAIN Existing Initiatives Meet-Ups. The interviews were made in English and recorded digitally. In both of the meet-ups, we followed the same procedure. First, the initiatives presented their motivation to start the initiatives and their initiative's work. Then we started the focus group interviews. During the interviews, we asked semi-structured interview questions and probe questions to deepen the participants' answers. We created two semi-structured questions: "What are the barriers you experienced with girls in informatics?", "What are the effective strategies you have experienced to overcome these barriers?". We also asked probe questions to deepen the participants' answers. The second researcher played both the moderator and interviewer roles. The first researcher helped with the probe questions and the recording. The interviews took 60–70 min.

The interview data were analyzed inductively. Therefore, the recordings of the interviews were transcribed as a first step. Then, the transcribed data were coded into smaller and more meaningful parts. After the coding, the themes were created in line with the codes. Then, data is organized and defined according to the codes and the themes. Finally, all the findings were interpreted in a holistic way by including the quotations of participants. The interrater reliability was used for the reliability.

3 Findings

3.1 What Are the Barriers for Girls in Informatics?

The analysis of the interviews revealed the themes and sub-themes about the most common barriers for girls to study informatics. The list of themes and sub-themes is below.

- Confidence
- Unsupportive Environment
  - Teachers
  - Parents
- Lack of Interest
- Learning Environment
  - Classmates
  - Teaching Methods

We found that one of the most common barriers for girls to study informatics is confidence. This theme covered the girls feeling uncomfortable in informatics class, answering questions in line with boys and letting them speak up, their feeling not good enough. ["... the idea women are not good enough with informatics."]. ["...When the boys spoke first, they said, no, that's bullshit that's not real computing. We don't want that. And if girls spoke second, they repeated the same. They just repeated what the boy said. If girls spoke first, they said yeah, that's interesting...")

The second most common barrier for girls to study informatics is an unsupportive environment. This theme divides into the subthemes of teachers and parents. Teachers sub-theme covers teachers' discouraging girls from informatics unintentionally, or they aren't being relatable role models for informatics. ["...the teachers who demotivate, sadly, because as the statistic shows, till year six girls are really interested in informatics and some teachers don't even know. It's sad. Some of them are just like no, you are not good enough..."]. ["...when a little child enters a classroom at their age of like 6, 7 or 8, the teachers make too harsh navigation of like you are a good fit and you are a bad fit and the teacher has like no idea what IT industry is about."]. Parents sub-theme covers unsupportive parents due to gender role beliefs or lack of information about informatics. ["...Gender role beliefs need to change, including aspects like what kind of career paths are appropriate for girls. Parents are extremely influential for the future jobs of their girls.]. [...parents play a great role in our life. So, so, so the parents are the ones that are extremely important in our childhood who can give us a win in the back and tell us, you know, go for it, you can do that, you are the best, etc. So parents are extremely important... 33% of girls do not think that their family would encourage them to to to go in the technology field that to to build their careers in the IT."].

The third most common barrier for girls to study informatics is a lack of interest. This theme covers late contact with informatics and the lack of information about informatics. ["... even people have computers at their homes, if a girl has brothers they generally use the computer..."]. ["... girls think that informatics equals coding. They don't know how wide the IT sector is..."].

The fourth most common barrier is a learning environment. This theme divides into the sub-themes of classmates and teaching methods. Classmates sub-theme covers the boys thinking the informatics is "boys' club" and the messages boys unintentionally send to the class. ["...when you are the only girl in the class, this really hard to stand the glass and you're looked upon like a miracle, like a Unicorn and Got taken a bit..."]. ["...when it comes to technical or digital skills, in usual classroom there is always like a very dominant boy or two that takes over the conversation. And kind of maybe not directly bullied the girls, but kind of pushes them away. I remember a girl was talking that she's the only girl in the robotics club, so she's not coming to our courses. I met her in some research interview and she said that she really struggles because she is interested actually in robotics, but they keep her, they keep pushing her away because it's a boys' club so it's it's really a challenge for her."]. And teaching methods sub-theme covers not teaching informatics as a part of daily life. ["...We need to present IT as a part of daily life. So multidisciplinary projects make them see IT as a part of life"]. ["...we need to, like change the view of like how we teach computing and kind of like, merge it and combine it with like other disciplines. ... if you could like combine it with other things and really just show that coding and technology is a tool"].

3.2   What Are the Effective Strategies You Have Experienced to Overcome These Barriers?

The analysis of the interviews revealed the effective strategies to overcome the barriers we determined. The effective strategies for the themes of barriers are in Table 1.

Table 1. Effective strategies to overcome the barriers

Themes (Barriers on girls to study informatics)	Effective strategies to overcome
Confidence	- Mentorship programs - Role models
Unsupportive environment	- Aware teachers - Collaboration with parents
Lack of interest	- Early contact with computing - Creating interest by challenges - Broader knowledge about informatics
Learning environment	- Educating boys - Multidisciplinary approach in teaching

The first strategy to overcome the "confidence" barrier is to develop mentorship programs for girls. ["...we have mentorship program and I will, I will tell you very very short story about a girl. She's a student, she wanted to apply for many internship positions but her CV did not pass any of of IT companies and she was not called on interview either. And she had her mentor, she was working with her on on writing CV on on some kind of programming languages on the side and she was talking with her constantly, giving her you know, motivation, constantly telling her not to give up. And she told her that she can put, she can imagine whatever she was thinking before she, she met her and before they basically joined in a mentorship pair to put everything what her thoughts in one folder and then to use that folder and put it in the recycle bin and that they will be working together on developing new documents etc., etc. So we we saw amazing confidence. It was in that girl who got internship position when she finished the mentorship program. So basically that is a very, very important to see to see the change in in their confidence."]. The second strategy for the confidence problem is relatable role models. ["...take students to events and excursions, taking motivational women and placing them and showing them yes, there is women in this field."]. ["A role model should be someone approachable in their close environment like University students, not any famous "far away" personalities. For example, include first-year University female students and let them share their personal experiences which will improve the younger girls confidence. Also share moments when they struggled to be real and show that they understand the thoughts the younger girls eventually have."].

The first strategy to overcome the "unsupportive environment" barrier is "aware teachers." ["The new teachers and the teachers with motivation making themselves some courses asking the girls to join them. When the school is really progressive, then the girls are joining and working together and so it's also really from the school if you look around and see. But you need to propagate this to the education and change the education to reflect this."]. ["... Teachers are extremely important because after we leave our House, teachers are are the ones that that we listen to carefully, that we somehow take their advices, take their beliefs on what we can do. So they should be careful and be aware their impact on girls."]. Second strategy to overcome the "unsupportive environment" barrier is a collaboration with parents. ["...we have all the parents that bring their, their daughters like age of 10, 11 years and they they are there with them on the workshop and they're really working with them and they're enjoying this. Parents play a great role in our life. So, so, so the parents are the ones that are extremely important in our childhood who can give us a win in the back and tell us, you know, go for it, you can do that, you are the best, etc. etc. So parents are extremely important..."]. ["...Girls tend to reflect on their parents' (!!) thoughts and thinking. Work and address the collaboration with moms and dads."].

The first strategy to overcome the "lack of interest" barrier is "early contact with computing". ["...If girls grew up with technology at home they had more interest in informatics."]. The second strategy to overcome this risk is "creating interest by challenges". ["...it helps us to realize one thing, it's actually that like the way how boys rather tend to interact with technology when they are new to it is that they challenge it, they challenge the technology, they try to break it, they try to bring it to its limits. And by that they are actually the, the thing that they don't need, safe, safe, you know, like if they break it, even better, you know, like this, this, this kind of like where is the limit? Like, how much I can push it to the limit. They they learn quicker, they learn quicker about how it works internally. While girls think about like OK for which purpose, like how this, like what this can help me with like and and if they need to configure the stuff so that it's helpful, they will. They can do very hard things, but if they don't need to configure it and it's prepared to work for their purpose, they will just use it as it is. And it's a very interesting finding that actually maybe we shouldn't do technology is so ready made and ready to use right? Like because if if the if those girls like have a plan and they need the technology they will go inside and they will they will reprogram it to meet that purpose. But but if it's just like ready there is no need to you know like go inside why why should I do it and it's like I have a friend who has who has a mobile app developer she's a she's a founder of a company on mobile app development and when I asked her how how she studied computing, she told me that she had the game as a little girl and she hated the clothes of those little, you know, like, figures in that she wanted nicer clothes, but she didn't know how to do it, so she did. She needed to find, like, where to change the code of that game so that she can, you know, like draw her own clothes and like, put it on those figures because she hated those, those clothes. That was ugly. And this is how she started, because she she was basically she had she known she wanted this like nice, you know, like scene, and she didn't like it and there wasn't a way to change it like by configuration. So she needed to go inside and dig deeper and reprogram it. And this is actually very interesting, you know, like that maybe this path can also lead to, like kind of like engaging girls more into, you know, like getting their hands dirty in the code."]. The third strategy to overcome the "lack of interest" barrier is "broader knowledge about informatics". ["...it's extremely important to to to mention I I wrote in my notes to mention, to mention how wide the IT sector is. So it's not about programming. You have many different varieties, varieties of many girls can find themselves in it..."].

The first strategy to overcome the "learning environment" barrier is "educating boys". ["...we are using now specialists and slowly making programs that through them, through the mail programmers, IT specialists showing that the equality is needed, how to speak in a natural and nice manner. But teaching boys that this is also for girls and the other way around, it's real. It's also very important."]. ["We call it breaking into men's club, so basically really showcasing to them that girls can do, not better, not worse, but but the same as as, as boys can do as well."]. Second strategy is "multidisciplinary approach in teaching". ["...like change the view of like how we teach computing and kind of like merge it and combine it with like other disciplines."]. ["For example with our product image change we have like a I know geography teacher has been using it like they're always like coding different flags and that has been like extremely successful. So they're learning about flags but like they're doing it with coding. in Sweden they introduced coding first as a part of mathematics and like mathematics is already like stigmatized against girls. So they like became that coding was also sort of like stigmatized and the idea if you could like combine it with other things and really just show that coding and technology is a tool."]. ["Project-based activities make girls see what they achieve and make them understand better. It also help them with confidence"]. ["Hands-on activities are great because they can see the results. And make them feel to be successful on the project"].

4   Discussion

The gender gap in informatics can be addressed through various means, including promoting the visibility of female role models in the field, creating a more inclusive and supportive learning environment for girls, and challenging gender stereotypes and biases in society and the family. These efforts can help to counter the negative attitudes and assumptions that many female students hold towards informatics and encourage greater participation and success in the field.

In this research, we have identified four primary barriers that hinder girls to study computer science, namely confidence, unsupportive environment, lack of interest, and learning environment. Our findings suggest that while confidence and lack of interest are more individual in nature, unsupportive environments and learning environments are social factors that involve other individuals who interact with students. Specifically, unsupportive environments refers to the absence of assistance and encouragement from teachers, and family members, whereas the learning environment encompasses classmates and methods.

Compeau and Higgins's [19] model gives a huge information about the relationship between confidence and computer anxiety. In our research confidence is the most common barrier reported by participants and our findings totally align with and reinforce this assertion. This barrier is also affected by previous experience, social persuasion, and vicarious experience of computer use [26]. To support this, unsupportive environment is our second barrier that, includes family and teacher support. Literature has shown that individuals' immediate social surroundings, especially family [8, 27] and teachers' support [10, 28], significantly impact their attitudes and achievement across various fields. There are also studies specifically on computer science classes and gender. According to Yates and Plagnol's research, an individual's self-efficacy beliefs and cultural background are significant factors that influence their career choices [12]. In a study conducted in 1998, it was revealed that the opinions of girls about participating an outdoor programming where boys' participation is thought to be more than girls are more abstaining when it comes to boys' participation [29]. Our findings also support this for informatics.

Secondly, we identified nine effective strategies for those barriers. Mentorship programs and meeting with role models could be effective for our most common barrier, confidence. Lack of female role models affects girls to choose informatics as a career [13–15, 17]. Similarly, mentorship programs can be beneficial in providing girls with information about a particular field and increasing their confidence. If chosen strategically, mentorship programs can provide girls also role models who can offer guidance and advice on navigating the challenges they may face in pursuing their goals. By having access to a mentor who has experience and expertise in a particular field, girls can learn about the opportunities available to them and develop the skills and knowledge they need to succeed. In addition to providing practical support and advice, mentorship encourages girls [30] and can also be a source of emotional support for girls. By having someone to turn to when they are facing challenges or feeling unsure of themselves, girls can develop a sense of belonging and confidence in their abilities and understand that abilities can be improved [17]. To overcome unsupportive environment barriers, collaboration with parents and raising awareness among teachers can be effective strategies. Thus this helps to change the views of parents and teachers. This strategy about teachers also supports the literature [31] The reason why girls don't contact with computing early is also about stereotypes. When we change the unsupportive environment, this will start to change automatically. In addition, if families will spend equal time with their daughters in technology-related situations, this also helps girls to contact with computing early, engage girls and via these give more time to broader their knowledge about informatics. Lastly educating boys and teaching with a multidisciplinary approach, we can overcome the learning environment barrier. It is not possible to solve the under-representative of women in the IT sector and inadequate participation of girls in informatics by only educating girls. This is a problem that will be solved by changing stereotypes and society's points of view. Boys are also part of this problem and an important part of the change. In addition, multidisciplinary teaching methods will support girls to discover and understand their own potential. Research shows that by educating teachers [32] or encourage them to use multidisciplinary methods girls can find different ways to understand and connect informatics.

As can be seen, the existence of certain barriers and strategies are strongly connected, even though they are distinct from each other. These barriers can harm an individual's self-confidence, which is considered to be one of the core barriers. This self-confidence can be negatively impacted by unsupportive family members or teachers. Additionally, exposure to negative behaviors from male peers in a classroom setting or experiencing failures due to ineffective teaching methods can also have a similar effect on self-confidence. Conversely, an individual who receives support from their family and/or teachers in their decision-making can strengthen their self-confidence and become more resilient against potential negative experiences in the classroom. All of those barriers also include strategies on their own and all those strategies effects each other.

5   Conclusion

This study aimed to identify effective strategies to encourage girls to pursue study informatics. The study was designed with a qualitative approach to understanding the experiences of the participants better. Thus, it complements the prevailing literature, which is predominantly focused on quantitative research. To identify the effective strategies, first, we discussed the barriers with the participants and we determine four common barriers: confidence, unsupportive environment, lack of interest, and learning environment.

According to the results, mentorship programs and role models are effective strategies to overcome the confidence barrier. The implementation of mentorship programs within school settings can help girls as a means of bolstering their self-confidence regarding their ability to pursue careers in informatics and creating a pathway to pursue their informatics career. Females who have achieved success within the informatics industry can be highly effective in inspiring young girls and cultivating their self-assurance in their ability to attain success within this field. As such, these female professionals can serve as pivotal role models for young girls considering careers in informatics, enhancing their confidence levels in the process.

Results showed that aware teachers and collaboration with parents are effective strategies to overcome the unsupportive environment barrier. Educators who possess a comprehensive understanding of the benefits of informatics in relation to female students are pivotal in guiding them toward fulfilling career opportunities. Hence, arranging informative seminars and training sessions for teachers can foster an increased awareness of informatics and their pivotal roles in empowering female students. Furthermore, parents play a crucial role in shaping the career aspirations of their daughters. Therefore, forging partnerships with parents through the organization of seminars can serve as a pivotal strategy in promoting greater awareness and understanding of informatics. Additionally, facilitating workshops that encourage parental participation in informatics activities with their children can represent a viable approach to mitigating entrenched gender stereotypes regarding informatics career paths.

Based on the findings early contact with computing, creating interest through challenges, and broader knowledge about informatics are effective strategies to overcome the lack of interest barrier. Exposure to informatics at early ages can aid girls in identifying their interests in informatics and discovering their aptitudes at an earlier stage. This can potentially prevent the development of prejudices towards informatics and foster greater confidence in their abilities within this field. Interest in informatics also can be created by challenges. Girls can be presented with games that lack pre-designed features, thereby allowing them to create such features through the use of coding. This can prompt their curiosity and make them realize their interest in informatics. Inadequate familiarity with the field of informatics represents another contributing factor to the observed dearth of female interest in this domain. Often, girls associate informatics exclusively with coding, failing to recognize the broad range of areas within the field, encompassing not only coding but also design and other domains. Greater awareness of the diverse areas within informatics can enable female students to locate a sphere in which they can identify with and belong to.

The results demonstrated that educating boys and a multidisciplinary approach in teaching are effective strategies to overcome the learning environment barrier. Boys often display high levels of self-assurance in informatics, potentially engendering feelings of inadequacy and inhibition in girls in the learning environment. Additionally, boys may sometimes condescendingly offer assistance to girls, irrespective of whether they actually require any help. Thus, this behavior may further contribute to girls' questioning of their own competencies or capabilities. Accordingly, it may be beneficial to arrange seminars aimed at educating children regarding the fact that informatics is not exclusively a domain for males and offering guidance on effective modes of communication. The way of teaching is also an effective way to encourage girls to study informatics. Adopting a multidisciplinary approach can represent an efficacious means of enabling female students to comprehend that informatics constitutes an integral component of daily life. Encouraging hands-on projects, in particular, can help girls to recognize their own capacity for achievement, potentially increasing their perception of informatics as a viable career path.

6   Limitations and Future Work

The present study aimed to investigate the experiences of select initiatives, with participants being drawn from said initiatives. However, an examination of the experiences of a more diverse sample, encompassing both boys and girls, would likely augment our comprehension of the phenomenon under consideration. Additionally, as the current study drew participants from a dozen countries, it was not feasible to undertake a long-term investigation utilizing observational methodologies. Thus, future research should involve conducting long-term observational studies to permit a more comprehensive analysis of the impact of the strategies employed. Moreover, while there exist studies on effective strategies, there is currently a dearth of research investigating the effects of these strategies. Therefore, future research endeavors should be directed toward investigating the efficacy of said strategies.

References

1. Bianchi, T.: Distribution of Google employees worldwide in 2021. Statista research report. https://www.statista.com/statistics/311805/google-employee-gender-department-global/. Accessed 27 Nov 2022
2. Dixon, S.: Distribution of Twitter employees worldwide in 2021, by gender and department. Statista research report. https://www.statista.com/statistics/313567/twitter-employee-gender-department-global/. Accessed 27 Nov 2022
3. Pasquali, M.: Distribution of eBay employees worldwide as of December 2021, by gender and department. Statista research report. https://www.statista.com/statistics/315060/ebay-employee-gender-department-global/. Accessed 27 Nov 2022
4. Saxegaard, E., Divitini, M.: CITY: a game to raise girls' awareness about information technology. In: Pozdniakov, S.N., Dagienė, V. (eds.) ISSEP 2019. LNCS, vol. 11913, pp. 268–280. Springer, Cham (2019). https://doi.org/10.1007/978-3-030-33759-9_21
5. Simpkins, S.D., Davis-Kean, P.E., Eccles, S.: Parents' socializing behavior and children's participation in math, science, and computer out-of-school activities. Appl. Dev. Sci. **9**(1), 14–30 (2005)
6. Vekiri, I., Chnoraki, A.: Gender issues in technology use: Perceived social support, computer self-efficacy and value beliefs, and computer use beyond school. Comput. Educ. **51**(3), 1392–1404 (2008)
7. Eccles, J.S.: Gendered socialization of STEM interests in the family. Int. J. Gend. Sci. Technol. **7**(2), 116–132 (2015)
8. Eccles, J.S.: Understanding women's educational and occupational choices: applying the Eccles et al. model of achievement-related choices. Psychol. Women Q. **18**(4), 585–609 (1994)
9. Vekiri, I.: Boys' and girls' ICT beliefs: do teachers matter? Comput. Educ. **55**(1), 16–23 (2010)
10. Stoilescu, D., Egodawatte, G.: Gender differences in the use of computers, programming, and peer interactions in computer science classrooms. Comput. Sci. Educ. **20**(4), 283–300 (2010)
11. Cheryan, S., Master, A., Meltzoff, A.N.: Cultural stereotypes as gatekeepers: increasing girls' interest in computer science and engineering by diversifying stereotypes. Front. Psychol. **6**, 1–8 (2015)
12. Yates, J., Plagnol, A.C.: Female computer science students: a qualitative exploration of women's experiences studying computer science at university in the UK. Educ. Inf. Technol. **27**(3), 3079–3105 (2022)
13. Cheryan, S., Siy, J.O., Vichayapai, M., Drury, B.J., Kim, S.: Do female and male role models who embody STEM stereotypes hinder women's anticipated success in STEM? Social Psychol. Pers. Sci. **2**, 656–664 (2011)

14. van der Molen, J.H.W.: Why do Dutch girls do not choose for science and engineering? A focus on gender stereotypes and a lack of female role models. In: 48th SEFI Annual Conference on Engineering Education, SEFI 2020, pp. 1191–1199. University of Twente, Netherlands (2020)
15. Dasgupta, N.: Ingroup experts and peers as social vaccines who inoculate the self-concept: the stereotype inoculation model. Psychol. Inq. **22**, 231–246 (2011)
16. Happe, L., Buhnova, B., Koziolek, A., Wagner, I.: Effective measures to foster girls' interest in secondary computer science education. Educ. Inf. Technol. **26**, 2811–2829 (2021)
17. Boston, J.S., Cimpian, A.: How do we encourage gifted girls to pursue and succeed in science and engineering? Gift. Child Today **41**(4), 196–207 (2018)
18. Beyer, S., Rynes, K., Perrault, J., Hay, K., Haller, S: Gender differences in computer science students. In: Proceedings of the 34th SIGCSE Technical Symposium on Computer Science Education, pp. 49–53. ACM, USA (2013)
19. Compeau, D.R., Higgins, C.A.: Computer self-efficacy: development of a measure and initial test. MIS Q. **19**(2), 189–211 (1995)
20. Sáinz, M., Eccles, J.: Self-concept of computer and math ability: gender implications across time and within ICT studies. J. Vocat. Behav. **80**, 486–499 (2012)
21. Govender, I., Khumalo, S.: Reasoned action analysis theory as a vehicle to explore female students' intention to major in information systems. J. Commun. **5**, 35–44 (2014)
22. Skyllingstad, D.: An exploration into the lack of female high school students in computer science. www.cs.swarthmore.edu/-newhall/Sky.pdf. Accessed 21 Feb 2022
23. Creswell, J.W.: Qualitative Inquiry and Research Design, 2nd edn. Sage Publications, Thousand Oaks (2007)
24. Byers, P.Y., Wilcox, J.R.: Focus groups: a qualitative opportunity for researchers. J. Bus. Commun. **28**(1), 68–78 (1991)
25. Bogdan, R.C., Biklen, S.K.: Qualitative Research for Education: An Introduction to Theories and Methods, 5th edn. Pearson Education Inc., New York (2007)
26. Tellhed, U., Björklund, F., Strand, K.K.: Sure I can code (but do I want to?). Why boys' and girls' programming beliefs differ and the effects of mandatory programming education. Comput. Hum. Behav. **135**, 107370 (2022)
27. Engin, G.: An examination of primary school students' academic achievements and motivation in terms of parents' attitudes, teacher motivation, teacher self-efficacy and leadership approach. Int. J. Progress. Educ. **16**(1), 257–276 (2020)
28. Ryan, R.M., Patrick, H.: The classroom social environment and changes in adolescents' motivation and engagement during middle school. Am. Educ. Res. J. **38**, 437–460 (2001)
29. Culp, R.H.: Adolescent girls and outdoor recreation: a case study examining constraints and effective programming. J. Leis. Res. **30**(3), 356–379 (1998)
30. Zweig, E. S.: STEM Promotion to Empower and Support Girls and Women: A Cross-University Project in Austria (2023)
31. Nash, J.: Understanding how to interest girls in STEM education: a look at how LEGO® education ambassador teachers engage female students in stem learning. (Doctoral dissertation, University of Florida) (2017)
32. Brotman, J.S., Moore, F.M.: Girls and science: a review of four themes in the science education literature. J. Res. Sci. Teach. Off. J. Nat. Assoc. Res. Sci. Teach. **45**(9), 971–1002 (2008)

Peer-Mentoring for Students with Disabilities – A Preliminary Study in Norwegian Higher Education

Norun C. Sanderson[✉] and Weiqin Chen

OsloMet – Oslo Metropolitan University, P.O. Box 4 St. Olavs Plass, N-0130 Oslo, Norway
nsand@oslomet.no

Abstract. The number of students with disabilities in higher education is increasing. Despite governmental and institutional support, students with disabilities often have poorer progression and are at a higher risk of dropping out than their non-disabled peers. Peer mentoring has been practiced in higher educational institutions to help students with disabilities in successful transition to higher education, participating social activities, enhancing retention, and achieving academic success. However, there is a lack of research concerning different stakeholders involved in peer-mentoring process and their experiences and challenges, particularly in different social contexts. In this study we have carried out interviews with support service personnel, mentors and mentees in the Norwegian context. The results show positive outcomes from the mentoring process as well as challenges that need to be addressed, particularly in the organization of the mentor program and the responsibilities of the different stakeholders. Further research should focus on a wider spectrum of social contexts in which the mentoring programs are organized.

Keywords: Peer-mentoring · Students with disabilities · Higher education

1 Introduction

At a global level, inclusion in higher education is considered in the United Nations Convention on the Rights of Persons with Disabilities (UN CRPD) in Article 24 Education, points 1 and 5 [1]. Inclusive education is also the objective in Goal 4 on Education in the UN Sustainable Development Goals, and inclusive tertiary education particularly addressed in Target 4.3 [2]. In the European Union (EU), targeting inclusive higher education as a social right that needs to be worked towards is stated in Principle 1 of the 2021 European Pillar of Social Rights [3]. Building on this principle, inclusive education and training at European universities is also addressed in the EU 2022 strategy for European universities, particularly in Sect. 4.2 Foster diversity, inclusiveness and gender equality [4].

At the same time, the number of students with disabilities in higher education is increasing. For example, in Europe about 15% of students in higher education reported

M. Antona and C. Stephanidis (Eds.): HCII 2023, LNCS 14021, pp. 393–404, 2023.
https://doi.org/10.1007/978-3-031-35897-5_28

that they are limited in their studies due to a health impairment [5]. In the US it is estimated that about 19% of undergraduate students and 12% of graduate students have disabilities [6]. Most higher education institutions have a support center that provides accommodation to students with disabilities such as sign language interpreting, allowing extra time for completing exams, and providing materials in alternative formats.

However, according to the EUROSTUDENT survey, 36% of students with impairments in higher education rate the public and institutional support they receive as not (at all) sufficient [5]. Students with disabilities often have poorer progression and are at a higher risk of dropping out than their non-disabled peers [7, 8].

Literature has shown that although university services provide support for students with disabilities, peer support, such as buddy-systems and peer mentoring, can help students in participating social activities and achieving academic success [9]. Some studies have demonstrated positive effects of peer support on both students with disabilities [10, 11] and on mentors [12]. Although existing studies have investigated peer-mentoring for students with disabilities in higher education, most of them focused on the experiences and challenges of mentors and mentees. In order to gain a more complete picture of the peer-mentoring, it is important to investigate different stakeholders who are involved in the peer-mentoring process, including disability support services personnel, staff who design and organize the programs, as well as mentors and mentees. Their experiences will be able to provide us with a richer context and a deeper understanding of the peer-mentoring programs.

The goal of this study is to address this gap by carrying out interviews with support service personnel, mentors and student mentees in the Norwegian context. This study is a part of a larger international collaboration project "Peer Learning and Social Support for Students with Disabilities in Higher Education (PLE3SD)" funded by Firah with partners from France, Ireland, Greece, Norway, and UK.

1.1 The Norwegian Context

The right to accommodation for students in higher education in Norway are covered in the Norwegian Act relating to universities and university colleges, Section 4-3c Individual accommodation related to reduced functional ability and special needs[1], and in the Norwegian Act relating to equality and a prohibition against discrimination, Section 21 Right to individual accommodation of pupils and students[2]. The 2021 action plan Sustainability and equal opportunities – a universally designed Norway 2021–2025[3], has a section on Education covering all levels of education and presents some action points for ensuring inclusive education.

---

[1] Lov om universiteter og høyskoler (Act relating to universities and university colleges), §4-3c Individuell tilrettelegging ved funksjonsnedsettelse og særskilte behov, https://lovdata.no/lov/2005-04-01-15/§4-3c.

[2] Act relating to equality and a prohibition against discrimination (Equality and Anti-Discrimination Act) Section 21 Right to individual accommodation of pupils and students: https://lovdata.no/NLE/lov/2017-06-16-51/§21.

[3] Norwegian Ministries: Bærekraft og like muligheter – et universelt utformet Norge 2021–2025, https://www.regjeringen.no/contentassets/51369fe60a0240e4bbd554c54310048d/no/pdfs/handlingsplan-for-universell-utforming.pdf.

Most universities in Norway do not have a mentor program targeted at students with disabilities, as was the case at the university in this study. Many do, however, have university financed student mentor, or buddy, programs for all first-year students, and some also have a buddy-program for international students. In Norway, only students that are enrolled in a work capability assessment program from the Norwegian Labour and Welfare Administration (NAV) are eligible to have a mentor to support them during their studies. Unless the student's institution takes on the responsibility for the mentor initiative, i.e., handles all practical arrangements such as the hiring of a mentor, etc., NAV does not fund the mentor. A contract is made between the student (mentee), the mentor, the university, and NAV. The contract is usually a three-month contract and allows for a certain number of hours mentor-support per week, depending on the student's (mentee's) situation and the decision made by NAV. The mentors are paid by NAV, not the university. The role of the university in this is mainly to help students eligible for mentor support apply (to NAV) for this support and to facilitate hiring an appropriate mentor in cooperation with the student. The mentor is typically a peer student in the same study program, typically a year ahead in their studies than the student receiving support (mentee). After the mentor and mentee have met and the contract signed, they are free to organize their work together themselves. The university support office is available to be contacted in case the mentor and/or mentee have questions or need support during the time of the mentoring.

2   Related Research

Peer-mentoring has been practiced in many contexts such as workplaces and education. According to literature, peer mentoring programs in higher education were found to contribute to increasing levels of wellbeing, integration, and retention for students who received mentoring [13–15].

Regarding peer-mentoring for students with disabilities in higher education, research has also shown positive effects. A recent literature review [16] on evidence-based mentoring programs for students with disabilities shows many benefits for mentees, including facilitating transition and adjusting to universities, providing social and emotional support [17], and better opportunities to participating in social activities that further contribute to enhanced communication skills, self-esteem, and self-efficacy [9]. The improvements on social activities by peer mentoring are more evidenced for students with intellectual and developmental disabilities [18, 19]. The literature review by Cardinot and Flynn [16] has also identified benefits for mentors such as enhancing social and communication skills, building relationships with peers, and becoming more committed to their universities [12, 17, 20]. Some mentors also consider the experience as a way to increase their potential in the labor market [12].

In addition to the benefits for both mentors and mentees, studies have also found challenges in peer-mentoring for students with disabilities in higher education. For example, mentors reported that developing mentor-mentee relationship [17] and setting up boundaries are challenging, and they feel inadequate in their role as a mentor [12]. Some studies have identified challenges in designing a suitable evaluation plan and measuring the effectiveness of the mentoring program [12, 20–22].

3 Method

In this study we have adopted a qualitative method for collecting data concerning experiences in relation to peer-mentoring for students with disabilities in higher education. Semi-structured interviews were conducted with three groups of participants representing support services, mentors and mentees. The participants were recruited with help from staff at the university support service, forwarding a request for participation to students that were either employed as mentors or receiving support as mentees at the time. The interviews took place in September 2021. All interviews were conducted via Zoom and each interview lasted 20–25 min. The interview data was transcribed and analyzed using the conventional content analysis approach [23]. The participants in this study include

- two female employees (one works in the university support office and the other works in the faculty administration as contact point for students with disabilities in the faculty),
- two mentors (one female and one male) who were both students at Master level in health and social sciences disciplines,
- one disabled student who received support from a mentor (female) who was a student at Master level in health sciences.

When interviewing the support service personnel, the questions focused on the support services provided, responsibilities, the process when disabled students seek mentors, and peer-mentoring practices. For mentors, the questions concerned how the contact between mentors and mentees were established, if and what types of training they received, the types of support provided to mentees, the motivation for being a mentor, the benefits for mentors, and general experiences and challenges. For the mentee, we asked about the initial contact, the types of support received, comparing experiences and outcome with and without support from the mentor, and general experiences and challenges.

The procedure for recruitment of participants, data collection, and secure data storage was approved by the Norwegian Agency for Shared Services in Education and Research – SIKT[4] in August 2021, ensuring secure handling of personal data. The transcribed interviews were fully anonymized.

4 Results

The interviewed mentors and mentee all have an educational background within health or social science and were at master level (one had already completed their master's degree). All had been working for some years before going back to university for further study. Both mentors also had much previous work experience within health and caring professions. However, only one of them said they had known people with disabilities in their personal life. Thus, both mentors had much professional experience with people with disabilities or other health-related challenges, which they said they found to be

---

[4] Norwegian Agency for Shared Services in Education and Research – SIKT, https://sikt.no/en/home.

very useful in their role as peer mentors. One of the mentors had been a mentor for three students, while the other was mentor for the first time. The mentee had only experience with one mentor.

One of the mentors had previously (before becoming a mentor) experienced fellow students that struggled or that had disabilities and often had helped these students as their peer student without it being formally a mentor role. When the mentors were asked about why they chose to become a mentor, one explained that they felt they mastered the academic subjects well and had more to offer, and that being a mentor was something that could make their studies more meaningful, while the other mentor said that it was the mentee's need for support that they found compelling, and that they just wanted to contribute in some way if they could. The more experienced mentor commented that they found their first period as a mentor so rewarding that they immediately accepted when another opportunity to be a mentor came along.

4.1 Recruitment

The presented results are primarily based on the interviews with the two university- staff members, supplemented with information from the interviewed mentee and mentors.

The university in this study does not have a formal mentor program for students with disabilities, thus the only option available is to get funding for a mentor via NAV, as explained in the Norwegian context. Since the support service at the university in this study is relatively small, they are dependent on involving administrative staff at the faculty where the mentee is enrolled. Mentors are usually recruited the same way as student assistants, by advertising vacant positions for the students at the university. Sometimes, students that have been mentors or that are otherwise qualified, are contacted directly by the university support office.

When a decision has been made regarding who to hire as a mentor, a meeting is arranged between the faculty administration, the university support office, and the mentor and mentee for signing the contract. At this meeting, they go through the specifics of the arrangement, such as the number of weekly hours, and some practical information such as where to find relevant information and who to contact if they need help from the faculty administration or the university support office.

Recruitment Criteria. The criteria for becoming a mentor are academic accomplishments (grades) and they must have good social competence. It is also preferred that the peer mentor is enrolled in the same study program as the mentee, although that is not always possible. The university support office arranges interviews with qualified applicants. The student seeking a mentor takes part in the interviews, as the selection of the mentor is very much up to the student and how they feel they connect with the applicant.

Follow-up. After this first meeting, the university support office or faculty administration mainly follow up through monitoring the academic achievements (exam results) by the student that receives support (the mentee), and help the student apply for further funding, and similar, but they do not have the capacity to follow up the mentor and mentee relationship any further. The support office also investigates cases where either the mentor or mentee no longer wants to continue the arrangement to try to disclose what lies behind this decision.

Training. There is no formal training for mentors for students with disabilities at the university in this study, due to the lack of capacity at the university support office. There is however some general mentor training available from people at the university library for student mentors for first year students. The two mentors we interviewed had not been offered any training in conjunction with their positions as mentors for students with disabilities. One of them said that they just did what they thought were expected based on what they discussed at the first meeting where representatives from the support office and faculty administration also were present.

4.2   The Interaction Between Mentor and Mentee

The mentor and mentee are free to organize their work together themselves, i.e., what kind of support is needed and when and where they meet, as long as they stay within the fixed number of hours per week in accordance with their contract. One mentor explained that they usually scheduled their meetings week by week, sometimes a couple of weeks ahead in time, and opted for flexibility so that a meeting quickly could be arranged if the mentee asked for this. However, the mentor emphasized that they took care to stay within the fixed number of hours per week. The mentee shared that the fixed hours of mentor support each week also covered time that the mentor needed to prepare for meetings, read through any written work sent by the mentee, and answer emails and questions, in addition to the time spent in the meetings. They also mentioned that some periods were more demanding than others and therefore more support was needed at those times, e.g., when an exam or an assignment deadline was coming up.

Communication Channels. Due to the COVID pandemic, most of the meetings between mentors and mentees had been online using Teams or Zoom, but all three students stated that if the situation had been different, they most likely would have had physical meetings, and one of the mentors said they now only had physical meetings with their mentee. The mentee shared that s/he initially had felt uncomfortable with online meetings and wanted to avoid it, but eventually got so accustomed to using it that s/he felt quite comfortable with it. They also mentioned communicating via phone calls and messages, e.g., using Messenger, mainly for scheduling meetings.

Type of Support. The type of support mentors give varies with the individual mentee's needs. Commonly, they need help with structuring their work as a student, getting started with tasks, reading, attend lectures, keep deadlines and appointments, plan their work with an assignment, required coursework, etc. Some may need academic support related to specific subjects, e.g., mathematics, or in conjunction with required practical training. While others may need a kind of study partner or someone to discuss academic subjects with or that can confirm that what they are doing is going in the right direction, e.g., related to coursework or preparing for an exam, as shared by one of the mentors. One mentor supporting a student during the required practical training said the support given concerned both the subject itself and the mentee as a professional in the field, and that s/he also had tried to provide some stability and strengthen the mentee's motivation in a situation where there had been much uncertainty concerning the required practical training.

The mentee shared that it was very helpful to discuss course-related topics with the mentor and that the mentor, when given a concrete issue, sometimes shared their own previous work on a similar issue as an example to read and discuss together in a meeting. The mentor also helped the mentee understand difficult topics from the required reading in a course and provided help to find Norwegian terms for some of the English terms in the course curriculum, because much of the required literature on higher levels of education in Norway are only available in English.

The Value of the Mentor Support Given. One of the staff members interviewed said that many students have had good results from having a mentor, and that sometimes the arrangement works very well, but it is difficult to identify what works well and not. Both mentors evaluated the support they provided as very important to the mentee, one also emphasized the importance of "having someone believe in you" and to communicate this to the mentee. One mentor shared that "one of them [mentee] said very, very clearly that it would not have been possible if there had not been such a mentor arrangement".

Experience with the Mentor-Mentee Relationship. The interviewed students said they experienced the interaction with their mentor/mentee(s) as mainly positive, with good rapport and without any major conflicts or misunderstandings. The mentee revealed that getting to know the mentor and discovering that s/he was "not an A-student ... [but] a bit like me" was a particularly positive experience. The mentee also appreciated that they in their meetings could share their experiences with the same courses, or even chat about what kind of jobs they wanted to apply for after their studies or what the topic of their master's theses was.

To ensure good communication and quality of support, one mentor explained that s/he actively tried to ask the mentee about their preferences when it came to how they communicated and how the mentee wanted to do things. The mentor emphasized that it is important to pause for a bit and check out if all is good, even ask "does this work well?" and to talk about these things, and if necessary, make some adjustments. The mentor that communicated with the mentee via a sign interpreter explained that s/he tried to adjust their way of communication to this new unfamiliar situation, through for example consciously using more body language and looking at the mentee when s/he talked via the interpreter.

Challenges in the Mentor-Mentee Interaction. One of the staff interviewed explained that they typically only get feedback when the mentor-mentee interaction does not work out well. For example, some mentors experience that mentees are very inconsistent and do not do what they agreed on or just disappear, or similar, and sometimes mentees do not really want a mentor because they feel it is too demanding, too many requirements. One mentor shared that s/he was feeling uncertain of what the mentee "really wants" and that s/he has offered support, but the mentee seemed reluctant to accept the support. This mentor also sometimes experienced the mentee a bit evasive, keeping things to herself/himself and suddenly cancelling meetings without giving a reason, etc. The mentor however emphasized that the contact and communication was good between them.

Another challenge experienced by one of the mentors was that the mentee and mentor needed a sign interpreter to communicate during meetings, which was unfamiliar to the mentor and took some time to get used to. One issue mentioned by the mentee is that the exam periods for the mentors and mentees usually coincided, and it would take a bit longer before the mentor responded in these periods, which was not optimal since s/he experienced exam periods as being particularly stressful.

The interviews also revealed that a mentor can feel insecure about how to deal with or who to contact in cases where a mentee might need more support or different support than the peer mentor can give. And that in such cases, being aware of one's limits and being clear on what is within the mentor's role and what is not, can become important for the mentor. Examples presented in the interviews were amongst other situations where the mentee needed more hours of support than the mentor contract allowed, a case where the mentor felt s/he had to explain clearly to the mentee that s/he was not their therapist, and what to do if the mentor fears the mentee's challenges are too great to complete the study or course. "Who to contact about all these issues, I am not quite sure about that," one of the mentors said.

4.3 Potential Improvements

Based on the interviews, we have found several areas with potential for improvement.

Good Mentors Can be Difficult to Find, and Sufficient Training is Essential. The university in this study at times had struggled to find suited mentors and did not currently offer training to mentors. One interviewee said that ideally, there should be a pool of mentors that could be contacted, and mentors should get the appropriate training, but it seemed clear that due to limited resources this was currently difficult to achieve at the university in this study. It was also clear from the interviews that some students may be better suited for a mentor role than others, which is something that could be related to age and life experience as well as to relevant educational background or previous professional experience. "I don't think just any student can be a mentor, I don't think so!", one interviewee said.

Ensuring Continuity in the Mentor-Mentee Relationship and Support. Partly because peer-mentors complete their studies and leave university and start working, but also because of a mismatch between the NAV contract and the university semester. The current length of the NAV contract (number of months) is much shorter than the length of the contract given to student assistants and the length of the university semester.

Systematic Recruitment, Training, Follow-up, and Evaluation. Although some feedback reaches the university support office, particularly when things do not work out well between the mentor and mentee, there is no systematic evaluation of all mentor-mentee co-operation at the university in this study. Evaluation only takes place in cases where the mentor and mentee continue their cooperation for more than one semester. It was expressed through the interviews that gathering information for evaluation should be done regularly. The importance of methodical and planned recruitment, training, follow-up, and evaluation was emphasized by the interviewees, as one interviewee said, "It is important to emphasize the significance of working with this in a systematic way."

Need for a Supporting Group for Mentors and Mentees. The interviews revealed that there can be many large and small challenges in the interaction between the mentor and mentee, and that the mentor (and perhaps also the mentee) sometimes can feel insecure about how to handle some situations. And in some cases, being aware of one's role and limits as a mentor may be important. Having a support group that gives the opportunity to share experiences and good advice with other peer mentors and students receiving support might be valuable for both mentors and mentees during their work together.

Information to Eligible Students Regarding the Possibility for a Peer Mentor. It also became clear through the interviews that students did not know that this kind of (mentor) support existed until they were in contact with the university support office either as an applicant for a mentor position or seeking support in their studies. Ensuring that information about this option is available might be good to ensure students that are eligible for this kind of support know about it.

5   Discussion

This preliminary study has confirmed many findings from previous studies, such as the benefits for mentees and challenges faced by mentors. This study has also contributed to new understanding of the roles and challenges of different stakeholders in mentoring process.

The support office and the mentor program staff play an important role in ensuring the success of peer-mentoring. They manage and oversee the whole process from program design, recruitment (strategy, criteria and screening), and training to soliciting feedback from both mentors and mentees and providing support and guidance for mentors [12, 17]. The university in this study does not have a formal mentor program for students with disabilities. The limited resources do not allow support service staff to carry out many of the important management, monitoring and supporting tasks. This challenge was addressed in Hillier et al. [12] where a graduate student was recruited to manage the day-to-day logistics of the program. In addition, mentor programs often involve different faculties working together with the support office, such as the Faculty of Education and Department of Psychology in Roberts & Birmingham [17]. Such partnership is valuable for the quality of the program, in the meantime, could also help to address the resource challenge in the support services.

In our study, mentees were found to often play a leading role in mentor-mentee interaction. First, a mentee participates in the interviews with potential mentors identified by the support service and decides which of them is most suitable. During the mentoring process, it is the mentee's needs that decide the types of help a mentor provides, whether it is about course work, motivation, or time management. In other words, the mentors adapt their activities according to the mentee's needs. The support services also try their best to accommodate the needs of the students with disabilities who seek mentors. This could be considered as a mentee-centered approach [17]. Such an approach requires that mentees are able communicate their needs and wishes to their mentors and support service staff, which in itself is a skill that mentees may develop through interacting with mentors.

In Norway, different from many other countries, understanding the different responsibilities between the Norwegian Labour and Welfare Administration (NAV) and support services in higher education institutions is important for students with disabilities who need mentors. This difference is not always clear for students, particularly first-year students. In our study, we have also found the duration for funding (3 months) provided by NAV does not match the semester length, which caused confusion and challenges for students with disabilities who expect to have a mentor throughout the whole semester. According to [24], mentor programs with significant outcomes were often longer in duration (over 6 months).

One of the limitations of this preliminary study is the small number of participants who are all from the same higher education institution in south of Norway. This limitation has a negative effect on the generability of the results. Nevertheless, the data we have collected provided us with a good understanding of the mentoring process and challenges in the Norwegian context. After we completed the interviews, the Directorate for Higher Education and Skills (HKDir) published a more comprehensive study aiming at understanding the benefits and the organization of the mentor program in NAV for students with disabilities in higher education. The study has confirmed many of our findings concerning organizational and practical challenges [25].

6 Conclusion and Future Work

In this preliminary study we have conducted interviews with different stakeholders including two disability support staff, two mentors and one mentee. We have identified positive outcomes from the mentoring process as well as challenges that need to be addressed. Several of the challenges could be attributed to the lack of a formal peer-mentoring program in the university. A carefully designed program with suitable structure, recruitment strategies, matching mechanism, and appropriate training for mentors as well as good supporting groups that can facilitating the mentoring process and providing timely supports for both mentors and mentees, will be able to address many of identified challenges and contribute to the success of the program [16].

As this preliminary study and the study by HKDir [25] have shown, the social context and the organization of mentoring programs play an important role for the success of programs. It involves not only support service, mentors and students with disabilities in higher education, but also national policies, agencies and other organizations such as NGOs. Therefore, future studies should investigate a wider spectrum of social contexts in which the mentoring programs are organized.

Acknowledgement. We would like to thank the funding agency Firah and all partners in the PLE3SD project. Thanks also to all participants of the study for their valuable input.

References

1. United Nations. Convention on the Rights of Persons with Disabilities, Article 24 Education. https://www.un.org/development/desa/disabilities/convention-on-the-rights-of-persons-with-disabilities/article-24-education.html. Accessed 10 Feb 2023
2. United Nations, Sustainable Development Goal 4 Education, Target 4.3, https://sdgs.un.org/goals/goal4. Accessed 10 Feb 2023
3. European Commission/EACEA/Eurydice. Towards equity and inclusion in higher education in Europe. Eurydice report. Publications Office of the European Union, Luxembourg (2022)
4. European Commission. Commission Communication on a European strategy for universities, January 2022 (2022). https://education.ec.europa.eu/sites/default/files/2022-01/communication-european-strategy-for-universities.pdf
5. Hauschildt, K., Gwosć, C., Schirmer, H., Wartenbergh-Cras, F.: Social and Economic Conditions of Student Life in Europe: Eurostudent VII 2018–2021 Synopsis of Indicators. wbv (2021)
6. National Center for Education Statistics. U.S. Department of Education: Digest of Education Statistics, 2017(2018–070) (2019)
7. Weedon, E.: The construction of under-representation in UK and Swedish higher education: Implications for disabled students. Educ. Citizenship Soc. Justice 12(1), 75–88 (2017). https://doi.org/10.1177/1746197916683470
8. Hubble, S., Bolton, P.: Support for disabled students in higher education in England. Commons Library Briefing, 28 July 2020 (2020)
9. Hillier, A., Goldstein, J., Tornatore, L., Byrne, E., Johnson, H.M.: Outcomes of a peer mentoring program for university students with disabilities. Mentor. Tutor. Partnership Learn. 27(5), 487–508 (2019). https://doi.org/10.1080/13611267.2019.1675850
10. Lucas, R., James, A.I.: An evaluation of specialist mentoring for university students with autism spectrum disorders and mental health conditions. J. Autism Dev. Disord. 48(3), 694–707 (2018)
11. Siew, C.T., Mazzucchelli, T.G., Rooney, R., Girdler, S.: A specialist peer mentoring program for university students on the autism spectrum: A pilot study. PLoS ONE 12(7), e0180854 (2017)
12. Hillier, A., Goldstein, J., Tornatore, L., Byrne, E., Ryan, J., Johnson, H.: Mentoring college students with disabilities: experiences of the mentors. Int. J. Mentor. Coach. Educ. 7(3), 202–218 (2018). https://doi.org/10.1108/IJMCE-07-2017-0047
13. Collings, R., Swanson, V., Watkins, R.: The impact of peer mentoring on levels of student wellbeing, integration and retention: a controlled comparative evaluation of residential students in UK higher education. High. Educ. 68(6), 927–942 (2014). https://doi.org/10.1007/s10734-014-9752-y
14. Chester, A., Burton, L.J., Xenos, S., Elgar, K.: Peer mentoring: Supporting successful transition for first year undergraduate psychology students. Aust. J. Psychol. 65(1), 30–37 (2013)
15. Crisp, G., Cruz, I.: Mentoring college students: A critical review of the literature be-tween 1990 and 2007. Res. High. Educ. 50(6), 525–545 (2009)
16. Cardinot, A., Flynn, P.: Review of evidence-based mentoring programmes for students with disabilities from 2010 to 2021. Galway: Centre for Pedagogy and Public Engagement Research, School of Education, NUI Galway (2022). https://doi.org/10.13025/w9ta-9770
17. Roberts, N., Birmingham, E.: Mentoring university students with ASD: A mentee-centered approach. J. Autism Dev. Disord. 47(4), 1038–1050 (2017)
18. Ames, M.E., McMorris, C.A., Alli, L.N., Bebko, J.M.: Overview and evaluation of a mentorship program for university students with ASD. Focus Autism Other Develop. Disab. 31(1), 27–36 (2016)

19. Culnane, M., Eisenman, L.T., Murphy, A.: College peer mentoring and students with intellectual disability: Mentors' perspectives on relationship dynamics. Inclusion **4**(4), 257–269 (2016)
20. Krisi, M., Nagar, R.: The effect of peer mentoring on mentors themselves: A case study of college students. Int. J. Disab. Develop. Educ. 1–13 (2021)
21. Suciu, M.: Une mentoring program for students living with autism spectrum disorders (ASDS). JANZSSA **44**, 55–59 (2014)
22. Tobajas, F., De Armas, V., Cabello, M.D., Grijalvo, F.: Supporting students with special needs at university through peer mentoring. In: 2014 IEEE Global Engineering Education Conference (EDUCON), pp. 701–705. IEEE (2014)
23. Hsieh, H.-F., Shannon, S.E.: Three approaches to qualitative content analysis. Qual. Health Res. **15**(9), 1277–1288 (2005). https://doi.org/10.1177/1049732305276687
24. Lindsay, S., Hartman, L. R., Fellin M.: A systematic review of mentorship programs to facilitate transition to post-secondary education and employment for youth and young adults with disabilities. Disab. Rehabilit. **38**(14), 1329–1349 (2016). https://doi.org/10.3109/096 38288.2015.1092174
25. Olaussen, E.J., Jørgensen, L.: Mentor for studenter med funksjonsnedsettelse: En kartlegging av nytteverdi og organisering av ordningen. Tungesvik, R. (ed.), Rapport nr. 14/2022, HK-Dir (2022). ISSN 2703-9102

Application of RFID Technology to Create Inclusive Educational Resources

Aías Sentíes Maqueda, José Manuel Olais-Govea, Daniel Alejandro Cuellar-Reynaga,
Exal Julián Rosales Salas, Elizabeth Torres Zafra, Yoxann Yakmeni Flores Sayavedra,
José Rafael Aguilar-Mejía, and Cristina G. Reynaga-Peña[✉]

Tecnologico de Monterrey, Av. Eugenio Garza Sada 2501, Monterrey, NL, México
cristina.reynaga@tec.mx

Abstract. Educational inclusion is a growing challenge faced by the various educational systems in the world. Providing quality education to students who encounter barriers due to physical, cognitive, or psychosocial disabilities is a major stumbling block, according to the Sustainable Development Goals.

In the Latin American context, a current area of opportunity is the shortage of didactic resources to support inclusive education for the teaching-learning process of elementary school children. Nevertheless, these resources must be low-cost, engaging, and universally accessible to all students. The use of technology facilitates autonomy and independence during the interaction of students with learning objects and is highly attractive for youth who nowadays are technology natives; then, incorporating technological elements to inclusive didactic resources is a must in today's classrooms.

Previously, we have reported the use of an academic makerspace to promote the involvement of students of engineering and other disciplines in the development of technology-based inclusive didactic resources upon the principles of Universal Design for Learning (UDL). The project initially focused on inclusion for visually impaired students and eventually derived into a continuous social service program called *Edumakers for inclusion*, which currently extends to three campuses of Tecnologico de Monterrey in Mexico. This program relies on the multi-disciplinary nature of the collaboration between students, which enriches the generation of ideas, development, and final products.

This paper reports on the incorporation of radio frequency identification (RFID) technology to create tactile 3D-printed representations of scientific concepts in the form of didactic resources. Using this technology, an RFID reading system was built to identify and respond to specific NFC tags, triggering the reproduction of pre-loaded audio with information about the object to which the tag is attached. To show the incorporation of this concept, we present two examples of the didactic resources we have produced with the RFID technology. They consist of three-dimensional representation of maps of Mexico and the human body's internal organs. Organs were 3D-printed from curated files found in open-source 3D model repositories, using criteria such as scientific accuracy and appropriateness for educational purposes at the elementary school level. Audios describing the organ's structure and functioning were elaborated for each organ. Each piece of the featured organs possesses an NFC tag that, when the organ is approximated to the RFID reader, signals the reproduction of the audio.

This material sets an example of how the technological basis of RFID allows the generation of a structural set of materials of inclusive nature. In this case, it was applied to elementary school topics, but it can extend to any other subject of varied areas of knowledge. The resulting products can be engaging for any student while they are also accessible to visually impaired users, facilitating teacher's work. But furthermore, their characteristics also help envisioning a new format of teaching intervention that permits decentralization of the teacher and gives way to more autonomy for students with disabilities. In the near future, as more didactic resources of this type are produced and inserted in UDL-designed didactic sequences, it will be possible to see their effects toward reaching the education goals for all.

Keywords: Educational innovation · Inclusive education · RFID Technology · 3D printing · UDL · Higher education

1   Introduction

Today, achieving sustainable economic development characterized by integral growth is becoming a global concern [1]. This deficiency is sharply exacerbated in developing countries, where inequalities increase for populations in a vulnerable situation; among them, people with physical, cognitive, and/or psychosocial disabilities are some of the most affected [2]. The notion of inclusive growth [3] is widely seen as a key ingredient for sustainable development. This contemplates an education that pursues equity-based access to the curricula to protect and foster a higher educational level of students who may present barriers to quality education [4]. Promoting successful learning in this group, at risk of being excluded from upward socioeconomic mobility [5], is particularly challenging even for inclusive schools [6].

A possible strategy to advance education issues based on equity lies in the use of new information and communication technologies (ICT) [7] if they are inclusive and accessible to all. The role of ICTs in general education is limitless: they can be included as part of the curriculum, may constitute a teaching system, serve as a didactic resource or can be a powerful tool to improve the pedagogy of the teaching-learning process [8]. This way, the incorporation of ICTs into school processes can turn education to be more interactive and inclusive instead of passive and restrictive.

In the Latin American context, inclusive scholarly attention for children up to secondary education is still in progress and has become a priority, as this formative stage is part of the fundamental education to which every citizen has a right [9]. Because nowadays most children have an intrinsic knowledge of the use of technology, ICTs can be a powerful tool to support the teaching in inclusive education, enhancing the learning experience of children with disabilities. This is in line with the idea that technological developments can allow them to improve their quality of life [10].

Although contemplating an ICT-based curriculum that favors the development of ICT skills for inclusive education is still a distant goal in developing countries, there is room for, and interest in the use of didactic resources for inclusive education which design has a technological base that allows the students with disabilities a free interaction with them

[11]. The autonomy that governs this type of interaction with educational resources induces a self-regulated metacognitive process that generates significant learning in students with a disability [12]. In fact, it has been reported that the successful application of such technologies can make classrooms more inclusive, physical environments more accessible, and teaching and learning content and techniques more in tune with learners' needs [13]. Therefore, designing inclusive educational materials focused on using new technologies has the potential of increasing the attention and enthusiasm of teachers for their use. However, these designs, to be inclusive, face challenges such as the selection of which new technologies can be incorporated to address specific topics of the disciplines that are the subject of study in primary education [14]. Here is where Universal Design for Learning (UDL) principles must be taken into consideration for the design and manufacture of low-cost materials that are universally accessible to all students [15]. The need for engineering sciences to participate in the development of this type of materials is essential since, par excellence, technological developments lie in engineering [16]. So, a natural route to generate inclusive educational materials is to promote engineering design processes that consider the principles of UDL from their inception [17]. This has the potential of generating a platform of educational material resources that fulfills the primary learning objectives of autonomy, inquiry, creativity, and innovation.

We recently presented academic maker spaces as creative spaces in which undergraduate students with different backgrounds coexist and interact immersed in an active learning process that involves fostering inclusion practices [18]. In that space, students are supervised by specialists and learn to use various technologies such as 3D printing, additive manufacturing, programming, mechatronic elements, and cyber-physical systems, among others that are available in this collaborative space. We have also reported how in this environment students are free to generate novel and engaging projects using the available materials, prioritizing their technical knowledge and skills as well as their collaborative teamwork, developing problem-solving and complex thinking capabilities [19]. Under the slogan of problem-solving learning, this technical and intellectual coexistence is fertile for the design of inclusive materials with a robust technological base, pursuing the principles of UDL. This environment and interactions provide a competence development approach that fits professional-level students perfectly, using challenge-based learning as the backbone of this process.

In the present work, we are interested in reporting the design process of two didactic projects that incorporate RFID technology: one is a map of regions and topography of Mexico, and the second one is the human body as a didactic material for learning human anatomy. Both were designed based on radio frequency identification (RFID) technology to create 3D-printed tactile representations of scientific concepts as teaching resources.

2   Theoretical Framework

The Universal Design for Learning (UDL) framework provides guidelines to improve and optimize teaching, so the curriculum is accessible and engaging for all students [20]. It is based on scientific insights on how humans learn. By considering all elements of the curriculum, UDL aims to provide all individuals with equal learning opportunities. One of the three UDL principles is to present information making use of multiple forms of representation, which can be accomplished by employing multi-sensory teaching/learning materials and multi-modal resources. For example, a UDL didactic object can present features such as being visually attractive, providing audible information or videos, incorporating a variety of textures, or activities that include the use of smell. UDL proposes that providing multiple forms of representation in conjunction with multiple forms of action and expression, and multiple forms of engagement, stimulates in students the interest and motivation for learning, makes the student resourceful, strategic and goal directed.

Our group has previously designed and produced kits of technology-based three-dimensional didactic materials based on UDL guidelines. Some of those materials were described elsewhere [18, 19, 21] and have characteristics like contrasting colors, tactile features such as textures, and audible information. In this paper, we have continued improving those features during the creation of tactile 3D-printed representations of scientific concepts for their use as didactic resources, with the incorporation of RFID technology.

3   Methods

This work relies on the involvement of students of engineering and other disciplines in the development of technology-based inclusive didactic resources [18, 19]. The maker space where this work took place is the *Innovaction Gym*, a makerspace within Tecnologico de Monterrey. The engineering students who participated were formally enrolled in a curricular space that, within their study plan, corresponds to their social service, where they collaborate for at least 400 h each of them. Among multiple options, they chose to be part of this on-going project, called *Edumakers for inclusion* where they team with students from various professional backgrounds and can register each school period.

The selection of topics on which didactic resources were to be made depended entirely on the interest of the participants and based on an identified need of the target population in the Mexican education context.

3.1   The Design Processes

For the design of all didactic materials, we used an approach following the RIP + Mix method [22] in the understanding of this method as a way of choosing and mixing steps of different methodologies into something "new(ish)" that fits the needs of this project and of its target users. As previously described, the *Edumakers for inclusion* project has involved students and professors from different backgrounds and expertise along its different stages. Then, using a mixing method facilitated taking elements of Design Thinking [23] and Human-Centered Design [24] to allow the involvement of non-designers within the design team, and seeking to take the design intellectual processes away from the design software by moving in into sketching and collaborative working.

For the resources described below, the focus was to assure accessibility for blind learners while UDL features aimed to be engaging for everyone. Then, participants of *Edumakers* worked in multi-disciplinary teams, and each work team proposed and matured ideas through iterative prototyping along the entire process, until a functional advanced prototype was produced. Throughout the various design phases, feedback from experts and potential users was crucial to obtain didactic resources with higher potential to be accessible and inclusive; nevertheless, team participants had a major role in decision-making steps along the way.

Because of the continuous participation of active students, the *Edumakers* group has built and matured as a strong community of makers, where the experience of veterans is strengthened through the involvement in various consecutive projects and sharing of their skills and knowledge is a genuine and unrestricted practice.

Following this methodology and activities, two didactic resources were built with RFID technology. The first didactic resource consisted of a set of two puzzle-like maps of the regions and topographic features of Mexico. Although there are many didactic maps, most are not accessible to blind students, one of our target users. A second didactic resource developed was the human body project, where internal organs are represented for students to learn about basic biology of living organisms. In both cases, the inclusion of RFID technology was chosen to deliver the information it was meant to convey and to make resources interactive and engaging.

3.2 Use of 3D Printing Technology and Open-Source Files

For the didactic set of two map of Mexico, all pieces were designed from two-dimensional images of the concepts represented herein, using a design software to obtain suitable STL files that served for rapid prototyping using 3D printing technology. To facilitate identification of all elements, pieces had textures and contrasting colors. Further copies of the puzzle-like pieces were made of epoxy resin using the original 3D printed pieces as molds.

For the human body project, organs were 3D-printed from curated STL files found in open-source 3D model repositories such as *Thingiverse* and others, using criteria such as scientific accuracy and appropriateness for educational purposes at the elementary school level. In contrast to the map, selection of color did not occur at the printing of pieces but was part of a post-processing procedure.

3.3 Integration of RFID Technology

The didactic resources generated by *Edumakers* incorporate low-cost technologies to make them inclusive and economically accessible. In the products to be described here, radio frequency identification (RFID) technology was selected as the technology of choice that would support interactivity and inclusiveness of the teaching materials. This technology serves to uniquely identify an object using electromagnetic or electrostatic coupling in the radio frequency part of the electromagnetic spectrum. An RFID system consists of tags and readers to exchange information, frequently triggering a previously programmed response.

An RFID reading system was built to identify and respond to specific NFC tags, specifically triggering the reproduction of pre-loaded audios with information about the object to which the tag is attached. Given that the resin pieces for the map were relatively fragile, NFC tags were placed in the bottom of each of the map pieces, which made it possible to be replaced with minimum effort.

Several considerations were taken when designing the RFID reader box, due to the characteristics and context of its use, as the target users were elementary school children. Then, the box had to be robustly built, as it was intended to be transported and utilized in regular classrooms within schools located either in urban or rural contexts. Another important aspect was to take into consideration that, if more materials were further developed using this technology, the same reader could be used without the need to be replaced when new models were generated.

The first version of the RFID reader circuit developed for the Map didactic resource consists of three main electronic components that make up all the functions. Inside of the reader box there is an Arduino Nano, a PN532 RFID reader sensor, a DFPlayer Mini as well as a printed circuit board that connects the components together and supplies power using 4 AA batteries. The PN532 RFID reader can detect and write values on the NFC tag when it is in proximity to the component depending on which mode is selected. The Arduino Nano is the main processing unit that is programmed and distinguishes between each value that is sent and executes the corresponding code that is associated to such a number. The DFPlayer Mini module works as an SD card reader that receives a signal from the Arduino Nano to start reproducing, pause, or increase the volume of the chosen MP3 file that is saved inside of the SD card.

This circuit was enclosed inside of a 3mm acrylic box that was elaborated using the substrative manufacturing method of laser cutting. Each side was designed by CAD Software Fusion 360, with the consideration of being able to use M5 Allen screws to secure the structure as well as the electronic components inside of it. Another important aspect considered was ease of access, so that teachers could be able to switch SD cards without tools and change the batteries using a Philipps screwdriver. The position of the components inside of the box had the RFID sensor on the top part, the volume control knob and power switch on the front, the audio jack and SD card slot on the side and the stop/pause button on the opposite side.

The working mechanism of the RFID reading box is simple. Since each RFID tag contains a different number than the other pieces of the system, the RFID reading sensor reads the number and sends that data to the Arduino. Then, the Arduino is programmed to send a signal to the MP3 player module to start reproducing the audio cue that corresponds to the number identified by the RFID reader module. For example, the 3D printed model of the North region of Mexico has an RFID tag that contains a number "1"; so, when it is placed on top of the RFID reader, it triggers the reproduction of the audio file with the same name. This file naming system and program code allows the user to switch the SD card and utilize another material containing NFC tags easily.

4 Results

4.1 Didactic Maps of México

Following the methodology described above, a set of two puzzle-like maps of Mexico were fabricated (Fig. 1). Each map set consists of pieces representing a) the eight geographical regions of Mexico or b) the fifteen topographic features of the country, such as plains, plateaus, mountain ranges, sierras, and peninsulas. On the latter, a smaller map of Mexico with topographic features was included to facilitate understanding of the overall topography, this map was printed in white resin and inserted next to the larger map. In both map sets, additional pieces were incorporated to hold the NFC tag for pieces that were too small, mainly to avoid interfering with the puzzle assembly.

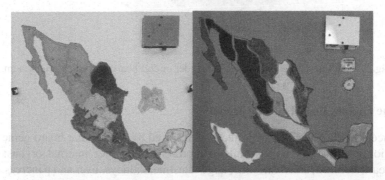

Fig. 1. Interactive maps of Mexico showing the Geographical regions (left), the topography (right).

A single RFID reader box was included in the map set, which was able to reproduce informative audios of both maps. The map pieces and the RFID reader box were held in place using a custom-made support of thick washable foam in contrasting color. The entire set was contained in a larger box for easier transportation.

4.2 Improvements in Electronics and Programming

Modifications in the RFID system (electronic circuit and components) were made to solve frequent but minor inconveniences observed during functioning of the map didactic resource with unexperienced users. Among those changes, some were critical, and others serve to fabricate more efficient prototypes that will better serve target users.

First, in a post-pandemic context, all educational materials touched by children require frequent cleaning. Therefore, to avoid the possibility of damaging the NFC tag that was originally positioned under the map pieces, it was convenient to "hide" the tag inside the pieces.

To improve the efficiency of the microcontroller performance, it was decided to use a Muon Pico microprocessor that operates with a modified CircuitPython open-source software, using libraries to integrate the DF player and the RFID/NFC pair. Such a combination resulted in a seamless and more powerfully built arrangement of the new RFID tag-reader system. Consequently, a new circuit board was also developed, that also allowed incorporation of new components that facilitated its functioning (Fig. 2).

Finally, to avoid the need to change batteries, which implied accessing the interior of the RFID box, the original battery-dependent power supply was substituted by a 5V wall charger. This modification did not have an impact on the efficiency of use of the didactic resource, given that the dimensions of the human body project were larger than the maps, making it less portable than the maps.

All modifications described above were incorporated into the human body project.

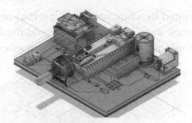

Fig. 2. Diagram of the modified RFID reader circuit board and electronic system.

4.3 The Human Body Didactic Model

The concept of the human body project was inspired by the popular board game called "Operation" (©Hasbro). It was built to represent the major internal organs: brain, lungs, heart, stomach, small intestine, large intestine, kidneys, liver and pancreas, topics reviewed in the elementary school curricula. The reproductive organs were not included, given that the target population was pre-school and elementary school children from first to third grade, and the topic of human reproduction is addressed until 6th grade.

Once the STL files were curated from open-source repositories, the next step of the process for designing the human body consisted of adjusting the scales for printing the organs, so it resembles the proportion and size of an average 10-year-old child. A major modification made before the printing of the scaled models was to digitally segment the object by transforming its STL file, so that each organ was manufactured in two pieces; this allowed attachment of the NFC tag in the interior to be successfully hidden.

After printing and assembling, the entire organs were subjected to post-processing that included applying a soft plastic coat to give a more organic texture, and/or applying color. The organs of the digestive system were complemented by positioning a flexible plastic hose in the beginning of the stomach to represent the esophagus; the flexible hose was also used to connect other organs of the digestive system to give a better understanding of the system's physiology.

As Fig. 3 shows, in the first functional prototype of the human body project, the organs were positioned within a box that was digitally designed to fit their shapes. An underneath support was also built to hold the pieces in their presumed place while allowing exploration by young users.

4.4 Incorporation of Auditory Information

An important feature of the didactic resources produced by *Edumakers* is the addition of audible information related to topics presented in the three-dimensional materials; in fact, this was the main reason for including low-cost technology in their design and manufacturing. The information to be presented had to be scientifically correct and aligned with the learning goals of the object itself, according to the targeted school levels. This information was loaded into the electronic system in the form of audio files which were delivered reproduced by the electronic system as response of the RFID/NFC pair activation.

Fig. 3. The human body internal organs didactic resource.

For the creation of the audio files both projects roughly followed the same pipeline. First, a script was developed by an interdisciplinary team of students that carried out research about representative and fun facts about the didactic model to be described, making sure the information was as concise as possible to avoid long audio durations. Next, the script was revised by education students and professors to make sure that the information was pedagogically adequate, sufficiently descriptive and engaging for both visually impaired and non-visually impaired students at the intended school level. After the script was approved, the audio was recorded using any free recording software or digital application, taking into consideration quality aspects such as the intonation of the narrator's voice, reduction of background noise and clearness of the narration. Next, the recording files were edited using free audio editing software tools such as Audacity, making sure to export the final product in an MP3 format for the files to be compatible with the audio reproducing electronic components. Finally, a last validation occurred with special education teachers to identify if modifications were necessary for better understanding of the information contained.

In the map project, special attention was paid to best representing features of the regions of Mexico. This was accomplished by adding music and sound effects evoking unique characteristics of those places; others were related to the regional culture, such as regional music and dances, with the final goal of providing an enriched and meaningful experience for the users. For the human body, audios describing the organ's structure and functioning were elaborated for each organ.

A unique characteristic of the didactic resources presented in this work is the seeming flexibility of presenting audible information in any language and for any elementary school level, as the storage card can be loaded with different audios, provided that the files are numbered in the respective order within the SD card.

4.5 Future Perspectives and Improvements

Because the design process and technology use have been positively evolving through each project of our work group, it is possible to facilitate the creation of didactic resources for teaching topics in other disciplines in the immediate future. At latter stages, end-users should be more actively involved in the Rip + Mix method for proposing concepts that are difficult to access and for the generation of ideas, not only during the user evaluation stages along the process.

It is also relevant to notice that the functional prototypes produced here are products of a step within a continuous iterative process and, therefore, are still susceptible to more improvements. Particularly, as they will be taken to a diversity of final users who are learning in regular classrooms. Such is the case of the human body project. Also, further work is required to design corresponding didactic sequences for the integration of these and other didactic materials into an inclusive pedagogy, where all children can learn together, verifying that barriers of access to information are reduced.

Although the description of the learning process of higher education students is beyond the scope of this work, it is essential to consider that inclusive didactic materials are scarce in the Latin-American context and their creation is a win-win process where we all learn. Thus, questions are born that are of great interest for educational research in this line, and those related to the participation of higher education students might give light on the impact of this work. For example, (i) How do these type of learning spaces promote the mutual development of didactic and technical skills related to inclusive technologies? (ii) How does the design of technology-based educational materials foster the theories of autonomy, inquiry, creativity, and innovation for higher education students? (iii) What aspects of participating in the project will have an effect in the future professional life of participants?

5   Conclusions

The success of this project and the *Edumakers* work products relies on the multi-disciplinary nature of the collaboration between members of the maker community composed by higher education students. Such diversity enriches the generation of ideas, development, and final products.

RFID has been reported to be useful to enhance visitor's experience in museums [25], or to guide students in laboratory activities [26]. There are clear advantages of using this technology in contrast with other technologies. One of them is its low cost, but also, in contrast to QR codes, it does not need an internet connection to operate, which makes it accessible in many ways, especially for underserved populations.

In the work reported here, the incorporation of RFID technology was applied to generate resources for elementary school topics within Geography and Biology disciplines, such as the regions and topography of Mexico and the Human Body, but the versatility of its use can extend to any other subject or areas of knowledge. One of the strengths of the system developed is that the new Muon Pico-Phyton programmed device is robust enough to read several sets of didactic materials using a single reading device. In addition, the system, from its conception, provides high flexibility, as it is possible to provide audible information in any language by just changing the SD cards. We aim that teachers can make their own audios for children in different school grades, or to adjust to the curricular objectives, when applicable.

Both examples of UDL didactic resources presented in this work can be engaging for any student while they are also accessible to visually impaired users, facilitating the teacher's work in inclusive classrooms. But furthermore, their characteristics also help envision a "new format" of teaching intervention that permits decentralization of the teacher and gives way to more autonomy for students with disabilities. Although autonomous, self-regulated learning with interactive resources is not novel in regular classrooms, in the Latin American context it is in those settings where children with disabilities are included. Soon, as more didactic resources of this type are produced and inserted in UDL-designed didactic sequences, it will be possible to see their effects toward reaching the education goals for all.

Acknowledgement. This work has been financed through Novus project number N21-218 of Tecnológico de Monterrey. The authors wish to acknowledge the financial support of the Writing Lab, Institute for the Future of Education, Tecnológico de Monterrey, Mexico, in presenting this work. Our special thanks to students who participated in the conceptual design and the fabrication of the maps and the human body, especially to Laura Angélica Valadez Rojas, José Antonio Rosales Medina, and Germán E. Flores Cabral. We also want to acknowledge Patricia Torres Sánchez and all past and current members of the community of *Edumakers for inclusion*; their engagement, passion and sharing spirit has been crucial to keep creating inclusive teaching/learning resources for underserved children. Finally, we thank the *Innovaction Gym* colleagues, particularly to Lilia Gómez Flores, Luis Fernando Garza Vera, Alvaro Cheyenne de Jesús Valdez, and Azael Jesús Cortés Capetillo for providing a fertile space to materialize ideas, their enlightening discussions and accompaniment during this work.

References

1. Ziolo, M., Bak, I., Cheba, K.: The role of sustainable finance in achieving Sustainable Development Goals: Does it work? Technol. Econ. Dev. Econ. **27**(1), 45 (2021)
2. Uleanya, C.: Reconceptualising disabilities and inclusivity for the postdigital era: Recommendations to educational leaders. Educ. Sci. **13**(1), 51 (2023)
3. Samans, R., Blanke, J., Corrigan, G., Drzeniek, M.: The Inclusive Growth and Development Report 2015, vol. 13. World Economic Forum, Geneva (2015)
4. Gordon-Gould, P., Hornby, G.: Inclusive education at the crossroads: Exploring effective special needs provision in global contexts. Routledge (2023)
5. Chatzitheochari, S., Velthuis, S., Connelly, R.: Childhood disability, social class and social mobility: A neglected relationship. Br. J. Sociol. **73**(5), 959–966 (2022)
6. DeMatthews, D.E., Serafini, A., Watson, T.N.: Leading inclusive schools: Principal perceptions, practices, and challenges to meaningful change. Educ. Adm. Q. **57**(1), 3–48 (2021)

7. Sarasola Sanchez-Serrano, J.L., Jaén-Martínez, A., Montenegro-Rueda, M., Fernández-Cerero, J.: Impact of the information and communication technologies on students with disabilities. A systematic review 2009–2019. Sustainability **12**(20), 8603 (2020)
8. Mikropoulos, T.A., Iatraki, G.: Digital technology supports science education for students with disabilities: A systematic review. Educ. Inf. Technol. **28**, 3911–3935 (2023)
9. Eleweke, C.J., Rodda, M.: The challenge of enhancing inclusive education in developing countries. Int. J. Incl. Educ. **6**(2), 113–126 (2002)
10. Simpson, C.G., McBride, R., Spencer, V.G., Lodermilk, J., Lynch, S.: Assistive technology: Supporting learners in inclusive classrooms. Kappa Delta Pi Record **45**(4), 172–175 (2009)
11. Nepo, K.: The use of technology to improve education. Child Youth Care Forum **46**(2), 207–221 (2016)
12. Perry, N.E., Mazabel, S., Yee, N.: Using self-regulated learning to support students with learning disabilities in classrooms. In: Handbook of Educational Psychology and Students with Special Needs, pp. 292–314. Routledge (2020)
13. Masih, A.: Effective use of ICT in teacher education for inclusive environment in classroom. Educ. Quest-An Int. J. Educ. Appl. Soc. Sci. **9**(3), 247–251 (2018)
14. Anderson, S.E., Putman, R.S.: Special education teachers' experience, confidence, beliefs, and knowledge about integrating technology. J. Spec. Educ. Technol. **35**(1), 37–50 (2020)
15. Pennazio, V., Bochicchio, F.: From technologies for a few to technologies for all: analysis of inclusive technologies perception in teachers in training. J. e-Learn. Knowl. Soc. **18**(1), 23–33 (2022)
16. Steinfeld, E., Smith, R.O.: Universal design for quality of life technologies. Proc. IEEE **100**(8), 2539–2554 (2012)
17. Bigelow, K.E.: Designing for success: Developing engineers who consider universal design principles. J. Postsecond. Educ. Disab. **25**(3), 211–225 (2012)
18. Reynaga-Peña, C.G., Myers, C., Fernández-Cárdenas, J.M., Cortés-Capetillo, A.J., Glasserman-Morales, L.D., Paulos, E.: Makerspaces for inclusive education. In: Antona, M., Stephanidis, C. (eds.) HCII 2020. LNCS, vol. 12189, pp. 246–255. Springer, Cham (2020). https://doi.org/10.1007/978-3-030-49108-6_18
19. Olais-Govea, J.M., Preval, D.T. Aguilar-Mejía, J.R., Reynaga-Peña, C.G.: Developing soft skills in engineering students through the design and production of educational materials for inclusion. In: 2022 International Conference on Inclusive Technologies and Education (CONTIE), Cartago, Costa Rica, pp. 1–6 (2022)
20. CAST. https://www.cast.org. Accessed 11 Feb 2023
21. Cuellar-Reynaga, D.A., Mendoza-Córdova, M.Y., Ramírez-Marrujo, A.G., Granados, U., Santamaría, D., Reynaga-Peña, C.G.: Touch and learn: Turning simple objects into learning materials. In: International Conference on Inclusive Technologies and Education (CONTIE), San Jose del Cabo, Mexico, 2019, pp. 135–140 (2019)
22. Press, M., Bruce, F., Chow, R., White, H.: Rip+mix: Developing and evaluating a new design method in which the designer becomes a DJ. Presentation for the 9th International European Academy of Design Conference "The Endless End", 4–7 May 2011, Porto, Portugal (2011)
23. Brown, T.: Design thinking. Harv. Bus. Rev. **86**(6), 84 (2008)
24. IDEO. The field guide to human-centered design. IDEO.org. (2015)
25. Hsi, S., Fait, H.: RFID enhances visitors' museum experience at the exploratorium. Commun. ACM **48**, 60–65 (2005)
26. Kao, M.C.: Pedagogical application of RFID technology for hard of hearing children during mathematics and science learning activities. In: 2013 IEEE Frontiers in Education Conference (FIE), pp. 1954–1955. IEEE (2013)

E-Inclusion of People with Disabilities in Vocational and Professional Education and Further Training Organisations in Switzerland: First Results of a Quantitative Survey

Olivier Steiner(✉) and Fabienne Kaiser

University of Applied Sciences Nordwestern Switzerland, Muttenz, Switzerland
olivier.steiner@fhnw.ch

Abstract. This paper presents first results of the quantitative part of the currently running NRP77 project "E-inclusion of people with disabilities in vocational and professional education and further training in Switzerland" (No.: 197423). In the framework of an explorative online survey, 431 professionals from 289 educational organisations assessed the digitalisation, inclusion of people with disabilities (PwD) and digital accessibility of their organisation and, in particular, of their educational offer. The results allow first conclusions to be drawn about the status quo of e-inclusion in vocational and professional education and further training (VPET) organisations in Switzerland and indicate that the type of organisation has a significant influence on in this regard. PwD in VPET organisations in Switzerland often encounter barriers regarding e-accessibility. Inclusion of PWD in VPET organisations is therefore to be sustainably strengthened. At the methodological level the results of a principal component analysis (CATPCA) suggest that the conceptualisation of e-inclusion along the dimensions of *structures*, *practices* and *cultures* proposed by Booth and Ainscow can be a good starting point for further studies on e-inclusion.

Keywords: Digitalisation · Disabilities · E-inclusion · Vocational and Professional Education and Further Training

1 Introduction

Digital technologies[1] are changing the economy and society, organisations, professions and everyday communication in many complex ways and represent a fundamental technical, economic and social challenge of the 21st century [1, 2]. Similarly vocational

---

[1] In the following, digital technologies are understood as all electronic systems operating based on binary code [3]. These include, for example, internet technologies, digital end devices, networked objects, robots and software applications.

© The Author(s), under exclusive license to Springer Nature Switzerland AG 2023
M. Antona and C. Stephanidis (Eds.): HCII 2023, LNCS 14021, pp. 417–433, 2023.
https://doi.org/10.1007/978-3-031-35897-5_30

and professional education and training (VPET)[2] organisations, their infrastructures, arrangements of teaching and support for students are also being profoundly transformed by the implementation of digital technologies. Studies show that digital technologies simplify access to lifelong learning and qualification and thus ultimately to the world of work [4–6]. These potentials can also apply to people with disabilities (PwD). However, we must not assume that the mere presence of digital technologies in VPET organisations is sufficient to ensure digital participation. As the ITU report states: "Maximizing the potential benefit of ICTs [information and communication technologies] requires a proper understanding of the full range of challenges and barriers faced by persons with disabilities in each local context" [7]. For the context of Switzerland the "Civil society report on the First State Report Procedure before the UN Committee on the Rights of Persons with Disabilities" [8] criticises that necessary adaptation measures for the accessibility of information are not sufficiently implemented either at state or cantonal level. Also the vast majority of cantons have not specified the obligation under Art. 21 CRPD to make their information accessible and have not yet implemented it. Accordingly, there is no legal basis at the level of the education ordinances regarding e-accessibility.

Although much is already being done to develop integrative educational offers, research on vocational training and higher education only deals sporadically with the subject of disability, closure mechanisms and the exclusion of PwD as learners or teachers [9–11]. Historical analysis of practical developments in the field refers to the central question of who is defined as in need and capable of education, and who is consequently included in (further) training programs [12]. Still, relevant to the Swiss case is a study by Kobi/Pärli [13] that shows how numerous obstacles make it difficult for students with disabilities to participate equally in higher education. Obstacles in the field of ICT though are not dealt with separately in the study (except for Websites).

Digital elements are increasingly being integrated into concepts of VPET: Education institutions are developing digital offers as supplements to their face-to-face courses in order to respond to the needs of participants and to tap into new target groups [14–16]. Most studies on digitalisation in the education and training for PwD focus on access to and use of the Internet [17–22]. Yet the tendency, observed by Seale et al. [23], to see "digital inclusion in higher education [...] solely in terms of accessibility" persists. Papadopoulos [24] concludes, that for comprehensive participation in (further) training, there must be technical and organisational prerequisites that have an impact on the participation at a teaching sequence or a further education event. These arguments point to the need to analyse inclusion as well as e-inclusion in VPET organisations with a concept encompassing different organisational dimensions.

Such a concept has been provided with the Index for Inclusion by Booth and Ainscow [25] to help schools develop inclusion in their organisation. The Index was developed by the authors in dialogue with experts, teachers and governors and is a resource designed for practical organisational development processes. The Index for Inclusion distinguishes the dimensions of cultures, policies and practices. According to Booth and Ainscow, the

---

[2] *Vocational and professional education and training (VPET)* is a joint task of the Swiss Confederation, the cantons and organisations in the world of work. It is regulated by the Vocational Training Act (Berufsbildungsgesetz) and the Vocational Training Ordinance (Berufsbildungsverordnung).

dimension of cultures contains in particular inclusive attitudes and values of employees of an educational organisation, which guide the decisions on structures (policies) and the actions of employees in everyday educational life. Inclusive policies include support services for teachers and students with disabilities, concepts and strategies for inclusion, and structural measures to ensure accessibility. The dimension of practices further reflects the inclusive cultures and policies in educational action. This includes, for example, actively involving students in the educational process, enabling collaborative learning, developing and sharing inclusive material resources and organising social support.

However, the issues of digitalisation, accessibility to information and e-inclusion are not included in the existing Index for Inclusion. This article aims to describe the operationalisation and analysis of the Index for Inclusion with regard to e-inclusion in VPET organisations.

2 Methods

2.1 Starting Point and Questionnaire Development

The results presented in this paper were developed within the framework of the second work package of the currently running NRP77 project "E-inclusion of people with disabilities: Digital participation in vocational and professional education and further training in Switzerland" (No.: 197423). The project is being carried out at the University of Applied Sciences Northwestern Switzerland, School of Social Work, and it's five work packages address questions at the intersection of *digitalisation, inclusion* and *vocational education and training*. While in the first work package the perspectives on digital participation of PwD and professionals from the field of VPET were reconstructed based on qualitative interviews, the second work package aimed to record the *status quo* regarding e-inclusion in the context of VPET in Switzerland. For this purpose, a trilingual online survey was conducted from June to October 2022, in which professionals from all types of organisations that can be assigned to VPET in Switzerland were surveyed. This includes organisations at upper-secondary level (regular and separative VET organisations) and at tertiary level (colleges of higher education, universities of applied sciences and universities of teacher education), as well as continuing education and training organisations (CET).

As there are currently no comparable instruments for surveying the *status quo* of e-inclusion in the context of vocational education, we developed an instrument specifically for this purpose. In developing the questionnaire, we made use of the Index for Inclusion, which was first published in 2000 by Booth and Ainscow [25] with the subtitle "developing learning and participation in schools"[3]. The Index for Inclusion was developed

---

[3] Although the Index for Inclusion is based on a broad understanding of inclusion, it was used as a framework for this project. For example, it is also recommended by the Monitoring Committee for the Implementation of the UN Convention on the Rights of Persons with Disabilities (CRPD) in Triol for inclusive school development [26]. This suggests that the Index for Inclusion can also be used to foster the inclusion of PwD in educational organisations based on a narrow understanding of inclusion.

by the authors in dialogue with experts, teachers and governors and is thus a resource designed for practical processes of inclusive organisational development. By transferring and adapting Booth and Ainscow's dimensioning of inclusion into *cultures, policies*, and *practices*, we aimed to capture the status quo regarding e-inclusion of learners with disabilities in the context of VPET as holistically as possible. Compared to Booth and Ainscow's index of inclusion, we attempted to complement all three dimensions with items on digital aspects that are relevant to the e-inclusion of PwD. For this purpose, the results of the first work package were used, which provide indications of what currently promotes or hinders the e-inclusion of PwD in the VPET context in Switzerland.

In the operationalisation of the Index for Inclusion, adjustments were made especially in the dimension *policies*: Booth and Ainscow understand this in particular as concepts, strategies and support that are intended to ensure inclusion. In this dimension, however, aspects of the infrastructure of an organisation that enable, or hinder inclusion are missing (except in relation to architectural measures), e.g. – with regard to e-inclusion – ensuring the accessibility of digital platforms and documents for PwD. In the following, this dimension is therefore not called policies but *structures*, as policies in this understanding are contained in structures, e.g., in the form of concepts.

A first version of the conceptualized instrument was presented to two rounds of experts (practical and scientific advisory board). Based on the experts' assessments, some items were reworded or rewritten, and others were excluded. The adapted instrument for assessing e-inclusion was then presented to experts from different types of organisations and language regions in Switzerland for a pre-test ($n = 18$) to finally check the wording, comprehensibility, and acceptance of the items. Based on the comments received, final minor modifications were made.

2.2 Data Collection and Sample Description

The full survey covered around 1280 educational organisations throughout Switzerland. The online survey was sent to the heads of the organisations with the request that they fill it out themselves and forward it within their organisation to people who have a management function in education or training or who deal with the topics of diversity, inclusion of people with disabilities, disadvantage compensation, accessibility, or e-learning.

Within the framework of the survey, extensive assessments on the topics of digitalisation, inclusion of PwD and digital accessibility were collected from 431 professionals. In relation to the population, the response rate is about 23%. For the organisation-specific evaluations, the answers of the professionals surveyed were first assigned to the corresponding organisations[4]. In total, the 431 professionals could be allocated to 289 different organisations. While in three quarters of the organisations one professional completed the survey, in 16% of the organisations two professionals took part. More than three professionals per organisation could be reached rarely.

Regular VET organisations are the most common in the sample, accounting for just over a third. Separate VET organisations for PwD make up a quarter of the sample. Universities of applied sciences account for 17% and colleges of higher education for

---

[4] For this purpose, the respondents created a code at the beginning of the survey, which made it possible to anonymously assign their answers to the corresponding organisation afterwards.

13% of the sample. While CET organisations represent 7% of the sample, universities of teacher education make up the smallest part of the sample with 3%.

Slightly more than half of the professionals surveyed work as (deputy) organisational leaders. Around one third of the professionals have a teaching position and/or are responsible for the coordination of training. Professionals who work in the field of coordination of continuing education represent 14% of the sample. Around every tenth professional surveyed is responsible for a position around digital learning/e-learning, diversity and/or disability-specific concerns. Every twentieth professional is responsible for IT.

2.3 Analyses

Group comparisons were made using inferential statistics. Two statistical tests were performed. The Chi^2 test was used to perform group comparisons for nominal scaled dependent variables. Comparisons of ordinal scaled dependent variables were performed using the Kruskal-Wallis test. To test the model developed in accordance with the Index for Inclusion, Nonlinear Principal Components Analysis (CATPCA) and a Two-Step Cluster Analysis were carried out for the dimension's *structures, practices,* and *cultures* (see Sect. 3.5).

3 Results

3.1 Digitalisation in the Context of VPET in Switzerland

We wanted to know from the respondents how much importance is attached to *digitalisation* in their organisation. In around two-fifths of the organisations surveyed, digitalisation is given a high priority and in around half a rather high priority (89% agreement). It emerges that in VET organisations for PwD, digitalisation is given a significantly lower priority than currently in regular VET organisations ($z = 3.863$, $p = .002$) and universities of applied sciences ($z = -3.781$, $p = .002$). Nevertheless, at 57%, the majority of the VET organisations for PwD surveyed also attribute a rather high priority to digitalisation.

The organisations were also asked how many *communication and information processes* in their organisation are already digitalised and whether they are continuously expanding their *technical-digital infrastructure.* While in half of the organisations surveyed many communication and information processes are already digitalised and in two-fifths rather many (91% agreement), around half of the organisations surveyed are continuously expanding their technical-digital infrastructure and two-fifths rather continuously (89% agreement). It is interesting that the communication and information processes in universities of applied sciences are digitalised significantly more often than in VET organisations for PwD ($z = -3.710$, $p = .003$).

In addition, the respondents' assessments of *innovativeness regarding the use of digital media* in their education and training were recorded. Around a quarter of the organisations surveyed describe themselves as innovative and half as rather innovative regarding the use of digital media in their education and training (74% agreement). In contrast, three out of ten organisations surveyed see themselves as rather or not at all innovative regarding the use of digital media in their education and training.

What relevance do VPET attribute to *digital learning formats* and how do they evaluate their *hardware and software equipment* for this purpose? Regardless of the type of organisation, digital learning formats are becoming increasingly important in the VPET organisations surveyed (88% agreement). About three quarters of the organisations surveyed have the necessary hardware and software. The statement that their organisation has the necessary hardware and software for digital learning is only completely agreed with by about one fifth of the organisations surveyed, with 55% of the majority agreeing rather more reservedly. It is noteworthy that especially VET organisations for PwD assess their equipment with hardware and software for digital learning significantly worse than regular VET institutions ($z = 3.589, p = .005$).

If the ratings of the *equipment of the classrooms* with various devices provided for selection are considered, it becomes apparent that most of the organisations surveyed are very well equipped with beamers, large screens, and visualizers. In detail, however, technologies that increase the accessibility of the educational offers are significantly less frequently available in the surveyed organisations. Thus, the equipment with devices for visual and/or auditory recording and transmission of lessons is rated as rather very poor by about one third of the organisations surveyed. Half of the organisations surveyed also criticize the provision of hearing aids respectively induction loops. It is interesting that a quarter of the professionals surveyed do not know whether hearing aids respectively induction loops are available at their organisation.

In terms of the *digital availability of learning materials,* the majority of organisations surveyed (just over two-thirds) make 51–75% of their learning materials available to learners digitally. Less than a quarter of the organisations surveyed make 76–100% of learning materials digitally available. About one fifth of the organisations surveyed provide 0–25% and 26–50% of their learning materials digitally. The extent of digitally available learning materials is heavily influenced by the type of organisation ($\chi^2(5) = 35.02, p > .000$, see Fig. 1). The extent of digitally available learning materials in VET organisations for PwD is significantly lower than in regular VET organisations ($z = 3.554, p = .006$), colleges of higher education ($z = -3.313, p = .014$), universities of applied sciences ($z = -4.798, p = .000$) and universities of teacher education ($z = -3.671, p = .004$).

What percentage of all learning materials are you estimating to be
digitally available to learners in your organisation?

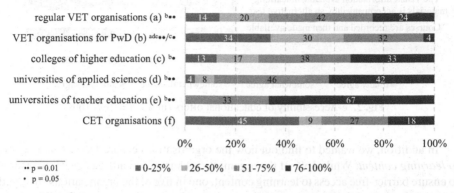

Fig. 1. Digital availability of learning materials (in %), n = 180

Finally, the results of two statement assessments are discussed, which are interesting
regarding the e-inclusion of PwD in the VPET context. The statement that the use of
digital technologies improves the *possibilities for individual support of PwD* was agreed
with by around three-fifths of the organisations surveyed to some extent and around one-
fifth to all intents and purposes (76% agreement). In contrast, it became apparent, not
least during the COVID-19 pandemic, that the digital technologies used are very difficult
to access for learners with disabilities in 5% of the organisations surveyed and rather
difficult in a quarter (30% agreement).

3.2 E-inclusion Structures

In the following, the results on e-inclusion located in the dimension *structures* are presented. As can be seen from the results already outlined, the majority of the educational
organisations surveyed are digitalised in their everyday education. This is also reflected
in the *forms of use of digital technologies in the classroom*. Only about every tenth
organisation surveyed (still) offers predominantly traditional, rather technology-free
face-to-face teaching. While the focus of 16% of the organisations surveyed is on a
combination of online and face-to-face teaching, around three quarters of the organisations surveyed state that they mainly provide face-to-face teaching, but frequently use
digital technologies.

The respondents were presented with various statements for assessment, which allow
conclusions to be drawn about the *digital accessibility* of their educational offers (cf.
Fig. 2). Films shown in class are consistently subtitled in around 5% of the organisations
surveyed and partially subtitled in 24%. In 3% of the organisations surveyed, the visual
information available in learning materials is consistently and in 13% partially provided with an alternative text. Providing recorded course to the learners is implemented
consistently in 3% of the organisations surveyed and partially in 12%.

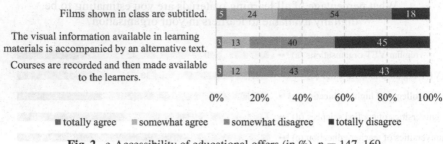

Fig. 2. e-Accessibility of educational offers (in %), n = 147–169

In addition, we wanted to find out how the organisations ensure *barrier-free access to learning content*. While 16% of the organisations surveyed hardly take any measures to ensure barrier-free access to learning content, one in five of the organisations surveyed strives for universal design and, according to the professionals, tries to make all learning content available to learners without barriers. However, the majority of the organisations surveyed (64%) only provide barrier-free access to learning content when required, which in eight out of ten organisations is the responsibility of the teachers.

Against this background, we wanted to know from the respondents whether the creation of accessible learning content is associated with *additional work for teachers*. In most of the organisations surveyed the creation of accessible learning content means a high additional effort for teachers. In about two-fifths of the organisations surveyed, the additional workload for teachers associated with the creation of accessible learning content is estimated to be rather high.

We were also interested in whether the organisations surveyed have *concepts* for the various topics they are asked to choose from. While the majority of the organisations surveyed (just over two thirds) have conceptual documents on the topic of digitalisation, those on the topics of inclusion (49%), education or training for people with disabilities (40%) and accessibility (39%) are significantly less common in the organisations surveyed. With regard to conceptual documents on the topic of accessibility, it can be seen that universities of applied sciences have them significantly more often than regular VET organisations and colleges of higher education ($\chi^2(5) = 23.869$, p > .000). In the context of conceptual documents on the topic of digitalisation, disability-specific concerns (such as accessibility) are only addressed in about one in three organisations surveyed.

If we look at the topics on which the organisations surveyed have offered *training for employees* in the last three years, it is noteworthy that the use of digital media was by far the most frequently addressed in training courses (90%). While around two fifths of the organisations offered training on the topics of compensation for disadvantages and diversity in the educational context, the topics of education and training for PwD and digital accessibility (e.g. design of accessible documents) were the subject of training in slightly less than one third of the organisations.

We also asked the respondents whether their organisations have contact persons or points of contact for disability-specific concerns and explicitly for questions related to digital accessibility. The majority of the organisations surveyed (around three quarters) have a defined contact point or contact person for disability-specific concerns. For questions related to digital accessibility, such contact persons or contact points are available in slightly less than half of the organisations.

3.3 E-inclusion Practices

In this section, the results on e-inclusion attributed to the dimension *practicies* are presented. First, we were interested in *how the organisation's management addresses inclusion-specific concerns*. According to the respondents, in about a quarter of the organisations surveyed, such concerns are addressed appropriately by the organisation's management, and in three fifths of the organisations surveyed, such concerns are addressed rather appropriately. In less than one in five organisations, inclusion-specific concerns are addressed rather inappropriately by the organisational management, and in one in twenty they are addressed completely inappropriately. The appropriateness of the organisational leadership's addressing of inclusion-specific concerns is influenced by the type of organisation. According to the professionals surveyed, the management of VET organisations for PwD address inclusion-specific concerns significantly more often than the management of regular VET organisations ($z = -5.014, p = .000$), colleges of higher education ($z = 4.538, p = .000$) and universities of applied sciences ($z = 2.948, p = .048$).

We also wanted to know the professionals' assessment of *teachers' knowledge of implementing inclusive teaching*. In 12% of the organisations teachers consistently have the necessary knowledge to implement inclusive teaching, and in 44% they have some knowledge (56% agreement). Teachers in two out of five of the organisations surveyed have rather little such knowledge. Only in about one in twenty of the organisations surveyed do the teachers do not know at all how to implement inclusive teaching, according to the professionals surveyed. Teachers' knowledge of how to implement inclusive teaching depends on the type of organisation. This shows that teachers from VET organisations for PwD seem to have such knowledge significantly more often than teachers from regular VET organisations ($z = -5.597, p = .000$), colleges of higher education ($z = 3.857, p = .002$) and universities of applied sciences ($z = 4.538, p = .000$).

The professionals were also asked whether, in their opinion, the teachers in their organisation can provide educational offers in such a way that PwD can participate in them without any problems. In 12% of the organisations surveyed, nothing should stand in the way of such a participation of PwD in the educational offer on the part of the teachers, and in about half of them rather nothing. In about one in three organisations, such problem-free participation of PwD on the part of the teachers is rather questionable, and in about one in ten it is very questionable. In relation to the type of organisation, in regular VET organisations ($z = -3.592, p = .005$) and universities of applied sciences ($z = 3.917, p = .001$) something seems to stand in the way of the participation of PwD on the part of teachers significantly more often than in VET organisations for PwD.

In addition, the professionals were asked about the frequency with which the *implementation of the UN CRPD* is addressed. In less than one fifth of the organisations surveyed, this is regularly discussed and in slightly more than one fifth it is discussed rather regularly (41% agreement). In about one third of the organisations surveyed, the implementation of the UN CRPD is rarely discussed, and in one in four organisations surveyed, it is not discussed at all (cf. Fig. 3). Differentiated by type of organisation, it can be seen that in VET organisations for PwD, the implementation of the UN CRPD is significantly more often a cause for discussion than in regular VET organisations ($z = -6.874, p = .000$), colleges of higher education ($z = 4.688, p = .000$) and universities of applied sciences ($z = 4.673, p = .000$).

The implementation of the UN CRPD is a regular topic at our organisation.

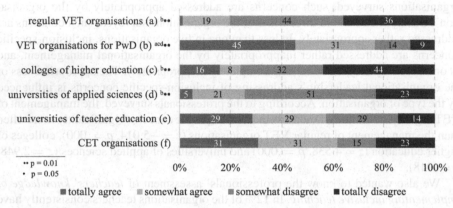

Fig. 3. Frequency of addressing the implementation of the UN CRPD (in %), n = 223

Furthermore, we wanted to know from the professionals whether their organisation provides teachers *with information materials for creating accessible learning content*. These are provided to teachers in slightly more than two-fifths of the organisations surveyed. It is interesting that about a quarter of the professionals surveyed – although all of them sometimes or often deal with accessibility – could not assess whether such information materials are available in their organisation.

3.4 E-inclusion Cultures

In the context of the *cultures* dimension, we first recorded the professionals' assessments of the general *attitude of employees towards the inclusion of PwD*. While the employees in two fifths of the organisations surveyed are rather open to the inclusion of PwD and in about half very open, the employees in one in ten of the organisations surveyed are rather critical. It is interesting that the type of organisation does not seem to have any influence on the general attitudes of employees towards the inclusion of PwD.

We also wanted to find out from the respondents how much *importance* is attached to the inclusion of PwD in their organisation. In one third of the organisations surveyed, the inclusion of PwD is given a high priority and in two fifths a rather high priority (73% agreement). Differentiated by type of organisation, it can be seen that in VET organisations for PwD the importance of inclusion is rated significantly higher than in regular VET organisations ($z = -6.280, p = .000$), colleges of higher education ($z =$

6. 144, $p = .000$) and CET organisations ($z = 3.074$, $p = .032$). It is also noteworthy that the inclusion of PwD is almost twice as often given a high or rather high priority in universities of applied sciences than in colleges of higher education ($z = -3.543$, $p = .006$). The exact assessments of the importance of the inclusion of PwD by type of organisation can be found in Fig. 4.

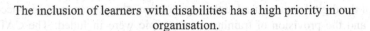

The inclusion of learners with disabilities has a high priority in our organisation.

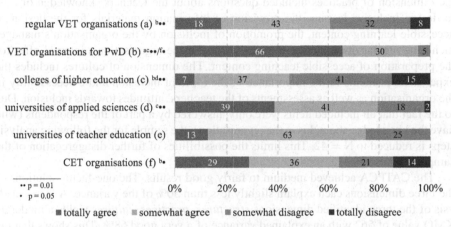

Fig. 4. The importance of inclusion of PwD in the organisations (in %), n = 236

In addition, we were interested in the *importance attached to digital accessibility* in the organisations surveyed. Regardless of the type of organisation, digital accessibility is considered to be of high importance in about one in ten organisations and of rather high importance in about two fifths. In two fifths of the organisations, digital accessibility is attributed a rather low value and in one in ten a very low value.

3.5 Testing Booth and Ainscow's Index for Inclusion

As there are no valid instruments on the realisation of e-inclusion in VPET organisations, the analysis presented below is an exploratory attempt to explore the potential of using the Index for Inclusion to investigate the realisation of e-inclusion in VPET organisations. The approach was as follows: In a first step, Nonlinear Principal Components Analysis (CATPCA) was undertaken to identify suitable items for describing the dimensions of *structures*, *practices* and *cultures* of e-inclusion. CATPCA is well suited to identify factors in data containing ordinal and nominal variables [27]. In a second step, a factor analysis was used to test whether the three dimensions of *structures*, *practices* and *cultures* can be reduced to one dimension that can theoretically be understood as e-inclusion of VPET organisations. In a third step, further analyses were carried out with the identified factors of *structures*, *practices* and *cultures*, including a two-step cluster analysis, in order to investigate whether certain types of organisations differ from each other with regard to the dimensional characteristics.

Nonlinear Principal Components Analysis of the Dimensions of E-inclusion. Figure 5 shows the procedure and the statistical parameters for the CATPCA on the dimensions of the Index for Inclusion in the operationalisation for e-inclusion. For the CATPCA in the *structures'* dimension, respondents' assessments of the accessibility of the digital content used at the organisation, the existence of an e-accessibility concept and the provision of training on the topic were included. The CATPCA for the dimension of practices included questions about the teachers' knowledge of how to design inclusive lessons, the provision of information materials for the design of accessible learning content, the promotion of inclusion by the organisation's management, the regular discussion of the UNCRPD and the organisation's internal offer for the preparation of accessible teaching content. The dimension of cultures includes the experts' assessments of the importance of the topic of inclusion and e-accessibility in the organisation as well as assessments of the teachers' attitudes towards inclusion. Due to the fact that all included items were only answered by a part of the respondents (who have the knowledge about this in the organisation), the sample for the following analysis steps is reduced to N = 42. This limits the possibilities of further disaggregation of the sample.

The CATPCA achieved medium to fairly good results. The one-factor solutions of the three dimensions each explain slightly less than 50% of the variance. A factor analysis of the three identified dimensions *structures*, *practices*, *cultures* yields a moderate KMO value of .562 with an explained variance of a very good 68%. This shows that the dimensions *structures*, *practices* and *cultures* refer to a factor that can theoretically be described as the realised e-inclusion of VPET organisations.

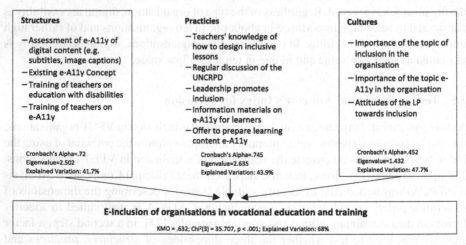

Fig. 5. Model of e-inclusion in VPET organisations

In the following, the organisations were classified by a two-step cluster analysis based on their characteristics in the dimensions. This clearly identified two groups (with a good silhouette measure of 0.5 for cohesion and separation). On closer examination, these two groups can be described as highly developed (N = 22) and less developed (N = 20) organisations in terms of realising e-inclusion. Highly developed organisations are those that stand out clearly (T-tests, all p < .001) in all dimensions from the less highly developed organisations. Figure 6 shows the distribution of the clusters in the dimensions *structures, practices, cultures*. The values are standardised (0–4), higher values mean higher development in the dimensions studied.

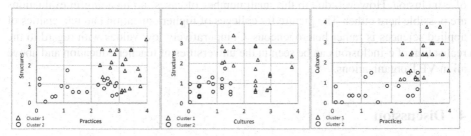

Fig. 6. Distribution of clusters in the dimensions structures, practices, cultures

It is interesting to look at the cluster affiliation by organisation type. However, it should be noted with regard to the results shown in Fig. 7 that the disaggregation to the types of organisation only results in very small numbers of cases that can no longer be processed in terms of inferential statistics. The data presented are thus in part more of methodological interest than informative in terms of content.

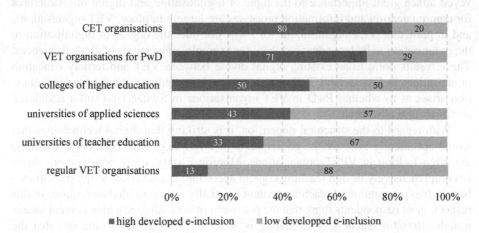

Fig. 7. Allocation of types of VPET organisations according to the state of e-inclusion realisation (in %), n = 44

For example, 80% of the CET organisations are in the cluster of highly developed organisations. This is due, among other things, 1. to the fact that more CET organisations took part in the survey that are engaged in the topic of disability and 2. that questions on the topic of inclusion and accessibility were only answered by employees with knowledge of this. This resulted in a double selection, which is reflected in the available data. The results on the other types of organisations are more comprehensible in terms of content: The majority (70%) of VET organisations for PwD have a highly developed implementation of e-inclusion. It would be interesting to have a breakdown of the types of disabilities covered by the VET organisations for PwD in order to identify in more detail separative educational organisations that have a need for development in terms of e-inclusion. However, due to the small number of cases, no meaningful evaluations are possible here either. The picture for colleges of higher education and universities of applied sciences is rather heterogeneous. Comparatively low values with regard to the realisation of e-inclusion can be seen in the universities of teacher education and above all in VET organisations.

4 Discussion

Digital technologies are profoundly changing VPET organisations, their infrastructures, teaching and support services. Although digital technologies have the potential to facilitate accessibility to content and support, the implementation of digital technologies does not automatically improve accessibility. The results of the quantitative part of the NRP77 project "E-inclusion of people with disabilities: Digital participation in vocational and professional education and further training in Switzerland" make it clear that e-accessibility and, in a broader sense, e-Inclusion of PwD are still poorly developed in some VPET organisations in Switzerland. Even though the VPET organisations surveyed attach great importance to the topic of digitalisation and digital infrastructures for communication and information processes are largely in place, VET organisations, and in particular VET organisations for PwD, consider the degree of digitalisation in the organisation to be less advanced than, for example, universities of applied sciences. These results point to an existing digital divide between VET and tertiary education organisations in Switzerland. Following on from these findings, the fundamental question arises as to whether PwD in VET organisations in Switzerland suffer additional disadvantages as a result.

With regard to the structural dimension, it is striking that digital technologies that would specifically improve the participation of PWD (e.g. induction loops, subtitles) are often lacking in VPET organisations. Moreover, only a few organisations strive to comprehensively design teaching content according to universal design principles – barrier-free preparation of teaching content is usually only provided on request. In this respect, most respondents think that the provision of accessible teaching content means a high effort for teachers. This finding is worrying, as it points to the fact that the responsibility for accessibility usually lies with the teachers, for whom this service means an additional effort.

Policies and concepts are an important basis for cultural development and professional action in educational organisations [28]. In view of the results reported, it is not surprising that accessibility concepts are only found in some of the organisations and much less often in VET organisations. Even though the respondents consider the topics of inclusion and digital accessibility to be highly significant for the organisations, this is conspicuously not reflected in the infrastructures and policies of the organisations. Accordingly, the organisations surveyed also characterise the practice of teaching as rather less inclusive and the knowledge of teachers about accessible teaching as low.

Overall, the findings outlined in this paper suggest that if the inclusion of people with disabilities in VPET organisations is to be sustainably strengthened and their exclusion countered, both digital opportunities and digital barriers to learning and participation should be identified and addressed – and this in all dimensions identified by Booth and Ainscow [25].

4.1 Towards a Model of E-inclusion in Higher Education

The operationalisation of the Index for Inclusion by Booth and Ainscow for studies on e-inclusion can be regarded as promising on the basis of the present results. The principal component and factor analysis indicate that an operationalisation in the dimensions *structures*, *practices* and *cultures* represent a coherent analytical framework for the realisation of e-inclusion in VPET organisations. However, the example of counselling services for teachers affecting the structure's one-factor solution shows that the structure dimension is not a coherent construct in practice. These findings indicate that just because guidance services exist, VPET organisations do not have to be well developed in all (infra-)structural areas. Finally the cluster analysis shows that VPET organisations can be classified very well according to their state of realisation of e-inclusion in the dimensions of *structures*, *practices* and *cultures*.

Limitations. Due to the small number of cases generated by the questionnaire selection, the content analyses on the described clusters are not to be considered representative for the population of VPET organisations in Switzerland. The corresponding analyses are more of a methodological character and are to be replicated in follow-up studies with larger samples. The indicators of the dimensions of e-inclusion described here represent the first operationalisation and analysis of a model of e-inclusion according to the knowledge of the authors. Further studies should further develop and standardise the operationalisation of the model.

References

1. Hepp, A., Krotz, F., Moores, S.: Connectivity, Networks And Flows: Conceptualizing Contemporary Communications. Cresskill, NJ (2008)
2. Stalder, F.: The Digital Condition. Polity Press, Cambridge (2018)
3. Evens, A.: Logic of the Digital. Bloomsbury Publishing, USA (2015)
4. BMAS Bundesministerium für Arbeit und Soziales: Forschungsbericht zu den Auswirkungen der Digitalisierung auf die Beschäftigung von Menschen mit Behinderung. https://www.bmas.de/SharedDocs/Downloads/DE/PDF-Publikationen/Forschungsberichte/fb-467-digitalisierung-behinderung.pdf;jsessionid=AB7646F3601DB36822884F9AA1C68DA9?__blob=publicationFile&v=3. Accessed 12 Mar 2020

5. Hümbelin, O., von Bergen, M., Luchsinger, L.: Technologischer Wandel: Chancen und Risiken für Menschen mit Behinderungen. Impuls: Magazin des Departements für Soziale Arbeit (3), pp. 32–34. Berner Fachhochschule BFH, Soziale Arbeit (2019)

6. Engels, D.: Chancen und Risiken der Digitalisierung für die Beschäftigung von Menschen mit Behinderung. In: Skutta, S. (ed.). Digitalisierung und Teilhabe. Mitmachen, mitdenken, mitgestalten, pp. 223–234. Nomos, Baden-Baden (2019)

7. ITU 2013: 35 ITU International Telecommunication Union: The ICT Opportunity of a disability-inclusive development frame-work. https://www.itu.int/en/action/accessibility/Documents/The%20ICT%20Opportunity%20for%20a%20Disability_Inclusive%20Development%20Framework.pdf. Accessed 12 Mar 2020

8. Hess-Klein, C., Scheibler, E.: Aktualisierter Schattenbericht. Bericht der Zivilgesellschaft anlässlich des ersten Staatenberichtsverfahrens vor dem UN-Ausschuss für die Rechte von Menschen mit Behinderungen. Editions Weblaw, Bern (2022)

9. Klein, U., Schindler, C.: Inklusion und Hochschule: Eine Einführung. In: Klein, U. (ed.) Inklusive Hochschule. Neue Perspektiven für Praxis und Forschung, pp. 7–18. Weinheim/Basel, Beltz (2016)

10. Corby, D., Cousins, W., Slevin, E.: Inclusion of adults with intellectual disabilities in postsecondary and higher education: a review of the literature. In: Jones, P., Storan, J., Hudson, A., Braham, J. (eds.) Lifelong Learning: Community Development, pp. 69–86. Berforts Information Press (2012)

11. Buys, N., Kendall, E., Ramsden, J.: Vocational education and training for people with disabilities: review of research. NCVER, Kensington Park (1999)

12. Schreiber-Barsch, S.: Ist Dabei sein alles? Inklusive Lernorte der Erwachsenenbildung und die Dialektik von Zugang und Barrieren. In: Dollhausen, K., Muders, S. (eds.) Diversität und Lebenslanges Lernen, pp. 217–229. Bertelsmann, Bielefeld (2016)

13. Kobi, S., Pärli, K.: Bestandesaufnahme hindernisfreie Hochschule: Schlussbericht. ZHAW Zürcher Hochschule für Angewandte Wissenschaften (2010). https://doi.org/10.21256/zhaw-1787

14. Weber, H.: Increasing inclusive capacity of vocational education and training (VET) organizations with digital media and ICT. In: Miesenberger, K., Kouroupetroglou, G. (eds.) ICCHP 2018. LNCS, vol. 10896, pp. 345–352. Springer, Cham (2018). https://doi.org/10.1007/978-3-319-94277-3_54

15. Burchert, J., Grobe, R.: Herausforderungen bei der Implementierung digital gestützter beruflicher Weiterbildung. Magazin erwachsenenbildung.at (30), Books on Demand GmbH, Nordstedt, 02-1–02-9 (2017)

16. Rohs, M.: Diversität und Lernen mit digitalen Medien in der Erwachsenenbildung. In: Dollhausen, K., Muders, S. (eds.) Diversität und Lebenslanges Lernen, pp. 191–206. Bertelsmann, Bielefeld (2016)

17. Borg, K., Smith, L.: Digital inclusion and online behaviour: five typologies of Australian internet users. Behav. Inf. Technol. 37(4), 367–380 (2018). https://doi.org/10.1080/0144929X.2018.1436593

18. Tuikka, A.-M., Vesala, H., Teittinen, A.: Digital disability divide in Finland. In: Li, H., Pálsdóttir, Á., Trill, R., Suomi, R., Amelina, Y. (eds.) WIS 2018. CCIS, vol. 907, pp. 162–173. Springer, Cham (2018). https://doi.org/10.1007/978-3-319-97931-1_13

19. Scholz, F., Yalcin, B., Priestley, M.: Internet access for disabled people: Understanding sociorelational factors in Europe. Cyberpsychol. J. Psychosoc. Res. Cybersp. 11(1) (2017). Article 4. https://doi.org/10.5817/CP2017-1-4

20. Newman, L., Browne-Yung, K., Raghavenra, P., Wood, D., Grace, E.: Applying a critical approach to investigate barriers to digital inclusion and online social networking among young people with disabilities. Inf. Syst. J. 27(5), 559–588 (2017)

21. Jaeger, P.T.: Disability and the Internet: Confronting a Digital Divide. Lynne Rienner Publishers, Boulder/London (2012)
22. Anderson, N.: Equity and Information Communication Technology (ICT) in Education. Peter Lang Publishing, New York (2009)
23. Seale, J., Draffan, E., Wald, M.: Digital agility and digital decision-making: conceptualising digital inclusion in the context of disabled learners in higher Education. Stud. High. Educ. 35(4), 445–461 (2010)
24. Papadopoulos, C.: Barrierefreiheit als didaktische Herausforderung. DIE Zeitschrift für Erwachsenenbildung 2, 37–39 (2012). https://doi.org/10.3278/DIE1202W037
25. Booth, T., Ainscow, M.: Index for Inclusion: Developing Learning and Participation in Schools, 4th edn. Centre for Studies on Inclusive Education, United Kingdom (2016)
26. Booth, T., et al. (eds.): Index für Inklusion. Ein Leitfaden für Schulentwicklung, 2nd edn. Weinheim/Basel, Beltz (2019)
27. Linting, M., van der Kooij, A.: Nonlinear principal components analysis with CATPCA: a tutorial. J. Pers. Assess. 94(1), 12–25 (2012)
28. Bell, L., Stevenson, H.: Education Policy: Process, Themes and Impact. Routledge, London/New York (2006)

Plagiarism in AI Empowered World

Aiste Steponenaite[1]([✉]) [iD] and Basel Barakat[2] [iD]

[1] Medway School of Pharmacy, University of Kent, Chatham, UK
A.Steponenaite@kent.ac.uk

[2] School of Computer Science, University of Sunderland, Sunderland, UK
Basel.Barakat@sunderland.ac.uk

Abstract. The use of Artificial Intelligence (AI) has revolutionized many aspects of education and research, but it has also introduced new challenges, including the problem of students using AI to create assignments that cannot be detected by plagiarism checkers. The proliferation of AI tools that can generate original-sounding text has made it easier for students to pass off the work of others as their own, making it more difficult for educators to identify and prevent plagiarism. This paper identifies the problem of plagiarism in the AI empowered world by comparing ChatGPT written assignments for biology and computer science. We have tested the plagiarism of those assignments in freely available tools online as well as in trusted and widely used Turnitin. We show that although the original ChatGPT written assignments sometimes result in relatively high plagiarism level, adding just one additional step of paraphrasing the work with free AI tools online significantly reduces the detected plagiarism with similarity levels laying within the acceptable range. This suggests that educational facilities should rethink of how they are assessing students' knowledge.

Keywords: Artificial Intelligence · ChatGPT · Plagiarism · Education

1 Introduction

Continuously evolving technology has provided various tools to assist with educational process. The tools range from simple methods for sharing documents, to sophisticated tools, like Virtual Learning Environments (VLEs). The last few years had a massive increase in 'smart' technologies that can learn from past data and make decisions without the need to be specifically programmed to do so, simply by applying Artificial Intelligence (AI) algorithms. AI has played a major role in several industries by automating tasks that usually require humans time and effort. It also has a great potential for enhancing the academia experience and the future of education, as using the AI tools can assist with various tasks and processes related to both education and research. These tools are designed to help educators and researchers to improve efficiency, accuracy, and productivity in their work.

Widely used AI tools in academia and teaching include tools for grading and evaluating student work, generating personalized learning materials, and supporting research and data analysis. And although these AI tools have the potential to revolutionize the way we approach education and research, it is important to carefully consider the limitations and ethical implications of them, and to ensure that they are used in a responsible and transparent manner.

ChatGPT - AI powered chatbot from San Francisco company OpenAI - has raised a lot of concerns since its launch on 30th November 2022. It is currently using GPT-3 and later in 2023 it will start using GPT-4, which is the largest language model yet that has 1 trillion parameters. ChatGPT chatbot is able to generate human-like text writing articles, emails, computer codes with little to no input from the users. Because of its high language capabilities and the quality of outputs it can present, ChatGPT, and AI tools in general, are seen as a threat to the education sector and academic integrity in online learning [1, 2].

Generating a high-quality essay with ChatGPT takes only seconds. In this paper we investigated the efficiency of plagiarism detection tools in assignments generated using AI tool ChatGPT (Dec 15 Version, OpenAI, 2022) for biology and computing fields. To add a level of complexity, we paraphrased the generated essays using free to use website paraphrasingtool.ai to test how likely students might succeed in cheating on their assessments with the help of AI and tested the plagiarism in paraphrasingtool.ai, smallseotools.com and Turnitin. We have also tested the written essays in AI generated text detection tool GPTZero [6].

2 Methods

We have created two assignments – biology and computer science based – and generated answers using the ChatGPT Dec 15 Version. First, we copied the exact assignment information, then we paraphrased the question and in both cases used the option to "regenerate response". This way we obtained four responses for each question and used paraphrasingtool.ai to paraphrase each of the answers. This gave us 8 essays per subject which we then tested in free to use plagiarism checkers: paraphrasingtool.ai plagiarism checker, SmallSEOTools as well as Turnitin. We have used the detected plagiarism percentage to report our results. To test if the generated assignments were likely to have been written by AI, we used the free AI generated text detection tool GPTZero API version 2.0.0.

The created assignments briefs were (Table 1):

Table 1. The tested assignments.

Major	Assignment Brief
Biology	Critically evaluate the physiology and pathophysiology of Alzheimer's disease and available treatments. Consider disease cause, progression, visible and diagnostically detectable symptoms and possible prognosis. Use scientific papers to write your essay and present your results in 1800–2000 words
Computer Science	Write a report critically evaluating five machine learning for image classification algorithms. The report should be no more than 2000 words and it should include an introduction, evaluation metrics, methodology and conclusion with 10–15 references

Data was plotted as mean ± SEM using GraphPad Prism (version 9.5.0) and significance was assessed using two-way ANOVA with Tukey multiple comparisons test.

3   Results

3.1   Plagiarism Detection

Assignments written using the ChatGPT were relatively well written and covered all the aspects requested in the original assignment. However, ChatGPT generated responses did not meet the word limit requirements, references were not always to the best academic standard and in some cases, there were no references at all, and the content was shallow. Nevertheless, if a student would submit an assignment of similar quality, it would deserve a pass mark.

The plagiarism score was the highest in the text written by ChatGPT only. However, detectable text similarity was significantly reduced after using paraphrasingtool.ai in both assignment groups as shown in Fig. 1 and Fig. 2. Two-way ANOVA results for the biology assignment (see Fig. 1) showed that there is a statistically significant interaction between a text source (original ChatGPT vs paraphrased) and the tool used to check for plagiarism ($F_{(2, 18)} = 4.83$, $P = 0.021$). Simple main effects analysis showed that a text source $F_{(1, 18)} = 15.12$, $P = 0.0011$) and a plagiarism detection tool ($F_{(2, 18)} = 8.58$, $P = 0.0024$) had a statistically significant effect on plagiarism levels.

The same trend was observed in the computing assignment (see Fig. 2). There is a statistically significant interaction between a text source and plagiarism detection tool ($F_{(2, 18)} = 9.82$, $P = 0.0013$) with significant effects on plagiarism arising from a text source ($F_{(1, 18)} = 14.79$, $P = 0.0012$) and plagiarism detection tool ($F_{(2, 18)} = 35.16$, $P < 0.0001$).

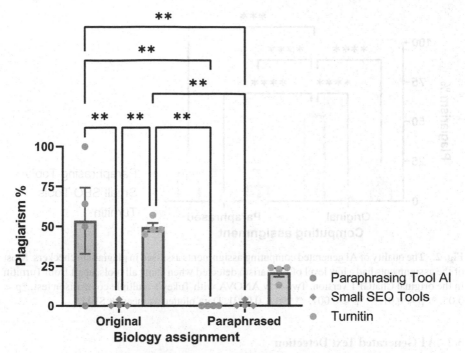

Fig. 1. The quality of AI generated biology assignments assessed in plagiarism checkers. Text generated using ChatGPT had the highest plagiarism results when tested with Paraphrasing Tool AI plagiarism detection website and Turnitin. Running the essays through paraphrasingtool.ai. Has significantly reduced plagiarism. Two-way ANOVA with Tukey's multiple comparison test, *p < 0.05, **p < 0.01, ***p < 0.001, ****p < 0.0001. Data plotted as mean ± SEM.

When comparing original ChatGPT generated text versus the paraphrased version in both assignment groups, paraphrasing the text resulted in acceptable plagiarism levels with similarity values <25% when tested using Turnitin – a plagiarism drop from 49.5% to 21% for biology and 54% to 18.5% drop for computing assignments. This plagiarism drop is evident when assessing the reports with highlighted sections that were plagiarised in biology (Fig. 3) and computing (Fig. 4) assignments.

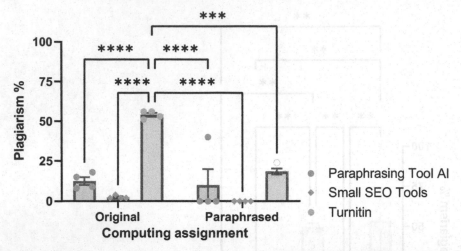

Fig. 2. The quality of AI generated computing assignments assessed in plagiarism checkers. Most of the assignments had a low level of plagiarism detected when using all tools, apart from Turnitin in the original ChatGPT version. Two-way ANOVA with Tukey's multiple comparison test, *p < 0.05, **p < 0.01, ***p < 0.001, ****p < 0.0001. Data plotted as mean ± SEM.

3.2   AI Generated Text Detection

Any written text can be assessed by measuring the content's perplexity and burstiness. Perplexity tests how well a language model can predict a sequence of words. The lower the value, the better the language model at predicting the next word. This perplexity score can then be used to find out burstiness – variation in the randomness in the text.

All of the biology assignments written by ChatGPT had low perplexity and burstiness scores, strongly indicating that the text is entirely written by AI (see Table 2). Only one of the assignments (paraphrased ChatGPT text with the regenerated response from original assignment question) was suggested to be only partially written by the AI.

It was surprising to see that all computing assignments written by ChatGPT (without paraphrasing the text) had much higher scores for perplexity and burstiness compared to biology assignments. It was also suggested that all assignments were only partially written by the AI. Paraphrasing the text resulted in even higher scores, with "paraphrased ChatGPT + paraphrased assignment + regenerate response" assignment tricking even the AI detection tool, as it was suggested that the work is likely to be written entirely by a human.

A

Alzheimer's disease (AD) is a progressive neurodegenerative disorder characterized by the loss of memory and cognitive function. It is the most common cause of dementia in older adults and is estimated to affect over 50 million people worldwide.

The cause of AD is not fully understood, but it is believed to be a combination of genetic, environmental, and lifestyle factors. One of the key risk factors for AD is age, as the risk of developing the disease increases with age. Other risk factors include a family history of AD, high blood pressure, high cholesterol, and a sedentary lifestyle.

The progression of AD is gradual, with early symptoms often including memory loss, difficulty with problem-solving, and confusion. As the disease progresses, individuals may experience more severe memory loss, disorientation, and difficulty with language and communication. They may also experience changes in personality and behavior, such as becoming anxious or aggressive.

B

Memory and cognitive function loss are two symptoms of Alzheimer's disease (AD), a progressive neurodegenerative disorder. It is thought to affect more than 50 million people worldwide and is the most common cause of dementia in older adults.

While the physiology of AD is complicated and poorly understood, it is characterized by the buildup of the proteins tau and amyloid beta in the brain, which results in the death of neurons and the destruction of connections between brain cells. Memory loss, confusion, and other hallmark symptoms of AD, such as changes in behavior and personality, start to emerge as a result of the decline in cognitive function.

Although the exact cause of AD is unknown, a number of genetic, environmental, and lifestyle factors are thought to contribute to the disease. The risk of developing AD rises with advancing age, making age one of the main risk factors. A sedentary lifestyle, high blood pressure, high cholesterol, and a family history of AD are additional risk factors. A number of genes have been linked to an increased risk of developing AD, suggesting that genetic factors also play a part in the disease's onset.

Fig. 3. A snippet of plagiarism report from Turnitin for biology assignment highlighting all the copied sections in the original ChatGPT text (A) and the paraphrased version of the same assignment (B).

A

Introduction:

Image classification is a fundamental task in the field of machine learning, with a wide range of applications such as facial recognition, object detection, and medical image analysis. In this report, we will critically evaluate five machine learning algorithms for image classification: k-Nearest Neighbors (k-NN), Support Vector Machines (SVM), Decision Trees, Random Forests, and Convolutional Neural Networks (CNN).

Evaluating Metrics:

There are several metrics that can be used to evaluate the performance of a machine learning algorithm for image classification. The most commonly used metric is accuracy, which is defined as the percentage of correct predictions made by the model. However, accuracy can be misleading if the data is imbalanced, meaning that there are significantly more samples of one class compared to the others. In such cases, it is important to also consider other metrics such as precision, recall, and F1 score.

Precision is defined as the number of true positive predictions divided by the total number of positive predictions made by the model. Recall is the number of true positive predictions divided by the total number of positive samples in the dataset. The F1 score is the harmonic mean of precision and recall, and it is a good metric to use when we want to balance precision and recall.

B

Machine learning's core task is image classification, which has numerous applications in areas like facial recognition, object detection, and medical image analysis. k-Nearest Neighbors (k-NN), Support Vector Machines (SVM), Decision Trees, Random Forests, and Convolutional Neural Networks (CNN) are five machine learning algorithms for image classification that we will evaluate critically in this report.

Metric Evaluation:

A machine learning algorithm for image classification can be measured using a variety of metrics. Accuracy, which is the percentage of accurate predictions made by the model, is the most frequently used metric. But if the data are unbalanced—that is, if one class of samples is represented by a disproportionately large number of samples—accuracy can be deceptive. In such circumstances, it is crucial to also take other metrics into account, such as precision, recall, and F1 score.

The ratio of the number of accurate positive predictions to all the positive predictions the model made is known as precision. Recall is calculated by dividing the total number of positive samples in the dataset by the proportion of true positive predictions. When we want to balance precision and recall, the F1 score, which is the harmonic mean of the two, is a useful metric to use.

Fig. 4. A snippet of plagiarism report from Turnitin for computing assignment highlighting all the copied sections in the original ChatGPT text (A) and the paraphrased version of the same assignment (B).

Table 2. Perplexity, burstiness and likely text source analysis of all assignments. Tested with GPTZero API.

Text source	Biology			Computing		
	Average Perplexity Score	Burstiness Score	Likely text source	Average Perplexity Score	Burstiness Score	Likely text source
ChatGPT + original assignment	19	12	AI	38	44	partially AI
ChatGPT + original assignment + regenerate response	17	19	AI	81	163	partially AI
ChatGPT + paraphrased assignment	17	17	AI	43	36	partially AI
ChatGPT + paraphrased assignment + regenerate response	18	17	AI	93	184	partially AI
paraphrased ChatGPT + original assignment	24	15	AI	116	255	partially AI
paraphrased ChatGPT + original assignment + regenerate response	30	18	partially AI	289	868	partially AI
paraphrased ChatGPT + paraphrased assignment	28	18	AI	188	517	partially AI
paraphrased ChatGPT + paraphrased assignment + regenerate response	23	12	AI	452	1174	human

4 Discussion

Artificial intelligence (AI) will likely continue to play an increasingly important role in academia in the future as we are seeing a rapid increase in the tools available in the market. Just in one week since the release of ChatGPT, one million people have tried it out [3]. However, it might negatively impact students' learning experience as AI might make cheating more accessible and harder to detect than ever before. Writing essays or online exams with AI requires minimal effort and it results in high quality outputs.

As seen in the results, using AI powered tools can generate human like essays that are hard to detect as plagiarized. We used three plagiarism detection websites - paraphrasingtool.ai plagiarism checker, SmallSEOTools and Turnitin - to test the plagiarism of essays written by ChatGPT in the fields of biology and computer science. In both cases, the essays could easily pass plagiarism detection tools after they were paraphrased with an AI tool paraphrasingtool.ai and when testing with free to use SmallSEOTools, there was almost no plagiarism detected in all of the tested assignments.

Much to our surprise, running the assignments through AI generated text detection tool GPTZero API did not always detect that all the text is written entirely by the AI. With the improvements in the language models used in AI text generation (the launch of GPT-4 later in 2023), it will likely become harder and harder to detect works written entirely by chatbots.

As argued by [4], using ChatGPT can put an end to the way academics assess student's progress. It is predicted that more sophisticated tools will be developed, which will make it harder to detect plagiarism and AI generated text. Having an easy way to produce high quality essays, reports, and coding assignments will affect the integrity of education and the learning process.

For now, academics might need to reconsider how they assess student learning and increase the use of in-class and skills-based assessments. Changing the assignments by incorporating personal opinion part would also require more input from students minimising the use of AI chatbots, as the AI cannot generate answers for such questions.

Although AI tools might sometimes be seen as a danger very rapidly invading academia, correct use of them can bring great benefits. The use of AI can improve the quality of educational processes through increased quality of educational resources with reduced need for human power and resources, by helping students to learn some basic concepts of the topics they are studying, encouraging them to explore additional resources, or even assisting with career choices [5]. Seeing that AI is getting more and more integrated into our daily lives, our role as educators should be to teach students how to remain critical when using AI tools, as very often they can provide wrong information, how to check if the information provided by AI chatbot is right and where to look for reliable, scientific, peer reviewed information.

It is worth remembering that the role of education is not about memorizing information, but about building the professional skills needed to succeed in life as an individual. Time management, critical thinking, communication, research and interpersonal skills are just a few examples of skills that employers are looking for, and these skills require a range of activities and experiences for their development. As educators, we should use a wide range of tools that are out there to prepare students for their future success and teaching them the best practice of safe and critical AI tool use should be part of the curriculum.

References

1. Surahman, E., Wang, T.H.: Academic dishonesty and trustworthy assessment in online learning: a systematic literature review. J. Comput. Assist. Learn. **38**, 1535–1553 (2022). https://doi.org/10.1111/jcal.12708
2. Abd-Elaal, E.S., Gamage, S.H.P.W., Mills, J.E.: Assisting academics to identify computer generated writing. Eur. J. Eng. Educ. **47**, 725–745 (2022). https://doi.org/10.1080/03043797.2022.2046709
3. Stokel-Walker, C.: AI bot ChatGPT writes smart essays—should professors worry? Nature (2022). https://doi.org/10.1038/d41586-022-04397-7
4. Susnjak, T.: ChatGPT: The End of Online Exam Integrity? (2022)
5. Chen, Y., Jensen, S., Albert, L.J., Gupta, S., Lee, T.: Artificial Intelligence (AI) student assistants in the classroom: designing chatbots to support student success. Inf. Syst. Front. (2022). https://doi.org/10.1007/s10796-022-10291-4
6. GPTZero. https://gptzero.me/. Accessed 9 Feb 2023

Chatbots and Children with Special Educational Needs Interaction

Juan Carlos Torrado[1], Caroline Bakke[2], and Elia Gabarron[2,3](✉)

[1] Department of Computer Science and Communication, Østfold University College, Halden, Norway
juan.c.torrado@hiof.no
[2] Department of Education, ICT and Learning, Østfold University College, Halden, Norway
egabarron@gmail.com
[3] Norwegian Centre for E-health Research, Tromsø, Norway

Abstract. Introduction and aim. Chatbots could have a strong potential for competence training, overcoming barriers, and wellbeing management for individuals with special educational needs. We carried out a review to describe the existing knowledge on design characteristics, and user involvement in research on chatbots related to individuals with special educational needs. **Methods.** We searched for publications on the topic in ACM Digital Library, Web of Science, PubMed, ERIC, Education Source, and proceedings from conferences on special needs education, and on health informatics. **Results.** A total of 9 studies were included in this review. Most of the studies used authoring tools to implement the chatbots or parts of them. Smartphones, tablets and PCs were the most common target devices for chatbots. End-users participated in the research mostly as experimental subjects to test the chatbot. Only one study involved participants as co-designers. **Conclusions.** Research on chatbots for individuals with special education seems to be in earlier stages. More high-quality research is needed, involving individuals with special educational needs in all stages of development and incorporating evidence-based training strategies.

Keywords: Chatbots · Human-Computer Interaction · Special Needs Education · Autism Spectrum Disorder · ADHD

1 Introduction

Unlike other software programs, chatbots are computer programs that engage directly with people in a natural way. Evidence suggests that people respond to chatbots as though they are human beings [1]. Chatbots are being used to provide services that require a person talking or assisting the user such as customer service, information search, and for general purposes in the case of home-based devices like Google Home or Alexa [2]. Because of its ease of use, chatbots could have a strong potential for competence training, overcoming barriers and wellbeing management for individuals with special educational needs [3].

© The Author(s), under exclusive license to Springer Nature Switzerland AG 2023
M. Antona and C. Stephanidis (Eds.): HCII 2023, LNCS 14021, pp. 443–452, 2023.
https://doi.org/10.1007/978-3-031-35897-5_32

Many individuals with special educational needs are diagnosed with conditions such as attention deficit/hyperactivity disorder –ADHD-, autism, or dyslexia, among others, and experience difficulties with their learning [4]. Research shows that digital technologies could be beneficial for these individuals: they can positively impact on the academic performance [5, 6]; and they also seem to be effective for overcoming barriers [6, 7]. Research also shows that individuals with special educational needs are barely involved in research on technology [8] thus, potentially limiting its meaningfulness.

The objective of this review is to describe the existing knowledge on design characteristics, and user involvement in research on chatbots for individuals with special educational needs. Therefore, we aim to answer the following research questions:

- RQ1. What types of chatbots have been investigated for people with special educational needs?
- RQ2. How have end-users been involved in research on chatbots for special educational needs?

2 Methods

In order to describe the existing knowledge on chatbots for individuals with special needs we carried out a scoping review. The scoping review followed the Preferred Reporting Items for Systematic Reviews and Meta-Analysis, extension for scoping reviews (PRISMA-ScR) [9]. This scoping review includes a secondary analysis of a broader review on the use of chatbots in special needs education.

2.1 Search Strategy

We conducted a search across 5 databases: ACM Digital Library, Web of Science, PubMed, ERIC, and Education Source. We used several keywords related to chatbots in combination with a sample of relevant keywords related to special needs education. The used search query is presented in Fig. 1. Additionally, we searched for grey literature published in available conference proceedings during the period 2015 to 2022. We searched the conference proceedings from three major congresses in special education field (World Congress on ADHD; International Meeting for Autism Research/International Society for Autism Research IMFAR/INSAR; and International Association of Special Education); and one major conference on Health Informatics (World Congress on Medical and Health Informatics, MedInfo). No year or language limitations were used.

2.2 Inclusion Criteria

We included in our review primary studies reporting results that referred to 1) chatbots, and 2) individuals with special educational needs. Reviews, opinion papers. Editorials, letters to editor, and study protocols not reporting results were excluded. Additionally, we excluded scattered literature belonging to the same authors when they did not contribute with relevant added findings in later studies.

keywords related to chatbots (Chatbot OR Conversational agent OR Relational agent OR Dialog system)

AND keywords related to special needs education (Special needs OR Special education OR Learning difficulties OR Learning differences OR ADHD OR Hyperactiv* OR Hyperkin* OR Attention deficit OR Attention deficit hyperactivity disorder OR Impulsivity OR Autis* OR ASD OR Asperger OR Pervasive developmental disorder)

Fig. 1. Search query.

2.3 Eligibility and Data Extraction

All identified references were uploaded to EndNote 20. After removing duplicates, two independent reviewers (CB and EG) assessed their eligibility. Discrepancies were discussed until we reached agreement. One reviewer (JCT) extracted the following data from the selected articles: chatbot technology; device target; and user involvement. A second reviewer (EG) verified the appropriateness of the extracted data.

2.4 Quality Assessment

The quality of the included studies was assessed by one reviewer (EG) by drawing on the GRADE guidelines [10].

3 Results

3.1 Sample Description

A total of 43 references were identified in the database search, and 1 in the conference proceedings. After removing 5 duplicates, a total of 39 records were assessed for eligibility. Thirty-four references were excluded during the title and abstract screening. A total of 9 publications dealing with chatbots and special needs education were reviewed in full text and were included in this review [11–19]. See Fig. 2.

3.2 Description of Included Studies

The included studies used very different technologies to implement their chatbots. Aside from commercial devices at global level like Amazon's Alexa [17] or regional level like NUGU CANDLE [11] or Todaki [14], the rest of the studies employed what is usually called an "authoring tool" to implement the whole chatbot [12, 15, 16] or parts of it [13, 18, 19].

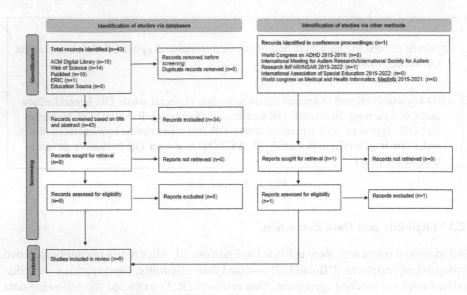

Fig. 2. Flowchart of the selection process.

Smartphones, tablets and PCs were the most common target devices for the chatbots: in two of the included studies, it was Windows PC [18, 19]; in two were tablets [15, 16]; and in two were smartphones [12, 14]. In the rest of the studies, the target device was a web browser (hence PC or tablet) [13]; Alexa from Amazon Echo [17]; and NUGU CANDLE [11]. See Table 1.

End-users participated in the research as experimental subjects to test the chatbot in six of the nine included studies [13–16, 18, 19]. Individuals with special educational needs evaluated the chatbot by participating in in-depth interviews in one study [17]; and in focus groups and surveys in another study [16]. One of the included studies involved parents of children with special educational needs as proxies to inform the design [12]. Only one study explicitly mentioned the use of participatory design workshops for involving end-users as co-designers of the chatbot [11].

Regarding the quality of the included studies, only one of the studies was considered of high quality [14]; the remaining studies were weighted as being of low or low quality according to GRADE guidelines [11–13, 15–19].

Table 1 shows a brief description of the included studies.

Table 1. Summary of the included studies (n = 9)

Article	Technology	Device target	User involvement	GRADE points*
Jang et al., 2021 [14]	"Todaki" chatbot application, developed by Korean company Medimind Co	Smartphone	Experimental subjects in a randomized pilot study. After the intervention evaluated the chatbot by answering a survey	4
Ramadan et al., 2021 [17]	Amazon's Alexa	Alexa from Amazon Echo	Consumers with special needs participated in in-depth semi-structured interviews	2
Tanaka et al., 2017 [18]	MMDAgent (Japanese spoken dialogue system) and facial expression analysis using Japanese Female Facial Expression and NOCOA + Database	Windows PC	As experimental subjects within a social skills training program replacing the human assistant with the chatbot	2
Tanaka et al., 2015 [19]	MMDAgent and MikuMikuDance (human-like behavior for the dialogue agent like blinking and nodding)	Windows PC	As experimental subjects within a social skills training program replacing the human assistant with the chatbot	2
Hayashi et al., 2015 [13]	A Web-based tutoring system comprising a Web server, database, and rule-based scripts. In-house	Web browser (hence PC or tablet)	Experimental subjects within a social skills training program	2

(continued)

Table 1. (*continued*)

Article	Technology	Device target	User involvement	GRADE points*
Massaro, 2006 [15]	"Baldi", a 3D computer-animated talking head, in-house design and development	Tablet	As experimental subjects in a within-subject performance test	2
Park et al., 2022 [16]	NAVER CLOVA chatbot builder	Tablet	As experimental subjects in an observational field study with post-session surveys and focus-group	1
Gagan et al., 2022 [12]	"Amy" mobile conversational agent, in-house design and development	Smartphone	Parents and domain expert used as proxies for children with ASD to inform the design of the software and its content	1
Cha et al., 2021 [11]	Benchmark study of Kakao Mini vs Google Home vs NUGU CANDLE	NUGU CANDLE: candle-shaped, commercial Korean device by SK Telecom	Participatory design workshops, participants with ASD as co-designers, repurposing of mainstream technologies	1

* Quality of the evidence (GRADE) 4 = High; 3 = Moderate; 2 = Low; 1 = Very low

4   Discussion

4.1   Summary of Main Findings

There is not much published research on chatbots for individuals with special educational needs yet. We have identified that the existing research focuses on three main areas of interest regarding the use of chatbots by people with special educational needs. First, there is a need for personalization that takes care of the social skills of the individual, as well as special language and speech features that might affect the interaction with the conversational agent. Second, conversational agents have a demonstrable potential to address emotion regulation for individuals with autistic features, and work in this regard is therefore needed. Lastly, we found out that there is a demand across studies for realism in chatbots, since the users make a more advantageous use of this technology when they feel they are having a believable interaction. Overall, even though these first chatbots seem to have a great potential for individuals with special educational needs, further research is needed.

Most of the included papers in this review were considered of low or very low quality according to GRADE guidelines [10]. These low scores are mostly explained because GRADE assigns a higher score to randomized studies. In our review, only one of the included studies was randomized. More high-quality research, based on different research methods, and especially using randomized experiments testing different effects of chatbots for benefiting individuals with special educational needs are needed.

4.2 Technology and Targeted Device

We observed a common characteristic across the papers when it comes to use: none of them chose to explore these devices as general-purpose assistants. This contradicts the use this technology is given for the general population. Actually, the only device that is commercially widespread among the ones targeted in the studies was Amazon's Alexa [17]. The authors repurposed Amazon's Alexa according to the requirements of people with special needs, either as a friend, a companion, a provider of functional benefits or a full relied-on caregiver [17]. Another mainstream commercial device found in the results was NUGU CANDLE [11], but it has a more limited scope, since it is only sold in Korea. Its functionality is similar to Alexa's, and the authors explored its use from a co-design perspective to tailor it to the individual needs of adolescents with autism spectrum disorders. Again, not as a general-purpose device, but as a provider of functional benefits, as Ramadan et al. called it. The Todaki chatbot used by Jang et al. [14] is a mobile app that can be obtained in the Google Store, but it is already tailored for ADHD participants, so the general purpose was not even considered from a study design perspective. The rest of the chatbots are in-house developments that target a specific kind of training, such as social skills training [13, 16, 18, 19]. This leads us to the conclusion that more research needed to study how the repurposing of commercial chatbots and the use of customized chatbots can help individuals with special needs, in a way that complements or challenges the results obtained in these studies. But, in addition, there is a knowledge gap about how commercial chatbots work if used for their intended purpose for these individuals that should be addressed.

Regarding the use of these devices, we observed another phenomenon that might concern practitioners. As we just mentioned, many of the studies target a specific training within special education such as social skills training. However, we did not find any study mentioning how this training relates to, differs from, or replaces current practices. Tanaka et al. [18] describe ad-hoc training sessions that follow the instruction, modeling, role- playing, feedback, and homework by Bellack [20], and mention that they appear to have potential to be used by teachers. And Tanaka et al. [18, 19] refer to the use of the social skills training model by Liberman [21]. Although these proposals relate to existing, theoretical training models, we suggest that researchers in this area will have to explore the possibility of a stronger connection between these innovative training sessions using chatbots and current practices in special education schools and individual assistance. Questions such as "how can we adapt current effective training models to chatbots to improve the logistic performance of special education programs?", "to what extent does the use of chatbots instead of the currently used materials improve the training of these individuals in social skills training", or even "what are the perks of using commercial chatbots to carry out this training versus using customized agents developed by researchers on the targeted areas" point at the knowledge gaps that we found in this review.

4.3 User Involvement

In our review we have found that the most common approach to involve end-users in research was as experimental subjects to test the chatbot. End-users were able to evaluate the chatbot by answering surveys and participating in interviews and focus groups in two studies; and in one additional study there were parents (acting as proxies of future chatbot end-users) who assessed the chatbot. Only one of the included studies actively involved individuals with special education needs as co-designers. Previous research has highlighted the low involvement of individuals with special educational needs in research on technology [8]. Our review, specifically focused on chatbots, confirms these findings.

Future research on chatbots for individuals with special educational needs must consider a more active involvement of end-users during all stages of development. It is well known that involving end-users in all stages of development and evaluation of technologies play an important role on innovation [22], and positively contributes to the system success [23]. Besides, it contributes to empower participants and meaningfully involve them [8].

4.4 Study Limitations and Future Directions

We have used only four keywords related to chatbots on our search engine. Although these might be the most common keywords related to conversational agents, we might have missed relevant research on the field. Our search was limited to databases, and some of the main conference proceedings in special education field, and only one conference on health informatics. The use and testing of chatbots for individuals with special educational needs is an emerging field. Therefore, future review papers could benefit from searching further sources where novel research projects are presented, such as trials registries, PhD and master theses, research reports, or additional conference proceedings, among others.

5   Conclusions

This scoping review aims to ascertain which technologies are being used to implement chatbots targeting users with special educational needs and what use they are given to help them. The search strategy yielded nine studies ranging from repurposing of commercial technologies to in-house implementation of custom chatbots. Most of the studies included the final users as experimental subjects, except for one study that discussed co-design.

In summary, research on chatbots for individuals with special education seems to be in the early stages. On one hand, the user involvement in the resulting studies is very limited, and more participatory approaches might improve the repurposing or design of these technologies for this population. On the other hand, the uses that these chatbots are given are mostly ad-hoc training sessions or usability inquiries, with no mention of factual practice change or potential connection to evidence-based training strategies for individual needs of individuals with special educational needs like hyperactivity and attention deficit disorders or autism spectrum disorders. More high-quality research is needed, involving individuals with special educational needs in all stages of development, and incorporating evidence-based training strategies.

References

1. Miner, A.S., Milstein, A., Hancock, J.T.: Talking to machines about personal mental health problems. JAMA **318**(13), 1217–1218 (2017)
2. Adam, M., Wessel, M., Benlian, A.: AI-based chatbots in customer service and their effects on user compliance. Electron. Mark. **31**(2), 427–445 (2020). https://doi.org/10.1007/s12525-020-00414-7
3. Federici, S., et al.: Inside pandora's box: a systematic review of the assessment of the perceived quality of chatbots for people with disabilities or special needs. Disabil. Rehabil. Assist. Technol. **15**(7), 832–837 (2020)
4. Nadeau, M.F., et al.: Education for students with neurodevelopmental disabilities-resources and educational adjustments. Handb. Clin. Neurol. **174**, 369–378 (2020)
5. Benavides-Varela, S., et al.: Effectiveness of digital-based interventions for children with mathematical learning difficulties: a meta-analysis. Comput. Educ. **157**, 103953 (2020)
6. Pontikas, C.M., Tsoukalas, E., Serdari, A.: A map of assistive technology educative instruments in neurodevelopmental disorders. Disabil. Rehabil. Assist. Technol. **17**(7), 738–746 (2022)
7. Khan, K., et al.: The effectiveness of web-based interventions delivered to children and young people with neurodevelopmental disorders: systematic review and meta-analysis. J. Med. Internet Res. **21**(11), e13478 (2019)
8. Spiel, K., et al.: ADHD and Technology Research – Investigated by Neurodivergent Readers. In: CHI'22, New Orleans, LA, USA (2022)
9. McGowan, J., et al.: Reporting scoping reviews-PRISMA ScR extension. J. Clin. Epidemiol. **123**, 177–179 (2020)
10. Guyatt, G., et al.: GRADE guidelines: 1. Introduction-GRADE evidence profiles and summary of findings tables. J. Clin. Epidemiol. **64**(4), 383–94 (2011)
11. Cha, I., et al.: Exploring the use of a voice-based conversational agent to empower adolescents with autism spectrum disorder. In: CHI'21, Yokohama, Japan (2021)
12. Gagan, I.T., et al., Designing a virtual talking companion to support the social-emotional learning of children with ASD. In: IDC'22, Braga, Portugal (2022)
13. Hayashi, Y.: Influence of social communication skills on collaborative learning with a pedagogical agent: investigation based on the autism-spectrum Quotient. In: HAI 2015, Daegu, Republic of Korea (2015)
14. Jang, S., et al.: Mobile app-based chatbot to deliver cognitive behavioral therapy and psychoeducation for adults with attention deficit: A development and feasibility/usability study. Int. J. Med. Inform. **150**, 104440 (2021)
15. Massaro, D.W.: Embodied agents in language learning for children with language challenges. In: Miesenberger, K., Klaus, J., Zagler, W.L., Karshmer, A.I. (eds.) ICCHP 2006. LNCS, vol. 4061, pp. 809–816. Springer, Heidelberg (2006). https://doi.org/10.1007/11788713_118

16. Park, D., et al.: Conversational agent for creating regularity in children with ADHD. In: MobileHCI'22, Vancouver, BC, Canada (2022)
17. Ramadan, Z., Farah, M.F., El Essrawi, L.: From Amazon.com to Amazon.love: how Alexa is redefining companion-ship and interdependence for people with special needs. Psychol. Market. **38**, 596–609 (2021)
18. Tanaka, H., et al.: Embodied conversational agents for multimodal automated social skills training in people with autism spectrum disorders. PLoS ONE **12**(8), e0182151 (2017)
19. Tanaka, H., et al.: Automated social skills trainer. In: IUI'15, Atlanta, GA, USA (2015)
20. Bellack, A.S.: Social Skills Training for Schizophrenia: A Step-by-Step Guide. Guilford Press (2004)
21. Wallace, C.J., et al.: A review and critique of social skills training with schizophrenic patients. Schizophr. Bull. **6**(1), 42–63 (1980)
22. Bosch-Sijtsema, P., Bosh, J.: User involvement throughout the innovation process in high-tech industries. J. Prod. Innov. Manag. **32**(5), 793–807 (2015)
23. Bano, M., Zowghi, D.: A systematic review on the relationship between user involvement and system success. Inf. Softw. Technol. **58**, 148–169 (2015)

The Use of Explainable Sensor Systems in Classroom Settings - Teacher, Student and Parent Voices on the Value of Sensor Systems

Zakia Batool Turabee[1]([✉]) [iD], Sean Haddick[1] [iD], David J. Brown[1] [iD],
Sarah Seymour Smith[2] [iD], Mufti Mahmud[1] [iD], Andrew Burton[1] [iD],
and Nicholas Shopland[1] [iD]

[1] Department of Computer Science, Nottingham Trent University,
Nottingham NG11 8NS, UK
zakia.turabee2021@my.ntu.ac.uk, {sean.haddick,david.brown}@ntu.ac.uk
[2] School of Social Sciences, Nottingham Trent University, Nottingham NG1 4FQ, UK
http://www.ntu.ac.uk

Abstract. AI-TOP is an ongoing project funded by the European Union's Erasmus+ program and is a collaboration between Nottingham Trent University and other universities throughout Europe. The intended outcome of the project is a platform that can be deployed in the learning environments of children with Autistic Spectrum Disorder in order to detect the early signs of oncoming behavioural dysregulation or meltdown and inform the supervising adult to enable them to try techniques to de-escalate these events.

This paper covers the Thematic Analysis of a series of interviews conducted by the partner institutions in order to investigate potential issues with the implementation and acceptance of a range of sensors and machine learning methods in order to predict the onset of an emotional dysregulation event.

Keywords: ASD · AI-TOP · Thematic Analysis · Rumble Moments · Emotional Dysregulation · Arousal · Tracking · Engagement · Cameras and Wearables

1 Introduction

Autism Spectrum Disorder (ASD) has been classified as a neurodevelopmental disorder by The Diagnostic and Statistical Manual of Mental Disorders, 5th Edition. An individual with ASD usually has difficulty in interacting socially and shows repetitive behaviour [14]. According to Autism and Education in England manual- 2017, at least 1 in 100 children in the UK are found to be on the Autistic Spectrum [2]. ASD is usually diagnosed in children at a young age, often because of their inability to socially interact [8]. Children with ASD usually

M. Antona and C. Stephanidis (Eds.): HCII 2023, LNCS 14021, pp. 453–468, 2023.
https://doi.org/10.1007/978-3-031-35897-5_33

have difficulty in expressing their mental and emotional state, and understanding that of others [16], which can lead to behaviour that their fellows and teachers can find challenging [12]. This challenging behaviour can be a result of sensory overload due to auditory, tactile, visual, or olfactory stimuli present in their surroundings, emotional overload caused by the frustration of unfulfilled needs or cognitive overload due to an inability to perform a task [1]. These episodes of escalating behaviour may manifest in the form of screaming, head banging, throwing objects, etc., which may cause harm to the child itself, or others in the vicinity [7].

An increasing amount of research has been taking place to identify the signals that a child with ASD might exhibit before becoming emotionally distressed. This phase of emotional transition is sometimes known as the 'rumbling stage' or 'rumble moments' [13], which can include covering their eyes and ears with hands, flapping, and pacing. Identification of rumble moments can assist parents, teachers, and caregivers in reducing or removing the offending stimuli where possible and to deescalate the situation before the child becomes emotionally dysregulated which is also commonly termed as a meltdown event. A recent study [10], has found that 72% parents' of children with ASD were willing to monitor physiological changes or behavioural patterns in order to avoid intense challenging behaviour.

2   Tracking Engagement and Arousal in Children with Autism

One possible approach to track engagement and arousal in children with autism is to use sensors including cameras to track the facial expressions, emotions, and actions of children. Salma et al. [7] studied the features of compound emotions expressed by children with autism before experiencing emotional transition. Video instances of children were recorded using Kinect Sensors under different circumstances. Recurrent Neural Networks (RNN) were utilised to analyse the subjects' facial spatio-temporal geometric features. Using Information Gain (IG) feature selection methods, challenging behavior was detected with an accuracy of 85.8%. This system was then used to warn the caregivers to take the necessary precautionary measures. Similarly, Hui-Chuan et al. [4] developed a facial expression-based emotion recognition system to improve the sensitivity of e-learning systems for High Functioning Autism (HFA). An emotion classifier was trained on facial feature data from video clips of individuals with autism using Support Vector Machine (SVM) supervised learning models, along with Information Gain (IG) and Chi-square which helped in achieving an accuracy of 92.4%.

Another method to detect intense episodes of distress is the use of non-invasive physiological signals [5,15]. Vikas et al. [9] proposed a deep learning-based meltdown detection system. Physiological signals such as temperature, Galvanic Skin Response (GSR) and heart rate were collected from a wristband and sent to an Internet of Things (IoT) server. After the pre-processing, deep learning was applied to train a classifier for meltdowns. The model was then deployed in a monitoring system that would alert the parents or caregivers in case of emotional distress. An accuracy of 96% was achieved in training and testing. On the other hand, Pradeep et al. [11] developed a VR platform for anxiety-sensitive social communication using gaze-based signals in real-time. Eye tracking indices were used to identify the social anxiety of people with autism which may lead to difficult communication. The eye gaze of participants with autism was traced while the participants completed different tasks of various complexity. Based on the indices, a rule generator was devised which was capable of adaptive task switching according to the level of anxiety.

However, not all children with autism may tolerate the use of wearable devices for the collection of physiological data, as they provide an unfamiliar tactile sensation. Alternatively, while tracking emotions through video surveillance, often by the time child starts exhibiting cues for the onset of a meltdown, it is too late to deescalate the situation and prevent the change in behaviour. Therefore, there is a need for a multimodal platform which is capable of gathering different types of sensor data such as eye gaze, facial expressions, heart rate variability, heart rate, skin temperature and conductivity, and body posture, and processing the data to detect early signs of meltdown which will help in early intervention and prevention of such events.

3   Context

AI-TOP-2020-1-UK01-KA201-079167 [6] is an ongoing study to predict the rumble moments in children with ASD. The aim of this project is to build a multimodal platform which will be able to detect early signs of a meltdown event and alert the relevant guardian or teaching staff member to minimise the trigger and prevent the situation from escalating further. This will not only help in increasing the engagement rate of children with autism in classrooms but also increase their overall quality of life and mental and emotional well-being. To do so, multiple sensors embedded in smartwatches, iPads and cameras (e.g., webcam, mobile phone camera, etc.) will collect various types of data such as eye gaze, facial expressions, heart rate variability, heart rate, skin temperature and conductivity, and body posture. This data will then be labelled by the parents/teachers/caregivers and machine learning models will be trained to predict the onset of emotional transition. Once trained, these models can be deployed in the classroom (and potentially beyond), where they can infer the onset of a rumble moment and alert the concerned person who can take necessary steps to mitigate the event in good time.

Since ASD can manifest very differently from child to child, every episode of challenging behaviour can also vary. However, there are some common traits that children show before the onset of the rumbling phase. In order to understand the nature of these distressing episodes, what events might trigger them from a behavioural perspective and what interventions can be used to mitigate them, we adopted a Thematic Analysis approach to analyse interview data. Interviews were conducted with key stakeholders, i.e. parents, teaching staff and caregivers to gather data and understand more about their first-hand experiences with the emotional transition in children with autism and also to elicit their views and opinions regarding developing a platform that can predict the potential rumble moments.

4   Method

4.1   Design

A series of structured interviews were conducted by the AI-TOP Project Partners, each interviewing a group of people either involved in the education and care of persons with ASD, or people with autism themselves, comprising teachers (8 of those working in mainstream education and 7 in specialist provision), 11 parents of persons with ASD, and 2 adults with autism. These interviews were either conducted with only one interviewee, or in small groups of no more than three associated interviewees - for example, staff at a single institution, or a child with ASD accompanied by their parent.

4.2   Participants and Procedure

In total, 28 unique persons were interviewed - 11 by Nottingham Trent University (NTU) in UK, 5 by the University of Thessaly in Greece, 8 from Bulgaria (SU Paisii Hilendarski and National Association Of Professionals Working With Disabled People-NARHU), and 4 from PhoenixKM BVBA in Belgium. The transcripts for these interviews were anonymised and, where required, translated into English. Whilst some members of the primary research team at NTU conducted the relevant interviews, it should be stressed that these persons were not directly involved in the thematic analysis in any form, nor did they provide the researchers involved with any additional context not provided by the transcripts. The said thematic analysis was primarily conducted by two researchers in tandem, with oversight from the rest of the Interactive Systems Research Group at NTU. Sarah Seymour-Smith, an experienced qualitative researcher, ensured that the Thematic Analysis was conducted correctly and rigorously.

Participants were interviewed on the following aspects in order to collect all the relevant information.

- Profile of the children the interviewee teachers/parents/cares for such as age, gender, diagnosis etc.
- What are the triggers which stimulate the children and make them emotionally dysregulated?
- How rumble moments and meltdown phases are manifested in their behaviour?
- What strategies are used by parents/teachers/caregivers to minimize those triggers, redirect the child or diffuse the meltdown?

- Information regarding the school settings i.e. specialized facility or mainstream schools.
- How comfortable children are using technology in classrooms, engaging in digital activities and attention span while using them?
- Views on tracking engagement and signs of meltdown in students with autism using the devices and the sensors identified.
- Expected attitude of children while tracking their behaviour using different sensors such as cameras, smart watches, chest straps, eye trackers (eye tracking device), microphones or sensor prompts - heart rate variation, movement data, electrodermal activity, audio and body pose. etc.
- What type of feedback would they prefer from a platform tracking engagement and early signs of meltdown?
- Concerns about how the sensor data is stored, analyzed or transferred.

4.3   Analytic Procedure

The main goal of the interviews was to explore a range of issues relevant to the development of a platform that will help in the early identification of rumble moments and an exploration of the evidence-based well-being interventions that can be used for their mitigation. As such, a realist approach to thematic analysis was employed (Braun & Clarke, 2006) [3] and the themes identified typically followed from the structure of the interview questions rather than a more interpretative analysis of the data.

Two researchers, who were largely uninvolved in the interview process, conducted the majority of the process. One of these researchers conducted a thematic analysis based solely upon a transcript of the interview, which was translated where needed. The second researcher then performed a second round of coding, verifying and adding to the list of codes created. Then, with consultation from other researchers, the codes were condensed into the themes listed below, and representative quotes were found for each.

The Thematic Analysis highlighted multiple areas of interest to the project (themes), which will guide the development of sensor-based platform to infer rumble moments. Broadly, these are: How rumble moments and episodes of arousal itself are manifested in behaviour, the factors that can cause these events to manifest, privacy and security issues connected to potential technological deployments, and general acceptance factors with the technology.

After analyzing the identified themes and sub-themes in detail, conclusions have been drawn on how the technology can be used in the best possible ways to help teachers, parents, and caregivers in identifying the onset of a rumble moments, along with consideration of data privacy and security issues.

5   Results

The Thematic Analysis highlighted multiple focal areas of interest to the project, and the research group's interests at large. Broadly, they are: How emotional transition (rumble moments) and emotional dysregulation (meltdown events) are manifested in behaviour, the factors that can cause these events to manifest, legal and ethical issues with potential deployments, and general acceptance factors with the technology.

Original transcripts are referred using conventions (partner country + interview number) (Fig. 1)

UK: Nottingham Trent University, United Kingdom
BG: SU Paisii Hilendarski, Bulgaria
BG(N): National Association Of Professionals Working With Disabled People
    (NARHU), Bulgaria
GR: University of Thessaly, Greece
BL: PhoenixKM BVBA, Belgium

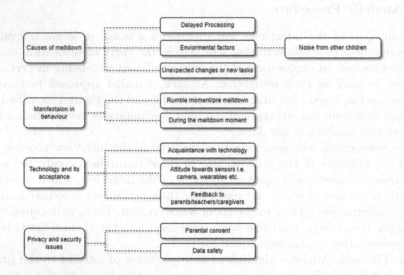

Fig. 1. Thematic Map: key themes and sub-themes identified from interviews

5.1   Factors that Trigger Rumble Moments

One common theme identified across the interviews conducted was how the events of meltdown are caused in children. Interviewees discussed multiple factors which may trigger arousal in children leading to severe behavioral problems which are identified and categorized below.

Unexpected Changes in Routine. Interviewees frequently highlighted the need for children with ASD to have a clear, defined, and regular schedule with expected stimuli. Any unexpected changes that are introduced without proper preparation are likely to cause an escalation in behaviour.

"The plan for the day is fine. It's got to have make sure he knows what he's doing for that day and if the if it changes, then it then he'll get stressed out won't you? but it you just depends on what pops up to cause the problem."
-UK11 (Parent)

It was specifically highlighted that outdoor settings increased the probability of such events occurring.

"More often when we are outdoors, rarely at home and occurs when there is a change in the normal rhythm of the day and daily routine tasks."
-BG(N)02 (Parent)

Focus was also drawn to responses to changes in staffing and supervision.

"Yes, I think there is a change anyway, stress, trying new things, uh, those are new colleagues, those are all things that cause a problem here." - BL04 (Teacher)

The three extracts above illustrate the need for a fairly rigid schedule. Deviance from this with things that "pop up" (extract 1) and change the "normal rhythm" (extract 2) are likely to cause a problem. Additionally, this change does not necessarily rest with activities but extends to new teaching staff (extract 3).

It was also suggested that having a planned timetable makes it easier for children to go through their day with a minimal chance of any distressing episodes.

"And really, just being proactive rather than reactive where we can, in terms of... visual timetables are up every morning, everybody's got symbols in place so they know what's happening and so it's just that really. And I mean, in terms of sometimes we can pre-empt it. Sometimes it it's unavoidable because it's unexpected change that even we were not expecting, such as a fire alarm or something like that." -UK01 (Teacher)

While talking about how teachers take a preemptive approach in classrooms, one of the teachers also mentioned how having a timetable helps children to go through the day and a little deviation can be very stressful.

"For all human beings, doesn't it? But yeah, a lot of structured timetable in my class there has got to be the most incredible structure. And constantly because one of my children absolutely can not cope unless they knew they know exactly what's happening and if we vary from the timetable one iota, then you know dysregulation is huge." -UK02 (Teacher)

Both the above extracts illustrate the lengths that are taken to be proactive and mitigate any chance of disruption which could lead to disturbances in routine primarily based on clear timetables.

Environmental Factors. Another important factor connected to the onset of a meltdown event according to the interviewees was found to be different environmental factors such as the texture of foods, clothing labels, or repetitive noises from the surroundings.

"He was mainly bothered by the textures in the fabrics, for example he did not have any clothes with a label when he was younger. I mean with the soft part of the tab. He was also disturbed by the repetitive noises or the repeated tones, voices etc. These mainly......and sometimes some smells." -GR02 (Parent)

Sometimes, one child having a difficult time can also cause knock-on effect, triggering meltdown in other children as well.

"We had, we had, we nearly had a meltdown this afternoon because of another student was having a tricky time. We had to come out the classroom. The timetable therefore changed and... and... that triggered quite a... difficult afternoon, So what you'd expect really. I would say change, sensory overload, perceived demands." -UK01 (Teacher)

In the extracts above it is clear that a range of things impact individuals with ASD, yet as seen in the last extract, sometimes things are out of staff/parental control.

Issues Due to Delayed Processing. Children with ASD usually have delayed cognitive functions e.g. such as perception, attention, memory and language [17] which can also lead to challenging behaviours as suggested by an interviewee.

"Well, we could say as well that the causes you know lots of our children have really delayed perception, so something might happen 2 hours, 5 hours 3 days beforehand and their processing time is is that long. So it might be that they're sitting in our classroom and they're actually worrying about something that happened 3 days ago, and you know, and it's playing over and over and over in their mind. And it has probably been playing over for three days. It suddenly gets the point where they can't cope with that anymore, and so that's when they become dysregulated." -UK04 (Teacher)

Children with autism can take longer to process emotions. So an event in past may continue bothering them resulting in a meltdown. The extract above outlines how challenging behaviour may resurface in children due to delayed processing.

5.2   Manifestations of Rumble Moments and Arousal in Behaviour

As soon as a child becomes stimulated, it affects their behaviour in a two phase manner, i.e. pre-meltdown which is also known as the rumbling stage and the actual escalating episode.

Rumbling Stage. Teachers and parents shed light on how the expressions of children change whenever they start feeling overwhelmed such as eye blinking at a different rate than usual, creases on face, sweating, or keeping their hands on their ears. Sometimes they start humming to cancel out the other noises in their surroundings.

"... You know, the way their blinking might be different. For example, I've got one child who develops creases on his face and the day before he's going to have a melt..., you know, meltdown as you call them..." -UK02 (Teacher)

"So a couple of them the one this afternoon he was having to he'd got hands on ears because it was too loud. A couple of them would have hoods and will pull hoods up again to do that. And a couple of mine make noises they will hum a make sounds to drown out some of the other noises." -UK05-06 (Teachers at special school)

The above extracts highlight that staff/parents are alert to warning signals yet these are often very slight changes, "blinking might be different".

Meltdown Stage. Past the rumbling stage, there is phase of challenging behaviour during which the children might start crying, screaming or hurting themselves or others in their surroundings.

"And so some of it will be physical. So we'll have we've got scratching, hitting, biting, kicking. Screaming, some of them will cry. I've got one or slam himself onto the floor. One he likes to try and abscond, spitting." -UK01 (Teacher)

"It can be crying and and self self harm. So one student will just keep biting himself or hitting his head lots of crying and just really distressed. Uh, another student to it could be lashing out at another." -UK05-06 (Teachers at a special school)

In contrast to the 'rumbling' stage, the meltdown stage is where individuals with ASD show fairly clear signs that all is not well.

5.3   Acceptability of Technology

Attitudes of children towards different technologies and wearables are also an important theme raised by teachers and parents.

Technology. According to the interviews, iPads appear to be the most popular device among children with autism.

"Yes. Our children know how to use such devices very well. They learn to use from a very young age. I think it's also a way for the family to be able to keep them a little calmer and, perhaps, to prevent meltdowns. So yes! most of them have a very good knowledge of technological devices." -GR03 (Teacher)

"iPads are by far the most popular. Everybody loves iPads, everybody fights over getting the iPads. I think teachers are very positive about them as well and. There, they're just. They're very intuitive because of the touch screen and children who really have no speech, no literacy, no ability to type or. Spell. They can operate iPads to quite an astonishing level in terms of, you know, navigating between different screens, open and closing apps, etc. And. And schools especially, I think have come on board because of all the AAC apps, the augmented of alternative communication, that's sort of brought up pedagogical use to them." -UK09 (Parent of 2 children with ASD who is also an expert and researcher into ASD)

In the extracts above, iPads are marked out as used from a young age demonstrating ease of usage and 'everybody' likes them.

Attitude Towards Mobile Phones, Cameras, Wearables. However, there were skeptical views regarding the use of wearable sensors, smart watches, mobile phone and cameras.

"...some children don't like labels or clasps, or buttons, or anything along those lines. My Fitbit has got, you know at buckle on it, that probably isn't gonna work. You also need to think about the weight for example. Could it be used as a weapon? And if they managed to get it off, is there anything like this pointy bit of my bit that goes through the buckle?." - UK02-UK04 (Teachers)

"I'm not sure how we would cope with sort of like anything like chest straps or things being stuck to our bodies. We might tolerate wristbands and watches, definitely iPads, microphones. I don't think they'd be overly aware of being there." - UK01 (Teacher)

"My personal opinion, speaking specifically about my child, is that it's nice to have something that's positioned away from him. Something that's not directly on his body, that's not touching him directly, because maybe he won't tolerate it. I think it's good to be something indirect, maybe the mobile phone?" -BG(N)02 (Parent)

From the extracts above, it appears that wearable sensors which are felt on the body have the least favorable approach due to the sensitivity of individuals with ASD.

One of the teachers also pointed out that being recorded using a camera might also make them feel unsafe.

"Yes, I think cameras are very difficult or very sensitive because we also have students here who say very clearly no I don't want to be photographed or yes and if there is a camera here I no longer feel safe here. So I don't think that's difficult, um I think a watch yes if they can handle it sensory to wear a watch, because that's another problem, I think it depends from student to student." - BL04 (Teacher)

However, there might be some acceptability as well due to social reasons.

"For my students personally, I think those smartwatches and those smartphones are because our students like to feel like everyone else and because that's generally accepted in society." -BL03 (Teacher)

The extracts above show that there could be varying responses toward wearable sensors.

Feedback. Further discussions also revealed that parents, teachers and caregivers are very particular about how a platform inferring rumble moments should inform in a way that children themselves are not triggered.

"I think it will be more important to inform those around him so that we can prevent an imminent crisis. A child may, in my opinion, be more upset with the sound [signal]. If this was visual we might be more covered. To reduce its processing in the stimulus a little at that moment. So, I think it's a little more important to inform those around [people] so that we can prevent a crisis and isolate the child or isolate the stimuli around the child." -GR03 (Teacher)

Having a traffic light system seemed helpful to the teachers.

"Yeah, probably not vibrating. I don't. I'm not sure that's really a good idea, but really as simple as possible because we just do not have time to read data and so something as simple as you know the child's initial and a traffic light system." -UK02 (Teacher)

Some of the interviewees indicated that having a detailed dashboard view would help them in assessing the situation of a child more easily.

"I think the best way is the application to signal through notifications so that we can react immediately and the parent or the teacher can access the information through a dashboard. Since I think that the dashboard information is very complete and detailed and one could receive it in the form of a diagram, we could immediately find out what is happening to the child." -BG01 (Teacher, who is also the parent of an atypical autistic child)

The design and development of sensor-based platform to infer rumble moments would need careful consideration so it can be successfully adopted by children, parents, teachers, and caregivers.

5.4 Privacy and Security Issues with Potential Deployment

In common with all technological solutions, this sensor-based platform will also have potential issues and challenges.

Parental Consent. Teachers strongly believed that before the deployment of such a platform, parents need to be thoroughly briefed about it.

"I think there'd certainly be a few parents that would be happy with that. There might be a few that'd want an in depth chat with you guys about what, it's in aid of... But yeah, I think generally there they they." -UK01 (Teacher)

"So we'd have to get GDPR permission for parents, and we've got parents who will not... you know you get one parent in a class that refuses and that's it for the class." -UK02 (Teacher)

Thus, it is very important to make parents understand how the implementation of such a platform would be beneficial for their child.

Data Safety. The safety of data that is being collected in classrooms is the utmost priority of parents, teachers, and caregivers.

"I think that's positive in itself, and I assume that privacy is protected as much as possible." -BL02 (Teacher)

"Personally no... not particularly. That's because I am in favor of using such data for research purposes only. So for me there has to be a recording in a safe context. It is necessary to record and to analyze the data and then little by little to have the system ready in order to put the appropriate tools." -GR03 (Teacher)

The extracts above highlight that data collected for the purpose of developing the platform should be managed and evaluated in an ethical manner as the privacy of participants is highly important.

6 Discussion

The main aim of this study was to understand the challenging episodes of children with ASD from a behavioural perspective and elicit views of parents, teachers, and caregivers on the implementation of a platform that can detect early stages of rumble moment and provide alerts. As the number of participants interviewed is relatively small, it is difficult to generalise to wider populations. However, through the thematic analysis of the interviews, deeper insights from a psychological, legal, and practical point of view on why and how children go through phases of meltdown and how this can be responded to by the use of sensor-based technologies was gained.

6.1 Consistent Signs of Meltdown Among all Children

Individuals with autism show distinct and identifiable signals before and during the meltdown which can be used in the timely introduction of preventive well-being measures. Most participants described similar precursors of a rumbling stage which included creases and changes in colour of their face, pacing in classrooms, becoming hyper-fixated on one thing, making different sorts of noises, pulling up their hoods or covering their ears, etc. Having visual timetables, pre-planned schedules, and informing the child what to expect next are the best strategies to avoid any rumble moments.

However, if the children are not redirected on time, their complex emotions may start resurfacing in the form of scratching, hitting, biting, kicking, screaming, or slamming on the floor. Such behaviours are extremely dangerous as they might hurt themselves or others in their surroundings. At this point, caretakers and teaching staff present usually try to remove the child from the environment to some safe space and make use of heavy blankets, physical touch, and pressure massages to calm the situation down. Sometimes, letting a child have a controlled explosion in a soft area also helps. Therefore, it is very important to have a platform that can potentially help in avoiding such circumstances and promote positive mental health outcomes for children with autism.

6.2 Tolerance Towards Potential Technology

This study was aimed at gathering views on a sensor-based platform to detect rumble moments from the lens of parents, teachers, and caregivers. While the participants seemed very confident regarding the use of iPads among children with autism, there were contrasting views on the use of wearable technology such as smartwatches. Children may not tolerate the touch of buttons, clasps, labels, or buckles with the skin and therefore, might feel overwhelmed. One of the interviewees raised the concern that any sensor used for tracking the children should be built in a way that it cannot be eaten or used as a tool by the children to harm themselves or others.

However, some children might accept wearing a smartwatch in order to fit in socially. One of the teachers mentioned that children with autism are more and more inclined to want to feel like their peers and therefore, the use of wearable technology might bring a sense of belonging and well-being to them.

6.3 Parental Consent and Data Security of Potential System

Teachers pointed out that parents might not always understand the motivation of the project and therefore, might need to have further explanation of objectives and outcomes of the project and how such a platform will be beneficial for their children in daily life. Along with the consent of the family, all the participants unanimously agreed that the data collected should be General Data Protection Regulation(GDPR) compliant. Recordings should be carried in a safe context with complete ethical evaluation and management of the data to create a sensor-based platform to infer rumble moments.

7   Conclusions

This study explores the possibility of adopting a system that will be able to detect early changes in the behaviour of children with autism when they are feeling overwhelmed. Early identification of symptoms can help the people in the surroundings to minimize the triggers and calm down the child in the best possible ways. Key stakeholders (parents, caregivers, and teachers) were interviewed about their experiences while dealing with meltdown events at home and school, along with views on the design and development of a sensor-based platform to infer rumble moments and the selection of evidence-based well-being interventions used for their mitigation. Analysis of the data collected supported previous studies showing how emotional transition can be predicted using different sensors such as cameras, smart watches, chest straps, eye trackers, microphones, or sensor prompts - heart rate variation, movement data, electrodermal activity, audio and body pose, etc. Important design aspects of the system were highlighted by the participants which would make the adoption of the technology easier given that children with autism are prone to a range of sensitivities. Interviewees also identified that in order to be like their peers, children with autism might accept the use of wearable technology for the purpose of tracking their engagement and behavioural changes. Moreover, given the varying tolerances of children to wearables, cameras, microphones, and sensors used for other data sources, supports the need for a multi-modal platform for the early identification of rumble moments in children with autism.

8   Impacts on Future Work

As well as highlighting requirements for the specification of the multi-modal platform to be developed by the AI-TOP project, the results of the thematic analysis also highlight the need for ongoing consultation and cooperation between the researchers and the wide range of stakeholders and end users that the specification of final system will involve. In particular, and in addition to the AI approaches needing to be explainable, the systems of data gathering, processing and storage also need to be designed so as to address stakeholders' concerns. The platform will require that audio and video data will be gathered, stored and analysed on the fly, but care must be taken to ensure that parents and other pupils in the vicinity of those being recorded are not monitored without permission. The system would have a number of legal and ethical requirements that would need to be satisfied regarding the handling of such data if it is used, particularly with regard to the gathering of consent under the regulations of GDPR and the equivalent Data Protection Act of 2018.

References

1. Alban, A.Q., et al.: Detection of challenging behaviours of children with autism using wearable sensors during interactions with social robots. In: 2021 30th IEEE International Conference on Robot & Human Interactive Communication (RO-MAN), pp. 852–857. IEEE (2021). https://doi.org/10.1109/RO-MAN50785.2021.9515459
2. AAPG on Autism: Autism and education in England 2017 (2017). https://www.autism-alliance.org.uk/wp-content/uploads/2018/04/APPGA-autism-and-education-report.pdf
3. Braun, V., Clarke, V.: Using thematic analysis in psychology. Qual. Res. Psychol. **3**(2), 77–101 (2006)
4. Chu, H.-C., Tsai, W.W.-J., Liao, M.-J., Chen, Y.-M.: Facial emotion recognition with transition detection for students with high-functioning autism in adaptive e-learning. Soft. Comput. **22**(9), 2973–2999 (2017). https://doi.org/10.1007/s00500-017-2549-z
5. Cibrian, F.L., Lakes, K.D., Tavakoulnia, A., Guzman, K., Schuck, S., Hayes, G.R.: Supporting self-regulation of children with ADHD using wearables: tensions and design challenges. In: Proceedings of the 2020 CHI Conference on Human Factors in Computing Systems, pp. 1–13 (2020). https://doi.org/10.1145/3313831.3376837
6. Erasmus+: An AI Tool to Predict Engagement and 'Meltdown' Events in Students with Autism - Erasmus+ (2020). https://www.ai-autism.eu/
7. Jarraya, S.K., Masmoudi, M., Hammami, M.: Compound emotion recognition of autistic children during meltdown crisis based on deep spatio-temporal analysis of facial geometric features. IEEE Access **8**, 69311–69326 (2020). https://doi.org/10.1109/ACCESS.2020.2986654
8. Jarraya, S.K., Masmoudi, M., Hammami, M.: A comparative study of autistic children emotion recognition based on spatio-temporal and deep analysis of facial expressions features during a meltdown crisis. Multimed. Tools Appl. **80**(1), 83–125 (2020). https://doi.org/10.1007/s11042-020-09451-y
9. Khullar, V., Singh, H.P., Bala, M.: Meltdown/Tantrum Detection System for individuals with autism spectrum disorder. Appl. Artif. Intell. **35**(15), 1708–1732 (2021). https://doi.org/10.1080/08839514.2021.1991115
10. Koo, S.H., Gaul, K., Rivera, S., Pan, T., Fong, D.: Wearable technology design for autism spectrum disorders. Arch. Des. Res. **31**(1), 37–55 (2018). http://www.aodr.org/xml/12876/12876.pdf
11. Krishnappa Babu, P.R., Lahiri, U.: Gaze-based anxiety sensitive virtual social communication platform for individuals with autism. In: CHI Conference on Human Factors in Computing Systems Extended Abstracts, pp. 1–7 (2022). https://doi.org/10.1145/3491101.3519855
12. Montaque, I., Dallos, R., McKenzie, B.: "It feels like something difficult is coming back to haunt me": an exploration of 'meltdowns' associated with autistic spectrum disorder from a parental perspective. Clin. Child Psychol. Psychiatry **23**(1), 125–139 (2018). https://doi.org/10.1177/1359104517730114
13. Myles, B.S., Hubbard, A.: The cycle of tantrums, rage, and meltdowns in children and youth with asperger syndrome, high-functioning autism, and related disabilities. In: Inclusive and Supportive Education Congress, CDROM ISEC 2005. [Online at www.inclusive.co.uk], vol. 10, p. 05 (2005). https://researchautism.org/the-cycle-of-tantrums-rage-and-meltdowns/

14. Posar, A., Resca, F., Visconti, P.: Autism according to diagnostic and statistical manual of mental disorders 5th edition: the need for further improvements. J. Pediatr. Neurosci. **10**(2), 146 (2015). https://doi.org/10.4103/1817-1745.159195
15. Puli, A., Kushki, A.: Toward automatic anxiety detection in autism: a real-time algorithm for detecting physiological arousal in the presence of motion. IEEE Trans. Biomed. Eng. **67**(3), 646–657 (2019). https://doi.org/10.1109/TBME.2019.2919273
16. Sarabadani, S., Schudlo, L.C., Samadani, A.A., Kushki, A.: Physiological detection of affective states in children with autism spectrum disorder. IEEE Trans. Affect. Comput. **11**(4), 588–600 (2018). https://doi.org/10.1109/TAFFC.2018.2820049
17. Szelag, E., Kowalska, J., Galkowski, T., Pöppel, E.: Temporal processing deficits in high-functioning children with autism. Br. J. Psychol. **95**(3), 269–282 (2004). https://doi.org/10.1348/0007126041528167

Easy Reading – Keeping the User at the Digital Original: Assessment and Potential Use of Easy Reading for Digital Accessibility

Miriam Wüst(✉) , Nele Maskut , Lukas Baumann , Vanessa Nina Heitplatz ,
Leevke Wilkens , Susanne Dirks , and Christian Bühler

Research Unit Rehabilitation Technology, TU Dortmund University, Dortmund, Germany
{miriam.wuest,nele.maskut,lukas.baumann,vanessa.heitplatz,
leevke.wilkens,susanne.dirks,christian.buehler}@tu-dortmund.de

Abstract. Digital access is essential to participation and everyday life in our digitized society and education [1]. Various laws and guidelines (e.g., UN-CRPD, WCAG) underline the importance of accessibility of new information and communication technologies and the Internet for independent living and full participation of people with disabilities. However, people with disabilities are often excluded from digital participation due to a lack of accessible websites, assistive technologies, and media literacy [2, 3]. Thus, strategies are needed to overcome these digital barriers [4].

In the "EVE4all – Easy understanding for all" project, Easy Reading, a digital software framework that helps users overcome digital barriers, is validated. Easy Reading enables users to individualize websites according to their special needs [5, 6]. Easy Reading was tested for a period of two and a half years (April 2020 to September 2022) by students at TU Dortmund University, aiming to identify the added value of the functions in Easy Reading and to collect more application possibilities and ideas for further adjustments of the software. The students assessed Easy Reading as a helpful tool with many potentials for usage in various contexts. Furthermore, additional target groups are identified, such as early readers.

Keywords: Digital Accessibility · Digital Participation · Digital Exclusion · Easy Reading

1 Introduction

Today's society is increasingly media-driven. Almost every aspect of life is in some way influenced by digital media usage [7]. Therefore, digital access has become an essential part of participation and everyday life in our digitized society including in education [1]. As new technologies influence social actions and interactions, professionals in nursing and education must deal with more technical tools and digital information in their professional work environment [8]. Also, the way of communicating and acquiring knowledge has fundamentally changed [9]. Thus, the European Commission has included digital competence as a key competence for lifelong learning [10]. Furthermore, the Covid-19

M. Antona and C. Stephanidis (Eds.): HCII 2023, LNCS 14021, pp. 469–487, 2023.
https://doi.org/10.1007/978-3-031-35897-5_34

pandemic has made digital learning settings more common in schools [9]. This sudden increase in digital learning has shown that access to the Internet and digital media is not equally distributed in our society. Pupils with little to no access to digital infrastructure or missing skills were often excluded from participating in school life. However, there is ambiguous information on how many persons with disabilities or special needs had access to those learning settings during the corona-related homeschooling [9]. In summary, people with disabilities are often excluded from digital participation due to a lack of accessible websites, assistive technologies, and media literacy [2, 3]. Thus, strategies are needed to overcome these digital barriers [4].

The project "EVE4all – Easy understanding for all", is one example of empowering users to overcome digital barriers with the help of a digital tool called Easy Reading. Easy Reading is a software framework that enables users to individualize websites according to their special needs [5, 6]. Easy Reading was tested for a period of two and a half years (April 2020 to September 2022) by students at TU Dortmund University, aiming to identify the added value of the functions in Easy Reading and to collect more application possibilities and ideas for further adjustments of the software. These results will be presented and discussed in this paper.

2   Challenges and Barriers for Digital Participation

Despite the growing importance of Internet access and usage for all aspects of life, such as work, social participation, or personal growth, there are marginalized groups, for instance, people with disabilities or elderly people, that are at risk of digital exclusion [11–19]. These marginalized groups show a significant difference in the development of digital competencies as well as general access to digital media [11, 20, 21]. For people with intellectual disabilities, it can be difficult to understand and use the navigation on websites [22]. In case of additional physical or sensory disability, navigation, operation, and interaction with websites can be even more complex [23, 24]. Furthermore, low literacy skills can make it difficult to access the Internet [25–29].

Even before the Covid-19 pandemic, people with low educational attainment, elderly people, and people with disabilities were affected by digital exclusion [22, 30, 31]. As Heitplatz, Bühler, Hastall [32] mentioned, educational professionals believe that people with disabilities should be guaranteed access to digital media. However, this access "should be overseen, legally secure and pedagogically supported" [32]. Furthermore, caregivers see the opportunities digital technologies offer to people with disabilities as very positive developments and are aware that their use is part of their clients' everyday lives.

In summary, new inequalities must be noticed due to the continuous shift of social processes into digital media and the inherent social change [33, 34]. Here the term digital divide describes the "gap" between people with access to ICT and those without access [15, 35]. The discussion on the digital divide focuses on more than just the access (first-level digital divide) but also the usage (second-level digital divide) of digital technologies [18]. In this context, various dimensions of inequalities have already been elaborated and discussed [17]. For example, people with disabilities lag behind the rest of the population in terms of both access and usage [16]. According to Vicente,

Lopez-Menendez [36], and Pelka [33], especially for people with disabilities, difficulties regarding technical access can result in less motivation to use them. Further aspects, such as the lack of media competence, handling skills [37], and the self-determined use or findability of accessible technologies [38], can play an essential role in the context of disability and other dimensions of inequalities. Additionally, these people benefit less from the advantages of digitalization, and on the other side, are more affected by the disadvantages. This leads to the fact that people with disabilities have hardly any say in the design of media and technologies [39, 40] and cannot help shaping the digital world of tomorrow [33]. In this context, it is particularly important to support the development of digital competencies so that disadvantaged groups can participate in digital transformation.

Through various digital assistive technology, people with different support needs can increase their independence and digital participation, for example, through more social interaction or individualized leisure activities. However, it has been shown that in addition to individual limitations (e.g., intellectual disability or low reading skills), a lack of support from caregivers limits the use of this technology and hinders digital participation [11, 22, 41, 42]. Therefore, so-called 'multipliers' have a significant share in the digital participation of disadvantaged groups.

Accordingly, the presented knowledge on digital exclusion implies that multipliers can play an important role for the digital participation of disadvantaged groups. Abel, Hirsch-Kreinsen, Steglich, and Wienzek [43] highlight the need to inform and involve employees systematically, so technologies are used in daily labor. The usage of technologies and digital media by people with disabilities is often influenced by professionals. For example, Rath and Tannrath [44] highlight that "Teachers' willingness to use digital media in class is highly dependent on teachers' attitudes towards digital media" [44]. Training and testing new technologies in the workplace can create digital experiences and skills to counteract subliminal rejections [43]. However, this can only succeed if feedback, suggestions for improvement and uncertainties are recognized and discussed. Attitudes and prejudices towards digital media on the part of the professional also affect the usage behavior of digital media on clients [32, 45]. Thus, the social environment plays a central role in end users' attitudes in the care context, both in their usage behavior and in the provision of digital services [46, 47]. Therefore, digital competencies of people who give and receive support are needed [33].

For technology usage among these groups, multipliers (such as teachers, professionals, and parents) must accept digital technologies. Acceptance means a positive decision, willingness, or attitude or approving attitude towards an activity, a state, or an idea, whereby this attitude is associated with a consequence of action [46, 48–52]. In this context, Petrie, Carmien and Lewis [53] highlight that technologies are often abandoned after purchase in rehabilitation practice. Accordingly, technology acceptance assumes that the usage of technologies depends not only on availability but on a variety of different factors [54–60]. Regarding the actual usage of assistive technologies Dirks and Bühler [61] assume that this can be increased if potential users' individual needs and living realities are recognized. This is confirmed by the findings of Ramsten, Martin, Dag, and Hammar [42], who describe ICT as useful in researching tips and information.

3   Digital Solutions and Technologies for Accessibility

To use digital technologies in the context of learning and education, technologies must be accessible [62]. The UN-CRPD describes accessibility as one of its principles and dedicates article 9 for further definition. It specifies elements which ensure equal access. In addition to physical environments and their accessibility, this also includes information and communication services, as well as technologies and systems, including access to the Internet [63]. The use of the Internet and digital content by people with disabilities can be supported by developing more accessible technology [22]. The World Wide Web Consortium (W3C) has developed web standards and guidelines (WCAG) to increase the accessibility of web content, non-web documents, and software. Strategies for web designers have also been developed to make websites and software more accessible [64].

It must be noted that although these specific laws and directives stipulate digital accessibility, websites show deficits in accessible design. According to a 2022 report on the accessibility of the top 1 million homepages, 96.8% of the websites studied are not WCAG 2.1 compliant [65]. The most frequently identified problem was the lack of design of high-contrast texts on the web pages examined, followed by the lack of alternative texts for images. The authors used an automated web accessibility evaluation tool for testing web accessibility called WAVE. Since such tools cannot detect all possible error types, it can be assumed that even more digital barriers could be identified. Due to these deficits, people with disabilities continue to be denied access to many websites, and their digital participation is restricted [5].

To counteract this, some solutions exist that try to break down digital barriers and create digital access. Website providers can for example incorporate specific software solutions into their websites to make them more accessible. IOS and Android systems and devices now have some settings for better readability. These customizations allow, for example, the adjustment of color contrasts, text sizes, or provide translation functions and text-to-speech. In addition to the adjustments that can be made in these systems and devices, the Eye-Able software [66], for example, can hide images and animations on web pages, has translation options in all languages, and can be integrated into all browsers, regardless of the end device.

Another software solution with a different approach is Easy Reading. This open-source software framework was developed in an EU-funded research project [5] (see www.easyreading.eu). The framework can be extended to meet specific customer needs, as tools could be easily added or removed [67]. The Easy Reading tools allow users to individualize the appearance of a website according to their special needs' independent of the website providers. With Easy Reading, different aspects, like any website's layout and content, can be simplified or reduced on the user side. The user stays at the original website and can always return to the original display. Easy Reading can be used anonymously or with a Google Account, where all configurations are stored. An overview of the main functions can be found in Fig. 1.

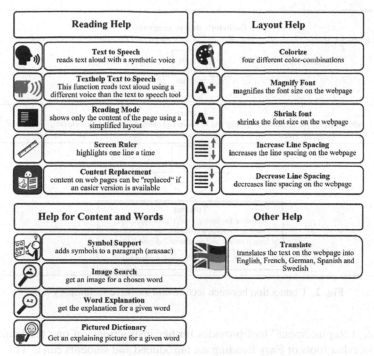

Fig. 1. Tools and Functions of Easy Reading

4 Methodology

Easy Reading was tested in the context of the lecture 'Fundamentals of rehabilitation technology and participation through technology and media' by a total of N = 581 students (non-probabilistic sample) for a period of two and a half years (April 2020 to September 2022) in the context of a course called Assistive Technology Lab ('Hilfsmittellabor'). Figure 2 illustrates the link between the lecture and the assistive technology lab. Due to technical problems with Easy Reading, 163 data sets had to be excluded. To represent a cross-section of all responses over the long period of time, 30% of the statements were evaluated. Therefore n = 127 feedbacks were evaluated.

In general, student teachers and students of rehabilitation pedagogy are identified as future professionals in pedagogical contexts. They will work in formal and informal educational contexts and have contact with people with different support needs, presenting them with different challenges as professionals. One of these challenges will be digital participation, as the Internet is an important part of today's society. Therefore, teachers and pedagogical professionals are multipliers for digital participation who could receive support with tools like Easy Reading.

From a selection of 21 stations, students who attend the lecture must complete eight stations in the lab. One station includes testing, evaluating, and reflecting on Easy Reading. Here, the students receive information on digital participation and Easy Reading. After that, they need to install Easy Reading and get familiar with the software. To do so,

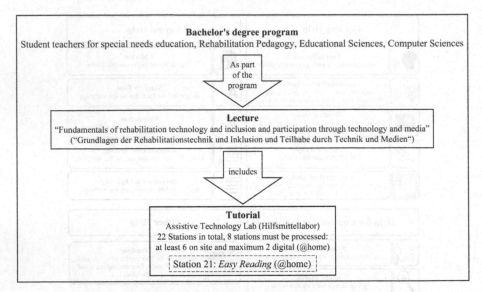

Fig. 2. Connection between lecture and assistive technology lab

the "Content Replacement" tool provides further instructions on one predefined web-page. Next, other tools of Easy Reading are introduced and students can test the tools on other websites. Finally, the students need to assess the added value for different target groups from a pedagogical point of view and indicate possibilities for using the "Content Replacement" tool in their future work environment. Furthermore, the students should develop ideas for additional tools within the framework.

The assessment ends with five questions. The answers are then checked to guarantee whether the station was carried out according to the instructions. The following list contains a translation of the five questions:

1. How would you evaluate your experience with Easy Reading?
2. Do you think that the software offers added values for the target groups? How would you evaluate the tool from a pedagogical perspective?
3. Which tools and functions worked well? Which functions and tools did not work properly? (Please give details of the tools and websites)
4. Can you think of other creative ways to use the tool content replacement in educational contexts?
5. What other useful tools could you imagine for Easy Reading in the future?

Due to contact restrictions during the corona pandemic, the station was developed as an at-home station so that students could complete the lab's stations. The task descriptions are provided via a digital learning platform.

In preparation for the analysis, the students' answers from the station processing were collected, and an overview was created in Excel. From this overview, the following research question was derived:

How is the use of the software Easy Reading evaluated by student teachers and students of rehabilitation pedagogy in everyday life of their target group?

To answer the research question, the answers to the reflection questions were analyzed and compared with the findings regarding the digital divide, technology acceptance and the importance of multipliers. Based on these, the following sub-questions were derived in order to answer the research question:

– Which target groups do students mention when evaluating the framework?
– Which inhibiting factors are named for the use of the framework?
– What added value do students identify for the mentioned target groups?
– What improvements do students suggest regarding the mentioned target groups?

The data was analyzed in MAXQDA 2022 using an exploratory-qualitative study design [68]. First, a category system was created based on the research question. Additionally, categories were inductively generated from the material. Various measures were undertaken to ensure relevant quality criteria, including transparent logging, trial coding, peer debriefing, and researcher triangulation [68–70]. Table 1 provides an overview of the sample.

Table 1. Sample Overview

Field of study of students	n
student teachers	101
rehabilitation pedagogy	15
computer science	2
educational sciences	1
no information	8
total	127

5 Results

Overall, the students gave varied and differentiated answers, which will be presented in the following section. The results can be divided into five subcategories. The different aspects within the categories are listed according to the frequency of mentioning.

5.1 Additional Value of Easy Reading

Empowerment. Some of the most frequently mentioned aspects were related to empowerment. Here the added independence was highlighted and includes aspects such as supporting help for self-help. Also, self-determination, self-efficacy or self-confidence, and self-esteem were suggested. As an example, research tasks in class were indicated. Other aspects noted regarding empowerment were maturity, relief, creation of a sense of achievement, freedom of action, freedom to make decisions (e.g., pupils are given the opportunity to work freely and independently with digital media), and personal responsibility.

Digital Participation. Another group of additional values can be assigned to digital participation, respectively participation in general. The most frequently mentioned aspect in this context is added accessibility. The software's ability to promote understanding was also suggested. Positively rated was also the usability of Easy Reading, mainly its simplicity. According to the students, Easy Reading also provides differentiated support and help for the users. Few students also mentioned the possible reduction of language barriers, social inequalities, and the enabling of equal opportunities.

Individualization. Added values mentioned were aspects regarding the possibilities of individualization. The most frequently named aspect was the focus on different target groups. The possibility of individual customizability or adaptability was also perceived positively. Other aspects mentioned as additional values refer to enabling differentiation (e.g., in educational contexts), supporting independent learning, and the possibility to combine the different tools. The focus on different types of learners and stimulus reduction were also mentioned sporadically.

Media Literacy. In addition, potentials in media literacy were also raised. The students often mentioned aspects of digitization in general, particularly the actuality of digital media. Repeatedly named was learning to handle the Internet and to navigate the Internet. Furthermore, some students mentioned the early use of the Internet (e.g., pupils learn early on how to handle the Internet) as well as the simplification of its handling. Using Easy Reading as a Scaffolding tool was indicated, as well as the added potential that only some technical knowledge is necessary.

Other. Other added values that cannot be classified into the other four subgroups were, for example, acquiring knowledge (including learning new words, and gaining information), the support in school contexts, or enabling to read in general. Sporadically mentioned were also simplification and reduction of content, process solution, protection, reaction to individual problems, and exploitation of current news.

5.2 Hindering Factors for the Use of Easy Reading

Nevertheless, the students also noted several aspects that could hinder the use of Easy Reading, or that could be understood as concerns regarding the use. Those factors can be sorted into four subgroups.

Resources, Knowledge, and Competencies. The biggest concern raised was the need for training to get used to the software and learn how to use it. This includes time and personal resources like the support of an additional person or training courses. Some students also stated that the software is not as self-explanatory as it should be to be able to use it right away. Especially the installation and setup of the software were mentioned as situations where additional support may be needed. Therefore, a quick introduction to the tools is considered useful. In addition, the students named a need for basic knowledge regarding, for example, symbol systems.

Easy Reading in Educational Contexts. While most students expressed added educational values, some noted that the software might tempt users into convenience, and thus, no individual development can occur. It was noted that Easy Reading offers no additional educational value since it is only an aid to use the Internet. Also mentioned was that the use of headphones is necessary.

Technical Aspects. Some students also noted some technical aspects that could hinder using Easy Reading. These aspects include that some tools do not function properly, which could lead to exclusion from using the software. It was also stated that Easy Reading is not usable with already highly structured web pages.

Other. Other aspects mentioned were that the usage needs to be well thought through so that users are neither over nor underchallenged. The use of Easy Reading also needs to be responsible. Easy Reading does not protect against the "dangers" of the Internet. In addition, the students raised the concern that Easy Reading might distract users from their actual task when they are not allowed to do so.

5.3   Usages of Content Replacement

The students were also asked about possible use scenarios for the content replacement tool. They named a wide range of different scenarios that can also be sorted in different subgroups.

Learning. The students see the most application possibilities in the learning context. This includes general tasks related to learning, such as learning independently (e.g., working independently, using different methods) or being able to give differentiated instructions, as well as researching different topics. Other usage scenarios were related to digital learning or, more specifically, pronunciation training. Further aspects mentioned were individualized use, for example, as a feedback tool. Also aspects regarding learning, specifically in the school context were indicated. In the context of learning in school, possible use cases were mostly related to the designing of lessons, such as the implementation of different learning methods, including station learning (e.g., project work, weekly schedule work) or WebQuests to discover the Internet. Other sporadically mentioned aspects include working with worksheets, peer learning, distance learning, or the possibility of hiding certain web pages. Moreover, the students stated usage in the context of learning German as a second language (DaZ) as well as using the content replacement tool to gamify learning (e.g., experimenting with the tool and comparing web pages). Also mentioned was the possibility of asking questions or using eBooks and digital material. Another aspect often mentioned regarding the understanding of texts was the possibility of working with Easy Reading to use it for difficult texts or to understand language (e.g., translating texts in easy-to-read). Using Easy Reading to adapt texts individually was also suggested.

Instructions and Explanations. According to the students, the content replacement tool can be used for different instructions or explanations. Examples of this are support (messages) or structural assistance. Instructions and warnings were also mentioned. Additionally, were application tips, notes, and to display the difficulty of a text.

Media Literacy. As already mentioned as possible added value, the content replacement tool might also be conducive to the acquisition of media skills, including the handling of computers or the general work with digital media. Working with PDF-Files were recommended.

Besides those contexts of usage, several other contexts were mentioned, including technical contexts (e.g., the use of apps), recreational activities such as recipes or entertainment, dealing with official matters, or communicational aspects (e.g., news and subtitles). This shows the wide range of possible scenarios of use.

5.4 Future Tools and Improvements

Since the Easy Reading software is a framework software, the students were asked about ideas on additional tools or improvements of already existing tools.

Additional Tools. Regarding additional tools, the students had various ideas on what to incorporate. One of the most named additional tools was some form of audio function, such as voice control or input. Another tool often mentioned was a marker function to highlight words or sentences. Overall, more than 30 different additional tools were suggested. Those tools can be divided into the following groups: general tools, alternative control options, tools to promote understanding, and tools to promote perception. Table 2 shows the variety of additional tools proposed by the students.

Improvements of existing Tools. The students had different ideas regarding possible improvements of already existing tools. General improvements, such as technical extensions, functions related to language barriers, instructions, and support, as well as layout and reading help improvements, were named. The technical aspects mentioned were the use of Easy Reading for other document types, e.g., PDF documents. The expansion of Internet browsers was also suggested so that Easy Reading can be used on different browsers. Regarding the language barriers, the students stated that the description of the tools should be available in different languages. Sporadically mentioned were additional instructions, especially when using Easy Reading with complex websites. Concerning layout help, the improvement of adding additional color-changing options was often indicated. As for reading help, improvements were often noted for the content replacement tool (e.g., content replacement on additional websites, using content replacement with other tools such as the layout functions) and for the read-aloud function. Another often-expressed improvement was translating into languages other than the ones already embedded. Regarding the tools that help with content and words some students saw improvements for the word explanation tool. Word explanations in easy-to-read language or the possibility of using the tool on the words within the word explanation were mentioned, as well as the possibility of having the explanation read aloud. The stated improvements as well as the ideas for additional tools will be considered in the further validation and adjustment of the software.

Table 2. Additional Tools

General Tools	Search function
	Bookmark function
	Explanation of symbols
	Note function
	Warnings/Blocking of websites
	Additional symbols
	Help with printing websites
	Button for additional information (e.g., for saving a website, printing a website etc.)
	Linkage to Social Media
	Locating further information/sources
	Writing support
	Screenshot tool
	General tips for the internet usage
Alternative control options	Eye Control
	Integrated mouse control
	Keypad control
	Head control
Tools to promote understanding	Text comprehension
	— easy-to-read language (e.g., translating into easy-to-read language, checking of texts in easy-to-read language)
	— Filtering and highlighting
	— Translation (e.g., automatic translation, translation of entire websites)
	— Suggesting synonyms
	— Keyword summary
	— Fill-out-the-blanks tool
	Other
	— Glossary function (e.g., individual lists of vocabulary)
	— Integrating explanatory videos
	— Scanner function
	— Solving math problems

(continued)

Table 2. (*continued*)

Tools to promote perception	Audio functions – Voice input/speech to text – Subtitles – Audio description – Audio translation – Voice-Over – Explaining colors – Converting language (e.g., to make it more understandable) – Screen reader function – Audio commentaries Alternative representations – Magnifying function – Alternative layouts – Brightness settings – Night mode – Converting websites to plain text – Overview function Pictures – Alternative texts – Enlarging pictures – Picture descriptions Other – Marker function – Integration of sign language – Marking hyperlinks – Converting music to text – Additional animated pictures – Syllabification – Hiding advertising

5.5 Additional Target Groups

The EVE4all project aims to identify additional target groups. Within the scope of the task, the students were asked for which additional target groups Easy Reading might be helpful. The answers can be categorized into three groups.

People with Comprehension Difficulties. The first target group can be summarized as people for whom Easy Reading helps with comprehension and understanding. Most often named were people with limited knowledge of German as well as people with little to no reading ability. Sporadically mentioned were also beginning readers, people with some form of dyslexia or analphabetism and people with ADHD or concentration difficulties. People with cognitive impairments or learning difficulties were not included in the listing since these groups were considered part of the original target group.

People with Perceptual Difficulties. Other target groups mentioned referred to people with sensory impairments. People with visual impairments were named most frequently.

According to the students, people with visual impairments might benefit, for example, from the color changes, the adjustment of the font size or the text-to-speech function. Also mentioned were people with hearing impairments (e.g., sign-language translation for deaf people) as well as people with perceptual difficulties.

Other Target Groups. In addition, other groups were identified. The most frequently named groups are children, especially school children. However, the students also identified older people as a target group. People with dementia, parents, children, and students were also mentioned.

6 Discussion

Internet usage presents some difficulties for people with disabilities, which must be addressed. Easy Reading is one tool to improve access to the Internet. In general, the use of the Easy Reading software is evaluated positively by the students for improving everyday life of their target group. Easy Reading can contribute to meeting the goals of the UN-CRPD, as it helps people to take an active part in a digitized world. This is promoted by the user-friendly design and simple usage. Therefore, it supports people with disabilities to become competent Internet users. The positive user experience reported by the students using Easy Reading indicates a high potential for being included in their future work contexts.

Even if the students emphasize the added value for the target group, they criticize the need for additional resources to understand the software and its functions, especially as some icons are not self-explanatory or do not function properly. Furthermore, students emphasize the necessity of a certain amount of training and the availability of technical support. The experience of other projects, such as the miTAS project, can also support these statements. The researchers pointed out that implementing new digital technologies in institutions depends on various factors, including support systems [71]. Based on these findings, further steps to implement the Easy Reading Software should include additional support systems such as training courses or technical support. These findings might also apply to the general implementation of new digital software or services and consolidate the statements of Abel et al. [43] and Chadwick, Chapman and Caton [22] that training and education are crucial for acceptance of media and that early contact with technologies helps to require experiential knowledge. In this regard, especially teachers can provide the necessary stimulus to strengthen the digital participatory skills of their pupils by providing, for example, dedicated learning spaces and actively helping to gain experience [33]. By involving the students, new ideas for digital learning and lesson planning focusing on digital participation can be created. However, teachers must be supported and trained using digital techniques and technologies because they are constantly developing. Training helps also to gather more knowledge about the structure of the Easy Reading framework to assess the possibilities of the software more realistically.

The usage of Easy Reading was emphasized, especially for the formal educational context. Especially the tool 'Content Replacement' offers an opportunity to design tasks individually for their pupils and promote independent work. As stated before, digital media and digital services can be beneficial when designing and implementing learning scenarios that are accessible to everyone [44]. The students provided many different ideas on how to use the Easy Reading software in class and in lessons. With Easy Reading, learning activities and materials can be designed to meet the different needs of pupils. This allows for differentiating learning levels in learning materials for the pupils while enabling collaborative learning in one classroom. Easy Reading addresses and supports the concept of Universal Design for Learning (UDL). According to the UN-CRPD "'Universal design' means the design of products, environments, programmes and services to be usable by all people, to the greatest extent possible, without the need for adaptation or specialized design. 'Universal design' shall not exclude assistive devices for particular groups of persons with disabilities where this is needed." [63]. Universal Design for Learning aims to apply the principles of Universal Design to teaching and lesson designing [72]. In this respect, digital technologies in the context of learning can positively affect the implementation of Universal Design for Learning. Digital Technologies can, for example, enable flexible modes of representation [73]. Therefore, Easy Reading can also facilitate UDL in educational contexts. Many students also mentioned the topicality of digital media in the school context. Easy Reading can create experiential opportunities for different target groups, as it shows broad potential, and targeted use, both in school and private context, is conceivable.

In addition to pupils, people with various disabilities were also mentioned as a possible target group. Originally Easy Reading was developed with and designed for people with intellectual disabilities. Other target groups mentioned were older people, people with a migration background, or people with low or no reading skills. Through the individualization of Easy Reading, these target groups might also derive added value from the software for their digital participation. The advantage of Easy Reading is that the different tools can be selected individually and combined with each other. This opens up new opportunities for the aforementioned target groups to participate comprehensively on the Internet. For example, older people with visual impairments can benefit from the layout changes, whereas people with little knowledge of German can use the word explanation or the translation. The EVE4all project aims to validate Easy Reading for other target groups. The results of this evaluation already suggest that diverse target groups are conceivable.

Overall, it can be said that the students positively evaluate the use of the Easy Reading software in everyday life. They highlight the increase in independence and autonomy of different target groups and describe a variety of potential use cases for the software and possible enhancements for improved use of Easy Reading. In addition, they highlight the individuality of the software and rate it as useful both for the educational context and for everyday use of the Internet.

This study aimed to investigate the added value of the Easy Reading tools in the education context and to collect other application scenarios and ideas for further adjustments in the software. Here methodological limitations need to be emphasized. It should be noted that the relatively large sample size affects the external validity positively. However, due to the nature of the data collection, only students were considered. To validate and generalize the results, further studies with different user groups need to be conducted. Additionally, students' internal motivation could be limited because of the educational setting of the evaluation. Furthermore, the functions of Easy Reading were partly over-estimated. It remains unclear whether the students assumed that there were more tools in Easy Reading or whether the functions were not understood Easy Reading, for example, cannot automatically translate texts into easy-to-read and does not have a function to generate sign language in videos automatically. It is to be noted that Easy Reading tools does work with html-based webpages. The benefits are certainly high enough for the target audience, the primary function of Easy Reading is to make existing webpages more accessible according to the individual needs of the users.

7 Conclusion

The analysis of the reflections has shown how important it is for multipliers to get in contact with assistive technologies early on in their training and studies. In this way, multipliers can ensure greater digital participation by their target group while keeping themselves up to date. To highlight further possibilities for multipliers connecting training with new technologies and software seems necessary in later everyday working life. In this way, multipliers are able to support digital participation of their target groups. Technologies and software should be equally understandable and easily integrated into the respective context (e.g., education, work, or private). To ensure this, the development of new assistive technologies and software should not ignore the context in which it will be used. Therefore, practitioners, as well as end-users, should be involved already during the development. The results of this study reveal further potential of Easy Reading as well as possible applications for educational professionals for different target groups.

During the EVE4all project, a training concept will be developed to introduce multipliers and users to Easy Reading. In addition, a concept for a possible sustainable further development of the Easy Reading software is to be elaborated continuously adapt the framework to future technical conditions.

References

1. Kutscher, N.: Digitalität, Digitalisierung und Bildung. In: Bauer, U., Bittlingmayer, U.H., Scherr, A. (eds.) Handbuch Bildungs- und Erziehungssoziologie. Springer Fachmedien Wiesbaden, Wiesbaden, pp 1–17 (2020). https://doi.org/10.1007/978-3-658-30903-9_59
2. Dobransky, K., Hargittai, E.: Unrealized potential: exploring the digital disability divide. Poetics **58**, 18–28 (2016). https://doi.org/10.1016/j.poetic.2016.08.003
3. Seeman, L., Lewis, C.: Cognitive and learning disabilities. In: Yesilada, Y., Harper, S. (eds.) Web Accessibility. HIS, pp. 49–58. Springer, London (2019). https://doi.org/10.1007/978-1-4471-7440-0_4
4. Leopold, M., Ertas-Spantgar, F., Müller, S.V.: Digitale assistive Technologien als Chancengeber für eine gleichberechtigte Teilhabe in der Gemeinschaft. In: Luthe, E.-W., Müller, S.V., Schiering, I. (eds.) Assistive Technologien im Sozial- und Gesundheitssektor. Springer Fachmedien Wiesbaden, Wiesbaden, pp. 225–243 (2022). https://doi.org/10.1007/978-3-658-34027-8_12
5. Dirks, S.: Persona design in participatory agile software development. In: Stephanidis, C., Antona, M., Gao, Q., Zhou, J. (eds.) HCII 2020. LNCS, vol. 12426, pp. 52–64. Springer, Cham (2020). https://doi.org/10.1007/978-3-030-60149-2_5

6. Heumader, P., Miesenberger, K., Murillo-Morales, T.: Adaptive user interfaces for people with cognitive disabilities within the easy reading framework. In: Miesenberger, K., Manduchi, R., Covarrubias Rodriguez, M., Peňáz, P. (eds.) ICCHP 2020. LNCS, vol. 12377, pp. 53–60. Springer, Cham (2020). https://doi.org/10.1007/978-3-030-58805-2_7
7. Schorb, B.: Medienkompetenz und Inklusion. In: Bosse, I., Schluchter, J.-R., Zorn, I. (eds.) Handbuch Inklusion und Medienbildung, pp 65–76. Beltz Juventa, Weinheim Basel (2019)
8. Hastall, M.R., Heitplatz, V.N.: Soziotechnische Systemgestaltung für Therapie und Pflege. In: Posenau, A., Deiters, W., Sommer, S., et al. (eds.) Nutzerorientierte Gesundheitstechnologien: Im Kontext von Therapie und Pflege, 1st edn., pp. 101–112. Hogrefe, Bern (2019)
9. Heitplatz, V., Wilkens, L., Bühler, C.: Gestaltungskonzepte und Beispiele zu digitalen Bildungsangeboten für heterogene Zielgruppen. In: Luthe, E.-W., Müller, S.V., Schiering, I. (eds.) Assistive Technologien im Sozial- und Gesundheitssektor, pp. 311–335. Springer Fachmedien Wiesbaden, Wiesbaden (2022). https://doi.org/10.1007/978-3-658-34027-8_16
10. European Union: Proposal for a COUNCIL RECOMMENDATION on Key Competences for LifeLong Learning (2019). https://eur-lex.europa.eu/legal-content/EN/TXT/PDF/?uri=CELEX:52018SC0014&from=EN. Accessed 21 Feb 2023
11. Chadwick, D., Wesson, C., Fullwood, C.: Internet access by people with intellectual disabilities: inequalities and opportunities. Fut. Internet 5, 376–397 (2013)
12. Chadwick, D., Fullwood, C.: An online life like any other: identity, self-determination, and social networking among adults with intellectual disabilities. Cyberpsychol. Behav. Soc. Netw. 21, 56–64 (2018). https://doi.org/10.1089/cyber.2016.0689
13. Carretero Gomez, S., Vuorikari, R., Punie, Y.: DigComp 2.1: The Digital Competence Framework for Citizens with eight proficiency levels and examples of use (2017). https://publicati ons.jrc.ec.europa.eu/repository/handle/JRC106281
14. Mayerle, M.: "Woher hat er die Idee?": Selbstbestimmte Teilhabe von Menschen mit Lernschwierigkeiten durch Mediennutzung: Abschlussbericht der Begleitforschung im PIKSL-Labor. ZPE-Schriftenreihe/Zentrum für Planung und Evaluation Sozialer Dienste der Universität Siegen, Nr. 40. universi - Universitätsverlag Siegen; Zentrum für Planung und Evaluation Sozialer Dienste, Siegen (2015)
15. Rawat, P., Morris, J.C.: The Effects of Technology and Institutions on E-participation: Across-National Analysis. Rutledge Research in Public Administration and Public Policy, vol. 30. Routledge, New York, NY (2021)
16. Rudolph, S.: Digitale Medien, Partizipation und Ungleichheit: Eine Studie zum sozialen Gebrauch des Internets. Springer Fachmedien Wiesbaden (2019). https://doi.org/10.1007/978-3-658-26943-2
17. Witting, T.: Digitale Ungleichheiten. In: Huster, E.-U., Boeckh, J., Mogge-Grotjahn, H. (eds.) Handbuch Armut und soziale Ausgrenzung. Springer Fachmedien Wiesbaden, Wiesbaden, pp. 457–478 (2018). https://doi.org/10.1007/978-3-658-19077-4_20
18. Verständig, D., Klein, A., Iske, S.: Zero-Level Digital Divide: Neues Netz und neue Ungleichheiten. Siegen: Sozial 21, 50–55 (2016)
19. Jenaro, C., Flores, N., Cruz, M., et al.: Internet and cell phone usage patterns among young adults with intellectual disabilities. J. Appl. Res. Intellect. Disabil. 31, 259–272 (2018). https://doi.org/10.1111/jar.12388
20. Initiative D21: D21 Digital Index 2021/2022 – Jährliches Lagebild zur Digitalen Gesellschaft (2022)
21. Scholz, F., Yalcin, B., Priestley, M.: Internet access for disabled people: understanding socio-relational factors in Europe. Cyberpsychol. J. Psychosoc. Res. Cybersp. 11 (2017). https://doi.org/10.5817/CP2017-1-4
22. Chadwick, D., Chapman, M., Caton, S.: Digital inclusion for people with an intellectual disability. In: Attrill-Smith, A., Fullwood, C., Keep, M., et al. (eds.) The Oxford Handbook of Cyberpsychology, pp. 261–284. Oxford University Press (2019)

23. Johnson, R., Hegarty, J.R.: Websites as educational motivators for adults with learning disability. Br. J. Edu. Technol. **34**, 479–486 (2003)
24. Lee, Y., Wehmeyer, M.L., Palmer, S., et al.: The effect of student-directed transition planning with a computer-based reading support program on the self-determination of students with disabilities. J. Spec. Educ. Technol. **19**, 7–22 (2004)
25. Holmes, K.M., O'Loughlin, N.: The experiences of people with learning disabilities on social networking sites. Br. J. Learn. Disabil. **42**, 1–7 (2014)
26. Keskinen, T., Heimonen, T., Turunen, M., et al.: SymbolChat: a flexible picture-based communication platform for users with intellectual disabilities. Interact. Comput. **24**, 374–386 (2012)
27. Kydland, F., Molka-Danielsen, J., Balandin, S.: Examining the use of social media tool "Flickr" for impact on loneliness for people with intellectual disability. In: Fallmyr, T., Bygstad, B., Fog, J., et al. (eds.) Proceedings of the 2012 Norsk konferanse for organisasjoners bruk av informasjonsteknologi. Akademika forlag, NOKOBIT 2012, Trondheim, Norway, pp. 253–264 (2012)
28. Löfgren-Mårtenson, L.: Love in cyberspace: Swedish young people with intellectual disabilities and the internet. Scand. J. Disabil. Res. **10**, 125–138 (2008). https://doi.org/10.1080/150 17410701758005
29. McClimens, A., Gordon, F.: Presentation of self in everyday life: how people labelled with intellectual disability manage identity as they engage the blogosphere. Sociol. Res. Online **13**, 40–52 (2008). https://doi.org/10.5153/sro.1774
30. Bengesser, C.: Digitale Teilhabe – Im Blickpunkt (2015). https://imblickpunkt.grimme-ins titut.de/digitale-teilhabe/. Accessed 15 Feb 2023
31. Solga, H., Dombrowski, R.: Soziale Ungleichheiten in schulischer und außerschulischer Bildung: Stand der Forschung und Forschungsbedarf. Bildung und Qualifizierung, Arbeitspapier 171 (2009)
32. Heitplatz, V.N., Bühler, C., Hastall, M.R.: Usage of digital media by people with intellectual disabilities: contrasting individuals' and formal caregivers' perspectives. J. Intellect. Disabil. (JOID) **26**, 420–441 (2021). https://doi.org/10.1177/1744629520971375
33. Pelka, B.: Digitale Teilhabe: Aufgaben der Verbände und Einrichtungen der Wohlfahrtspflege. In: Kreidenweis, H. (ed.) Digitaler Wandel in der Sozialwirtschaft: Grundlagen - Strategien - Praxis, 1. Auflage. Nomos, Baden-Baden, pp. 57–80 (2018)
34. Altmeppen, K.-D.: Teilhabe: Grundbegriffe der Kommunikations-und Medienethik (Teil 16). ComSoz **52**, 187–192 (2019). https://doi.org/10.5771/0010-3497-2016-2-191
35. van Dijk, J.A.: Digital divide: impact of access. In: Rössler, P., Hoffner, C.A., Zoonen, L. (eds.) The International Encyclopedia of Media Effects, pp. 1–11. Wiley (2017)
36. Vicente, M., Lopez-Menendez, A.: A multidimensional analysis of the disability digital divide: some evidence for internet use. Inf. Soc. **26**, 48–64 (2010). https://doi.org/10.1080/016154 40903423245
37. Heitplatz, V.N.: Digitale Teilhabemöglichkeiten von Menschen mit intellektuellen Beeinträchtigungen im Wohnkontext. TU Dortmund (2021)
38. Haage, A.: Informationsrepertoires von Menschen mit Beeinträchtigungen: Barrieren und Förderfaktoren für die gleichberechtigte Teilhabe an öffentlicher Kommunikation, 1. Auflage. Lebensweltbezogene Medienforschung, vol. 9. Nomos, Baden-Baden (2021)
39. Pelka, B.: Digitalisierung als soziale Innovation verstehen und umsetzen. In: Ückert, S., Sürgit, H., Diesel, G. (eds.) Digitalisierung als Erfolgsfaktor für das Sozial- und Wohlfahrtswesen. Nomos, pp. 263–278 (2020)
40. Reidl, S., Streicher, J., Hock, M., et al.: Digitale Ungleichheit: Wie sie entsteht, was sie bewirkt … und was dagegen hilft (2020). https://www.femtech.at/sites/default/files/Reidl%2C%20S treicher%2C%20Hock%2C%20Hausner%2C%20Waibel%2C%20G%C3%BCrtl%20%282 020%29%20Studie_Digitale_Ungleichheit_barrierefrei_final.pdf. Accessed 21 Feb 2023

41. Lussier-Desrochers, D., Normand, C.L., Romero-Torres, A., et al.: Bridging the digital divide for people with intellectual disability. Cyberpsychol. J. Psychosoc. Res. Cybersp. **11** (2017). https://doi.org/10.5817/CP2017-1-1

42. Ramsten, C., Martin, L., Dag, M., et al.: Information and communication technology use in daily life among young adults with mild-to-moderate intellectual disability. J. Intellect. Disabil. **24**, 289–308 (2018)

43. Abel, J., Hirsch-Kreinsen, H., Steglich, S., et al.: Akzeptanz von Industrie 4.0

44. Rath, M.O., Tannrath, M.: Teaching in digital societies as a topic of an ethically informed media pedagogy (2019)

45. Ramsten, C., Hammar, L.M., Martin, L., et al.: ICT and intellectual disability: a survey of organizational support at the municipal level in Sweden. J. Appl. Res. Intellect. Disabil. **30**, 705–713 (2017). https://doi.org/10.1111/jar.12265

46. Parsons, S., Daniels, H., Porter, J., et al.: Resources, staff beliefs and organizational culture: factors in the use of information and communication technology for adults with intellectual disabilities. J. Appl. Res. Int. Dis. **21**, 19–33 (2008). https://doi.org/10.1111/j.1468-3148.2007.00361.x

47. Seale, J., Chadwick, D.: How does risk mediate the ability of adolescents and adults with intellectual and developmental disabilities to live a normal life by using the Internet? Cyberpsychol. J. Psychosoc. Res. Cybersp. **11** (2017). https://doi.org/10.5817/CP2017-1-2

48. Caton, S., Chapman, M.: The use of social media and people with intellectual disability: a systematic review and thematic analysis. J. Intellect. Dev. Disabil. **41**, 125–139 (2016). https://doi.org/10.3109/13668250.2016.1153052

49. Jockisch, M.: Das Technologieakzeptanzmodell. In: Bandow, G., Holzmüller, H.H. (eds.) "Das ist gar kein Modell!": Unterschiedliche Modelle und Modellierungen in Betriebswirtschaftslehre und Ingenieurwissenschaften, pp. 233–254. Gabler, Wiesbaden (2010)

50. Krüger, S., Berberian, A.P.: Augmentative and alternative communication system (AAC) for social inclusion of people with complex communication needs in the industry. Assist. Technol. **27**, 101–111 (2015). https://doi.org/10.1080/10400435.2014.984261

51. Raghavendra, P., Newman, L., Grace, E., et al.: 'I could never do that before': effectiveness of a tailored Internet support intervention to increase the social participation of youth with disabilities. Child Care Health Dev. **39**, 552–561 (2013). https://doi.org/10.1111/cch.12048

52. Simon, B.: Wissensmedien im Bildungssektor: Eine Akzeptanzuntersuchung an Hochschulen. Dissertation, Wirtschaftsuniversität Wien (2001)

53. Petrie, H., Carmien, S., Lewis, A.: Assistive technology abandonment: research realities and potentials. In: Miesenberger, K., Kouroupetroglou, G. (eds.) ICCHP 2018. LNCS, vol. 10897, pp. 532–540. Springer, Cham (2018). https://doi.org/10.1007/978-3-319-94274-2_77

54. Davis, F.D.: A technology acceptance model for empirically testing new end-user information systems: theory and results (1986)

55. Davis, F.D.: Perceived usefulness, perceived ease of use, and user acceptance of information technology. MIS Q. **13**, 319 (1989). https://doi.org/10.2307/249008

56. Davis, F.D., Bagozzi, R.P., Warshaw, P.R.: User acceptance of computer technology: a comparison of two theoretical models. Manage. Sci. **35**, 982–1003 (1989). https://doi.org/10.1287/mnsc.35.8.982

57. Venkatesh, V., Davis, F.D.: A theoretical extension of the technology acceptance model: four longitudinal field studies. Manage. Sci. **46**, 186–204 (2000). https://doi.org/10.1287/mnsc.46.2.186.11926

58. Venkatesh, V., Morris, M.G., Davis, G.B., et al.: User acceptance of information technology: toward a unified view. MIS Q. **27**, 425 (2003). https://doi.org/10.2307/30036540

59. Venkatesh, V., Bala, H.: Technology acceptance model 3 and a research agenda on interventions. Decis. Sci. **39**, 273–315 (2008). https://doi.org/10.1111/j.1540-5915.2008.00192.x

60. Venkatesh, V., Thong, J.Y.L., Xu, X.: Consumer acceptance and use of information technology: extending the unified theory of acceptance and use of technology. MIS Q. **36**, 157 (2012). https://doi.org/10.2307/41410412
61. Dirks, S., Bühler, C.: Akzeptanz von assistiven Softwaresystemen für Menschen mit kognitiven Beeinträchtigungen. Gesellschaft für Informatik, Bonn (2017)
62. Quante, A.: Förderbedarfe und digitale Möglichkeiten. In: Haider, M., Schmeinck, D. (eds.) Digitalisierung in der Grundschule: Grundlagen, Gelingensbedingungen und didaktische Konzeptionen am Beispiel des Fach Sachunterrichts, pp. 98–108. Verlag Julius Klinkhardt, Bad Heilbrunn (2022)
63. Convention on the Rights of Persons with Disabilities: UN-CRPD (2006)
64. W3C: Web Content Accessibility Guidelines (WCAG) 2.1. (2018). https://www.w3.org/TR/WCAG21/. Accessed 21 Feb 2023
65. The WebAIM Million: The 2022 report on the accessibility of the top 1,000,000 home pages (2022)
66. Homepage Eye-Able. https://eye-able.com/en/. Accessed 24 Feb 2023
67. Meyer, A.: Standardsoftware. In: Meyer A (ed) Softwareentwicklung. De Gruyter, pp. 121–132 (2018)
68. Kuckartz, U., Rädiker, S.: Qualitative Inhaltsanalyse: Methoden, Praxis, Computerunterstützung, 5. Auflage. Grundlagentexte Methoden. Beltz Juventa, Weinheim, Basel (2022)
69. Creswell, J.W.: Research Design: Qualitative, Quantitative, and Mixed Method Approaches, 3rd edn. SAGE, London (2009)
70. Kuckartz, U., Rädiker, S.: Fokussierte Interviewanalyse mit MAXQDA. Springer Fachmedien Wiesbaden, Wiesbaden (2020). https://doi.org/10.1007/978-3-658-31468-2
71. Heitplatz, V., Nellen, C., Sube, L., et al.: Implementing new technological devices in social services: introducing the miTAS project. In: Miesenberger, K., Petz, A. (eds.) Future Perspectives of AT, eAccessibility and eInclusion, vol. 1, pp. 109–118 (2020)
72. Wember, F.B., Melle, I.: Adaptive Lernsituationen im inklusiven Unterricht: Planung und Analyse von Unterricht auf Basis des Universal Design for Learning. In: Hußmann, S., Welzel, B. (eds.) DoProfiL – Das Dortmunder Profil für inklusionsorientierte Lehrerinnen- und Lehrerbildung. Waxmann, Münster, New York, NY, pp. 57–72 (2018)
73. Fisseler, B.: Inklusive Digitalisierung, Universal Design for Learning und assistive Technologie. Sonderpädagogische Förderung heute **1**, 9–20 (2020)

Assistive Environments and Quality of Life Technologies

Communication Needs of Individuals with Aphasia and Caregivers in Unplanned Activities

Lula Albar[1](✉), Vitaveska Lanfranchi[1], and Suvodeep Mazumdar[2]

[1] Department of Computer Science, University of Sheffield, Sheffield S1 4DP, UK
lhalbar1@sheffield.ac.uk
[2] Information School, University of Sheffield, Sheffield S1 4DP, UK

Abstract. People with Aphasia (PWA) have communication difficulties that affect their daily activities and ability to live independently and increase the risk of social isolation. Most of their daily activities are planned and primarily performed in familiar settings or with familiar people. Augmented and Alternative Communication (AAC) devices can support communication for PWA and their family and carers during everyday life. However, managing new activities in an unfamiliar setting with unfamiliar people would subject PWA to stressful situations in which they could feel less confident and unable to communicate. In these situations, the benefits of AAC devices can be diminished. Therefore, a new approach is needed that can support individuals with aphasia and their families or carers in unplanned activities, but to be effective, this approach must be grounded in the unmet needs of PWA and co-designed with them. For this purpose, we conducted user studies to understand our users' information and communication needs. Our results show that (1) the most used and appreciated communication aid amongst PWA is photos; (2) personal photos reflect people's favourite locations, events they enjoy discussing, and friends they enjoy spending time with; (3) they are therefore the ideal starting point for a context-aware AAC. This work contributes to the literature on the design of context-aware systems for individuals with aphasia, and the results will help inform the design of a new AAC.

Keywords: Aphasia · Augmented and Alternative Communication · Context-Aware Computing · Aphasia · Unplanned Activity

1 Introduction

Aphasia is one of the most severe consequences of a stroke or head injury and can affect memory, speed of reasoning, and the ability to communicate [1]. People with Aphasia (PWA) face communication challenges that interfere with their daily activities and ability to live independently and increase the risk of social isolation [2, 3]. Eventually, PWA adapt to their new lives, which are heavily reliant on Augmented and Alternative Communication (AAC) devices and carers as a support system while communicating [4]. Caregivers play a crucial role in configuring AAC devices with information (e.g., symbols and functional sentences) relevant to the user's plans and training them to use the devices in natural conversational situations [5, 6]. Thus, the daily activities of PWA are structured around plans with familiar people and places. Generally, these are indoor activities (e.g., at home or in a therapy clinic) and mostly passive (e.g., watching TV) [4]. Managing new activities in an unfamiliar setting with unfamiliar people, on the other hand, would place PWA in stressful situations where they could feel inadequate in social settings, leading to frustration, alienation, and a feeling of being a burden on their carers [7, 8]. In these situations, the benefits of AAC devices can be diminished, which leads to high abandonment rates [9].

PWA expect AACs to meet their needs in different settings, whether in familiar or unfamiliar environments or with different conversation partners. However, there is a gap between the users' expectations and the available AACs, which is the major reason for the high abandonment rates [10–13]. AAC interfaces adhere to two forms of content organisation: grid displays with symbols in semantic categories (e.g., Lingraphica) and visual scene displays (VSD) that provide photos in context (e.g., Talkabout) [14, 15]. The typical hierarchical organisation of symbol-based AAC tools makes it difficult for users to locate the desired words [16–18] and time-consuming for carers to select and pre-programme helpful words [5]. Therefore, tools are frequently programmed with a limited vocabulary that cannot be used for unanticipated activities. Recent research [19] evaluated the effects of the two displays on communicative characteristics such as conversational turns among PWA. The study revealed that visual scene presentation enhanced participants' communication by reducing frustration, decreasing navigational errors, and increasing conversational turns.

Accordingly, a new approach is needed that can support PWA and their family members when participating in unplanned activities. Our objective in this paper is to understand the information and communication needs of AAC users to support them with a rich contextual information and communication aid that enables PWA in any conversational setting, especially an unplanned one, and does not limit them to a list of vocabulary and prepared sentences for planned activities. To design an AAC that is adaptable to new situations, we designed user studies to identify (1) the difficulties that PWA face when communicating in unplanned activities and (2) the needs and require-ments of PWA when using AAC in unplanned activities. In future, we would like to use these findings to develop AAC that can assist self-expression using contextual infor-mation for unexpected social interactions that go beyond pre-planned interactions or functional communication tasks.

This paper presents the findings of the user requirements study. First, we conducted focus groups and interviews with PWA, clinical staff, and family and carers to understand their experiences and unmet needs. From these, we derived examples of unplanned activities, AAC usage patterns, and communication styles. The main finding from the focus groups and interviews was the use of photo content as communication clues for PWA, who identify a person, a location, or an event by using photos on their mobile phone or iPad. That led to a photo content study to better understand what photos they use and how they could influence our design direction for future work in developing adaptive communication aid applications. We also present the lessons learned about how to communicate with and approach participants with aphasia, develop trust, and deal with unexpected circumstances. We learned that PWA are willing to participate in research if the research team provides the necessary support. Tailoring the approach process to recruit PWA and obtain their consent is required, such as providing visual information sheets and large fonts [20, 21].

This paper is organised as follows: we initially discuss the related literature (Sect. 2) on AAC and aphasia, VSD and context-aware AACs for PWA, followed by a description of our first focus group study and key findings. In Sect. 3, we discuss our photo content study and present our findings. In the discussion section, we present our broad findings and lessons learned. We conclude the paper with a summary of the research conducted and some ideas about future work.

2 Related Work

In this section, we briefly discuss relevant work on the design and usage of AACs, how changes in the field of AAC influence AAC use, and prior context-aware AAC technologies.

2.1 AAC and Aphasia

Despite the high abandonment rate of AAC [9], the appeal of AAC technology as the ultimate solution for compensatory communication is still strong. Communication competency for AAC users has been defined by Light in 1989 with four domains: operational, linguistic, social and strategic [22]. Prior AAC rehabilitation efforts for aphasia emphasised linguistic and operational skills with little focus on the social and strategic domains [23–25]. The original definition of communication competency for AAC users was reviewed by Light and McNaughton in 2012 and 2014 to reflect on the changes in the AAC area and the challenges for users to master the four domains [26, 27]. Light and McNaughton discussed how the range of communication requirements has expanded. The realisation is growing that AAC systems must accommodate complex communication. It is no longer sufficient to convey desires and needs, but there is an understanding that AAC users' systems must go beyond functional communication into extensive discourse.

2.2 Visual Scene Displays for Aphasia

AAC technology interfaces follow two types of content organisation: grid displays with symbols in semantic categories (e.g., Lingraphica) and VSD that present photos in contextual reference (e.g., Talkabout) [14, 15]. A recent study compared the impact of the two displays on many communicative variables (e.g., conversational turns) among PWA [19]. The study showed that visual scene presentation improved participants' communication with fewer frustrations and navigational blunders and more conversational turns. PWA can use VSDs to help with both their therapy activities and their communication with other people. The use of personal photos has a greater impact because photographs of people, objects, and activities that are personally significant for users rely primarily on autobiographical memory and visual cognitive skills rather than linguistic processing as the basis for representing messages and navigating AAC systems [28]. VSDs also provide a basis for establishing a shared communication space between a person with aphasia and their communication partners [29]. Photographic content is a rich data source that reflects places, objects, actions, people, and daily life activities more than line-drawing symbols [17].

2.3 Context-Aware AAC

Using contextual information for developing AAC can improve the design in terms of simplicity and effectiveness for the end users [30]. We argue that communication aids for PWA should not require the user to experience lengthy navigation tasks to find a vocabulary or a phrase. A communication aid should provide the user with an informative presentation and services to improve communication quality based on their current context, whether it is planned or not. Context-awareness computing can provide these features and improve the quality of communication. We observed several context-aware AAC systems designed for people with communication impairments [15, 31–34]. MyVoice and Talkabout are two studies that provide PWA with conversation topics based on the user's location [15, 33]. Sánchez designed an AAC device for visually impaired users that supports users in an unplanned activity [35]. While prior studies have not used context-aware technology to support PWA in unplanned activities, we believe that our study findings could support that design direction to support users in any conversational setting.

3 Study 1: How PWA Communicate in Unplanned Activity

We began our inquiry with a qualitative study that included focus groups and interviews that were perfectly appropriate for investigating the complex communication experiences of PWA [36]. The aim is to have rich data that reflect contextual details about complicated stories of PWA communicating in unplanned activities. Due to COVID-19, the study started with a focus group in Sheffield, UK, with the Geriatric and Stroke Medicine (GSM) department at Sheffield Teaching Hospitals, then moved to Jeddah, KSA, to continue with interviews at the rehabilitation centre at Abdul Latif Jameel Hospital. We received ethics approval from The University of Sheffield with reference number 031173 to conduct the study in Sheffield and KSA. There were no significant changes to recruitment processes, methods, or any specific ethical considerations or risks (to participants and researchers) of conducting the research in a new location.

3.1 Focus Group

Participants. We recruited eight participants, five individuals with aphasia and three caregivers. Table 1 presents details of their demographic information and AAC usage. Participants were approached through the GSM group, who offers continuous care for elderly patients with dementia and stroke survivors. We identified participants with aphasia from this group that might have used or are still using AAC and their caregivers.

Individuals with severe cognitive impairments or visual disabilities were not qualified for this study because of the visual materials presented within the study.

Procedures. The focus group was scheduled as a one-and-a-half-hour session that took place at the Graves Health and Sports Centre. The session was designed to present participants with a structured scenario, following which they were asked a series of questions. The structured scenario was presented as a pictorial storyboard of an unplanned activity example based on our discussion with a speech therapist to stimulate participants' engagement in the discussion (see Fig. 1). The first author and a speech therapist facilitated the session by illustrating questions and ideas, pausing the conversation if any participants were confused, and writing keywords on the board to assist participants in understanding the discussion. We used the storyboard example to motivate participants to share similar experiences and answer the following questions:

- What would Peter do in this situation?
- Do participants face similar unplanned communication situations?
- Does it help to have a communication aid in this situation?
- What technologies do participants use to support communication in similar situations?

Table 1. Focus Group Participants

P	Sex	Age	Aphasia Severity	Communication Aid
P1	F	55	Mild comprehension and Severe expressive ability	iPhone app Lingraphica
P2	M	47	Mild expressive ability	Rarely used iPhone app Lingraphica
P3	M	67	Mild comprehension and Severe expressive ability	iPhone app Lingraphica
P4	M	62	Mild expressive ability	Stopped using it a while ago
P5	F	51	Severability to express (aphonia)	Paper and pen for drawing/writing small words

3.2 Interviews

To complement and confirm the breadth offered by the focus group, we conducted a second user study to examine the nature of communication in unplanned activities as semi-structured interviews.

Participants. We recruited nine participants, seven PWA and two caregivers. Table 2 presents details of their demographic information and AAC usage in planned and unplanned activities if any. The rehabilitation centre at Abdul Latif Jameel Hospital, introduced us to 15 patients who were approached through an invitation letter and information sheet in an aphasia-friendly format, followed by a phone call from the researcher to their caregivers. If the participant consented, we scheduled a date and time for the

Fig. 1. A scenario used as an example of unplanned activity. Peter is a person with aphasia who loves photography. He planned his day to attend his speech therapy session by himself, but while on the bus, he received a text saying, "Your therapy appointment is cancelled." He got off the bus confused and had no idea what to do with his free time without his wife's support.

interview. We also interviewed two speech therapists who work closely with aphasic individuals.

Design. We asked participants for a single interview that took place at the rehabilitation centre in a familiar environment where they felt comfortable. The face-to-face semi-structured interview was designed to take approximately one and a half hours. Interviewing participants with aphasia requires the researcher to adopt different strategies for questioning [37]. It is essential to use communication support strategies for PWA to capture the full extent of information available from participants. The speech therapist reviewed interview questions and recommended a few wording changes to improve the language used. The speech therapist suggested simple grammar and visual cues; thus, we used a communication style suitable to the need of PWA. Pictorial vocabulary allows participants to express their answers such as using the visual analogue scale that was inspired by (see Fig. 2) [38]. The interviews were conducted in Arabic, as all participants were more familiar with conversing in the local language.

Fig. 2. Using a visual analogue scale to answer interview questions such as "Do you use AAC?

Table 2. Participants' demographic information and AAC usage in planned/unplanned Activity

P	Sex (Age)	Years post stroke	Comprehension/Naming	AAC	Planned/Unplanned
P1	M (54)	2	Near regular/often poor	Application on iPhone	Yes/No
P2	M (62)	2	Mild ability/often poor	Stopped using it a while ago	Yes/tried with difficulties
P3	M (58)	4	Mild ability/often poor	Rarely used	Yes/tried with difficulties
P4	F (62)	5	Mild/always poor	Rarely used	Yes/No
P5	F (56)	2	Severability to express (aphonia)	Application on iPhone	Yes/tried with difficulties
P6	F (48)	1	Normal/Varied	Application on iPhone	Yes/Yes
P7	M (66)	1	Mild/always poor	Rarely used/Paper and pen	Yes/No

3.3 Findings

1. **Suggested Scenarios.** Participants shared similar scenarios that they faced and struggled with:

Shopping. P1 shared a story of shopping in a clothing store and trying to communicate with the sales assistant to find the right size of a shirt in a different colour. She described that as an exhausting experience that she would not do again without her support system.

Conversation While Driving. P3 and his spouse shared one of their daily life activities that becomes stressful for both. The spouse complained about how it is hard to communicate while driving with her husband, especially when they pass a location he wants to talk about or is interested in visiting. P3 described it as a tedious conversation when she cannot understand what he wants to say. She said he uses the palms down gesture with both hands to show he gives up on their conversation. This couple showed interest in finding an easier way to make the conversation accessible and fun, affecting the relationship positively.

2. Communication Style

Participants responded to the first question, "How much do your current communication skills affect your life?" They agreed on the difficulties they faced in accomplishing daily life tasks such as grocery shopping. They elaborated that they must have a plan for completing a specific task to be equipped with the right communication aids.

We asked our participants about their communication styles and what type of AAC they use. All participants had used AAC tools to support communication, such as Lingraphica, Grid 3, and TouchChat, with an extra cost for the Arabic language interface [39, 40]. Participants mentioned how useful these tools were for communication during their therapy sessions. P1: "I can point to an image, and my therapist would understand what I want to say." However, they rarely used it outside their homes or with new conversation partners. This was due to the constant need for customising AAC devices to a user's needs, a difficult task for which participants mainly depend on their therapist or partner.

Slow Conversation: Another issue the participants highlighted was difficulties finding the appropriate word, making the conversation slow. One of the participants pointed to a Lingraphica that he liked, saying, "I can use this for small talk and questions." However, participants did not consider AAC tools as conversation support because it takes time to find the word.

Attention: Our two caregiver participants showed the need for complete attention while conversing with their partners. They described the experience of talking with their aphasic partners as a task that needs all senses to have a successful conversation. However, giving full attention in a situation such as talking while driving is not easy. People with CI mostly use gestures, facial expressions, and pointing at objects, and photos as communication supports.

Conversation Partners: Our participants mentioned that, after the stroke, they had limited social contact. All participants were looking for a patient con- versation partner who urged them to talk. Participants depended on their partners to communicate with caregivers: "I have to go with him everywhere."

Guessing Games: We learned that PWA have communication keys with their caregivers. They create a style that makes essential functional communication more accessible for them to perform, such as using gestures and pointing for essential communication. Our caregiver participants described the guessing games they play with their partners. They mentioned that using this game is not always practical, and it depends on the situation. For example, in a home setting playing the guessing game is more productive than playing it with a group of friends and family. Also, the caregiver or the conversation partner must be patient and can support the conversation with cues known cues to both of them.

The Use of Photos: The use of photos as a communication style was mentioned several times during the focus group and interviews Participants find that using photos makes the experience more interactive, especially if they work with their own photos. The group elaborated that using photos makes telling stories to their conversation partners more interesting.

3. Professional Interview Insights

To better understand how PWA currently communicate, we conducted semi-structured interviews with two experienced speech therapists. We gained strong design ideas by working with experts in the aphasia field. The speech therapists understood the research goal and were able to contribute based on their knowledge. They work with aphasia daily; thus, they have a much broader knowledge of aphasic needs and abilities. The interview objectives were: (a) to comprehend the potential role of contextual information to improve communication aids; and (b) to understand current barriers to using AAC applications in face-to-face communication in planned or unplanned activities. The therapist mentioned that PWA use visual materials as an educational tool in almost every activity at the centre. PWA may become more open over time and start sharing stories using their photos. They mentioned that many members at the centre become excited and interactive when they work with photos associated with events and locations they love. We also discussed the employment of AAC applications and how an aphasic person perceives them. They mentioned that configuration is the main barrier to every member having one-to-one sessions to customise his or her AAC application. Another problem while using AAC applications observed by therapists is the complexity of AAC applications that have a long list of words a user must browse to find the right word.

4   Study 2: Photo Content Study

The usage of images as a communication aid by PWA is one of the primary insights we gained from Study 1. Participants shared stories about how they used images from their phones to carry on a conversation during unplanned activities. They used the content of photos as communication cues, such as recognising an object while shopping, a favourite area while driving, or a person while telling a story. That is a user-driven communication experience that should be investigated while designing AAC that supports unplanned activity communication. As a result, we designed the photo content analysis study, which has long been used as a research instrument in visual studies [41]. Visual tools are becoming more popular as alternative qualitative ways of complementing and enriching quantitative investigations, but they have their own set of research advantages [42]. In recent years, the use of photo interpretation as a significant research methodology has expanded in different research areas, such as context awareness, artificial intelligence, and tourism [43, 44].

4.1 Approach

We manually examined participants' photos, looking for data related to their activities. These data indicate the possibility for a person's existing photo collection to be used to enrich the AAC's underlying database. This research is based on the concept that meaningful information can be extracted from a collection of personal photographs. We anticipated being able to collect data on the following topics: individuals, locations, objects, events, and tags. Rich data sources, such as photographs, depict a person's location (e.g., vacation spots), memorable events they prefer to recall, or objects that demonstrate their hobbies (e.g., fishing). To better comprehend photo usage, we conducted a study consisting of two tasks: (1) a photo content analysis and (2) a photo sorting exercise. The objective was to analyse digital photo albums on the mobile devices of individuals with aphasia to answer the following questions regarding photo content and communication usage:

Task 1. Photo content analysis: What are the subjects of the photos taken by aphasic individuals? What is the information that human judges can collect?

Task 2. Understanding photo use in communication: How do PWA use photographs to communicate? What elements of images are most crucial for participants?

4.2 Participants

To explore these questions, we contacted participants from the interview study to obtain a photo sample for another research activity, with the same ethics approval from The University of Sheffield with reference number 031173, to conduct a photo content analysis study. The rehabilitation centre of Abdul Latif Jameel Hospital conducts a storytelling activity where PWA practice talking about their families and hobbies. Speech therapists help PWA in creating posters using printed personal photos to make a family tree or describe a trip as a communication skill practice. During this activity, we collected a set of photos to explore what data exists and what can potentially be extracted. These photos were gathered by the staff of the rehabilitation centre and examined by the researcher with permission from the participants.

4.3 Task 1: Photo Content Analysis

Procedure and Analysis. We employed grounded theory to code (i.e., categorise) a sample of 714 photos [45, 46]. The rehabilitation centre staff collected these photos, and then the researcher and the speech therapist examined them. Photos were taken from nine PWA (5 male, 4 female) average age of 61.7 (SD = 11.3, minimum 48, maximum 66). First, the researcher and speech therapist independently analysed each photo using a coding scheme, where each photo belonged to only one category. The initial coding categories are people, locations, objects, selfies, nature, and text. Then, to improve the quality of this manual categorisation, we asked the speech therapist to examine photos in each category. Through discussion, the researcher and speech therapist analysed the affinity of the themes within and across categories and manually adjusted categories if necessary (moving photos to a more appropriate category). This coding process was conducted by human judges and will potentially be automated in the future.

Findings

Size of Photo Collections: The average size of an individual's photo collection was 79.3 (SD = 56.8).

Subjects of the Photos: 397 photos (6%) were of people, 240 photos (33.6%) were of objects, 161 photos (22.5%) were scenes, 129 photos (18.1%) were of nature, and 33 photos (4.6%) were text. The observation showed many pictures of boats, ships, signs, and buildings. Also, the participants' photos showed a high appearance of animals (e.g., pets) and flowers. Among photos with people in them, the average number of people in the photos was 1.2 (SD = 1.4). 153 photos (21.4%) had only one person, and 135 photos (18.9%) had two people.

Locations of the Photos: 473 photos (66%) were taken outside, 214 photos (30%) were taken inside, and 25 photos (3.5%) were from unknown locations. The observation showed several indoor locations, such as the participants' homes. Outdoor locations were mostly trip photos such as boat trips and the city downtown.

Filenames: 28 photos (3.9%) had a date, eight photos (1.1%) named an object, 67 photos (9.4%) named people, 36 photos (5.0%) named locations, and 20 photos (2.8%) named events. Two participants had descriptive file names for their photos, e.g., names of people in the photo or a combination of data, events, and people's names (see Fig. 3).

Faces in the Images: 346 photos (48.5%) had recognisable human faces, and 105 photos (14.7%) had unrecognisable human faces.

Photo Sources: 216 photos (30.3%) were scanned, and 498 photos (69.7%) were not. Photos were taken with a Nikon camera, a Fujifilm camera, and an iPhone 4s. We saw details of several devices and models. Also, most of the participants scanned some of their printed photos (e.g., old family portraits) to be able to browse them on their portable devices or took a photo of a printed image to convert it to digital.

4.4   Task 2: Photo Sorting Activity

This activity aims to answer these questions: How do PWA organise or group their photos? How do they order photos (e.g., chronologically)? How do they describe or tag their photos?

Procedure. The activity was conducted at the rehabilitation centre of Abdul Latif Jameel Hospital with six members (five male, one female) with an average age of 59.2 (SD = 13.6, minimum 42, maximum 76). We randomly selected 20 of each member's photos with the participants' permission. We designed the activity with two different tasks: The first task was to cluster and sort their 20 printed personal photos. The second task was to indicate the most important data for their photos. We asked participants to

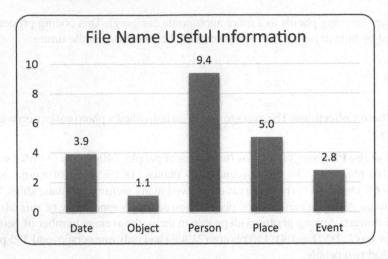

Fig. 3. Data extracted from photos filenames

view all their photos in the clustering task and start grouping them. We observed participants while they were grouping their photos and sorting them. In finding the most important data in the photo task, the researcher reviewed each photo with the participants and asked them to point out the most important data or what caught their eye first. The second task was done in two rounds.

Findings. Participants started looking at each photo and finding an appropriate group for each one; they took less than two minutes to group their photos. All the participants started with their newest image of the entire collection to create the first group. The average group number was 3.7 (SD = 0.8).

Table 3. Photo grouping preferences

	P1	P2	P3	P4	P5	P6	%
Spatial	2	2	3	2	3	1	59%
Content	3	1	0	2	1	2	40.9%

Photo Grouping Preferences: 13 groups (59%) were spatially formed, and nine (40.09%) groups were formed by content (Table 3). The spatial group had photos of trips or locations they attend regularly (e.g., rehabilitation centre, supermarket). Four out of six participants sorted their photos within the same group chronologically, and the rest did random sorting. Two out of six participants lined up the groups according to time (e.g., when photos were taken, Day 1 of a trip). Participants used a map to identify every spatial group they formed to determine where the photo was taken. The content group had photos of people (e.g., family, friends), nature, and objects (e.g., cars, motorcycles). Participants had random organisation within content groups. Participants did not hesitate or reform any created group and found the task easy to do independently. That also helped them tell stories and talk about their trips or the people in the photo.

Regions of Interest: All our participants identified one important piece of data in the first round. They recognised six data subjects: 42.9% were people, 20.2% were objects, 17.8% were places, 10.7% were events, 4.8% were nature, and 1.2% were text data. In the second round, 27 photos (32.1%) did not have recognisable data for participants. The highest percentage of data identified was place data at 22.6%, with 20.2% people, 10.7% objects, 9.5% nature, 2.4% events, and 1.2% text (Table 4).

Table 4. Personal photos region of interest with two rounds

	People	Event	Place	Nature	Object	Text
Round 1	42.9%	10.7%	17.8%	4.8%	20.2%	1.2%
Round 2	20.2%	2.4%	22.6%	9.5%	10.7%	1.2%

Pointing out the most important piece of data was easy for our participants in the first round and made them talk more about the story behind the photo, referring to the person or object in the photo. The second round was slow, and participants had difficulty finding another interesting subject in their photos.

5 Discussion

The study found that PWA are keen to enhance their communication abilities and adjust to their new condition; most participants used AAC or aphasia therapy programmes at home. Outside of their homes or rehabilitation centres, none of the participants used AAC. Participants stated that they required assistance in using these programmes. For other individuals who had never used computer treatment or an AAC, the most difficult challenge was a lack of assistance in training and customising the AAC device. These findings indicate that speech therapists and AAC developers must improve AAC to balance aphasics' desire for independent AAC use with their need for support. We believe that striking this balance will increase the success of AAC applications while also making users happier.

AAC Use
A tiny number of people expressed negative thoughts concerning AAC apps. These negative judgements, according to the analysis, were often based on a mismatch between a communication aid system and the participant's expectations regarding task difficulty, diversity, or overall effectiveness. It emphasises the need for speech therapists to direct and support PWA who use AAC, preferably beginning with the initial selection of AAC and activities based on the user's language and movement skills and continuing with AAC suitability, diversity, and effectiveness monitoring. The conclusions of the interviews

support the findings of the preceding section's focus group in terms of using contextual information as a clue to stimulate face-to-face dialogue.

Photo Content-Driven Data

Overall, the photo content study highlighted interesting data that could be extracted from the photosets. Over 89.2% had an identifiable subject. While the current analysis was conducted manually, we believe that some aspects of this analysis can be fully or partially automated.

From working with PWA, we learned that family members and friends are some of the most frequent conversational topics. However, participants have difficulty remembering or saying their names and their relationships. Our analysis showed that 55.6% of the collected photo sets were of people, and 48.5% of these photos had at least one recognisable human face, making face detection feasible. Applying facial recognition technology can identify familiar faces and label them once. This would make it accessible for an aphasic person to participate in a conversation and answer questions, e.g., Who are the people in this photo? Who went with you on this trip?

Object data were contained in 33.6% of the collected photosets. Their frequent activities and objects of interest can be learned by applying object detection techniques. Starting a conversation and using labelled objects would be more enjoyable if everyday objects could be recognised. P3 liked to talk about boats and ships, and his photo set contains many photos of his favourite topics. Another example is that P1 enjoys music and attends musical performances. His photo set contains 15 out of 56 photos of a band playing music; a guitar was the most common object in this photo set.

Lessons Learned from Working with PWA

Working with communication-impaired participants to collect data is challenging because of their difficulties expressing their experiences and needs [39]. We recommended that the participant's partner or a speech therapist be present during interviews to overcome these issues. We asked questions, and the carer or speech therapist assisted in clarifying the question when it was needed. If the caregiver or therapist answers a question without consulting the participant, we asked the participants to con- firm. Also, tailoring the approach process to recruit and obtain consent is required for PWA, such as by providing visual information sheets and large fonts [38].

We believe it is important for the researchers to educate themselves on communication strategies with PWA. In our case, working as a volunteer in the aphasia rehabilitation centre, the first author gained practical experience and built trust with potential participants for future studies. This helped with preparing the necessary research materials (e.g., consent forms) and documentation. Not having the right communication aids would subject the research project to a slow recruitment process. Also, reviewing the research materials (e.g., interview questions) with a speech therapist would increase participants' engagement and reduce their frustration.

6   Conclusion

We hypothesised that individuals with aphasia would be more independent while engaged in spontaneous discussions and capable of doing a variety of daily tasks. However, present AAC devices do not provide the intended users with applicable tools for use in such environments. We believe that incorporating contextual information into the AAC application would enhance the user experience. To create a successful AAC product, we must satisfy the demands and requirements of the user. Therefore, in this user study, user-centred design framework was used to enhance the quality and effectiveness of the final product. We used the following techniques to gather user requirements: 1) Focus groups reflected the perspectives of a variety of communication aid users. 2) We then conducted interviews with aphasic individuals, their caretakers, and experts. 3) These investigations led us to the application of picture study in aphasia patients' conversations.

This study triangulated three data sources to acquire a better understanding. The triangulation of data strengthens the research's evidence and links it to design, analysis, and interpretation. The variety of data sources shows how contextual data can improve the AAC app user experience. The focus group and interviews with aphasics discussed their AAC application use and issues. They also described their communication methods by using photographs to make the impromptu discussion more participatory. The photo content study demonstrated that by identifying persons, things, and places in users' photographs, we could provide aphasic individuals with conversation subjects and memory cues for forgotten words. Finally, we offer a new method for enhancing the database underlying communications tools by scanning digital photographs of persons for information about their actions. The AAC system can then incorporate recognisably named people and locations from the photo database into a standard AAC menu. This can assist the user in instances such as determining their preferred shopping locations. For future work, we will rely on the data collected from the previous study to identify requirements for building a context-aware AAC application. The main goal of this tool is to increase the number of communication tasks that would improve the quality of life for people with aphasia and support them in an unplanned circumstance. The objective of this study is to evaluate the use of contextual information in AAC devices to augment communication abilities for people with aphasia in natural settings.

Due to the low response rate, the current study may not be representative of all individuals with aphasia. While participants responded to questions regarding their experiences with AAC applications, some had trouble recalling the pros and cons due to memory difficulties. A further restriction of the interview and focus group is that we eliminated the perspectives of participants with severe aphasia due to their poor communication and comprehension abilities. Instead, we talked to their caretaker, but that did not give us a full picture of how they had trouble communicating.

Acknowledgement. We want to thank our participants from the Geriatric and Stroke Medicine (GSM) department at Sheffield Teaching Hospitals and the rehabilitation centre at Abdul Latif Jameel Hospital, with special thanks to Philippa Hedley-Takhar for the support in recruiting aphasic individuals and Shaun Kane for assisting with this project.

References

1. Keil, K., Kaszniak, A.W.: Examining executive function in individuals with brain injury: A review. Aphasiology **16**(3), 305–335 (2002)
2. Dykstra, A.D., Hakel, M.E., Adams, S.G.: Application of the ICF in reduced speech intelligibility in dysarthria. In: Seminars in Speech and Language, vol. 28, no. 04, pp. 301–311 (2007). © Thieme Medical Publishers
3. Finkelstein, E., Corso, P.S., Miller, T.R.: The Incidence and Economic Burden of Injuries in the United States. Oxford University Press, USA (2006)
4. Sjöqvist, N.B.: A new life with aphasia: Everyday activities and social support. Scand. J. Occup. Therapy **17**(2), 117–129 (2010)
5. Ball, L., et al.: AAC outcomes studies for persons with acquired communication disorders. In: Seminar Presented at the Annual Convention of the American Speech-Language-Hearing Association, Atlanta (2002)
6. Goossens', C.: Aided communication intervention before assessment: A case study of a child with cerebral palsy. Augment. Altern. Commun. **5**(1), 14–26 (1989)
7. Hjelmblink, F., Bernsten, C.B., Uvhagen, H., Kunkel, S., Holmström, I.: Understanding the meaning of rehabilitation to an aphasic patient through phenomenological analysis–A case study. Int. J. Qual. Stud. Health Well Being **2**(2), 93–100 (2007)
8. Parr, S.: Living with severe aphasia: Tracking social exclusion. Aphasiology **21**(1), 98–123 (2007)
9. Johnson, J.M., Inglebret, E., Jones, C., Ray, J.: Perspectives of speech language pathologists regarding success versus abandonment of AAC. Augment. Altern. Commun. **22**(2), 85–99 (2006)
10. Moorcroft, A., Scarinci, N., Meyer, C.: 'We were just kind of handed it and then it was smoke bombed by everyone': How do external stakeholders contribute to parent rejection and the abandonment of AAC systems? Int. J. Lang. Commun. Disord. **55**(1), 59–69 (2020)
11. Lasker, J., Bedrosian, J.: Promoting acceptance of augmentative and alternative communication by adults with acquired communication disorders. Augment. Altern. Commun. **17**(3), 141–153 (2001)
12. Waller, A., Dennis, F., Brodie, J., Cairns, A.Y.: Evaluating the use of TalksBac, a predictive communication device for nonfluent adults with aphasia. Int. J. Lang. Commun. Disord. **33**(1), 45–70 (1998)
13. Reiter, E., Turner, R., Alm, N., Black, R., Dempster, M., Waller, A.: Using NLG to help language-impaired users tell stories and participate in social dialogues. In: Proceedings of the 12th European Workshop on Natural Language Generation (ENLG 2009), pp. 1–8 (2009)
14. About lingraphica. https://www.aphasia.com/about-lingraphica/
15. Kane, S.K., Linam-Church, B., Althoff, K., McCall, D.: What we talk about: designing a context-aware communication tool for people with aphasia. In: Proceedings of the 14th International ACM SIGACCESS Conference on Computers and Accessibility, pp. 49–56 (2012)
16. Beukelman, D., McGinnis, J., Morrow, D.: Vocabulary selection in augmentative and alternative communication. Augment. Altern. Commun. **7**(3), 171–185 (1991)
17. Beukelman, D., Light, J.: Augmentative and alternative communication for children and adults. Paul H., Baltimore (2020)
18. Schlosser, R.W., Shane, H.C., Allen, A.A., Abramson, J., Laubscher, E., Dimery, K.: Just-in-time supports in augmentative and alternative communication. J. Dev. Phys. Disabil. **28**, 177–193 (2016)
19. Brock, K., Koul, R., Corwin, M., Schlosser, R.: A comparison of visual scene and grid displays for people with chronic aphasia: A pilot study to improve communication using AAC. Aphasiology **31**(11), 1282–1306 (2017)

20. Jayes, M.J., Palmer, R.L.: Stroke research staff's experiences of seeking consent from people with communication difficulties: Results of a national online survey. Top. Stroke Rehabil. **21**(5), 443–451 (2014)

21. Jayes, M., Palmer, R.: Initial evaluation of the Consent Support Tool: A structured procedure to facilitate the inclusion and engagement of people with aphasia in the informed consent process. Int. J. Speech Lang. Pathol. **16**(2), 159–168 (2014)

22. Light, J.: Toward a definition of communicative competence for individuals using augmentative and alternative communication systems. Augment. Altern. Commun. **5**(2), 137–144 (1989)

23. Hough, M., Johnson, R.K.: Use of AAC to enhance linguistic communication skills in an adult with chronic severe aphasia. Aphasiology **23**(7–8), 965–976 (2009)

24. Koul, R., Corwin, M., Hayes, S.: Production of graphic symbol sentences by individuals with aphasia: Efficacy of a computer-based augmentative and alternative communication intervention. Brain Lang. **92**(1), 58–77 (2005)

25. Purdy, M., Dietz, A.: Factors influencing AAC usage by individuals with aphasia. Perspect. Augment. Alternat. Commun. **19**(3), 70–78 (2010)

26. Light, J., McNaughton, D.: Communicative competence for individuals who require augmentative and alternative communication: A new definition for a new era of communication? Augment. Altern. Commun. **30**(1), 1–8 (2014)

27. Light, J., McNaughton, D.: The changing face of augmentative and alternative communication: Past, present, and future challenges. Augment. Altern. Commun. **28**(4), 197–204 (2012)

28. Dietz, A., Weissling, K., Griffith, J., McKelvey, M., Macke, D.: The impact of interface design during an initial high-technology AAC experience: A collective case study of people with aphasia. Augment. Altern. Commun. **30**(4), 314–328 (2014)

29. Beukelman, D.R., Hux, K., Dietz, A., McKelvey, M., Weissling, K.: Using visual scene displays as communication support options for people with chronic, severe aphasia: A summary of AAC research and future research directions. Augment. Altern. Commun. **31**(3), 234–245 (2015)

30. Judge, S., Hawley, M.S., Cunningham, S., Kirton, A.: What is the potential for context aware communication aids? J. Med. Eng. Technol. **39**(7), 448–453 (2015)

31. Hossain, M.S., Takanokura, M., Sakai, H., Katagiri, H.: Using context history and location in context-aware AAC systems for speech-language impairments. In: Proceedings of the International Multi Conference of Engineers and Computer Scientists, vol. 1 (2018)

32. Krishna, S., Little, G., Black, J., Panchanathan, S.: A wearable face recognition system for individuals with visual impairments. In: Proceedings of the 7th International ACM SIGACCESS Conference on Computers and Accessibility, pp. 106–113 (2005)

33. McGrenere, J., Sullivan, J., Baecker, R.M.: Designing technology for people with cognitive impairments. In: CHI'06 Extended Abstracts on Human Factors in Computing Systems, pp. 1635–1638 (2006)

34. Wisenburn, B., Higginbotham, D.J.: An AAC application using speaking partner speech recognition to automatically produce contextually relevant utterances: Objective results. Augment. Altern. Commun. **24**(2), 100–109 (2008)

35. Sánchez, J., de la Torre, N.: Autonomous navigation through the city for the blind. In: Proceedings of the 12th International ACM SIGACCESS Conference on Computers and Accessibility, pp. 195–202 (2010)

36. Simmons-Mackie, N., Lynch, K.E.: Qualitative research in aphasia: A review of the literature. Aphasiology **27**(11), 1281–1301 (2013)

37. Luck, A.M., Rose, M.L.: Interviewing people with aphasia: Insights into method adjustments from a pilot study. Aphasiology **21**(2), 208–224 (2007)

38. Della Sala, S., Cocchini, G., Beschin, N., Cameron, A.: VATA-m: Visual-analogue test assessing anosognosia for motor impairment. Clin. Neuropsychol. **23**(3), 406–427 (2009)
39. Ward-Kear, J.: Grid3. https://thinksmartbox.com/product/grid-3/
40. PRC-Saltillo: Discover the Joy of Communication. https://touchchatapp.com/
41. Rose, G.: Visual methodologies: An introduction to researching with visual materials. Vis. Methodol. 1 (2022)
42. Gotschi, E., Freyer, B., Delve, R.: Participatory photography in cross-cultural research: A case study of investigating farmer groups in rural Mozambique. In: Doing Cross-Cultural Research: Ethical and Methodological Perspectives, pp. 213–231 (2008)
43. Hu, Y., Manikonda, L., Kambhampati, S.: What we instagram: A first analysis of instagram photo content and user types. In: Eighth International AAAI Conference on Weblogs and Social Media (2014)
44. Hao, X., Wu, B., Morrison, A.M., Wang, F.: Worth thousands of words? Visual content analysis and photo interpretation of an outdoor tourism spectacular performance in Yangshuo-Guilin, China. Anatolia **27**(2), 201–213 (2016)
45. Charmaz, K.: Constructing Grounded Theory: A Practical Guide Through Qualitative Analysis. Sage (2006)
46. Corbin, J.M., Strauss, A.: Grounded theory research: Procedures, canons, and evaluative criteria. Qual. Sociol. **13**(1), 3–21 (1990)

Software Architecture for Safety, Ergonomics, and Interaction for Industrial Mobile Robotic Platforms

Omar Eldardeer[1]([✉]), Jonathan Bar-Magen[1], and Francesco Rea[2]

[1] CONTACT Unit, Istituto Italiano di Tecnologia, Genova, Italy
omar.eldardeer@iit.it
[2] RBCS, Istituto Italiano di Tecnologia, Genova, Italy

Abstract. Robots in industrial scenarios are having growing roles. Industrial scenarios are the most applied scenarios in the robotics field. Among the different scenarios of robots, many of them are having different interactions with human workers. Industrial robotics offers a very competitive economic advantage as it can perform a wide range of tasks. However, the main challenge comes to insure the safety and engagement of the human worker in the context of human-robot interaction. In this paper we propose a novel software architecture to monitor and analyze the safety, ergonomics, and social interaction of the human worker and the surrounding environment. And based on the analyzed scenario, the architecture is executing the required action to optimize and achieve the designed behavior for the required task. The architecture is using the state of the art visual sensory (neuromorphic cameras) and is designed for a mobile robotic platform that interacts physically with a human worker in different scenarios. Safety, ergonomics, and social interaction are three crucial factors that insures the workers' well-being and avoid injuries in the work environment. The paper is presenting the overall designed architecture and the software implementation of the communication system that processes multiple visual processes to get a high-level understanding of the situation and further execute actions by the robot.

Keywords: Human-Robot Interaction · Software Architecture · Industrial Robotics · Mobile Robotics

1 Introduction

In industrial scenarios, robotics platforms support production activities in collaborative interaction with human workers [4] guaranteeing at the same time the necessary levels of safety and ergonomics [2]. This is one of the main required activities in industrial scenarios as humans are restricted by physical capabilities including speed, stamina, and strength, especially for repetitive tasks [6]. These restrictions are affecting the quality of the output and efficiency of the processes [8]. Robots can fulfill these gab by assisting the human worker in such activities [5]. To assess the optimal assistance during the interaction and high level of safety and collaborative ergonomics, the robotic platforms require closing

M. Antona and C. Stephanidis (Eds.): HCII 2023, LNCS 14021, pp. 509–517, 2023.
https://doi.org/10.1007/978-3-031-35897-5_36

the perception-action interaction loop with unprecedented sensorial and motor action skills [9]. Such skills once developed guarantee an advanced level of coordination and in general more natural interaction between the interactive parts. In particular, collaborative robots that better sense the human counterpart's intentionality and style of action can better instantiate natural and easy-to-interpret actions. The fundamental component for effective interaction is enabled by an accurate architectural design. Optimal design generates a software framework that has to comply with specific constraints of natural human-robot interaction: a) reliable interpretation of the human intentions with the robot's perceptual skills and b) generation of motor actions that can naturally coordinate with human's actions. The real-time robotic platforms that sense the environment, and human individuals in it, and promptly react to assure safety and ergonomics interaction activities are the most challenging scenario for industrial mobile robotic platforms [3]. The challenge can be addressed with success if very specific aspects of software engineering are taken into consideration [1]. Aspects such as algorithmic redundancy and short response time often investigated in software engineering find an interesting application in the context of industrial collaborative tasks involving both human workers and robotic platforms in joint activities. In this study, we propose a software architecture that includes most of the relevant guidelines in software engineering necessary to guarantee collaborative activities in safe and ergonomic environments. We present a modular approach that distributes the computational demand through two components: the social interaction module (SIM) that takes into account the natural communication between robot and worker and the safety and ergonomics module (SEM) that monitors the human's activities to promptly intervene to prevent safety and ergonomics accidents. Whereas the first component monitors the human operator (e.g.: attentive inner state, intentionality, etc.), the second proactively maintains a high level of safety and ergonomics. The two components coordinate in real-time exchanging information between them and with the other software layers. The robust and reliable between modules rely on the adopted and widely used middleware: ROS [7].

2   The Architecture

Our proposed architecture consists of two main modules. The first module is the social interaction module (SIM), and the second module is the safety and ergonomics module (SEM). Both modules are doing high-level monitoring and analysis for different visual processing. Based on the analysis results, the modules communicate action commands based on a defined protocol. The implementation of the architecture is using the Robot Operating System (ROS) [7], more specifically ROS2.

In this section, we will explain both of the modules.

2.1   SIM: Social Interaction Module

Figure 1 is showing the software architecture of the social interaction module (SIM). There are five visual input processes that the module receives as the following:

- **Grasping Strategy Classification.** The grasping strategy classification module is looking visually at the hand of the worker (perception) and assesses the optimal behavior of the grasp. It is a machine-learning module. The grasping strategy adopted by the robotic system is crucial for complex interactions such as object handover. As one of the most complex interactions between a robot and a human worker, handover requires precise temporal and spatial coordination. The module of environmental and human states is where the process that tracks the state of workers and the environment is done. This includes the position of the worker in the environment with respect to the position of the robot and the state of the process stages.
- **Environmental and human states.** The precise monitoring of the behavior of the worker has to be performed with low latency. In fact, the body movements detected by the cameras might be completed in short time frames, and still, the robot has to compute details of the movement in space and time. Sometimes the use of specific high-frame-rate cameras or innovative chips (e.g.: neuromorphic cameras [10]) might give raw data with sufficient throughput rate but software has to reduce at minimum (sometimes to less than a few milliseconds) the latency in order to process all the information available. In terms of software design, this is a critical and important aspect.
- **Neuromorphic Pose/velocity Estimation.** The neuromorphic pose and velocity estimation are achieved by processing the information provided by the neuromorphic chip for vision. In software design, it is engineered as a module that takes the events from the neuromorphic cameras and transfers a processed output as the human pose and the velocities of the human body joints. The main advantage, but also a challenge, of using this approach is to have a faster response with low computational power. This is due to the fast response of the neuromorphic cameras and the low required processing power of these cameras. In the presented architecture, this is achieved with specific and carefully designed software in C++. The compiled software allows for real-time but still requires careful design in the interpretation of input data. For example, the careful interpretation of the body joint movements with the interpretation of the velocity profile for every single joint is conditioned to the faster interpretation of the pose. If the body pose is of immediate interpretation and relevant risk the priority is biased towards fast communication of intervention as module output.
- **Fatigue Detection.** The fatigue detection process has been designed differently with respect to the other modules. The objective of the module is to rely less on a model-based interpretation of the sensorial input but rather to exploit a data-driven approach. The modules is designed as machine-learning detection module based on the human pose extracted from both the neuromorphic camera together with the RGB camera. After accurate supervised

training the system autonomously figured out the regularities in the data that mark the presence of fatigue and stored the interpretation of these regularities as deep network weights. Successively, when presented with new data the systems try to generalize and infer the presence of fatigue. The advantage of this solution is that it remains relatively fast but the data-driven approach during training requires labeling.

– **Gesture Recognition**. The gesture recognition module shows yet another possible implementation in typical architecture for human-robot interaction. This module is not another machine-learning module that recognizes a defined set of gestures that are specified for the use case scenario and it is not resulting from a model-based approach where behavior is modeled using theories. In the gesture recognition module the preference goes in using specific matching between what is measured and what is expected.

For each of these 5 inputs, a corresponding block is responsible for getting a high-level understanding of the perceived stream of data. This is happening through the interfaces. The interfaces integrate the information from the streams and create a high-level explanation for the streamed data. For example, transforming the joint velocities to walking directions, or standing state. Generally, there are three kinds of interfaces. The first one is (what) interface which analyses what the worker is doing with respect to the robot and the environment. Therefore, there are three interfaces for the Sensing-What block which are understanding the physical interaction (Grasping strategy), the environment and the worker states, and finally the worker movement interface. The information from these three interfaces is integrated together in the sensorial inference block to finally create a defined state for the interaction of the worker with the robot.

The second category of interfaces is Sensing-How. This has only one interface that analysis the fatigue state of the worker.

Finally, the third category is non-verbal communication. It takes the recognized gestures as an input stream. The gestures are then analyzed and based on the pattern of the gestures the robot understands the message. Thanks to the defined communication protocol which is part of the social requirement block in the architecture.

The last point to mention in this part is the engine. The engine is the master of the whole process. It receives the analysis from the different interfaces and based on the social requirement, it sends high-level requests for executing actions. The executed actions are under two kinds, a communication action, and a monitoring action. The communication action is to communicate a certain piece of information to the human worker, while the monitoring action is to indicate the states which is some kind of showing of what the robot is perceiving. Based on the design of the robot, and the monitoring and communication devices, the action is defined which can be through a screen, or LEDs, or audio.

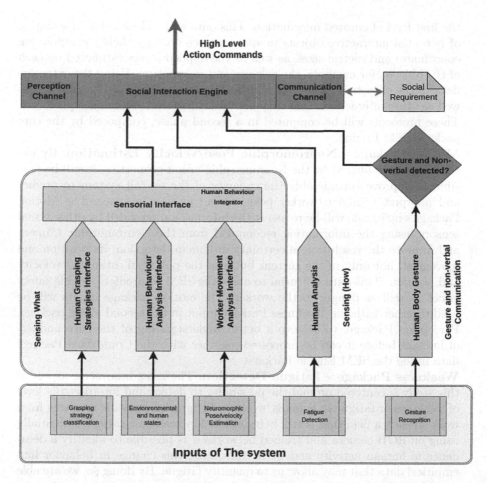

Fig. 1. The Software architecture for the social interaction module (SIM)

2.2 SEM: Safety and Ergonomics Module

Safety and Ergonomics software architecture is strongly linked to the role it plays in the overall system. Its functionality is of upmost importance for it supervises the safety working environment for the human in a variety of use cases scenarios. The number of inputs, three in total which are less than in the Social Interaction Module implies that it will require less data sources to operate, allowing for a broader adaptability. From the architectural scheme, Fig. 2, we can extract the inputs that at the same time, for development purposes under ROS as independent packages, and act as a first level process phase before proceeding to the next sub modules inside SEM. These inputs/packages are:

- **Contextual Package - Object Recognition** The first phase package contains the nodes which gather from a variety of input topics data to create the first level of curated information. This data will include a broad scanning of potential interactive objects in space, represented by their corresponding coordinates and metric sizes, as well as the applied forces estimated on each of the objects, for example, the velocity and momentum. Using the extensive data of the objects in space, we will be able to predict possible collisions as well as other interactions that may activate safety and ergonomics protocols. These protocols will be computed in a second phase, composed by the core package SEM Engine.

- **Motion Package - Neuromorphic Pose/velocity Estimation**. By use the advantages offered by the Neuromorphic vision properties, it will be possible to improve considerably the capacity of the overall system to predict and interpret a human/worker position and motion in space. The Motion Package's main role will be to assert the information provided by other visual sensors, using the information recompiled from the Neuromorphic Camera and improve the resolution of certainty in human detection, its position and movement, not only in the current but also the potential estimated velocity and position. This data is crucial to allow the SEM to predict possible safety issues as well as danger to the worker. The motion package inputs will be used together with the Weakness Package input in the second phase package, Perception Package, to achieve a better understanding of the surroundings of humans before it can be processed together with the Contextual Package data inside the SEM Engine Package.

- **Weakness Package - Fatigue Detection**. The most innovative aspect of this study is centered around the possibility to detect and interpret the level of weakness or fatigue in humans/workers. Fatigue information resulting from work stress is a field that is still being studied in academic society. Potentially using an RGB camera and trained networks it is possible to identify a decadence in human activity and by it translating this change in behavior into empirical data that may allow us to quantify fatigue. By doing so, we are able to add another variable to our Perception Package equations, improving the system's capacity to predict potentially dangerous situations, and allowing the SEM Engine package to act as soon as possible in case of an emergency. This package will also allow the system to gradually control passively the worker's conditions, and inform of his status to the rest of the system.

From the scheme, we can identify two more core packages: Perception Package and SEM Engine Package. While Perception Package will combine the information acquired from Motion and Weakness, it will later pass this information in a quantified format to the SEM Engine package, which in turn will combine the Perception Package and the Contextual Package, allowing not only to extract information from the worker condition, but also cross it with the position of the object in the working area, ensuring that there is no potential dangerous situation.

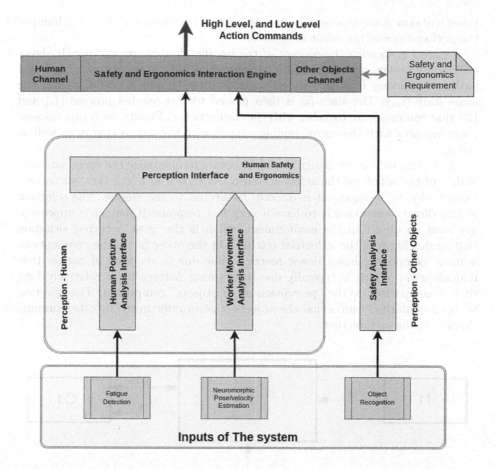

Fig. 2. The Software architecture for the safety and ergonomics module (SEM)

3   The Architecture in Relation to International Standards

ISO 13489-1:2015 is the international safety standard that is applied to the control system of machines including robots. It provides detailed safety requirements for the design and implementation of the control system to ensure that the minimizes risks to people and property. The standard has different categories. Category 3 is the one related to the SEM component of our architecture. The conclusion of the analysis regarding this category states that a parallel doubled architecture is required. This means that two different processes run together in parallel and check their output. This requires two computers or two chips or a multicore software architecture.

Regarding this, the use of two computers or two ships and comparing their outputs slow down the reaction time of the system. Thus the movement of the robot will slow down as a consequence of a slower reaction time. This will hamper the performance of the robot in general.

Figure 3 is showing the concept of the parallel double architecture. It shows the required safety design. The safety implementation has to rely on two parallel pathways starting from two independent inputs (I1 and I2) that stream the same state (i_m). The state i_m is then passed to two parallel process (L1 and L2) that communicate together with the connection c. Finally, each process sent communicates with the corresponding output with the connection m as well as the state i_m.

According to this, we design our architecture to maximize the speed and reliability of the robot for the safety scenario. As shown in Fig. 2 the "perception - other objects" component is directly connected to the engine. The selection of this direct connection is to have a very fast response if danger is approaching from an object in the environment which is the most occurred situation that causes harm in the industrial setting. On the other hand, the "perception-human" component has a slower reaction time due to the kind of danger that it deals with. Which is typically due to a wrong pattern for a relatively long time in comparison to the "perception-other objects" component. The selection of this modularity ensures that the process is never interrupted by other running threads in the architecture.

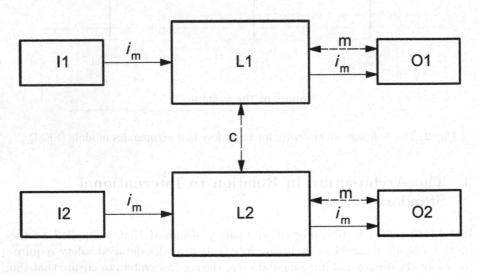

Fig. 3. The Parallel Requirement of the software architecture

4   Conclusion and Future Work

With the growing use of robots in the industrial environment, it is essential to have a safe operating environment, especially in human-robot interaction scenarios. In this paper, we proposed a software architecture that consists of two components. The first component is for the social interaction module (SIM) and the second component is the safety and ergonomics module (SEM). SIM monitors the social states of the human operators to ensure the socially required characteristics of the human operator. On the other hand, SEM is responsible for monitoring the physical characteristics of both the humans and the surrounding environment with respect to the robot and insures the safety of physical and ergonomic aspects. Both architecture's components interact with the interfaces of the robot, and the user by sending communication commands and response signals respectively. The framework of the proposed software has been developed in its labs and preliminary results. iI the very near future, the internal nodes of the software will be developed and the software will be tested in different real-world use cases in the facilities of our industrial partners and SMEs.

References

1. El Zaatari, S., et al.: Cobot programming for collaborative industrial tasks: an overview. Robot. Auton. Syst. **116**, 162–180 (2019)
2. Faccio, M., et al.: Human factors in cobot era: a review of modern production systems features. J. Intell. Manuf. **34**(1), 85–106 (2023)
3. Heinzmann, J., Zelinsky, A.: Quantitative safety guarantees for physical human-robot interaction. Int. J. Robot. Res. **22**(7–8), 479–504 (2003). https://doi.org/10.1177/02783649030227004
4. Heyer, C.: Human-robot interaction and future industrial robotics applications. In: 2010 IEEE/RSJ International Conference on Intelligent Robots and Systems, pp. 4749–4754. IEEE (2010)
5. Matheson, E., et al.: Human-robot collaboration in manufacturing applications: a review. Robotics **8**(4), 100 (2019)
6. Müller, R., Vette, M., Mailahn, O.: Process-oriented task assignment for assembly processes with human-robot interaction. Procedia CIRP **44**, 210–215 (2016)
7. Quigley, M., et al.: ROS: an open-source robot operating system. In: ICRA Workshop on Open Source Software, vol. 3, p. 5, Kobe, Japan (2009)
8. Rüßmann, M., et al.: Industry 4.0: the future of productivity and growth in manufacturing industries. Boston Consult. Group **9**(1), 54–89 (2015)
9. Zacharaki, A., et al.: Safety bounds in human robot interaction: a survey. Saf. Sci. **127**, 104667 (2020)
10. Zalevsky, Z., et al.: Super-resolved imaging with randomly distributed, time-and size-varied particles. J. Opt. A: Pure Appl. Opt. **11**(8), 085406 (2009). https://doi.org/10.1088/1464-4258/11/8/085406

Accessible and Inclusive Mobile Application for Social Support and m-Health in Forced Isolation: SAFE TALK

Luciano Gamberini[1,2], Patrik Pluchino[1,2(✉)], Federica Nenna[1,2], Valeria Santus[2], Filippo Zordan[2], Anna Spagnolli[1,2], Alessandro Lorenzin[4], Andrea Munari[4], Gianluca Bacchiega[5], Valentina Campagnaro[6], and Andrea Zanella[1,3]

[1] Human Inspired Technologies (HIT) Research Centre, University of Padova, Padova, Italy
patrik.pluchino@unipd.it
[2] Department of General Psychology, University of Padova, Padova, Italy
[3] Department of Information Engineering, University of Padova, Padova, Italy
[4] Rawfish s.r.l., Vicenza, Italy
[5] I.R.S. s.r.l., Padova, Italy
[6] Cooperativa "L'Incontro", Castelfranco Veneto, Treviso, Italy

Abstract. The condition of forced isolation due to the Covid-19 Pandemic clearly highlighted the importance of social support. Indeed, the absence of interaction with families and friends in the presence can lead to feelings of loneliness, abandonment, psychological discomfort, anxiety, and depression, especially for the elderly. On this premise, adopting a user-centered approach, an app for social and professional support SAFE TALK was created and evaluated recruiting end users. The participatory activities involving elderly informed the design of the app prototypes, while at a second stage two samples of target users (i.e., elderly and psychologists) were considered in the evaluations of the SAFE TALK app. The performance, usability, accessibility, and user experience of the app were tested. Findings showed that despite a slightly lower performance of the elderly, both groups of individuals positively evaluated the usability, accessibility, and user experience of the app. SAFE TALK was appreciated by the elderly as a potential supportive tool in case of forced isolation to reach their social sphere and eventually a professional. Psychologists reported the relevance of the app as a tool to remotely support people in conditions of need.

Keywords: m-health · accessibility · elderly

1 Introduction

1.1 Impact of Forced Isolation

The Pandemic has brought to evidence the need for social support in case of forced isolation related to lockdowns. The maintenance of relationships that matter with family members and friends helps to face these adverse situations. The same type of speech applies to long-term care. Besides, loneliness can exacerbate mild anxiety and depression symptoms, and forced isolation can prevent the possibility of asking for help from professional figures.

L. Gamberini and P. Pluchino equally contributed to this work and share first authorship.

M. Antona and C. Stephanidis (Eds.): HCII 2023, LNCS 14021, pp. 518–530, 2023.
https://doi.org/10.1007/978-3-031-35897-5_37

1.2 Mobile Applications for Psychological and Social Support

Several mobile applications have been designed and developed to remotely support people's psychological health even before the Covid-19 Pandemic [1, 2]. These tools are also called telehealth technologies [3]. In some cases, these apps comprised thematic group interventions with psychotherapists during the Covid-19 Pandemic [4], which showed how this kind of assistance effectively ameliorated the overall psychological state of participants. A recent paper [5] focused on the future of mental health services mentioning digital mental health and hybrid systems referring to remote mental health when there was a lack of this type of service in specific areas (e.g., rural). Besides, the authors reported the quick acceleration in adopting these digital services related to the recent Pandemic. Information and communication technologies are promising for reducing isolation among the elderly. Czaja and colleagues [6] suggested that access to digital technologies can improve social connectivity, reduce loneliness among old individuals, and change their attitudes toward technology.

Jarvis and collaborators [7] highlighted the prevalence of a sense of loneliness among the elderly in residential care facilities. Isolation is often accompanied by maladaptive cognition that can affect the establishing and maintaining meaningful social connections [7]. A review conducted by Abbaspur-Behbahani and colleagues [8] explored the use of mobile health (i.e., m-health) solutions in the elderly population during the Pandemic. These digital instruments provided real-time communication channels and video calls to support a more comprehensive interaction as the exchange includes verbal and non-verbal communication [9] differently from text messaging. Perdana and collaborators [10] underlined that these digital tools are already widespread among the elderly. However, it could be further encouraged by family members and peer groups [10]. Regarding m-health solutions, their acceptance, i.e., the degree to which an individual intends to adopt these tools continuously, plays a crucial role. Indeed, a lower acceptance will result in a reduced intention of technologies/digital services' usage, overall experience and satisfaction, and an unlikely actual use [11]. In the following sections, there will be a description of the user-centered approach adopted to develop a mobile application, i.e., SAFE TALK, created mainly for the elderly and people weakened by long periods of hospitalization to support the maintenance of active interpersonal relationships with their own social sphere (i.e., family, friends). Besides, the app will also allow contacting caregivers and or psychologists.

2   SAFE TALK

The application SAFE TALK was designed and developed, involving final users by adopting a user-centered design approach in the context of the SAFE PLACE project [12, 13]. This project designs and develops smart living and environments based on the paradigm of the Internet of Things characterized by salubrity and safety to fight pandemics. SAFE TALK aims at reflecting the highest standard of usability (e.g., ease of use), accessibility, and user experience.

2.1 Participatory Design

Sessions of participatory design were organized to involve end users (i.e., the elderly) to gather their needs, expectations, and desires. The objective was to incorporate such elements in the design of the application. Two Focus Groups (FG) were conducted using Zoom, due to the pandemic situation and since the involved users were all elderly. The participants were recruited by the ninth author of the manuscript.

Method

Participants. Thirteen elderly were recruited on a voluntary basis ($Range_{age} = 68$–89; $M_{age} = 78.15$; $F = 6$). All participants did not report physical or cognitive disabilities. Only one participant reported having an experience with long-term care.

Procedure. On the days of the FGs, participants were welcome in one quiet room set up to allow the remote connection with the Human Inspired Technology (HIT; University of Padova) research group considering using a good quality web camera and microphone. Both zoom sessions were recorded to permit the subsequent transcription of the group discussions to integrate the notes taken by the observer during the FGs. In Figs. 1 and 2, the setting of both FGs is depicted. It is possible to observe that all participants followed the anti-Covid 19 safety regulations, and they were wearing masks. The second author led the FGs, while the fourth author was the observer. During the Focus Groups, different questions were asked concerning the usage of communication tools (e.g., phone, tablet, etc.) and which kind of applications (es., WhatsApp, Skype, Zoom) were used to stay connected with their social sphere (i.e., family, friends) during the Pandemic lockdowns. Besides, the moderator asked questions about the psychological experience of forced isolation and if they felt the need to contact a professional (e.g., a psychologist). In the second phase of the FG, the moderator asked the elderly to imagine a mobile app that could support the maintenance of social relationships when it is not possible to communicate and interact in the presence with their social sphere or a professional figure and report which kind of features and functionalities this application needed.

At the end of the FGs, the moderator summarized the activities and the outcomes and asked the participants for any additional comments that they may have.

Analysis and Results. Considering the usage of communication tools, all the elderly use a mobile phone (100%) to call and/or send messages (86.61%), and around half of the sample utilized the phone to make video calls, surf the web and watch videos (46.15%).

Regarding how the participants felt during the forced isolation, five participants (38.46%) reported a feeling of sadness linked to the lack of physical contact with relatives and friends (i.e., "*...I missed the hugs...*"), and two participants reported the anxiety connected to the risk of new Pandemic waves that could come.

To what pertains the characteristics and functions that an app to support the maintenance of important relationships in forced isolation, the following information emerged (in parenthesis the percentage of participants): a) the app needs to be easy to use (100%); b) the presence of simple and clear information (100%); c) the app permits to contact family (100%) and emergency numbers (100%) rapidly; and d) having the opportunity to contact a psychologist for support (33,33%).

Fig. 1. First Focus Group (Zoom).

Fig. 2. Second Focus Group (Zoom).

The outcomes of these research activities informed the design and development of various mock-ups (Fig. 3).

As can be seen in Fig. 3, for instance, based elderly's needs and expectations collected in the FGs, in the second mock up designer and developers added on the home screen the possibility to quickly contact selected numbers (e.g., family members, friends) in a "favorites section" (i.e., *Preferiti*) and a red button was inserted (must be pressed for a specific time to avoid errors) to call for an emergency in the second mock-up (Fig. 3

Fig. 3. First (left) and Second Mock-ups (right).

right). In addition, the need to quickly contact families and friends (i.e., video calls) and the desire to contact a psychologist and the possibility of video calls to caregivers were maintained across mockups.

Based on the FGs and the first design and developing phases (i.e., mockups) the SAFE TALK app was created. As it was stated in Introduction of the manuscript, this application is intended mainly for elderly individuals, people in long-term care or home residences, and those with mild cognitive impairment to maintain interpersonal relationships with their family, friends, and colleagues, and to contact caregivers and psychologists. The final prototype of SAFE TALK that was released meets the latest standards of accessibility and usability. It will provide novel support for video communication and spending quality time with loved ones. It presents an intuitive and straightforward interface and different services. Indeed, end users can video call their contacts, select caregivers to speak with someone freely, and psychologists in case they need professional support. The app provided only video calls to reduce the complexity of usage related, for example, to writing text messages or recording audio messages.

In addition, one simple versions of the app (i.e., *professionals*) have been realized respectively for caregivers and psychologists that will have the opportunity to provide their availability with times and days. Finally, the application could be used by single individuals and/or in wider programs to avoid isolation considering nursing homes, long-term hospital services, and residential facilities for people with mild mental disabilities.

2.2 Preliminary Evaluation Involving End Users and Stakeholders

An experiment was conducted with the purpose of evaluating the usability, accessibility, and user experience of the first release of SAFE TALK involving elderly and psychologists.

Method

Participants. Ten participants were recruited on a voluntary basis. Five elderly ($Range_{age}$ = 70–76; M_{age} = 74; F = 3) and five psychologists ($Range_{age}$ = 25–53; M_{age} = 36.8; F = 3) of the SCUP - University Centre for Psychological University Clinical Services of the University of Padova. All participants did not report physical or cognitive disabilities.

Equipment and Materials. The following equipment was used in the experiment:

- a smartphone with installed the app SAFE TALK for the elderly (i.e., Samsung Galaxy A13; 6,6" screen; display resolution: 2408 × 1080 pixels);
- a smartphone with installed the app SAFE TALK for the psychologists (i.e., Samsung S8; 5.8" screen; display resolution: 1440 × 2960 pixels);
- a GoPro Hero 5 to allow the video recordings of the experimental sessions for the subsequent video analysis;
- a laptop was utilized to present the questionnaire and instructions for the experimental tasks (i.e., Huawei MateBook X Pro; 13.9" screen; display resolution: 3000 x 2000 pixels).

Considering the materials:

- Demographic questionnaire. This tool was used to collect general information about the participants (i.e., age, gender, education).
- Usability and accessibility checklist. To assess SAFE TALK usability, some of the Nielsen's heuristics were considered (Nielsen & Molich, 1990; Nielsen, 1994; Nielsen & Norman, 2014). Furthermore, the accessibility was evaluated with *ad hoc* items. In total, the checklist included 19 items and the following usability dimensions:

  - Aesthetic and minimalist design (e.g., sufficient colors contrast, absence of irrelevant information, etc.);
  - Match between system and the real world (e.g., presence of clear and accurate information, familiar language, etc.);
  - Recognition over recall (e.g., presence of icons and labels immediately recognizable, etc.);
  - Navigation (e.g., ability to easily navigate between the various screens, etc.).
    The possible responses were "Yes", "No", and "N/A" (i.e., not applicable). Besides, in the case of "Yes"/"No" responses, participants were asked to provide comments. The checklist was administered only after the interaction with the version of SAFE TALK for elderly.

- Ad Hoc User Experience (UX) questionnaire. The tool was exploited to assess the user experience related to both versions of SAFE TALK. The dimensions of pleasantness, engagement, satisfaction, and support were considered. For the support dimension, the items were slightly different, referring respectively to support the maintenance of the relationships with families and friends (i.e., app version for elderly) or to support their work (i.e., app version for psychologists). A 5-point scale was used for the responses (from 1 = not at all to 5 = completely).

Experimental Tasks. To assess the participants' interaction with the SAFE TALK app for elderly the following experimental tasks were administered:

1. Favorites. Adding Patrik Pluchino to the favorites section by selecting him among your numbers;
2. Invite to SAFE TALK. Inviting Carlo Di Sarli to use SAFE TALK by selecting him among your numbers;
3. Video call. Video calling Patrik Pluchino by selecting him among your numbers. Turn off the video camera. Then, ending the video call;
4. "Ti senti solo?" service. Using the service and video calling Filippo Zordan by selecting him among the list of available operators. Then, ending the video call;
5. Personal Information. Accessing the personal information screen. Inserting the personal data and taking a picture. Saving the changes;
6. Receiving a video call. Answering a video call. Then, terminating the call;
7. "Ti serve aiuto?" service. Activating the service allowing the localization. Setting Padova as the city of residence and choosing the 10-day subscription;
8. SOS. Utilizing the SOS button to access the screen in which is possible to contact the emergency number.

Besides, to evaluate the participants' interaction with the SAFE TALK app for psychologists the following tasks were considered:

1. Personal Information. Accessing the personal information screen and verifying that the name and last name are Filippo Zordan;
2. Biography. Accessing the biography section and modifying the text by inserting "This is a test";
3. Availability. Accessing the profile screen to insert some time availability (e.g., Monday morning, 9:00–12:00 a.m.; Friday afternoon, 2:30–4:30 a.m.) and save the changes.

At the end of all tasks, participants were asked to return to the Home screen.

In Fig. 4, there are some SAFE TALK screens.

Procedure. The experimental sessions were conducted in the presence. The sample of psychologists was tested at the Department of General Psychology, while the elderly in one of the venues of Cooperativa "L'Incontro".

At the beginning of the experiment, the participants were administered an informative note (which contained general details about the research, the procedure, etc.), informed consent, and the demographic questionnaire. Then, considering both versions of the SAFE TALK apps (i.e., elderly and psychologists), the tasks were presented in a randomized order except for the SOS task, while using the elderly version, which led participants to exit the application. Besides, considering only the psychologists, which

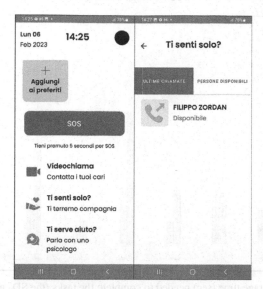

Fig. 4. SAFE TALK Home Screen and screen for the "Ti senti solo?" service.

interacted with both versions, the presentation of SAFE TALK apps was randomized. The researcher read the instruction for each task to the participants. However, the instructions were always available for participants as they were presented on the screen of the experimental laptop.

Considering the version for the elderly, after the experimental tasks, the usability and accessibility checklist and the UX questionnaire were administered. Regarding the version for psychologists, after the experimental tasks, only the UX questionnaire was completed.

The experimental sessions lasted 35–40 min for the elderly and 45–50 for the psychologists.

Measures. The following quantitative measures were analyzed:

- time needed to complete each task (i.e., average time on task);
- number of interactions to complete a task (i.e., average number of taps);
- responses to the usability and accessibility checklist (i.e., mean percentage);
- responses to the UX questionnaire (i.e., mean scores).

Analyses and Results. Overall, the statistical analyses were performed using RStudio [14]. The independent variable was the group (i.e., elderly vs. psychologists). In case of multiple comparisons, the *p*-values were adjusted using BH correction [15].

Performance (time on task in sec). Considering the time necessary to complete a task, a series of Mann-Whitney tests were conducted. The elderly appeared to be slower than the psychologists in carrying out the tasks, but due to the variability in the data, no differences emerged between the groups (all $p_s > .05$) (Fig. 5).

Performance (number of taps). Regarding the number of taps needed to accomplish a task, a series of Mann-Whitney tests were run. Similarly, to the time on task variable, the

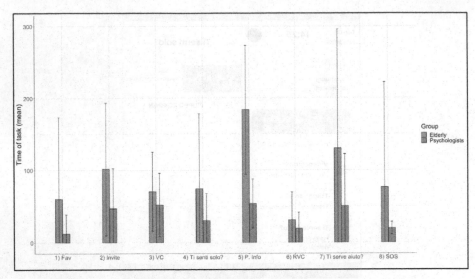

Fig. 5. Average time (sec) needed to complete the tasks (the SD$_S$ are plotted).

mean number of taps was not different between the two samples (all $p_s > .05$), although some tasks showed higher differences (e.g., task Personal Information) (Fig. 6).

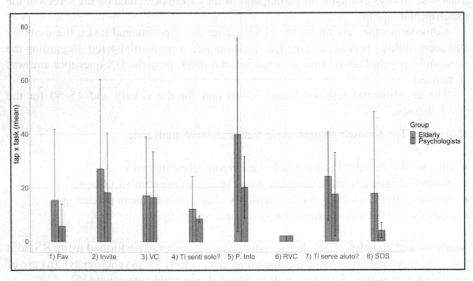

Fig. 6. Mean tap to accomplish the tasks (the SD$_S$ are plotted).

Usability and accessibility. To evaluate the difference in the percentage of the usability and accessibility scores, a series of beta regressions were conducted. Overall, differences between groups were not shown (all $p_s > .05$) (Fig. 7).

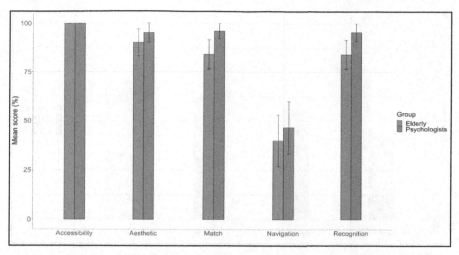

Fig. 7. Mean scores (in percentage) to the usability and accessibility checklist (se_s are plotted).

User experience (elderly app). To evaluate the difference in the scores, a series of Mann-Whitney tests was carried out. No differences were highlighted between groups (all $p_s > .05$) considering all the UX dimensions (Fig. 8).

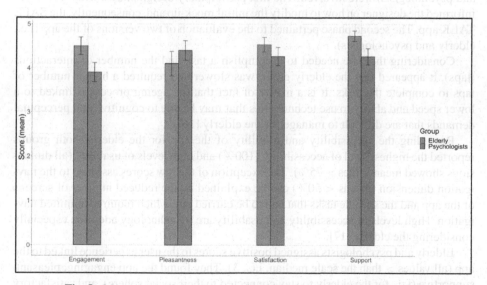

Fig. 8. Mean scores to the user experience questionnaire (app for elderly).

User experience (psychologists app). The scores assigned to the user experience related to the SAFE TALK app for psychologists reported a low level of engagement (i.e., ~ 2), and intermediate levels of pleasantness and satisfaction (i.e., ~ 3). Differently, the support dimension was evaluated positively (~3.5) (Fig. 9).

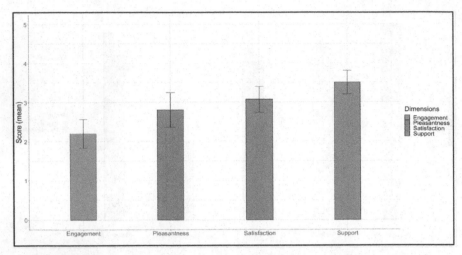

Fig. 9. Mean scores to the user experience questionnaire (app for psychologists).

General Discussion. The paper described the process of design, development, and evaluation of an app SAFE TALK, created to support people in forced isolation in maintaining the relationship with their social sphere. Different target users (i.e., elderly and psychologists) were involved. The first participatory design phases with the elderly informed the designer on how to modify the initial mock-up and, consequently, the SAFE TALK app. The second phase pertained to the evaluation of two versions of the app (i.e., elderly and psychologists).

Considering the time needed to accomplish a task and the number of interactions (taps), it appeared that the elderly group was slower and required a higher number of taps to complete the tasks. It is a matter of fact that the ageing process is linked to a lower speed and ability to use technologies that may be due to cognitive and perceptual demands that are difficult to manage for the elderly [16].

Regarding the accessibility and usability of the app for the elderly, both groups reported the highest level of accessibility (100%) and high levels of usability (all dimensions showed mean values > 75%). The exception of the low scores assigned to the navigation dimension (means < 50%) can be explained by the reduced number of screens of the app and the specific tasks that had to be carried out, which required a limited navigation. High levels of accessibility and usability are to technology adoption especially considering the elderly [17].

Elderly and psychologists assigned positive scores to the user experience linked to the app (all values > than the scale median, i.e., 3). They found the app engaging, pleasant, supportive (i.e., for the elderly to stay connected to their social sphere), and satisfactory to use. These findings are also related to the design elements that were included in the SAFE TALK [18].

Regarding the app for psychologists, the low number of screens and the absence of many aesthetic features (i.e., colors, pictures, menu, etc.) negatively affected the levels of engagement, pleasantness, and satisfaction. Nevertheless, the supportive dimension (i.e., to remotely support people in conditions of need) was positively evaluated by the professionals.

The limited number of participants involved in the evaluation phase has certainly affected the performed analyses. The authors planned have already planned to recruit more individuals of both target groups (i.e., elderly and psychologists) for more consistent results.

Acknowledgements. This work was supported by the POR FESR 2014–2020 Work Program of the Veneto Region (Action 1.1.4) through the project No. 10288513 titled "SAFE PLACE. Sistemi IoT per ambienti di vita salubri e sicuri".

References

1. Price, M., et al.: mHealth: A mechanism to deliver more accessible, more effective mental health care. Clin. Psychol. Psychother. **21**(5), 427–436 (2014)
2. Naslund, J.A., et al.: Digital technology for treating and preventing mental disorders in low-income and middle-income countries: A narrative review of the literature. Lancet Psychiatry **4**(6), 486–500 (2017)
3. Luxton, D.D., Pruitt, L.D., Osenbach, J.E.: Best practices for remote psychological assessment via telehealth technologies. Prof. Psychol. Res. Pract. **45**(1), 27 (2014)
4. Parolin, L.A.L., Benzi, I.M.A., Fanti, E., Milesi, A., Cipresso, P., Preti, E.: Italia Ti Ascolto [Italy, I am listening]: an app-based group psychological intervention during the COVID-19 pandemic. Res. Psychotherapy: Psychopathol. Process Outcome **24**(1) (2021)
5. Rosen, A., Gill, N.S., Salvador-Carulla, L.: The future of community psychiatry and community mental health services. Curr. Opin. Psychiatry **33**(4), 375–390 (2020)
6. Czaja, S.J., Boot, W.R., Charness, N., Rogers, W.A., Sharit, J.: Improving social support for older adults through technology: Findings from the PRISM randomized controlled trial. Gerontologist **58**(3), 467–477 (2018)
7. Jarvis, M.A., Padmanabhanunni, A., Chipps, J.: An evaluation of a low-intensity cognitive behavioral therapy mHealth-supported intervention to reduce loneliness in older people. Int. J. Environ. Res. Publ. Health **16**(7), 1305 (2019)
8. Abbaspur-Behbahani, S., Monaghesh, E., Hajizadeh, A., Fehresti, S.: Application of mobile health to support the elderly during the COVID-19 outbreak: A systematic review. Health Policy Technol. 100595 (2022)
9. Dürst, A.V., et al.: Fighting social isolation in times of pandemic COVID-19: The role of video calls for older hospitalized patients. Aging Clin. Exp. Res. **34**(9), 2245–2253 (2022)
10. Perdana, A., Mokhtar, I.A.: Seniors' adoption of digital devices and virtual event platforms in Singapore during Covid-19. Technol. Soc. **68**, 101817 (2022)
11. Venkatesh, V., Bala, H.: Technology acceptance model 3 and a research agenda on interventions. Decis. Sci. **39**(2), 273–315 (2008)
12. Gamberini, L., et al.: IoT as non-pharmaceutical interventions for the safety of living environments in COVID-19 pandemic age. Front. Comput. Sci. **3**, 733645 (2021)
13. Capuzzo, M., et al.: IoT systems for healthy and safe life environments. In: 2022 IEEE 7th Forum on Research and Technologies for Society and Industry Innovation (RTSI), pp. 31–37. IEEE (2022)
14. R Core Team. R: A language and environment for statistical computing. R Foundation for Statistical Computing, Vienna, Austria (2022). https://www.R-project.org/

15. Benjamini, Y., Hochberg, Y.: Controlling the false discovery rate: a practical and powerful approach to multiple testing. J. Roy. Stat. Soc. Ser. B (Methodol.) **57**(1), 289–300 (1995). R Core Team (2022). R: A language and environment for statistical (1995)
16. Czaja, S.J., Lee, C.C.: The impact of aging on access to technology. Univ. Access Inf. Soc. **5**, 341–349 (2007)
17. Paiva, J.O., et al.: Mobile applications for elderly healthcare: A systematic mapping. PloS One **15**(7), e0236091 (2020)
18. Kalimullah, K., Sushmitha, D.: Influence of design elements in mobile applications on user experience of elderly people. Procedia Comput. Sci. **113**, 352–359 (2017)

Designing a Multimodal Application for People with Brain Injuries to Manage Their Daily Routine: A User-Centered Approach

Bruno Giesteira[1], Andreia Pinto de Sousa[2]([✉]) [iD], Tiago Salgueiro dos Santos[3], and Carolina Vaz-Pires[4]

[1] University of Porto/ID+: HEAD, Health +Design Lab, Porto, Portugal
bgiesteira@fba.up.pt
[2] Lusófona University/HEI-Lab: Digital Human-Environment Interaction Lab, Lisboa, Portugal
andreia.pinto.sousa@ulusofona.pt
[3] University of Porto, Engineering Faculty, Integrated Master in Informatics and Computational Engineering, Porto, Portugal
[4] University of Porto, Engineering Faculty, Specialization Interaction Design, Web and Games, Porto, Portugal

Abstract. Centro de Reabilitação Profissional de Gaia (CRPG) is a Portuguese public association that promotes the social, educational, occupational, and rehabilitation aspects of people with disabilities. The CRPG project presented in this paper is directly related to the Rehabilitation and reintegration of labor accidents and occupational diseases (RAC/LCA) victims. The solution presented in this paper heavily relied on user research of the institution's procedures and the patients themselves. Their habits, goals, needs, and mental models allowed a better understanding of the heterogeneity of patient's injuries, which usually affected memory, motion, and cognition in different ways and severity. The User Centered-Design methodological approach also encompasses a comparative analysis of mobile applications in Google Play and Apple App Store related to disabilities and features some main features identified by CRPG; interviews with patients and with CRPG stakeholders; personas and contextual scenarios development, requirements, and features definition, workflow, wireflows, lo and high fidelity prototype, formative evaluation with end users. The usability and accessibility test results suggest the viability and efficacy of multiple interaction modalities in improving the accessibility of the application, ensuring a broader reach to the CRPG community with future implications as good practices in the inclusiveness of applications in other contexts.

Keywords: Brain injury · User Centered-Design · mHealth

1 The Context

How human society has faced differences has significantly influenced the development of educational policies essentially aimed at the inclusion of disability [1].

© The Author(s), under exclusive license to Springer Nature Switzerland AG 2023
M. Antona and C. Stephanidis (Eds.): HCII 2023, LNCS 14021, pp. 531–548, 2023.
https://doi.org/10.1007/978-3-031-35897-5_38

Brain injuries can affect both genders and people with different professional backgrounds. Accordingly to a study by Ponte (2016), the average age when the injury happened was 48.7 years old, and the gender balance. Most of them (62.5%) did not finish elementary school. Although more than 90% would like to return to work after the incident, only 6.3% returned to their previous work, and 47.9% retired.

Technology can support these patients in the rehabilitation process, cognition levels, and doctors' involvement in these treatments. In addition, patients suffering from brain injuries hampered their ability to perform their daily routines, implying specific requirements to design a solution that can give them that support.

XX	SEG	TER	QUA	QUI	SEX
09h00 10h30	Oficina	Oficina	Psicologia	Oficina	Autonomia 1.16
10h45 12h30	Relações Interpessoais 1.26	Autonomia 1.26	Treino Cognitivo 1.16	Act Física Adaptada 1.14	
	ALMOÇO	ALMOÇO	ALMOÇO	ALMOÇO	ALMOÇO
13h30 15h15	Act Física Adaptada 1.14	Treino Cognitivo 1.16	TIC 1.16	Relações Interpessoais 1.16	
15h30 17h00	Treino Cognitivo 1.26	"Atenção Plena" 1.16	Empregabilidade 1.16	Autonomia 1.16	

Fig. 1. Example of CRPG patient scheduling with text and colors

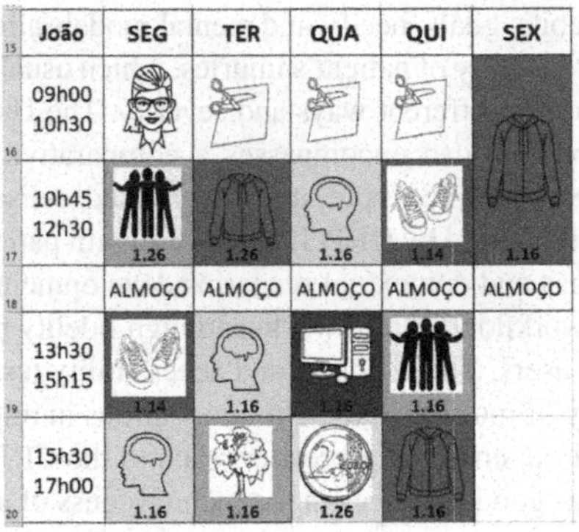

Fig. 2. Example of CRPG patient schedule with icons and colors

In their recovery process, these patients develop strategies to deal with memory loss and control impulsiveness, such as recording repetition and planning[1]. The CRPG

---

[1] Shirley Ryan AbilityLab, (2019, April 1). Brett's Story: Back to College after a Traumatic Brain Injury. Retrieved from https://www.youtube.com/watch?v=pJlEwRPrI04 and Attitude, (2016, October 30). Broken Part 1: Living with a Brain Injury. Retrieved from: https://www.youtube.com/watch?v=qbzd7Zp70UU

approach to addressing the disabilities of their patients includes the adaptation of daily resources used by the patients, such as the examples represented in Figs. 1 and 2.

They have two different representations for their patients of a daily agenda. One has text and colors referring to activities (Fig. 1), and the other relies on a graphical representation (icons and colors) of the different activities (Fig. 2) for the patients who had lost their ability to read. Based on this, we identified some of the specificities of these patients and how technology can help them. The biggest challenge in designing this solution is how to show the information so that the majority of these patients would better perceive it. Therefore, in Fig. 1 and Fig. 2, the need for content adaptation could be challenging in the designing phase. The main objective of this project was to design a solution to help brain injury patients in their daily lives after the 5-month[2] rehabilitation treatments.

2 Methodological Approach to Understanding the Context

The methodological approach to designing a digital artifact that can improve CRPG patients' daily routine heavily relied on user research. In the observing phase, besides visiting the space and getting to know the strategies as the agenda to overcome patients' disabilities, we also conducted a comparative analysis and semi-structured interviews with patients and stakeholders.

Based on user research, they were able to develop three different personas as representative users, scenarios that explore the daily use of the solution. Requirements and the knowledge acquired in the User Research phase were the foundation for the prototype and to conduct several evaluation and iteration moments.

2.1 Comparative Analysis

A comparative analysis was made to gain further insight into the solutions that address these health issues in the Android and iOS mobile application markets. Nine different mobile applications related to other disabilities and also related features that CRPG wanted to implement were analyzed. In addition, the applications were analyzed in terms of functionalities' simplicity, weaknesses, and advantages.

The comparative analysis allowed us to identify the necessity to design the user experience as frictionless as possible, without extra elements that would not address the user's actual needs.

This analysis also raised our awareness regarding the proposed system's user interface and visual design, particularly in color, contrast, and font. Due to the various disabilities that can afflict patients with brain injuries, our application needed to be easily read and understood. It also showed the importance of having an initial guide that helps the user familiarize themselves with the new interface when they see it for the first time.

---

[2] Time spent having treatments every weekday in CPRG to recover from the brain injury.

2.2 User Research and Concepts

The user research started in tandem with defining the problem. By analyzing the previously mentioned resources, we better understood this app's future users, characteristics, and difficulties. The comparative analysis revealed some experience and functional requirements. However, we needed a more profound knowledge of brain injuries to understand better the reality of those suffering from them. As such, we conducted interviews with representative users and relevant stakeholders.

Semi-structured Interviews. Accordingly to Cooper et al. [2], having the possibility of doing one-to-one interviews is one of the most efficient ways to gather data about the user and their goals. Ku & Lupton [3] reinforce the importance of referring to interviews to build empathy and reveal insights.

The main goals of these interviews were to discover the patients' objectives, motivations, pain points, and skills and to understand in depth how the stakeholders are involved in these users' routines. For this, we conducted eleven semi-structured interviews, five with patients in RAC/LCA treatment for five months and with six stakeholders: Trainers, Physiotherapists, and Neuropsychologists. Among the patients, three were men and two women, and the stakeholders were four women and three men. The questions approached both the user's and stakeholders' realities. The interviews were held online due to the unexpected spreading of the new SARS-CoV-2 virus, using the online tools Zoom and WhatsApp between the 25th and 30th of March 2020.

Our results showed that, on average, these patients were 42 years old, and their jobs varied from university to high school studies. In addition, most of them were either unemployed or couldn't return to their previous jobs due to their brain injury consequences.

Knowing more about their routines in CRPG, motivations, pain points, and skills made us understand that these patients want to regain the independence they lost after the injury, and the role of family/caretakers is essential. Some accepted the new life reality, while others are still in the process of accepting it. Concerning technology use, all of them have a smartphone and use them every day.

We likewise observed that these patients were very heterogeneous. e.g., their condition is very different depending on whether they had an accident or a stroke. In some, it was possible to see that their motion was affected, but to others, it was more their cognition or memory. Some patients had both movement and cognition affected.

The data analysis at this depth level was fundamental to prepare ourselves for the following design phases better, as we could better compare and contrast the different CRPG patients, their specificities, and necessities. Furthermore, it also became evident that the information presented in the application should be designed in an accessible and understandable way by all these users.

2.3 Personas and Scenarios

Based on the knowledge acquired through patient interviews, we create three distinct personas to showcase user behavior patterns and necessities [2]. We assigned them Goals, Motivations, Pain Points, and Skills to quantify their Focus and Anxiety connection to

Technology. Considering their heterogeneity and needs, we created two primary and one secondary persona to represent the majority of patients. The primary personas represent the patients and are the main target of our application. Furthermore, the secondary persona represents the stakeholders who have different needs.

Fig. 3. Primary persona (Maria) (I"O" by prefabu is licensed under CC BY-NC-ND 2.0.)

One of the primary personas is a 28 years old woman named Maria (Fig. 3). She is facing cognitive and memory issues, changes in right-side eye vision, and aphasia (inability to understand or produce speech) after a stroke. Her goals are not missing tasks or medicines anymore and to be able to go to any place herself. Her primary motivations are being more independent, getting a job, and helping others. Her pain points are remembering things, organizing her daily life, performing complex tasks, and depending on others since she has problems staying focused and a high level of anxiety. However, she can write, read, and use computers, tablets, and smartphones, so she is familiar with the technology. The other primary persona is Fernando, a 35 years old man who had a stroke from stress at work (Fig. 4). His left hand is moving poorly, and the movement is out of sync. He is also dealing with some memory issues. His goals are organizing all information in one application and improving his communication with CRPG. His motivations are being independent, having a job, returning to full mobility, and physically active. However, it is hard for him to tie shoelaces, cook, change his cat's toilet container, and play sports. Despite that, Fernando has a Master's degree and additional qualifications. He can use all mobile devices, social networks, and messaging apps, buy online tickets, use online transport websites, and even play games.

The interviews with the CRPG stakeholders raised awareness of the patient's connection with caretakers, and based on that, we created a secondary persona. Our secondary persona is Raquel, 39 years old; she works as a Neuropsychologist in CPRG (Fig. 5). Her goals are teaching and evaluating patients and groups, supporting patients to be more independent, and helping them decrease their emotional and cognitive issues. Her motivations are helping people and keeping human contact between her and the patients. Her pain points are doing the same tasks twice in the CRPG software platform, communicating with some patients due to their cognitive and memory issues, and dealing with heterogeneous groups.

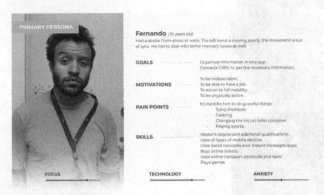

Fig. 4. Primary persona (Fernando) ("skeptical man" by jseliger2 is licensed under CC BY 2.0.)

Fig. 5. Secondary persona (Raquel) ("Woman with glasses and Women's suit 1.jpg" by ukieiri-999636 is licensed under CC0 1.0.)

Scenarios are a powerful tool to develop experience. Context scenarios Cooper et al. [2] allow us to develop the pragmatic relationship between the user and the object and determine the experience's context [4]. As referring to a solution to daily routines, the Scenarios developed in this context describe a day in these patients' lives, from waking up to bed. Table 1 samples one of the scenarios developed.

Based on scenarios, we could find the application's main functionalities: Calendar, Reminders, Meals, Transports, Notes, and Meditation. For each functionality, there was a group of correlated features and tasks that users should be able to perform to be more organized in their daily life inside the center.

In Calendar, the users should be able to see, create and edit their activities at CRPG. For that, the application should: (i) show the current day and time, daily activities,

Table 1. Scenarios for one of the primary CRPG Personas

Marias's Scenario
Maria takes her morning medicine straight after hearing her waking-up alarm on her phone. Her father brings her to the metro stop near their home by car. Afterward, she arrives at Casa da Música station, where she takes the CRPG bus. Maria listens to calm music on her smartphone during the bus ride
Regarding her stroke, Maria arrives at CRPG but needs to remember where her classroom is. So, she gets anxious about it, but luckily, she finds some colleagues at the entrance, and they all wait for their Morning trainer
Maria did not understand what she needed to do at first, but her Trainer exemplified it, so it was easier for her to follow and repeat afterward
It is 12h30 - lunchtime in CRPG. Everyone goes to the CRPG canteen
Maria should have booked her meal one day before, so she asked her class Trainer to email the canteen with her card number during her session. She usually chooses the Fish menu
She sees the menu for the next day while waiting in line to have her food and books it for the next day, passing her card on the machine
In the afternoon, Maria has a Cognitive Training session. She learns some methodologies not to forget things, such as: preparing the supermarket items list, so she never fails any item
It is 5 PM, and the day is over in CRPG
Maria goes home the same way she arrived, by the CRPG bus. Maria goes to the supermarket with the list she had prepared before
She cooks dinner and afterward listens to some meditation music before she goes to bed

activity details, Staff member's picture of the activity, user's medicine and its time, the meal chosen for the day, and a timeline for completed/remaining activities; (ii) be integrated with MS Outlook API so the CRPG Staff could help and interact with the user's agenda feed to customize it considering each patient's needs.

For Reminders, users should be able to see, create and edit their reminders. For that, the app should: (i) allow setting the reminder name, time, type of alarm, type of reminder, and customized frequency.

In Meals, users should: (i) choose between four options (Meat, Fish, Diet, Vegetarian) that would be the next day's choice; (ii) be able to see the chosen meal for the current day and their meals history.

The Transports functionality should consider the two types of users, represented as Maria and Fernando, our primary personas: those that go there by themselves or by public transportation and those that take the CRPG bus to the treatments. Therefore, the application should: (i) have Google Maps API to get the public transport schedules and trace possible user routes. For that, access to the smartphone's location would be mandatory; (ii) have CRPG transport schedule, stop sites, and the driver's picture.

For the Notes feature, users should be able to: (i) type text, save a note, see their list of notes, add images, and send the note to someone; (ii) allow users to save notes by voice so users can save their notes faster. For that, the app must access the smartphone's microphone.

The Meditation application should contain: (i) classes and exercises in audio files provided by CRPG. The users should be able to see the meditation classes list and hear them.

To meet the deadlines for presenting and reporting all phases of the project, we discussed with CRPG the priority of the features and the tasks regarding their impact on the user's daily life. For example, Agenda and Reminders functionalities were in higher priority, meals and transport medium priority, and meditation and notes low priority.

3 Prototypes and Evaluation

With the requirements and features defined, we started the defining phase. First, we focused on the information architecture, drawing the flow, and a preliminary interface design (wireflows) based on the priority tasks and possible interactions. In this process, we were always aware of the importance of limiting unnecessary steps, keeping their memory alive, and not being disrupted by users by their natural navigation flow [5].

3.1 Navigation and Interaction Definition

The information organization process led us to the workflow (Fig. 6), where the user's main screen allows access to Calendar, Reminders, Meals, Transports, Free notes, and Meditation Class features.

From the Calendar screen, users start in the daily view and can go to the weekly view. They can also see activity details and create/edit a new activity. In Reminders, the initial screen is the list of reminders where users can go to the reminder detail screen or create/edit a reminder.

Users can navigate between the public transport screen and the CRPG transport screen from the Transports screen. Similar to the Reminders screen, in Notes, users can go to the note's details or create a new note. Lastly, the Meditation screen gives access to meditation details and plays the audio file for the meditation classes (Fig. 7).

Since the first sketches, the screens considered mobile accessibility and design guidelines such as Mobile Accessibility Principles from w3.org[3] and Material Design[4] from Google. As a result, some of the screens integrated some principles, such as the elevated cards concept[5]: a shadow was added to the card to indicate that element displays content and is good to focus the user's attention[6].

This exercise revealed that navigation, such as closing buttons, needed to be improved. In addition, the bottom navigation menu could be more prominent to make

---

[3] Guideline for accessible mobile web content considering the perceivable, operable, understandable and robust principles. https://www.w3.org/TR/mobile-accessibility-mapping/

[4] Components based on the best practices of user interface design. https://material.io/components

[5] Material Design from Google. Cards. https://material.io/components/cards

[6] Material Design from Google. Elevation. https://material.io/design/environment/elevation.html#elevation-in-material-design

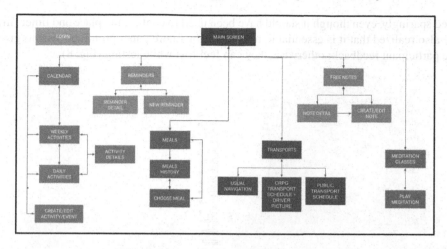

Fig. 6. Site map including apps' main features

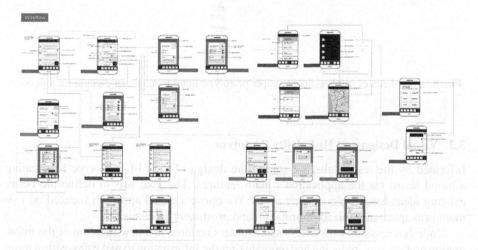

Fig. 7. The first wireflow study of the application.

it easier for the users to interact. Finally, we developed a low-fi prototype to test with users and see if our proposal was on the right track.

3.2 Navigation and Interaction Validation Through a Paper Prototype

Due to COVID-19 circumstances, we conducted these tests with our relatives and closest friends to ensure the navigation and information were simple and well communicated. As a result, this first evaluation cycle shows that: (i) the clock feature had to be simplified since it needed to be more prominent, and the users needed clarification about what they were supposed to do; (ii) There were also some difficulties at the beginning of creating the activity. The add button needed to be clarified for all the users. The OK button was used sparingly, even though it should have been used to confirm the place and time; (iii) we also realized that it is essential to remember for future paper prototype tests to give the participant feedback; otherwise, they can feel lost while testing (Fig. 8).

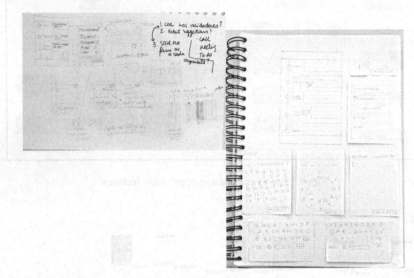

Fig. 8. First sketches and low-fidelity paper prototype items to create an event in the calendar.

3.3 Visual Design and Hi-Fidelity Prototype

Informed by the test results, we started the design of the hi-fi prototype by creating a mood board for the application's main features. The goal was to define the better existing ideas based on our target needs. We chose a visual approach focused on two main principles: minimized information and prominent elements.

Codesign sessions with CRPG stakeholders resulted in a new iteration of the information architecture, reducing and reorganizing the information to make navigation more accessible. As Meals and Transport were based on previous planning and remember, they should be under Reminders functionality. This new organization was also beneficial for the bottom navigation menu so that it could have four buttons, and the icons in it could be more prominent.

The visual layer of the interface also represented a challenge as we have to comply with accessibility guidelines and CRPG brand identity. We started to verify the color combination in the color blind simulation tool[7], the results showed that the contrast between the CRPG identity color palette wasn't good enough to fit our user's needs. To overcome this, we seek to follow identity guidelines, such as typography and icon styles and study different colors to combine with the primary identity color and grant the minimum contrast suggested in W3C principles of accessibility.

---

[7] Stark is a plugin for Adobe Xd that includes color blind simulations and a contrast checker. https://www.getstark.co/

Fig. 9. Agenda screens iteration trying several forms of present information

We did several iterations to figure out a better way to show and interact with the information (Fig. 9). For example, other colors and time controls were added to the layouts (Fig. 10).

In Figs. 9 and 10, it is possible to see different graphical solutions of the same Agenda screens. There was the need to create some options using different colors and displaying the same information until arriving at a solution that would be comfortable for the user. An iteration was designed, including improved features: the activity card and its style.

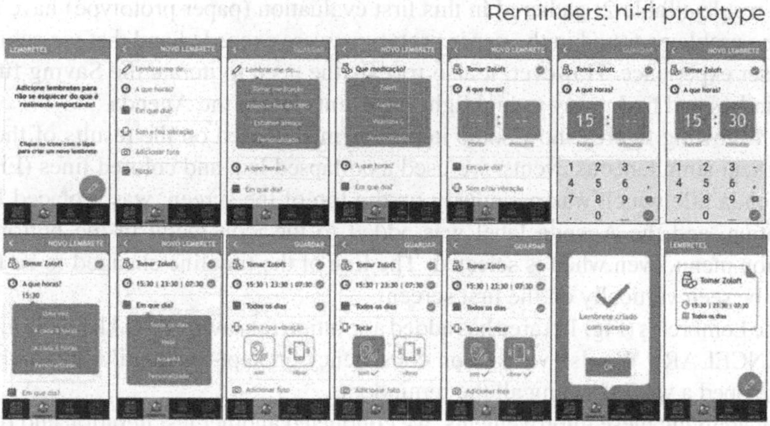

Reminders: hi-fi prototype

Fig. 10. Reminders screens iteration trying several solutions to present information.

The size, pictures, icons, and texts were more prominent. As they already use post-its in their daily life and therapies, and to make it easier to recognize it, the style of the card was adapted to a post-it metaphor adjusting the card to the user's mental model.

From this stage, we developed a prototype supported by the previous contextual scenarios and some validation scenarios to ensure we thought about unexpected situations to improve our prototype.

3.4 High-Fidelity Prototype and Implementation Validation

Users Evaluation. The Hi-fidelity prototype evaluation was pre-tested with CRPG staff and conducted with five final users. Due to COVID-19 pandemic restrictions, the tests were conducted remotely through Microsoft Teams. Participants were asked to complete two tasks and answer a questionnaire with ten closed and two open questions where they could share their suggestions and personal opinions about the application. Among our participants were four men and one woman between 26 and 50. All of them had finished their five-month rehabilitation process. The main objectives of this first evaluation were to verify the following aspects.

1. Easiness: in the navigation, such as moving from screen to screen, scrolling inside the app, etc.;
2. Simplicity: of the information displayed (textual and graphical);
3. Comfort: in the sense that the users would not feel lost inside the application;
4. Readability: if they read all the information displayed on each screen without any difficulty;
5. Recognition of graphical elements: if each icon would have its meaning immediately recognizable;
6. Quickness: how sharp images, texts, and icons were perceived.

The results (Table 2) gathered in this first evaluation (paper prototype) have shown that some problems found in the paper prototype were exceeded and that we achieved a better user experience. However, it also reveals the need to iterate the Saving function in Reminders and find a way to highlight the events inside the Agenda.

The following figures show some iterations made based on the results of the tests. To represent simultaneous events: we used a collapsed list, and colored lines (Fig. 10). The Agenda title which was previously on the top of the screen, was replaced by day information, and the Agenda label was added to the icon menu in the bottom blue navigation menu, even when is selected. The line of the timeline changed to be thicker and can be seen vertically on the first screen;

In the Lembretes (Fig. 11) area has added a solution for saving (GUARDAR) and cancel (CANCELAR). We also worked on consistency on kept-in sound/vibration buttons and developed a way of seeing all the reminders.

After applying these improvements, we conducted another test iteration and realized the user experience was smoother and faster when requesting to perform both tasks.

Accessibility Assessment. After this iteration informed from tests with users, this project followed to an implementation phase and has been submitted again to different evaluation moments. Given the purpose and context of this paper, we will focus on the functional tests, namely: graphic user interface and non-functional tests concerning accessibility, which were on system and accessibility testing.

Table 2. Summary of the results with CRPG users evaluation

Categories	Positive feedback	Improvements to be made
Easiness and Simplicity	The application has a simple and convenient navigation	Make the save function in reminders more convenient and obvious
Comfort and Readability	The navigation menu is intuitive enough to be comfortable for these users to use it. The size and style of the text were chosen correctly, which allowed the users to read without any difficulties	–
Recognition of graphical elements	The icons and photos are clear and help the user understands the meaning without reading the text	Highlight the following events inside the agenda more clearly with a different color
Quickness	The navigation menu is intuitive enough to be comfortable for these users to use. To decrease the time of tasks, an initial guide that explains how to use the application will help these users. Also, onboarding screens guide them better across the app	–
Open answers/ suggestions	The patients that evaluated the app were quite happy about what they saw. Personalization was very valuable: having this app for CRPG-related activities and their life outside the center. They would add a sports component related to physical exercises	

Fig. 11. Agenda and Lembretes screen iteration after the high-fidelity prototype's first evaluation

The application tests on three different devices: (i) Motorola G (2015/Android 6.0); (ii) Xiaomi 7 (2018/Android 10.0); (iii) Xiaomi Redmi Note 9 (2020/Android 11.0). Each device has a distinct Android release installed.

Regarding the assessment of accessibility, we analyzed the application, four topics: (i) Screen Readers; (ii) Colour Ratio Analyzers; (iii) Inbuilt Accessibility Settings; (iv) WCAG 2.1 Guidelines.

Screen Readers. To assess the suitability of Talkback integration with the app, we performed a test to ensure that the specified content descriptions were working as intended.

Due to time constraints, the screen readers were not tested with users. Instead, the test was done manually following the recommendations presented in the Android documentation[8]. The documentation recommends swiping through each visual element and analyzing the following topics:

1. Does the verbal feedback for each element convey its content or purpose appropriately?;
2. Are announcements succinct, or are they needlessly verbose?
3. Can the main workflows be completed efficiently?
4. Can every element be reached by swiping?
5. If alerts or other temporary messages appear, are they read aloud?

After verifying if the app follows all screens' guidelines, the results were satisfactory overall. The labels are succinct and clear in describing each element's purpose, and all relevant elements have their content description done. The workflows were all completed, and every interaction element was reached. The Talkback service could also read when an error message is shown on the screen.

Color Ratio Analysers. The application uses a relatively reduced number of colors; the text in the application is mostly black if on a white background or white, if in a dark-colored element. Apart from the background, which is always white (#FFFFFF), the following colors were used (color code below each example) (Fig. 12):

| #F9B401 | #002345 | #00BBF2 | #87B700 |

Fig. 12. Colors present in the color scheme of the application.

---

[8] Test your app's accessibility: https://developer.android.com/guide/topics/ui/accessibility/testing

To guarantee the suitability of the color scheme and the contrast between colors, we used a Color Contrast Analyzer (CCA)[9]. As a result, we obtained a value regarding the contrast between the two colors, and it's possible to compare their suitability.

The application background color is always white, and text varies between white, black, or one of the four colors of the color schema depending on the background element color. Based on our color schema, we analyzed four combinations of colors: (i) dark blue on white background; (ii) light blue on white background; (iii) green on white background; (iv) orange on white background. Black on white is, by default, the highest contrast possible, so the test was unnecessary.

Table 3 .

	Normal Text		Large Text	
	WCAG AA	WCAG AAA	WCAG AA	WCAG AAA
dark blue on white background	Pass	Pass	Pass	Pass
light blue on white background	Pass	Fail	Pass	Pass
green on white background	Pass	Fail	Pass	Pass
orange on white background	Pass	Pass	Pass	Pass

The results (Table 3) were satisfactory overall. Despite two combinations (light blue and green) with normal text failing to pass the more demanding WCAG AAA test, the color scheme proved a good choice. These results are a valuable recommendation to add to the application design system.

Inbuilt Accessibility Settings. Android provides several native accessibility tools by default. Stock Android 11.0 release integrates (among others) the following tools:
High contrast text: This feature fixes the text color as either black or white, depending on the original text color. High contrast should improve the readability of text, improving user experience;
Color correction: allows specific colors to be corrected to make visibility easier for colorblind users;
Magnifier: Allows the user to zoom in and out of specific areas of the screen, improving the visibility of specific visual elements.

The first test was with the High Contrast Text tool. All screens were explored using this tool, with a 100% success rate, as no inconsistencies or visual issues were identified.

Due to reasons that were not fully identified, usage of the Color Correction tool was inconsistent. In some screens, the tool could not be activated, and in other cases, visual elements were not present. Because the tool would cause glitches even when the application was not being run, it is possible that the experimental nature of this tool,

---

[9] Contrast checker https://webaim.org/resources/contrastchecker/

or the specific release which was used for testing, did not work entirely as expected. In the future, these tests could be performed again using different Android releases and an improved version of the tool to pinpoint the origin of the issues.

All the screens/features were also explored with the Magnifier tool test, with a 100% success rate. The magnifier could zoom in on any specific screen area, improving visibility.

WCAG 2.1 Guidelines. As mentioned previously, WCAG 2.1 is a very extensive document that covers many different topics on accessibility. It is impossible to cover every single one in detail, so a paraphrased summary from the official documentation is used to check the accessibility points of the app. Table 4 presents each of the key[10] topics, as well as the approach during development to fulfill the requirements.

Table 4. WCAG topics and approaches/features used to meet all requirements

ID	Topics	Approach
1	Text alternatives for non-text content should be provided	All buttons and icons have a description tag that describes their use
2	Captions and other alternatives should be provided for multimedia	The meditation media player has content description tags
3	Created content should be presented in different ways, including by assistive technologies, without losing meaning	All of the created notes are described in the consult reminder/note screens, following the format in which Talkback describes them is recommended by the official documentation
4	Make it easier for users to see and hear content	Attention was directed to the size of visual elements and text in order to improve readability, as well as using concise content descriptions for the Talkback service to make comprehension easier
5	Make all functionality available from a keyboard	Not implemented
6	Give users enough time to read and use content	There are no timed messages or pop-ups, so the user is free to take the time needed to read any content
7	Content that causes seizures or physical reactions should not be used	None of the screens/features integrate content that flickers, flashes, or blinks, which could trigger photosensitive epilepsy
8	Help users navigate and find content	The bottom bar icon and labels have increased in size to help the users find the desired feature

(continued)

---

[10] Extracted from https://www.w3.org/WAI/standards-guidelines/wcag/glance/

Table 4. (*continued*)

ID	Topics	Approach
9	Make it easier to use inputs other than the keyboard	The use of speech recognition commands, as well as gesture recognition by Talkback, provide the user input alternatives
10	Text should be readable and understandable	Android recommends the minimum font size to be 12px for users with no impairment to the vision. Given the context, the minimum text size in the platform is 14px, but most text in the app ranges from 16-22px for normal text and 25-35px for titles and subtitles
11	Make content appear and operate in predictable ways	The presentation of content follows the guidelines of accessible mobile apps design, as well as input from the end users from the CRPG community
12	Help users avoid and correct mistakes	Most screens allow the user to return to a previous screen using both the app bar arrow, and screens which require considerable input from the user (such as create new Reminder) provide a button which allows all fields to be cleared
13	Maximize compatibility with current and future user tools	The platform was designed with the most modern Android's accessibility guidelines, and as such future Android updates should maintain or even improve the accessibility level of the app

4   Final Considerations

Increasing the accessibility of mobile devices and applications is essential to increase their reach to a more significant number of users, namely people with special needs. Assistive technologies allow the user to overcome obstacles when interacting with these devices. Multimodal input/output combinations increase the options available to the user, reducing the barriers encountered in single-modal applications. The assistive technologies field is vast and complex. Many factors have an impact on the way individuals with disabilities interact with smartphones. Some assistive technologies are purpose-built to the necessity of a single user, which makes ensuring accessibility for these cases even more difficult. These circumstances make achieving total accessibility for 100% of the users virtually impossible. The implemented interaction modalities were the one's CRPG clients identified as answering their primary needs. The requests were primarily related to memory and visual limitations instead of hardware technologies. Future iterations of this project include increased compatibility with different kinds of devices and other alternative assistive technologies.

The mobile application integrates multiple modes of interaction and features related to daily tasks that customers perform, such as selecting meals, checking transport schedules, or meditating. Users can interact with the app using the touchscreen or voice commands, and audio cues have also been implemented. Contextual notifications serve as reminders for events and provide shortcuts to specific application features. The users well received the integrated interaction modalities. The tests suggest that the multiple modalities are adequate to allow the participants to fulfill the tasks. Younger participants, more experienced with smartphone applications, performed better when interacting using the touchscreen. Older participants, who self-diagnosed their skill in using the devices as being lower, seemed to benefit from using audio cues and voice commands. Some tasks were performed in less time, raising fewer doubts when using the device's touch screen.

Including users in the application development process allowed a more effective response to the needs of the CRPG community, raising obstacles and issues that would only be identified if they placed them as potential final users. The test results suggest the feasibility and effectiveness of multiple interaction modalities in improving the application's accessibility, ensuring that the application can reach the maximum number of people in the community. All participants use smartphones daily and did not use any assistive technology to help perform tasks. Different interaction modes may be integrated to ensure that even more CRPG customers can use the application across a broader range of devices.

Acknowledgements. Special thanks to CRPG's patients and stakeholders, the students and supervisors Pedro Cardoso e Rodrigo Assaf involved in the project, and also the ID+ Research Center, Group HEAD Health + Design Lab.

This study was funded by the Foundation for Science and Technology – FCT (Portuguese Ministry of Science, Technology and Higher Education), under the grant UIDB/05380/2020.

References

1. Ribeiro, A., Giesteira, B.: Universidade inclusiva: retrospetiva e prospetiva no contexto da UP, pp. 229–241 (2014). Novas tecnologias e educação: ensinar a aprender, aprender a ensinar. Biblioteca Digital da Faculdade de Letras da Universidade do Porto, pp. 229–241 (2014)
2. Cooper, A., Reimann, R., Cronnin, D., Noessel, C., Csizmadi, J., LeMoine, D.: About Face, 4th Edn. John Wiley & Sons. Inc. (2014)
3. Ku, B., Lupton, E.: Health Design Thinking: Creating products and services for better health. In: MIT Press Paper Knowledge. Toward a Media History of Documents (2019)
4. Zagalo, N.: Engagement Design. Designing for Interaction Motivations, Tan, D. (ed.). Springer (2020). https://doi.org/10.4018/978-1-4666-4916-3.ch002
5. Nielsen, J.: Workflow Expectations: Presenting Steps at the Right Time. https://www.nngroup. com/articles/workflow-expectations/. Accessed 18 July 2020

Building an Online Platform for Speech and Language Therapy in Germany: Users Needs and Requirements

Katharina Giordano[✉], Manja Wonschik, and Juliane Leinweber

University of Applied Sciences and Arts Hildesheim/Holzminden/Göttingen, Faculty of
Engineering and Health, Health Campus Göttingen, Göttingen, Germany
{katharina.giordano,manja.wonschik1,juliane.leinweber}@hawk.de

Abstract. The aim of the HiSSS project is to develop a hybrid teletherapy system
for people with speech and language disorders after stroke. This system should
cover both face-to-face and video therapy and also enable patients to do independent exercises at home. This paper describes the analysis of the requirements and
needs for such a system. The requirements analysis is based on literature and app
research on the one hand and on the results of a focus group with speech and language therapists (SLTs) on the other. The literature research includes publications
on the development and evaluation of technology for speech and language therapy
for people after stroke. The app research aimed to derive requirements from the
feedback on existing apps used in speech and language therapy. This was followed
by a focus group with 3 SLTs who have previous experience of delivering video
therapy. The results show overlaps, but also their own main areas of focus: While
the literature research revealed more general requirements, the app research and
the focus group indicated concrete wishes for specific functions. The synthesis
of the results of the literature and app research and the focus group was essential to comprehensively collect and specify the requirements and user needs for a
teletherapy system. The comparison between the results of the literature review
and results of the focus group demonstrated the need for user involvement in technical development as early as possible. The amount of implementation ideas and
the commitment shown by the therapists highlights the relevance for a teletherapy
system in Germany that integrates three elements: (1) face to face therapy, and (2)
video therapy and (3) home exercises.

Keywords: Teletherapy · Aphasia · Co-Design · Speech and Language Therapy

1 Background

Stroke is one of the most common causes of disability in adulthood [1]. Speech and
language functions are often affected, with 20% of stroke patients suffering from chronic
aphasia, dysarthria and/or central facial paresis [2, 3]. These disorders directly affect
communication and often lead to social isolation [4, 5]. Thus, aphasia leads to a massive
reduction in quality of life, resulting in a significantly lower quality of life in the long

M. Antona and C. Stephanidis (Eds.): HCII 2023, LNCS 14021, pp. 549–565, 2023.
https://doi.org/10.1007/978-3-031-35897-5_39

term than in the case of cancer or Alzheimer's disease, a stroke without a speech disorder or in healthy people [6]. Speech and language therapy aims to counteract these negative consequences by reducing the symptoms of speech and language disorders, as well as their negative impact on psychosocial factors.

Breitenstein et al. [2] were able to show for patients with chronic aphasia that the therapy frequency is the decisive success factor in speech therapy on verbal communication and quality of life. This was confirmed in a study with self-organised additional training with a commercially available application. The therapy effects increased with each additional day of exercise per week [7]. Although the relevance of high-frequency therapy is well known, it is difficult to implement due to staff and cost shortages in healthcare. Innovative approaches are needed that complement the therapy process and thereby increase the frequency of speech and language therapy to improve the quality of life of patients in the long term.

One possibility to facilitate access to therapy and increase the frequency of therapy is the use of teletherapy [8]. Teletherapy has great potential for speech and language therapy, for example by maintaining access to therapy despite long distances and limited mobility of patients, but also as the chance to connect with patients in their everyday environment [9]. Teletherapy can be conducted synchronously and asynchronously, whereby synchronous teletherapy usually corresponds to an exchange via video conference with a therapist in an individual or group setting. Evidence is still insufficient, but the data to date suggest that synchronous teletherapy for aphasia leads to comparable outcomes as face-to-face therapy [10]. Similar results are available for the teletherapeutic implementation of the intensive LSVT LOUD programme for people with dysarthria in Parkinson's disease [11, 12].

In addition to synchronous teletherapy, there is also asynchronous teletherapy. This is the provision of information or material that enables the patient to perform exercises independently without simultaneous support from the therapist. These include web- or app-based therapy exercises for independent working. Clients can access these for the intended purposes on devices of their choice and use them as needed and desired. In recent years, with the progress of digitalisation, specific programmes for use in speech therapy have been developed and studied for their usability and effectiveness. For example, Stark & Warburton [13] investigated the use of a therapy app compared to a language-nonspecific app. The results showed language-specific improvements that remained stable over a period of six months. Further studies confirm that remote technology-assisted aphasia training is acceptable [14, 15] and beneficial to patients [16–18].

The different forms of teletherapy can be combined with each other and with face-to-face therapy and are mostly meant to complement rather than replace usual care. The combination of usual care, in this case face-to-face therapy, with self-administered tablet-based tasks for people with aphasia was investigated by Palmer et al. [19]. Word finding improved significantly higher in the experimental group than in the control group, which received only usual care. The combination of usual care and computerised speech and language therapy also led to higher improvements in word finding than the combination of usual care and computerised attention training. The combination of synchronous teletherapy and additional asynchronous online language exercises was also investigated [20]. Twelve people with chronic aphasia took part in teletherapy services in individual and group settings over a period of 12 weeks and performed additional online language exercises on the computer between therapy appointments. Analysis of the results shows that the mean scores on most measurements improved after treatment. Individual analyses of the usage data of the online exercises showed that the exercise time increased over the course, which could indicate an increasing self-confidence in using the exercises or also an increased motivation. The advantage of this combination is that the contents practised by the patient independently can be controlled and adjusted by the therapist from a distance. Finally, the digital implementation made it possible to maintain the regularity of the therapy despite possible distances.

Since in the long term the different forms of therapy, teletherapeutic and face-to-face, can be most usefully combined in everyday practice, a platform that supports the different forms would be useful. At this point, the project HiSSS (Hybrid and Interactive Speech and Language Therapy after Stroke) takes up, which aims on adding a hybrid interactive format to the therapy of speech and language disorders after stroke. The core of the project is a complex, web-based speech therapy care that integrates existing and innovative both synchronous and asynchronous therapeutic elements. The innovative elements include the automatic speech recognition (ASR) and automatic face recognition (AFR) via the sensors of the user device and the use of these analysis results in the therapy. All elements are part of a speech therapy interaction, which can be applied in face-to-face and video therapy, but also in asynchronous self-administered exercises.

In order to achieve a sustainable and user-relevant result, a co-creation development process is carried out. Co-creation is characterised by involving different stakeholders in the process of problem identification and solution finding and evaluation [21, 22]. The end user's experiences are incorporated during the development process in order to create solutions that are more suited to the end-users' situation and thus provide meaningful support. This paper is dedicated to the first step of this development, a requirements analysis for the targeted hybrid system. User perspective, app and literature research will serve as the basis for deriving specific requirements for the development of a teletherapy system that integrates all elements.

2 Methods

2.1 Design

The requirement analysis is based on a two-step approach: in a first step a literature and app research is done. This includes literature on the development and evaluation of technologies for speech and language therapy for people after stroke and ratings and reviews of speech therapy apps already in use. In a second step, the user perspective is illuminated by conducting a focus group with speech and language therapists. Combining the results of the research and the focus group provides an overview of the requirements and user needs. This should create a basis for the following co-design process. The realisation of these steps is described in more detail in Sects. 2.2 and 2.3. The study was approved by the ethics committee of University of Applied Sciences and Arts Hildesheim/Holzminden/Göttingen and is registered in the German Register of Clinical Trials (DRKS00030430).

2.2 Research

The research was divided into a systematic literature research and an app research. The literature research aimed to identify evidence-based requirements for a teletherapy platform. For this purpose, publications on the development or evaluation of digital technologies for speech and language therapy for people after stroke were included in order to derive requirements from them. The literature research was conducted in the databases Medline, Cinahl, Pedro, Cochrane, PsycInfo, PsycNet. The following search terms were used: Stroke OR dysarthria OR aphasia OR apraxia AND SLT OR SLP AND teletherapy OR technology OR videotherapy OR telerehabilitation OR telepractice AND evaluation OR development OR experiences OR feasibility. According to the different search functions, these search terms were applied to the databases. No additional filter regarding the publication period was used. Articles in English and German were included. In addition to this systematic approach, individual articles were discovered through the bibliography of included articles and were also included if their content was suitable. The app research aimed to derive requirements from the feedback on existing apps used in speech and language therapy. For this purpose, the ratings in the App Store or forums of apps used in German-speaking countries were examined and requirements were derived.

2.3 Focus Group

Procedure. The focus group was organized to identify the requirements for a hybrid and interactive therapy system from the user's perspective, in this case speech and language therapists (SLTs). Due to the Covid-19 pandemic and to increase the recruitment range, the focus group was conducted via videoconferencing. Zoom served as the platform for the videoconference. The focus group lasted one and a half hours and covered two main topics: previous experiences with teletherapy and wishes and suggestions for a hybrid therapy system.

To begin with, the participants were welcomed by the facilitators and a short round of introductions followed in which each person introduced themselves with their name and professional focus. This was followed by a short presentation of the HiSSS project with its main objective and the aim and procedure of the focus group. In order to ensure a balanced and respectful atmosphere, short rules for communication were presented and asked to be respected. After this introduction, the two content-related blocks followed. First, existing experiences with teletherapy were collected in order to derive requirements from these. For this purpose, an initial open question was asked (*What are your experiences with teletherapy so far?*) to which the participants could respond. In case no further comments followed, more specific questions were prepared (e.g. *What did you particularly like about the teletherapy? What problems did you encounter?*). At the same time, a student assistant documented the mentioned aspects on a prepared Miro-Board. The Miro-Board was shared on the screen for the participants providing an overview of the aspects mentioned and serving as an impulse for further experiences. The facilitators explicitly asked about the different settings (face-to-face, synchronous and asynchronous teletherapy) in order to get appropriate feedback for all formats. In the next block, a creative method was used to collect wishes and suggestions. The participants were supposed to write down at least five ideas on how a technology-supported system could usefully support speech therapy after stroke in the future (within five minutes). The participants were encouraged not to think about the feasibility of their idea, but to freely write down what they thought would be useful or necessary, regardless of the technical possibilities they were aware of. After the five minutes, each participant was given the opportunity to present their ideas. Questions could be asked or additions and subsequent ideas could be expressed. After these two thematic blocks, the participants had the opportunity to ask any remaining questions before the facilitators concluded the focus group by thanking the participants.

Participants. The aim was to include five SLTs for the focus group. The inclusion criteria was that they should be a SLT who regularly treats speech and language disorders after stroke. At the same time, they should have already gained experience with the realisation of teletherapy. Recruitment was done through cooperating speech therapy practitioners and professional associations. Contact was initially made in writing by email with a project presentation and details of the focus group. This was followed by an additional contact by telephone to provide detailed and personal information and to answer potential queries. After giving their consent to participate, the participants received an invitation to the focus group and the link to the video conference by email.

Data Collection. For data collection, the focus group was video recorded. With the help of the video recording, the entire session was transcribed. In addition, the Miro Board filled live during the focus group was saved. Before the focus group, the participants filled out a questionnaire on technology affinity [23]. Technology affinity is understood as a person's attraction to technical devices. The TA-EG refers to general electronic devices from everyday life. The four subscales of the TA-EG (Enthusiasm: a $= 0.843$; Competence: a $= 0.863$; Positive Consequences: a $= 0.767$; Negative Consequences: a $= 0.732$) show satisfactory to good internal consistency. It is a reliable and valid questionnaire that has been validated on a large, heterogeneous sample [23]. The questionnaire consists of 19 items, statements on the subscales. The respondents rate the extent to which the individual statements apply to them using a five-point Likert scale (1 = "does not apply at all", 5 = "applies completely"). The achievable score ranges from 19, indicating a low affinity for technology, to 95 points.

Data Analysis. In order to evaluate the focus group and derive requirements, experiences and wishes expressed were filtered from the transcript and the notes on the Miro Board. In a next step, these were reformulated into requirements for a teletherapy system. Table 1 shows examples of this step for three aspects.

Table 1. Exemplary transformation of expressed conditions into requirements for the teletherapy system

Statements of the participants	Resulting requirement for the tele-therapy system
Passing on material is currently a difficulty in the digital setting, as this has to be done via an additional channel (e-mail or post)	Easy sharing and sending of documents via the system should be possible
Through video therapy, the creation of audio/video recordings was increasingly used (e.g. for self-reflection) and was very positively received by both sides (patients and SLTs)	It should be possible to create and save sound and video recordings within the system
In synchronous teletherapy, focus control is more difficult, i.e. clarifying the common centre of attention (Which item are we currently on?)	Possible function for SLTs: "Highlighter" function; therapist has a light circle around her own cursor, which she can use to draw attention to certain aspects of an exercise

3   Results

The aim was to compile a catalogue of requirements for a teletherapy platform for people with speech and language disorders after stroke. This should be based on literature, the user's perspective and the technical possibilities from the developer's point of view. The results of these three areas are presented in detail below.

3.1   Research

The literature research identified 53 articles that were considered appropriate based on the abstract. In a second step, ten of these were excluded due to duplication. Of the remaining articles, the full text was checked for compliance with the inclusion criteria, which led to the exclusion of a further twelve articles. Finally, 31 articles were found that met the inclusion criteria, an overview of which is given in the appendix (Fig. 1).

The included articles comprise study protocols [24, 25], intervention studies [7, 13, 19, 20, 26–37], review papers [10, 38–43], qualitative and quantitative surveys [44–47], as well as feasibility and usability studies [14, 48] and one practical guide [49]. The majority are intervention studies, five of those are randomised controlled trials (RCTs) [19, 28, 29, 31, 34]. Other intervention studies are crossover, pre-post or cohort studies. The included studies show predominantly quantitative investigations that serve to demonstrate the effectiveness of teletherapy. Only two qualitative studies were included, each capturing SLTs' perspectives on teletherapy [45, 47]. A total of six reviews could be included that address teletherapy in speech therapy [38–41, 43], after stroke or even specifically teletherapy for people with aphasia [10]. There is also a trend in the target group. Half of the included studies explicitly refer to people with aphasia. People with apraxia or dysarthria are addressed far less often. However, since these disorders rarely

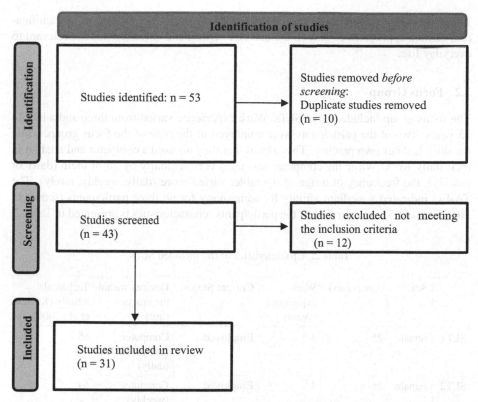

Fig. 1. Flowchart on the literature research process

occur in isolation, they are also not excluded as concomitant disorders in most studies focusing on aphasia.

The requirements that could be derived from these studies are in particular general preconditions for a teletherapy system. For example, intuitive operation is expected [45, 49] and there should be sound and image transmission that is also of sufficiently high quality [20, 30, 35, 47, 49]. It is also emphasised several times that a system should be customisable [28] so that additional exercises can be created [49] and feedback mechanisms can be adapted to the needs of the patient [19]. Support options, such as the availability of multiple communication channels [35], temporary remote access in case of technical difficulties [25, 30], guidance and technical support, are also an important focus [43].

Requirements could also be derived by researching the app reviews. Some of these duplicate those of the literature research. Here, too, the need for technical support and intuitive operation emerged in order to keep user frustration to a minimum. Special reference was also made to usability in different operating systems (e.g. iOS, Android). Additional requirements are a user-friendly design (large buttons, low stimulus) and a theoretical foundation of the content offered. In addition to these general requirements, it was also possible to derive exercise-specific requirements from the app research.

These include the individualisation of the solution time, the integration of gamification elements, progress display in the exercise setting and exercises that are relevant to everyday life.

3.2 Focus Group

The focus group included three SLTs. Work experience varied from three and a half to 35 years. Two of the participants were employed at the time of the focus group, while the third had her own practice. They stated that they all used a computer and a tablet in their daily work. While the computer was used very regularly by all of them (daily or weekly), the frequency of usage of the tablet varied more (daily, weekly, rarely). The TA-EG indicated a medium affinity for technology for all three participants (scores of 50–65 out of 95). An overview of the participants' characteristics is presented in Table 2.

Table 2. Characteristics of the included SLTs

	Sex	Age (years)	Work experience (years)	Current Status	Devices within the practice (use)	Technical affinity (Karrer et al., 2009)
SLT1	female	25	3,5	Employed	Computer (daily), Tablet (daily)	65
SLT2	female	26	4	Employed	Computer (weekly), Tablet (rarely)	64
SLT3	female	58	35	Practice owner	Computer (daily), Tablet (weekly)	50

Some of the requirements derived from the focus group discussion also duplicate those of the research. Thus, the requirements for intuitive operation, technical support, a large pool of images and exercises that are close to everyday life also emerged here. In addition, many specific functional requirements could also be added through the focus group. For example, the therapists would like to have a live measurement of volume and pitch, as well as a recording function in synchronous teletherapy. When replaying the recordings made, they should be adjustable in speed to facilitate the reflection of what is seen. For synchronous teletherapy, a whiteboard function can be very helpful to visualise discussed content and bring it into common focus. Additional functions desired by therapists for a whiteboard are double-sided editing and access to numbers and letters, as these are often used symbols. In order to simplify directing the attention in synchronous therapy, a highlighter function would be helpful for the therapist. This could highlight the cursor in colour so that it can be used for orientation. The material included should be searchable by relevant filters (target sound, complexity, type of exercise, semantics). In order to supplement the built-in material with their own ideas, the therapists would like to have the possibility to create their own tasks or connect to the internet or other apps, as also mentioned in the literature [28]. For varied asynchronous teletherapy, a function with modules for creating worksheets would be useful, as well as the use of various aids and specific feedback during technical independent exercises. To facilitate communication and sharing of documents, it should be easy to share and send documents via the platform.

4 Discussion

The aim of this article was to conduct a requirements analysis for a hybrid teletherapy system based on literature and app research as well as the experiences of the target group, in this case SLTs. In the following, the resulting implications for the further development process of the teletherapy system are discussed, before concluding with a reflection on the procedure.

4.1 Implications for the Development Process of a Teletherapy Platform

The results demonstrated that the literature and app research and focus group complemented each other well. Apart from some overlaps in the requirements captured, the two methods revealed their own focal points. While the literature and app research mainly uncovered general system requirements, the focus group resulted in very concrete ideas for additional functions. The requirements derived from the research therefore represent more of a macro level and the requirements from the user involvement more of a micro level (see Fig. 2).

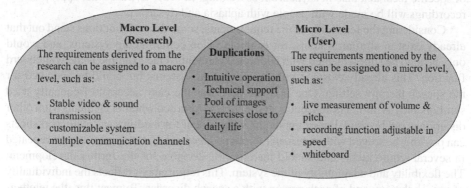

Fig. 2. The focus of the derived requirements depending on the method and their overlaps

The requirements analysis was conducted in the sense of a divergent collection. Thus, the participants of the focus group were also guided to express their ideas freely without thinking about feasibility. This resulted in a rich and detailed picture of SLTs' requirements and wishes for a teletherapy platform. For the further development process, these requirements must now be bundled and filtered in a convergent process in order to obtain sensible and realistically implementable approaches to solutions for this development.

In order to select requirements that are as relevant as possible, we will first look at the duplications. One of these is the requirement for intuitive operation. This requirement should be met in the further development process, especially through the co-creation approach. In addition to therapists, people with speech and language disorders will also be included. It should be considered that the different disorders (aphasia, dysarthria, apraxia) are represented, as the research has shown that mainly the requirements of people with aphasia could be mapped. Including the other disorders makes it possible to identify possible additional requirements or barriers and to adapt them in the course. The operation of the system will be tested for intuitiveness through test runs with the target group. Involving users in the development steps and carrying out usability tests can particularly increase user-friendliness [50].

Usability comes along with the demand for technical support. Should technical difficulties arise despite high usability, there should be easy-to-reach support tools. One possibility for this is temporary remote access to the patient's end device by the therapist, as already exemplified by Øra et al. [25]. Another requirement evolved from the app research and the focus group was the inclusion of exercises that are close to everyday life. Everyday life exercises in speech therapy usually involve some form of spontaneous speech, as used in everyday situations. This can be evoked, for example, by imitating an everyday situation (e.g. re-enacting a shopping situation at the bakery). In order to enable asynchronous exercises of this kind, the integration of automatic speech recognition (ASR) is a possibility. Automatic speech recognition can also identify incorrectly spoken language and even identify the errors and point them out as feedback [51]. However, the technology is not yet fully developed and the quality of the feedback depends on parameters such as phoneme recognition, speech continuity, speaker and environmental differences [52]. The use of ASR is planned in the HiSSS project to meet the requirement of specific feedback also in asynchronous training. In order to train ASR appropriately, recordings will be made with people with aphasia and dysarthria.

Considering the feasibility of the requirements, some desired functions stand out that already exist in similar systems, for example video conferencing systems, and would only need to be supplemented with additional elements. One example is the whiteboard function. This already exists in videoconferencing systems, but could be specified for the speech therapy setting. One example here was the easy access to frequently used symbols such as numbers and letters. It should also be noted whether elements from other disciplines can be used. For example, the requirement for modules to create worksheets can possibly be solved with experiences from pedagogy [53]. One core idea was repeated in several requirements and should therefore be decisive for the further development: The flexibility and adaptability of the system. This requirement reflects the individuality of speech therapy and of each person with a speech disorder. To meet this, the teletherapy platform as a whole should have customization capabilities, such as creating own exercises, adjusting the level of difficulty, and selecting appropriate aids.

4.2 Methodological Reflection

The results showed that the research and the focus group together produced diverse requirements. At this point, it should be noted that the inclusion of persons with speech and language disorders might have resulted in further requirements at this stage. In particular, the perspective of people with dysarthria and apraxia should be taken into account in the future. Only a small number of therapists were involved, but they were already able to bring in a rich and productive wealth of experience. Due to the proportionate overlaps and yet clearly recognisable focal points, the methods for literature and app research as well as the conduct of the focus group proved to be relevant. Together they form a good starting point to continue with the further development process.

5 Conclusion

The synthesis of the literature review and focus group results was essential to comprehensively collect and specify the requirements and user needs for a teletherapy system. The comparison between the results of the literature review and results of the focus group demonstrated the need for user involvement in technical development as early as possible. User involvement in early stages can lead to better requirement quality and thus increase sustainable system success [54]. The amount of implementation ideas and the commitment shown by the participating therapists highlights the relevance for a teletherapy system in Germany that integrates three elements: (1) face to face therapy, and (2) video therapy and (3) home exercises. For the constant linking of the user and developer perspectives, the HiSSS project will involve iteratively therapists and people with speech and language disorders after stroke in the development process by conducting co-creation workshops.

Appendix

Author(s)	Topic	Study Type	Target Group
Barthel et al. (2021)	Recommendations for video therapy in SLT	Practical guide	All SLT target groups
Bhattarai et al. (2022)	Challenges in Telepractice for SLTs & Audiologists	Cross-sectional survey	Audiologists & SLTs
Bilda et al. (2014)	Teletherapy in Aphasia	Study protocol	Adults with aphasia
Brennan et al. (2004)	Effect of Telerehabilitation on Story Retelling	Comparative Study	Brain-Injured Subjects
Cacciante et al. (2021)	Telerehabilitation for people with aphasia	Review & Meta-analysis	Adults with aphasia

(continued)

(*continued*)

Author(s)	Topic	Study Type	Target Group
Cherney et al. (2021)	Web-based Oral Reading for Language in Aphasia	Randomized Controlled Trial (RCT)	Adults with aphasia
Cordella et al. (2022)	Dosage frequency effects in self-managed digital therapy	Retrospective Cohort Study	individuals with poststroke speech, language, and cognitive deficits
Gerber et al. (2019)	Development & evaluation of an tablet-based telerehabilitation system	Usability Study	Adults with aphasia
Guo et al. (2017)	Aphasia assessment via an iPad-based app	RCT	Adults with aphasia
Hill et al. (2009)	Using telerehabilitation to assess apraxia of speech in adults	Comparative Study	Adults with acquired apraxia of speech
Keidel et al. (2017)	Poststroke telerehabilitation	Review	Adults with poststroke aphasia/dysarthrophonia
Kesav et al. (2017)	Effectiveness of an add-on computer-based therapy software	RCT	Adults with early poststroke aphasia
Kurland et al. (2014)	Effectiveness of a tablet-based home practice program	Pre-post-study	Adults with aphasia
Kurland et al. (2018)	Effectiveness of a tablet-based home practice program	Pre-post-study	Adults with aphasia
Knepley et al. (2020)	Telerehabilitation for stroke-related deficits	Review	Stroke survivors
Lauer (2020)	SLTs' experiences with teletherapy	Qualitative study	SLTs
Laver et al. (2020)	Telerehabilitation services for stroke	Review	Stroke survivors

(*continued*)

(*continued*)

Author(s)	Topic	Study Type	Target Group
Liu et al. (2022)	Effectiveness of a computer-assisted executive function training	RCT	Adults with aphasia
Macoir et al. (2017)	Synchronous telespeech therapy on functional communication	Quasi-Experimental study	Adults with aphasia
Mallet et al. (2016)	Feasibility of a Tablet-Based Rehabilitation Intervention	Feasability study	Adults with poststroke communication deficits
Øra et al. (2018)	Telerehabilitation for aphasia	RCT protocol	Adults with aphasia
Palmer et al. (2019)	Evaluating self-managed computerised SLT	RCT	Adults with aphasia
Peñaloza et al. (2021)	Telerehabilitation for Word Retrieval Deficits	Retrospective comparative study	Bilinguals with aphasia
Ruiter et al. (2016)	Evaluation of the teletherapy application e-REST	Single subject study	Adults with aphasia
Sarfo et al. (2018)	Telerehabilitation poststroke	Systematic review	Stroke survivors
Schwinn et al. (2020a)	Video therapy in outpatient SLT	Review & quantitative survey	SLTs
Schwinn et al. (2020b)	Video therapy in outpatient SLT	Quantitative survey	SLTs
Stark & Warburton (2022)	Self-delivered iPad speech therapy	Crossover study	Adults with expressive aphasia
Steele et al. (2014)	Combining teletherapy and online language exercises	Pre-post-study	Adults with aphasia
Tar-Mahomed et al. (2022)	Perspectives of SLTs on providing teletherapy	Qualitative study	SLTs

(*continued*)

(*continued*)

Author(s)	Topic	Study Type	Target Group
Weidner & Lowman (2020)	Review of the literature regarding adult SLT telepractice services	Systematic review	Adult SLT patients

References

1. Lozano, R., et al.: Global and regional mortality from 235 causes of death for 20 age groups in 1990 and 2010: a systematic analysis for the global burden of disease study 2010. The Lancet **380**(9859), 2095–2128 (2012). https://doi.org/10.1016/S0140-6736(12)61728-0
2. Breitenstein, C., et al.: Intensive speech and language therapy in patients with chronic aphasia after stroke: a randomised, open-label, blinded-endpoint, controlled trial in a healthcare setting. The Lancet **389**(10078), 1528–1538 (2017). https://doi.org/10.1016/S0140-673 6(17)30067-3
3. Winstein, C.J., et al.: Guidelines for adult stroke rehabilitation and recovery: a guideline for healthcare professionals from the American Heart Association/American Stroke Association. Stroke **47**(6), e98–e169 (2016). https://doi.org/10.1161/STR.0000000000000098
4. Dickson, S., Barbour, R.S., Brady, M., Clark, A.M., Paton, G.: Patients' experiences of disruptions associated with post-stroke dysarthria. Int. J. Lang. Commun. Disord. **43**(2), 135–153 (2008). https://doi.org/10.1080/13682820701862228
5. Nätterlund, B.S.: A new life with aphasia: Everyday activities and social support. Scand. J. Occup. Therapy **17**(2), 117–129 (2010). https://doi.org/10.3109/11038120902814416
6. Lam, J.M., Wodchis, W.P.: The relationship of 60 disease diagnoses and 15 conditions to preference-based health-related quality of life in Ontario hospital-based long-term care residents. Med. Care **48**(4), 380–387 (2010). https://doi.org/10.1097/MLR.0b013e3181ca 2647
7. Cordella, C., Munsell, M., Godlove, J., Anantha, V., Advani, M., Kiran, S.: Dosage frequency effects on treatment outcomes following self-managed digital therapy: Retrospective cohort study. J. Med. Internet Res. **24**(7), e36135 (2022). https://doi.org/10.2196/36135
8. Munsell, M., De Oliveira, E., Saxena, S., Godlove, J., Kiran, S.: Closing the digital divide in speech, language, and cognitive therapy: Cohort study of the factors associated with technology usage for rehabilitation. J. Med. Internet Res. **22**(2), e16286 (2020). https://doi.org/10. 2196/16286
9. Cason, J., Cohn, E.R.: Telepractice: An overview and best practices. Perspect. Augment. Alternat. Commun. **23**(1), 4–17 (2014)
10. Cacciante, L., et al.: Telerehabilitation for people with aphasia: A systematic review and meta-analysis. J. Commun. Disord. **92**, 106111 (2021). https://doi.org/10.1016/j.jcomdis. 2021.106111
11. Levy, E.S., et al.: The effects of intensive speech treatment on intelligibility in Parkinson's disease: A randomised controlled trial. EClinicalMedicine **24**, 100429 (2020). https://doi.org/ 10.1016/j.eclinm.2020.100429
12. Ramig, L.R., Halpern, A., Spielman, J., Fox, C., Fremman, K.: Speech treatment in Parkinson's disease: Randomized controlled trial (RCT). Mov. Disord. **33**(11), 1777–1791 (2018). https:// doi.org/10.1002/mds.27460

13. Stark, B.C., Warburton, E.A.: Improved language in chronic aphasia after self-delivered iPad speech therapy. Neuropsychol. Rehabil. **28**(5), 818–831 (2018). https://doi.org/10.1080/096 02011.2016.1146150

14. Mallet, K., et al.: RecoverNow: A patient perspective on the delivery of mobile tablet-based stroke rehabilitation in the acute care setting. Int. J. Stroke **14**(2), 174–179 (2019). https:// doi.org/10.1177/1747493018790031

15. Mortley, J., Wade, J., Davies, A., Enderby, P.: An investigation into the feasibility of remotely monitored computer therapy for people with aphasia. Adv. Speech Lang. Pathol. **5**(1), 27–36 (2003)

16. Choi, Y.H., Park, H.K., Paik, N.J.: A telerehabilitation approach for chronic aphasia following stroke. Telemed. e-Health **22**(5), 434–440 (2016). https://doi.org/10.1089/tmj.2015.0138

17. Des Roches, C.A., Balachandran, I., Ascenso, E.M., Tripodis, Y., Kiran, S.: Effectiveness of an impairment-based individualized rehabilitation program using an iPad-based software platform. Front. Hum. Neurosci. **8**, 1015 (2015). https://doi.org/10.3389/fnhum.2014.01015

18. Routhier, S., Bier, N., Macoir, J.: Smart tablet for smart self-administered treatment of verb anomia: Two single-case studies in aphasia. Aphasiology **30**(2–3), 269–289 (2016)

19. Palmer, R., et al.: Self-managed, computerised speech and language therapy for patients with chronic aphasia post-stroke compared with usual care or attention control (Big CACTUS): a multicentre, single-blinded, randomised controlled trial. The Lancet Neurol. **18**(9), 821–833 (2019). https://doi.org/10.1016/S1474-4422(19)30192-9

20. Steele, R.D., Baird, A., McCall, D., Haynes, L.: Combining teletherapy and on-line language exercises in the treatment of chronic aphasia: An outcome study. International Journal of Telerehabilitation **6**(2), 3 (2014). https://doi.org/10.5195/ijt.2014.6157

21. Vargas, C., Whelan, J., Brimblecombe, J., Allender, S.: Co-creation, co-design, co-production for public health: a perspective on definition and distinctions. Publ. Health Res. Pract. **32**(2) (2022). https://doi.org/10.17061/phrp3222211

22. Endter, C.: Assistiert Altern. Die Entwicklung digitaler Technologien für und mit älteren Menschen. Wiesbaden, Springer (2021)

23. Karrer, K., Glaser, C., Clemens, C., Bruder, C.: Technikaffinität erfassen – der Fragebogen TA-EG. ZMMS Spektrum **29**, 194–199 (2009)

24. Bilda, K., Fesenfeld, A., Leienbach, M., Meyer, E., Riebandt, S.: Teletherapie bei Aphasie: Eine Therapiestudie zur Akzeptanz und Effektivitt eines internet basierten Sprachtrainings mit integriertem Videokonferenzsystem. Forum Logopädie **28**(2), 34–39 (2014)

25. Øra, H.P., Kirmess, M., Brady, M.C., Winsnes, I.E., Hansen, S.M., Becker, F.: Telerehabilitation for aphasia - protocol of a pragmatic, exploratory, pilot randomized controlled trial. Trials **19**(1), 208 (2018). https://doi.org/10.1186/s13063-018-2588-5

26. Barthel, M., Schwinn, S., Borgetto, B., Leinweber, J.: Digitalisierungschancen - Spurensuche nach Evidenz: Ergebnisse der Videointeraktionsanalyse aus dem Forschungsprojekt "ViTaL." Forum Logopadie **35**(1), 34–39 (2021)

27. Brennan, D.M., Georgeadis, A.C., Baron, C.R., Barker, L.M.: The effect of videoconference-based telerehabilitation on story retelling performance by brain-injured subjects and its implications for remote speech-language therapy. Telemed. J. E Health **10**(2), 147–154 (2004)

28. Cherney, L.R., Lee, J.B., Kim, K.Y.A., van Vuuren, S.: Web-based Oral Reading for Language in Aphasia (Web ORLA®): A pilot randomized control trial. Clin. Rehabil. **35**(7), 976–987 (2021). https://doi.org/10.1177/0269215520988475

29. Guo, Y.E., et al.: Assessment of aphasia across the international classification of functioning, disability and health using an iPad-based application. Telemed. J. E-Health: Off. J. Am. Telemed. Assoc. **23**(4), 313–326 (2017). https://doi.org/10.1089/tmj.2016.0072

30. Hill, A.J., Theodoros, D., Russell, T., Ward, E.: Using telerehabilitation to assess apraxia of speech in adults. Int. J. Lang. Commun. Disord. **44**(5), 731–747 (2009). https://doi.org/10. 1080/13682820802350537

31. Kesav, P., Vrinda, S.L., Sukumaran, S., Sarma, P.S., Sylaja, P.N.: Effectiveness of speech language therapy either alone or with add-on computer-based language therapy software (Malayalam version) for early post stroke aphasia: A feasibility study. J. Neurol. Sci. **380**, 137–141 (2017). https://doi.org/10.1016/j.jns.2017.07.010

32. Kurland, J., Wilkins, A.R., Stokes, P.: iPractice: Piloting the effectiveness of a tablet-based home practice program in aphasia treatment. Semin. Speech Lang. **35**(1), 51–63 (2014). https://doi.org/10.1055/s-0033-1362991

33. Kurland, J., Liu, A., Stokes, P.: Effects of a tablet-based home practice program with teleprac-tice on treatment outcomes in chronic aphasia. J. Speech Lang. Hear. Res. JSLHR **61**(5), 1140–1156 (2018). https://doi.org/10.1044/2018_JSLHR-L-17-0277

34. Liu, M., et al.: Improvement in language function in patients with aphasia using computer-assisted executive function training: A controlled clinical trial. PM R **14**(8), 913–921 (2022). https://doi.org/10.1002/pmrj.12679

35. Macoir, J., Sauvageau, V.M., Boissy, P., Tousignant, M., Tousignant, M.: In-home synchronous Telespeech therapy to improve functional communication in chronic poststroke aphasia: Results from a quasi-experimental study. Telemed. J. E Health **23**(8), 630–639 (2017). https://doi.org/10.1089/tmj.2016.0235

36. Peñaloza, C., et al.: Telerehabilitation for word retrieval deficits in bilinguals with aphasia: Effectiveness and reliability as compared to in-person language therapy. Front. Neurol. **12**, 589330 (2021). https://doi.org/10.3389/fneur.2021.589330

37. Ruiter, M.B., Rietveld, T.C., Hoskam, V., Van Beers, M.M.: An exploratory investigation of E-rest: Teletherapy for chronically aphasic speakers. Int. J. Telerehabil. **8**(1), 21–28 (2016). https://doi.org/10.5195/ijt.2016.6191

38. Keidel, M., et al.: Telerehabilitation nach Schlaganfall im häuslichen Umfeld. Der Nervenarzt **88**(2) (2017)

39. Knepley, K.D., Mao, J.Z., Wieczorek, P., Okoye, F.O., Jain, A.P., Harel, N.Y.: Impact of telerehabilitation for stroke-related deficits. Telemed. J. e-health: Off. J. Am. Telemed. Assoc. **27**(3), 239–246 (2021). https://doi.org/10.1089/tmj.2020.0019

40. Laver, K.E., Adey-Wakeling, Z., Crotty, M., Lannin, N.A., George, S., Sherrington, C.: Tel-erehabilitation services for stroke. Cochrane Datab. System. Rev. **1**(1), CD010255 (2020). https://doi.org/10.1002/14651858.CD010255.pub3

41. Sarfo, F.S., Ulasavets, U., Opare-Sem, O.K., Ovbiagele, B.: Tele-rehabilitation after stroke: An updated systematic review of the literature. J. Stroke Cerebrovasc. Dis. **27**(9), 2306–2318 (2018). https://doi.org/10.1016/j.jstrokecerebrovasdis.2018.05.013

42. Schwinn, S., Barthel, M., Leinweber, J., Borgetto, B.: Digitalisierungschancen in der Krise. Erste Ergebnisse zur Umsetzung der Videotherapie in der ambulanten Logopädie (ViTaL). Forum Logopädie **35**(4), 18–21 (2020)

43. Weidner, K., Lowman, J.: Telepractice for adult speech-language pathology services: A systematic review. Perspect. ASHA Spec. Interest Groups **5**(1), 326–338 (2020)

44. Bhattarai, B., Sanghavi, T., Abhishek, B.P.: Challenges in delivering tele-practice services for communication disorders among audiologists and speech language pathologists. Indian J. Otolaryngol. Head Neck Surg. (2021). https://doi.org/10.1007/s12070-021-03032-7

45. Lauer, N.: Teletherapie – hat die Logopädie eine digitale Zukunft?. Ergebnisse eines qual-itativen Forschungsprojekts des Studiengangs Logopädie der OTH Regensburg. Forum Logopädie **34**(5), 12–17 (2020)

46. Schwinn, S., Barthel, M., Leinweber, J., Borgetto, B.: Digitalisierungschancen–Umsetzung von Videotherapie im Lockdown. Ergebnisse der Online-Befragung aus dem Forschungspro-jekt "ViTaL". Forum Logopädie **34**(6), 36–40 (2020)

47. Tar-Mahomed, Z., Kater, K.A.: The perspectives of speech-language pathologists: Providing teletherapy to patients with speech, language and swallowing difficulties during a COVID-19

context. S. Afr. J. Commun. Disord. **69**(2), e1–e7 (2022). https://doi.org/10.4102/sajcd.v69 i2.902

48. Gerber, S.M., et al.: Therapist-guided tablet-based telerehabilitation for patients with aphasia: Proof-of-concept and usability study. JMIR Rehabilit. Assist. Technol. **6**(1), e13163 (2019). https://doi.org/10.2196/13163

49. Barthel, M., Schwinn, S., Einfeldt, A., Borgetto, B., Leinweber, J.: Digitalisierungschancen nutzen! Kernaussagen und Empfehlungen für die Nutzung von Videotherapie in der ambulanten logopädischen/sprachtherapeutischen Versorgung (Kurzfassung). Forum Logopädie **35**(2), 49–50 (2021)

50. Gradinger, F., et al.: Values associated with public involvement in health and social care research: A narrative review. Health Expect. **18**(5), 661–675 (2015). https://doi.org/10.1111/hex.12158

51. Kitzing, P., Maier, A., Åhlander, V.L.: Automatic speech recognition (ASR) and its use as a tool for assessment or therapy of voice, speech, and language disorders. Logoped. Phoniatr. Vocol. **34**(2), 91–96 (2009). https://doi.org/10.1080/14015430802657216

52. Jamal, N., Shanta, S., Mahmud, F., Sha'abani, M.N.A.H.: Automatic speech recognition (ASR) based approach for speech therapy of aphasic patients: A review. AIP Conf. Proc. **1883**(1), 020028 (2017). AIP Publishing LLC

53. Schulz, L. (2021). Differenzierte Arbeitsblätter für den Deutschunterricht erstellen. In: Schulz, L., Krstoski, I. (Eds.) Diklusive Lernwelten. Zeitgemäßes Lernen für Schüler:innen. Visual, Dornstadt

54. Kujala, S., Kauppinen, M., Lehtola, L., Kojo, T.: The role of user involvement in requirements quality and project success. In: 13th IEEE International Conference on Requirements Engineering (RE'05), pp. 75–84. IEEE (2005)

Toward a Shared Experience of Uncertainty of Interpersonal Communication Through an Immersive Virtual Reality Serious Game

Shirin Hajahmadi[1] and Gustavo Marfia[2(✉)]

[1] Department of Computer Science and Engineering,
University of Bologna, Bologna, Italy
[2] Department of the Arts, University of Bologna, Bologna, Italy
gustavo.marfia@unibo.it

Abstract. Ordinary life without uncertainty is unimaginable. Uncertainty is experienced daily almost by everybody in tasks such as choosing, and solving problems, and mostly it appears in the context of interpersonal communications. Past research highlights that perceived uncertainty of information in a communication system has high effects on the quality of information transfer between sender and receiver and may follow cognitive, emotional, and behavioral responses in people involved. In this paper, we extend the previous work of the authors. Similar to the previous work the aim is to create an enjoyable experience supporting the investigation of how different levels of uncertainty affect the ways participants manage uncertain features of interpersonal communications in a workplace scenario, but this time they are accompanied by an assistant. In the design of our proposed system we create uncertainty of interpersonal communications in terms of ambiguity, probability, and complexity. We also report the result of a within-subject user study with 6 participants aged between 20 and 40, and their behavioral responses to two levels of uncertainty with subjective and objective measures. Through our study, we found that the proposed application successfully created a pleasant experience, received good usability evaluation scores from the participants, and meaningfully measured some behavioral responses related to exposure to different levels of uncertainty in this social experience.

Keywords: Human-computer interaction · Virtual Reality · Serious game · Interpersonal communications · Uncertainty · Shared experiences and social VR · Behavioral responses

1 Introduction

Uncertainty is a ubiquitous concept. It means we can find it everywhere and everybody can experience it or at least be affected by it [7]. Each person perceives uncertainty with most of the things about the past and present, and almost everything about the future [17,25,31]. The relationship between the person and

© The Author(s), under exclusive license to Springer Nature Switzerland AG 2023
M. Antona and C. Stephanidis (Eds.): HCII 2023, LNCS 14021, pp. 566–580, 2023.
https://doi.org/10.1007/978-3-031-35897-5_40

the environment characterizes the kind and degree of uncertainty that is experiencing [34]. There would be self, others, and relationships that create uncertainty that results in cognitive and behavioral responses to it. This introduces interpersonal communications as a potential context for the study of uncertainty since the study of social interaction between people and the way they used verbal and written dialogues, as well as nonverbal actions are the main focus of this field [3]. In this regard, uncertainty appears closely connected with the concept of information [4,19]. A conceptualization proposed by [15] suggests inducing the uncertainty of information into a communication system can be done in three ways: creating any kind of information deficit that makes the target message unclear for the receiver, creating some requested changes that the receiver could not predict, and creating the content of the message so interconnected and complex that limits understanding. In these situations, one may perceive uncertainty when not sure about the content of a message but accepts it assuming that having enough information would resolve this doubt. The person may try to reduce this kind of uncertainty by referring to the information sources that could be accessed through available information channels [14]. This is where information-seeking behaviors may appear.

Human information behavior (HIB) studies have been focused on investigating different aspects of human information-seeking behaviors such as the kind of choices, searching performance, and emotions of the users, when exposed to a variable of interest [18,29]. Belkin [2] suggests that someone experiencing the uncertainty of information first recognizes an anomaly in the state of knowledge that could only be resolved in the process of information seeking by communicating information with others. In this way, uncertainty may trigger information-seeking actions like asking questions. In this regard, a systematic study of the relationship between uncertainty and information-seeking behavior is highlighted [11,13,16,26,37]. Such a study will concern the investigation of whether uncertainty will be perceived by people in a situation and how it influences their information-seeking behaviors.

Virtual reality experiences traditionally have been restricted to being experienced by only one user at a time interacting with the environment [27]. Recent studies have focused more on creating a virtual multi-user experience that gives multiple persons the possibility of experiencing the same content together and interacting with each other similar to what one experiences in the real world [10,22]. On the other hand, when experiencing a shared experience, an important way to measure if a communication system is successful in providing a proper platform for the user to have social interactions is to measure the degree of experienced co-presence. Co-presence is a variable that has been used to measure the degree that the participants think they are not alone [21].

Considering this domain, we propose the design and development of an immersive virtual reality experience to create an enjoyable shared experience. Also, it supports the investigation of how uncertainty affects the performance and information-seeking behavior of the person performing tasks in a social workplace scenario that is characterized by the elements of uncertainty.

With this work, we try to examine these hypotheses:

- **H1:** Participants rate the perceived uncertainty of experience in office 2 more than in office 1.
- **H2::** Participants show more information-seeking behavior like asking questions in the experience in office 2 compared to office 1.
- **H3::** Participants spend more time executing the task in office 2 in comparison to office 1.
- **H4::** Participants give a different score to the presence and co-presence of the experience in office 2 compared to office 1.
- **H5:** Participants will have a good evaluation of the usability of the system.

In this paper, we present the related work in Sect. 2, describe the design and development of the system in Sect. 3, describe the result of a usability study that evaluates the user experience of the proposed VR system and report some behavioral responses, in Sect. 4. discuss the main findings of the experiment in Sect. 5. and finally conclude the paper and discusses future opportunities for research in Sect. 6.

2   Related Work

Applying the concept of uncertainty in game design could potentially improve the user's experience by holding his/her attention and interest during the experience [8]. For example, "Gone Home" [39] and "Don't Starve" [9] are two examples that incorporate uncertainty in their gameplay to increase tension and keep players engaged. This creates a sense of unpredictability and adds to the overall experience of playing the games. In "Gone Home," uncertainty is created through the mystery surrounding the disappearance of the family. As the player explores the house and learns more about what happened, they are faced with a sense of uncertainty and unease, which adds to the suspense of the game. In "Don't Starve," uncertainty is created through the unpredictability of the game's randomly generated wilderness. The player never knows what challenges or dangers they might face, and must constantly adapt to new situations in order to survive. This creates a sense of uncertainty and keeps the player on edge, as they must always be prepared for the unexpected.

Uncertainty also has been the subject of study in virtual reality games. For example, Xu et al. [38] in their studies explore the effect of different factors such as gameplay uncertainty, display type, and age on the players' enjoyment, motivation, and engagement when playing their designed VR game. The study's results suggest that gameplay uncertainty, or the unpredictability of the game, has a positive effect on player motivation and engagement, while display type, or the type of VR headset used, has a relatively small effect on player experience. Additionally, the study found that age did not significantly affect player experience with the experienced VR game. In RelicVE [24] the authors aim to create an experience that is both engaging and educational, and uncertainty is used as a tool to increase player engagement and promote learning. In the "RelicVR" game, uncertainty is introduced in several ways. For example, players are given limited information about the relics they are exploring, and they must use their knowledge and skills to uncover the history and cultural significance of the relics.

Social VR is also a potential context that could target the study of uncertainty, especially in interpersonal communications. Since it targets the study of multi-user platforms that allow two or more users to co-experience and interact with one another in a virtual space and social scenario [34]. For example, such applications may target social activities like co-experiencing virtual mortality [1], dancing [32], puzzle-solving task [33], prototyping procedure of a product [20], and learning experience [23,30].

A recent previous study by the authors of the current paper, [12], suggested the design, development, and evaluation of a first version of a VR platform that challenged users to accomplish tasks with two levels of uncertainty. Their results showed that they created a pleasant virtual experience and reported some meaningful measures related to the participants' behavioral responses about the frequency, time of actions, and user position when exposed to uncertainty. In the above-mentioned version, the user was alone in the virtual office during the experience and did not have any possibility to communicate with somebody to express his/her doubts during the experience. Since, to the best of our knowledge, no previous work targeted a study of the effects of the elements of uncertainty in the interpersonal communication of a social VR experience, we will take this step and propose an extended version of our previous application. This extension suggests the design and development of such an application by adding the possibility of the user being able to communicate with an assistant during the experience. Also, we added to the complexity of the previous environment by creating more spaces that give the possibility for the objects to be hidden and as a result could not be found easily. In addition, we created two office rooms each with a different representative task, which gives us the possibility of conducting a better comparison between the variables of interest in two different situations.

3   Experimental Setting

In this section, we describe the experiment we conducted to study the behavioral responses of participants to perceived uncertainty in two virtual offices.

3.1   Participants

We recruited 6 participants (1 female, 5 males, age:20–40, M=26.33, SD=5.28)) who are master's students at the university of Bologna to participate in our study. We asked them to rate (1=never, 5=every day) any previous experience with virtual reality using a head-mounted display (M = 2.83, SD=0.75) and their level (1=low, 5=high) of English proficiency (M = 3.17, SD= 1.17) through a demographic questionnaire.

3.2   Materials

In this section, we will provide more details to explain the design and implementation choices of the proposed virtual environment.

Setup. In our experiment, participants navigated in a virtual office via an HTC Vive Pro HMD (refresh rate: 90 Hz, resolution: 1440 × 1600 pixels, FoV 110°) connected to a workstation (Intel(R) Core(TM) i7-6850K CPU @ 3.60 GHz, 3.60 GHz) and an HTC Vive (refresh rate: 90 Hz, resolution: 1080 × 1200 pixels, FoV 110°) connected to a workstation ("Intel(R) Core(TM) i7-9750H CPU @ 2.60GHz, 2.59 GHz"). The environment was developed using Unity version 2019.4.35 f1 and the avatars were designed with the "Ready Player Me" tool [28]. The data analysis was performed using R version 4.2.2 and RStudio version 2022.07.2+576. To build our multiplayer experience we used the Photon software development kit (SDK) which was developed by Photon Engine, a leading provider of cloud-based network infrastructure to help game developers and application builders reduce the complexity of networking and simplify the process of building and deploying online experiences. Also, this experience required a woman who played the role of assistant in the experience.

Design of the Experience. In the experiment described in this paper, we utilize a VR system that creates a shared experience between the participants and an assistant in a workplace scenario. They are each represented by a virtual humanoid body and they can see virtual representations of the other people present in the virtual world. Data communication is shared across a network, and consistency of the shared world is maintained, so that all involved perceive the same environment from their unique viewpoints, and can interact with one another. We uploaded three photographs of three people (two women and a man) randomly collected online and uploaded them into the "Ready player me" platform to create three half-body avatars with facial features similar to those photographs. These avatars were used in our experiment representing an assistant and two participants (Please see the Fig. 1 to see the avatars which are used in our experience).

The experience includes the familiarization room, office room 1, and office room 2. It starts first with the user login into the system by selecting the "Start my experience" button (Please see the Fig. 2) leading to the familiarization phase. The familiarization room (Please see Fig. 3) is furnished with simple items of furniture, some interactive and non-interactive objects, two boards for communicating instructions, and a mirror that helps the user to feel more present in the experience representing his/her movements and actions in the familiarization room [36]. The left board shows the how-to instructions and the right one the task instructions. When the user enters, first the boss's voice will be played introducing himself, explaining that this is the first day of work for the participant, telling that he (the boss) could not be present in the office, and asking him to follow the instructions from the boards to execute some tasks during the experience. Then, the experience will proceed first by experiencing office room 1 and then office room 2. For all the room experiences, there would be an assistant which accompanies the user in the experience by standing near a desk, watching the user, and answering his/her questions.

For accomplishing tasks, inside the rooms the user rays a cast on the object and presses a trigger to remove an interactive object. For each room, the user is asked to press the blue button on the table when finishing the task (Please see the Fig. 4 for some screenshots of the participant's experience in room 1).

The presented task in each room amounts to sequences of instructions to search and remove objects which are expressed in written form and will be communicated by the blackboard on the left wall of the room. Inspired by the definition of Hillen et al. [15], uncertainty in our experience appears in terms of ambiguity, probability, and complexity. Ambiguities result from incomplete guides and instructions. Probable situations, such as unexpected task changes, can also increase the uncertainty of the user's experience, and complexity can increase uncertainty by adding a large number of causal factors or elements that must be considered in the instructions. This can make it more challenging for the user to understand the situation and make decisions.

Following this guide we proposed two office room experiences each representing a different level of uncertainty (Please also see Fig. 5 for the placements of objects in both offices in seven different areas of the environment with their associated rugs):

- **Room1 (with a base task):** The instructions in this room experience express simple and clear task steps in which the number, place, and color of objects that should be removed could be understood easily.
Instructions for Task 1:

- Step 1: Remove the green mug and pink book from the white rug area.
- Step 2: Remove the bag and the sandwich from the blue rug area.
- Step 3: Remove the apple and the red book from the gray rug area.
- Step 4: Remove the tart and the blue mug from the red rug area.
- Step 5: Remove the red pillow and paper punch from the green rug area.
- Step 6: Remove the blue mug and glasses from the yellow rug area.

Room 2 (with an intermediate level of uncertainty): The instructions in this room are more complex compared to room office experience 1 including some uncertain elements like some missing information, and the possibility of change during the experience.

Instructions for Task 2:

- Step 1: Remove any foods not positioned on the plates from the pink rug area.
- Step 2: If there are two bags in the white rug area, just keep the blue and orange mugs and remove the others.

- Step 3: Remove all the glasses from the yellow rug area.
- Step 4: Remove only the pillows that are close to the shelves in the red rug area.
- Step 5: Remove any kind of bread from the gray rug area.
- Step 6: Remove all the glasses from the green rug area.

After the 30s, the task will be changed by adding some lines to the instruction requesting to also remove the orange mug from the white rug area and the blue mug from the gray rug area.

Fig. 1. Screenshots from the avatars; a. a female avatar representing a female participant. b. a male avatar representing a male participant. c. a female avatar representing a female assistant.

Fig. 2. An image from the login scene.

3.3 Methods

Procedure. First, the participants read the consent form and provide their informed consent form, Then, they will be asked to listen to a short tutorial about the HTC Vive headset, controllers, sensors, and their applications for this study. The participants then will experience the familiarisation phase, room office 1 and room office 2 in a sequence. Finally, they will answer some questionnaires related to their experience with the system.

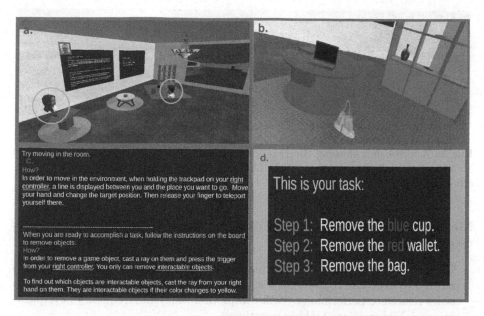

Fig. 3. Screen shots from the familiarization phase. a. showing the positions of the objects in the familiarization room, and the avatars in a moment of the experience. b. a close-up screenshot from the interaction of the user with an interactive object by casting a ray on it and pressing the trigger from the controller. c and d are close-ups of the boards instructions that are appeared in part a.

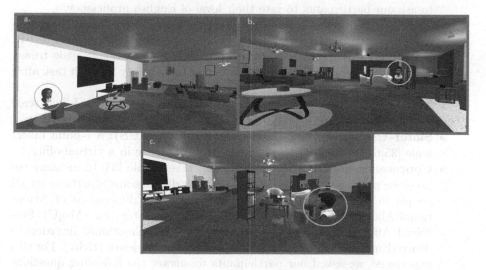

Fig. 4. Some screenshots from room 1 (a similar situation would happen also in room 2). a. shows the position of the assistant in the office room. b. shows the participants when accomplishing tasks in the office room 1. c. shows the participant when selecting an interactable object.

Fig. 5. A screenshot showing the two office rooms characterized by seven associated areas for accomplishing the steps of the task each with a different colorful rug; a. shows office room 1. b. shows office room 2.

Measures. In this Section, we describe the objective and subjective measures used to test our hypotheses.

- **Objective measures** In this experience, we captured behavioral responses related to exposure to different levels of uncertainty by measuring some variables related to performance (task completion time) and frequency of requesting social interactions (asking questions).
- **Subjective measures** We utilized multiple questionnaires to evaluate participants' subjective experience with the application as detailed below.
  - **Demographic questionnaire:** A questionnaire to ask our participants some demographic questions like sex and age.
  - **Level of English proficiency questionnaire:** A 5-point Likert scale to ask our participants to rate their level of English proficiency.
  - **Previous Experience with immersive VR:** A 5-point Likert scale to ask our participants to rate their previous experience with immersive VR.
  - **Perceived uncertainty questionnaire:** A 5-point Likert scale to ask participants to rate their level of perceived uncertainty for each task after the experiment.
  - **System Usability Scale (SUS) questionnaire:** A 5-point Likert scale [5] to provide a "quick and dirty" reliable tool for measuring usability.
  - **Slater-Usoh-Steed presence questionnaire (SUS):** A 7-point Likert scale [35]to assess participants' sense of being there in a virtual office.
  - **Copresence questionnaire:** A 7-point Likert scale [35] to measure copresence which people experience with their digital counterparts as actual people in a social VR experience measuring the dimensions of Attentional Allocation (Atn), Perceived Message Understanding (MsgU), Perceived Affective Understanding (Aff), Perceived Emotional Interdependence (Emo), and Perceived Behavioral Interdependence (Behv). For this experience, we asked our participants to answer the following questions measuring just the CoPresence (CoP), Attentional Allocation (Atn), and Perceived Message Understanding (MsgU) dimensions.

    * **CoP-Q1:** I noticed the other person.

* **CoP-Q2:** The other person noticed me.
* **CoP-Q3:** The other person's presence was obvious to me.
* **CoP-Q4:** My presence was obvious to the other person.
* **CoP-Q5:** The other person caught my attention.
* **CoP-Q6:** I caught the other person's attention.
* **Atn-Q1:** I was easily distracted from the other person when other things were going on.
* **Atn-Q2:** The other person was easily distracted from me when other things were going on.
* **Atn-Q3:** I remained focused on the other person throughout our interaction.
* **Atn-Q4:** The other person remained focused on me throughout our interaction.
* **Atn-Q5:** The other person did not receive my full attention.
* **Atn-Q6:** I did not receive the other person's full attention.
* **MsgU-Q1:** My thoughts were clear to the other person.
* **MsgU-Q2:** The other person's thoughts were clear to me.
* **MsgU-Q3:** It was easy to understand the other person.
* **MsgU-Q4:** The other person found it easy to understand me.
* **MsgU-Q5:** Understanding the other person was difficult.
* **MsgU-Q6:** The other person had difficulty understanding me.

4   Results

In this section, we present the objective and subjective results of our experiment concerning our research questions:

In order to compare the participants' ratings to the perceived uncertainty of two office room experiences we used the Wilcoxon Signed-Ranks test. The result found a significant difference between them ($v = 0$, $p = 0.035 < 0.05$). These results suggest that the perceived uncertainty of task 2 was rated significantly higher than office room experience 1 (See also Fig. 6 for a visual comparison of the ratings).

To find the effects of different degrees of induced uncertainty on the user's behavior, we were interested to investigate the effects of uncertainty on variables related to performance and information-seeking behavior. Related to performance we measured the effects on the task completion time of each room office experience. First, we confirmed the normality of the data with the Shapiro-Wilk test at the 5% level. Then, we conducted the Paired T-Test. The results did not find a significant difference between the task completion time in the two office room experiences ($t(5) = -3.2916$, $p = 0.9892$). However, the box plot in part (b) from Fig. 9 visually shows a higher task completion time for office room experience 2 when compared to office room experience 1. Also, we measured the effects on information-seeking behaviors like asking questions. First, we confirmed the normality of the data with the Shapiro-Wilk test at the 5% level. Then, we conducted the Paired T-Test. The results did not find a significant difference between the number of asking questions in the two office rooms ($t(5) = -1.1125$, $p = 0.8417$). However, the box plot in part (a) of Fig. 9 visually shows a higher number of asking questions in office room experience 2 when compared to office room experience 1.

Figure 7 presents a visual comparison of the data obtained from the SUS questionnaire (M=77.91, SD=12.84).

We calculated scores for finding a significant difference in a comparison of different co-presence dimensions. The results for co-presence ($V = 1$, $p = 0.05917$), attentional allocation ($V = 6$, $p = 0.4017$), and perceived message understanding ($V = 3$, $p = 0.1411$) did not show any significant difference. Also, we could not find any significant difference between the scores of presence in office room experience 1 and office room experience 2 ($V = 1$, $p = 0.1056$). Figure 8 shows a visual comparison between the results of social presence dimensions and presence in two different levels of experiences.

Bar charts of the means of rating for the perceived uncertainty of tasks by participants.

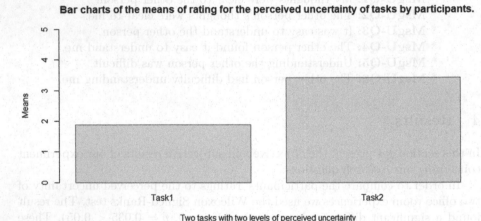

Fig. 6. A comparison between the scores participants gave to the perceived uncertainty of two office room experiences

5   Discussion

In this section, we present and discuss the main findings of the experiment in more detail. In this paper, we contributed to examine the following hypothesis:

– **H1:** Participants rate the perceived uncertainty of experience in office 2 more than in office 1. Our findings from a comparison of the post-experiment ratings of the participants to the perceived uncertainty of two tasks indicate the potential of the proposed design to successfully produce at least two levels of uncertainty in the experience of the system.

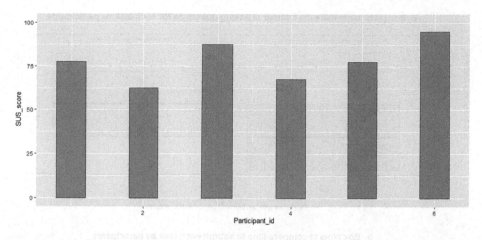

Fig. 7. A screenshot showing the scores that participants gave to the SUS questionnaire

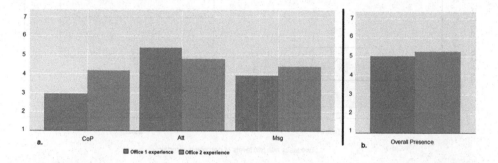

Fig. 8. Results for a comparison between the means of a. social presence dimensions and b. for Presence in office room experience 1 and office room experience 2.

- **H2::** Participants show more information-seeking behavior like asking questions in the experience in office 2 compared to office 1. We were expecting that with an increase in the perceived uncertainty, the information-seeking behavior will be increased. Although our statistical test could not find a significant difference.
- **H3::** Participants spend more time executing the task in office 2 compared to office 1. We were expecting that with an increase in the perceived uncertainty, the task completion time will be increased. Although our statistical test could find a significant difference.
- **H4::** Participants give a higher score to the presence and copresence of the experience in office 2 compared to office 1. We were expecting that with an increase in the perceived uncertainty, the level of perceived presence and co-presence will be increased. Although our statistical test could not find a significant difference.

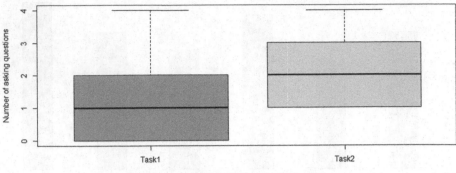

a. Box plots to compare the number of asking questions for each task by participants

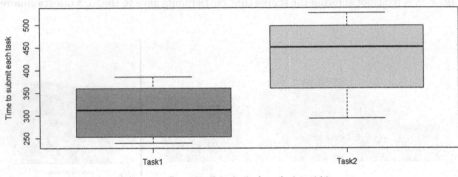

b. Box plots to compare time to submit each task by participants

Fig. 9. A comparison in the a. number of asking questions by participants and b. time to submit the task in office room experience 1 and office room experience 2.

- **H5:** Participants will have a good evaluation of the usability of the system. Another purpose of the study was to report the results of the participants' evaluation of their experience with the system. The mean score of our results from the System Usability Scale (SUS) (M = 77.91, SD = 12.85) reports an acceptable average score (the minimum acceptable average score is 68). This means that the system overall got a good usability score and needs some minor improvements [6].

6   Conclusions and Future Works

In this paper, we suggested the design and development of a shared VR experience and investigated the effects of uncertainty levels on the information-seeking behavior and performance of the user in a virtual office. We measured the participants' objective and subjective responses through a controlled human-subject study. The results did not convey any significant difference between the task completion time, the performance, the sense of presence, and the co-presence of the user in two different office rooms. But, we were able to confirm that the system can create two different levels of uncertainty and the participants gave a good score to the usability of the system. We plan to increase the sample size in a future study that gives us the possibility to have more statistical power to detect and report the behavioral responses from the proposed experience.

References

1. Barberia, I., et al.: Virtual mortality and near-death experience after a prolonged exposure in a shared virtual reality may lead to positive life-attitude changes". PloS one **13**(11), e0203358 (2018)
2. Belkin, N.J.: Anomalous state of knowledge. na (2005)
3. Berger, C.R.: Interpersonal communication. In: The International Encyclopedia Of Communication (2008)
4. Berger, C.R., Calabrese, R.J.: Some explorations in initial interaction and beyond: toward a developmental theory of interpersonal communication. Human Commun. Res. **1**(2), 99–112 (1974)
5. Brooke, J., et al.: Sus-a quick and dirty usability scale. Usability evaluation in industry. **189**(194), 4–7 (1996)
6. Brooke, J.: Sus: a retrospective. J. Usability Stud. **8**(2), 29–40 (2013)
7. Chödrön, P.: Living beautifully with uncertainty and change. Shambhala Publications (2012)
8. Costikyan, G.: Uncertainty in games. Mit Press (2013)
9. Entertainment, K.: Don't starve. In: Video game. PC, IOS, Android, Xbox, Playstation, Wii U. Klei Entertainment, Canada (2013)
10. Gigante, M.A.: Virtual reality: definitions, history and applications. In: Virtual reality systems, pp. 3–14. Elsevier (1993)
11. Goldsmith, D.J.: A normative approach to the study of uncertainty and communication. J. Commun. **51**(3), 514–533 (2001)
12. Hajahmadi, S., Marfia, G.: Effects of the uncertainty of interpersonal communications on behavioral responses of the participants in an immersive virtual reality experience: a usability study. Sensors **23**(4), 2148 (2023)
13. Hatch, S.: Uncertainty in medicine (2017)
14. Hertzum, M.: Collaborative information seeking: The combined activity of information seeking and collaborative grounding. Inform. Process. Manage. **44**(2), 957–962 (2008)
15. Hillen, M.A., et al.: Tolerance of uncertainty: Conceptual analysis, integrative model, and implications for healthcare. Social Sci. Med. **180**, 62–75 (2017)
16. Ingwersen, P.: Information retrieval interaction, vol. 246. Taylor Graham London (1992)
17. Kahneman, D., Tversky, A.: Variants of uncertainty. Cognition **11**(2), 143–157 (1982)
18. Keller, A.M., Taylor, H.A., Brunyé, T.T.: Uncertainty promotes information-seeking actions, but what information? Cogn. Res.: Principles Implicat. **5**, 1–17 (2020)
19. Klir, G.J.: Uncertainty and information. In: Foundations of Generalized Information Theory (2006)

20. Knöpfle, C.: Working together-a vr based approach for cooperative digital design review. In: Proceedings of the Working Conference on Advanced Visual Interfaces, pp. 361–362 (2002)
21. Kreijns, K., Xu, K., Weidlich, J.: Social presence: Conceptualization and measurement. Educ. Psychol. Rev. **34**(1), 139–170 (2022)
22. Ally Lee, S., Lee, M., Jeong, M.: The role of virtual reality on information sharing and seeking behaviors. J. Hospitality Tourism Manage. **46**, 215–223 (2021)
23. Liao, M.-Y., et al.: Embodying historical learners' messages as learning companions in a vr classroom. In: Extended Abstracts of the 2019 CHI Conference on Human Factors in Computing Systems, pp. 1–6 (2019)
24. Liu, Y., et al.: Relicvr: A virtual reality game for active exploration of archaeological relics. In: Extended Abstracts of the 2021 Annual Symposium on Computer-Human Interaction in Play, pp. 326–332, (2021)
25. March, J.G., Olsen, J.P.: The uncertainty of the past: Organizational learning under ambiguity. Europ. J. Political Res. **3**(2), 147–171 (1975)
26. Mousavi, S., Gigerenzer, G.: Heuristics are tools for uncertainty. Homo Oeconomicus. **34**, 361–379 (2017)
27. Rauschnabel, P.A., et al.: What is xr? towards a framework for augmented and virtual reality. Comput. Human Behav. **133**, 107289 (2022)
28. Readyplayerme. https://readyplayer.me/. Accessed 2d 06 (2023)
29. Rosen, N.O., Knäuper, B: A little uncertainty goes a long way: State and trait differences in uncertainty interact to increase information seeking but also increase worry. Health Commun. **24**(3), 228–238 (2009)
30. Saalfeld, P., et al.: Student and teacher meet in a shared virtual reality: a one-on-one tutoring system for anatomy education. In: arXiv:2011.07926 (2020)
31. Schwartz, P.: The art of the long view: planning for the future in an uncertain world. Currency (2012)
32. Sra, M., Mottelson, A., Maes, P.: Your place and mine: Designing a shared vr experience for remotely located users. In: Proceedings of the 2018 Designing Interactive Systems Conference, pp. 85–97 (2018)
33. Steed, A., et al.: Leadership and collaboration in shared virtual environments. In: Proceedings IEEE Virtual Reality (Cat. No. 99CB36316), pp. 112–115. IEEE (1999)
34. Unruh, D.R.: Characteristics and types of participation in social worlds. Symb. Interact. **2**(2), 115–130 (1979)
35. Harms, C., Biocca, F.: Internal consistency and reliability of the networked minds measure of social presence. In: Seventh Annual International Workshop: Presence, vol. 2004. Universidad Politecnica de Valencia Valencia, Spain (2004)
36. Waltemate, T., et al.: The impact of avatar personalization and immersion on virtual body ownership, presence, and emotional response. IEEE Trans. Visualiz. Comput. Graph. **24**(4), 1643–1652 (2018)
37. Wilson, T.: Exploring models of information behaviour: the 'uncertainty'project'. Inform. Process. Manage. **35**(6), 839–849 (1999)
38. Xu, W., et al.: Effect of gameplay uncertainty, display type, and age on virtual reality exergames. In: Proceedings of the 2021 CHI Conference on Human Factors in Computing Systems, pp. 1–14 (2021)
39. Yap, C.M., Kadobayashi, Y., Yamaguchi, S.: Conceptualizing player-side emergence in interactive games: Between hardcoded software and the human mind in papers, please and gone home. Int. J. Gaming Comput. Mediated Simul. (IJGCMS) **7**(3), 1–21 (2015)

Wrist View: Understanding Human Activity Through the Hand

Vishnu Kakaraparthi(✉)(iD), Morris Goldberg(iD), and Troy McDaniel(iD)

Arizona State University, Tempe, AZ 85281, USA
{vkakarap,troy.mcdaniel}@asu.edu, masmmlesbaux@me.com

Abstract. Understanding human-object interaction is important for recognizing the activity and the sequence of actions performed. Egocentric tracking of people's actions and interactions has long been a research topic in many fields. Humans use their hands to manipulate objects in their daily lives to perform various activities. We contend that it is possible to determine human activity by watching how the wrist, palm, and fingers move and how they affect objects in the immediate area. There is a need to recognize the sequence of human actions. This is the key to understanding the activities and inferring the success or failure of the activity when manipulating objects. In this paper, we present a new perspective view, the wrist-centric view, a view from the wrist of the person while performing activities of daily living (ADLs). We explored activities of daily living (ADLs) through the wrist-centric view to identify activities where this novel view is advantageous over other egocentric views. This paper explores the importance of understanding human-object interaction in identifying activities and recognizing ADLs in finer detail. ADLs such as cooking, laundry, eating, drinking, doing dishes, interacting with people, gesturing, shopping, reading, walking, and interacting with everyday objects such as keys, glasses, and medication were selected to depict the representational motions a person needs to perform to carry out daily tasks. We provide different perspectives on these activities, including chest-centric and wrist-centric views, and demonstrate which scenarios the wrist-centric view is most advantageous.

Keywords: Wrist-centric view · Wrist-worn Camera · Wearables · ADLs · Daily Activities

1 Introduction

Humans have remarkable manual dexterity and rely heavily on their hands for a wide range of activities in their daily lives. Our hands are essential tools that allow us to interact with our environment, manipulate objects, and perform complex tasks with ease. Our ability to reach, grasp, and manipulate objects within

Supported by National Science Foundation under Grant No. 1828010 and 2142774 and Arizona State University.

arm's reach with precision and finesse is a testament to the remarkable dexterity and functionality of our hands [1]. Moreover, our hands play a crucial role in gathering information about objects and our environment. Most human actions involve the hands; furthermore, we do this at the subconscious level, and we can recognize objects and gather a variety of information about them, including their shape, size, orientation, weight, compliance, surface texture, and thermal characteristics [1]. This information is processed by our brains and used to make informed decisions and actions, allowing us to interact with our environment with greater efficiency and precision.

The role of the hands in human manual dexterity and interaction with the environment is a testament to their importance and functionality. To fully capitalize on the potential of the human hands, a wrist-centric view has been developed that focuses on the wrist as the center of movement and activity. It also allows the device to track the user's movements and activities more accurately, as the hands are typically the most active part of the body during many activities [2]. The wrist-centric view is a valuable perspective that provides a wealth of benefits for the users by focusing on the wrist as the center of activity; it allows for accurate tracking of the user's movements and activities and allows for identification of the environment and objects of interest.

To effectively capture the movements and activities that take place, a new technology is essential. PERACTIV Fig. 1 is designed to meet these requirements, utilizing a wrist wearable camera that allows for accurate tracking of the user's movements and activities. This innovative technology makes it possible to capture and record daily experiences more conveniently and intuitively.

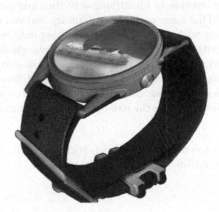

Fig. 1. PERACTIV Device showing the view during pill-taking activity.

The next step is activity understanding using the wrist-centric view to track and understand a person's movements and activities. By focusing on the wrist as the center of activity, the device can accurately monitor the user's movements and interpret them in the context of different activities. For example, a wrist-centric device can detect whether the correct pill has been picked up and placed in the mouth.

To gain deeper insight into the nuances of Activities of Daily Living (ADLs) from a wrist-centric perspective, we conducted research on multiple ADLs and their execution from different viewpoints. ADLs encompass the essential skills required for individuals to maintain independence and self-care, including activities like preparing food, eating and drinking, dressing, personal hygiene, transfers and mobility, orientation, medication management, using the telephone, communication, household tasks, shopping, managing finances, engaging in hobbies, and transportation [3]. The term "Activities of Daily Living" was first introduced by Sidney Katz in 1950 [4,5]. A person with a physical or mental impairment can have difficulty performing specific ADLs. The difficulties generally arise due to aging [6], musculoskeletal, neurological, circulatory, or sensory conditions [7], a cognitive or mental decline [8], side effects of medications, social isolation, or the patient's home environment can influence the ability to perform ADLs [9,10].

PERACTIV aims to leverage the wrist-centric view and computer vision to easily track and recognize activities involving hand and object manipulation, such as ADLs.

2 Literature Review

The idea of using exocentric views, or videos recorded from an external perspective, has also been explored in the field of computer vision and machine learning. Exocentric views capture the movements and activities of individuals from an external viewpoint. This information can be used for various purposes, such as activity recognition, video summarization, and object detection. Analyzing the visual information in exocentric views makes it possible to understand the relationships between individuals, objects, and their environment. This information can be useful in several applications, such as monitoring the movements and interactions of groups of people, detecting and analyzing patterns in crowd behavior, and more.

Egocentric views provide a different perspective on the world compared to exocentric views, as they capture the movements and activities of the individual from their own first-person perspective. This view allows for a more personal and intimate view of the world, providing a unique window into the individual's experiences and surroundings. In contrast, exocentric videos capture the movements and activities of individuals from an external viewpoint, allowing for a broader and more comprehensive view of the environment and interactions between individuals and objects.

The use of egocentric views or videos recorded from the first-person perspective has become increasingly popular for various applications, including activity recognition, video summarization, and object detection. The widespread availability of commercial and lightweight cameras like GoPros has made capturing and utilizing these types of views easier. The advantages of egocentric views are that they provide a unique perspective on the world, capturing a person's movements, activities, and surroundings from their own point of view. This information can be used to improve our understanding of daily activities. The idea of using egocentric views for these purposes has been broadly explored and continues to be an active area of research and development. These large amounts of first-person or egocentric views, which are recorded from the point of view of the camera wearer have large, non-linear, and unpredictable head and body motions as well as a lack of global context. This unpredictable motion poses a challenge for machine learning algorithms [11].

UCF-11 [12], HMDB-51 [13], Sports-1M [14] and Hollywood2 [15] are a few of the popular Exocentric datasets. UCF-11 consists of 1600 videos and 11 actions and is the YouTube Action dataset. HMDB-51 Human Motion Database dataset provides three train-test splits, each consisting of 5100 videos containing one action each. These clips are labeled with 51 classes of human actions. The Hollywood2 Human Actions dataset consists of 1707 video clips collected from movies. These clips are labeled with 12 classes of human actions and have multiple actions associated with them. Other exocentric datasets such as ActivityNet [16], Kinetics [17], and MPII-Cooking [18] discuss fine-grained and composite activities. MPII-Cooking consists of 67 fine-grained activities and 59 composite activities made of 14,105 clips and 273 videos. The ActivityNet has 203 classes, 137 untrimmed videos per class, and 1.41 activity instances per video. The Kinetics dataset is a YouTube Action dataset consisting of 400/600/700 classes with at least 400/600/700 clips per class.

A few well-known egocentric datasets are Charades-Ego [19] and EPIC-KITCHENS [20]. Charades-Ego: Actor and Observer: Joint Modeling of First and Third-Person Videos consists of 4000 paired videos belonging to 157 action classes from 112 people. EPIC-KITCHENS uses a head-mounted camera and is an egocentric dataset consisting of 100 h, 37 participants, 20M frames, 90K action segments, 700 variable-length videos, 97 verb classes, 300 noun classes, and 4053 action classes.

Although activity understanding from various different views has been explored previously and using hand-centric features was investigated [18] for understanding human actions, the wrist-centric view has yet to be widely studied. Previous studies [21–23] have explained the utility of wrist-worn cameras in tracking activities of daily living. Still, work has yet to study a comparative analysis of the wrist-centric view compared to other egocentric views when performing different activities. In the last couple of years, there has been a surge of interest in developing wearable systems that can assist older adults living independently, people with memory deficits, and dementia in performing their everyday activities. To leverage the wrist-centric view and understand actions performed with hands, we developed PERACTIV - **Per**sonalized **Activ**ity Monitoring [24] as seen in Fig. 1. It is a wrist-worn wearable device that tracks hand and finger movements and generates a video stream of the activities and the immediate environment. It is lightweight, inexpensive, scalable, and simple to use.

3   Understanding the Wrist-Centric View from Dorsal and Ventral Views

The wrist-centric view offers unique insights into human activities by capturing the movements and interactions of the hands and wrist with the environment. It can be viewed from two distinct perspectives - the dorsal and the ventral view. The dorsal view refers to the view when the camera is situated on the back of the wrist Fig. 2a, where the bones of the wrist and hand are visible. This view is useful to identify the immediate surroundings.

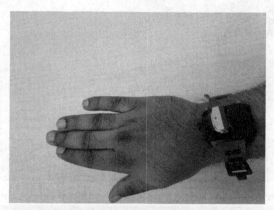

(a) Camera placed on the Dorsal side of the wrist.

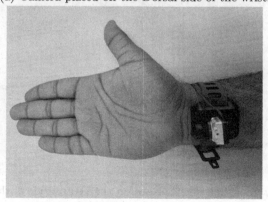

(b) Camera placed on the Ventral side of the wrist.

Fig. 2. Camera placed on both the Dorsal (a) and Ventral (b) side of the wrist.

The ventral view refers to the view when the camera is placed on the palm side of the wrist Fig. 2b, where the tendons and muscles that control the wrist and hand are visible and captures the fingers, palm, object of interest and object interactions during various activities.

As illustrated in the activity of pill taking in the kitchen shown in Fig. 3, the dorsal view (Fig. 3a) offers information about the surrounding environment and enables the inference of location and action. In this scenario, the kitchen setting can be deduced from visual cues. Meanwhile, the ventral view (Fig. 3b) provides insight into the movements of the fingers, the interactions with objects, and the activity being performed. In the example of pill taking, we can gather information about the pill box, the type of pill, the action of picking up the pill, and more.

(a) View from the camera placed on the Dorsal side of the wrist.

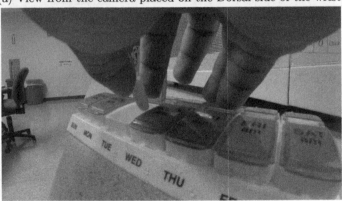

(b) View from the camera placed on the Ventral side of the wrist.

Fig. 3. Views from the camera placed on both the Dorsal (a) and Ventral (b) side of the wrist.

4   Understanding Activities of Daily Living from Wrist-Centric View

In this section, we classify activities of daily living into four categories based on various parameters, including the nature of the activity (stationary vs. non-stationary), location (in or outside the home), and interaction with others. This systematic categorization helps better understand the wrist-centric view and analyze different types of activities.

4.1   Performing Stationary Activities at Home

A few examples of stationary activities performed at home include eating, drinking, taking medication, using a telephone or mobile phone, reading, and interacting with common household objects such as television remotes.

In the example seen in Fig. 4, the wrist-centric view captures the precise actions performed on a television remote, allowing us to gain a deeper understanding of the activity being carried out, including the specific button presses and movements. Additionally, in reading Fig. 5, the wrist-centric view allows us clearly see the object of focus, providing us with a comprehensive understanding of the activity being performed. Despite not involving hand movements, the wrist-centric view can easily identify all the activities performed at home while stationary. In activities such as reading, it might be necessary to supplement the wrist-centric view with a chest-centric view to achieving a more comprehensive understanding of the activity being performed. But the wrist-centric view is highly advantageous for tracking and identifying fine-grained details, such as which medication was taken, what action has been performed using the remote, and more.

Fig. 4. Wrist camera view while interacting with a television remote.

(a) Chest camera view while Reading.

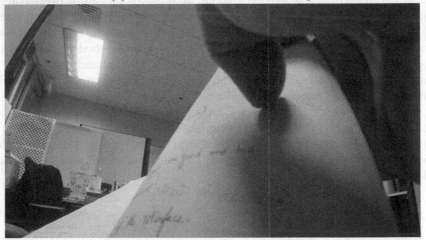

(b) Wrist camera view while Reading.

Fig. 5. Chest-centric and wrist-centric views while reading.

4.2 Performing Non-stationary Activities at Home

Preparation of food, doing laundry, personal hygiene, other housework, and interacting with daily objects such as keys, glasses, and more are a few examples of ADLs performed at home while not being stationary. As seen in the chest-centric view (Fig. 6) and wrist-centric view examples of cooking and cleaning dishes (Fig. 7), the wrist-centric view provides a wealth of information such as ingredients used, interactions with the gas knob, dishes cleaned, and placement of dishes, etc. while the chest camera can miss some of these interactions.

The interaction with the gas knob can be clearly seen in the wrist-centric view, Fig. 8 but not in the chest-centric view.

Fig. 6. Chest camera view while cooking and doing dishes.

Fig. 7. Wrist camera view while cooking and doing dishes.

The wrist-centric view offers a unique advantage over traditional methods of monitoring. Unlike other approaches that only identify the task being performed, the wrist-centric view provides a more detailed insight into the finer details of the interactions and information involved in the task. For instance, in a cooking scenario, the wrist-centric view captured from a wearable device can clearly display the state of the gas knob, whether it is on or off (Fig. 8), and whether the flame is lit or not. This kind of detailed information can give a more comprehensive understanding of the task being performed, enabling a better assessment of the individual's ability to perform activities of daily living.

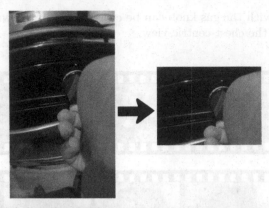

(a) Ventral View while turning the gas knob to On state.

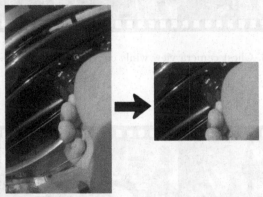

(b) Ventral View while turning the gas knob to Off state.

Fig. 8. Ventral views during cooking.

4.3   Performing Activities Outside Home

The wrist-centric view provides a detailed understanding of activities performed outside the home, such as shopping, games, physical activities, hobbies, travel, and transportation. It provides a continuous view of shopped items, as seen in Fig. 9. For example, during shopping, it captures finer interactions with objects, like items picked and placed in the basket. It can also track what items have been put in the basket and removed from (Fig. 9).

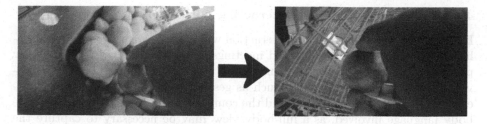

Fig. 9. Wrist-centric camera view with object interactions.

In contrast, the chest-centric view may miss some critical information like placing the item in the cart, as seen in Fig. 10a. Activities performed outside the home for example shopping, we can clearly see the advantage of the wrist-centric view over the chest-centric view, the item shopped for was always in view from picking it up to placing it in the cart (Fig. 10b), whereas in the chest-centric view, placing the item shopped for in the cart is not captured (Fig. 10a). The wrist-centric view proves to be a valuable tool in accurately tracking and documenting the user's movements and interactions with the environment.

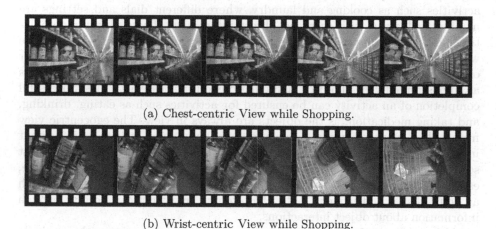

(a) Chest-centric View while Shopping.

(b) Wrist-centric View while Shopping.

Fig. 10. Chest-centric and Wrist-centric views during Shopping.

The wrist-centric view has limitations in capturing complex activities, such as fast-paced sports, requiring a holistic understanding of the body and the environment to comprehend the activity accurately. In these scenarios, additional cameras or sensor data may be necessary to provide a complete understanding of the activity performed in finer detail.

4.4   Performing Activities Interacting with People

Examples of activities involving interaction with people are speech and comprehension, such as conversations and meetings. Although the wrist-centric view primarily focuses on hand movements and object manipulation, it can still provide insight into these activities, such as gesturing during conversations. However, it struggles to fully understand the complexities of these activities and the body language involved, as a full-body view may be necessary to capture the complete picture. In activities where the individual's full body posture and movements are important, the wrist-centric view may not accurately capture human activity completely. In such cases, a combination of different viewpoints, including wrist-centric and other body-centric views, may be necessary to understand the full context of the activity.

5   Discussion

The wrist-centric view captured by a camera mounted on the wrist provides a clear and unobstructed view of hand and object interactions during activities of daily living (ADLs). The wrist-centric view excels in clearly identifying object manipulations performed by hand; this is especially useful during activities such as cooking and laundry, where different dials and settings are manipulated along with everyday object interaction. These object manipulations are clearly observed compared to a camera mounted on the body. The wrist-centric view also excels in activities where a person interacts with smaller objects, such as those employed in ADLs. The wrist-centric view Fig. 7 provides an unobstructed view of object manipulations during these activities. Successful completion of an activity can be ensured for activities such as eating, drinking, and taking medication, as the objects are always in view. The egocentric view from a chest-mounted camera (egocentric view) gives very little to no important information about the actions performed by the hands and activities in most scenarios. It is better suited for understanding interactions with other people, especially during leisure activities like reading or watching TV. In activities such as doing dishes and laundry, both chest-centric and wrist-centric give enough information about object interactions.

Although activities such as walking, reading, and interacting with people do not involve object manipulation with hands, they can still be monitored and analyzed through the wrist-centric view, especially hand gestures during conversations. In these cases, it might be advantageous to complement the wrist-centric view with a chest-centric view in order to obtain a more complete understanding of the activity being performed.

The wrist-centric view, although beneficial in tracking and monitoring activities of daily living, can face some limitations such as occlusion from the palm and fingers during interaction with small objects, as shown in Fig. 11.

However, despite these limitations, the wrist-centric view approach still provides a unique and comprehensive understanding of an individual's daily activities, and thus, remains a valuable tool in tracking and monitoring of ADLs.

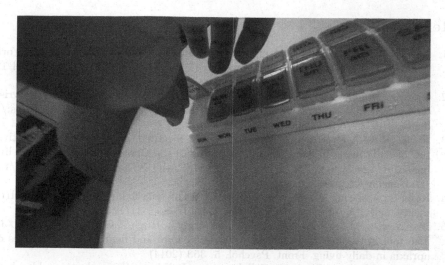

Fig. 11. Occlusion in wrist-centric view while taking a pill.

6   Conclusion

Focusing on the wrist as the center of activity allows for accurate and comprehensive monitoring of the user's movements and activities and the ability to provide valuable insights and feedback to the user. The wrist-centric view approach allows for more precise tracking of ADLs, providing valuable insights into daily living patterns and habits such as cooking, shopping, laundry, and more. By focusing on the wrist as the center of activity, the wrist-centric view, as provided by PERACTIV, has been proven to be a valuable tool in providing a unique and valuable perspective for tracking and better understanding activities of daily living.

In addition, the wrist-centric view can also be beneficial in monitoring elderly or disabled individuals, providing family members and caregivers with peace of mind and a better understanding of the individual's daily activities. This technology can help to ensure the individual's safety, well-being, and independence while providing the caregiver with valuable information about the individual's daily habits and routines.

The wrist-centric view has a wide range of potential applications, and its influence on technology and human interaction is expected to be substantial. This groundbreaking method of tracking and analyzing activity can transform our activity understanding, bringing about new possibilities for enhancing health, well-being, and autonomy.

References

1. Jones, L.A., Lederman, S.J.: Human Hand Function. Oxford Academic, New York (2006). https://doi.org/10.1093/acprof:oso/9780195173154.001.0001. Accessed 12 Aug 2022
2. Gjoreski, M., Gjoreski, H., Luštrek, M., Gams, M.: How accurately can your wrist device recognize daily activities and detect falls? Sensors **16**, 800 (2016). https://doi.org/10.3390/s16060800
3. Bucks, R.S., Ashworth, D.L., Wilcock, G.K., Siegfried, K.: Assessment of activities of daily living in dementia: development of the Bristol activities of daily living scale. Age Ageing. **25**(2), 113–120 (1996). PMID: 8670538. https://doi.org/10.1093/ageing/25.2.113
4. Katz, S.: Assessing self-maintenance: activities of daily living, mobility, and instrumental activities of daily living. J. Am. Geriatr. Soc. **31**(12), 721–7 (1983)
5. Bieńkiewicz, M.M., Brandi, M.L., Goldenberg, G., Hughes, C.M., Hermsdörfer, J.: The tool in the brain: apraxia in ADL: behavioral and neurological correlates of apraxia in daily living. Front. Psychol. **5**, 353 (2014)
6. Geriatric Medicine Research Collaborative. Delirium is prevalent in older hospital inpatients and associated with adverse outcomes: results of a prospective multi-centre study on World Delirium Awareness Day. BMC Med. **17**(1), 229 (2019). PMID: 31837711; PMCID: PMC6911703. https://doi.org/10.1186/s12916-019-1458-7
7. Edemekong, P.F., Bomgaars, D.L., Sukumaran, S., et al.: Activities of Daily Living. In: StatPearls [Internet]. Treasure Island (FL). StatPearls Publishing (2022). https://www.ncbi.nlm.nih.gov/books/NBK470404/
8. Farias, S.T., et al.: Everyday cognition in older adults: associations with neuropsychological performance and structural brain imaging. J. Int. Neuropsychol. Soc. **19**(4), 430–441 (2013). PMID: 23369894; PMCID: PMC3818105. https://doi.org/10.1017/S1355617712001609
9. Farias, S.T., Harrell, E., Neumann, C., Houtz, A.: The relationship between neuropsychological performance and daily functioning in individuals with Alzheimer's disease: ecological validity of neuropsychological tests. Arch. Clin. Neuropsychol. **18**(6), 655–72 (2003). PMID: 14591439
10. Chu, N.M., et al.: Functional independence, access to kidney transplantation and waitlist mortality. Nephrol. Dial. Transplant. **35**(5), 870–877 (2020). PMID: 31860087; PMCID: PMC7849992. https://doi.org/10.1093/ndt/gfz265
11. Li, Y., Ye, Z., Rehg, J.M.: Delving into egocentric actions. In: Proceedings of the IEEE Conference on Computer Vision and Pattern Recognition (2015)
12. Soomro, K., Amir, Z., Mubarak, S.: UCF101: A Dataset of 101 Human Actions Classes From Videos in The Wild. CoRR (2012)
13. Kuehne, H., Jhuang, H., Garrote, E., Poggio, T., Serre,T.: HMDB: a large video database for human motion recognition. In: 2011 International Conference on Computer Vision, Barcelona, Spain, pp. 2556–2563 (2011). https://doi.org/10.1109/ICCV.2011.6126543
14. Karpathy, A., Toderici, G., Shetty, S., Leung, T., Sukthankar, R., Fei-Fei, L.: Large-scale video classification with convolutional neural networks. In: 2014 IEEE Conference on Computer Vision and Pattern Recognition, Columbus, OH, USA, pp. 1725–1732 (2014). https://doi.org/10.1109/CVPR.2014.223
15. Marszalek, M., Ivan, L., Cordelia, S.: Actions in context. In: Proceedings CVPR, IEEE Computer Society Conference on Computer Vision and Pattern Recognition, pp. 2929–2936 (2009). https://doi.org/10.1109/CVPR.2009.5206557

16. Heilbron, F.C., Escorcia, V., Ghanem, B., Niebles, J.C.: ActivityNet: a large-scale video benchmark for human activity understanding. In: 2015 IEEE Conference on Computer Vision and Pattern Recognition (CVPR), Boston, MA, USA, 2015, pp. 961–970 (2015). https://doi.org/10.1109/CVPR.2015.7298698
17. Smaira, L., Carreira, J., Noland, E., Clancy, E., Wu, A., Zisserman, A.: A Short Note on the Kinetics-700-2020 Human Action Dataset (2020)
18. Rohrbach, M., et al.: Recognizing fine-grained and composite activities using hand-centric features and script data. Int. J. Comput. Vision **119**(3), 346–373 (2015). https://doi.org/10.1007/s11263-015-0851-8
19. Alahari, K.: Actor and observer: joint modeling of first and third-person videos. In: Proceedings of the 1st Workshop and Challenge on Comprehensive Video Understanding in the Wild (CoVieW 2018), vol. 3. Association for Computing Machinery, New York (2018). https://doi.org/10.1145/3265987.3265995
20. Damen, D., et al.: Rescaling egocentric vision: collection, pipeline and challenges for EPIC-KITCHENS-100. Int. J. Comput. Vision **130**(1), 33–55 (2021). https://doi.org/10.1007/s11263-021-01531-2
21. Tavakolizadeh, F., Gu, J., Saket, B.: Traceband: locating missing items by visual remembrance. In Proceedings of the Adjunct Publication of the 27th Annual ACM Symposium on User Interface Software and Technology (UIST 2014 Adjunct), pp. 109–110. Association for Computing Machinery, New York (2014)
22. Maekawa, T., Kishino, Y., Yanagisawa, Y., Sakurai, Y.: WristSense: wrist-worn sensor device with camera for daily activity recognition. In: 2012 IEEE International Conference on Pervasive Computing and Communications Workshops (2012)
23. . Vardy, A., Robinson, J., Cheng, L.T.: The WristCam as input device. In: Digest of Papers: Third International Symposium on Wearable Computers, pp. 199–202 (1999). https://doi.org/10.1109/ISWC.1999.806928
24. Kakaraparthi, V., McDaniel, T., Venkateswara, H., Goldberg, M.: PERACTIV: personalized activity monitoring - ask my hands. In: Distributed, Ambient and Pervasive Interactions. Smart Living, Learning, Well-being and Health, Art and Creativity: 10th International Conference, DAPI 2022, Held as Part of the 24th HCI International Conference, HCII 2022, Virtual Event, Proceedings, Part II, 26 June–1 July 2022, pp. 255–272. Springer, Heidelberg (2022). https://doi.org/10.1007/978-3-031-05431-0_18

Body-Focused Expression Analysis:
A Conceptual Framework

João M. F. Rodrigues[(✉)] 🆔 and Pedro J. S. Cardoso 🆔

LARSyS and ISE, Universidade do Algarve, 8005-226 Faro, Portugal
{jrodrig,pcardoso}@ualg.pt

Abstract. Humans are prepared to comprehend others' emotional expressions
from subtle body movements or facial expressions, and they change the way
they communicate in the function of those interactions/responses. Emotions influence sentiment and sentiment influences emotions. To transition from the traditional human-computer interaction to a human-machine collaboration, where the
machine delivers relevant information and functionalities in a timely and appropriate manner, machines, user interfaces, and robots need to be equipped with
such capabilities. The current state-of-the-art in methods and models for body
emotion and sentiment classification, as well as existing datasets, are reviewed in
this position paper. In this context, it also suggested the creation of a database for
body expression analysis and a framework for emotion and sentiment prediction.

Keywords: Affective Computing · Human-Centred AI · Body Emotions · Body
Expression · Computer Vision

1 Introduction

Human-Centred Artificial Intelligence (HCAI) [1] focuses on promoting human values
such as rights, justice, and dignity, and on developing tools that support humans in different daily functions. Additionally, HCAI looks to balance human control with automation, using thoughtful design strategies, by supporting human autonomy, well-being, and
control over emerging technologies.

Affective Computing (AC) combines the areas of emotion recognition and sentiment
analysis, being a multidisciplinary field of computer science, psychology, and neuroscience. Throughout its development, AC can use a variety of data sources including
physical information such as text, audio (speech), or visual data (e.g., facial expression,
body posture, or environment), as well as physiological signals like EEGs (Electroen-
cephalography) or ECGs (Electrocardiograms), i.e., AC is built on either unimodal or
multimodal data [2].

HCAI and AC are deeply connected, in the sense that a machine, in *lato sensu*, must
be designed to cooperate or learn to cooperate with human beings, like in an interpersonal relationship between two humans. But interpersonal relationships are dependent
on emotions and sentiments. In this context, the detection of facial expressions (emotions and sentiments) is a widespread topic in the literature [3], with a huge number

of public and commercial libraries and methods that can be used in different applications. Conversely, body expressions classification [4], including emotion and sentiment classification, is still a subject that needs fundamental and systematic research. Body expression classification is and will be a fundamental tool for human expression classification [5], in a stand-alone mode, or in connection with other methods from different data sources (such as the already mentioned, speech, text, environment etc.).

There are several examples of the use of this technology. For instance, AC is used in commercial stores to recognize the consumer's expressions while shopping [6], i.e., to figure out the person's emotion (e.g., happy, sad, or angry), sentiment (positive, negative, or neutral), or deducing its buying intention. Another straightforward example is brand activation. AC is also applicable to adaptive interfaces [7], interfaces that adapt the layout in the function of the user's emotions (as well as other factors, such as gender, age etc.). More examples are shown when applying this technology to Socially Assistive Robot (SAR) technologies, including in elderly care [8].

This position paper presents a body expression framework that can be used for brand activation, covering three main topics:

- An overview of the current state-of-the-art in methods and models for body emotion and sentiment classification, as well as existing datasets that are used to develop Artificial Intelligence (AI)/Machine Learning (ML) detectors and classifiers for body expression.
- A proposal for the development of a database for body expression analysis, including considerations for the types of data to be collected and the methods for collecting, storing, and organizing the data.
- A preliminary concept for a framework for body emotion and sentiment classification, including an explanation of how it can be integrated with other models for expression classification (e.g., speech, environment etc.).

The paper structured into five sections. Following this introduction, the second section addresses the contextualization, the state-of-the-art associated with body expression analysis, and respectively available datasets. Section three addresses how to develop a dataset for body expression analysis, and the proposed prototype for body emotion and sentiment classification is established in the fourth section. In the final section, the conclusions and recommendations for future work are presented.

2 Contextualization and State-of-the-Art

The interpersonal relationship defines the association, warmth, friendliness, and dominance between two or more people, it manifests when one establishes, reciprocates, or deepens relationships with one another [5]. On the other side, since interactions in digital communication, namely in Human-Machine Interaction (HMI), are impersonal, which hinders communication, there are no reciprocal or close ties between humans and machines (devices and/or interfaces). In this context, emotion and sentiment analysis methods are the automated processes of analyzing information to estimate the emotion (typically limited to happiness, sadness, fear, surprise, disgust, anger, and neutral), or sentiment (typically limited to positive, negative, and neutral) [9].

One another influence both the emotion and the sentiment. People are equipped to read one other's emotions through subtle body language, expressions on the face, words that are spoken, or even just tone of voice. They use this ability when they communicate between themselves, changing the way they pass the message based on those responses/emotions/sentiments. In this sense, machines should/must be designed to cooperate or learn to cooperate with human beings, usually termed as Human-Machine Cooperation (HMC) [10]. The interfaces (machines) must be able to evaluate human's behaviors and adapt to human's goals and behaviors [10, 11], in the same way, it occurs in interpersonal relationships. For the HMC, the goal is to support the user's individual characteristics, tasks, contexts, and feelings so the machine provides the "correct" information and functionality at the "right" time and in the "right" way [10].

Overall, user emotions and sentiments classification go beyond the traditional facial expression recognition that analyzes facial motions and facial feature changes of a single subject. This classification aims for a higher-level interpretation of fine-grained and high-level relational clues extracted from facial expressions, body posture, environment etc. In fact, it can combine facial expression and head pose with other visual clues, such as, body posture, age, race, and gender, although, the face can, in general, reveal much richer information.

2.1 Body Expression Analysis

There are many ways to go from Facial Expression Recognition (FER) to Interpersonal Relation Prediction. In this context, to improve accuracy, some models update the traditional FER methods with auxiliary attributes, such as, gender, age, or head pose [5]. Despite this improvement and outputs, more information can be retrieved by the classifiers if we connect the above attributes with other body attributes, such as actions and/or expression analysis.

A survey presented in 2021 by Naroozi et al. [9] focused on emotional body gesture recognition, introducing emotional body gestures as a part of what is commonly known as "body language" and commenting on general aspects, such as, gender differences and cultural dependence. The work also introduces person detection and comment on static and dynamic body pose estimation methods, as well as on recent literature related to representation learning and emotion recognition from images of emotionally expressive gestures. Moreover, the discussion on multi-modal approaches, that combine speech or face with body gestures for improved emotion recognition, is discussed in the survey, concluding that for emotion recognition the quantity of labelled data is scarce.

Filntisis et al. [12] propose a method of recognizing affect in child interaction by combining body posture and facial expressions. Leiva et al. [13] studied the dissociation between facial and bodily expressions in emotion recognition. The authors evaluated a patient with autism spectrum disorder who was 30 years old and did not have an intellectual disability, using four tasks for basic and complex emotion recognition, through face and body movements, as well as two non-emotional control tasks. With a modified one-tailed t-test they compared the patient and control group's performance while analyzing the dissociation between facial and body expressions. They concluded that a profile of impaired emotion recognition through body expressions and intact performance with facial expressions.

Ahmed *et al.* [14] introduced a novel two-layer feature selection framework for emotion classification from a comprehensive list of body movement features, accurately recognizing five basic emotions, namely: happiness, sadness, fear, anger, and neutral. In the first layer, a unique combination of analysis of variance and multivariate analysis of variance was used to drop irrelevant features. In the second layer, a binary chromosome-based genetic algorithm was used to select a feature subset, from the relevant list of features, which maximizes the emotion recognition rate. Score and rank-level fusion were then applied to further improve the accuracy of the system. Yang *et al.* [4] also proposed a two-stage system. In the first stage, the process generates sequences of body language predictions based on human poses estimated from input videos. These predictions are computed using OpenPose for pose estimation and a Spatio-Temporal Convolutional PoseFeature (ST-ConvPose) to encode the spatial-temporal relationships among the joints. With the learned pose representation, the authors use a K-Nearest-Neighbors based classifier for body language[1] recognition. In the 2nd stage, the predicted sequences are fed into a temporal network for emotion recognition, such that the model predicts the emotion based on the predicted body language sequences. The authors mentioned that the proposed framework outperforms other methods on their dataset (URMC).

To better use gesture data for emotion recognition, Wu *et al.* [15] used an emotion category as a collection of many body gesture types. With the aid of semantic information, a Generalized Zero-Shot Learning (GZSL) framework is presented to recognize both seen and unseen body gesture categories. Moreover, emotion predictions are estimated based on the correlation between gestures and emotions. There are two branches in this framework: the first branch is a Hierarchical Prototype Network (HPN) that learns body gesture prototypes and applies them to the calculation of emotion-aware prototypes, being the predictions on examples of the observed gesture categories the goal of this branch; The second branch is a Semantic Auto-Encoder (SAE), which forecasts samples of unseen-gesture categories using semantic representations. Thresholds are trained to select the right branch result. Also interesting is the work of Blythe *et al.* [16] which concluded and proved that emotion is perceived accurately from isolated body parts, especially hands.

Wang *et al.* [2] presented a more recent (July 2022) systematic review of emotional computing, including emotion models, databases, and recent advancements. In this article, AC is reviewed with a focus on single- and multi-modal analysis using benchmark databases. A taxonomy of state-of-the-art methods that take into account ML-based or DL-based (Deep Leaning based) techniques is also presented, along with a comparative breakdown of the characteristics and quantitative performance of key methods. The authors examine issues and potential influences on affect recognition and analysis in their final section, dividing facial expression recognition and body gesture emotion recognition, both of which are directly related to the current paper, as sub-branches of the single model affect recognition, a branch of visual emotion recognition. Both sub-branches are then further divided into conventional ML- and DL-based methods. Another even

---

[1] Examples of body language and their meanings can be found at this website: https://www.enk iverywell.com/body-language-examples.html.

more recent (January 2023) systematic review on multimodal emotion recognition using learning algorithms is presented in [17].

Finally, it is important to mention, there are three main categories of emotion models in affective computing [9]: (a) *categorical*, supported on a universal set of emotions as defined by Ekman, (b) *dimensional* as defined by Russell's model, and (c) *componential models* as defined by Plutchik's model (see **Error! Reference source not found.**). A detailed definition of the categories is presented in [9].

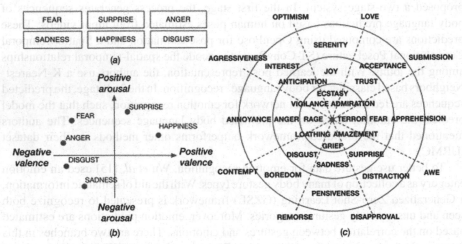

Fig. 1. Three main categories of emotion models in affective computing. Figure created by Narozzi et al., available in [9].

2.2 Datasets

A survey on databases for multimodal emotion recognition can be found in [18]. In this context, there is a staggering number of datasets for recognizing facial expressions and emotions. For instance, in [2], 19 databases specifically devoted to faces were identified. In that same work, the datasets were split into datasets where faces were collected in a laboratory environment and datasets where faces were collected in the wild (real-world or similar to real-world conditions). When discussing body/gesture emotion databases, the same authors [2] only identified 5 databases, with extra 8 multimodal databases which are far more scarce.

Nevertheless, several databases exist (for body and/or gesture emotion classification). For example, the (i) EmoTV (2005) [19] holds interview video sequences from French TV channels. EmoTV has multiple types of annotations but is not publicly available. Authored by Ma *et al.* (2006) [20], (ii) the Body Movement Library – BML[2] is a library that is an attempt to systematically represent the wide range of personal properties,

---

[2] BML - Body Movement Library: https://paco.psy.gla.ac.uk/?page_id=14973 (accessed 2022/12/29).

such as identity, gender, and emotion, which are available in a person's movements. The movements from a total of 30 nonprofessional actors were captured in the video while they performed walking, knocking, lifting, and throwing actions, as well as their combination of angry, happy, neutral, and sad affective styles. These authors use 8 cameras to capture the motion. The (iii) Bimodal Face and Body Gesture Database – FABO[3], developed by Gunes & Piccardi (2006) [21], is a bimodal database consisting of combined face and body expressions recorded simultaneously, with 23 subjects and 60 min *per* subject. The authors used 2 RGB cameras focusing upper torso, hands, and face, with 9 emotion classes, neutral, uncertainty, anger, surprise, fear, anxiety, happiness, disgust, boredom, and sadness.

The (iv) Interactive Emotional Dyadic Motion Capture – IEMOCAP[4], released by Busso *et al.* (2008) [22], presents a database with 10 actors who performed selected emotional scripts and improvised hypothetical scenarios designed to elicit 5 specific types of emotions. The face, heads, and hands of actors are marked to supply detailed information about their facial expressions and hand movements while performing. (v) THEATER Corpus (2009) [23] consists of two movie sections. The emotion annotation was performed by the authors on the speech segments and was coded with eight affective states.

The (vi) Geneva Multimodal Emotion Portrayals – GEMEP[5], presented by Bänziger *et al.* (2012) [24], is a database of body postures and gestures collected from the perspectives of both an interlocutor and an observer. The GEMEP database is one of the few databases that have frame-by-frame labels. The (vii) Multi-Modal Movie Opinion – ICT-MMMO[6], by Wollmer *et al.* (2013) [25], is a database that has 308 YouTube videos and 78 movie review videos from ExpoTV, with five emotion labels. From Fourati & Pelachaud (2014) [26], (viii) EMILYA presents a database of emotional body expression in daily actions, where 11 actors express 8 emotions in 7 actions. The (ix) Modeling Creative and Emotive Improvisation in Theatre Performance – CreativeIT[7], proposed by Metallinou *et al.* (2016) [27], is a database having detailed full-body motion visual-audio and text description data collected from 16 actors, during their affective interactions, ranging from 2–10 min each. Two kinds of interactions (two-sentence and paraphrases exercises) are set as improvised.

The (x) CMU Multimodal Opinion Sentiment and Emotion Intensity – CMU-MOSEI[8], created by Zadeh *et al.* (2018) [28], is considered one of the largest databases for sentiment analysis and emotion recognition, consisting of 23,453 sentences and 3,228

---

[3] FABO - The Bimodal Face and Body Gesture Database: https://www.cl.cam.ac.uk/~hg410/fabo.html (accessed 2022/12/29).

[4] IEMOCAP - Interactive Emotional Dyadic Motion Capture: https://sail.usc.edu/iemocap/ (accessed 2022/12/29).

[5] GEMEP - GEneva Multimodal Emotion Portrayals: https://www.unige.ch/cisa/gemep/coreset/ (accessed 2022/12/29).

[6] ICT-MMMO - Multi-Modal Movie Opinion: http://multicomp.cs.cmu.edu/resources/ict-mmmo-dataset/ (accessed 2022/12/29).

[7] CreativeIT - Modeling Creative and Emotive Improvisation in Theatre Performance: https://sail.usc.edu/CreativeIT/index.html (accessed 2022/12/29).

[8] CMU-MOSEI - CMU Multimodal Opinion Sentiment and Emotion Intensity: http://multicomp.cs.cmu.edu/resources/cmu-mosei-dataset/ (accessed 2022/12/29).

videos collected from more than 1,000 online YouTube speakers. Each video has a manual transcription. The (xi) Baby Robot Emotion Database – BRED[9], by Filntisis *et al.* (2019) [12], presents a children's robot emotion database which includes two different kinds of recordings with the Zeno and Furhat robots: pre-game recordings during which children were asked by a human to express one of six emotions, and game recordings during which children were playing a game called "Express the feeling". (xii) Ahmed *et al.* (2020) [14] presented a private dataset with 30 subjects, each subject performed five different motion-expressive walking sequences, including a separate neutral walking sequence. The authors focus on the subjects' structural and physical properties of body shape, dynamic quality of movement, and surrounding space use during movement. Each emotional walking sequence was recorded for 20 s with a Microsoft Kinect v2. A total of 3,000 s of recorded video data holding approximately 90,000 frames were recorded. The emotion classes were happiness, sadness, fear, anger, and neutral.

Not being an exhaustive enumeration, this section shown that a reasonable number of databases devoted to affective computing is available in the literature. Nevertheless, as far as the authors could find, these databases do not cover all the conditions to allow the development of realistic emotion models, such as how emotions change with gender, age, and culture, as well as in different environments, from those more formals, like in a meeting, to the ones more informal, like in vacations.

3   Develop a Dataset for Body Expression Analysis

The constitution of human activities (emotions and sentiments) depends on the age, gender, culture, and even physical (health) conditions of the subjects. Therefore, the human subject's diversity is therefore essential for an action recognition emotion benchmark.

The dataset must at the very least include the following elements: (a) a full-body person with a frontal to 3/4 view; (b) persons standing and sitting; (c) culture-dependency; (d) age; (e) gender; (f) visible facial expression; (g) body posture; (h) gestures; (i) eye movement; (j) personal space; and (g) various environments/contexts (format/informal). The collection should include both video (with all frames labelled) and static photos. Real-world and chromakey should be used for images and videos. Videos and images created with chromakey should support the insertion of various backgrounds.

As widely known, Deep Neural Networks (DNN) for emotion and sentiment recognition/classification can be trained using databases, but this process requires careful planning and execution of those databases. The main steps to creating such a database are listed below:

(a) *Identify the emotions and sentiments to be detected* – the dataset should include at least 6 (categorical) basic emotions and basic sentiments [9]. These emotions and sentiments should be clearly defined beforehand and considering the diversity of cultures that will be addressed.

(b) *Collect images and videos* – collect a diverse set of images and videos of a diversity of people expressing emotions and sentiments. The images and videos should include

---

[9] BRED - Baby Robot Emotion Database: https://zenodo.org/record/3233060#.Y_SwvnbP1D8 (accessed 2022/12/29).

full-body persons with frontal to 3/4 view, people standing up and sitting down, culture-dependent, age, gender, facial expression visible, body posture, gestures, eye movement, head pose, personal space, and environmental context. The images and videos should be filmed in real-world conditions and should include people moving around alone and interacting in groups.

(c) *Chromakey videos and images should be taken* – to allow for the insertion of different backgrounds. This will help to increase the diversity of the dataset and will also help to make the dataset more robust.

(d) *Annotate the dataset* – the collected images and videos should be annotated, i.e., each image, video (frame-by-frame), and the complete video (recorded scene), should be labeled with the corresponding emotion or sentiment. The annotation process should be conducted by multiple annotators with the same cultural background to ensure consistency and accuracy.

(e) *Split the dataset into training, validation, and test set* – the annotated dataset should be split into three sets, namely: training, validation, and test. The training set should be used to train the AI algorithm (for instance a DNN), the validation set should be used to evaluate the performance of the algorithm, and the test set should be used to evaluate the final performance of it.

(f) *Store the dataset* - the final dataset should be stored in a database, in a format that is easy to use and can be easily loaded by the AI algorithms. This may include storing the images and videos in a specific folder structure, creating a CSV file with the labels, and creating a JSON file with the metadata.

(g) *Data pre-processing* – the dataset should always be pre-processed before being used to train the AI algorithm. This may include cropping images, resizing images, normalizing images, and removing any irrelevant information.

By following these steps, a comprehensive database for emotion and sentiment detection can be created, which can be used to train, for instance, a DNN for accurate and robust emotion and sentiment detection.

4   Body Emotion and Sentiment Classifier Framework Prototype

A description of the user is fundamental in Brand Activation or SAR. In an initial paper [29], authors describe the user by age, gender, height, object carried, and facial emotion. In a following publication, a facial emotion classification method was improved [30]. Nevertheless, it was clear - and Sect. 2 confirms this - that information about the body, including gestures and actions, is fundamental for a reliable emotion classifier, particularly in circumstances like Brand Activation or SAR, situations where the user's face is/can be often occluded.

Figure 2 shows a simplified block diagram of the framework that the authors are presently implementing to describe the user. Independent of the input being a video or an image, of course different processing methods apply, the temporal or static information is used to detect the user's age, gender, height, objects carried, as well as the environment or the prediction of the users' cultural background. The later one, can be computationally achieved by the framework combining the types of clothes, images background, and other information available in the video or image, like localization. Having this information, a first user description is established and identification is given: *Person ID#*.

The user description can now be used by the method to further fine-tune the user description (e.g., child vs. adult) or select the emotion classes available (e.g., supported on a formal vs informal environment; or different cultures). This tuned information is then combined with the information of the video or images as inputs for the (i) *Face Analysis*, (ii) the *Body Analysis*, (iii) the *Gesture Analysis*, and (iv) the *Action Analysis* emotion and sentiment classification modules.

Having these 4 initial classifications, or the ones available (the available classification are dependent on things, such as, occlusions, body parts framing, etc.), the next step is to combine them in the *Emotion/Sentiment Ensemble* module, returning the final decision for emotion and sentiment classification.

The user's information, with *Person ID#*, and complementary information from the module *Other Detectors* (see Fig. 2 and also [29]) can be used to have a final description of the user - *Person IDf#* module. The final description allows to decide which action to take (e.g., how the machine should react), and when to take it.

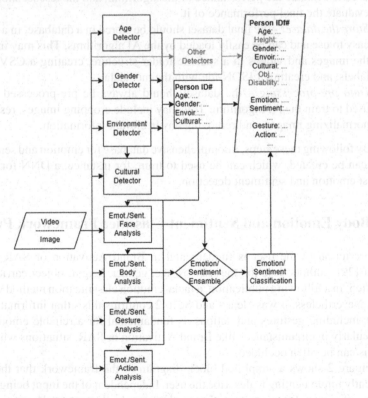

Fig. 2. Block diagram of the framework for user description.

In the case of the *Body Analysis* module, one of the articles' focus, it is important to stress that our present work in body emotion analysis follows the general principles presented in [4] (see Fig. 1). Further, Fig. 3 shows a general diagram block for the body emotion classifier, which can be described as follows. The video or streaming acquired is processed by the MediaPipe Library [31, 32], which returns the human body joints *per* frame, not including the face (which is processed in a different module – *Face Analysis*; see Fig. 2). There are 22 joints, which can be increased by 20 × 2 joints if the hands are detected. These joints are (i) divided into upper- and lower-body, and each (ii) body part's lengths, (iii) orientations, and (iv) inner angles are also calculated. All this information, (i)-(iv), is fed to two DNNs classifiers ("upper" and "down" classifier), and the results are then fed to a final temporal DNN classifier, returning the final emotion prediction.

It is important to explain the reason for the two paths, which is: men and women behave differently, thus there should be separate paths for the upper- and lower-body parts of the body. For example, ladies typically move their arms more through their hair and ears than men do, males typically sit with their legs open, while the ladies with their legs crossed etc. This separation into two paths is also used for the *Gesture Analysis* and *Action Analysis* presented in Fig. 2.

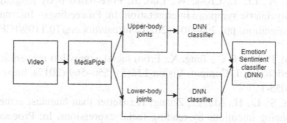

Fig. 3. Block diagram for the body emotion classifier.

Finally, it is also important to point out that the described framework is based on zero/few-shot learning or unsupervised learning methods (e.g., self-supervised learning), as also mentioned in [2]. This is mainly due to the lack of reliable ground-truth data (for this particular topic), as well as particularly to their potential to enhance the robustness and stability of affective analysis under limited or biased emotion/sentiment databases.

5 Conclusions and Future Work

The present position paper focuses on body expression analysis for Brand Activation and SAR. With this purpose a conceptual framework for user description was presented, being one of the blocks of this framework a *Body Analysis* emotion and sentiment classification module, which conceptually was also presented.

Further, an overview of the current state-of-the-art in methods, models, and databases for body emotion and sentiment classification was presented, as well as a proposal for developing a database for body expression analysis.

Finally, following the same principles described in [30] and [33], it is possible to integrate ensembles body emotion and sentiment classification with speech, text etc., allowing the development of a user descriptor with more information.

Future work consists of the completion of the development of the body emotion classifier following the conceptual principles presented in Fig. 3 as well as the development of the framework following the conceptual principles presented in Fig. 2.

Acknowledgements. This work was supported by the Portuguese Foundation for Science and Technology (FCT), project LARSyS - FCT Project UIDB/50009/2020.

References

1. Shneiderman, B.: Human-Centered AI. Oxford University Press, Oxford (2022)
2. Wang, Y., et al.: A systematic review on affective computing: emotion models, databases, and recent advances. Inf. Fusion **83–84**, 19–52 (2022). https://doi.org/10.1016/j.inffus.2022. 03.009
3. Li, S., Deng, W.: Deep facial expression recognition: a survey. IEEE Trans. Affect Comput. **3045**, 1–20 (2020). https://doi.org/10.1109/TAFFC.2020.2981446
4. Yang, Z., Kay, A., Li, Y., Cross, W., Luo, J.: Pose-based body language recognition for emotion and psychiatric symptom interpretation. In: Proceedings - International Conference on Pattern Recognition, pp. 294–301 (2020). https://doi.org/10.1109/ICPR48806.2021.941 2591
5. Zhang, Z., Luo, P., Loy, C.C., Tang, X.: From facial expression recognition to interpersonal relation prediction. Int. J. Comput. Vision **126**(5), 550–569 (2017). https://doi.org/10.1007/ s11263-017-1055-1
6. Chen, X., Sun, S., Li, H., Ma, Z., Zhang, K.: Better than humans: a method for inferring consumer shopping intentions by reading facial expressions. In: Proceedings - 2021 14th International Symposium on Computational Intelligence and Design, ISCID 2021, pp. 142–147 (2021). https://doi.org/10.1109/ISCID52796.2021.00041
7. Miraz, M.H., Ali, M., Excell, P.S.: Adaptive user interfaces and universal usability through plasticity of user interface design. Comput. Sci. Rev. **40**, 100363 (2021). https://doi.org/10. 1016/j.cosrev.2021.100363
8. Abdollahi, H., Mahoor, M., Zandie, R., Sewierski, J., Qualls, S.: Artificial emotional intelligence in socially assistive robots for older adults: a pilot study. IEEE Trans. Affect Comput. (2022). https://doi.org/10.1109/TAFFC.2022.3143803
9. Noroozi, F., Corneanu, C.A., Kaminska, D., Sapinski, T., Escalera, S., Anbarjafari, G.: Survey on emotional body gesture recognition. IEEE Trans. Affect Comput. **12**(2), 505–523 (2021). https://doi.org/10.1109/TAFFC.2018.2874986
10. van Maanen, P.P., Lindenberg, J., Neerincx, M.A.: Integrating human factors and artificial intelligence in the development of human-machine cooperation. In: Proceedings of the 2005 International Conference on Artificial Intelligence, ICAI 2005. vol. 1, pp. 10–16 (2005)
11. Crandall, J.W., et a.: Cooperating with machines. Nat. Commun. **9**(1), 233 (2018). https:// doi.org/10.1038/s41467-017-02597-8
12. Filntisis, P.P., Efthymiou, N., Koutras, P., Potamianos, G., Maragos, P.: Fusing body posture with facial expressions for joint recognition of affect in child-robot interaction. IEEE Robot Autom. Lett. **4**(4), 4011–4018 (2019). https://doi.org/10.1109/lra.2019.2930434
13. Leiva, S., Margulis, L., Micciulli, A., Ferreres, A.: Dissociation between facial and bodily expressions in emotion recognition: a case study. Clin. Neuropsychologist **33**(1), 166–182 (2019). https://doi.org/10.1080/13854046.2017.1418024
14. Ahmed, F., Bari, A.S.M.H., Gavrilova, M.L.: Emotion recognition from body movement. IEEE Access **8**, 11761–11781 (2020). https://doi.org/10.1109/ACCESS.2019.2963113

15. Wu, J., Zhang, Y., Sun, S., Li, Q., Zhao, X.: Generalized zero-shot emotion recognition from body gestures. Appl. Intell. **52**(8), 8616–8634 (2022). https://doi.org/10.1007/s10489-021-02927-w

16. Blythe, E., Garrido, L., Longo, M.R.: Emotion is perceived accurately from isolated body parts, especially hands. Cognition **230**, 105260 (2023). https://doi.org/10.1016/j.cognition.2022.105260

17. Ahmed, N., al Aghbari, Z., Girija, S.: A systematic survey on multimodal emotion recognition using learning algorithms. Intell. Syst. Appl. **17**, 200171 (2023). https://doi.org/10.1016/j.iswa.2022.200171

18. Siddiqui, M.F.H., Dhakal, P., Yang, X., Javaid, A.Y.: A survey on databases for multimodal emotion recognition and an introduction to the viri (visible and infrared image) database. Multimodal Technol. Interact. **6**(6), 47 (2022). https://doi.org/10.3390/mti6060047

19. Abrilian, S., Devillers, L., Martin, J.-C., Stéphanie, B.: EmoTV1: Annotation of real-life emotions for the specifications of multimodal a ective interfaces (2005). https://www.researchgate.net/publication/244425428

20. Ma, Y., Paterson, H.M., Pollick, F.E.: A motion capture library for the study of identity, gender, and emotion perception from biological motion. Behav. Res. Methods **38**(1), 134–141 (2006). https://doi.org/10.3758/BF03192758

21. Gunes, H., Piccardi, M.: Bimodal face and body gesture database for automatic analysis of human nonverbal affective behavior. In: Proceedings - International Conference on Pattern Recognition. vol. 1, pp. 1148–1153 (2006).https://doi.org/10.1109/ICPR.2006.39

22. Busso, C., et al.: IEMOCAP: interactive emotional dyadic motion capture database. Lang Resour. Eval. **42**(4), 335–359 (2008). https://doi.org/10.1007/s10579-008-9076-6

23. M. Kipp., Martin, J.C.: Gesture and emotion: Can basic gestural form features discriminate emotions?. In: Proceedings - 2009 3rd International Conference on Affective Computing and Intelligent Interaction and Workshops, ACII 2009 (2009). https://doi.org/10.1109/ACII.2009.5349544

24. Bänziger, T., Mortillaro, M., Scherer, K.R.: Introducing the Geneva Multimodal expression corpus for experimental research on emotion perception. Emotion **12**(5), 1161–1179 (2012). https://doi.org/10.1037/a0025827

25. Wollmer, M., et al.: You tube movie reviews: sentiment analysis in an audio-visual context. IEEE Intell Syst **28**(3), 46–53 (2013). https://doi.org/10.1109/MIS.2013.34

26. Fourati, N., Pelachaud, C.: Emilya: Emotional body expression in daily actions database (2014)

27. Metallinou, A., Yang, Z., Lee, C.-C., Busso, C., Carnicke, S., Narayanan, S.: The USC CreativeIT database of multimodal dyadic interactions: from speech and full body motion capture to continuous emotional annotations. Lang. Resour. Eval. **50**(3), 497–521 (2015). https://doi.org/10.1007/s10579-015-9300-0

28. Zadeh, A., et al.: Multimodal language analysis in the wild: CMU-MOSEI dataset and interpretable dynamic fusion graph. Assoc. Comput. Linguist. (2018). https://github.com/A2Zadeh/CMU

29. Turner, D., Rodrigues, J.M.F., Rosa, M.: Describing people: an integrated framework for human attributes classification. In: Monteiro, J., et al. (eds.) INCREaSE 2019, pp. 324–336. Springer, Cham (2020). https://doi.org/10.1007/978-3-030-30938-1_26

30. Novais, R., Cardoso, P.J.S., Rodrigues, J.M.F.: Facial emotions classification supported in an ensemble strategy. In: Universal Access in Human-Computer Interaction. Novel Design Approaches and Technologies: 16th International Conference, UAHCI 2022, Held as Part of the 24th HCI International Conference, HCII 2022, Virtual Event, June 26–July 1, 2022, Proceedings, Part I, pp. 477–488 (2022). https://doi.org/10.1007/978-3-031-05028-2_32

31. Papandreou, G.: MediaPipe. https://mediapipe.dev/ 27 Dec 2022

32. Lugaresi, C.: et al.: MediaPipe: A Framework for Building Perception Pipelines. (2019). http://arxiv.org/abs/1906.08172

33. Novais, R., Cardoso, P.J.S. Rodrigues, J.M.F.: Emotion Classification from Speech by an Ensemble Strategy. In: 10th International Conference on Software Development and Technologies for Enhancing Accessibility and Fighting Info-exclusion (DSAI 2022) (2022)

Co-creating an Object Recognition
Exergame with Hospital Service Users
to Promote Physical Activity

Kieran Woodward(✉), Eiman Kanjo, and Will Parker

Department of Computer Science, Nottingham Trent University, Nottingham, UK
{kieran.woodward,eiman.kanjo,william.parker}@ntu.ac.uk

Abstract. It is challenging to encourage hospital service users with
mental health conditions to engage in physical activity despite its proven
benefits. Technological implementation, such as mobile games could offer
a method of improving healthcare delivery without significant cost. Co-
design helps create a sense of empowerment and a feeling of competence,
which benefits the participants as they derive satisfaction and fun while
feeling useful through their participation. Therefore, we propose the co-
creation of objects using papier-mâché for use within an AI exergame
whereby hospital service users and staff construct co-created models that
are placed along a mile long walk around the grounds for use within the
game. This enables a novel approach to gamify exercise and promote
physical activity by developing a smartphone app that encourages hospital service users to search for and scan co-created objects around the
hospital grounds. The game has successfully engaged hospital service
users as they both enjoyed the active gamified experience and took ownership of the co-designed objects used within the game.

Keywords: Co-Deign · Mental Wellbeing · App · Object
Recognition · AI · Exergame · Physical Activity · Gamifiction

1 Introduction

Mental health problems constitute a global challenge that affects a large number
of people of all ages and socioeconomic backgrounds. According to the Mental
Health Foundation, about a quarter of the population will experience some form
of mental health problem in the course of a year [22]. Physical activity's (PA)
health benefits are proven and wide-ranging. However, people with mental health
challenges tend to be less physically active and it is even more so challenging to
encourage hospital service users with mental health conditions to engage in PA
[4]. Technological implementation, such as mobile health (mHealth), could offer
a method of improving healthcare delivery without significant cost. Specifically,
Exergames are video games that require physical movement to play. Exergames
make physical activity more enjoyable for users by providing a fun gaming environment with gamification that motivates and engages people to participate in
physical activity. The goal of exergames is to create games that are fun but

M. Antona and C. Stephanidis (Eds.): HCII 2023, LNCS 14021, pp. 609–619, 2023.
https://doi.org/10.1007/978-3-031-35897-5_43

also motivate players to be more physically active therefore the development of fun, sustainable physical activities that people with mental health conditions will be motivated to participate in consistently and frequently would be highly beneficial.

Technological advancements such as Artificial intelligence (AI), in particular object recognition, is becoming an increasingly popular but its uses for entertainment have thus far been limited. With the ubiquity of smartphones capable of running AI models, interactive apps utilising object recognition is an ideal method to blend the virtual and physical worlds whilst promoting exercise. AI applications present many opportunities for the future of Human-Computer Interaction (HCI), by revolutionizing the way users seamlessly interact with the real world using a real-time camera feed. Object recognition presents many opportunities for promoting exercise as it can be used to engage players and encourage exploration. The vast majority of existing implementations of object recognition are not for entertainment purposes. This may be because that until recently small devices such as smartphones were not capable of classifying a real-time camera feed.

Co-designing an AI exergame is a vital step for actively engaging people who have mental health conditions, allowing them to make a meaningful contribution to the design process [1,2,8]. Co-design helps to solve real-world problems by bringing together people from different backgrounds into the design process, resulting in more inclusive solutions. We propose the co-creation of sculptures and objects using papier-mâché whereby hospital service users and staff construct co-created models that are utilised within an object detection treasure hunt exergame.

This research outlines the development of a smartphone app that utilises advances in deep learning to detect the co-designed objects in real-time. We have worked with occupational therapists at Highbury mental health Hospital, Nottingham to help engage patients in the design and development of the casual exergame and co-designed models to promote physical activity. The hospital currently have a mile long walk around the grounds which service users are actively encouraged to engage with, but a lack of motivation and the mundane nature of walking around hospital grounds prevented many from exercising despite the benefits of PA. Therefore, this research focuses on the co-design of objects with hospital service users for use within an exergame demonstrating the ability to engage people with SMI in the solutions to help them become more physically active.

2   Background of Exergames

Physical inactivity is a significant issue for people with serious mental illness (SMI), including psychotic disorders such as schizophrenia spectrum disorders, bipolar disorder, and major depressive disorder [4]. Lack of motivation is a key factor contributing to this inactivity, and therefore, new ways to encourage individuals with mental health conditions to engage in physical activity are needed. Smartphone apps, specifically game-inspired apps, have emerged as a potential solution to this issue.

Exergames, or games that require physical activity to play, have been developed and tested by researchers in the past. Examples include World of Workout [5], a mobile exergame that uses a user's steps to play a role-playing game and complete quests by walking a certain number of steps, and PiNiZoRo [18], in which players walk to locate enemies and then complete puzzle games to defeat them. Most popularly, the Pokemon Go platform [11], which combines augmented reality, exergaming, and location-based multiplayer features, gained widespread attention on smartphones in the summer of 2016.

Most previous exergames have been developed for individuals without SMI. However, a study using a Wiimote with individuals who have schizophrenia [13] found that an exergame had a positive impact on patients' mood and motivation. Another study using a Microsoft Kinect-based exergame with individuals suffering from schizophrenia [3] also found that exergames can have a positive effect on physical activity levels. These findings suggest that exergames may be a promising solution for promoting physical activity in individuals with mental illness.

In order to encourage players with SMI to be physically active on a regular basis, it is important to engage players whilst being physically active. An approach should also be utilised that does not block the player if they are not sufficiently active, to avoid discouragement. However, more research is needed to determine the effectiveness and feasibility of using smartphone apps and exergames specifically for this population.

3   Methodology

The concept of the developed game is a virtual treasure hunt completed using a smartphone in which users must walk to find the indicated co-designed object and then scan the object using the smartphone camera. The exergame has been implemented at Highbury hospital, Nottingham, where players will walk around the hospital grounds as shown in Fig. 1 searching for the locations. However, In order to develop the exergame, a number of unique objects are first required for the object recognition activity. A co-design approach has been adopted as it offers a unique opportunity to engage service users and enable them to take ownership in the objects and exergame which will hopefully promote continued engagement.

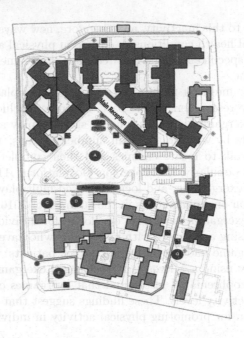

Fig. 1. Map of the Highbury Mile route.

3.1 Co-designing Objects

Co-design is the methodology for actively engaging people directly involved in an issue, place or process in its design, allowing them to make a meaningful contribution to the design process [1,2,8]. Co-design enables the reduction of the gap in knowledge between end users and researchers, allowing non-designers to become equal members of the design team, ensuring designer subjectivity is removed and the technologies developed are suitable for the target population [14,24]. During the process, design tools are used to empower all of the participants to facilitate a 'joint inquiry' where 'problem and solution co-evolve' [19]. Co-design brings many benefits to the design of the project by helping the researcher better understand the challenges faced by users and any potential solutions [17,20].

We have adopted a participatory approach to co-design objects to use within the exergame. This enables the design of products directly with the final users including those with SMI in order to help them take ownership of the product. Co-design helps create a sense of empowerment and a feeling of competence, which benefits the participants as they derive satisfaction and fun while feeling useful through their participation [6,10]. We therefore involved adults with SMI throughout the co-design process with the assumption that their inclusion will positively impact the quality of the final product in addition to their own experience. The co-design process was conducted with the same occupational

Fig. 2. The co-design process where the papier-mâché models were created.

therapists and researchers. All participants were service users at Highbury hospital, Nottinghamshire with varying mental illnesses but no participants had significant motor skill impairments that would impact their participation.

With very little around the Highbury mile to engage the users, a co-design element was the most engaging method to support and develop the game. Various papier-mâché sessions were set-up by staff members to involve the service users with the creation of multiple 3D objects that would later be water-proofed and placed securely in designated areas. Over 10 service users participated in the activity designing their own unique 3D models with each having a different shape and colour in order for the AI models to be trained with increased accuracy. Service users were divided into small groups and guidance was provided on how to create the papier-mâché models. The service users were then able to design and create their own models as shown in Fig. 2. After the initial models were created they were then painted by the service users under supervision.

With the co-design models in place, a large number of photos were captured for each of the objects. These photos were specifically taken to capture different angles ensuring the object recognition would function reliably for users. Each of the initial objects are displayed in Table 1.

Table 1. Description of the 5 models that were co-designed by hospital service users.

Model Name	Image	Description
Hot Air Balloon		One of the first papier-mâché objects implemented in the the Highbury Mile was a hot air balloon created by a service user.
Pinocchio		Pinocchio is another creation by one of the service users. This object was placed in an area that would get the user to search for it before they could complete the activity.
Robin		A robin was also created. The service user suggested that this model to be placed in a tree.
Mars		One of the service users wanted to create a more simple object that represented Mars.
Triceratops		One of the final objects to be created by the service users was a Triceratops. Similarly to the model of Pinocchio, this object was placed in an area that would require the user to have a look around in order to complete the activity.

3.2 Object Recognition

Advances in AI, in particular deep learning have resulted in the capability to classify images with increasing accuracy. However, the use of AI and object recognition for entertainment purposes within a game to promote physical activity has not had much consideration. Object recognition presents many opportunities and is becoming increasingly used in consumer apps such as enabling automated photo tagging [7]. The developed exergame utilises advances in object recognition as players are tasked with finding the co-designed objects identified through AI.

Convolutional Neural Networks (CNNs) are frequently used for object recognition. These are feed forward networks that are constructed of numerous layers including an input layer, an output layer and hidden layers that includes convolutional layers making use of a set of learnable filters, pooling layers, fully connected layers and normalisation layers. Transfer Learning (TL) [12] is a common approach in machine learning to improve the learning of a target task by improving initial performance, producing sharp performance growth and resulting in higher training performance [23]. It is based on the ability to learn new tasks relatively fast, alleviating the need for large datasets by relying on previous, similar data from related problems. TL capitalises on a large dataset stemming from a related problem to pre-train a model, and then adapting the model for the smaller target dataset [25]. CNNs are commonly used in TL approaches, being initially trained on a vast dataset and then having the last fully-connected layer removed and re-trained on a smaller target dataset. A pre-trained CNN alleviates the need for a large dataset while simultaneously decreasing the time required to train the model.

TL has most commonly been used to train images as large ImageNets have been used to developed pre-trained models such as VGGNet [16], Inceptionv3 [21] and mobileNetv3 [9] that contain pre-trained object classification models. TL has facilitated training new models in the visual domain using pre-trained CNNs [15] and has been utilised to learn the papier-mâché objects for the AI object recognition activity. The accuracy of the model (using hold-out validation) is 99%, demonstrating the ability of the model to infer each of the objects with high precision. The model was exported as a tflite file and embedded within the mobile app.

3.3 Smartphone Exergame

A mobile App that integrates the object recognition of the co-designed objects has been developed to increase physical activity with hospital service users. The app was developed using Flutter, a cross-platform programming language and is compatible with Android and iOS operating systems. The app is currently available on both Google Play and Apple Store.

As users approach different objects, the camera turns on for the players to find the nearby sculpture which then gets identified by the pre-trained AI model embedded in the app, enabling frames from the camera to be classified in real-time, if the accuracy is above 85% the location has then been 'found' and the user moves on to find the next object. During the gameplay players can view the current inference accuracy displayed as a progress bar. Players are able to find the objects in any order with the aim of the game being for players to find as many objects as possible. Figure 3 shows screenshots of the camera-based AI activity and the progress of the AI model detecting the sculpture.

Fig. 3. Screenshots of the developed exergame showing the inference of a co-designed object using the camera feed.

To ensure the app has high replayability, in some areas of the Highbury mile multiple co-designed objects are placed within a small area and the app randomly selects one of the objects for the user to find and scan. This random element ensures walks around the mile are dynamic and more engaging for hospital service users who may complete this walk daily. The game remains simple to play in nature with users simply having to point the app to the correct object as outlined within the app. This ensures the vast majority of service users will be able to use the app and by having a non-punishing gameplay whereby there are no punishments for scanning the incorrect object along with no time pressure it enables the game to be relaxing and not stressful which may otherwise harm service users' mental health.

4   Discussion and Conclusion

We completed the co-creation of objects with hospital service users and implemented an AI exergame at Highbury hospital in Nottingham. Although PA has been proven to be beneficial for all, motivating it for people with disabilities, especially people with intellectual disabilities, is challenging and requires specialised and individualised intervention. After the co-design sessions the occupational therapists who led the sessions provided their feedback. One said "the freedom in design was encouraging for the service users and it really helped them be more creative", another said "the sense of ownership meant that they took pride in their creations and they want to see users interacting with their model when development is complete". This feedback shows the co-design approach was successful in engaging service users in the creation of the exergame.

The designed objects were all unique and had clear designs ranging from dinosaurs to birds. This shows the time and effort service users placed when designing their objects resulting in the pride they felt when the objects were displayed and used within the app. The outstanding quality of the objects further shows the benefits of involving users in the co-design process as it creates a unique, rewarding experience that benefits the service users and the exergame. Participants stated they would like to design additional objects with possible new objects being created for different seasons of the year, showing how much they enjoyed this creative element and the invaluable addition of being part of the design process.

A preliminary trial was conducted where hospital staff took group of 3–5 service users around the Highbury mile to use the app. All service users successfully managed to use the app and found the Highbury Mile much more engaging than previously, making sure to find the objects as the app instructed. Participants took ownership in the co-designed objects making the app and associated physical activity moreso appealing. Participants both enjoyed the visual nature of having colourful co-design objects placed around the walk as well as the gamified element of using the app to search for and scan the correct object. Technically, the object recognition worked well with the phones correctly identifying the objects quickly. Overall, this shows the potential for the developed exergame and co-design process to successfully help increase PA in service users with SMI.

The co-design element of the production of the app enabled Highbury Hospital to host a variety of sessions that engaged the service users in creating objects that would later be implemented within the game. Although the co-design had benefits such as increasing creativity and engagement with the exergame, there was one issue that arose after some time of testing. Due to the quality of the materials used and the UK's adverse weather conditions, some of the models struggled to stay in tact when placed into the environment. At first thought, this was a concerning issue for the integrity of the treasure hunt, but having discussed the issues, it turned out to be a minor issue, and it was suggested to be positive as it will encourage the continuation of the papier-mâché co-design sessions. These constant sessions will keep benefiting the services users as previously mentioned, but will also regularly improve the treasure hunt. It will ensure that the content get's less repetitive as new models can be implemented regularly and it also opens up the opportunity to offer specified content such as seasonal or holiday features.

Overall, we have conducted a co-creation process with hospital service users and developed a novel object recognition exergame to promote physical activity. This research provides an overview of the developed AI exergame from a co-design perspective. It also discusses how the game extends the current scope of object recognition to gamify the walking experience. These advances help to promote the mass adoption of AI technologies for social good.

In the future we aim to continue trialling the exergame to gather further feedback and explore the impact the app has on service users physical activity as well as mental wellbeing. We will also continue working with Highbury hospital to include new co-designed objects within the app.

References

1. Binder, T., De Michelis, G., Ehn, P., Jacucci, G., Linde, P., Wagner, I.: Participation in design things. In: Design Things (2019). https://doi.org/10.7551/mitpress/8262.003.0011
2. Burkett, I.: An Introduction to Co-design. Technical report (2016). http://www.csi.edu.au/
3. Campos, C., Mesquita, F., Marques, A., Trigueiro, M.J., Orvalho, V., Rocha, N.B.: Feasibility and acceptability of an exergame intervention for schizophrenia. Psychol. Sport Exerc. **19**, 50–58 (2015). https://doi.org/10.1016/J.PSYCHSPORT.2015.02.005
4. Daumit, G.L., et al.: Physical activity patterns in adults with severe mental illness. J. Nerv. Mental Dis. **193**(10), 641–646 (2005). https://doi.org/10.1097/01.NMD.0000180737.85895.60
5. Doran, K., Pickford, S., Austin, C., Walker, T., Barnes, T.: World of workout: towards pervasive, intrinsically motivated, mobile exergaming. In: Meaningful Play 2010 Conference (2010)
6. Frauenberger, C., Good, J., Alcorn, A., Pain, H.: Supporting the design contributions of children with autism spectrum conditions. In: ACM International Conference Proceeding Series, pp. 134–143 (2012). https://doi.org/10.1145/2307096.2307112
7. Fu, J., Mei, T., Yang, K., Lu, H., Rui, Y.: Tagging personal photos with transfer deep learning. In: WWW 2015 - Proceedings of the 24th International Conference on World Wide Web, pp. 344–354 (2015). https://doi.org/10.1145/2736277.2741112
8. Holmlid, S.: Participative, co-operative, emancipatory: from participatory design to service design. In: First Nordic Conference on Service Design and Service Innovation (2009)
9. Howard, A., et al.: Searching for MobileNetV3. Technical report (2019)
10. Malinverni, L., Mora-Guiard, J., Padillo, V., Mairena, M.A., Hervás, A., Pares, N.: Participatory design strategies to enhance the creative contribution of children with special needs. In: ACM International Conference Proceeding Series (2014). https://doi.org/10.1145/2593968.2593981

11. Niantic: Pokémon GO (2021). https://pokemongolive.com/en/
12. Pan, S.J., Yang, Q.: A survey on transfer learning (2010). https://doi.org/10.1109/TKDE.2009.191
13. Patsi, C., Antoniou, P., Batsiou, S., Bebetsos, E., Lagiou, K.: Exergames and their effect on emotional state in people with Schizophrenia. Balkan Milit. Med. Rev. **15**(4), 275–281 (2012)
14. Sanders, L.: An evolving map of design practice and design research. Interactions (2008). https://doi.org/10.1145/1409040.1409043
15. Singh, M.S., Pondenkandath, V., Zhou, B., Lukowicz, P., Liwicki, M., Kaiserslautern, T.: Transforming sensor data to the image domain for deep learning-an application to footstep detection. https://doi.org/10.1109/IJCNN.2017.7966182
16. Simonyan, K., Zisserman, A.: Very deep convolutional networks for large-scale image recognition. In: 3rd International Conference on Learning Representations, ICLR 2015 - Conference Track Proceedings (2015)
17. Skliarova, I., Sklyarov, V.: Hardware/software co-design. In: Lecture Notes in Electrical Engineering (2019). https://doi.org/10.1007/978-3-030-20721-2_6
18. Stanley, K.G., Livingston, I., Bandurka, A., Kapiszka, R., Mandryk, R.L.: PiNiZoRo: a GPS-based exercise game for families. In: Future Play 2010: Research, Play, Share - International Academic Conference on the Future of Game Design and Technology, pp. 243–246 (2010). https://doi.org/10.1145/1920778.1920817
19. Steen, M.: Co-design as a process of joint inquiry and imagination. Des. Issues (2013). https://doi.org/10.1162/DESI_a_00207
20. Steen, M., Manschot, M., de Koning, N.: Benefits of co-design in service design projects. Int. J. Des. **5**, 1–8 (2011)
21. Szegedy, C., Vanhoucke, V., Ioffe, S., Shlens, J., Wojna, Z.: Rethinking the inception architecture for computer vision. In: Proceedings of the IEEE Computer Society Conference on Computer Vision and Pattern Recognition (2016). https://doi.org/10.1109/CVPR.2016.308
22. The Mental Health Foundation: Fundamental facts about mental health. Technical report (2015)
23. Tommasi, T., Orabona, F., Caputo, B.: Safety in numbers: learning categories from few examples with multi model knowledge transfer. In: Proceedings of the IEEE Computer Society Conference on Computer Vision and Pattern Recognition (2010). https://doi.org/10.1109/CVPR.2010.5540064
24. Vines, J., Clarke, R., Wright, P., McCarthy, J., Olivier, P.: Configuring participation: on how we involve people in design. In: Conference on Human Factors in Computing Systems - Proceedings (2013). https://doi.org/10.1145/2470654.2470716
25. Wang, J., Chen, Y., Zheng, V.W., Huang, M.: Deep transfer learning for cross-domain activity recognition. In: ACM International Conference Proceeding Series (2018). https://doi.org/10.1145/3265689.3265705

Research on the Design Narrative for Medical Popular Science Serious Games: A Case Study of AIDS Prevention Game "Bluebridge Cafe"

Xu Yang[1], Xin Sun[2], and Jianhua Yang[3(✉)]

[1] School of Design Art and Media, Nanjing University of Science and Technology, Nanjing, China
[2] Kaixin Culture Communication Co. Ltd., Nanjing, China
[3] College of Communication, Qingdao University of Science and Technology, Qingdao, China
jianhua2111@163.com

Abstract. The primary aim in the present study was to investigate the design narrative expression in the medical popular science serious games. Methods of integrating the relevant content of disease prevention and treatment into the challenging, interesting, and interactive game segments in serious games, and how to present it through the narrative and design methods were key areas of investigation. Firstly, the relevant theoretical background was reviewed. After theoretical research, the relationships between content, vision, and interactive experiences in the AIDS prevention game "Bluebridge Cafe" developed by Tencent were investigated and analyzed. The focuses in the present study were the design and expression of content related to AIDS prevention and post infection disease treatment in the game, how to guide users to change their attitudes and behaviors in storytelling, and how to combine the content with the functions of the game segments. The results of the present study can help improve the design of functional games for medical science popularization, so as to enhance the transmission of health information and improve the effects of medical knowledge popularization.

Keywords: Medical Serious Game · Narrative · AIDS education

1 Introduction

1.1 A Subsection Sample

At present, games are used to undertake and solve social problems, and have played a positive role [1]. In the field of health, the gamification of applications has become increasingly used to address issues such as chronic disease management, mental health promotion, lifestyle intervention, and auxiliary treatment [2]. Gamification has become significant tool for medical science popularization and education. The number of people infected with AIDS has continued to increase in recent years, and with the inequality of regional resources producing huge regional differences, AIDS not only causes health problems, but many social problems too [3]. Since there is currently no effective vaccine or cure, providing education to the public regarding AIDS prevention is one of the most significant steps in the fight against AIDS [4]. The AIDS prevention and control regulations issued by government agencies clearly emphasize the need to teach AIDS prevention and control to key groups, especially in public and educational settings within medical institutions and schools. The government agencies also aim to encourage and support relevant organizations and individuals to complete consultation, guidance, publicity, and educational work on the prevention and control of AIDS [5].

Due to the increase in new media, the traditional AIDS prevention education model is now too simple and only possesses a small scope of influence [6]. For the current growing population infected with AIDS, on the one hand, it is necessary to shift the target population of publicity and education from high-risk groups to the general population [7]. On the other hand, because the infection of AIDS is difficult to notice, education for AIDS prevention needs to be updated in regard to scale, methods, effect, and other aspects in order to meet the needs of current publicity and education. The innovative development of AIDS prevention education models under the new media environment is a new topic [8]. Digital games are an effective method to improve health behaviors and attract public participation and attention. The use of digital games increases opportunities for interactive learning. To promote the formation of positive health behaviors, educational games relating to AIDS can be utilized as a tool for broader medical science education and to conduct education and communication in a more dynamic, immersive and attractive way [9].

The key focuses in popular science serious games are scientific knowledge and content. When designing a game, the purpose of knowledge dissemination and whether the contents also promote entertainment, functionality [10], and experience all need to be considered. Consequently, the narrative design in medical popular science games has become a significant focus. In the present paper, the key discussion is the design narrative expression in medical popular sicence serious games, especially methods of integrating the relevant content of disease prevention and treatment into the challenging, interesting, and interactive game links, and how to display the relevant content through the design narrative and aesthetic methods. In the present study, China's AIDS prevention and control science popularization requirements were used to explore the design narrative of China's first AIDS prevention science popularization game "Bluebridge Cafe". Further, the specific method of combining science popularization content and design in medical popular science games was analyzed, providing reference for future research into promoting health science popularization through games.

2 Literature Review

2.1 Medical Serious Game

Serious games usually refer to carefully designed games with an educational purpose [11], which are not only for entertainment, but also for public health, public policy and corporate strategy, as well as other purposes [12]. The concept thereof is broad, but serious games generally encompass the following characteristics: (1) serious games have certain goals, such as education, training, publicity and others; (2) serious games still retain the entertainment characteristics of traditional video games [13]; (3) serious games contain specific communication content; (4) the educational content of the games is attached to the entertainment content [12]. Recently, serious games have received widespread attention, having been adopted as important tools in numerous fields, including national defense, education, scientific exploration, medical care, emergency management, urban planning, engineering, religion and politics. Such games have also been a positive factor in the acceptance and effectiveness of knowledge [14].

Serious games have also been extensively used in the field of health and medical treatment. As an example, such games can assist in clinical skill training and theoretical knowledge learning in the study of medical majors. Such games possess the advantages of improving students' interest in learning professional knowledge, increasing practical practice opportunities, and reducing the cost of learning skills [15]. Secondly, serious games have also been applied to such fields as adjuvant therapy and play intervention. To be specific, several content elements with educational purposes have been designed for various medical applications, and games are being used to encourage users to participate in activities to gain certain experience, thereby influencing human behavior and motivation [2]. Thirdly, there are serious popular science games targeted at the spread of health knowledge, particularly popular science health-related or disease-related knowledge. Users can experience, simulate, learn relevant knowledge and obtain useful information during the game process [1].

2.2 AIDS Preventive Educational Games

The emergence of serious games provides a new path for AIDS publicity and education. In sexual health education, serious games are attractive, confidential and convenient, thereby allowing for embarrassment or boredom to be avoided when discussing such issues with others or health promotion educators [16]. At the same time, the game is a voluntary activity, often accompanied by a pleasant experience [17]. Most people are familiar with and have been exposed to a game environment [18], which is easier for the education and dissemination of AIDS knowledge [19]. Additionally, video games also possess the advantage of convenient dissemination, and the intervention scope thereof is broader, with the ability to also facilitate the implementation of actions [20].

The educational mechanism of popular science games on AIDS mostly involves fostering the Knowledge, Attitude, Practice (KAP) mode through games. Among such objectives, the primary objective is cognition and understanding of relevant knowledge, which is also the premise of forming attitudes and actions. Secondly, AIDS popular science knowledge is disseminated through entertainment education, and effective dissemination is achieved through narrative. The affinity, fun and immersive experience of game narratives are also conducive to the dissemination of knowledge, thereby forming positive attitudes and influencing behavior [21]. The games also provide a personalized learning environment for promoting knowledge learning opportunities, such as effective transformation of necessary information through storylines, role plays and avatars. Meanwhile, through challenging game activities, learners can cultivate problems such as cognition, criticism, choice, memory, evaluation, and solution of AIDS knowledge to achieve strong internal motivation and achievement [22].

To summarize, the content of serious games regarding AIDS science popularization education is crucial, that is, the type of science popularization content that is transmitted in the games. After referring to the latest version of the < Core information of AIDS prevention publicity and education for young students (2021 version) > [23] revised by the China Center for Disease Control and Prevention in addition to other publications from relevant institutions on AIDS publicity and education knowledge points, the main content of AIDS science popularization education was found to include the following: (1) Basic knowledge: what AIDS is, and the basic knowledge that needs to be understood; (2) Prevention knowledge: safe sex, drug refusal, and others. (3) Detection and treatment: how to receive treatment. (4) Relevant laws and regulations (Core information of AIDS prevention publicity and education for young students, 2021). In addition, research has been conducted on the demand for AIDS health education games. The results have shown that the demand for popular science information about helping people infected with AIDS is the highest in the selection of game content, followed by the desire to learn AIDS related knowledge and prevention and control skills [24].

2.3 Design Aesthetics of Medical Serious Games

By creating virtual scenes, serious games stimulate learners' curiosity, imagination, learning and exploration [25]. Computer games based on digital media allow for medical science knowledge to be combined with games, while games create a space environment that is alienated from reality and is a form of skill training and optimization experience. As such, appropriate strategies should be adopted in game design to achieve the goal of the game activity [26].

Common types of medical science games include role playing games, episodic experiential games, simulation games and knowledge quiz games [1]. Role playing games are games in which role-playing is the main way to advance the plot by completing tasks according to the game plot and acquiring knowledge or skills in the process of interaction [27]. Episodic experiential games are a common category in the game genre, being designed to tell a story to the player and interact with them. When players enter a set game world, choices need to be made in relation to themselves, and the player will ultimately receive feedback through the game that is personal to them [28]. In simulation games, players can choose certain characters to control and manage the set world and unlock scientific knowledge through the simulation mode [1]. Knowledge-based quiz games are games in which the main mode is to answer questions, which are designed based on scientific knowledge, and to acquire knowledge by answering questions. Being simple to operate, knowledge quiz games can be played by answering questions to obtain corresponding scores and achievements [29].

To fully consider how to create a game experience in a virtual environment where the content to be communicated is naturally embedded in the game and can be perceived by the players, the integration of knowledge content and game scenarios is the end point of discussion regardless of the form of medical science serious games, especially in game design [25]. Narratives and games are two complementary modes of perception and experience. Stories can act as scripts for potential games, while games can also be potential stories. A cycle can be formed between the two [26]. In serious games with narrative interactions, the theme of the story is usually present throughout, and the player is the controller of the game, can choose the direction of the game or cooperate with others, and is more easily integrated into the game and drives the plot [30].

The story content of medical science games is important, but the design and level of performance also play a crucial role in bringing the game to life. This includes the use of artistic language, which can evoke emotions, creativity, and thought. Specifically, the game's ability to create an impactful artistic experience, its level of innovation in presentation, and its ability to evoke memories and insights in the audience, are significant factors in determining its success. [31]. Next is the emotional performance, when the complex emotions and stories shown in the game reach the reflective level, they can be accompanied by higher intellectual activities generated to trigger the emotional resonance of the players [32]. Again, this is reflected in the visual presentation, where the storyline is used as a guide to increase interest [33], and player-friendly presentation is used [34]. Finally, game interaction experience is judged according to the immersibility, joviality, playability and replayability[35].

3 Analysis on the AIDS Prevention Game "Bluebridge Cafe"

3.1 Game Structure

"Bluebridge Cafe" is an episodic experiential game developed by Tencent to popularize AIDS knowledge [36]. The game focuses on the story of a coffee shop owner and three AIDS patients in the form of a theater and intersperses the story with knowledge about AIDS prevention and treatment [1], with the aim of popularizing AIDS knowledge (Fig. 1).

Fig. 1. "Bluebridge Cafe" Game Promotional Image (from the Internet)

The game consists of two primary sections: the story section and the knowledge and science section. The story section, which is the heart of the game, follows the tale of AGan, the manager of Bluebridge Cafe, and three AIDS patients. The story highlights the lives of AIDS patients and interweaves relevant prevention and treatment knowledge, providing a realistic portrayal of the everyday lives of AIDS patients. AGan serves as the central character and the key link between the story and its message. He cares for the AIDS patients and enters the lives of three different AIDS patients by listening and accompanying them, and from the beginning, he is difficult to approach to the later, he opens up his heart. In the game, players mainly act as listeners and witnesses of the story, interspersed with interactive links to advance the story, which is different from the traditional didactic game form. However, the form of the story is used as a tool to promote understanding of the relevant knowledge. The knowledge section is supplemented by an "HIV Prevention Knowledge Manual", which complements and completes the lack of

HIV-related knowledge in the story section. Additionally, there is also a sharing board, where scenes and knowledge points from the game can be shared to enhance interactivity and publicity (Fig. 2).

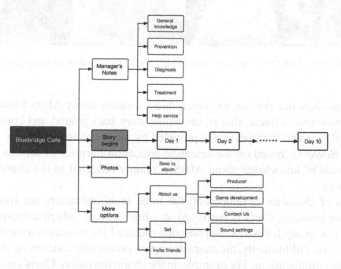

Fig. 2. "Bluebridge Cafe" Game Information Structure Diagram

3.2 AIDS Preventive Education Content

The Bluebridge Cafe is an episodic game, in which the main message of the game is told through the story and simple interactions [37]. The story is set in a cafe where the cafe manager, AGan, unwittingly meets CiWei who has AIDS, and then hires him as a sales clerk before teaching him how to become a barista. Chris, a singer and regular customer of the cafe, is also an AIDS patient who has been infected with AIDS and has developed other illnesses that have caused him to break up with a man he was dating. ShuYi is a mother who had to leave her family and children because she was accidentally infected with AIDS. She visits the cafe every afternoon to observe her daughter returning from school through the window. Several main characters are linked together because of the existence of the cafe. CiWei regains his confidence in life because of the help of the shopkeeper, AGan, and learns barista skills. He also finds his birth mother while helping ShuYi to see her child. Chris, a singer, and AGan, the cafe manager, are friends. With the support of his friends at the cafe, Chris regains confidence and continues to receive treatment for his complications. With the help of AGan and CiWei, ShuYi was able to see her child again and get a chance to spend time with her. In addition, there are some secondary characters for the advancement of the story, such as the coffee shop chef AKang, the man Chris was dating Dolphin, Shu Yi's daughter Nan Nan, Nan Nan's father, CiWei's mother, a kindergarten teacher, a doctor, and other characters. The player mainly serves as an observer of the story and participates in making a cup of coffee at pivotal moments in the plot, helping to advance the story (Fig. 3).

Fig. 3. The Main Characters of "Bluebridge Cafe" (screenshot of game interface)

The game does not contain too much direct content about AIDS knowledge, and the overall narrative is linear, that is, the whole story background and context are laid out for the player, and the storyline is provided by means of scrolling bars to drive the game [38]. However, based on the scientific education purpose of serious games, the communication of knowledge about AIDS is mainly reflected in the character setting and plot design.

In terms of character development, the three main characters are linked to HIV infection. For instance, Chris is portrayed as a homosexual, which corresponds to the actual high-risk group for AIDS, emphasizing the need for increased awareness among high-risk groups. Additionally, the character development also touches on the themes of treatment and complications. For example, in the characterization, Chris's own condition worsens and causes complications such as tumors, which is also related to the knowledge of AIDS complications. Once again, one of the core ideas of the game is to appeal to the public to take note of the problem of AIDS while enhancing understanding and tolerance, which is a theme that is also reflected in the characters' backgrounds. For example, AGan, the cafe manager, is a non-judgmental person who is able to face and help people with AIDS. Moreover, several secondary characters also convey knowledge about AIDS, such as the doctor who teaches the public about the need to receive treatment after contracting AIDS.

Regarding the plot, the game mainly establishes a story of helping the AIDS community: AGan, teaches CiWei how to become a barista and reintegrate into society again, the characters help ShuYi and her daughter to return to normal life again, and Chris is encouraged by AGan to undergo oncology treatment again, all of which involve the theme of "help". The plot is interwoven with AIDS knowledge, as seen when a character discusses their own experience of infection with AGan. They mention not knowing about a 24-h blocking drug, highlighting the importance of seeking effective treatment. This message is conveyed through the characters' dialogue. Then, there is the episode in which the store manager AGan tells CiWei and Chris to stick to their medication, which also conveys the knowledge about AIDS treatment (Fig. 4).

Since it is not possible to integrate the entirety of relevant knowledge into the game's storyline, an interactive learning section called "Store Manager's Notes - HIV Prevention Manual" was added to the game. AIDS knowledge is presented in the form of notes from the perspective of the store manager, Agan. The knowledge in this section is also combined with the main content of AIDS education and publicity requirements, subdivided into general knowledge, prevention, diagnosis, treatment, institutional help

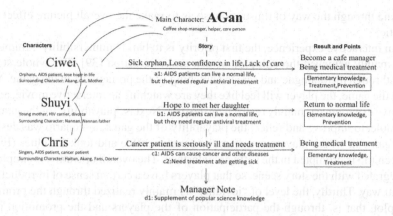

Fig. 4. Story Frame Diagram

and so on. Through such means, the game is supplemented with knowledge that should be understood and mastered (Fig. 5).

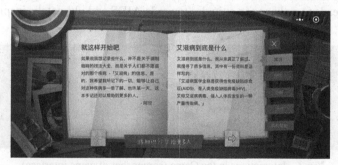

Fig. 5. Story Frame Diagram (screenshot of game interface)

3.3 Game Design

According to the theme and plot of the story, the overall visual design of the game presents a storytelling style that encourages healing. Through character design that adopts non-player characters [39] there is more freedom in visual expression. Combined with the theme of the story, a more realistic illustration style was chosen, which can make the plot more introverted, but also help portray the personality and details of the characters. The overall color scheme is unified and warm, avoiding excessive color contrasts, while the painting style is realistic. The aim of the game is also to restore the scene of the story, set off the atmosphere of the story, and enhance the immersive experience. Especially in video games, the sense of personal experience should be provided as much as possible, so as to create a feeling as vivid as the practice of real life, making players become more immersed [34]. Therefore, in the visual aspect, attempts should be made to restore the plot scene through the way of illustration, so as to make the overall picture effect more cinematic.

In an interactive experience, the first priority is to build "immersibility". Immersion here is mainly achieved through plot, screen and interaction [39]. The whole story is formed through the dialogue and screen switching of the protagonist in the game. When playing the game, the player will feel like they are watching an interactive movie, and the immersive experience is mainly realized by the plot. Next is "playability" of the game. As an example, to improve and reflect the playability of the game, a scenario was designed for the game in which players can operate to make coffee and look for clues (Fig. 6). Such scenario is prompted in the software interface. The overall operation is simple, and it is integrated with the story scene, so that players have a certain sense of introduction in a natural way. Thirdly, the level of "joviality" is mainly realized through the promotion of the plot, that is, through the participation of the players and the promotion of the character story, a good ending is finally achieved, and a good "achievement" is provided at the end. The players are both spectators and participants of the whole story. Finally, the game's artistry is reflected in the thought-provoking and impactful experience it leaves with players after playing, which is also the embodiment of the emotional level of the game. The game employs the use of images, music, camera angles, and storytelling to guide players to think about AIDS and to proactively acquire knowledge [39]. This shift in thinking leads to a change in attitudes towards AIDS and ultimately, inspires action.

Fig. 6. Interactions in the Game (screenshot of game interface)

4   Research Conclusion and Future Prospect

In the era of new media, the initiative of users is becoming enhanced. Compared with passive preaching, users are more willing to take the initiative to obtain information in an interesting way according to their preferences and needs [40]. Serious games provide an alternative path for medical knowledge science education. The functional game of AIDS science popularization education can be used as an auxiliary tool for AIDS prevention and has a certain educational effect [41]. As such, integration of [33]. Different from traditional didactic games, formal innovation is necessary in the design of such serious games. Attention should be paid to the narration of knowledge content and integration into the game process in a reasonable and acceptable way. The case of the game "Bluebridge Cafe" gives a new design narrative scheme, that is, to integrate the rich medical science knowledge into the game plot, and to convey the disease knowledge through the immersive story experience, so as to achieve the goal of raising public awareness.

In the game design, based on the purpose of the game story, the setting of the characters, the plot, and the design of the interaction are all closely related to the theme. The purpose is to strengthen the coherence of the narrative plot, guide the players to obtain useful information along with the plot, and reduce the difficulty of understanding the simple preaching information transmission. Additionally, the combination of vision and effect can deepen the five-sense experience from the perspective of vision and hearing, and facilitate knowledge experiences through imperceptible influence. This is also the inspiration and thinking obtained from the case analysis of the game "Bluebridge Cafe".

There are many factors to be considered in the game design. For instance, in the game "Bluebridge Cafe", there is still room for discussion in terms of the fun of the interactive links, reward mechanism, game level setting, multi-dimensional experiential interaction, and the full realization of all content presentation in a limited game. Thus, such serious medical games require further investigation. In the present study, there was a failure to make certain experiments and evaluation on the actual effect of the game, and thus, the plan is to supplement and further explore in a follow-up study.

Acknowledgement. This research was supported by the Key Project of the National Social Science Fund (22AC003).

References

1. Pan, J.Y., Jiang, P.: Review of health science popularization game based on plot+H5 mode. Sci. Educ. Mus. **8**(05), 22–29 (2022)
2. Jiang, F., et al.: Application status of gamification in medical and health field abroad. Mil. Nurs. **37**(11), 63–66 (2020)
3. UNAIDS: IN DANGER: UNAIDS Global AIDS Update 2022 (2022)
4. Liu, T.T., et al.: Practice and challenge of AIDS prevention and control publicity and education. Chin. J. AIDS STD **27**(11), 1179–1181 (2021)
5. Regulations on AIDS Prevention and Treatment. http://www.gov.cn/zhengce/2020-12/27/con tent_5573544.htm23,Last. Accessed 23 Jan 2023
6. Ma, S.M.: Effect evaluation about AIDS health education for floating population in Huajing town community of Shanghai. Health Educ. Health Promot. **0**(02), 105–107 (2015)
7. Ge, X.M., et al.: Analysis on epidemiological characteristics and trends of HIV/AIDS in Guangxi During 2010–2015. Chin. J. AIDS STD **23**(1), 40–43 (2017)
8. Yang, W.M., et al.: Establishment and application of new mode of "Internet+" HIV/AIDS warning publicity and education in Guangxi. Appl. Prev. Med. **24**(6), 421–428 (2018)
9. Hightow-Weidman, L.B., Muessig, K.E., Bauermeister, J.A., Sara, L., Fiellin, L.E.: The future of digital games for HIV prevention and care. Curr. Opin. HIV AIDS **12**(5), 1–7 (2017)
10. Kwon, J.H., et al.: Game design strategy for medical serious game. J. Korean Soc. Comput. Game (KSCG). **23**, 295–303 (2010)
11. Göbel, S., Ma, M., Baalsrud Hauge, J., Oliveira, M.F., Wiemeyer, J., Wendel, V. (eds.): JCSG 2015. LNCS, vol. 9090. Springer, Cham (2015). https://doi.org/10.1007/978-3-319-19126-3
12. Zhang, S., Sheng, Y.: Serious games in disease management of patients with type 2 diabetes: a review of the progress in research. Mod. Clin. Nurs. **21**(3), 62–66 (2022)

13. Lu, H., et al.: Analysis of the current situation of serious games and its application prospect in medical education. Comput. Knowl. Technol. **17**(19), 199–200 (2021)
14. Connolly, T.M.: A systematic literature review of empirical evidence on computer games and serious games. Comput. Educ. **59**(2), 661–686 (2012)
15. Luo, X.L.: Research progress in application of serious games in medical professional learning. Chin. J. Libr. Inf. Sci. Tradit. Chin. Med. **45**(01), 69–73 (2021)
16. Chu, S.K.W., et al.: Promoting sex education among teenagers through an interactive game: reasons for success and implications. Games Health J. **4**(3), 168–174 (2015)
17. Wei, T.: A study on the factors of stimulating and sustaining students' learning-motivation in educational games and motivational design strategies. Mod. Educ. Technol. **19**(01), 55–58 (2009)
18. McGonigal, J.: Reality Is Broken: Why Games Make Us Better and How They Can Change the World; Penguin: London, UK, vol. 22 (2011)
19. Kashibuchi, M., Sakamoto, A.: The educational effectiveness of a simulation/game in sex education. Simul. Gaming **32**(3), 331–343 (2001)
20. Li, G.X., et al.: Study on internet-based HIV intervention targeted on men who have sex with men. Chin. J. AIDS STD **19**(08), 599–601+614 (2013)
21. Zhang, X.X., Lai, E.M.: Hot knowledge and cold knowledge: game intervention and experiment evaluation of HIV/AIDS knowledge awareness. Visual Commun. Res. **00**, 34–48 (2022)
22. Haruna, H., et al.: Improving sexual health education programs for adolescent students through game-based learning and gamification. Int. J. Environ. Res. Public Health **15**(9), 1–26 (2018)
23. NCAIDS/STD. Core information of AIDS prevention publicity and education for young students. https://ncaids.chinacdc.cn/zxzx/zxdteff/202112/t20211207_253553.htm. Accessed 23 Jan 2023
24. Xie, H., et al.: Investigation on the needs of AIDS health educational games and influencing factors among adolescent students. Chin. J. AIDS STD **27**(9), 956–959 (2021)
25. Wei, T., Li, Y.: Review of educational game design at home and abroad. J. Distance Educ.**17**(03), 67–70 (2009)
26. Zhang, X.J.: Story and game: toward a digital narratology. Wuhan Univ. Technol. (Soc. Sci. Ed). **23**(02), 248–252 (2010)
27. Liu, Q.: Design and Development of RPG Science Education Game. Huazhong University of Science and Technology, Wuhan (2018)
28. Sun, S.J., Li, D.N.: On narrative goal design of plot games based on herman's interpretation model. Des. Res. **12**(02), 66–69 (2022)
29. Jiang, J.F., et al.: Assumption on the application of question-answering games in histology and embryology teaching. Basic Med. Educ. **20**(11), 933–936 (2018)
30. Gao, Q.: Interactive narrative design of digital games. Mod. Educ. Technol. **19**(07), 82–85 (2009)
31. Huang, S.: From game to art : on the artistic language and visual style of independent games. Zhuangshi **04**, 38–41 (2017)
32. Huang, S., Zhu, Z.T.: Core artistic evaluation criteria of digital games. Ind. Eng. Des. **2**(01), 11–21 (2020)
33. Wang, T., Li, J.: Research on ecological education game design under the framework of flow experience. Design **23**, 28–31 (2022)
34. Yang, Y., Ji, L.W.: Research on interactive experience of children's science popularization serious games: design practice of bird atlas app in Shedao Laotieshan nature reserve. Zhuangshi **10**, 133–135 (2022)
35. Huang, S.: Gameplay evaluation based on player interactive experience. J. Beijing Inst. Technol. (Soc. Sci. Ed.) **12**(04),102–104+108 (2010)

36. Tencent Games Dreaming Plan. Blue Bridge Cafe | There is no distance between Ai and being loved. https://zhuimeng.qq.com/web201904/detail-news.html?newsid=8995232. Accessed 25 Jan 2023
37. Pan, Q.X., et al.: The design of interactive game of Miao folk story "Snail-Girl" based on Codemao. Comput. Era **11**, 113–116 (2022)
38. Guan, P.P.: The narrative interpretation in digital games. J. Huaiyin Teachers Coll. Soc. Sci. **32**(01), 110–114 (2010)
39. Huang, S.: Game Characters Design based on Users' Psychology. Zhuangshi **06**, 76–77 (2010)
40. Zeng, W.J.: The status quo and development strategy of medical science popularization cartoons in the context of new media: a case Study of Xiaodaifu Cartoon, Tencent Medpedia and Hunzhi health. Stud. Sci. Popularization **17**(3), 54–61 (2022)
41. Tang, J., et al.: Gamification design of AIDS educational software based on IBM theory. Chin. J. AIDS STD **26**(11), 1230–1233 (2020)

Author Index

Printed in the United States
by Baker & Taylor Publisher Services